Fourth Edition

Essentials of Psychology

Kenneth S. Bordens, Professor Emeritus
Purdue University at Fort Wayne

Josh R. Gerow, Professor Emeritus
Purdue University at Fort Wayne

Nancy K. Gerow, MS, LMFT
Psychological Service Associates, Inc.
Fort Wayne, IN

Academic Media Solutions

Affordable - Quality Textbooks, Study Aids, & Custom Publishing

Dedications

To my wife, Ricky Karen Bordens,
and to my children and grandchildren.
Kenneth S. Bordens

To Josh
Nancy Gerow

Essentials of Psychology, 4th Edition, Bordens/Gerow/Gerow

Cover image: © Lucky Team Studio/Shutterstock

Paperback (color):	ISBN-13: 978-1-942041-88-7
	ISBN-10: 1-942041-88-8
Paperback (black/white):	ISBN-13: 978-1-942041-89-4
	ISBN-10: 1-942041-89-6
Loose-leaf version:	ISBN-13: 978-1-942041-90-0
	ISBN-10: 1-942041-90-X
Online version:	ISBN-13: 978-1-942041-91-7
	ISBN-10: 1-942041-91-8

Printed in the United States of America by Academic Media Solutions.

Brief Contents

Contents

9 Human Sexuality and Relationships 189

10 Personality 209

11 Stress and Health Psychology 231

12 Psychological Disorders 257

13 Treatment and Therapy for Psychological Disorders 277

Preface

Essentials of Psychology, 4th edition, is a concise and balanced introduction to psychology and its applications created specifically for courses in basic psychology. This student-friendly text embraces the latest perspectives on traditional concepts and current theories to provide students with insight into human behavior. The authors have minimized complex explanations and illustrations to maximize straightforward understanding and application.

This comprehensive text presents the core topics in psychology in a clear and concise manner. New chapters in this edition cover consciousness, human sexuality, social psychology, and developmental psychology. *Essentials of Psychology* has been thoroughly updated to reflect recent examples, research, and scholarship from across the discipline.

Text features include a broad range of examples and applications that increase the relevance of key concepts and issues for a wide range of students, such as the Psychology in Action and Focus on Diversity boxes that are found in every chapter. This edition has a contemporary design with numerous graphs, figures, and tables that reinforce the text discussions by providing a visual guide to key concepts. *Essentials of Psychology* also includes specific student- and instructor-oriented features.

STUDENT-ORIENTED FEATURES

This book includes many time-tested features that enhance the accessibility of the material for students and will facilitate learning. In addition to the following features, see "Student Supplements and Upgrades" for a complete list of the available student supplements.

- ■ *Chapter Outline and List of Questions to Be Answered*: Each chapter begins with a chapter outline, followed by a list of questions that students will be able to answer after reading the chapter. These questions will cue students to the central topics they should focus on as they read the chapter, with Study Checks throughout highlighting the relevant questions for each section of the chapter. The questions appear once more in the Chapter Summary, with answers provided so that students can check their understanding.

- ■ *Preview*: The Preview gives a concise overview of each chapter, listing the issues to be addressed and providing a sense of direction and focus for what to expect in each chapter.

- ■ *Thinking Critically Boxes and Study Checks*: Each chapter has several Thinking Critically boxes with questions that encourage critical reflection and prompt students to apply examples to their own lives, further enhancing the learning experience. The Thinking Critically and Study Checks features provide "resting places" within each chapter to pause and reflect on the material. As a review, the Study Checks help promote elaborative rehearsal of what has been read. Students can self-test and reread a particular section if they need more time with a concept.

- ■ *Glossary Terms*: For the beginning student, vocabulary development is vital to learning about psychology. To assist in that process, key words and concepts are printed in the text in a colored, boldface type and defined immediately. Each term is then defined again in a running marginal glossary. All key terms are assembled in a Key Terms list at the end of the chapter, with a page reference to indicate where each term may be found in the chapter. Key terms are repeated in a glossary at the back of the book.

CHAPTERS INCLUDED IN THE BOOK

This book is organized into 15 chapters. The content of each chapter is summarized as follows:

- *Chapter 1, Psychology Is in Our Lives*: Chapter 1 is an introductory chapter with information intended to familiarize students with the field of psychology. Topics include definitions of psychology and its subject matter, the science and practice of psychology, scientific methods in psychology, a brief history of psychology, and careers in psychology. The chapter concludes with a discussion of key principles that guide us in understanding topics in psychology (e.g., explanations for behavior are complex and involve interactions; there are individual differences in behavior).

- *Chapter 2, The Biological Foundations of Behavior*: Chapter 2 introduces students to the biological underpinnings of behavior, cognition, and affect. The chapter starts by looking at these underpinnings at the microlevel and includes information on neurons (structure and function), synaptic transmission, and neural thresholds. Next, the bigger picture is provided with a discussion of how the human nervous system is organized and what each element does. Then, the spinal cord is explored. Finally, there is a discussion of brain structures, starting with structures in the brainstem, then moving to the limbic system, and ending with the cortex.

- *Chapter 3, Sensation and Perception*: Chapter 3 explores the related processes involved in sensation and perception. The major senses are covered (vision, hearing, cutaneous senses, kinesthetic senses, position senses, and the pain sense). The discussion of perception includes the topics of perceptual selection, how the perceptual world is organized, the perception of depth and distance, and perceptual constancies.

- *Chapter 4, Learning*: Chapter 4 introduces students to the main approaches to learning: classical conditioning, operant conditioning, and cognitive approaches. The basics of classical conditioning are covered, including the components of classical conditioning (e.g., unconditioned and conditioned stimuli) and information on generalization, discrimination, and extinction. Additional discussion focuses on how classical conditioning applies to our everyday lives. Similarly, the basics of operant conditioning are covered, including positive reinforcement, negative reinforcement, and punishment. The section on cognitive approaches includes discussions of latent learning, cognitive maps, and social learning theory.

- *Chapter 5, Memory*: Chapter 5 begins with a discussion of the nature of memory and the processes of encoding, storage, and retrieval. A discussion of sensory memory follows. Next, short-term memory is discussed. This discussion includes information on the nature of short-term memory and its capacity. The section on long-term memory includes discussions of semantic, episodic, and procedural memory. There is also information on the accuracy of long-term memory, including recovered memories and eyewitness testimony. The chapter concludes with discussions of how memory can be improved (e.g., practice strategies, mnemonics).

- *Chapter 6, Consciousness*: Chapter 6 opens with a definition of consciousness and a presentation of James's characteristics of normal waking consciousness. Next, sleep is covered, including discussions of the stages of sleep and dreaming. The next main section covers alterations of consciousness through hypnosis, meditation, and the use of psychoactive drugs.

- ***Chapter 7, Thinking, Language, and Intelligence***: Chapter 7 includes discussions of thinking and problem solving. The section on thinking covers thinking processes, concepts, and types of reasoning. The discussion of problem solving includes information on how problems are defined and the distinction between well-defined and ill-defined problems. Language is covered next. Language is contrasted with communication, and the structure and functions of language are discussed. The chapter concludes with a discussion of approaches to intelligence, intelligence testing, and the extremes of intelligence (i.e., giftedness and intellectual disability).

- ***Chapter 8, Motivation and Emotion***: The chapter opens with a definition of motivation and then discusses instincts, needs, and drives. Physiological (e.g., need for food) and psychological needs (e.g., need to achieve) are discussed. The next section covers emotions, including discussions of how emotions are classified, the physiology of emotions, and how emotions are expressed.

- ***Chapter 9, Human Sexuality and Relationships***: The chapter begins with a discussion of sexual motivation and human sexuality. The next major section covers the varieties of human sexuality. In this section, the various sexual orientations (e.g., heterosexual, same sex, and transgender) are defined and discussed. In-depth coverage is provided on the same-sex and transgender orientations. The final section of the chapter discusses how relationships are formed and covers the roles of proximity, similarity, and physical attractiveness. The chapter ends with a discussion of love relationships.

- ***Chapter 10, Personality***: Chapter 10 first defines personality and then covers the major theories and approaches to personality. Information is presented on psychoanalytic theory (Freudian and neo-Freudian), the behavioral/learning approach, the cognitive approach, and humanistic theory. Trait theories are covered next, including information on the HEXACO model, which is an extension of the Big Five approach. The chapter concludes with a discussion of the various ways in which personality is measured.

- ***Chapter 11, Stress and Health Psychology***: Chapter 11 begins with a definition of stress and stressors. Information is provided on frustration-induced, conflict-induced, and life stress. Sections on effective and ineffective coping strategies are included as well. The chapter concludes with sections on health psychology, including such topics as unhealthy lifestyles, promoting healthy behaviors, and coping with HIV/AIDS.

- ***Chapter 12, Psychological Disorders***: A definition of the term *abnormal* and a description of how psychological disorders are classified open Chapter 12. A distinction is made between the concepts of psychological disorders, insanity, and competence. The remainder of the chapter is devoted to covering a range of psychological disorders, including anxiety disorders, obsessive-compulsive disorder, posttraumatic stress disorder, autism, dissociative disorders, personality disorders, depressive disorders, bipolar disorder, and schizophrenic spectrum disorder.

- ***Chapter 13, Treatment and Therapy for Psychological Disorders***: Chapter 13 covers various methods for treating psychological disorders. The chapter begins with a discussion of biomedical treatments (psychosurgery, electroconvulsive therapy [ECT], and drug therapy). Next, psychotherapy techniques are discussed, including psychoanalytic therapy, humanistic approaches, behavioral approaches, cognitive approaches, and group approaches. The chapter closes with a section on evaluating psychotherapy.

- ***Chapter 14, Social Psychology***: Chapter 14 presents several topics in social psychology. The chapter opens with a discussion of social cognition, followed by a section on attitudes and attitude change via persuasion. Next, prejudice, stereotyping, and discrimination are defined and discussed. Topics related to social influence (e.g., conformity and obedience) are then covered. Sections on bystander intervention, social loafing, and decision making in groups follow.

■ ***Chapter 15, Development Throughout the Life Span:*** Chapter 15 discusses the development process from birth to death. The chapter begins with a discussion of prenatal development and the factors (e.g., nutrition, alcohol, and drugs) that can affect the normal course of development. The chapter then covers cognitive development in childhood (Piaget's theory and the information-processing approach) and the development of gender identity. Next, the chapter covers the biological and psychological aspects of adolescence. The chapter then discusses development during early, middle, and late adulthood.

FOCUS ON DIVERSITY AND PSYCHOLOGY IN ACTION BOXES

In the modern era, it is becoming increasingly important for students to understand how diversity issues relate to behavior, cognition, and affect. To this end, *Essentials in Psychology* integrates multicultural content throughout and provides discussions of specific diversity issues in each chapter in the form of Focus on Diversity boxed features. Each of the Focus on Diversity boxes includes discussion of an important diversity issue relating to the main themes of the chapter. The material included in these boxes presents students with a sketch of what we know about gender, ethnic, cultural, and racial differences based on research. The selected topics are intended not only to inform students on these issues but also to spark their curiosity and encourage them to further explore these topics.

As important as diversity issues are, students often want to know how all of the "theoretical stuff" applies to everyday life and experience. To show students how many of the topics covered in the text apply to real life, a Psychology in Action box is included in each chapter. Like the Focus on Diversity boxes, these boxes show students how issues directly relating to them or people they know can be informed by research in psychology. Once again, these boxes are intended to spark curiosity among students and encourage them to think about how psychology relates to their everyday lives.

The Focus on Diversity and Psychology in Action boxes, organized by chapter, are as follows:

Chapter 1
   Psychology in Action: Distinguishing Science from Pseudoscience
   Focus on Diversity: Pioneering Women and Minorities in Psychology

Chapter 2
   Psychology in Action: The Neuropsychology of Addiction
   Focus on Diversity: Gender Differences in the Brain

Chapter 3
   Psychology in Action: Personal Listening Devices and Hearing Loss
   Focus on Diversity: Culture and Perception

Chapter 4
   Psychology in Action: The Training and Use of Service Dogs
   Focus on Diversity: Ethnic and Racial Differences in Parenting

Chapter 5
   Psychology in Action: Hypnosis and Memory Improvement
   Focus on Diversity: Gender Differences in Memory

ONLINE AND IN PRINT

Student Options: Print and Online Versions

This fourth edition of *Essentials of Psychology* is available in multiple versions: online, in PDF, and in print as either a paperback or loose-leaf text. The content of each version is identical.

The most affordable version is the online book, with upgrade options including the online version bundled with a print version. The benefit of the print version is that it offers you the freedom of being unplugged—away from your computer. Academic Media Solutions recognizes that it is difficult to read from a screen at length and that most of us read much faster when reading printed materials. The print version is particularly useful when you have extended print passages to read.

The online edition allows you to take full advantage of embedded digital features, including search and notes. Use the search feature to locate and jump to discussions anywhere in the book. Use the notes feature to add personal comments or annotations. You can move out of the book to follow Web links. You can navigate within and between chapters using a clickable table of contents. These features allow you to work at your own pace and in your own style as you read and surf your way through the material. (See "Harnessing the Online Version" for more tips on working with the online version.)

Harnessing the Online Version

The online version of *Essentials of Psychology* offers the following features to facilitate learning and to make using the book an easy, enjoyable experience:

- *Easy-to-navigate/clickable table of contents*—You can surf through the book quickly by clicking on chapter headings, or first- or second-level section headings. The table of contents can be accessed from anywhere in the book.

- *Key terms search*—Type in a term, and a search engine will return every instance of that term in the book, then jump directly to the selection of your choice with one click.

- *Notes and highlighting*—The online version includes study apps such as notes and highlighting. Each of these apps can be found in the tools icon embedded in the Academic Media Solutions/Textbook Media's online eBook reading platform (www.academicmediasolutions.com).

- *Upgrades*—The online version includes the ability to purchase additional study apps and functionality that will enhance the learning experience.

SUPPLEMENTS FOR INSTRUCTORS

In addition to the student-friendly features and pedagogy, the variety of student formats available, and the uniquely affordable pricing options, *Essentials of Psychology*, 4th edition, also includes a number of ancillaries and supplements that instructors will find useful when teaching their courses:

- *Test-Item File*—The extensive Test-Item File includes a bank of multiple-choice questions for each chapter for use in creating original quizzes and exams. Each item indicates the page(s) on which the material covered in a question appears in the text.

- *Instructor's Manual*—For each chapter, the Instructor's Manual contains a chapter outline, chapter preview, learning objectives, key terms, a lecture outline, a practice quiz, ideas for class demonstrations and discussions, and links to online videos. The Instructor's Manual has been developed to facilitate a quick review of the chapter and provide insights into the best use of the text's features.

- *PowerPoint Presentations*—Each chapter has an accompanying PowerPoint presentation that instructors can use to help organize lectures. The slides summarize the key concepts and material in each chapter, and include all of the numbered figures and tables from each chapter.

- *Online Video Labs with Student Worksheets*—This collection of high-quality, dynamic, and sometimes humorous video segments (contemporary and classic), produced by a variety of media, academic, and entertainment sources, is accessed via the Web. Organized by chapter, the video segments illustrate key topics and issues discussed in the text. Each video segment is accompanied by a student worksheet that consists of a series of discussion questions that help students connect the themes presented in the video segment with key topics discussed in the specific chapter.

STUDENT SUPPLEMENTS AND UPGRADES (ADDITIONAL PURCHASE REQUIRED)

- *Lecture Guide*—This printable lecture guide is designed for student use as an in-class resource or study tool. Note: Instructors can request the PowerPoint version of this guide, which can be used as developed or customized.

- *Quizlet Study Set*—Quizlet is an easy-to-use online learning tool built from all the key terms in the textbook. Students can turbo-charge their studying via digital flashcards and other types of study apps, including tests and games. Students are able to listen to audio clips and create their own flashcards. Quizlet is a cross-platform application and can be used on a desktop, tablet, or smartphone.

- *Study Guide*—The Study Guide is available online, and a printable version is available via downloadable PDF chapters for easy self-printing and review. The Study Guide provides several additional learning aids for each chapter and includes the following features:
  - The chapter outline lists the main topic headings for each chapter.
  - The list of questions to answer is provided at the beginning of each chapter, with space included for students to add their own answers. Students can use this feature to help review and study material.
  - The key terms for each chapter are listed, with space provided for students to add definitions for each term. This feature allows students to rehearse key term definitions, aiding in recall and retention.
  - Practice multiple-choice questions with answers can be used for review and self-testing.
  - Active Internet links that relate to the chapter content are organized in a "Cyber-Psychology" section. These links are keyed to the major sections of every chapter. Students can use these links to learn more about the content discussed in the text.

ACKNOWLEDGMENTS

We wish to thank the staff at Academic Media Solutions (AMS) who worked with us to publish this new edition of *Essentials of Psychology*: Daniel C. Luciano, president/founder of AMS, and Victoria Putman of Putman Productions. We appreciate the support and assistance they provided throughout the development and production of this book.

About the Authors

Kenneth S. Bordens (Professor Emeritus of Psychology) received his bachelor of arts degree in psychology from Farleigh Dickinson University (Teaneck, New Jersey, campus) in 1975. He earned a master of arts (1978) and a doctor of philosophy (1979) degree in social psychology from the University of Toledo. After receiving his Ph.D., he accepted a position at Purdue University Fort Wayne, formerly Indiana University-Purdue University Fort Wayne (IPFW), where he taught psychology for 37 years before retiring in 2016. Dr. Bordens's main research interest was psychology and the law. He published several studies on juror and jury decision making in criminal and civil trials. His most recent research focused on stereotyping and prejudice on the Left of the political spectrum. He has co-authored several textbooks in psychology, including *Social Psychology* (5th ed.), *Research Design and Methods: A Process Approach* (10th ed.), *General Psychology* (5th ed.), and *Psychology and the Law: Integrations and Applications* (2nd ed.). Dr. Bordens taught classes on social psychology, child development, research methods, the history of psychology, and introductory psychology during his tenure at Purdue University Fort Wayne.

Josh R. Gerow (1941–2015) began his college training at Rensselaer Polytechnic Institute, where he majored in chemistry. He earned his bachelor of arts in psychology at the University of Buffalo and his Ph.D. in experimental psychology at the University of Tennessee. His graduate area of specialization was developmental psycholinguistics. After teaching for two years at the University of Colorado, Denver, he joined the faculty of Purdue University Fort Wayne, formerly Indiana University-Purdue University Fort Wayne (IPFW), in 1969. Dr. Gerow conducted research and published articles in the field of instructional psychology, focusing on factors that affect performance in the introductory psychology course. During his more than 40 years as a college professor, he taught courses on the psychology of learning, memory, and the history of psychology, as well as his favorite course, general psychology. He brought college-level introductory psychology classes to high school students and made frequent presentations at regional and national conferences on the teaching of psychology. He authored (or co-authored) a large number of editions of introductory psychology textbooks and the supplements that accompany those texts. Dr. Gerow died on December 4, 2015.

Nancy K. Gerow, MS, earned her bachelor of arts degree in psychology from Indiana University and her master of science in psychology from Purdue University. As a personal counselor of college students, she assisted college students with decision making, stress management, short-term therapy, and assessment and referral. She co-authored a text on achieving success in college, focusing on personal and social adjustment issues. She also has prepared ancillary materials for a number of introductory psychology textbooks. Ms. Gerow participated in the field trials for the 5th edition of the *Diagnostic and Statistical Manual of Mental Disorders (DSM-5)*. As a clinician in private practice, Ms. Gerow provides individual, marital, family, and group therapy services. She also provides short-term assessment and counseling services as an employee assistance provider to businesses as well as for members of the military. Under the supervision of a health service provider in psychology (HSPP) psychologist, she has been responsible for testing and assessment in a variety of clinical settings. She is a licensed marriage and family therapist in the states of Indiana and Florida. She is a Clinical Fellow of the American Association of Marriage and Family Therapists and a Life Status member of the American Psychological Association.

Psychology Is in Our Lives

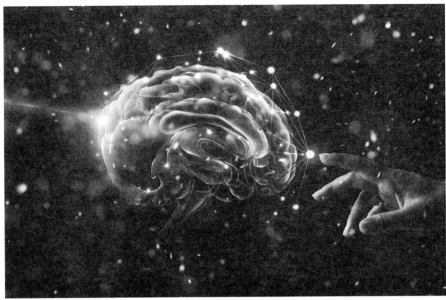

Source: PopTika/Shutterstock

Questions You Will Be Able to Answer

After reading Chapter 1, you should be able to answer the following questions:

- What is the subject matter of psychology?
- What are affect and cognitions?
- Why does psychology qualify as a science?
- In general terms, what are scientific methods?
- What are the typical activities of scientist-practitioners in psychology?
- What are reliability and validity?
- What distinguishes correlational and experimental methods?
- What are the three major variables involved in an experiment?
- What were the contributions of some of the persons who shaped psychology's early years, mentioning in particular, Wundt, James, Watson, Freud, and Rogers?
- For what jobs or careers is the study of psychology a relevant experience?
- What are the three major principles that will appear repeatedly throughout this text?

Preview

Psychology may well be the best class you'll take. After all, it is about you, your family, and your friends. It's about why people think and feel and behave as they do. It's about how all of us find out about the world and how we learn and remember things. It's about facing problems and stress and finding ways to cope. This book will cover all sorts of issues you've wondered about for a long time. It may not answer all of your questions, and it may even raise a few new ones, but it will set you off on a new path of discovery.

This first chapter is necessarily quite general. It seems logical to start off with everyone coming to a general agreement about what psychology is and what psychologists do. In many ways, you can think of this first chapter as an outline, with details to be filled in as we go along. We begin with a standard "textbook" definition of psychology, looking at what it is that psychologists study and why we may call their endeavors scientific. We will take a very brief look at some of the high points of psychology's past, and consider a few of the pioneers who helped shape the discipline as it developed. We will examine some of the careers that are available to psychologists and to people with training in psychology. You will find us constantly reminding you that psychology is a science. To reinforce that notion, we'll take a few pages to examine some of the major methods used in the science of psychology. We end the chapter by listing a few major, over-arching themes or ideas that will guide our study of the science of psychology.

Psychology's Subject Matter: You and Me and More

Psychology—the science that studies behavior and mental processes.

Behavior—what organisms do—their actions and reactions.

Cognitions—mental events, such as beliefs, perceptions, thoughts, ideas, and memories.

We will expand on it throughout the rest of this text, but here is a definition of psychology that we can work with for now: **Psychology** is the science that studies behavior and mental processes. This rather simple definition may not tell us a lot just yet, but it does raise a couple of points worthy of our time.

This definition claims that the subject matter of psychology is behavior and mental processes. Before we get into what it means to say that psychology is a science, let's take a closer look at just what it is that psychologists study.

Psychologists study behavior. **Behavior** is what organisms do—their actions and reactions. The behaviors of organisms are observable and measurable. If we wonder whether a rat will press a lever in some situation, we can put a rat in that situation and watch to see what it does. If we are interested in Jason's ability to draw a circle, we can ask him to draw one and observe his efforts. Observable, measurable behaviors offer an advantage as objects of study. Several observers can agree on the behavior or event being studied. We can agree that the rat pressed the lever (or didn't) and even measure the extent, speed, and force with which it did so. We can agree that Jason correctly drew a circle and not a triangle or an oval. If you were interested in the extent to which violent movies contribute to aggression, you would most likely focus on observable, aggressive behaviors, rather than on how such movies make a viewer feel or think.

Psychologists also study mental processes. There are two kinds of mental processes: cognitions and affect. **Cognitions** are mental events, such as beliefs, perceptions, thoughts, ideas, and memories. Cognitive (cog´-ni-tiv) processes, then, include activities such

Cognitive processes are "intellectual" mental processes, such as perceiving, remembering, or—in this case—reading.

as perceiving, thinking, knowing, deciding, and remembering. For example, if you read a news story on Facebook, what you think about it is a cognitive process, and you may choose to agree or disagree with it. Affect (af´-ekt) is a term that refers to feelings, emotions, or moods. How you feel about the news story would determine your affect regarding that story (e.g., Does it make you angry, happy, or sad?). For just about anything you do or encounter in your world, you will likely have cognitions (thoughts) and affect (feelings). It is important to understand that your thoughts and feelings may or may not relate directly to your behavior. For example, if you read a news story about hungry children, it may make you sad and angry. These feelings might lead you to donate money to a charity to help hungry children or volunteer to help directly. In this case, your affect motivated you to behave in a certain way. On the other hand, just because the story makes you sad and angry, you may not necessarily do anything different behaviorally.

Source: ESB Professional/Shutterstock.

Affect is the term that psychologists use when referring to the mental state related to a person's emotional state or mood, such as happiness.

Here we have a scheme we will encounter repeatedly: the **ABC**s that make up the subject matter of psychology. Psychology is the science that studies **a**ffect, **b**ehavior, and **c**ognition. To say that we understand a person at any given time, we must understand what that person is feeling (A), doing (B), and thinking (C).

Affect (af´-ekt)—a term that refers to feelings, emotions, or moods.

The major difference between behaviors and mental processes is that while behaviors are directly observable, mental processes are not. A person's affect or cognitions have to be inferred from the observation of behaviors. For example, we may infer that someone is sad (an affective state) if we see him sitting slumped over and crying. We may infer that jurors used certain pieces of evidence when coming to their decision (a cognitive process) on the basis of what they tell us in a post-trial interview. Remember, we can observe directly what people are doing (e.g., slumping over, finding a defendant guilty), but we cannot observe directly how they are feeling or thinking (e.g., feeling sad, using certain evidence).

Here's a point often overlooked: Most of the time, psychologists do focus their study on the behaviors and/or the mental processes of their fellow humans. Although unstated in our definition, psychologists often study non-human animals as well. We will see many examples of psychological research that use animals in an effort to help us understand human behaviors or mental processes. At the same time, some psychologists study the behavior and mental activity of animals simply because they find them interesting and worthy of study in their own right.

People in many walks of life can be said to "study behavior and mental processes." Scholars and laypersons alike have studied human nature for centuries. What makes psychology's study unique is its reliance on the methods of science. It is to this issue that we turn now.

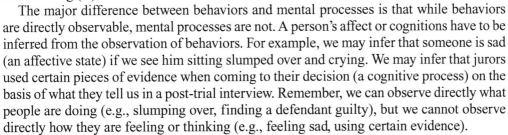

STUDY CHECK

What is the subject matter of psychology?
What are affect and cognitions?

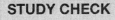

THINKING CRITICALLY

If you want to know how someone really feels, or what someone really thinks about some issue, what are some of the problems that might arise from simply asking them how they feel or what they think?

Psychology: The Science and the Practice

Our beliefs about ourselves and the world in which we live have come from many different sources. Some are formed as a matter of faith (for example, there is a God—or there isn't). Some beliefs come through tradition, passed from generation to generation, accepted because "they say it is so." (For example, you may believe that if you get your feet wet in the winter, you'll catch pneumonia—because that's what your grandmother told you.) Occasionally, our beliefs about the human condition are credited to common sense (for example, "absence makes the heart grow fonder"—but then that same common sense tells us "out of sight, out of mind"). Some of our beliefs derive from art, literature, poetry, and drama (for example, some of our ideas about romantic love may have roots in Shakespeare's *Romeo and Juliet* or the latest song from today's hottest recording star). Although all of these ways of learning about behaviors and mental processes have value, psychologists maintain that there is a better way: by applying the values and methods of science.

Memories of previous biology or chemistry classes notwithstanding, the goal of science is to make the world easier to understand (Mitchell & Jolley, 2001). Scientists do this by generating scientific laws about their subject matter. Simply put, scientific laws are statements about one's subject matter that one believes to be true—not on the basis of faith, tradition, or common sense, but through logical reasoning and observation. A science is a discipline with two characteristics: (1) an organized body of knowledge (published research articles), and (2) the use of scientific methods. How does psychology rate on these two criteria?

Over the years, psychologists have accumulated a great deal of information about the behaviors and mental processes of organisms. Granted, many intriguing questions remain unanswered. Some of the knowledge that psychologists have accumulated about some very important, relevant questions is incomplete and tentative. And not having all the answers can be frustrating, but that is part of the excitement of psychology today—there are still so many things to discover! The truth remains, however, that psychologists have learned a lot, and what they know is reasonably well organized.

Psychology also meets the second requirement of a science because what is known in psychology has been learned through scientific methods—methods that involve observing a phenomenon, formulating hypotheses about it, making more observations, and refining and re-testing hypotheses (Bordens & Abbott, 2018). The scientific method reflects an attitude or an approach to discovery and problem-solving. It is "a process of inquiry, a particular way of thinking," rather than a prescribed set of procedures that must be followed rigorously (Graziano & Raulin, 1993, p. 2). Science involves an attitude of being both skeptical and open-minded about one's work.

When doing science, there might not be specific rules to follow, but there *are* guidelines. The process goes something like this: The scientist (psychologist) makes some observations about her subject matter. For example, she notices that her son and his close friends seem to be doing better in first grade than are most of the other students. On the basis of that preliminary observation, the scientist develops a hypothesis—a tentative explanation of some phenomenon that can be tested and then either accepted or rejected. It is essentially an educated guess about one's subject matter. In our example, the psychologist might hypothesize that the reason that her son and his friends are doing so well in school is because they spent at least two years in a daycare center. In this case, a causal factor (time in daycare) is tentatively linked to behavior (success in first grade).

Science—a discipline with two characteristics: (1) an organized body of knowledge (published research articles), and (2) the use of scientific methods.

Scientific methods—methods that involve observing a phenomenon, formulating hypotheses about it, making more observations, refining and re-testing hypotheses.

Hypothesis—a tentative explanation of some phenomenon that can be tested and then either accepted or rejected.

Source: Brian A. Jackson/Shutterstock.

Some of the beliefs (cognitions) that we acquire about the world, such as "If you get your head wet, you'll catch a cold!" come from tradition, passed on from one generation to another.

No matter how reasonable this hypothesis may sound to the scientist—or to others—it cannot be accepted as an explanation. The hypothesis must be tested under carefully controlled conditions. First, how much time *did* her son and his friends spend in daycare? How will performance in first grade be measured? New observations need to be made.

Let us assume for a moment that the psychologist's son and his friends did indeed spend significantly more time in daycare than did their classmates. Let us assume further that these children performed at a higher level on each of the tests of academic achievement used in this study. It looks as though the psychologist's hypothesis has been confirmed: At least two years of daycare produces superior academic achievement in first grade.

An interesting reality about scientific research is that once a scientist finds evidence supporting her hypothesis, the research process does not stop. In fact, more questions are often raised than are answered, and these new questions serve as a basis for generating new hypotheses and new research. In our example, for instance, are there any other characteristics of those students who did well in first grade other than the fact that they had similar daycare experiences? What factors other than daycare might account for these results? Will the differences in achievement hold up through second grade? Can these results be replicated with any other group of youngsters? What is there about being in daycare that might account for superior academic achievement at any level? Many new hypotheses could be developed and tested. In this way, the acquisition of knowledge becomes an on-going process of trying to refine explanations of behavior and mental processes.

Here is an important point to remember about science, the scientific method, and hypotheses. A scientific hypothesis may be rejected because there is no evidence to support it. On the basis of evidence, a hypothesis may be supported, but it cannot be "proven" as true. No matter how much evidence one finds to support a hypothesis, scientists—always open-minded—realize that new hypotheses may come along that can do a better job of explaining what has been observed. It is important to understand that in true science, there is no such thing as "settled science." Thus, psychologists avoid statements or claims that their research proves something or indicates that the final word on behavior has been written. As an example, evidence—based on some pretty good science of the day—once indicated that stomach ulcers were caused by stress and stress alone. We now understand that many types of ulcers are caused by infection, not stress at all.

The goal of many psychologists is to use scientific methods to learn about their subject matter. But, while psychologists are scientists, most are *scientist-practitioners*. Sometimes these psychologists are called "service providers." This means that they are not so much involved in discovering new laws about behavior and mental processes as they are in applying what is already known. Of those psychologists who are practitioners, most are clinical or counseling psychologists. Their goal is to apply what is known to help people deal with problems that affect their ability to adjust to the demands of their environments, including other people.

Psychological practitioners can be found in many places, not just clinical settings where therapy and treatment are conducted. Even before the dust settled after the World Trade Center collapsed on September 2001, psychologists (and other mental health professionals) were rushing to New York City to try to offer some relief from the pain and suffering of that horrendous trauma (Boss, Beulien, & Wieling, 2003).

Other scientist-practitioners apply psychological principles to situations that arise in the workplace. These are industrial-organizational, or I/O, psychologists. Sports psychologists use what they know about affect, behavior, and cognition to improve the performance of athletes. Educational and school psychologists work to apply what they know about learning and memory, and other cognitive processes to make student-teacher interactions as effective as possible. Other practitioners advise attorneys on how to present arguments in the courtroom or select jurors. Some intervene to reduce ethnic prejudice or to teach others how differing cultural values affect behaviors. Some establish programs to reduce litter or to increase the use of automobile safety belts, while others help people train their pets.

Thus, we can say that, as a discipline, psychology has two inter-related goals: (1) to use scientific methods to understand the behaviors and mental processes of organisms, and (2) to apply that understanding to help solve problems in the real world. The science of psychology and the practice of psychology are not mutually exclusive. Many practitioners in clinical, industrial, or educational settings are also active scientific researchers. And much of the research in psychology originates as a response to problems that arise in the real world.

STUDY CHECK

Why does psychology qualify as a science?
In general terms, what are scientific methods?
What are the typical activities of scientist-practitioners in psychology?

THINKING CRITICALLY

In what ways have you seen psychology applied to problems or issues in your own life?

More on the Scientific Methods of Psychology

Reliability—the consistency, dependability, or repeatability of an observation.

Validity—the extent to which an observation reflects what is actually happening.

Before psychologists can explain what people do (much less why they do it), they first must make reliable and valid observations of just what it is that people do. Reliability is the consistency, dependability, or repeatability of an observation. For observations to be worthwhile, they must be reliable. They must be stable, and a number of people have to agree on the observations under study. If you observe today that Tommy is actively aggressive, but others do not see that aggressiveness, or if he never appears aggressive again, then your observation lacks reliability. A test that indicates today that Rolanda's intelligence is well below average, but next week indicates that she is almost mentally gifted is not a reliable test.

Validity is the extent to which an observation reflects what is actually happening. A test, for example, is said to be valid if it measures what it claims to be measuring. Several observers notice Jamal acting in a very friendly, supportive, caring manner in the presence of members of another racial or ethnic group. The observers conclude that Jamal has little or no prejudice toward that ethnic group. It may be, of course, that Jamal's behaviors were shaped by that particular social situation—and the fact that he knew that he was being watched. He may, in fact, have extreme prejudices toward that group. In such a case, the original observation lacks validity.

Sometimes having good, reliable, valid observations about peoples' affect or cognitions or behaviors is an acceptable end in itself. It may be valuable to know, for example, just how many registered voters intend to vote for a given candidate. It might make a difference if the cafeteria on your campus had reliable and valid information about the food preferences of the student body. How many hours a week, on average, *do* children watch television, and how many hours *do* they spend playing outside? How many times a month *do* most married couples engage in sexual intercourse? How many Iraqi civilians *have* been wounded in the current conflict? Good questions—questions that can be answered with carefully made, reliable, valid observations.

Source: Africa Studio/Shutterstock.

Collecting valid observations about how many people use cell phones while driving is a first step in understanding how cell-phone use relates to automobile accidents.

Ways of Doing Research

Although the range of specific research techniques available to psychologists is vast, in general terms, we can divide methods into two categories: correlational or experimental. **Correlational research** is research involving the search for a relationship between variables that are observed and measured but not manipulated. A *variable* is anything that can take on different values—as opposed to a *constant*, which has but one value. For example, if you were to have 100 people take an intelligence test, do you think everyone would achieve the same score? Of course not! Although some may have the same score, more likely than not there will be a range of different scores. The fact that you would observe different scores in your 100 respondents shows *variability* in intelligence scores.

Correlational research depends on measuring the values of variables and looking for relationships between or among them. It's not all that complicated. For example, if you were interested in the play patterns of boys and girls in a daycare center, you could observe their play times and categorize their behaviors (e.g., being aggressive or helping, playing with others or alone). Correlational methods could then tell you if there were lawful relationships between those variables you observed. You might find that boys tend to engage in aggressive play with others, while girls tend to be non-aggressive and play alone.

This sort of study can be useful in many situations. If it is not possible (or proper) to manipulate (change the value of) a variable of interest, then correlational research is the way to go. For instance, in a study of the relationship between birth defects and alcohol consumption during pregnancy, you surely would not want to encourage pregnant women to drink alcohol—particularly if it were your own hypothesis that doing so would have negative consequences! But you might be able to find women who *did* drink to varying degrees during their pregnancies and use that information to see if it is related to birth defects. Correlational research is often used in the early stages of an investigation just to see if relationships between selected variables do exist. For example, based on the early correlational studies concerning alcohol consumption and birth defects, subsequent experimental research (using animal subjects) might further explore the biological link between alcohol and birth defects. Research that involves the characteristics of people (e.g., age, gender, race, and ethnicity) is correlational by necessity. After all, you cannot manipulate (change) a person's age, gender, race, or ethnicity for research purposes.

Because of the prevalence and importance of correlational research, let's work through an example in some detail. A correlational study of the relationship between talking on a cell phone while driving (variable 1) and frequency of traffic accidents (variable 2) was conducted by Seo and Torabi (2004). Samples of college students from five universities completed a questionnaire including questions about how often they talked on a cell phone while driving and their driving history (accidents or near accidents). Seo and Torabi found a statistically significant relationship (that is, the observed relationship is not likely due to chance) between the frequency of cell phone use while driving and accidents/ near accidents. As expected, the more frequently a participant reported talking on a cell phone while driving the greater the number of accidents/near accidents. Interestingly, they also found a higher accident rate among respondents reporting that they used hands-free phones than handheld phones.

Whenever you encounter correlational research, there are two very important points to keep in mind:

1. No matter how strongly two variables are correlated, one cannot make predictions for individual cases; there always will be exceptions. For example, there is a very strong correlation between high school grades and college grades, but that relationship is not perfect. As you may know from your own experience, some students who do well in high school flunk out of college, while other students who did poorly in high school end up performing very well in college. That is, there are exceptions, even though it is generally true that students who earned good high school grades will tend to earn good college grades.

Correlational research—research involving the search for a relationship between variables that are observed and measured, but not manipulated.

2. No matter how logical it may be, if all you know is that two variables are correlated, you cannot infer a cause-and-effect relationship between them. After all, good high school grades do not *cause* good college grades—they simply are related to each other, or co-related (correlated). If all you know is that there is a correlation between cell-phone use and car accidents, you cannot conclude that cell-phone use actually *causes* accidents, as logical as your argument may be.

Experimental research—
research in which investigators actually manipulate a variable and then look for a relationship between that manipulation and changes in the value of some other variable.

Experimental research is research in which investigators actually manipulate a variable and then look for a relationship between that manipulation and changes in the value of some other variable. Now that is quite a mouthful, but the actual procedures are not that difficult to understand. Say, for example, that a researcher was interested in factors that influence children's willingness to donate candy to needy children. The researcher has one group of children watch a pro-social television program (say an episode of *SpongeBob SquarePants* portraying generosity). At the same time, a second group made up of different children watches a "neutral" show, perhaps a series of standard cartoons. Afterward, all the children are asked to play a game in which part of their winnings is donated to needy children. In this case, the researcher manipulates one variable (the nature of a television show children watched) and measures another (the number of pieces of candy donated in a game) to see if there is a relationship between the two.

When researchers perform an experiment, they are no longer content just to discover that two measured observations are related; they want to be able to claim that, at least to some degree, one *causes* the other. To determine if such a claim can be made, researchers manipulate the values of one variable to see if those manipulations cause a measurable change in the values of another variable. An **independent variable** is a variable that the experimenter manipulates. The experimenter determines its value, and nothing the participant in the experiment does will affect its value. In our previous example, the type of show children watched is the independent variable. It is important to understand that it was the experimenter who determined which show a child watched. The experimenter did not simply ask parents what types of shows their children watched. Instead, the researcher actually assigned children to watch either a pro-social or neutral show. On the other hand, a **dependent variable** is a variable providing a measure of the participants' behavior. In the previous example, the number of pieces of candy children donated is the dependent variable. Because the dependent variable is the measure of what a research participant does, it is sometimes referred to as a *dependent measure*. In general, an experimental hypothesis is that the values of the dependent variable will, indeed, *depend* upon the independent variable manipulation the participants received.

Independent variable—a variable that the experimenter manipulates.

Dependent variable—a variable providing a measure of the participants' behavior.

Experimental group—a group of participants exposed to some value of the independent variable.

In its simplest form, an experiment has two groups of participants: an experimental group and a control group. The **experimental group** is a group of participants exposed to some value of the independent variable. For example, in an experiment on the effects of alcohol on the driving ability of college students, 10 students in the experimental group could be given an amount of alcohol equivalent to three mixed drinks. We ask these students to then "drive" a course using a driving simulator—like a video game. We discover that these students average seven accidents in a 15-minute testing session. Is there any way we can claim that the alcohol they drank before driving had anything at all to do with those accidents? No, not really. Why not? There are lots of reasons. For one thing, these 10 students might be among the worst drivers ever and be prone to accidents whether they drink or not. To show that it was the alcohol causing the poor performance, you need a second group of students—with comparable driving skills—who receive a nonalcoholic beverage that tastes exactly like the alcoholic one. Participants in this group comprise the control group. In general terms, a **control group** is a group of participants receiving a zero level of the independent variable. You may think of the control group as the baseline against which the performance of the experimental group is judged. Even in the simplest of experiments, one must have at least two levels of the independent variable, where one will be zero.

Control group—a group of participants receiving a zero level of the independent variable.

Now let's work through an example, just to be sure we have our terminology straight. Across the United States, there are campaigns to discourage people from texting while they drive. These campaigns rest on the assumption that texting distracts drivers and will ultimately lead to more traffic accidents. Is there evidence to back up this assumption? An experiment by Bendak (2015) helps answer this question. Bendak had participants drive in a driving simulator under one of two conditions. In one condition, participants navigated the simulated course while sending text messages. In the other condition, participants navigated the same course while not sending text messages. Bendak measured the number of crashes that occurred under these two conditions. Before we look at the results, can you identify the independent and dependent variables and the experimental and control conditions? If you said that the independent variable is whether the participant drove while texting or not, you are correct! If you said that the number of crashes is the dependent variable, you also are correct. If you said that driving while texting is the experimental group and driving while not texting is the control group, you are once again correct. Bendak found that there were five times as many crashes when participants drove while texting than when not texting. So, it might be a good idea not to text while driving.

Before we get too carried away, there is yet one more type of variable to consider. An **extraneous variable** is a factor, other than the independent variable, that can influence the dependent variable of an experiment. To conclude that changes in the dependent variable are caused by the manipulations of the independent variable, extraneous variables need to be controlled for or eliminated. Such factors should be considered and dealt with before an experiment begins. In Bendak's study, for example, all participants were allowed to practice on the driving simulator for the same amount of time before beginning the experiment, the simulated driving test was the same for all participants in all conditions, and the same simulator was used for all participants. So, we can safely rule those variables out as possible factors in the number of crashes observed in the two conditions.

Extraneous variable—a factor, other than the independent variable, that can influence the dependent variable of an experiment.

Source: Monkey Business Images/Shutterstock.

An experiment can support or refute the hypothesis that taking a "study skills" course will improve classroom performance.

Distinguishing Science from Pseudoscience

We have taken great pains to point out that psychology is a science because it adheres to the rules and methods employed by a science to acquire knowledge. Does this mean that everything you encounter relating to psychology and its phenomena is based on careful scientific scrutiny? Unfortunately, the answer to this question is "no." There is a great deal of dross out there ("dross" means "worthless, commonplace, or trivial" matters), especially in the popular media that is not based on careful scientific research. For example, is it really possible that you will experience greater physical and psychological well-being if you tape a patch to the bottom of your foot at night to draw out toxins from the body? Will you actually get more and higher quality sleep if you take a pill with a special blend of herbs and enzymes before you go to bed? And, can autistic children learn to communicate effectively through a "facilitator"? Does moving your eyes back and forth rapidly during therapy help you get better faster? Many of the claims made in commercials and by seemingly legitimate psychologists are simply false because they are based on pseudoscientific claims and not on carefully conducted scientific studies.

What exactly is *pseudoscience*? Well, the term literally translates to "false science." However, we really need a more formal definition to better understand exactly what this means. One definition that we particularly like states that "pseudoscience is [a] set of ideas based on theories put forth as scientific when they are not scientific" (Carrol, 2006). Scott Lilienfeld (2005) enumerates several characteristics that comprise pseudoscience. For example, in pseudoscience disconfirmed ideas are not adjusted based on new information. The burden of proof to falsify a claim is shifted to the critic from the person making the claim. Claims are largely based on anecdotal evidence (e.g., My aunt sleeps better after wearing a magnetic bracelet), and published findings are not reviewed by experts before publication. Additionally, impressive-sounding jargon is often used to give credibility to dubious claims. It is important to understand that not every instance of pseudoscience will have all of Lilienfeld's characteristics. However, the more of them present, the more likely a claim or finding is the product of pseudoscience.

Why is it important for you to understand the difference between a true science and pseudoscience? The answer is relatively simple. Understanding this distinction can help you better critically analyze what appear to be scientific claims made in sales pitches, on your newsfeed, or in an article you might read online. By critically thinking about claims made in these and other sources, you will be in a better position to separate the gold from the dross and make more informed decisions about your world. Also, it can possibly save you money! You might not shell out your hard-earned money on those pads for the bottoms of your feet or that magnetic bracelet. How can you distinguish real science from pseudoscience? It takes work. However, a place to start is with the information in **Table 1.1**, which presents some clues you can use to distinguish science from pseudoscience.

TABLE 1.1 Real Science versus Pseudoscience

Real Science	Pseudoscience
Findings published in scientific, peer-reviewed journals.	Findings published in publications for the general public that do not involve peer review.
Methods used in experiments must be specified clearly, and results must be reproducible.	Vague descriptions of methods are provided, and results cannot be easily reproduced.
Failures in prediction are scrutinized carefully.	Failures are downplayed, rationalized away, hidden, ignored or avoided.
With time, more and more is learned about a phenomenon being studied.	Little, if any, progress, is made over time with respect to a phenomenon or claim.
Persuasion is based on scientific evidence, and old ideas are discarded when they are shown to be incorrect.	Persuasion is often through belief or faith. Conversion is sought rather than convincing others with evidence. Ideas are adhered to, regardless of conflicting evidence.
No advocacy of unproven products or claims.	Person making claim or advocating product likely to make money based on unproven claims or products.

Based on Corker (2001).

STUDY CHECK

What are reliability and validity?
What distinguishes correlational and experimental methods?
What are the three major variables involved in an experiment?

THINKING CRITICALLY

A TV ad tells you that "Four out of five doctors surveyed preferred Brand X medicine for the treatment of backache." Is Brand X *necessarily* the best for treating back pain? Why or why not? What uncontrolled variables might be reflected in this claim?

Where Psychology Has Been—A Brief History

The questions and concerns of modern psychology are ancient. Long before there were psychologists, people had wondered about the affect, the cognitions, and the behaviors of others and themselves. "Why do I *feel* this way?" "I wonder what he is *thinking* about right now?" "Why did they *do* that?" For centuries, dealing with such issues fell to philosophers—and to theologians—who struggled to understand human nature.

By the late 1800s, scientists had made major strides in explaining how the human body works. Philosophers were discussing the nature of human consciousness, and the qualities and origins of mental life. The stage had been set for someone trained in philosophy and in science, for someone with a burning desire to know more about the human mind, about consciousness, to begin a new science, psychology.

That someone was Wilhelm Wundt. Wundt had been trained to practice medicine, was familiar with the methods of science, and also held an academic position in philosophy. In 1879, Wilhelm Wundt realized his life-long dream of opening a psychology laboratory (at the University of Leipzig in Germany) to use scientific methods to try to understand human mental processes. His laboratory studied many of the topics we will study in this text: sensation, perception, word-associations, and emotions. The over-riding goal of Wundt's laboratory was to understand the structure of the human mind. This approach to psychology became known as *structuralism*. What are the elements of thought? (In the same sense that chemists of that day were seeking to list all the chemical elements.) How are the elements of the mind related to each other? How do feelings become associated with some words, but not to others? These were all questions addressed by Wundt and other early psychologists. Psychology as a separate science was under way.

Wundt's laboratory was an exciting place. He had, after all, just begun a brand-new science—and called it psychology. His lab attracted many students from all over Europe and the United States. One American who visited Wundt at his laboratory was William James, a Harvard University philosophy professor. He was most impressed with what he saw there. He was convinced that mental processes *could* be studied with scientific methods. He was not convinced, however, that Wundt was asking the right questions. James argued that it is not the *structure* of human consciousness that matters; it is the *function* of human conscious that psychology should take as its focus. This approach is known as *functionalism*. Drawing largely from Charles Darwin, James saw mental life—consciousness—as a monumental advantage that humans have over all other species. Humans are, after all, far from being the fastest or the strongest of the animals populating the planet, but my how humans have managed to survive and thrive. It is because of their intellect, their minds, their cognitive abilities. He suggested that we should care less about the structure of the mind and more about how the mind functions to help us get along. James never professed to be a psychologist, but his approach to the study of mental life found favor at American universities, and many psychology laboratories sprung up—all using scientific methods to study the human mind.

By the early 1900s, the center of the science of psychology had moved from Europe to the United States. Attracted by this new science, John B. Watson left his South Carolina home to travel to Chicago to study this new science of the mind. He soon was frustrated and disappointed. Watson (1913) began to argue that if psychology ever hoped to be a mature, productive science, it had to give up its preoccupation with consciousness and mental life and concentrate instead on events that could be observed and measured, *behaviors*. Watson's argument was convincing. For nearly fifty years (roughly 1920–1970), psychology was defined simply as "the science of behavior." But mental processes, affect and cognitions, were too interesting, and too important to be ignored for long. By the 1970s, the definition of psychology became what it is today, the science of behavior and mental processes.

Early in the twentieth century, as American scientific psychology flourished, a Viennese physician, Sigmund Freud became intrigued with what were then called "nervous disorders." He was struck by how little was known about these disorders and decided to specialize in the diagnosis and treatment of nervous disorders—a discipline now called

Sigmund Freud (1865–1939)

Everett Historical/Shutterstock.

psychiatry. Freud declared that we are often subject to forces of which we are not aware. Our feelings, behaviors, and thoughts (our A, B, and C, again) are often under the influence of the *unconscious mind*, wrote Freud, and many of our behaviors are expressions of instinctive strivings. Freud's views became known as *psychoanalytic psychology*, and we shall encounter Freud time and again in the chapters that follow.

In many respects, *humanistic psychology* arose as a reaction against both Watson's behaviorism and Freud's psychoanalysis. The leaders of this approach were Carl Rogers and Abraham Maslow. Humanistic psychology takes the position that the individual, the *self*, should be the focus of psychology. Matters such as caring, intention, love, hate, and will are worthy of scientific investigation. Humanists believe that psychology should try to understand personal growth and achievement—not just instincts and the influence of environmental forces.

Please understand that this list of psychologists who helped shape the discipline since Wilhelm Wundt opened that first psychology laboratory in 1879 is only provided as a small glimpse of psychology's past. We will find many other classic contributions as we move through the rest of this text. It is also important to note that although a vast majority of the early pioneers of psychology were men, women also played an important role. An overview of the role of some pioneering women and minorities in psychology is provided in our Focus on Diversity section.

STUDY CHECK

What were the contributions of some of the persons who shaped psychology's early years, mentioning, in particular, Wundt, James, Watson, Freud, and Rogers?

THINKING CRITICALLY

Suppose that Wilhelm Wundt, William James, John Watson, and Sigmund Freud met by chance on a train. What do you think they might have talked about? On what would they have agreed, and on what would they have disagreed?

Pioneering Women and Minorities in Psychology

A reading of our brief sketch of psychology's past might give the impression that the only pioneers who mattered were white males. Not so. In truth, because of stereotypes and prejudice, the major players in psychology's early years *were* white males. In the later 1800s and early 1900s, it was very difficult for women or minorities to get into college, much less graduate school programs. But against great odds, many did, and their contributions were significant. Francis Sumner was the first African American to earn a Ph.D. in psychology—from Clark University in 1920. Perhaps his greatest influence was expanding opportunities for more young black students to pursue graduate training. Kenneth Clark and his wife, Mamie, published groundbreaking research on the development of self-esteem and self-perceptions of young children, both black and white (Clark & Clark, 1939). Although his college career was interrupted by military service, *Robert Guthrie* finally earned his Ph.D. in psychology in 1970. Six years later he published, *Even the rat was white: A historical view of psychology* (Guthrie, 1976/2004). Few texts have had such an impact on so many students of color. It has been hailed as an "excellent piece of historiography that offers a good, hard look at racism in the development of psychology" (Cross, Parham, & Helms, 1998). Charles H. Turner (1867–1923) was another pioneering African American. Turner received his Ph.D. in Zoology from the University of Chicago in 1906. Because of racism, Turner was denied a position at a university. So, he took a job at a small, underfunded African American high school in Georgia. Although Turner did not receive his Ph.D. in psychology, he conducted some of the earliest studies on perception and learning in insects. Among his discoveries were that bees saw patterns and color, that experience could modify "instinctive" behaviors, and that ants were capable of complex learning.

The first woman to earn a Ph.D. in psychology was *Margaret Floy Washburn*. She was instrumental in opening psychology to the study of nonhuman animals, publishing *The Animal Mind* in 1908. This text addressed questions of animal consciousness and intelligence. *Mary Calkins* was a student of William James, although Harvard would not allow her to officially enroll in classes (nor would they award her a Ph.D., for which she had met all the requirements). Calkins went on to do significant research on human learning and memory, and, in 1905, was the first woman elected president of the American Psychological Association. *Christine Ladd-Franklin* received her Ph.D. from Johns Hopkins University forty years after it had been earned and the university lifted its ban on awarding advanced degrees to women. Among other contributions, she authored an influential theory on how humans perceive color. *Mary Ainsworth* received her Ph.D. from the University of Toronto in 1939. Her best-known work is on the attachments—and the sense of security—that develop between infants and those who care for them. *Anne Anastasi* earned her Ph.D. (in just two years) from Columbia University, in 1930. She was interested in how culture and experience affect one's intellectual development. Published in 1954, her text *Psychological Testing* is a classic. There were many other pioneering women in the early days of psychology. For example, Florence Mateer who conducted the first experiment in the United States on what we now call classical conditioning. Her classmate, Elizabeth Dooley, received a Ph.D. in clinical psychology and became the first woman to head Saint Elizabeth's Hospital in Washington, D.C.

Careers in Psychology Today—Psychology in Your Career

Psychology has come a long way since those few students gathered around Wilhelm Wundt in his laboratory back in the late 1800s. At the end of the twentieth century, there were over 500,000 psychologists at work in the world, and approximately 166,000 were employed in the United States in 2017 (Bureau of Labor Statistics, 2018b). The Bureau of Labor Statistics projects a 14 percent growth in job opportunities in psychology between 2016 and 2018. Organized in 1892, the American Psychological Association (APA) is the oldest professional organization of psychologists. The APA claims about 175,000 members and lists 54 divisions, including General Psychology, Teaching of Psychology, Military Psychology, Psychotherapy, Health Psychology, International Psychology, Aesthetics and the Arts, and the like, to which its members may belong (American Psychological Association, 2018). The Association for Psychological Science (APS), formed in 1988, currently has approximately 30,000 members dedicated to the advancement of scientific psychology (Association for Psychological Science, 2018). In addition to these general national organizations, there are also a number of specialized professional organizations, such as the Society for Personality and Social Psychology (SPSP) and the Society for Research in Child Development (SRCD).

There are many jobs or careers for which a knowledge of psychology is a real benefit. Nursing is just one.

Most careers in psychology require a graduate degree. In fact, in most states, a person cannot publicly claim to be "a psychologist" unless he or she has an earned doctorate degree. That certainly does not mean that decent, fulfilling jobs are available only to persons with a Ph.D. in psychology—to the contrary.

With a baccalaureate or an associate degree, there are several career options within psychology, but they are likely to be in supportive roles. You will not be able to open your own office as a psychotherapist, but you may find relevant employment in a psychological clinic, rehabilitation center, nursing home, or hospital. You may not get a job as a school psychologist, but there are several places within most school systems that would love to have someone with any background in psychology. You may not get hired as an industrial/organizational psychologist, but most human resources offices of most companies look for people with training in psychology.

As with most generalizations, it is not fair to divide careers in psychology into only specialty areas of "researcher" and "practitioner." As we said earlier, many psychologists in applied settings engage in scientific research, and many research psychologists become involved in projects that are applied or practical in nature. Still, for the sake of generating a list of subfields in psychology, let's start with those that are *primarily* scientific/research oriented and then move to those that are *primarily* applied or practical in focus.

Scientific/Research Areas in Psychology

- *Cognitive psychologists* study how people perceive the world and form memories of their experiences. They do research on matters such as thinking, problem-solving, language development, and intelligence.
- *Physiological psychologists* (sometimes *neuropsychologists*) focus on the biological organism, filled with tissue, fibers, nerves, and chemicals that underlie all of our thoughts, feelings, and behaviors.
- *Social psychologists* look at how a person's psychological functioning is influenced by others. They are concerned about people as they really live, as social organisms in a world of others.

- *Health psychologists* are concerned with how psychological processes influence physical health, and vice versa, how one's physical health influences one's affect, behavior, and cognition.
- *Developmental psychologists* study the psychological development of the individual throughout the life span, looking for milestones of development at all age levels.
- *Psychometric psychologists* explore how best to measure the subtleties of psychological functioning, developing and evaluating psychological tests and devising ways to analyze experimental and correlational data.

Applied/Practitioner Areas in Psychology

- *Industrial/organizational psychologists* aim to improve both the quality of work life and worker productivity, dealing with issues such as personnel selection, training, and motivation.
- *Rehabilitation psychologists* tend to work with persons with disabilities, both physical and mental, in an effort to help such people function at the best possible level.
- *Educational, or instructional, psychologists* apply psychological principles to the processes of teaching and learning in an effort to maximize the efficiency of both.
- *Clinical psychologists* have a Ph.D. in psychology from a program that provides practical, applied experience in therapeutic techniques, as well as research. Clinicians complete a one-year internship, usually at a mental health center or psychiatric hospital, and have extensive training in psychological testing and assessment. Some clinical psychologists have a Psy.D. (pronounced "sigh-dee"), which is a Doctor of Psychology, rather than the Doctor of Philosophy degree. Psy.D. degree programs take as long to complete as Ph.D. programs, but tend to emphasize more practical, clinical work.
- *Counseling psychologists* usually have a Ph.D. in psychology. The focus of study (and required one-year internship) is generally with patients with less severe psychological problems. For instance, rather than spending an internship in a psychiatric hospital, a counseling psychologist is more likely to spend time at a university's counseling center.
- *Licensed professional counselors* usually have a degree in psychology, marriage and family therapy, or education at the Master's level, and have met state requirements for a license to practice psychotherapy. Counselors are found in schools and in private practice; they also work in mental health settings, specializing in family counseling, marriage counseling, and drug abuse counseling.
- *Occupational therapists* usually have a master's degree (less frequently, a bachelor's degree) in occupational therapy, which includes many psychology classes and internship training in aiding the psychologically and physically handicapped.
- *Psychiatric nurses* often work in mental hospitals and clinics. In addition to their R.N. degree, psychiatric nurses have training in the care of mentally ill patients.
- *Pastoral counseling* is a specialty of those with a religious background and a master's degree in psychology or educational counseling.
- *Mental health technicians* usually have an associate degree in mental health technology (MHT). MHT graduates seldom provide unsupervised therapy, but they may be involved in the delivery of many mental health services.
- *Psychiatry* is a specialty area in medicine. In addition to work required for the M.D., the psychiatrist does a psychiatric internship (usually one year) and a psychiatric residency (usually three years) in a hospital where psychological disorders are treated. A psychiatrist is permitted to use biomedical treatments.

Even if you pursue a career in some area not directly related to psychology, you will find that training in psychology is relevant for nearly *every* job you can imagine. Think about it: Psychology seeks to understand feelings, beliefs, and behaviors. For what position is even a basic understanding of such matters not a relevant skill or talent? Psychology may be most valuable for careers in which you would interact with others—as clients, customers, or fellow workers. And no matter what your chosen line of work, the better you can understand yourself, your own affect, cognitions, and behaviors, the better off you will be.

The workplace today is significantly different from what it was when your parents—much less your grandparents—entered the world of work. Manufacturing jobs, or work that requires sitting or standing alone in assembly lines, are becoming fewer and fewer. Most jobs today are "service industry" positions and require an interaction with (servicing) the public (customer). They are positions that require active listening, tact, interpersonal communication skills, and empathy. In short, they require good psychology.

The workplace today also requires self-understanding, flexibility, and stress management. Seldom can a young adult enter the workforce with any reasonable expectation of retiring in the same position at the same company. In many companies, large and small, *flextime* allows workers to schedule their work shifts to accommodate personal needs—at least up to a point. Job-sharing is becoming a recognized way for employers to keep valued workers who do not want full-time employment. The nature of one's job can change. Companies change: Some expand; some downsize. Being open and ready for change is a powerful asset—as is being open to retraining.

STUDY CHECK

For what jobs or careers is the study of psychology a relevant experience?

THINKING CRITICALLY

Generate a list of 10 jobs or occupations, none of them as "psychologist," "therapist," or "counselor," in which the top 5 are heavily involved in matters psychological and the bottom 5 have virtually no relation to psychology.

Some Key Principles to Guide Us

Over the years, a few over-arching principles have emerged that seem to touch upon nearly every area of psychological investigation. If you get these points firmly in mind now, at the start, you will see them again and again as you read on.

1. ***Explanations in psychology often involve INTERACTIONS.*** This is another way of saying that nothing is simple. In case after case, we find that a psychological explanation involves the interaction of powerful underlying forces. How much of our identity (our affect, behaviors, and cognitions) is the result of inheritance, or our biological *nature*? How much of our identity reflects the influences of the environment and our experiences with it, or our *nurture*? Is intelligence inherited (nature) or the result of experience with the environment (nurture)? Is aggressiveness inborn (part of one's nature), or is it learned (an aspect of one's nurture)? Does alcoholism reflect a person's innate nature, or is it a learned reaction to events in the environment? Why do some people react to stress by becoming depressed, while others develop physical symptoms, and yet others seem not to be bothered?

The position that psychologists take is that most behaviors and mental processes result from the interaction of both inherited predispositions and environmental influences. That is, a psychological characteristic is not the result of either heredity or experience, but reflects the interaction of both. "For all psychological characteristics, inheritance sets limits on, or sets a range of potentials for, development. Environment determines how near the individual comes to developing those potentials" (Kimble, 1989, p. 493).

Another case of interaction that we'll encounter later is that between a person's internal dispositions, or personality, and the situation in which that person finds himself or herself. Which determines what a person will do, the situation, or personality? Both. They interact. For example, Bob may be a very out-going, extroverted, sociable sort of person. It's just the way he is. But it is easy to imagine situations (surrounded by "important," powerful employers, perhaps) in which Bob may act far more reserved and less social.

2. *There are individual differences*. No two people are exactly alike. This is psychology's most common and well-documented observation. Given the diversity of genetic make-ups and environments—which include social and cultural pressures—it is not surprising that people can be so different from one another. Not only is each organism unique, but also no organism is exactly the same from one point in time to another. You are not the same person today that you were yesterday. Learning and experience have changed you, probably not in any great, significant way, but what may have been true of you yesterday may not be true of you today. Do you see the complication this causes for the science of psychology? Because of the variability that exists among people, virtually all psychological laws are statements made "in general, in the long run, and more often than not."

3. *Our experience of the world often matters more than what is in the world*. What we perceive and what we remember are surely dependent upon events as they occurred. But, as we shall see, they are also influenced by many previous experiences as well. The main idea here is that, as active agents in the world, we each select, attend to, interpret and remember different aspects of the same world of events. That is, our view of the world comprises two forms of reality: objective and subjective. *Objective reality* is what is actually there. For example, when a crime occurs, certain events take place: There is a perpetrator, some incident occurs in a specific way (e.g., a robbery), and there are consequences of that action (e.g., stolen money, personal injury, and the like). Your *experience* of these objective events comprises *subjective reality*. Point of view, personal expectations and prejudices, stress levels, and other factors determine what aspects of any event are processed and stored in memory. This is why eyewitness accounts of a crime so often differ, sometimes drastically. Witnesses construct their own versions of subjective reality that becomes, for them, "what happened." More often than not, it is one's subjective reality that determines one's reactions and behaviors.

STUDY CHECK

What are the three major principles that will appear repeatedly throughout this text?

THINKING CRITICALLY

Granted that scientific laws in psychology are made "in the long run" and "in general," how might you proceed if you really wanted to understand one individual and make a prediction about that person's behaviors in a given situation?

What is the subject matter of psychology?

Psychologists study the behavior and mental processes of organisms (human and non-human), where mental processes are categorized as affect and cognitions.

What are affect and cognitions?

In psychology, "affect" refers to feelings, moods, and emotional states, whereas cognitions are understood to be ideas, beliefs, perceptions, knowledge, and understanding. You may know that a high-fiber cereal is good for you (a cognition), but you may hate the taste of such a cereal (affect). Sometimes your emotions (affect) may be so powerful that you find it difficult to express those feelings in words (a cognitive process).

Why does psychology qualify as a science?

Psychology is a science because it meets the two defining conditions: (a) an organized body of knowledge and (b) the application of scientific methods.

In general terms, what are scientific methods?

Not so much a list of rules, scientific methods reflect an attitude to discovery and problem-solving. Science involves observing, forming hypotheses, testing hypotheses and observing some more, being both skeptical and open-minded.

What are the typical activities of scientist-practitioners in psychology?

Scientist-practitioners take present knowledge—as incomplete and possibly flawed as it may be—and apply that knowledge in the real world in attempts to solve real-world problems. Many are clinical or counseling psychologists, helping people deal with personal problems, but psychological service providers can be found in many other settings, including law, sports, education, business, and industry.

What are reliability and validity?

An observation, measurement, or event is reliable if it is consistent, repeatable, or stable. It is said to be valid if it truly reflects what it claims to be observing or measuring.

What distinguishes correlational and experimental methods?

Correlational methods seek reliable relationships between measured observations. If two variables are correlated, one can be used to predict the other. High school grades can be used to predict college grades, for instance. Predictability will never be perfect, however, because exceptions are always present. Importantly, no matter how well two variables may be correlated, we cannot reach any cause-and-effect conclusions about them. Experimental methods do allow for cause-and-effect conclusions. If an experiment is well done, it may be said that changes in the independent variable have caused measured changes in the dependent variable.

What are the three major variables involved in an experiment?

Your hypothesis is that learning is enhanced by the use of audio-visual (AV) aids. You have three third-grade classes. One gets all the AV aids you can find. A second gets videotapes and movies, while the third gets no AV aids. You have manipulated the amount of AV aids; therefore, it is the independent variable. After six weeks of instruction, the three classes are given a test, and you find that the first class gets the best (average) score, while the third class gets the worst score. You have measured learning with a test; the test scores, then, are the dependent variable. In order to conclude that the AV aid differences caused the measured differences in test scores, you have to show that you have eliminated or controlled all extraneous variables—any other events (like differences in the skill of the teachers involved) that might have produced the differences in test scores.

What were the contributions of some of the persons who shaped psychology's early years, mentioning, in particular, Wundt, James, Watson, Freud, and Rogers?

We can claim that the science of psychology began in 1879 when Wundt opened the first psychology laboratory at Leipzig University. He was most interested in how best to describe the structure of the human mind or consciousness. Harvard philosopher, William James, argued that psychology should focus on the function of consciousness in helping organisms survive and thrive, not the structure of the mind. John Watson believed that psychology should give up the study of consciousness altogether and focus on that which was observable—behavior. Sigmund Freud, the father of modern psychiatry, became interested in nervous disorders and claimed that the unconscious mind and instinctive forces could explain a great deal of a person's actions and reactions. Carl Rogers believed that psychology's main concern should be the self, one's perception of one's self, and personal growth. In the early years of psychology, it was very difficult for minority students and women to gain access to graduate education. Still, many did, and they provided significant contributions to the emerging science of psychology.

For what jobs or careers is the study of psychology a relevant experience?

The study of psychology will surely be required for anyone wanting a job as a scientist-practitioner, either in a clinical setting, an educational setting, or an industrial or organizational setting. One could also argue the case that the study of psychology is relevant for every job or career imaginable—particularly for those that involve interacting with others.

What are the three major principles that will appear repeatedly throughout this text?

Some findings in psychology are so common, so overarching that they may be referred to as key principles. Three such major ideas are: (1) Many explanations of affect, behaviors, and cognitions involve interactions (e.g., between one's nature and one's nurture, between one's personality and the situation in which one happens to be). (2) Making specific predictions for individuals is difficult because in so many ways, no two persons are alike. Moreover, no one person is exactly the same over two points in time. (3) Objective reality (what really happened in the world) is often much less important than subjective reality (one's experience of what happened, flavored by beliefs and values already stored in memory).

Key Terms

Psychology (p. 2)
Behavior (p. 2)
Cognitions (p. 2)
Affect (af´-ekt) (p. 3)
Science (p. 4)
Scientific methods (p. 4)
Hypothesis (p. 4)
Reliability (p. 6)

Validity (p. 6)
Correlational research (p. 7)
Experimental research (p. 8)
Independent variable (p. 8)
Dependent variable (p. 8)
Experimental group (p. 8)
Control group (p. 8)
Extraneous variable (p. 9)

The Biological Foundations of Behavior

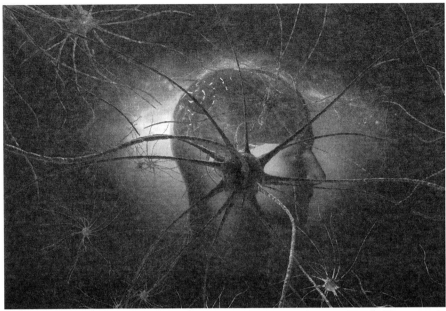

Source: vitstudio/Shutterstock.

Questions You Will Be Able to Answer

After reading Chapter 2, you should be able to answer the following questions:

- What are the major parts of a neuron?
- What is myelin, and what functions does it serve?
- What is the nature of a neural impulse?
- What is the all-or-none principle, and what are neural thresholds?
- What is the synapse, and in general terms, what happens there?
- What are the major divisions of the human nervous systems, and what do they do?
- What is the function of the endocrine system in general and the pituitary gland, thyroid gland, and adrenal glands in particular?
- What are sensory neurons, motor neurons, and interneurons?
- What is the basic structure of the spinal cord, and what are its two functions?
- Where are the medulla and the pons, and what do they do?
- What is meant by cross laterality?
- What are the major functions of the cerebellum and the reticular formation?

- What are the basal ganglia, and what is their relation to Parkinson's disease?
- What are the major structures of the limbic system, and what are their functions?
- What are the functions of the thalamus, and where is it located?
- What is the location of each of the four lobes of the cerebral cortex?
- What are the functions of the sensory areas, the motor areas, and the association areas of the cortex?
- What is the split-brain procedure, and what has been learned from it?

Preview

As you first look through this chapter, it may look a lot more like biology than what you expected in a psychology text. Perhaps it does, but here is the point: All of your behaviors, from the simple blink of an eye to typing a text on your phone; every emotion you have ever experienced, from mild annoyance to extreme fear; your every thought, from the trivial to the profound—all of these can be reduced to molecules of chemicals racing in and out of the tiny cells that comprise your nervous system.

Every day, a huge array of sights, sounds, smells, tastes, and tactile (touch) stimuli bombard you. Some go unnoticed; some are ignored; some elicit a response on your part. Most of the time, we take these reactions for granted. Now, they are the focus of this chapter. The processes of getting information to and from the brain (and other parts of your body) involve a beautifully complex set of actions on a cellular level.

We will take a building-block approach to this discussion of the biological underpinnings of psychological functioning and behavior. We will begin by considering the structures and functions of the individual nerve cell. As remarkable as these microscopically tiny cells are, they would have little impact without their ability to pass information from one part of the body to another in nerve fibers. We will see that nerve cells communicate with one another through a remarkable set of chemical actions. Before we go on, we will survey how scientists organize their discussion of nervous systems, and we will briefly examine a system of glands and hormones that can significantly affect psychological functioning—the endocrine system.

Then, we can put together what we have been discussing into the truly complex structures of the central nervous system, or the CNS. The CNS is composed of the spinal cord and the brain. In our discussion of the spinal cord, we see the first indication of how stimuli from the environment produce behaviors—simple reflexive reactions.

Then, there is the brain. No more complex structure exists in nature than the human brain. It is in the brain that conscious, voluntary actions begin, emotions are experienced, and cognitions are formed, manipulated, and stored. Because of the brain's complexity, it is necessary to study its structures and their functions one at a time. Although we will examine the parts of the brain one at a time, we must keep in mind that all of these structures are part of an integrated, unified system in which all the parts work together and influence one another in complex ways.

Neurons—The Building Blocks of the Nervous System

Neuron—a microscopically small cell that transmits information—in the form of neural impulses—from one part of the body to another.

Our exploration of the nervous system begins with the nerve cell, or neuron. A neuron is a microscopically small cell that transmits information—in the form of neural impulses—from one part of the body to another. Neurons were not recognized as separate structures until around the end of the 19th century. To underscore how small neurons are, consider that there are approximately *125 million* light-sensitive neurons that line the back of each of your eyes, an estimated *1 billion* neurons in your spinal cord, and about *100 billion* neurons

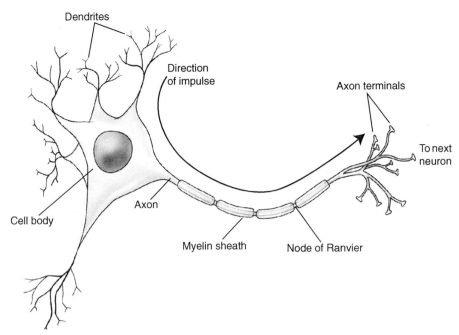

FIGURE 2.1 The Neuron

The main structures of the neuron are the dendrites, the cell body, and the axon. The dendrites receive neural impulses from other neurons; the soma regulates neuronal functions; and the axon conveys signals to other neurons, skeletal muscles, or internal organs. When a neuron receives sufficient stimulation from other neurons, it transmits an electrical-chemical neural impulse along its entire axon.

in your brain (Zillmer & Spiers, 2001). Add to these staggering numbers that a single neuron may, on average, establish 10,000 connections with other neurons (Beatty, 1995).

Even though, much like snowflakes, no two neurons are exactly alike, there are some commonalities among neurons. **Figure 2.1** illustrates these shared features.

All neurons have a **cell body**, the largest concentration of mass in the neuron, containing the nucleus of the cell and other structures necessary for the neuron's life. Protruding from a neuron's cell body are several tentacle-like structures, called dendrites, and one particularly long structure called the axon. Typically, a **dendrite** is the part of a neuron reaching out to receive messages, or neural impulses, from nearby neurons. Also extending from the cell body is an **axon,** the part of a neuron that sends messages along its length to other neurons, muscles, or glands. Some axons are quite long—as long as two to three feet in the spinal cord, whereas others are microscopic (such as those in your brain). Within a neuron, impulses go *from dendrite to cell body to axon*, and most of the distance traveled is along the axon.

The neuron in Figure 2.1 has a feature not found on all neurons. This axon has a cover, or sheath, made of myelin. **Myelin** is a white substance composed of fat and protein, and is found on about half of the axons in an adult's nervous system. Myelin is not an outgrowth of the axon itself but is produced by other cells throughout the nervous systems. Myelin covers an axon in lumpy segments, separated by gaps (Nodes of Ranvier) rather than in one continuous coating. It is largely the presence of myelin that allows us to distinguish between the gray matter (dendrites, cell bodies, and bare, unmyelinated axons) and white matter (myelinated axons) of nervous-system tissue. We tend to find myelin on axons that carry impulses relatively long distances. For instance, most neurons that carry messages up and down the spinal cord have myelin on their axons, whereas most of those that carry impulses back and forth across the spinal cord do not.

Myelin serves several functions. It protects the long and delicate axon. It also acts as an insulator, separating the activity of one neuron from those nearby. Myelin speeds impulses

Cell body—the largest concentration of mass in the neuron, containing the nucleus of the cell and other structures necessary for the neuron's life.

Dendrite—the part of a neuron reaching out to receive messages, or neural impulses, from nearby neurons.

Axon—the part of a neuron that sends messages along its length to other neurons, muscles, or glands.

Myelin—a white substance composed of fat and protein; found on about half of the axons in an adult's nervous system.

along the length of the axon. Myelinated neurons carry impulses nearly ten times faster than unmyelinated ones—up to 150 yards per second, or well over 300 miles an hour!

Whether covered with myelin or not, axons end in a branching series of bare end points called **axon terminals**. So to review: Within a neuron, impulses travel from the dendrites to the cell body, to the axon (which may be myelinated), and then to axon terminals.

Axon terminals—a branching series of bare end points of an axon.

Have you noticed that discussing the structure of the neuron is nearly impossible without referring to its function: the transmission of neural impulses? We have seen that neural impulses are typically received by dendrites, passed on to cell bodies, then to axons, and ultimately to axon terminals. We know that myelin insulates some axons and speeds neural impulses along, but what exactly is a neural impulse? We will explore the neural impulse next.

The function of a neuron is to transmit neural impulses from one place in the nervous system to another. A **neural impulse** is a rapid, reversible change in the electrical charges within and outside a neuron. When a neuron transmits an impulse (when a neuron "fires"), this change in electrical charge travels from the dendrites to the cell body, to the axon, to the axon terminal. Even as you sit quietly reading your textbook, millions of neurons are transmitting impulses to and from various parts of your body. Some are moving (incredibly fast) from your eyes to your brain, which is trying to make sense of these invisible processes. Some are racing from your brain to your arms and hands, directing you to go to the next page or shift your weight in your chair.

Neural impulse—a rapid, reversible change in the electrical charges within and outside a neuron.

Neurons don't fire every time they are stimulated. That is to say, they don't always transmit a neural impulse when they are stimulated. The **all-or-none principle** states that a neuron either fires or it doesn't. There is no such thing as a weak or strong neural impulse; the impulse is there or it isn't. This raises an interesting psychological question: How does the nervous system react to differences in stimulus intensity? How do neurons react to the difference between a bright light and a dim one, a soft sound and a loud one, or a tap on the shoulder and a slap on the back? Remember, neurons do not fire partially, so we cannot say that a neuron fires partially for a dim light and fires to a greater extent for the brighter light. Part of the answer involves neural thresholds.

All-or-none principle—a principle stating that a neuron either fires or it doesn't.

Indeed, neurons do not generate impulses every time they are stimulated. In fact, each neuron has a level of stimulation that must be reached to produce an impulse. The minimum level of stimulation required to fire a neuron is the **neural threshold**. This concept, coupled with the all-or-none principle, is the key to understanding how we process stimuli of varying intensities. High-intensity stimuli (bright lights, loud sounds, etc.) do not cause neurons to fire more vigorously; they stimulate *more* neurons to fire. And, as it happens, those neurons will fire more frequently as well. High-intensity stimuli are above the neural threshold of a greater number of neurons than are low-intensity stimuli. The difference in our experience of a flash going off near our faces and how we see a candle at a distance reflects the number of neurons involved and the rate at which they fire, not the degree or extent to which they fire.

Neural threshold—the minimum level of stimulation required to fire a neuron.

Now that we have examined the individual nerve cell in detail, we are ready to learn how neurons communicate with each other—how impulses are transmitted from one cell to another. How impulses travel between neurons is as remarkable, but quite different from how impulses travel within neurons.

The location at which a neural impulse is relayed from one neuron to another is called the **synapse**. At these synapses (see **Figure 2.2**), neurons do not touch each other. Instead, there is a microscopic gap (the *synaptic cleft*) between the axon terminal of one neuron and the dendrites (or cell body) of another neuron. At the end of an axon, there are many branches which themselves end at axon terminals. Concentrated at the axon terminal are **vesicles**, incredibly small containers that hold complex chemicals called neurotransmitters. **Neurotransmitters** are chemicals released into the synapse that act to excite or inhibit the transmission of a neural impulse in the next neuron. Notice that across the synaptic cleft, there are *receptor sites* that receive the neurotransmitter molecules. Receptor sites are specialized areas that accept molecules of particular neurotransmitters. Think about neurotransmitters as being tiny keys that fit into tiny locks at the receptor sites.

Synapse—the location at which a neural impulse is relayed from one neuron to another.

Vesicles—incredibly small containers that are concentrated at axon terminals and hold neurotransmitters.

Neurotransmitters—chemicals released into the synapse that act to excite or inhibit the transmission of a neural impulse in the next neuron.

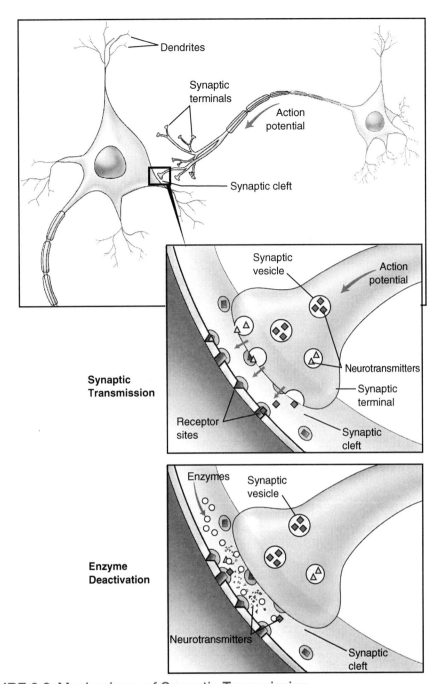

FIGURE 2.2 Mechanisms of Synaptic Transmission

When a neural impulse reaches the end of an axon, it stimulates synaptic vesicles to release neurotransmitter molecules into the synaptic cleft. The molecules diffuse across the fluid in the synaptic cleft and interact with receptor sites on another neuron. The molecules then disengage from the receptor sites and are either broken down by enzymes or taken back into the axon in a process called reuptake.

When an impulse reaches the axon terminal, the vesicles burst open and release the neurotransmitters they have been holding. Then what happens? Actually, any number of things can happen. Let's look at two. The most logical scenario is that the neurotransmitters float across the gap between neurons, enter into receptor sites in the next neuron in a chain of nerve cells, and excite that neuron to fire a new impulse down to its axon terminals. Some neurotransmitters are excitatory in nature. An **excitatory neurotransmitter** stimulates the next neuron in a sequence to fire.

Excitatory neurotransmitter— a neurotransmitter that stimulates the next neuron in a sequence to fire.

Inhibitory neurotransmitter— a neurotransmitter that prevents the next neuron from firing.

As it happens, there are many places throughout our nervous systems where the opposite effect occurs. An **inhibitory neurotransmitter** prevents (inhibits) the next neuron from firing. One final note: Impulse transmission also occurs at the synapse of neurons and other kinds of cells. For instance, when a neuron forms a synapse with a muscle cell the release of a neurotransmitter from the neuron's axon terminals may excite that muscle to contract momentarily. Similarly, neurons that form synapses with the cells of a gland may cause that gland to secrete a hormone when stimulated by the appropriate neurotransmitter. After the neurotransmitter has done its job there are mechanisms that eliminate them so they will not have a long-term effect.

> **STUDY CHECK**
>
> What are the major parts of a neuron?
> What is myelin, and what functions does it serve?
> What is the nature of a neural impulse?
> What is the all-or-none principle, and what are neural thresholds?
> What is the synapse, and in general terms, what happens there?

> **THINKING CRITICALLY**
>
> Neural impulses may begin when stimuli activate one's sense receptors. In what other ways might neural impulses begin? Once neurons begin to fire and send impulses on to other neurons, what do you suppose stops the process, i.e., when does neural transmission stop?

Human Nervous Systems: The Big Picture

Now that we know how neurons work individually and in combination, let's consider the context in which they function. Behaviors and mental activities require large numbers of integrated neurons working together in complex, organized systems. **Figure 2.3** depicts these systems.

The major division of the nervous systems is determined wholly on the basis of anatomy. The **central nervous system (CNS)** includes all neurons and supporting cells found

Central nervous system (CNS)—a division of the nervous system that includes all neurons and supporting cells found in the spinal cord and brain.

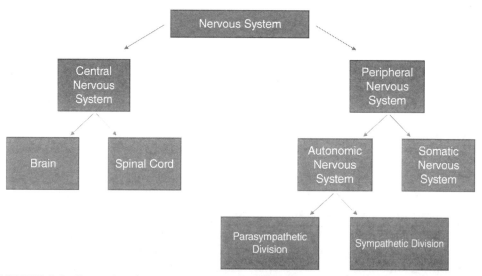

FIGURE 2.3 Organization of the Nervous System

in the spinal cord and brain. This system of nerves is the most complex and most intimately involved in the control of behavior and mental processes. The **peripheral nervous system (PNS)** consists of all neurons in the body not in the CNS—the nerve fibers in the arms, face, fingers, intestines, and so on. Neurons in the peripheral nervous system carry impulses from the central nervous system to the muscles and glands or to the CNS from receptor cells.

The peripheral nervous system is divided into two parts, based largely on the part of the body being served. The **somatic nervous system** includes those neurons that are outside the CNS and serve the skeletal muscles and pick up impulses from our sense receptors, such as the eyes and ears. The other part of the PNS is the autonomic nervous system (ANS). "Autonomic" essentially means "automatic." This name implies that the activity of the ANS is largely independent of central nervous system control. The nerve fibers of the **autonomic nervous system** are involved in activating the smooth muscles, such as those of the stomach and intestines, and the glands. The ANS provides feedback to the CNS about this internal activity.

The ANS also consists of two parts: the sympathetic division and the parasympathetic division. These two components commonly work in opposition to each other. The **sympathetic division** is active when we are emotionally aroused or excited, as we might be when riding up that first incline of a roller coaster. The **parasympathetic division** is active when we are relaxed and quiet, as we might be after a long day at the amusement park, half asleep in the back seat on the drive home. Both divisions of the ANS act on the same organs, but they do so in opposite ways.

There is good reason to categorize the various organizations of neurons: It makes a very complex system easier to understand, and it reminds us that not all neurons in our body are doing the same thing for the same reason at the same time. Note that the outline of the nervous system in Figure 2.3 is very simplified to this extent: The nerve fibers in each of the systems have profound influences on one another. They are not at all as independent as our diagram might imply.

The **endocrine system** is a network of glands that affect behaviors by secreting chemicals called *hormones*. All hormones travel through the bloodstream and can affect organs far from where the hormones are produced. Many hormones produced by the glands of the endocrine system are chemically similar to neurotransmitters and have similar effects. The endocrine system's glands and hormones are controlled by parts of the brain and by the autonomic nervous system. Although not composed of neurons and synapses, the endocrine system is relevant to our discussion for two reasons. First, its function is like that of the nervous system: to transmit information from one part of the body to another. Second, hormones exert a direct influence on behavior.

Consider the so-called sex hormones, testosterone and estrogen. These hormones are found in both males and females, but testosterone is much more common in males, while estrogen is more common in females. High levels of testosterone in males have long been associated with increased aggression (Booth et al., 2003; Dabbs et al., 1995); but the relationship between testosterone and aggression is quite complex. The connection between testosterone and aggression is complicated by findings that aggression (particularly the activation of aggressive behaviors) is influenced not just by the "male" testosterone, but also by the "female" estrogen. Other research indicates that what seems to matter most is the relative levels or balance of the two hormones.

Let us consider three endocrine glands—the pituitary, the thyroid, and the adrenal glands. Perhaps the most important endocrine gland is the pituitary gland. The **pituitary gland** is often referred to as the master gland, reflecting its direct control over the activity of many other glands in the system. The pituitary is nestled under the brain and secretes many different hormones. One hormone released by the pituitary is *growth hormone*, which regulates the growth of the body during its fastest physical development. Extremes of overproduction or underproduction cause the development of giants or dwarfs. The so-called "growth spurt" associated with early adolescence is due to the activity of the pituitary gland. It is the pituitary gland that stimulates the release of hormones that regulate the amount of water held within the body. It is the pituitary that

Peripheral nervous system (PNS)—a division of the nervous system that consists of all neurons in the body not in the CNS—the nerve fibers in the arms, face, fingers, intestines, and so on.

Somatic nervous system—consists of those neurons that are outside the CNS and serve the skeletal muscles and pick up impulses from our sense receptors, such as the eyes and ears.

Autonomic nervous system—consists of neurons involved in activating the smooth muscles, such as those of the stomach and intestines, and the glands.

Sympathetic division—division of the autonomic nervous system that is active when we are emotionally aroused or excited.

Parasympathetic division—division of the autonomic nervous system that is active when we are relaxed and quiet.

Endocrine system—a network of glands that affect behaviors by secreting chemicals called hormones.

Pituitary gland—a gland often referred to as the master gland, reflecting its direct control over the activity of many other glands in the endocrine system.

directs the mammary glands in the breasts to release milk after childbirth. In its role as master over other glands, the pituitary regulates the output of the thyroid and the adrenal glands, as well as the sex glands.

The **thyroid gland** is located in the neck and produces a hormone called *thyroxin*. Thyroxin regulates the pace of the body's functioning—the rate at which oxygen is used and the rate of body function and growth. When a person is easily excited, edgy, having trouble sleeping, and has lost weight, a person may have too much thyroxin in his or her system, a condition called *hyperthyroidism*. Too little thyroxin leads to a lack of energy, fatigue, and an inability to do much, a condition called *hypothyroidism*.

The **adrenal glands**, located on the kidneys, secrete a variety of hormones into the bloodstream. The hormone *adrenaline* (more often referred to as epinephrine) is very useful in times of stress, danger, or threat. Adrenaline quickens breathing, causes the heart to beat faster, directs the flow of blood away from the stomach and intestines to the limbs, dilates the pupils of the eyes, and increases perspiration. When our adrenal glands flood epinephrine into our system during a perceived emergency, we usually feel the resulting reactions; but, typical of endocrine-system activity, these reactions may be delayed.

For example, as you drive down a busy street, you see a child dart out from behind a parked car and race to the other side of the street. You slam on the brakes, twist the steering wheel, and swerve to avoid the child. As the child scampers away, oblivious to the danger, you proceed down the street. Then, about a block later, your body reacts to the near miss: your heart pounds, a lump forms in your throat, your mouth dries, and your palms sweat. Why does your reaction come when the incident is over and you are out of danger? The delay in your body's reaction is because your reaction is largely hormonal. Your body's adrenal glands secrete epinephrine, and it takes time for this substance to travel through the bloodstream to the heart, pupils of the eyes, and the brainstem. You begin to feel effects once the epinephrine reaches these places.

> **Thyroid gland**—a gland located in the neck that produces a hormone called thyroxin. Thyroxin regulates the pace of the body's functioning.
>
> **Adrenal glands**—glands located on the kidneys that secrete a variety of hormones into the bloodstream.

STUDY CHECK

What are the major divisions of the human nervous systems, and what do they do? What is the function of the endocrine system in general and the pituitary gland, thyroid gland, and adrenal glands in particular?

THINKING CRITICALLY

Imagine you are walking barefoot in the dark and step on a tack. Which of your various nervous systems might be involved, and how?

The Spinal Cord

The central nervous system consists of the brain and the spinal cord. In this section, we consider the structure and function of the spinal cord, reserving our discussion of the brain for the next section.

The spinal cord is a mass of interconnected neurons within the spinal column that looks rather like a section of rope or thick twine. It is surrounded and protected by the hard bone and cartilage of the vertebrae. A cross-sectional view of the spinal column and the spinal cord is illustrated in **Figure 2.4**. A few structural details need to be mentioned. Note that the spinal cord is located in the middle of the spinal column, which extends from the

The Neuropsychology of Addiction

If you have been following the news, you probably know that the United States is in the midst of a serious problem: addiction to opioids. Opioids belong to a class of drugs called opiates that includes heroin, cocaine, codeine, and an array of prescription pain-reducing drugs (e.g., *Oxy-Contin*). A principal effect of taking an opiate is an intense feeling of euphoria and well-being, which causes many people to use these drugs. Unfortunately, these drugs are highly addictive. Many people who are addicted to illegal drugs like heroin and cocaine started on the path of addiction by taking legally prescribed pain medications for medical conditions. This has led in recent years to an explosion in the number of people who become addicted to and may even die as a result of abusing opiate drugs.

The statistics on opioid addiction are grim. According to the U.S. Department of Health and Human Services (2018), in 2016, 11.5 million people misused prescription opioids, and 2.1 million did so for the first time. The reasons for this abuse are many and include relieving pain, helping one to sleep, relieving tension, to see what doing the drug feels like, and to get high (Lipari, Williams, & Van Horn, 2017). Alarmingly, 42,249 Americans died from opioid-related causes in 2016, a rate of around 116 per day. The economic costs of this epidemic amount to approximately $504 billion per year. So, becoming addicted to prescription drugs and later illegal drugs is a major problem. Two interesting questions are: What do these drugs do in the brain, and how does that relate to addiction?

As you just learned, communication between neurons in the brain involves impulses being transmitted between nerve cells via the synapse. When a neural impulse gets to the end of a neuron, a chemical is secreted (neurotransmitter) that affects receptor sites on the next neuron. The key to understanding how opioids work in the brain centers on the neurotransmitter dopamine and its receptor sites. Opioids operate on these receptor sites in many parts of the brain, spinal cord, and bodily organs. These receptor sites are intimately involved in pleasure and pain. The opioids act to block pain signals, and with higher doses, they arouse feelings of euphoria and pleasure (National Institute on Drug Abuse, 2018a). Opioids affect the brain on all levels, including brain cells, the circuits in the brain, and the general system (Evans & Cahill, 2016). Essentially, according to Evans and Cahill, the drug creates a "new normal" in the user's brain. In short, what happens is that when the opioid is present in an addicted person's brain, the brain operates "normally" for that person. When the drug is not there, the brain does not operate in this new normal manner (Kosten & George, 2002). Addiction appears to involve a change to the reward circuitry in the brain leading to a strong desire for the opioid. According to one theory, changes in the reward circuity relate to positive reinforcement from drug use and loss of inhibitory controls (Evans & Cahill, 2016).

Withdrawal from an opioid addiction involves physical symptoms that are unpleasant. Treatment can be effective, but relapse can occur.
Source: Oksana Mizina/Shutterstock.

A big problem with opioid use is that as a person uses them more and more, the brain needs higher doses to produce the same effects. This is referred to as *tolerance*. Tolerance develops because the receptors involved become less responsive to the drug over the period of drug use, requiring higher and higher doses to obtain the same effect (Kosten & George, 2002). Once tolerance occurs, a person becomes drug *dependent*, which means that he or she will be susceptible to negative withdrawal symptoms when the opioid is not taken. As drug dependence becomes stronger, the addicted person keeps taking the drug to avoid the negative consequences of not taking the drug (withdrawal) (Kosten & George, 2002).

As you might expect, breaking an opioid addiction is extremely difficult. When the person stops taking the drug, it triggers *withdrawal*. Withdrawal typically involves some physical symptoms (e.g., sweating, tremors, and diarrhea) that go away relatively quickly and others (e.g., dysphoria, anxiety, and insomnia) that can last for months (Evans & Cahill, 2016). Treatment typically involves some form of drug therapy. Drugs such as Methadone and LAAM (a long-acting Methadone derivative) are used to treat the short-term symptoms of addiction. These drugs act on the same receptors as the opioid, but in a different way (Kosten & George, 2002). Another drug, Naltrexone, is used in the longer term to help avoid relapse. These drugs may be combined with other forms of psychological therapies (e.g., cognitive-behavioral therapy or contingency management [see Chapter 13]) to help break addiction. Although treatment can be effective, many people relapse and start using drugs again. It is widely known that individuals addicted to opioids are susceptible to stress. When stress is encountered, it triggers a desire to return to drug use (Kosten & George, 2002).

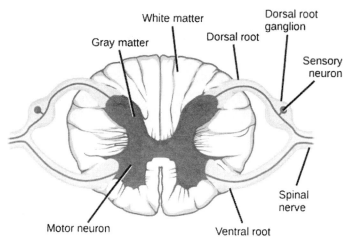

FIGURE 2.4 Cross-Sectional Diagram of the Spinal Column and Spinal Cord

Sensory neurons—nerve fibers that carry impulses toward the brain or spinal cord.

Motor neurons—nerve fibers that carry impulses away from the spinal cord and brain to the muscles and glands.

Interneurons—neurons within the spinal cord and central nervous system that transmit information between neurons.

lower back to high in the neck just below the brain. Note also that nerve fibers enter and leave the spinal cord from the side. In fact, there are three types of neurons in the spinal cord. **Sensory neurons** or nerve fibers carry impulses toward the brain or spinal cord. **Motor neurons** or nerve fibers carry impulses away from the spinal cord and brain to the muscles and glands. **Interneurons** are neurons within the spinal cord and central nervous system that transmit information between neurons.

Notice also that the center area of the spinal cord consists of gray matter, while the outside area is light white matter. This color difference means that the center portion is filled with cell bodies, dendrites, and unmyelinated axons, while the outer section is filled with myelinated axons. These observations about the structure of the spinal cord are the key to understanding its functions.

The spinal cord has two major functions. One involves transmitting impulses rapidly to and from the brain. When sensory impulses originate in sense receptors below the neck and make their way to the brain, they do so through the spinal cord. When the brain transmits motor impulses to move or activate parts of the body below the neck, those impulses first travel down the spinal cord. For example, if you stub your toe, pain messages travel up the spinal cord and register in the brain. When you decide to reach for that cup of coffee and bring it toward your mouth, impulses originating in your brain move to the muscles in your back, arm, and hand by traveling first down the spinal cord.

Impulses to and from various parts of the body leave and enter the spinal cord at different points. Impulses to and from the legs, for example, enter and leave at the very base of the spinal cord. If the spinal cord is damaged, communication may be disrupted. The consequences of such an injury are disastrous, resulting in a loss of feeling and a loss of voluntary movement (that is, paralysis) of the muscles in those parts of the body served by the spinal cord below the injury. The higher in the spinal cord that damage takes place, the greater is the resulting loss.

Spinal reflexes—simple, automatic behaviors that occur without conscious, voluntary action of the brain.

The second major function of the spinal cord involves spinal reflexes. **Spinal reflexes** are simple, automatic behaviors that occur without conscious, voluntary action of the brain. To understand how these reflexes work, see **Figure 2.5**. In this drawing of the spinal cord, you can see that impulses are sent from the finger to the spinal column via sensory neurons. Interneurons then connect the sensory neurons to motor neurons. Finally, motor neurons carry impulses back to the hand to withdraw the finger.

Let's trace your reaction to holding the tip of your finger over a burning candle. Receptor cells in your fingertip respond to the heat of the flame, sending neural impulses racing along sensory neurons, up your arm and shoulder, and into the spinal cord. Then

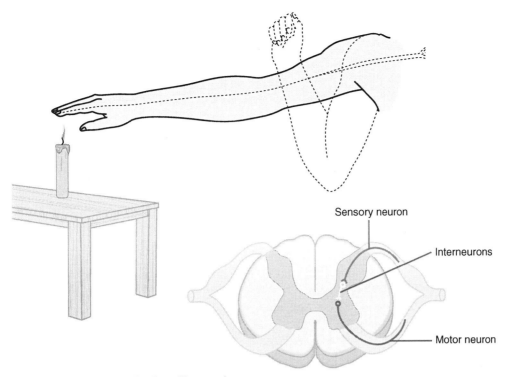

FIGURE 2.5 Spinal Reflex Example

Example of a spinal reflex involving only sensory and motor neurons. **Top:** Sensory neurons detect the heat of the flame, and motor neurons signal the arm to withdraw. **Bottom:** Impulses travel along sensory neurons to the spinal cord and then out via motor neurons to activate muscles to withdraw the hand.

two things happen at almost the same time. Impulses rush up the ascending pathways of the spinal cord's white matter to your brain (very quickly you learn how silly putting a finger near a flame was). Impulses also travel on interneurons and leave the spinal cord on motor neurons to your arm and hand, where muscles are stimulated to contract, and your hand jerks back.

This is a simple spinal reflex. Impulses travel *in* on sensory neurons, *within* on interneurons, and *out* on motor neurons. Here we have an environmental stimulus (a flame), activity in the central nervous system (neurons in the spinal cord), and an observable response (withdrawal of the hand). Notice that, for this sequence of events of the spinal reflex, the involvement of the brain is not at all necessary.

There are a few observations we must make about the reflex of the type shown in Figure 2.5. First, the fact that impulses enter the spinal cord and immediately race to the brain is not indicated in the drawing. In a situation such as the candle example, you may jerk your hand back "without thinking about it," but very soon thereafter you are aware of what has happened. Awareness occurs in the brain, not in the spinal cord. It is also true that some reflexes are simpler than the one in Figure 2.5. Some reflexes involve three types of neurons—sensory, motor, and interneurons. Other spinal reflexes involve only sensory neurons and motor neurons, which directly interact within the spinal cord. The common knee-jerk reflex is an example—sensory neurons and motor neurons synapse directly with no interneurons involved.

A spinal reflex: Stimulation of receptor cells in the skin stimulates sensory neurons, interneurons, and motor neurons without the conscious voluntary action of the brain. You don't have to think about moving your hand after hitting your thumb with a hammer!

Chapter 2 The Biological Foundations of Behavior   31

"Lower" Brain Centers and What They Do

Perched atop your spinal cord, encased in bone, is a wonderful, mysterious organ: your brain (see **Figure 2.6**). Your brain is a mass of neurons, supporting cells, blood vessels, and ventricles (interconnected cavities containing fluid). Your brain accounts for a small fraction of your body weight, but due to its importance, it receives almost 20 percent of the blood in your body. Your brain contains a storehouse of memories and is the seat of your emotions and motivation. It regulates your breathing and the beating of your heart.

For convenience, we will divide the brain into two major categories of structures. We first discuss the role of some of the "lower" brain centers, which are involved in several important aspects of behavior. Then we will examine the role of the cerebral cortex, the outer layers or covering of the brain that controls higher mental functions.

The "lower" centers of the brain contain vital structures involved in crucial, involuntary functions like respiration and heartbeat. Although we may call these structures "lower," they are by no means unimportant. Lower brain centers are "lower" in two ways. First, they are physically located beneath the cerebral cortex. Second, these brain structures

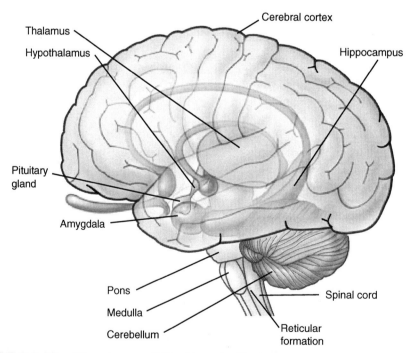

FIGURE 2.6 The Structures of the Human Brain

The structures of the brain serve a variety of life-supporting, sensory, motor, and cognitive functions.

develop first—both in an evolutionary sense and within the developing human brain. The lower brain structures are those we most clearly share with other animals and upon which our very survival depends.

If you look at the spinal cord and brain, you cannot tell where one ends and the other begins. There is no abrupt division of these two aspects of the central nervous system. Just above the spinal cord, there is a slight widening of the cord that suggests the transition to brain tissue. At this point of widening, two structures form the brainstem: the medulla and the pons.

The lowest structure in the brain is the medulla. In many ways, the medulla acts like the spinal cord in that its major functions involve involuntary reflexes. The **medulla** controls such functions as heart rate, respiration, blood pressure, coughing, sneezing, tongue movements, and reflexive eye movements. You do not think about blinking your eye as something rushes toward it, for example; your medulla produces that eye blink reflexively.

The medulla contains neurons that control breathing reflexes, mediate blood pressure levels, and regulate the muscles of the heart to keep it beating. We can control some of the neurons of the medulla, but only within limits. For example, the medulla controls our respiration (breathing), but we can override the medulla and hold our breath. We cannot, however, hold our breath until we die, as some children occasionally may threaten. We can hold our breath until we lose consciousness, which is to say until we give up voluntary control; then the medulla takes over and breathing resumes.

At the level of the medulla, most nerve fibers to and from the brain cross from right to left and vice versa. That is, motor neurons from the left side of the brain cross over to control the right side of the body. Motor neurons from the right side of the brain cross to control the left side of the body. Similarly, sensory nerve fibers from each side of the body cross over to carry information to the opposite side of the brain. This crossover explains why electrically stimulating the correct area in the *left* side of the brain produces a movement in the *right* arm. It also explains why a cerebral stroke in the left side of the brain causes loss of movement in the right side of the body. The arrangement of nerve fibers in the brainstem crossing from one side of the body to the opposite side of the brain is called **cross laterality**.

Just above the medulla is a structure called the pons. (The pons is one structure; there is no such thing as a "pon.") The **pons** serves as a relay station or bridge, sorting out and relaying sensory messages from the spinal cord and the face up to higher brain centers and similarly relaying motor impulses from higher centers of the brain down to the rest of the body. The cross laterality that begins in the medulla continues in the pons. Cells in the pons are also partially responsible for the rapid eye movement that occurs when we dream. Other centers in the pons are involved in determining when we sleep and when we awaken.

The cerebellum sits behind your pons, tucked up under the base of your skull. Your cerebellum (literally, "small brain") is about the size of your closed fist and is the second-largest part of your brain. Oddly, the cerebellum, as small as it is, contains nearly half of all the neurons in the human brain (Zillmer & Spiers, 2001). The major role of the **cerebellum** is to smooth and coordinate rapid body movements. Most intentional movements originate in higher brain centers (the motor area of the cerebral cortex) and are coordinated by the cerebellum. Because of the close relationship between body movement and vision, many eye movements originate in the cerebellum.

Your ability to stoop, pick a dime off the floor, and slip it into your pocket involves a complex series of movements smoothed and coordinated by your cerebellum. When athletes practice or rehearse a movement, such as a golf swing or a gymnastic routine, we may say that they are trying to "get into a groove," so that their trained movements can be made simply and smoothly. In a way, the athletes are training their cerebellums, which play such

Medulla—part of the brain that controls such functions as heart rate, respiration, blood pressure, coughing, sneezing, tongue movements, and reflexive eye movements.

Cross laterality—arrangement of nerve fibers in the brainstem crossing from one side of the body to the opposite side of the brain.

Pons—a structure in the brain serving as a relay station or bridge, sorting out and relaying sensory messages from the spinal cord and the face up to higher brain centers and similarly relaying motor impulses from higher centers of the brain down to the rest of the body.

Cerebellum—the part of the brain that smooths and coordinates rapid body movements.

Source: Beto Chagas/Shutterstock.

Catching a hard-hit baseball is an example of the cerebellum in action.

an important role in coordinating "automatic" movements. Examples would be catching a fast line drive hit right to you, playing a well-practiced piano piece, or quickly reaching out to save a priceless vase you just knocked off a table with your elbow. It appears that such movements are not reflexive, but rather the cerebellum learns to make them—a process that is the focus of research by neuroscientists interested in how one's learning experiences are represented in the brain.

Few behaviors are as well coordinated or as well learned as the movements needed to speak. The next time you're talking to someone, focus on how quickly and effortlessly your lips, mouth, and tongue are moving, thanks to the cerebellum. Damage to the cerebellum slurs speech. In fact, damage to the cerebellum disrupts all coordinated movements. Someone with cerebellum damage may shake and stagger when he or she walks. To the casual observer, such a person may appear to be drunk. (On what region of the brain do you suppose alcohol has a direct effect? Yes, the cerebellum.)

The reticular formation is hardly a brain *structure* at all. It is a complex network of nerve fibers that begins in the brainstem and works its way up through and around other structures to the top portions of the brain. What the reticular formation does, and exactly how it does so, remains something of a mystery, but we do know that the **reticular formation** is involved in determining our level of activation or arousal. It influences whether we are awake, asleep, or somewhere in between. Electrical stimulation of the reticular formation can produce patterns of brain activity associated with alertness. Classic research has shown that lesions of the reticular formation cause a state of constant sleep in laboratory animals (Lindsley et al., 1949; Moruzzi & Magoun, 1949). In a way, the reticular formation acts like a valve that either allows sensory messages to pass from lower centers up to the cerebral cortex or shuts them off, partially or totally. We don't know what stimulates the reticular formation to produce these effects.

A curious set of tissues is the basal ganglia. The basal ganglia are a collection of small, loosely connected structures deep within the center of the brain. Like the cerebellum, the basal ganglia primarily control motor responses. Unlike the cerebellum, the **basal ganglia** are involved in the planning, initiation, and coordination of large, slow movements. Although the basal ganglia are clearly related to the movements of some of our body's larger muscles, there are no direct pathways from the ganglia down the spinal cord and to those larger muscles.

Researchers have come to better understand the functions of the basal ganglia as they have come to better understand **Parkinson's disease**, a disorder involving the basal ganglia in which the most noticeable symptoms are impairment of movement and involuntary tremors. At first, patients with Parkinson's may have tightness or stiffness in the fingers or limbs. As the disease progresses, patients lose their ability to move themselves, or they are able to move but only with great effort. Walking, once begun, involves a set of stiff, shuffling movements. In advanced cases, voluntary movement of the arms is nearly impossible. Parkinson's is more common with increasing age, afflicting approximately 1 percent of the population.

The limbic system is more a collection of small structures than a single unit. It is particularly important in controlling the behaviors of animals, which do not have as well-developed cerebral cortexes as humans. In humans, the **limbic system** controls many of the complex behavioral patterns that are often considered to be instinctive. The limbic system is located in the middle of the brain. Figure 2.6 shows some of the limbic system's major structures: thalamus, amygdala, hippocampus, and hypothalamus. There are other structures in the limbic system not shown in Figure 2.6 (septum, basal ganglia, and the cingulate gyrus).

Parts of the limbic system are involved in the display of emotional reactions. One structure in the limbic system, the *amygdala*, produces reactions of rage or aggression when stimulated, while another area, the *septum*, has the opposite effect, reducing the intensity of emotional responses when it is stimulated. The influence of the amygdala and the septum on emotional responding is immediate and direct in non-humans. In humans, its role is more subtle, reflecting the influence of other brain centers. There is little doubt

Reticular formation—brain structure involved in determining our level of activation or arousal.

Basal ganglia—brain structures involved in the planning, initiation, and coordination of large, slow movements.

Parkinson's disease—a disorder involving the basal ganglia in which the most noticeable symptoms are impairment of movement and involuntary tremors.

Limbic system—a collection of brain structures controlling many of the complex behavioral patterns that are often considered to be instinctive.

that the amygdala is involved in most cases of depression, but exactly how is not yet clear (Davidson et al., 2002).

The amygdala also plays an important role in the emotion of fear (Davis et al., 2010). The authors of a case study of a woman (SM) with damage to her amygdala (Feinstein et. al., 2011) report that SM is incapable of experiencing fear to a wide range of stimuli (e.g., snakes, spiders, a haunted house, a scary film), nor does she report experiencing fear in her everyday life. SM is also not able to "read" the facial expression associated with fear in others. However, SM is fully capable of experiencing a range of other emotions including anger and happiness. So, the damage to her amygdala does not disrupt emotions generally, but rather only the emotion of fear. The amygdala is also important when deciding whether or not a stimulus is dangerous (Ekman, 1992; LeDoux, 1995), an ability that is also related to the experience of fear.

Another structure in the limbic system, called the *hippocampus*, is less directly involved in emotion and more involved with the formation of memories. (Vargha-Khadem et al., 1997). People with a damaged hippocampus are often unable to "transfer" experiences (e.g., a birthday party) into permanent memory storage (Wheeler & McMillan, 2001). They may remember events for short periods and may be able to remember events from the distant past, but only if these events occurred before the hippocampus was damaged.

The role of the hippocampus may differ according to the nature of the memory. Brian Witgen and his colleagues (2010) report that detailed memories require activity of the hippocampus, whereas less detailed memories do not. Another study demonstrated the role of the hippocampus in the formation of fear-related memories (McEwon & Treit, 2010).

The *hypothalamus* is a structure that plays a complex role in motivational and emotional reactions. Among other things, it influences many of the functions of the endocrine system, which, as we have seen, is involved in emotionality. The major responsibility of the hypothalamus is to monitor critical internal bodily functions. One subsection, for example, mediates feeding behaviors. Destruction of this nucleus in a rat results in a condition that causes the animal to lose its ability to regulate food intake and become obese. (As you can imagine, researchers who study the various eating disorders have been very interested in the hypothalamus (e.g., Polivy & Herman, 2002)). In a similar way, another area in the hypothalamus is involved in the detection of thirst and regulation of fluid intake.

The hypothalamus also plays a role in aggression. Stimulation of the lateral nucleus in a cat produces aggression that looks much like predatory behavior. The cat is highly selective in what it attacks and stalks its prey before pouncing. Stimulation of the medial nucleus results in an anger-based aggression (Edwards & Flynn, 1972). The cat shows the characteristic signs of anger (arched back, ears flattened, hissing and spitting) and will attack anything in its way. Interestingly, the role of the hypothalamus in hunger and aggression is not as simple as it may seem. For example, if you apply mild stimulation to the lateral nucleus, a cat will show signs of hunger (but not aggression). Increase the strength of the stimulation to the same site, and a cat will display aggression. Stress early in life can lead to changes in the hypothalamus that increase aggression in adulthood (Veenema et al., 2006). For example, separating rat pups from their mothers (a highly stressful event) produced changes in the levels of a hormone and a neurotransmitter in parts of the hypothalamus. These changes led to higher levels of aggression among adult male rats.

The hypothalamus also acts something like a thermostat, triggering a number of automatic reactions should we become too warm or too cold. It does this by integrating temperature information from the environment, the central core of the body, and the peripheral regions of the body. Scientists believe that the temperature regulation function of the hypothalamus may be linked to the aging process and longevity (Tabarean et al., 2010). This structure is also involved in aggressive and sexual behaviors. It acts as a regulator for many hormones. The hypothalamus has been implicated in the development of sexual orientations, an implication we'll discuss in later chapters when we study needs, motives, and emotions.

Thalamus—a brain structure acting as a relay station for impulses traveling to and from the cerebral cortex.

The thalamus sits below the cerebral cortex and is intimately involved in its functioning. Like the pons, the thalamus is a relay station for impulses traveling to and from the cerebral cortex. Many impulses traveling from the cerebral cortex to lower brain structures, the spinal cord, and the peripheral nervous system pass through the thalamus. Overcoming the normal function of the medulla (for example, by holding your breath) involves messages that pass through the thalamus. The major role of the thalamus, however, involves the processing of information from the senses.

In handling incoming sensory impulses, the thalamus collects, organizes, and then directs sensory messages to the appropriate areas of the cerebral cortex. Sensory messages from the lower body, eyes, and ears, (but not the nose) pass through the thalamus. For example, at the thalamus, nerve fibers from the eyes are spread out and projected onto the back of the cerebral cortex. It is believed by many neuroscientists that the thalamus "decides" what information will be sent to the cortex and enter consciousness, but empirical data to support this hypothesis have proven difficult to obtain.

STUDY CHECK

Where are the medulla and the pons, and what do they do?
What is meant by cross laterality?
What are the major functions of the cerebellum and the reticular formation?
What are the basal ganglia, and what is their relation to Parkinson's disease?
What are the major structures of the limbic system, and what are their functions?
What are the functions of the thalamus, and where is it located?

THINKING CRITICALLY

One way to study how the various structures in the central nervous system work is to contemplate what would happen if those structures were damaged or destroyed. For example, what would be the result of an accident that damaged the medulla? What if the pons were destroyed?

The Cerebral Cortex

The human brain is a homely organ. There is nothing pretty about it. When we look at a human brain, the first thing we are likely to notice is the large, soft, lumpy, creviced outer covering of the cerebral cortex (cortex means "outer bark," or covering). The cerebral cortex of the human brain is significantly larger than any other brain structure. It is the complex and delicate cerebral cortex that makes us uniquely human by giving us our ability to think, reason, and use language.

Cerebral cortex—the large part of the brain that makes us uniquely human by giving us our ability to think, reason, and use language.

Lobes and Localization

Figure 2.7 presents a lateral (side) view of the cerebral cortex. You can see that the deep folds of tissue provide us with markers for dividing the cerebrum into major areas. There is a deep crevice that runs down the middle of the cerebral cortex from front to back, dividing it into the left and right cerebral hemispheres.

Figure 2.7 allows us to see the four major divisions of each hemisphere, called "lobes." The *frontal lobes* (plural because there is one on the left and one on the right, as is the case for the other lobes) are the largest and are defined by two large crevices called the central fissure and the lateral fissure. The *temporal lobes* are located at the temples below the lateral fissure, with one on each side of the brain. The *occipital lobes*, at the back of the brain,

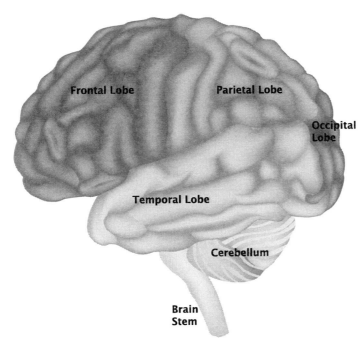

FIGURE 2.7 The Lobes of the Brain

The cerebral cortex covering each cerebral hemisphere is divided into four lobes: The frontal lobe, the temporal lobe, the parietal lobe, and the occipital lobe.

are defined somewhat arbitrarily, with no large fissures setting them off, and the *parietal lobes* are wedged behind the frontal lobes and above the occipital and temporal lobes.

Researchers have learned much about what normally happens in the various regions of the cerebral cortex, but many of the details of cerebral function are yet to be understood. Neuroscientists have mapped three major areas of the cortex: *sensory areas*, where impulses from sense receptors are sent; *motor areas*, where most voluntary movements originate; and *association* areas, where sensory and motor functions are integrated and where higher mental processes are thought to occur. We now review each of these in turn, referring to **Figure 2.8** as we go along.

Let's review for a minute. Receptor cells (specialized neurons) in our sense organs respond to stimulus energy from the environment. These cells then pass neural impulses along sensory nerve fibers, eventually to the cerebral cortex. Senses in our body below our neck first send impulses to the spinal cord. Then it's up the spinal cord, through the brainstem, where they cross from left to right and from right to left, on up to the thalamus, and beyond to the cerebrum. After impulses from our senses leave the thalamus, they go to a **sensory area**, an area of the cerebral cortex that receives impulses from the senses. Which sensory area gets involved depends on which sense was activated.

Large areas of the human cerebral cortex are involved with vision and hearing. Virtually the entire occipital lobe processes visual information (labeled "visual association area" in Figure 2.8). Auditory (hearing) impulses go to large centers ("auditory areas") in the temporal lobes. Bodily senses (touch, pressure, pain, etc.) send impulses to a strip at the very front of the parietal lobe (labeled "primary somatosensory cortex" in Figure 2.8). In this area of the parietal lobe, researchers have mapped out specific regions that correspond to the various parts of the body. Looking at such a "map," we find that some body parts—the face, lips, and fingertips, for example—are over-represented in the body sense area of the cerebral cortex, reflecting their high sensitivity.

Finally, let's remind ourselves of cross laterality, the crossing over of information from senses on the left side of the body to the right side of the brain, and vice versa, that occurs in the brain stem. When someone touches your right arm, that information ends up in your left parietal lobe. A tickle to your left foot is processed by the right side of your cerebral cortex.

Sensory area—the area of the cerebral cortex that receives impulses from the senses.

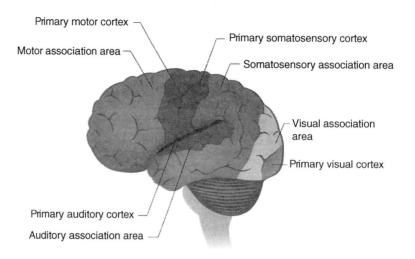

Primary motor cortex

Motor association area

Primary somatosensory cortex

Somatosensory association area

Visual association area

Primary visual cortex

Primary auditory cortex

Auditory association area

FIGURE 2.8 Association Cortex

The association cortex is involved in higher-order mental functions such as judgment, memory, and facial recognition.

Source: Alila Medical Media/Shutterstock.

Motor area—the area of the cerebral cortex located in strips at the very back of the frontal lobes that coordinates and initiates most voluntary activity.

We have seen that some of our actions, at least very simple and reflexive ones, originate below the cerebral cortex. Although lower brain centers, such as the basal ganglia, may be involved, most voluntary activity is initiated in the **motor areas** of the cerebral cortex in strips at the very back of the frontal lobes. These areas (again, there are two of them, left and right) are directly across the central fissure from the body sense areas in the parietal lobe (labeled "primary motor cortex" in Figure 2.8). We need to make the disclaimer that the actual *decision* to move probably occurs farther forward in the frontal lobes.

Electrical stimulation techniques have allowed neuroscientists to map locations in the motor areas that correspond to, or control, specific muscles or muscle groups. As is the case for sensory processing, some muscle groups (e.g., those that control movements of the hands and mouth) are represented by disproportionally larger areas of cerebral cortex.

As you know, cross laterality is also at work with the motor area. It is your right hemisphere's motor area that controls movements of the left side of your body, and the left hemisphere's motor area that controls the right side. Someone who has suffered a cerebral stroke (a disruption of blood flow in the brain that results in the loss of neural tissue) in the left side of the brain will have impaired movement in the right side of his or her body.

Association areas—areas of the cerebral cortex where sensory input is integrated with motor responses and where cognitive functions such as problem solving, memory, and thinking occur.

Once we have located the areas of the cerebral cortex that process sensory information and initiate motor responses, there is a lot of cortex left over. The remaining areas of the cerebral cortex are called **association areas**, which are areas of the cerebrum where sensory input is integrated with motor responses and where cognitive functions such as problem solving, memory, and thinking occur. There is an association area in each of the two frontal, parietal, and temporal lobes. The occipital lobes are so "filled" with visual processing that there is no room left for occipital association areas.

There is considerable support for the idea that the "higher mental processes" occur in the association areas. Frontal association areas are involved in many such processes (Schall, 2004). Normal speech functions are controlled by this portion of the brain (located on the left side of the brain in most people), now called *Broca's area* (see **Figure 2.9**). That is, it coordinates the actual functions needed to express an idea. A person with damage to Broca's area shows an interesting pattern of speech defects. If asked a question like, "Where is your car?" a person with Broca's area damage might be able to tell you, but only in broken, forced language. For example, the person might say, "Car . . . lot . . . parked by . . . supermarket."

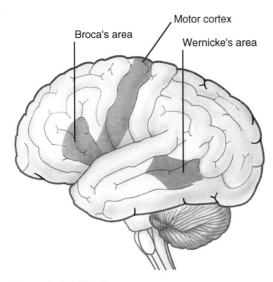

FIGURE 2.9 Speech and the Brain

Wernicke's area, Broca's area, and the motor cortex interact in producing speech.

Understanding language and organizing linguistic responses are functions of Wernicke's area (see Figure 2.9). If you asked a person with damage to Wernicke's area where his or her car was, the person might say, "The cat is sitting on the table." Notice that this response is well formed (because Broca's area is working fine) but makes no sense with respect to the question.

Damage to the very front of the right frontal lobe or to an area where the parietal and temporal lobes come together often interrupts or destroys the ability to plan ahead, to think quickly, reason, or think things through (Greene & Haidt, 2002). Interestingly, these association areas of the brain involved in forethought and planning nearly cease to function when one is feeling particularly happy (e.g., George et al., 1995) or one consumes alcohol (Pihl, Assad, & Hoaken, 2003).

We should not get too carried away with cerebral localization of function. Please do not fall into the trap of believing that separate parts of the cerebral cortex operate independently or that they have the sole responsibility for any one function. It is also true that the brain shows a remarkable degree of flexibility in both structure and function. Brain scientists refer to this as plasticity. *Plasticity* is the nervous system's "capacity to respond in a dynamic manner to the environment and experience via modification of neural circuitry" (Anderson, Spencer-Smith, & Wood, 2011, p. 2198). Tissue in the nervous system has the capacity to adapt and take on new functions because of environmental conditions. So, for example, if a part of the brain with a specific function is damaged, it is possible for other areas of the brain to take over its function.

The Two Cerebral Hemispheres: Splitting the Brain

The ancient Greeks knew that the cerebral cortex was divided into two major sections, or hemispheres. That the cerebral cortex is divided in half seems quite natural. After all, we have two eyes, arms, legs, lungs, and so forth. Why not two divisions of the brain? In the last decades, interest in this division into hemispheres has heightened as scientists have accumulated evidence that suggests that each half of the cerebral cortex may have primary responsibility for its own set of functions.

In most humans, the left hemisphere is the larger of the two halves, contains a higher proportion of gray matter, and is considered the *dominant hemisphere* (active to a greater degree in more tasks). We have already noted that the major language centers are housed in the left cerebral hemisphere. At least this is true for nearly all right-handed people. For some left-handers, language may be processed primarily by the right hemisphere. Because

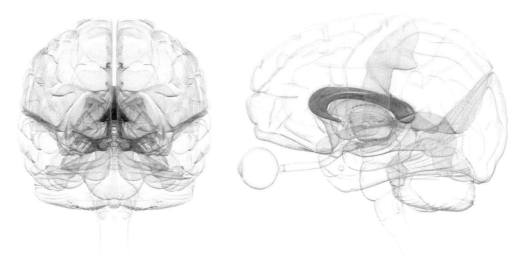

FIGURE 2.10 The Corpus Callosum

A frontal and lateral view of the brain showing the location and shape of the corpus callosum within the brain. The corpus callosum is a wide band of axons that connects the right and left hemispheres.

Source: decade3d—anatomy online/Shutterstock.

Corpus callosum—a network of hundreds of thousands of fibers connecting the two hemispheres of the cerebral cortex.

Split-brain procedure—a surgical technique used to separate the functions of the two cerebral hemispheres.

humans are so language-oriented, little attention was given to the right hemisphere until a remarkable surgical procedure performed in the 1960s gave us new insights about the cerebral hemispheres (Sperry, 1968, 1982; Springer & Deutsch, 1981).

Normally, the **corpus callosum**, a network of hundreds of thousands of fibers, connects the two hemispheres of the cerebral cortex (see **Figure 2.10**). Through the corpus callosum, one side of our cortex remains in constant and immediate contact with the other. Separating the functions of the two hemispheres is possible, however, through a surgical technique called a **split-brain procedure**, which is neither as complicated nor as dangerous as it sounds. The procedure was first performed on a human in 1961 by Joseph Brogan to lessen the severity of the symptoms of epilepsy. As a treatment of last resort, the split-brain procedure has been very successful. Although the procedure destroys the corpus callosum's connections between the hemispheres, it does leave intact other, smaller, connections between the two hemispheres.

Most of what we know about the activities of the cerebral hemispheres has been learned from split-brain subjects, both human and animal. One of the things that makes this procedure remarkable is that, under normal circumstances, split-brain patients behave normally. Only in the laboratory, using specially designed tasks, can we see the results of independently functioning hemispheres of the cerebral cortex (Corballis, Funnell, & Gazzaniga, 2002; Foerch, 2005; Gazzaniga, Ivry, & Mangun, 2002).

Experiments with split-brain patients confirm that speech production is a left-hemisphere function in most people. Imagine you have your hands behind your back. I place a house key in your left hand and ask you to tell me what it is. Your left hand feels the key. Impulses travel up your left arm, up your spinal cord, and cross over to your right cerebral hemisphere (remember cross laterality). You tell me that the object in your left hand is a key because your brain is intact. Your right hemisphere quickly passes the information about the key to your left hemisphere, and your left hemisphere directs you to say, "It's a key."

Now suppose that you are a split-brain patient. You cannot answer my question even though you understand it perfectly. Why not? Your right brain knows that the object in your left hand is a key, but without an intact corpus callosum, it cannot inform the left hemisphere, where speech production is located. Under the direction of the right cerebral hemisphere, you would be able to point with your left hand to the key placed among other objects before you. Upon seeing your own behavior, your eyes would communicate that information to your left hemisphere.

So, a major task for the left hemisphere is the production of speech and the processing of language. But we must remain cautious about making too much of the specialization of function. When the results of the first research efforts on split-brain patients were made public, many people, less skeptical than the researchers themselves, jumped to faulty, overly simplistic conclusions. We now know that virtually no behavior or mental process is the product of one hemisphere alone. For example, Gazzaniga (1998) reports of one split-brain patient who learned to speak from the right hemisphere 13 years after surgery severed the corpus callosum.

Still, what about the right hemisphere? The clearest evidence is that the right hemisphere dominates the processing of visually presented information (Bradshaw & Nettleton, 1983; Kosslyn, 1987). Putting together a jigsaw puzzle, for instance, uses the right hemisphere more than the left. Skill in the visual arts (e.g., painting, drawing, and sculpting) is associated with the right hemisphere. It is involved in the interpretation of emotional stimuli and in the expression of emotions. While the left hemisphere is analytical and sequential, the right hemisphere is considered better able to grasp the big picture—the overall view of things—and tends to be somewhat creative.

Yes, there are exceptions, but very often artistic, visual skills are processed more in the right cerebral hemisphere than the left.

Source: Golubovy/Shutterstock.

FOCUS ON DIVERSITY

Gender Differences in the Brain

There are obviously many anatomical differences between men and women. Can the same be said of the brains of men and women? As we explore the answer to this question, keep in mind that we are asking about general differences and not about the specific brains of one man and one woman. If there are differences in the anatomy of male and female brains, we then must ask if these differences are significant. Do they have a measurable impact on psychological functioning?

Research shows that there are some anatomical differences between the male and female brain. For example, the male brain is larger than the female brain (even after body size is controlled) but has a lower ratio of gray matter to white matter (Sacher, Neumann, Okon-Singer, Gotowiec, & Villringer, 2013). Additionally, females have more white matter in regions of the left hemisphere and men in the right hemisphere (Sacher et al., 2013). Other interesting anatomical gender differences are that the two hemispheres (halves) of women's brains are more highly connected, but there is more connectivity within the hemispheres in men (Ingalhalikar et al., 2013). This suggests that the two hemispheres of women's brains might work together more than the hemispheres of men's brains. There is also evidence that there are gender differences in the lateralization of the male and female brain. Research shows that the hemispheres of the cerebral cortex are more separate and distinct (more lateralized) in males than in females. This may account for the fact that women are more likely to recover from strokes than are men, perhaps because functions lost as a result of damage in one hemisphere can be taken over more easily by the other, undamaged hemisphere (McGlone, 1980).

Do the anatomical differences between male and female brains translate into any differences in function or behavior? Yes, they do—at least to some extent. Women recall or recognize emotional information better than men (Canli, Desmond, Zhao, & Gabrieli, 2002). Canli et al. found that women's recollections of emotionally stimulating photographs were 10 to 15 percent more accurate than men's recollections of similar photographs. The study also found that women's brains were more active than men's when looking at pictures of emotional stimuli. Another widely reported gender difference is that males show more interest in playing video games than females. This difference may relate to differences in brain functioning (Hoeft, Watson, Kesler, Bettinger, & Reiss, 2008). Using functional magnetic resonance imaging, Hoeft et al. found greater activity in parts of the limbic system associated with reward and addiction in males compared with females. The authors believe this may help explain why males are more likely than females to become "hooked" on video games.

So, there is enough evidence to show that there are anatomical and functional differences between the male and female brains. However, keep in mind that the differences found are small; only about 1 percent of lateralization differences are accounted for by gender (Boles, 2005). Despite this relatively small difference, researchers believe that continued research will give us a greater understanding of brain functioning and potential treatments for brain trauma and other disorders.

These possibilities are intriguing. While it seems that there are differences in the way the two sides of the cerebral cortex normally process information, these differences are slight, and many are controversial. In fact, the more we learn about hemispheric differences, the more we discover similarities. And let's not lose sight of the enormous ability of the human brain to repair itself. In 2003, the Associated Press published a story about Christina Santhouse, a 16-year-old high school student. When she was 9 years old, the entire right cerebral hemisphere of her brain was surgically removed. The treatment was for an advanced case of Rasmussen's encephalitis, a neurological disease that gradually eats away brain tissue. The surgery was done at Johns Hopkins Hospital, where over 100 such "hemispherectomies" have been performed. Yes, Christina suffers from side effects of the procedure (e.g., partial paralysis in her left arm and leg and the loss of peripheral vision in one eye), but in most ways, the fully functioning left hemisphere has managed to take over the functions of the missing right hemisphere. Christina, now an adult, is a speech pathologist.

STUDY CHECK

What is the location of each of the four lobes of the cerebral cortex?
What are the functions of the sensory areas, the motor areas, and the association areas of the cortex?
What is the split-brain procedure, and what has been learned from it?

THINKING CRITICALLY

Might it be possible to train or educate one hemisphere of the brain while ignoring the other? Imagine that you wanted to strengthen the abilities of your right cerebral hemisphere. How might you proceed?

Chapter Summary

What are the major parts of a neuron?
A neuron is the basic cell of the nervous system. Every neuron has three parts: the cell body, dendrites, and axon. The cell body contains the structures needed to sustain the life of the neuron. Dendrites extend from the cell body and receive messages from other neurons, while the axon extends from the cell body and carries the neural message away from the cell body. At their ends, axons branch out to form several axon terminals.

What is myelin, and what functions does it serve?
Myelin is a white fatty substance that coats the axons of some neurons of the nervous system. The myelin sheath covers the axon in segments, rather than in one continuous covering. The myelin sheath has several functions. First, it protects the delicate axon from damage. Second, it insulates the axon against signals from other neurons. Third,

it speeds the rate of the neural impulse as it travels down the axon.

What is the nature of a neural impulse?
A neural impulse is the electrical signal, or activity, that travels down the axon after a neuron has been stimulated.

What is the all-or-none principle, and what are neural thresholds?
The all–or–none principle is the name for the observation that if a neuron fires, the neural impulse occurs at full force, or not at all. Thus, there is no such thing as a strong or weak neural impulse; it is either present or not. Neural thresholds describe the minimal level of stimulation necessary to get a neuron to transmit an impulse of its own. Some neurons have very low thresholds (and, thus, are very sensitive), while some have high thresholds (and require considerable stimulation before they fire).

What is the synapse, and in general terms, what happens there?

A synapse is the location where two neurons communicate with each other. The neurons do not physically touch; there is a small gap separating the axon of one neuron from the dendrite or cell body of the next. Communication between neurons across the gap between neurons is accomplished chemically. When the neural impulse reaches the axon terminal, a neurotransmitter is released into the synaptic cleft. It is through this chemical that the neural impulse is communicated across the synapse.

What are the major divisions of the human nervous systems, and what do they do?

The central nervous system (CNS) includes all of the neurons and supporting cells found in the brain and spinal cord. It is a complex system involved in the control of behavior and mental processes. The peripheral nervous system (PNS) consists of all of the neurons in our body that are not in the central nervous system. It includes the nerve fibers in our arms, face, fingers, intestines, etc. Neurons in the peripheral nervous system carry impulses either from the central nervous system to the muscles and glands or to the central nervous system from receptor cells. The somatic and autonomic nervous systems are subdivisions of the peripheral nervous system. The somatic nervous system includes the neurons that serve the skeletal muscles and pick up impulses from our sense receptors. The autonomic nervous system (ANS) is composed of the nerve fibers that activate the smooth muscles, such as those of the stomach, intestines, and glands. The autonomic nervous system has two subsystems. The sympathetic system is activated under conditions of excitement or arousal, and the parasympathetic system is activated when a person is relaxed and calm.

What is the function of the endocrine system in general and the pituitary gland, thyroid gland, and adrenal glands in particular?

The endocrine system is a network of glands that influence behaviors through the secretion of chemicals called hormones. The hormones, which circulate through the blood system, can have an effect on behavior. The pituitary gland is often called the "master gland" because it controls many other glands in the endocrine system. It is located under the brain and secretes a variety of hormones. Pituitary hormones affect growth, lactation, regulation of the amount of water held in the body, and the regulation of other glands. The thyroid gland, located in the neck, produces a hormone, thyroxin, which regulates the body's "pace" (e.g., the rate at which oxygen is used). Hyperthyroidism occurs when too much thyroxin in the blood results in excitability, edginess, insomnia, and weight loss. Too little thyroxin leads to hypothyroidism, associated with fatigue and lack of energy. The adrenal glands, located on the kidneys, secrete a variety of hormones into the blood. One such hormone, adrenaline, is released during times of danger. It increases respiration and heart and perspiration rates, directs the flow of blood away from the digestive system toward the limbs, and causes pupils to dilate.

What are sensory neurons, motor neurons, and interneurons?

Sensory neurons carry information (in the form of neural impulses) from the body to the central nervous system. Motor neurons carry information from the central nervous system to muscles and glands in the body. Interneurons are those neurons located and functioning within the central nervous system.

What is the basic structure of the spinal cord, and what are its two functions?

The spinal cord, encased in the spinal column, is a mass of interconnected neurons resembling a piece of rope that extends from the lower back to just below the brain. It has nerve fibers that carry messages to and from the brain and to and from the body. The spinal cord also is involved in reflex actions. When a receptor is stimulated (e.g., your hand touches a hot surface) sensory neurons transmit the information to the spinal cord. There, interneurons form synapses with motor neurons that then send impulses to muscles in your arm and hand to withdraw your hand. At the same time, however, information is transmitted up the spinal cord, and you consciously experience the pain. Note that some reflexes do not involve interneurons to mediate sensory experience and motor response, and instead work through direct synaptic connections between sensory and motor neurons. These synapses are located within the spinal cord.

Where are the medulla and the pons, and what do they do?

Like the spinal cord, the medulla's major functions involve involuntary reflexes. There are several small structures in the medulla that control functions such as coughing, sneezing, tongue movements, and reflexive eye movements. The medulla also sends out impulses that keep your heart beating and your respiratory system breathing. The pons serves as a relay station, sorting and relaying sensory messages from the spinal cord and the face to higher brain centers, and reversing the relay for motor impulses coming down from higher centers. The pons is also responsible, at least in part, for the sleep/waking cycle and the rapid movement of our eyes that occurs when we dream.

What is meant by cross laterality?

Cross laterality means that the right side of your brain controls the left side of your body, while the left side of your brain controls the right side of your body. In the same fashion, sensory impulses from the right side of your body cross to be received by the left side of your brain, and sensory impulses from the left side of your body are registered in the right side of your brain.

What are the major functions of the cerebellum and the reticular formation?

The cerebellum is located under the base of the skull. The major function of the cerebellum is to smooth out and coordinate rapid body movements. Most voluntary movements originate in the higher brain centers and are coordinated by the cerebellum. Damage to the cerebellum can lead to a variety of motor problems including loss of coordination, tremors, and speech problems. The reticular formation is more a network of nerve fibers than a true brain structure. Most of the functions of the reticular formation remain a mystery. However, we know it is involved in alertness and the sleep/waking cycle.

What are the basal ganglia, and what is their relation to Parkinson's disease?

The basal ganglia are a collection of small, loosely connected structures deep in the middle of the brain. The basal ganglia primarily control the initiation and the coordination of large, slow movements. In Parkinson's disease, the cells in the basal ganglia that produce the neurotransmitter dopamine die, and the levels of dopamine in the basal ganglia drop. This loss of dopamine is thought to produce the characteristic motor problems associated with the disease.

What are the major structures of the limbic system, and what are their functions?

The limbic system is a collection of structures rather than a single one. The limbic system is composed of the amygdala, hippocampus, septum, and hypothalamus. The limbic system controls many of the behaviors that we consider instinctive. When stimulated, the amygdala evokes reactions of rage or aggression. It also helps you to decide whether or not a stimulus is dangerous. The septum reduces the intensity of emotional responses when it is stimulated. The influence of the amygdala and the septum on emotional responding is immediate and direct in non-humans. In humans, it is more subtle, which reflects the influence of other brain centers.

The hippocampus is involved with forming memories. Persons with damage to the hippocampus have difficulty transferring memories from temporary memory storage to permanent storage. The hypothalamus is a part of the limbic system involved in the mediation of motivation. It is not a unitary structure, but rather a collection of smaller structures called nuclei. Each nucleus plays a different role. The major function of the hypothalamus is to monitor and control internal body functions such as hunger, thirst, and body temperature, as well as to regulate many hormones.

What are the functions of the thalamus, and where is it located?

The thalamus is a lower brain structure located just below the cerebral cortex. It relays impulses traveling to and from the cortex. The primary function of the thalamus is to relay sensory information to the cerebral cortex, and perhaps to regulate access to consciousness.

What is the location of each of the four lobes of the cerebral cortex?

The cerebral cortex, also known as the cerebrum, is associated with those higher mental processes that make us human. The lobes of the cerebral cortex are divisions of each of the two cerebral hemispheres. The frontal lobes are defined by two large crevices called the central and lateral fissures, and are located at the front of the brain. The temporal lobes are located at the temples, below the lateral fissure on each side of the brain. The occipital lobes are located at the very back of the brain, and the parietal lobes are sandwiched between the frontal, occipital, and temporal lobes.

What are the functions of the sensory areas, the motor areas, and the association areas of the cortex?

The sensory areas of the brain are portions of the brain specialized for receiving neural impulses from the senses. Nearly all of the occipital lobe is dedicated to receiving information from visual stimuli. Impulses relating to hearing are directed to the temporal lobes. Information from the body senses goes to the body sense areas located in the parietal lobe. The motor areas of the cerebral cortex initiate and control most voluntary motor movements. The motor areas of the cortex are located at the back of the frontal lobes. The association areas of the cortex are the parts of the cortex not directly involved in the mediation of sensory and motor activities. The association areas make up a large portion of the cortex and are involved in the integration of sensory input, motor responses, and higher cognitive functions (e.g., problem-solving and memory).

What is the split-brain procedure, and what has been learned from it?

The split–brain procedure is a surgical technique performed to relieve the symptoms of severe epilepsy. The procedure involves severing the corpus callosum. The result is that the two hemispheres become disconnected and can be studied independently. In most people, the left hemisphere of the cerebrum is larger and is referred to as the "dominant hemisphere" because it is active in so many tasks and because it is the seat of language in most people. The differences in function of the two hemispheres of the cortex are quite minimal, but the right hemisphere seems to be specialized for visual and spatial information. Artistic skills like painting and sculpting are also associated with the right hemisphere, as is the interpretation of emotional stimuli.

Key Terms

Neuron (p. 22)
Cell body (p. 23)
Dendrite (p. 23)
Axon (p. 23)
Myelin (p. 23)
Axon terminals (p. 24)
Neural impulse (p. 24)
All-or-none principle (p. 24)
Neural threshold (p. 24)
Synapse (p. 24)
Vesicles (p. 24)
Neurotransmitters (p. 24)
Excitatory neurotransmitter (p. 25)
Inhibitory neurotransmitter (p. 26)
Central nervous system (CNS) (p. 26)
Peripheral nervous system (PNS) (p. 27)
Somatic nervous system (p. 27)
Autonomic nervous system (p. 27)
Sympathetic division (p. 27)
Parasympathetic division (p. 27)
Endocrine system (p. 27)
Pituitary gland (p. 27)

Thyroid gland (p. 28)
Adrenal glands (p. 28)
Sensory neurons (p. 30)
Motor neurons (p. 30)
Interneurons (p. 30)
Spinal reflexes (p. 30)
Medulla (p. 33)
Cross laterality (p. 33)
Pons (p. 33)
Cerebellum (p. 33)
Reticular formation (p. 34)
Basal ganglia (p. 34)
Parkinson's disease (p. 34)
Limbic system (p. 34)
Thalamus (p. 36)
Cerebral cortex (p. 36)
Sensory area (p. 37)
Motor area (p. 38)
Association areas (p. 38)
Corpus callosum (p. 40)
Split-brain procedure (p. 40)

Sensation and Perception

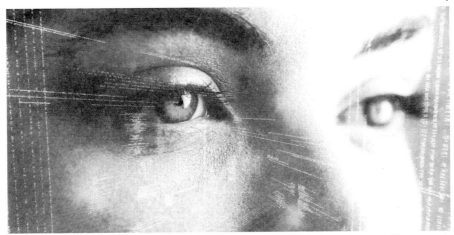

Source: vectorfusionart/Shutterstock

Chapter Outline

Questions You Will Be Able to Answer

After reading Chapter 3, you should be able to answer the following questions:

- What are the processes of information processing, sensation, and perception?
- How do the processes of sensation and perception differ?
- What are sensory thresholds?
- In sensation, what is a difference threshold?
- What is sensory adaptation?
- What are the three major characteristics of light, and what psychological experience does each produce?
- What are the structures of the eye that are involved in focusing images onto the back of the eye (the retina)?
- What are the structures of the retina, and what are the different functions of the rods and cones?
- What are the three main physical characteristics of sound, and what psychological experience is produced by each?
- What are the major structures of the human ear, and what are their roles in hearing?
- What are the stimuli and the receptors for the senses of gustation and olfaction?
- What are the characteristics of the cutaneous senses and the position senses?

- What is the pain sense?
- What stimulus factors influence which stimuli are attended to or selected for further processing?
- What personal factors can influence which stimuli are attended to or selected for further processing?
- What are the characteristics of stimuli that guide our bottom-up organization of information presented by our senses?
- How does top-down processing influence how incoming sensory messages are organized or grouped together?
- What are the cues that allow us to perceive depth and distance?
- What are the perceptual constancies?

Preview

This chapter on sensation and perception actually begins our discussion of learning and memory. Before you can learn about or remember some event in the world you must perceive that event. You must select, organize, and interpret the event. And before you can do that, you must first sense the event. That is, you must gather information about the event and put it in a form your brain can appreciate. Your senses take energy from the world around you (in the form of light, sound, tastes, smells, physical pressures, etc.) and change that energy into the only energy there is in your brain: the impulses of energy called "neural impulses."

In brief: We cannot remember what we have not learned, we cannot learn that which we have not perceived, and we cannot perceive that which we have not sensed.

Processing information begins with sensation. We'll review three important concepts that are relevant to all the human senses: transduction, thresholds, and adaptation.

The scientific study of the human senses—and your own personal experience—should tell you just how incredibly sensitive sense receptors are. Here is the problem that such sensitivity produces: Our senses are so good that they present to us much more information, more detail, than we can possibly process—and that is where perception comes in. Perception allows us to pay attention and react to only a small number of stimuli, selected from the massive amounts of incoming signals. Once attended to, these stimuli can be made meaningful; can be recognized, organized, interpreted, and remembered.

Much of the discussion that follows comes from the work of German psychologists, who began their study of perception at the beginning of the twentieth century. It was their insight that there is a difference between what we *sense* and what we *perceive*. Imagine a foggy evening. Imagine two very similar lights, only slightly separated, blinking on and off alternately (such as you might find on a railroad crossing signal). As one blinks on, the other goes off. We may *sense* the reality of two separate lights, but what we perceive, what we *experience*, is one light moving back and forth.

Perception is largely a matter of selection and organization. To select some aspects of sensory input while ignoring others relies on our paying attention to the world around us. Some of what we attend to is determined by characteristics of the stimulus events in our environment. Some of what we perceive is determined by who we are. Once information is attended to and selected for processing, we tend to organize that information in sensible, meaningful ways. The factors that guide that process are the subject matter of the remainder of the chapter.

A Preliminary Distinction

In this chapter, we begin our discussion of information processing, which is the process of finding out about the world, making judgments about it, learning from it, and remembering what we have learned. Although they are very much related and cannot be separated in our personal experience, we will divide our discussion of the initial stages of information processing into two sub-processes: sensation and perception.

Sensation is the act of detecting external stimuli and converting those stimuli into nervous-system activity. Sensation provides our immediate experience of the stimuli in our environment. For example, when you hear your phone ring, you detect the external stimulus of the ringtone. The psychology of sensation deals with how our various senses do what they do. Sense receptors are the specialized nerve cells in the sense organs that change physical energy into neural impulses. That is, each of our sense receptors is a transducer—a mechanism that converts energy from one form to another. A light bulb is a transducer. It converts electrical energy into light energy (and a little heat energy). Your eye is a sense organ with sense receptors that transduce light energy (light waves) into neural energy (neural impulses). Your ears are sense organs that contain receptors that transduce the mechanical energy of sound waves into neural energy. For example, your ear transduces the physical sound waves produced by your phone ringer into a form that your brain can understand (electrical and chemical neural information).

Compared to sensation, perception is a more active, complex, even creative, process. It acts on the stimulation that is received by the senses. Perception is a process that involves the selection, organization, and interpretation of stimuli. Perception is a more cognitive and central process than sensation. We may say that senses present us with information about the world in which we live, and that perception represents (re-presents, or presents again) that information, often flavored by our motivational states, our expectations, and our past experiences. That is, "we sense the presence of a stimulus, but we perceive what it is" (Levine & Shefner, 1991, p. 1). To continue our example of your phone ringing, you may have different ringtones for different people. Your ability to know that one ringtone is for your sister and another for your best friend depends on the information processing involved in perception.

> Information processing—the process of finding out about the world, making judgments about it, learning from it, and remembering what we have learned.

> Sensation—the act of detecting external stimuli and converting those stimuli into nervous-system activity.

> Transducer—a mechanism that converts energy from one form to another.

> Perception—a process that involves the selection, organization, and interpretation of stimuli.

STUDY CHECK

What are the processes of information processing, sensation, and perception? How do the processes of sensation and perception differ?

THINKING CRITICALLY

Other than our sense receptors and a light bulb, what are some of the common transducers we experience in our daily lives?

Basic Sensory Processes

Think about some electronic device that runs on a solar battery—a small calculator, for example. If you use it in the dark, it will not work. In dim light, you might see some signs of life from the calculator, but in bright light, the calculator functions fully. The display is bright and easy to read, and all of its features work properly. The calculator's power cell requires a minimal amount of light to power the calculator sufficiently. This is the *threshold* level of stimulation for that device. Light intensities below the threshold will not allow the electronics of the calculator to work. Light intensities at or above threshold allow the calculator to operate properly.

Your sense organs operate in a manner similar to the photoelectric cell in the calculator. A minimal intensity of a stimulus must be present for the receptor cells within the sense organ to transduce the external physical stimulus from the environment (for example, light, sound, pressure on your skin) into a neural impulse that your nervous system can interpret. This intensity is known as the **sensory threshold**, or the minimum intensity of a stimulus needed to operate a sense organ. Threshold levels are actually a measure of *sensitivity*. If a receptor has a *low* threshold, then—by definition—very little energy is needed to stimulate it. In other words, that receptor is very sensitive. As threshold levels go down, sensitivity increases. As threshold levels go up, sensitivity decreases.

What good is the concept of sensory threshold? Determining sensory thresholds is not just an academic exercise. Threshold levels as a measure of sensitivity are used to determine if one's senses are operating properly and detecting low levels of stimulation (which is what happens when you have your hearing tested, for example). Engineers who design sound systems need to know about sensory thresholds; stereo speakers that do not reproduce sounds above threshold levels aren't of much use. Warning lights must be well above the visual (sensory) threshold to be useful. How much perfume do you need to use for it to be noticed? How low must you whisper so as not to be overheard in a classroom? Did you feel your cell phone vibrate, or is it your imagination? Can one basil leaf in the tomato sauce be detected, or will two be required? These are questions about sensory thresholds that pertain to everyday experiences outside the laboratory. As it happens, our sense receptors are remarkably sensitive. For example, your sense of vision is capable of detecting a candle flame 30 miles away on a clear night, and your hearing can detect the ticking of a watch in a quiet room from 20 feet away.

There is another sort of sensory threshold that is important in our everyday lives. These are *difference thresholds*. We often are called upon to detect differences between stimuli that are above our sensory thresholds. The issue now is not whether the stimuli can be detected, but whether they are in some way *different* from each other. So, a **difference threshold** is the smallest difference between stimulus attributes that can be detected.

Here's an example: You are presented with two tones. You hear them both (they are above your sensory threshold), and you report that they are equally loud. If the intensity of one of the tones is gradually increased, it will reach a point (eventually) at which you can just detect that it has become louder. This difference is the amount of change in a stimulus that makes it just detectably different from what it was.

The concept of difference threshold is relevant in many contexts. A parent tells a teenager to "turn down that music!" The teenager reduces the volume, but not by a noticeable amount from the parent's point of view, and an argument could erupt. Does the color of the shoes match the color of the dress closely enough? Can you tell the difference between the ringtone on your cell phone and the one on your friend's phone? While painting a

Difference thresholds are relevant in everyday life, whether you are painting a wall ("Are those these really the same color?") or making a sauce ("Do you think that anyone will notice that we did not use the expensive ingredients?")
Sources: (*left*) dotshock/Shutterstock; (*right*) Rawpixel.com/Shutterstock.

room, you run out of paint. Does the newly purchased paint (from a different batch) match the old paint closely enough to be below the difference threshold?

Sensory adaptation occurs when our sensory experience decreases with continued exposure to a stimulus. There are many examples of sensory adaptation. When we jump into a pool or lake, the water may feel very cold. After a few minutes, we adapt and are reassuring our friends to, "Come on in; the water's fine." When we walk into a house in which cabbage is cooking, the odor is nearly overwhelming, but we soon adapt and then fail to notice it. When you turn on your dishwasher if seems to make a terribly loud noise. In a few minutes, we no longer notice the noise—until it stops and silence returns to the kitchen.

There is an important psychological insight in these examples of sensory adaptation: The ability to detect a stimulus depends largely on the extent to which our sense receptors are being newly stimulated or have adapted. In fact, sense receptors respond best to changes in stimulation (Rensink, 2002). The constant stimulation of a receptor leads to adaptation and less of a chance that the stimulation will be detected.

There is an exception to this use of the term "adaptation." What happens when you move from a brightly lit area to a dimly lit one? Say you enter a darkened movie theater on a sunny afternoon. At first, you can barely see and cannot even identify an empty seat, but in a few minutes, you can see reasonably well. What happened? We say that your eyes have "adapted to the dark." Here the term "adaptation" is being used differently. **Dark adaptation** refers to the process in which visual receptors become *more* sensitive with time spent in the dark.

Now it is time to look at some of our basic sensory processes. In each case, we will look at two questions: (1) What is the stimulus that gives rise to our experience? (2) What is the receptor that transduces that stimulation?

> **Sensory adaptation**—sensory experience decreases with continued exposure to a stimulus.

> **Dark adaptation**—the process in which visual receptors become *more* sensitive with time spent in the dark.

STUDY CHECK

What are sensory thresholds?
In sensation, what is a difference threshold?
What is sensory adaptation?

THINKING CRITICALLY

You are trying to explain sensory thresholds to someone who has never taken a psychology class. What examples can you generate to illustrate that sensory thresholds are relevant to everyday life?

Vision

If you could have only one of your senses, which one would you choose? Each of our senses helps us process different information about the environment. Many of us enjoy eating and might choose the sense of taste. Others delight in listening to music and might choose the sense of hearing. None of us would wish to give up the sense of touch during intimate moments. Perhaps the strongest case would be for the sense of sight. An entire lobe of the brain (the occipital) is given over to the processing of visual information, and we equate visual experience with truth or reality, as in the expression, "Seeing is believing."

The Stimulus for Vision: Light

The stimulus for vision is a form of electromagnetic energy we call light. Understanding the nature of light can help us understand how vision works. Light radiates from its source in waves. Light waves have three important physical characteristics, each related to psychological experience: wave amplitude, wavelength, and wave purity.

Light energy varies in its intensity. Differences in intensity correspond to physical differences in the *wave amplitude* of light. One of the physical differences between light A and light B is their amplitude. Our experience of wave amplitude, or intensity, is brightness. The difference between a bright and a dim light is due to the difference in wave amplitude.

Wavelength is the distance between any point in a wave and the corresponding point on the next wave, or cycle. It is difficult to imagine distances so small, but the length of a light wave can actually be measured. The unit of measurement is the *nanometer (nm)*, which is equal to one one-billionth of a meter.

Wavelength determines the hue, or color, of the light we perceive. The human eye responds only to radiant energy with a wavelength between roughly 380 nm and 760 nm (see **Figure 3.1**), which is a small part of the whole spectrum of light. This is the range of energy that constitutes the *visible spectrum*. As light waves increase from the short 380 nm wavelengths to the long 760 nm wavelengths, we experience these changes as gradually moving from violet, to blue, green, yellow-green, yellow, orange, and to red—the color spectrum. Waveforms of energy with wavelengths shorter than 380 nm (e.g., X-rays and ultraviolet rays) are too short to stimulate the receptors in our eyes and go unnoticed. Waveforms of electromagnetic energy with wavelengths longer than 760 nm (e.g., radar and microwaves) are too long to stimulate the receptor cells in our eyes.

Here is an apparently easy problem: We have two lights, one red (700 nm) and the other yellow-green (550 nm). We adjust the physical intensities of these two lights so that they are equal. Will the lights appear equally bright? Actually, they won't. Even with their amplitudes equal, and even though amplitude does determine brightness, the yellow-green light appears much brighter than a red one. It also appears brighter than a blue light of the same amplitude. Wavelength and wave amplitude interact to produce apparent brightness. Wavelengths in the middle of the spectrum (such as yellow-green) appear brighter than do wavelengths of light from either extreme if their amplitudes are equal. We *can* get a red light to appear as bright as a yellow-green one, but to do so, we will have to increase its amplitude, which requires more energy and is thus more expensive. Perhaps the lights on emergency vehicles should be yellow-green, not red. With everything else being equal, yellow-green lights appear brighter than red ones.

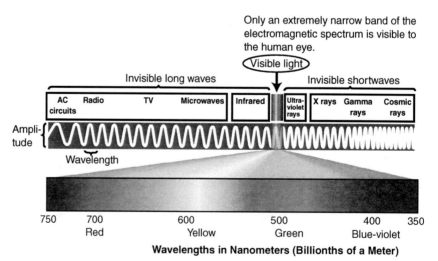

FIGURE 3.1 The Visible Spectrum

The human eye is sensitive to only a narrow slice (from about 380 to 760 nanometers) of the electromagnetic spectrum. This visible spectrum appears in rainbows, when sunlight is broken into its component wavelengths as it passes through raindrops in the atmosphere.

Chapter 3 Sensation and Perception

Now consider a third characteristic of light waves: their *saturation*—the degree of purity of a light. Imagine a light of medium amplitude with all of its wavelengths exactly 700 nm long. Because the wavelengths are all 700 nm, it would appear red. Moreover, it would appear as a pure, rich red. We call such a light *monochromatic* because it consists of light waves of one (mono) length or hue (chroma). Monochromatic light is said to be highly saturated. We seldom see such lights outside the laboratory because producing a pure, monochromatic, light is expensive. The reddest of red lights we see in our everyday experience have other wavelengths of light mixed with the predominant 700 nm red. (If the 700 nm wave did not predominate, the light would not look red.) Even the red light on top of a police car has some violet, green, and yellow light in it.

As different wavelengths are mixed into a light, it lowers in saturation and looks pale and washed out. Light of the lowest possible saturation, a light consisting of a random mixture of wavelengths, is white light. It is something of a curiosity that white light is in fact as *impure* a light as possible. A pure light has one wavelength; a white light contains many wavelengths. A true white light is as difficult to produce as is a pure monochromatic light. Fluorescent light bulbs generate a reasonable approximation, but their light contains too many wavelengths from the short or blue-violet end of the spectrum to be truly white. Light from incandescent bulbs contains too many light waves from the orange and red end of the spectrum, even if we paint the inside of the bulb with white paint. A prism can break a beam of white light into its various parts to produce a rainbow of hues. Where did all those hues come from? They were there all along, mixed together to form the white light.

White light—light of the lowest possible saturation, consisting of a random mixture of wavelengths.

STUDY CHECK

What are the three major characteristics of light, and what psychological experience does each produce?

THINKING CRITICALLY

The stimulus for vision is light, not paint. Why, then, do we see a red barn as red? What would we see if we were to cover the barn with green paint? For that matter, what is the difference between red and green paint?

The Receptor for Vision: The Eye

Vision involves transducing light-wave energy into the neural energy of the nervous system, i.e., causing neurons to transmit impulses to the brain. The sense receptor for vision is the eye. As shown in **Figure 3.2**, the human eye is a complex organ composed of several structures. Most of them are involved in focusing light on the back of the eye where the actual transduction of light energy into neural energy takes place.

We shall now describe the different structures of the eye and their functions. The cornea is the tough, virtually transparent outer shell of the eye. The cornea has two functions: to protect the delicate structures at the front of the eye and to bend light rays so that they can be focused at the back of the eye. In fact, the cornea does about three-fourths of the bending of light waves in the eye.

The pupil is an opening through which light enters the eye. The iris is the colored part of the eye that can expand or contract depending on the intensity of light striking the eye. In bright light, the iris contracts and lets only small amounts of light into the eye. Conversely, in dim light, the iris expands and allows more light to enter. The iris of the eye also enlarges when people view images of attractive members of the opposite sex (Tombs &

Cornea—the tough, virtually transparent outer shell of the eye.

Pupil—the opening through which light enters the eye.

Iris—the colored part of the eye that can expand or contract depending on the intensity of light striking the eye.

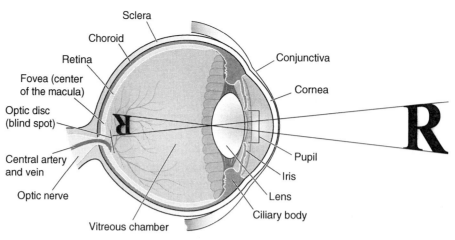

FIGURE 3.2 The Human Eye

The lens is behind the pupil and focuses light onto the retina in this cross section of the eye. The letter R is in the visual field and is projected upside down onto the retina. Our brain interacts with the visual system and corrects the flip, and we perceive a letter R in front of us.

Lens—a flexible structure in the eye that changes shape to focus an image on the back of the eye.

Ciliary muscles—powerful muscles that expand or contract to reflexively change the shape of the lens that brings an image into focus.

Accommodation—changing of the shape of the lens in the eye.

Aqueous humor—the fluid in the eye providing nourishment to the cornea and the other structures at the front of the eye.

Vitreous humor—the thick fluid filling the interior of the eye behind the lens.

Retina—the structure at the back of the eye where vision begins to take place. Light energy is transduced into neural energy here.

Rods—photoreceptors that are responsible for achromatic (not color), low light vision.

Cones—photoreceptors for color vision that operate best in daylight conditions.

Optic nerve—the collection of neurons that leaves the eye and starts back toward other parts of the brain.

Silverman, 2004). The **lens** is a flexible structure in the eye that changes shape to focus an image on the back of the eye. The **ciliary muscles** are powerful muscles that expand or contract to reflexively change the shape of the lens that brings an image into focus. The lens becomes flatter when we try to focus on an object at a distance and rounder when we try to view something up close. The changing of the shape of the lens is called **accommodation**. Often an image does not focus on the back of the eye as it should because of the shape of the lens or because of a failure of accommodation. Sometimes, even a healthy lens and ciliary muscles can't focus on an image because of the shape of the eyeball. The result is either nearsightedness or farsightedness. With age, lenses harden and ciliary muscles weaken, making it difficult to focus.

The eye is filled with two fluids. The **aqueous humor** (humor means fluid) provides nourishment to the cornea and the other structures at the front of the eye. The aqueous humor is constantly produced and supplied to the space behind the cornea, filtering out blood to keep the fluid clean. If the fluid cannot easily pass out of this space, pressure builds within the eye, causing distortions in vision or, in extreme cases, blindness. This disorder is known as *glaucoma*. The interior of the eye (behind the lens) is filled with a thicker fluid called **vitreous humor**. Its major function is to keep the eyeball spherical.

The **retina** is the structure at the back of the eye where vision begins to take place. Light energy is transduced into neural energy here. As you can see in **Figure 3.3**, the retina is really a series of layers of specialized nerve cells at the back surface of the eye. To describe the retina, let's move from the back of the retina toward the front. The layer of cells *at the very back* of the retina contains the receptor cells for vision, the transducers or "photoreceptors" of the eye. It is here that light wave energy is changed into neural energy. Photoreceptor cells come in two types: rods and cones. They are so named because they look like tiny rods and cones. Their tips respond to light-wave energy and begin neural impulses. **Rods** are photoreceptors that are responsible for achromatic (not color), low-light vision. **Cones** are photoreceptors for color vision that operate best in daylight conditions. Impulses travel down the rods and cones and pass on to—form a synapse with—other cells arranged in layers. Within these layers, there is considerable combination and integration of neural impulses. No rod or cone has a single direct pathway to the cerebral cortex of the brain. Impulses from many rods and cones are combined within the eye by *bipolar cells* and *ganglion cells* among others. Fibers from ganglion cells form the **optic nerve**, the collection of neurons that leaves the eye and starts back toward other parts of the brain.

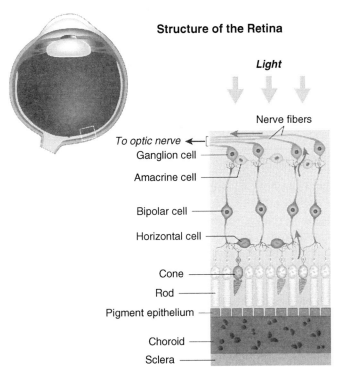

Structure of the Retina

Light

Nerve fibers

To optic nerve ←

Ganglion cell

Amacrine cell

Bipolar cell

Horizontal cell

Cone

Rod

Pigment epithelium

Choroid

Sclera

FIGURE 3.3 The Cells of the Retina

Light must first pass through layers of ganglion cells and bipolar cells before striking the rods and cones. The rods and cones transmit neural impulses to the bipolar cells, which in turn transmit neural impulses to the ganglion cells. The axons of the ganglion cells form the optic nerves, which transmit neural impulses to the visual processing areas of the brain.

Source: Alila Medical Media/Shutterstock.

The fovea and the blind spot are two main features of the retina. The fovea is a small area of the retina where there are few layers of cells between the entering light and the cone cells that fill the area. The fovea contains no rods but many tightly packed cones. It is at the fovea our visual acuity—or ability to discern detail—is best, at least in daylight or in reasonably high levels of illumination. When you thread a needle, you focus the image of the needle and thread on the fovea.

The **blind spot** is the place at which the nerve impulses from the rods and cones, having passed through many layers of cells, exit the eye. There are no rods or cones at the blind spot—nothing is there except the optic nerve threading its way back into the brain. Because there are no rods or cones, there is no vision there. You can demonstrate your blind spot using **Figure 3.4**. Close your right eye and focus your left eye on the black dot. Move your head around slightly, and eventually you will see the mouse disappear!

Let's continue our discussion about rods and cones—the two types of receptor cells in our retinas. Although they are both nerve cells, rods and cones are very different. In each eye, there are about 120 million rods but only 6 million cones. Rods and cones are distributed unevenly throughout the retina. Cones are concentrated in the center of the retina in the fovea, and rods are concentrated on the periphery in a band or ring around the fovea.

Cones function best in medium to high levels of light (as in daylight, for example) and are primarily responsible for our experience of color. On the other hand, rods operate best under conditions of reduced light (as in twilight). Rods are more sensitive to low-intensity light but do not discriminate among wavelengths of light, which means that rods do not contribute to our appreciation of color.

To a degree, you can verify these claims about cones and rods with your own experiences. Do you find it difficult to distinguish among colors at night or in the dark? The

Fovea—a small area of the retina where there are few layers of cells between the entering light and the cone cells that fill the area.

Blind spot—the place at which the nerve impulses from the rods and cones, having passed through many layers of cells, exit the eye.

Chapter 3 Sensation and Perception **55**

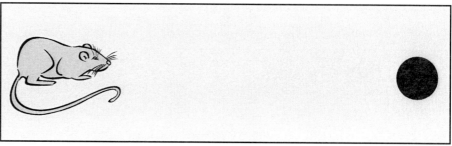

FIGURE 3.4 Finding Your Blind Spot

Because your retina has no rods or cones at the point where the optic nerve leaves the eye, the retina is "blind" at that spot. To find your blind spot, keep your eyes about an arm's length away from the figure, close your right eye, and focus your left eye on the black dot. Move your head slowly toward the figure. When your head is about a foot away, the image of the mouse should disappear. It disappears when it becomes focused on your blind spot. You do not normally notice your blind spot because your eyes see different views of the same scene, because your eyes constantly focus on different parts of the scene, and because your brain fills in the missing portion of the scene.

next time you are at the movies eating pieces of different-colored candy, see if you can tell them apart without holding them up to the light of the projector. You probably will not be able to tell a green piece from a red one because they all will appear black. You cannot distinguish colors very well in a dark theater because you are seeing them primarily with your rods, which are very good at seeing in the reduced illumination but unable to distinguish among wavelengths of light. It is important to understand that under the conditions just described, the cones do not stop functioning. The reason you cannot see the differing colors of candy is that the intensity of light reflected by the candy is too low to activate the cones. Your experience also tells you that this is true, but you can still see the colors of the film because the light is bright enough to stimulate your still-working cones. At night in your car, you can still see colored lights on your dashboard because they are bright enough to trigger the cones.

If you are looking for something small outside on a moonlit night, you probably won't see it if you look directly at it. Imagine changing a tire at night and losing a lug nut in the gravel. If you look directly at it, the image of the lug nut falls on your fovea. Remember, your fovea consists almost entirely of cones and cones do not operate well in relative darkness, so you won't see the nut. To increase your chance of finding it, you have to get the image of the nut to fall on the periphery of your eye, where rods are concentrated.

One of the reasons nocturnal animals (e.g., many varieties of owls) function so well at night is because their retinas are packed with rods, which enable them to see well in the dark. Usually, such animals have little or no fovea, far fewer cones, and are color-blind.

STUDY CHECK

What are the structures of the eye that are involved in focusing images onto the back of the eye (the retina)?
What are the structures of the retina, and what are the different functions of the rods and cones?

THINKING CRITICALLY

Think about the structures of the eye mentioned in this section. As you consider each in turn, describe the effect on vision if that structure were damaged or destroyed.

Audition: The Sense of Hearing

Vision is an important sense. Try this experiment on your own: Blindfold yourself and spend part of your day without your sense of sight. Try to do your normal everyday activities without your eyes. You will realize almost immediately just how heavily you rely on vision. But consider for a moment the quantity and quality of information you receive from your other senses. You may gain a new appreciation of how well they inform you of the wonder of your environment: the aroma and taste of well-prepared barbecue, the sounds of birds and music, the touch and feel of textures and surfaces, the sense of where your body is and what it is doing, the feedback from your muscles as you move. We now turn to these "lesser" senses, beginning with hearing, or audition.

The Stimulus for Hearing: Sound

As the stimulus for vision is light, the stimulus for hearing is sound. Sound is a series of air pressures (or other medium, such as water) beating against the ear. These pressures constitute sound waves. As a source of sound vibrates, it pushes air against our ears in waves. Like light waves, sound waves have three major physical characteristics: amplitude, frequency (the inverse of wavelength), and purity. And, as is the case for light, each is related to a different psychological experience.

As shown in Panel (a) of **Figure 3.5**, the amplitude of a sound wave depicts its intensity—the force with which air strikes the ear. The physical intensity of a sound determines the psychological experience of loudness—the higher its amplitude, the louder the sound. Quiet, soft sounds have low amplitudes.

The physical intensity of sound is measured in units of force per unit area (or pressure). Loudness, however, is a psychological characteristic, measured by people's experiences, not by instruments. The decibel scale is a scale of sound intensity measuring perceived loudness. Its zero point is the absolute threshold, or the lowest intensity of sound that can be detected. Our ears are very sensitive receptors and respond to very low levels of sound intensity. If our ears were any more sensitive, we would hear molecules of air bouncing against our eardrums. Individual receptor cells for sound, deep in our ears, need only to be displaced by the diameter of a hydrogen atom to produce the experience of sound (Hudspeth, 1997).

> Decibel scale—a scale of sound intensity measuring perceived loudness.

If sound intensities are high enough, we literally can "feel" sound. Sounds in the 90–120 decibel range (such as those produced by jet aircraft engines or fast-moving trains) are often felt as much as heard. Because sounds this loud are common in dance clubs and at concerts, the shift from hearing a sound to feeling it has been named "the

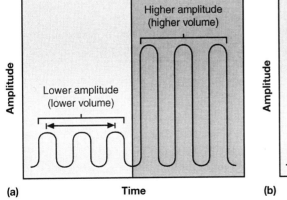
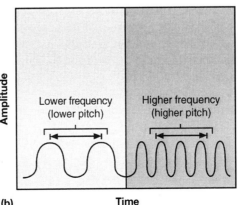

(a) Time   **(b)** Time

FIGURE 3.5 Sound Waves and Hearing

(*a*) The amplitude of a sound wave primarily affects loudness (volume), and (*b*) its frequency primarily affects pitch.

Source: Based on Seely, Stephens, and Tate, *Anatomy and Physiology*, 4th ed., McGraw-Hill, 1998.

rock and roll threshold" (McAngus-Todd & Cody, 2000). Prolonged exposure to very loud, high-intensity sounds can cause deafness.

Granting that long-term exposure to very loud sounds can cause hearing problems, a recent concern has focused on a problem that some people have with *quiet*. It is generally a good idea to get out of the path of a moving car or truck. We can see cars and trucks coming at us, and when they approach from behind, we can hear them. The problem: Today's hybrid and totally electric cars are so quiet that they often operate with virtually no sound being produced by the vehicle. This is a danger for all of us, but particularly for those of us who are visually impaired and rely heavily on their sense of hearing (Rosenblum, 2008). Technology is being added to many electric cars to make them audible to pedestrians (Tschampa, 2014). Currently, however, there are no standards for what these sounds are going to be and whether they will be emitted all of the time or just when pedestrians are present (Tschampa, 2014).

The second physical characteristic of sound is wave frequency (see Panel (b) of Figure 3.5), or the number of times a wave repeats itself within a given time period. For sound, frequency is measured in terms of how many waves of pressure are exerted every second. The unit of sound frequency is the hertz, which is abbreviated Hz. If a sound wave repeats itself 50 times in one second, it is a 50-Hz sound; 500 repetitions is a 500-Hz sound.

The psychological experience produced by sound-wave frequency is *pitch*. Pitch is our experience of how high or low a tone is. The musical scale represents differences in pitch. Low frequencies correspond to bass tones, such as those made by foghorns or tubas. High frequencies correspond to high-pitched sounds, such as the musical tones produced by flutes or the squeals of smoke detectors.

Just as the human eye cannot see all possible wavelengths of radiant energy, the human ear cannot hear all possible sound-wave frequencies. A healthy human ear responds to sound-wave frequencies between 20 Hz and 20,000 Hz. If air strikes our ears at a rate less than 20 times per second, we do not hear a sound. Nor can we hear sound vibrations faster than 20,000 Hz. Many animals can hear sounds with frequencies above 20,000 Hz, such as those produced by dog whistles.

A third characteristic of sound waves is wave purity or complexity. Just as we seldom experience monochromatic lights, we seldom experience pure sounds. A pure sound would be one in which all waves from the sound source vibrate at exactly the same frequency. Pure sounds can be produced electronically and approximated by tuning forks, but most real-world sounds are complex mixtures of many different sound-wave frequencies. A tone of middle C on the piano is a tone of 256 Hz. (The piano wire vibrates 256 times per second.) A pure 256-Hz tone consists of sound waves (vibrations) of only that frequency. As it happens, the piano's middle C has many other wave frequencies mixed in with the predominant 256-Hz wave frequency. (If the 256-Hz wave did not predominate, the tone wouldn't sound like C.)

Timbre is the psychological quality or character of a sound that reflects its degree of purity. For example, each musical instrument produces a unique variety or mixture of overtones, so each type of musical instrument sounds a little different from others. If a trumpet, a violin, and a piano play the same note, equally loudly, we can still tell the instruments apart because of our experience of timbre.

We learned that the opposite of a pure light is white light—a light made up of all wavelengths of the visible spectrum. Again we see the parallel between vision and audition. If a sound source produces all the possible sound-wave frequencies, it sounds similar to the buzzing noise one hears when a radio is tuned to a position between stations. This soft, buzzing sound, containing a range of many audible sound frequencies, is useful in masking or covering other unwanted sounds. We call a random mixture of sound frequencies white noise, just as we refer to a random mixture of wavelengths of light as white light.

Timbre—the psychological quality or character of a sound that reflects its degree of purity.

Personal Listening Devices and Hearing Loss

Earbuds and personal listening devices—they seem to be everywhere! Many of us listen to our favorite music over these devices with those tiny buds stuffed into our ears. Unfortunately, many also play their music at high volumes while plugged in. It is well known that prolonged exposure to very loud, high-intensity sounds can cause hearing loss and reduced ability to understand speech (Levey, Levey, & Fligor, 2011). Although such exposure can come from any number of sources, one area of concern is the use of headphones with personal listening devices (PLDs) such as smartphones.

Statistics show that over 90 percent of college students own a PLD (Torre, 2008). Research by Levey et al. (2011) notes that many college students listen to PLDs at sound levels that can potentially cause hearing loss. In their study, Levey et al. stopped college students entering a college campus and measured the volume levels of the music they were listening to on their PLDs. Participants also filled out a questionnaire on their PLD listening habits. Levey et al. found that 58.1 percent of the sound levels measured were above the level known to be associated with hearing loss and that 51.9 percent of PLD users reported exceeding weekly sound-exposure limits. They also found that males and females did not differ in their listening habits. Another study found that, on average, teenagers aged 13 to 17 listened to their PLDs at between 82 and 89 decibels (the equivalent of loud street noise or the cheering of 60,000 fans in a stadium), depending on listening conditions (Muchnik, Amir, Shabtai, & Kaplan-Neeman, 2012). College students report that the main reason for listening to their PLDs at high levels is that it is acoustically and emotionally pleasing (Serpanos, Berg, & Renne, 2016). Additionally, college students are well aware that those high levels are potentially damaging to their hearing (Hutchinson Marron et al., 2015). Interestingly, not all PLDs have the same sound characteristics, and some may be more dangerous to hearing than others. Gibbeum Kim and Woojae Han (2018) compared the sound pressures produced by six different smartphones (Galaxy S6, Galaxy Note 3, iPhone 5S, iPhone 6, LG G2, and the LG G3) with different types of music (dance-pop, hip-hop, pop-ballad, and Billboard pop). They measured the sound pressures produced through earbuds attached to the PLDs. Kim and Han found that the Galaxy S6 produced the lowest level of sound output and that the LG G3 produced the highest. They also found that dance-pop and hip-hop produced the highest sound levels.

So, it is pretty clear that listening to loud music using earbuds can potentially damage one's hearing. Is there anything that can be done? The answer is yes. Research shows that targeted messages to young children and adolescents can increase awareness of this problem and lead to behavior change (Punch, Elfenbein, & James, 2011). Punch et al. suggest that the effectiveness of such messages can be increased by disseminating them via age-appropriate media, focusing the message on the irreversible damage done, and stressing the effects of loudness and duration of listening on hearing. How about college students? In one of the studies cited earlier (Serpanos et al., 2016), participants were exposed to information concerning listening to loud music and hearing loss and asked if they would then reduce their listening volumes. A majority of participants agreed that they would reduce their listening volumes. Now, whether they actually *will* is another thing!

The Receptor for Hearing: The Ear

The energy of sound wave pressures is transduced into neural impulses deep inside the ear (see **Figure 3.6**). As is the case with the eye's, most of the ear's structures simply transfer energy from without to within. The pinna is the outer ear. Its function is to collect sound waves from the air around it and funnel them through the auditory canal toward the eardrum (see the top part of Figure 3.6). Airwaves push against the eardrum (technically, the *tympanic membrane*) setting it in motion so that it vibrates at the same rate as the sound source. The eardrum then passes vibrations to three very small bones (collectively called *ossicles*) in the middle ear. They are, in order, from the eardrum inward the *hammer* (or malleus), *anvil* (or incus), and *stirrup* (or stapes, pronounced stape-eez). The stirrup is, in turn, attached to a structure called the *oval window*. These bones then amplify and pass the vibrations to the oval window membrane, which is like the eardrum only smaller.

Pinna—the outer ear.

When sound waves pass beyond the oval window, the vibrations are in the inner ear (see the bottom part of Figure 3.6). The cochlea is the snail-like structure of the inner ear containing the actual receptor cells for hearing. As the stirrup vibrates against the oval window, a fluid inside the cochlea is set in motion at the same rate. When the fluid within

Cochlea—the snail-like structure of the inner ear containing the actual receptor cells for hearing.

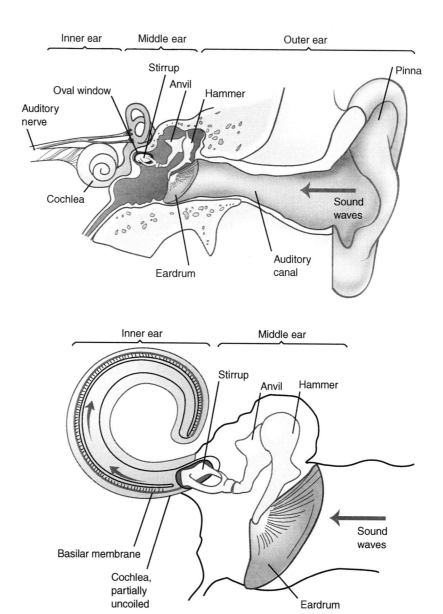

FIGURE 3.6 The Human Ear

The human ear is divided into an outer ear, middle ear, and inner ear. Sound waves pass through the outer ear and strike the eardrum, making it vibrate. This action produces vibrations in the bones (ossicles) of the middle ear (the hammer, the anvil, and the stirrup), which in turn convey the vibrations to the oval window of the inner ear. Vibrations of the oval window produce waves that travel through the fluid of the cochlea. The waves cause bending of hair cells that protrude from the basilar membrane, which stimulates the transmission of neural impulses along the neurons that form the auditory nerve. These impulses travel to the auditory cortex of the temporal lobes as well as to other regions of the brain involved in hearing.

the cochlea moves, the *basilar membrane* is bent up and down. The basilar membrane is a small structure that runs about the full length of the cochlea. Hearing takes place when tiny mechanical receptors called *hair cells* are stimulated by the vibrations of the basilar membrane. Through a process not yet fully understood, the mechanical pressure of the basilar membrane causes the hair cells to bend. The neural impulses leave the ears, traveling on the auditory nerves toward the temporal lobes. Thus, most of the structures of the ear are responsible for amplifying and directing waves of pressure to the hair cells in the cochlea where the neural impulse begins.

STUDY CHECK

What are the three main physical characteristics of sound, and what psychological experience is produced by each?
What are the major structures of the human ear, and what are their roles in hearing?

THINKING CRITICALLY

Loss of hearing often can be characterized as "conduction deafness" or "nerve deafness." What do you suppose the difference is, and which is more likely to be treatable with hearing aids?

The Other Senses

Taste and smell are referred to as the "chemical senses" because the stimuli for both are molecules of chemical compounds. For taste, the chemicals are dissolved in liquid (usually, the saliva in our mouths). For smell, they are dissolved in the air that reaches the smell receptors high inside our noses. **Gustation** is the technical term for the sense of taste. **Olfaction** is the technical name for the sense of smell.

Gustation—the technical term for the sense of taste.

Olfaction—the technical name for the sense of smell.

If you have ever eaten while suffering from a serious head cold, you appreciate the extent to which our experiences of taste and smell are inter-related. Most foods seem to lose their taste when we cannot smell them. This is why we differentiate between the *flavor* of foods (which includes qualities such as odor and texture) and the *taste* of foods. A simple test demonstrates this point. While blindfolded, eat a small piece of peeled apple and a small piece of peeled potato. See if you can tell the difference between the two. You shouldn't have any trouble. Now hold your nose very tightly and try again. Without your sense of smell, you will likely find telling the difference much more challenging.

Scientists have long claimed that taste has four basic psychological qualities (and many combinations of these four): sweet, salty, sour, and bitter. Most foods derive their special taste from a unique combination of these four basic taste sensations. You can easily generate a list of foods that produce each of these sensations. It is more difficult to think of sour and bitter-tasting foods because we do not like bitter and sour tastes and have learned to avoid them.

Neuroscientists have added a fifth taste quality to the list of basic tastes: *umami* (Chandrashekar et al., 2006; Soldo, Blank, & Hofmann, 2003; Palmer, 2007). The taste is difficult to describe, but is most often referred to as "savory-ness" or "meatiness." The experience of umami is created by a specific amino acid, glutamate. The recognition of umami as a basic taste became widespread with word of the discovery of a separate, independent receptor cell for glutamate in the taste buds (Chaudhari, Landin, & Roper, 2000; Nelson et al., 2002).

The **taste buds** are the receptor cells for taste located on the tongue. We have about 10,000 taste buds, and each one consists of several parts. When parts of taste buds die (or are killed by foods that are too hot, for example), they regenerate. This capacity to regenerate makes taste a unique sense because taste buds are nerve cells and most nerve cells do not regenerate when they die.

Taste buds—the receptor cells for taste located on the tongue.

Taste buds respond primarily to chemicals that produce one of the five basic taste qualities. These receptors are not evenly distributed on the surface of the tongue; receptors for sweet tastes are concentrated at the tip of the tongue, for example. Nonetheless, all five qualities of taste can be detected at all locations of the tongue. You may have seen drawings of the tongue that indicate the locations where the basic tastes are processed. We now know that such simplified drawings are simply incorrect. Another factor arguing against a simple model of the sense of taste is the fact that there is wide genetic variation in the sense of taste. Linda Bartoshuk and her colleagues have found that some individuals have a larger number of taste buds than others. These individuals are called *supertasters* (Bartoshuk, Fast & Snyder, 2005).

You might be surprised to learn that your sense of taste also plays a role in how you make moral judgments about behavior. When we learn that someone has done something reprehensible, it elicits a specific emotional response of disgust similar to the one we feel when we taste something disgusting. According to an experiment by Eskine, Kacinick, & Prinz (2011) if you taste something disgusting, you will judge a moral transgression by another person more harshly compared to if you taste something pleasant.

The sense of smell is not well understood. Receptors for smell are hair cells located high in the nasal cavity, very close to the brain itself. The pathway from these receptors to the brain is the most direct and shortest of all the senses. In humans, the sense of smell is very keen. That is, we can detect low levels of smell stimuli.

The sense of smell is very important for many animals. Many animals, including humans, emit pheromones. **Pheromones** are chemicals that produce distinctive odors affecting other members of the same species. Pheromones are sometimes released in urine, or by cells in the skin, or from special glands (in some deer, this gland is located near the rear hoof). One purpose of pheromones is to mark territory, to let others of the same species know of your presence. If you take a dog for a walk and he urinates on almost every signpost, he is leaving a pheromone message that says, "I have been here; this is my odor; this is my turf." As you might suspect, dogs have a significantly more sensitive sense of smell than humans (from 300 to 10,000 *times* more [Goldstein, 2017]), and the canine nose is more sensitive to pheromones than nearly anything else (Leinders-Zufall et al., 2000).

Recall that a foul taste can lead us to judge someone's bad behavior harshly. The same is true for the sense of smell. Schnall, Haidt, Clore, and Jordan (2008) report that participants exposed to a foul smell rated a transgression more harshly than those not exposed to a foul smell. It didn't matter if the foul smell was strong or weak. Interestingly, with the sense of smell, a more pleasant smell can promote positive behaviors (Liljenquist, Zohng, & Galinsky, 2010). Compared to a no-smell control, participants who were exposed to a clean smell showed higher levels of altruism (helping). Participants in clean smell conditions were willing to donate more money, expressed more interest in volunteering, and return more money mistakenly given to them.

Most of us don't often think about our skin. We scratch it, scrape it, cut it, and wash it, but we surely don't pay much attention to it. Each square inch of our multi-layered skin contains nearly 20 million cells, and among these cells are many special sense receptors. Skin receptor cells may be divided into those with *free nerve endings* and those with some sort of covering—called *encapsulated nerve endings*, of which there are many types. The special sense receptors in our skin somehow give rise to our cutaneous senses. These **cutaneous senses** provide the psychological experience of touch or pressure and of warm and cold.

We can easily discriminate between a light touch and a strong jab in the arm and between vibrations, tickles, and itches. An appealing hypothesis is that different receptors in the skin are responsible for each kind of sensation, but the facts do not support this hypothesis. Although some types of receptor cells are more sensitive to some types of stimuli, current thinking is that our ability to discriminate among types of cutaneous sensation is due to the unique combination of responses the many receptor cells have to various types of stimulation.

We take for granted our ability to know how and where our bodies are positioned in space. Without thinking, we seem to know how our bodies are positioned in regard to the pull of gravity. Our senses also let us know where parts of our body are in relation to one another. We can tell if we are moving or standing still. And, unless we have a special reason to pay attention to them (for example, being on a roller coaster), we usually adapt quickly to these sensory messages and virtually ignore them.

Our sense of sight gives us most of the information about where we are in space. If we need to know, we simply look around. However, even with our eyes closed, we have two systems to help us sense our position in space. One, the vestibular sense, tells us about balance, about where we are in relation to gravity, and about acceleration or deceleration.

The receptors for the vestibular sense are on either side of the head near the inner ears. When the vestibular receptors are over-stimulated, the result may be motion sickness.

The kinesthetic sense senses the position and movements of parts of the body and has receptors found in the joints, muscles, and tendons. The way the kinesthetic receptors operate is an excellent example of reflex action. Consider something as simple as bending your elbow. At the same time that muscles in the front of your upper arm (biceps) contract, the corresponding muscles in the back of your arm (triceps) automatically relax. Our kinesthetic receptors, operating reflexively through the spinal cord, take care of the details without our having to think about them. In fact, about the only time you notice your kinesthetic system is when it stops working well, such as when your leg "falls asleep" and you have trouble walking.

People who go on amusement park rides like this are putting a real strain on their vestibular sense, the ability to judge one's position with regard to gravity, acceleration, and deceleration.

Source: Jacob Lund/Shutterstock.

A special sense is the *pain sense*. Pain, or the fear of it, can be a strong motivator; people will do all sorts of things to avoid pain. Pain is surely unpleasant, but it is also very useful. Pain alerts us when a problem occurs somewhere in our bodies and prompts us to take steps to remove the source of the pain. We don't know much about the receptors for the pain sense. Our skin's surface has many receptors for pain, but they can also be found deep inside our bodies—consider stomachaches, headaches, and lower back pain. Researchers have long suspected that the brain plays a crucial role in the experience of pain, but only recently have they been able to find areas in the thalamus and the parietal lobe of the cerebral cortex that are intimately involved in the sensation of pain. Pain is the only "sense" for which they cannot find a specific center in the cerebral cortex (Loyd & Murphy, 2006). Each person's response to pain is unique. Many factors influence how each of us responds to pain, including prior experiences, memories of those experiences, and attitudes about pain. In addition, each person's tolerance for pain may be partly genetic. Researchers have isolated a gene that produces an enzyme called COMT involved in pain tolerance (Nielsen, Christrup, Sato, Drewes, & Olesen, 2017). According to Nielsen, et al. there are two versions of this gene (G and A). Individuals with the G version of the gene are more sensitive to pain than those with the A version.

Vestibular sense—the sense that tells us about balance, about where we are in relation to gravity, and about acceleration or deceleration.

Kinesthetic sense—senses the position and movements of parts of the body and has receptors found in the joints, muscles, and tendons.

STUDY CHECK

What are the stimuli and the receptors for the senses of gustation and olfaction?
What are the characteristics of the cutaneous senses and the position senses?
What is the pain sense?

THINKING CRITICALLY

Is cutaneous sensation the same all over your body, or are some areas more sensitive to touch and pressure than others? How might sensitivity to touch over different body areas be tested?

Perceptual Selection: A Matter of Paying Attention

To help guide our discussion of perceptual processes, consider the following story of a classroom demonstration observed by a colleague when he was in graduate school.

In a grand old lecture hall at the University of Tennessee, nearly 600 students settled down to listen to the day's lecture on perception. Suddenly a student burst through the closed doors at the rear of the hall. Unknown to the class, he was the lecturer's student assistant. This student stomped down the center aisle of the classroom, screaming obscenities at the professor. "You failed me for the last time, you so-and-so!" The class was stunned. No one moved as the student leaped over the lectern to grab the professor. The two struggled briefly, then—in full view of everyone—a chrome-plated revolver appeared. Down behind the lectern they fell. Kaboom! With no experience in school shootings as we presently have, the class sat frozen in their seats as the professor lay moaning on the floor. The student ran from the room through the same side door from which the professor had entered just minutes ago. At just the proper dramatic moment, the professor slowly drew himself up to the lectern. And in a calm, soft voice he said, "Now I want everyone to write down exactly what you saw."

You can guess what happened. The "irate student" was described as being from 5'4" to 6'3" tall, weighing between 155 and 230 pounds, wearing either a blue blazer or a gray sweatshirt. The most remarkable misperception had to do with the pistol. When the professor first reached the lectern, he reached into his suit-coat pocket, removed the gun, and placed it on top of his notes. When the "irate student" crashed into the room, the first thing the professor did was to reach for the revolver and point toward the student. In fact, the student never had the gun. It was the professor who fired the shot that startled the class, sliding the gun to the floor as he fell. In fact, fewer than 25 of the 600 students in class that day reported the events as they occurred. The overwhelming majority of witnesses claimed that a crazy student had burst into the classroom with a gun in his hand.

Try to imagine how you might have reacted if you had been in class that morning. You sit in class listening to your professor lecture, and from time to time, your mind wanders (we hope not too frequently). You think that wearing your new shoes was not a good idea. Your feet hurt. To your left, a student rips open a bag of chips. You turn your head, annoyed. You smell someone's perfume and think what a pleasant fragrance it is. You can feel the pen in your hand as you write. Your senses are being bombarded simultaneously by all sorts of information: sights, sounds, tastes, smells, even pain. Suddenly, someone enters the room and begins arguing with your professor. A scuffle breaks out. You see a gun and hear a shot. Your heart is pounding, you are breathing heavily, and you don't know what to do next.

What determines which stimuli attract our attention and which get ignored? One thing is for sure: You cannot attend to every stimulus at once. Typically, we select a very few details to which we attend. The competition among stimuli to be selected in or ignored is not just an academic exercise.

Now let's consider some of the important variables that influence what we attend to and what we ignore. These variables are of two general types: stimulus factors and personal factors. By *stimulus factors* we mean those characteristics that make some stimuli more compelling than others no matter who the perceiver is. By *personal factors* we are referring to those characteristics of the perceiver that influence which stimuli get attended to or perceived. Personal factors may be short-lived, such as the emotional arousal that accompanies witnessing an accident, or they can be more stable, such as poor vision or personal prejudices.

Stimulus Factors in Perceptual Selectivity

Contrast—the extent to which a stimulus is physically different from the other stimuli around it.

The most important stimulus factor in perceptual selection is contrast, the extent to which a stimulus is physically different from the other stimuli around it. One stimulus can contrast with other stimuli in a variety of ways. For example, we are more likely to attend to a stimulus if its *intensity* is different from the intensities of other stimuli. Generally, the more intense a stimulus, the more likely we are to select it for further processing. We are more likely to attend to an irate student in a classroom if he is shouting rather than whispering. In other contexts, a bright light is more attention-grabbing than a dim one; an extreme temperature is more likely to be noticed than a moderate one. This isn't always the case, however, as context can make a difference. A shout *is* more compelling than a whisper, unless everyone is shouting; then it may be the soft, quiet, reasoned tone that gets our attention. If we are faced with a barrage of bright lights, a dim one, by contrast, may be the one we process more fully.

The same argument holds for the stimulus characteristic of physical size. In most cases, the bigger the stimulus, the more likely we are to attend to it. There is little point in building a small billboard to advertise your motel or restaurant. You want to construct the biggest billboard you can in hopes of attracting attention. Still, faced with many large stimuli, contrast effects often cause us to attend to the one that is smaller. The easiest player to spot on a football field is often the place-kicker, who tends to be smaller and does not wear as much protective padding as the other players.

A third dimension for which contrast is relevant is motion. Motion is a powerful factor in determining visual attention. Walking through the woods, you may nearly step on a chipmunk before you notice it, as long as it stays still—an adaptive camouflage that chipmunks do well. If it moves to escape, you easily notice it as it scurries across the leaves. Again, it is the contrast created by movement that is important.

Although intensity, size, and motion are three characteristics of stimuli that readily come to mind, there are others. Indeed, any way in which two stimuli are different can provide a dimension that determines which stimulus we attend to. A red leaf on a tree of otherwise green leaves will "stand out" and get our attention. (Even a small grease spot can easily grab attention if it is right in the middle of a solid yellow tie.) Because contrast so often guides attention, key terms are printed in **boldface type** throughout this book—so you will notice them, attend to them, and recognize them as important stimuli. There is no doubt that every student in that Tennessee classroom the morning the "crazed" student rushed the lectern attended to several salient details of the situation. The events of that class session surely contrasted with normal classroom expectations.

There is another stimulus characteristic that determines attention, but for which contrast is not relevant: *repetition*. The more often a stimulus is presented, the more likely it will be attended to, with all else being equal, of course. Note that we have to say, "all else being equal," or contradictions will arise. If stimuli are repeated too often, we adapt to them, because they are no longer new or novel. Even so, there are many examples that convince us of the value of repetition in getting someone's attention. Instructors who want to make an important point seldom mention it just once; they repeat it. This is why we repeat the definitions of important terms in the text, in the margin, and again in the glossary. People who schedule commercials on television want you to attend to their messages, and obviously repetition is one of their main techniques.

There are many ways in which stimuli differ. The greater the contrast between any stimulus and others around it, the greater the likelihood that that stimulus will capture our attention. All else being equal, the more often a stimulus is presented, the greater the likelihood that it will be perceived and selected for further processing.

Source: Richard Laschon/Shutterstock.

If ever there were a situation in which we would want a stimulus to stand out as a figure against a background, it would be of a railroad-crossing signal as a train approaches. Those lights had better be bright and flashing.

STUDY CHECK

What stimulus factors influence which stimuli are attended to or selected for further processing?

You have been hired to design a billboard to advertise a new motel in town. What sorts of issues should you consider to make sure that a motorist will notice your billboard among all the other signs along the side of the road?

Personal Factors in Perceptual Selectivity

Sometimes attention is determined less by the physical characteristics of the stimuli present than by personal characteristics of the perceiver. Imagine two students watching a football game on television. Both are viewing identical stimulation from the same screen. One asks, "Wow, did you see that tackle?" The other responds, "No, I was watching the cheerleaders." The difference in perception here is hardly attributable to the nature of the stimuli because both students received the same sensory information from the same TV. The difference is due to personal factors, which can be categorized as motivation, expectation, or past experience.

After each classroom exam, an instructor collects answer sheets from the students and then goes over the multiple-choice test, sharing what she believes is the best answer. Students have marked their answers on the exams and thus can get immediate feedback. One student is particularly worried about item #2. It was a difficult item for which he chose alternative D. The instructor gets to item #2 and clearly says, "The answer to number two is B." The student responds, "Yes! I knew I got that one right!" But wait a minute! The instructor said "B." But the student wanted to hear her say "D" so badly that that was what he perceived. He selected (attended to) a stimulus that was not even there.

Just as we often perceive what we want to perceive, we often perceive what we *expect* to perceive. We may not notice, or process, stimuli when they are present simply because we did not "know" that they were coming—we didn't expect them. A **mental set** is a cognitive structure formed when we are psychologically predisposed or expect to perceive something.

The inability to change a mental set way of perceiving a problem can interfere with finding a solution to that problem. What we call "creative" problem-solving is often a matter of perceiving aspects of a problem in new or unexpected ways. Thus, even as complex a cognitive process as problem-solving can be, it often hinges on basic perceptual processes.

When we say that what we attend to is a result of motivation and expectation, we are claiming that what we perceive is often influenced by our past experiences. We are likely to perceive, or be set to perceive, what we have perceived in the past. For example, a student took a course in comparative psychology that focused on the behaviors of non-human organisms. One of the teachers of the course was an ornithologist (a scientist who studies birds). Participation in early morning bird watching was a requirement of the course. The student's memory is vivid: cold, tired, clutching a thermos of coffee, slopping through the marshland looking for birds as the sun was just rising. After 20 minutes of this unpleasantness, the instructor had identified 10 or 11 different birds. The student wasn't certain but thought he had seen a duck. The differences in perception between the instructor and the student that cold, wet morning can be explained in terms of motivation (he *did* care more than the student), but his ability to spot birds so quickly also reflected his past experience. He knew where to look and what to look for.

To review: Our perception of stimuli in the world usually happens without conscious effort. The process can be influenced by several factors, some of which depend on the stimuli themselves. What we perceive is determined to some extent by the bits and pieces of information we receive from our senses. We may attend to a particular stimulus because it is significantly larger, smaller, more colorful, louder, or slower than the other stimuli around it. There are two types of processing we can use. **Bottom-up processing** involves organizing, identifying, and storing stimuli in our memory centers based on information derived from our senses. On the other hand, how stimuli are perceived also can be influenced by the motivation, expectations, and experiences of the perceiver.

Mental set—a cognitive structure formed when we are psychologically predisposed or expect to perceive something.

Bottom-up processing—organizing, identifying, and storing stimuli in our memory centers based on information derived from our senses.

In this case, selection of stimuli is a matter of applying concepts and information already processed. **Top-down processing** occurs when what one selects and perceives depends on what the perceiver already knows.

Top-down processing—when what one selects and perceives depends on what the perceiver already knows.

STUDY CHECK

What personal factors can influence which stimuli are attended to or selected for further processing?

THINKING CRITICALLY

The American judicial system relies on the testimony of eyewitnesses in prosecuting crimes. Given what you have learned about perception and paying attention, what do you think about the wisdom of relying on such testimony?

Organizing Our Perceptual World

A basic task of perception is to select certain stimuli from among all those that strike our receptors for further processing. A related perceptual task is to organize and interpret those bits and pieces of experience into meaningful, organized wholes. We do not hear individual sounds of speech; we perceive words, phrases, and sentences. Our visual experience is not one of bits of color and light and dark, but of identifiable objects and events. We do not perceive a warm pat on the back as responses from hundreds of individual receptors in our skin. Our view of the world falls onto a two-dimensional surface at the back of our eyes, but our experience of that world is in three dimensions.

A basic principle of perceptual organization is the **figure-ground relationship**, in which well-defined objects stand out against a relatively formless background. As you focus your attention on the words on this page, they form figures against the ground (or background, if you'd prefer) provided by the rest of the page and everything else within your field of vision. When you hear your instructor's voice during a lecture, it is the figure against the ground of all other sounds in the room. The irate student who barged into the classroom to confront a professor became a perceptual figure rather quickly. When you go to a museum and look at a painting hanging on the wall, the painting is the figure, and the wall is the ground. It is important to note that the figure (e.g., the painting on the wall) dominates our perception and is remembered better than the ground (the wall behind the painting). **Figure 3.7** shows

Figure-ground relationship—well-defined objects stand out against a relatively formless background.

FIGURE 3.7 Figure-Ground Perception

As you view this picture, you will see that it seems to reverse. At one moment you see a vase, and at the next moment you see the profiles of two faces. What you see depends on what you perceive as figure and what you perceive as ground.

an example of a *reversible figure-ground relationship* where figure and ground can be reversed. Do you see two faces facing one another or a chalice?

Grouping Stimuli with Bottom-Up Processing

As with perceptual selection, many factors influence how we organize our perceptual world. Again, it will be useful to consider both stimulus factors (bottom-up processing) and personal factors (top-down processing).

Bottom-up processing occurs when we select stimuli as they enter our senses and process them on up "higher" into our cognitive systems by organizing them, interpreting them, making them meaningful, and storing them in our memories. When we talk about bottom-up processing in this context, we are talking about organizing stimuli together based solely on the characteristics of the stimuli themselves. These "stimulus factors" include closure, proximity, similarity, and continuity. **Figure 3.8** illustrates these four stimulus factors, described as follows:

Closure—the process by which we fill in gaps in our perceptual world.

1. **Closure**. One of the most commonly encountered principles of grouping, or organization, is **closure**, the process by which we fill in gaps in our perceptual world. Closure provides an excellent example of perception as an active process. It underscores the notion that we constantly seek to make sense out of our environment, whether that environment presents us with sensible stimuli or not. This concept is illustrated by Panel (a) of Figure 3.8. At a glance, we see a star and a circle but, of course, they are not. For example, that's not the way to make a star. Because of closure, however, we perceive a star.

    As an example of closure, make a recording on your phone of a casual conversation with a friend, and write down exactly what you both say. A truly faithful transcription will reveal that many words and sounds were left out. Although they were

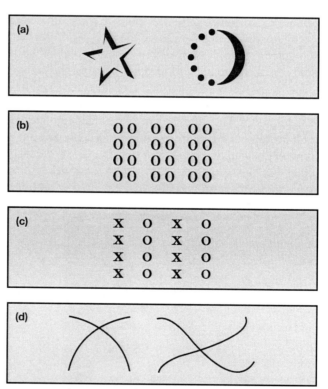

FIGURE 3.8 Gestalt Principles of Form Perception

These patterns illustrate the roles of (*a*) closure, (*b*) proximity, (*c*) similarity, and (*d*) continuity in form perception.

FIGURE 3.9 A Subjective Contour

Seeing a complete triangle when only its corners are displayed is an example of the Gestalt principle of closure. Feature-detector cells in the visual cortex respond to such illusory contours as if they were real. This finding supports the Gestalt position that the brain imposes organization on stimuli.

Source: Based on an image from the Wikimedia Commons; Kanizsa, G. (1955).

not actually there as stimuli, they were not missed by the listener because he or she filled in the gaps (closure), and you both understood what was being said.

A phenomenon that many psychologists believe to be a special case of closure is the perception of *subjective contours*, in which arrangements of lines and patterns enable us to see figures that are not actually there. If that sounds a bit strange, see **Figure 3.9**, in which we have an example of subjective contour. In this figure, you "see" a solid triangle that is so clear it nearly jumps off the page. There is no accepted explanation for subjective contours, but it seems to be another example of our perceptual processes filling in gaps in our perceptual world in order to provide us with sensible information.

2. ***Proximity***. Glance quickly at the portion of Panel (b) of Figure 3.8. Without giving it much thought, what did you see? A bunch of Os, yes, but more than that, there are three identifiable groups of Os, aren't there? The group of Os on the left seems somehow separate from the groups on the right, whereas the Os within each group seem to go together. This illustrates what psychologists call **proximity** (or contiguity)—events occurring close together in space or time are perceived as belonging together and part of the same figure.

> **Proximity (or contiguity)**—events occurring close together in space or time are perceived as belonging together and part of the same figure.

Proximity operates on more than just visual stimuli. Sounds that occur together (are contiguous) in speech are perceived together to form words or phrases. In written language, there are physical spaces between words on the printed page. Thunder and lightning often occur together, thunder following shortly after the lightning. As a result, it is difficult to think about one without also thinking about the other.

3. ***Similarity***. Now glance at Panel (c) of Figure 3.8 and note what you see there. These Xs and Os are clearly organized into a simple pattern: two columns of Xs and two of Os. Perceiving *rows* of alternating Xs and Os is possible, but difficult, which demonstrates the principle of similarity. **Similarity** involves grouping together in perception stimuli that are alike or share properties. Similarity underlies the old adage that "birds of a feather are perceived together." For example, most of us perceive Australian koalas as bears because they look so much like bears when, in fact, they are related to kangaroos and wallabies.

> **Similarity**—grouping together in perception stimuli that are alike or share properties.

4. ***Continuity***. The principle of **continuity** (or good continuation) is operating when we see things as ending up consistently with the way they started. Panel (d) of Figure 3.8 illustrates this point with a two simple line drawings. The clearest way to organize each of the drawings is as being made up of two separate but intersecting curved lines. It's difficult to imagine seeing this figure any other way.

> **Continuity (or good continuation)**—when we see things as ending up consistently with the way they started.

Continuity may account for how we organize some of our perceptions of people. Aren't we surprised when we hear that a hardworking, award-winning high school honor student does poorly in college and flunks out? That's not the way we like to view the world. We would not be as surprised to find that a student who barely made it through high school fails to pass in college. We want things to continue as they began, as in "as the twig is bent, so grows the tree."

STUDY CHECK

What are the characteristics of stimuli that guide our bottom-up organization of information presented by our senses?

THINKING CRITICALLY

For each of the stimulus factors listed above that influence the grouping of stimuli, generate an example different from the one in the text.

Grouping Stimuli with Top-Down Processing

Remember that when we refer to top-down processing, the implication is that we take advantage of motivations, expectations, and previously stored experiences in order to deal with incoming stimuli. In terms of perceptual organization, this means that we often perceive stimuli as going together, as part of the same figure, because we want to, because we expect them to, or because we have perceived them together in the past.

There may be few examples of this observation better than the one of the professor who was lecturing when an irate student barged into the room (actually the professor's assistant) and got into a heated argument with the professor. What happened next was the most interesting. Nearly 600 students claimed to have perceived something that did not really happen. They *saw* a student with a gun try to shoot their professor. In actuality, it was the professor who brandished the gun. The problem was not one of perceptual selection. Everybody saw the gun. The problem was one of organization—with whom did they associate the gun? No one was mentally set for the professor to bring a gun to class. No one wanted to see the professor with a gun. And no one had experienced a professor with a gun in class before. (Seeing crazed students with guns is not a common experience either, but with television, movies, and similar events showing up in the daily news, it is certainly a more probable one.)

Here is another simple example of how top-down processing can influence our perception of reality. Examine the short sentence presented in **Figure 3.10**. Even at a glance, you

THE CAT SAT
BY THE DOOR.

FIGURE 3.10 An Example of Top-Down Processing

have little difficulty with the meaning of this short phrase: The cat sat by the door. Now note that the "H" in both instances of the word "THE" and the "A" in the words "CAT" and "SAT" are identical. Your senses could not discriminate between these two figures, except that they occurred in a meaningful context. Without past experience with the English language and a passing knowledge of cats, doors, and sitting, the stimuli of Figure 3.10 would make little sense.

Hidden in all of these examples of perceptual selection and organization is one of the most important principles of psychology as it affects our lives. It is the central importance of perception in our everyday lives. Simply put: What matters most to you and me is not what actually happened in the world. What matters most is what we *perceive to have happened*. Yes, it was the professor who had the pistol. But—for many reasons—most of those people present saw the irate student with the gun. And *that* is what they processed. *That* is how they organized their worlds. And *that* is what they remembered—not what actually happened, but what they perceived to have happened.

STUDY CHECK

How does top-down processing influence how incoming sensory messages are organized or grouped together?

THINKING CRITICALLY

People in which jobs or professions are most likely to find issues of perceptual organization most important, and why?

Perceiving Depth and Distance

Perception requires that we select and organize stimulus information. One of the ways in which we organize visual stimuli is to note where they happen to be in the world. We perceive the world as three-dimensional. As long as we pay attention (surely a required perceptual process), we won't fall off cliffs or run into buildings. We know with considerable accuracy just how far we are from objects in our environment. What is remarkable about this ability is that light reflected from objects and events in our environment falls on two-dimensional retinas at the back of our eyes. Thus, the depth and distance in our world is not something we directly sense; it is something we perceive.

The ability to judge depth and distance accurately is an adaptive skill that plays an important role in determining many of our actions. Our ability to make such judgments reflects the fact that we are simultaneously responding to a large number of cues to depth and distance. Some cues are built into our visual systems, while others rely on our appreciation of the physical environment. It is also the case that one's culture plays a role in the perception of depth and distance.

Some of the cues we get about distance and depth reflect the way our eyes work. Cues that involve both eyes are called *binocular cues* (bi means "two"). For example, when we look at a nearby three-dimensional object, each eye gets a somewhat different view of it. Hold a pen with a clip on it a few feet in front of your eyes. Rotate the pen until the clip can be viewed by the left eye, but not by the right. (Just close one eye, then the other, as you rotate the pen). **Retinal disparity** is a binocular cue for depth in which each eye gets a different view of the same object. It is a cue that what we are looking at must be solid or three-dimensional. Otherwise, each eye would see the same image, not two disparate ones.

Convergence is another binocular cue for depth and distance and involves the eyes turning toward each other when viewing something up close. As we gaze off into the

Retinal disparity—a binocular cue for depth in which each eye gets a different view of the same object.

Convergence—a binocular cue for depth involving the eyes turning toward each other when viewing something up close.

distance, our eyes aim outward in almost parallel fashion. As we focus on objects up close to us, our eyes come together, or converge, and we interpret that convergence as an indication that what we are looking at is nearby. If you consider convergence and retinal disparity together, you get a hint about the depth-perception abilities of certain animals. Those with their two eyes located at the front of their heads (dogs, cats, frogs, and primates, for example) have significantly better depth perception than do those animals with one eye located on each side of their heads (such as horses, rabbits, birds, and fish).

The remaining depth-perception cues are monocular, implying that they require only one eye to have their influence. (Even the physical cues that follow are monocular cues because they can be appreciated with only one eye.) A unique monocular cue, at least for relatively short distances, is *accommodation*, which is, as noted earlier, the changing of the shape of the lens by the ciliary muscles to focus images on the retina. When we focus on distant objects, accommodation flattens our lens, but when we focus on nearby objects, our lens gets rounder or fatter. Although the process is reflexive and occurs automatically, our brains react to the activity of our ciliary muscles in terms of the distance of an object from our eyes. Accommodation does not function well as a cue for distances much beyond arm's length because the changes in the activity of the ciliary muscles are too slight to be noticed ("below threshold," right?). But it is within arm's length that decisions about distance are often critical.

The physical cues to distance and depth are those we get from the structure of our environment. These are sometimes called *pictorial cues* because artists use them to create the impression of three-dimensionality on a two-dimensional canvas or paper. Here are some of the most important.

1. *Linear perspective*: As you stand in the middle of a road, looking off into the distance, the sides of the road, which you know to be parallel, seem to come together in the distance. Using this pictorial cue in drawing takes some time and experience to develop. See Panel (a) of **Figure 3.11** for an example of linear perspective.

2. *Interposition*: This cue to distance reflects our appreciation that objects in the foreground tend to cover, or partially obscure, objects in the background, and not vice versa (Panel (b) of Figure 3.11). One of the reasons a professor knows that people sitting in the back of a classroom are farther away than people sitting in the front row is the information that he or she gets from interposition. People (and other objects) in the front partially block the view of the people sitting behind them.

3. *Relative size*: This is a commonly used cue to our judgment of distance. Very few stimuli in this world change their size, but a lot of things get nearer to or farther away from us. Objects that are near to you cast a larger image on your retina than objects that are farther away. So, all else being equal, we tend to judge the object that produces the larger retinal image as closer. Imagine standing behind a large truck. The image of that truck nearly fills your field of vision. As the truck pulls away and heads down the road, its image on the retina of your eye gets smaller and smaller. You know very well that trucks do not shrink in size, so you interpret the change in retinal image as a change in distance. See Panel (c) of Figure 3.11 for an example of relative size.

4. *Texture gradient*: Standing on a gravel road, looking down at your feet, you can clearly make out the details of the texture of the roadway. You can see individual pieces of gravel. As you look on down the road, the texture gradually changes, and details give way to a smooth blend of a surface without texture. We interpret this gradual change (gradient) in texture as a change in distance. Here is a related observation, known well by golfers: People tend to overestimate the distance of an object (e.g., a flag in the center of a golf course green) when it is observed across a gap, such as a steep ravine or valley. The same distance can be judged much more accurately if viewed over flat or even rolling terrain, where

FIGURE 3.11 Examples of Monocular Cues for Depth

(*a*) Linear perspective is a common and clear cue to distance. (*b*) With interposition, objects in the foreground (closer to us) partially obscure our view of objects farther away. (*c*) We all know that hot air balloons are about the same size and thus judge those that appear larger as being closer to us—relative size. (*d*) Texture gradient refers to the notion that we can discern up close the bits and pieces of small objects that gradually seem to become indistinguishable as they are farther away from us. (*e*) Motion parallax refers to the fact that when we move past a stable view (as does a passenger in a train), objects that are close or nearby seem to whiz by us quickly, while objects that are farther away remain in our sight line for a longer period of time. (*f*) Shadows cast by objects provide another cue for depth.

Source: (*a*) Skyimages/Shutterstock. (*b*) Marcio Jose Bastos Silva/Shutterstock. (*c*) topseller/Shutterstock. (*d*) Serov Aleksei/Shutterstock. (*e*) CebotariN/Shutterstock. (*f*) olies/Shutterstock.

the ground is continuously in view—allowing for texture gradient effects to operate (Sinai, Ooi, & He, 1998). See Panel (d) of Figure 3.11 for an example of texture gradient.

5. ***Motion parallax***: This rather technical label names something with which we are all familiar. The clearest example may occur when we are in a car, looking out a side window (as the passenger, not the driver). Even if the car is going at a modest speed, nearby utility poles and fence posts seem to race by. Objects farther away from the car seem to move more slowly, while mountains or trees way off in the distance seem hardly to be moving at all. This difference in apparent motion is known as motion parallax. Motion parallax is shown in Panel (e) of Figure 3.11.

6. ***Patterns of shading***: Drawings that do not use shading look flat and two-dimensional. Children eventually learn that if they want their pictures to look lifelike, they should shade in tree trunks and apples and show them casting shadows (See Panel (f) of Figure 3.1). Two-dimensional objects do not cast shadows, and how objects create patterns of light and shade tells us a great deal about their shape and solidity.

Culture and Perception

Sensation is a matter of physics and physiology. Energy levels above threshold initiate neural impulses in sense receptors. There is every reason to believe that everyone's sense receptors work in pretty much the same way. Perception, however, is a different matter altogether. Very often, perception depends on the person doing the perceiving. It should not be too surprising that how we perceive the world can be shaped by the culture within which we are raised and live.

Culture is related to how basic visual information is processed. Generally, European Americans tend to be analytical. They pay attention to things like category relationships (e.g., an apple is a fruit) and rules. East Asians tend to be holistic in their processing of information. That is, they tend to pay more attention to an entire stimulus rather than parts of it (Nisbett, Peng, Choi, & Norenzayan, 2001). European Americans are also more likely than Asians to focus on the central details of a stimulus (e.g., in a movie), and Asians are more likely to focus on aspects of the context in which the details are found (Masuda & Nisbett, 2001). Asians are also more likely to shift their gaze to aspects of a stimulus showing context (Chua, Boland, & Nisbett, 2005) and pay more attention to subtle changes in background information than European Americans (Masuda & Nisbett, 2006). These differences most likely relate to the different visual environments in which members of different cultures are raised. One study, for example, found that Japanese cities tend to be much more complex and confusing than Western cities. The more confusing environments in Japan lead Japanese people to rely more on contextual cues (Miyamoto, Nisbett, & Masuda, 2006).

Culture also relates to how people judge depth and distance. In a classic study, Colin Turnbull (1961) observed that members of the Bambuti people in the African Congo spend much of their lives in the dense Ituri Forest, where they seldom can see much farther than 100 feet. When Turnbull took his Bambuti guide out onto a grassy plain, he was visually confused and disoriented by the open spaces. The guide (Kenge)

thought that buffalo grazing a few miles away were tiny insects because they looked so small. Kenge was using retinal size rather than relative size as a cue to distance, as would a person more familiar with open spaces and great distances. In fact, when Turnbull told Kenge that the specs were actually buffalo, he laughed and was sure that Turnbull was lying to him!

Interestingly, culture can also affect how people produce pictorial representations. Vaid, Rhodes, Tosun, and Eslami (2011) had English-speaking and Arabic-speaking participants draw a picture showing two houses, one closer than the other. The cultural difference here was expected to be reflected based on the differences in how written language works in the two cultures. In English, language is read and written from left to right, whereas in Arabic, it is read and written from right to left. Vaid et al. found that participants from both language cultures drew the nearer house larger than the more distant house and drew the nearer house first. However, they found that English-speaking participants drew the nearer (larger) house on the left, and Arabic-speaking participants drew it on the right. Vaid et al. suggest that prolonged exposure to the different languages led to the differences in how objects are represented pictorially. Culture can also influence creative expression. Some evidence suggests that cultures that value autonomy and self-directed learning show greater creativity than those that do not value these characteristics (Palmiero, Nakatani, & van Leeuwen, 2017). To test the idea that culture influences artistic expression, Palmiero et al. had Japanese and Italian participants do several tasks to evaluate creativity. For example, participants added details to a common figure (e.g., a circle), such as shading. Palmiero et al. found that Italian participants added significantly more details. However, the two groups did not differ on a number of other tests of creative expression. This suggests that although some cultures may enhance creative expression more than others in some realms, cultural groups may not differ all that much from one another in terms of creativity.

Perceptual Constancies

Perceptual constancies help us organize and interpret the stimulus input we get from our senses. Because of the constancy of perception, we recognize a familiar object as being the same regardless of how far away it is, the angle from which we view it, or the color or intensity of the light reflected from it. You can recognize your textbook whether you view it from a distance or close up, straight on or from an angle, in a dimly or brightly lighted room, or in blue, red, or white light; it is still your textbook, and you will perceive it as such regardless of how your senses detect it. Were it not for perceptual constancy, you might perceive each sensation as a new experience, and little would appear familiar to you.

Size constancy is the tendency to see objects as unchanging in size regardless of the size of the retinal image they produce. A friend standing close to you may fill your visual field. At a distance, the image of the same person may take up only a fraction of your visual field. The size of the image on your retina may be significantly different, but you know very well that your friend has not shrunk but has simply moved farther away. Our ability to discern that objects remain the same size depends on many factors, but two of the more important are the quality of the depth-perception cues available to us, and our familiarity with the stimulus object.

Shape constancy is the perception that objects maintain their shape even though the retinal image they cast may change. You can demonstrate shape constancy with any familiar object, such as a door. As you look at a door from various angles, the shape of the image of the door on your retina changes radically. Straight on, it appears to be a rectangle; partially open, a trapezoid; from the edge or fully open, a straight line. However, despite the retinal image, shape constancy ensures you still see a door as a rectangle.

Brightness constancy is the perception that familiar objects retain their usual brightness regardless of the amount or type of light under which they are viewed. You might sense the white shirt or blouse you put on this morning as light gray when you pass through a shadow, or as even a darker gray when night falls, but it is still perceived as a white shirt and in no way darker than it was in the morning. Picture a brick wall on a sunny day. Upon it falls the shadows of nearby trees and shrubs. Although the brightness of the light presented to your eyes from the shaded part of the wall is considerably less than from the unshaded part, you still perceive the wall as all of the same brightness. The same principle holds for color perception.

Color constancy is the perception that the color of a familiar object is constant, despite changing lighting conditions. For example, if you know you put on a white shirt this morning, you would still perceive it as white even if we were to illuminate it with a red light. Under a red light, the shirt might appear red to someone else, but not to you because of color constancy.

Size constancy—the tendency to see objects as unchanging in size regardless of the size of the retinal image they produce.

Shape constancy—the perception that objects maintain their shape even though the retinal image they cast may change.

Brightness constancy—the perception that familiar objects retain their usual brightness regardless of amount or type of light under which they are viewed.

Color constancy—the perception that the color of a familiar object is constant, despite changing lighting conditions.

STUDY CHECK

What are the cues that allow us to perceive depth and distance?
What are the perceptual constancies?

THINKING CRITICALLY

Given what we know about cues to depth and distance, what would it be like to see the world with only one eye?

Chapter Summary

What are the processes of information processing, sensation, and perception?
Information processing refers to how we find out about the world, make judgments about it, learn from it, and remember what we have learned. Information processing is divided into two subtypes: sensation and perception. Sensation is the act of detecting external stimuli and converting those stimuli into nervous-system activity and provides our immediate experience of the stimuli in our environment. Perception is a process that involves the selection, organization, and interpretation of stimuli. Perception is a

more cognitive and central process than sensation, involving motivational states, expectations, and past experiences.

How do the processes of sensation and perception differ?
Sensation is the process of receiving information from the environment and changing it into nervous-system activity. The process of transforming external stimuli into a form that the nervous system can interpret is known as transduction. Perception is the process that involves selection, organization, and interpretation of stimuli. Sensation and perception differ in that perception is a more active, cognitive, and central process than sensation.

What are sensory thresholds?

Sensory thresholds refer to the minimum amount of stimulus intensity or energy necessary to trigger a reaction from a sense organ.

In sensation, what is a difference threshold?

A difference threshold is the minimal difference between stimuli that can be detected. Difference thresholds can be determined for any stimulus characteristic, not just intensity.

What is sensory adaptation?

Sensory adaptation occurs when sensory experiences decrease as a result of continued exposure to a stimulus. For example, when you first walk down a city street, the noise of the traffic may seem very loud. As you continue to stroll, even though the noise level is unchanged, you tend not to notice the sounds because of adaptation. Sense organs are best able to detect changes in stimulation, not continuous stimulation.

What are the three major characteristics of light, and what psychological experience does each produce?

Light is a form of energy that radiates from its source in waves. Light has three properties: wave amplitude (the height of the wave), wavelength (the distance between peaks of the wave, measured in nanometers), and wave purity (the number of different types of waves making up the stimulus). Differences in wave amplitude determine the brightness of light—the higher the wave, the brighter the light. Wavelength determines the hue or color of the light. The visual spectrum for the human eye ranges from 380 to 760 nanometers. The experience of hue gradually shifts from violet, to blue, to green, to yellow, and to red as wavelengths increase from 380 nm to 760 nm. Finally, wave purity refers to its saturation. The more saturated a light wave, the more pure its hue. The purest light is monochromatic and is made up of light waves of energy that are all of the same length. A random mixture of wavelengths produces the lowest saturation, or white light.

What are the structures of the eye that are involved in focusing images onto the back of the eye (the retina)?

The cornea is a tough, virtually transparent structure, and is the first to bend light to focus an image onto the back of the eye. The pupil (the opening through which light passes) and the iris (the colored part of the eye) work to expand or contract, letting in more or less light respectively. In dim light the pupil will be larger, and in bright light it will be smaller. The lens is a flexible structure whose shape is controlled by the ciliary muscles. The ciliary muscles change the shape of the lens to focus light as it enters the eye. The lens becomes flatter when we try to focus on a distant object and more round when we try to focus on a nearby object. This changing of the shape of the lens is called accommodation.

What are the structures of the retina and what are the different functions of the rods and cones?

The retina is a series of photosensitive layers located at the back of the eye. The layer of cells at the very back of the retina contains the photoreceptors, which actually transduce light energy into neural impulses. There are two types of photoreceptors: rods and cones. Rods are responsible for low-light vision and do not provide any information about color or hue. Cones are responsible for daylight vision and the experience of color. Signals from the rods and cones are processed through the bipolar cells and ganglion cells that begin to combine and integrate neural impulses. Fibers from the ganglion cells form the optic nerve. Cones are concentrated in the fovea (near the center of the retina) where there are few layers of cells between the light entering the eye and the cones. In the fovea, the cones are densely packed, and there are no rods. The rods are found outside the fovea, in the retina's periphery. Visual acuity is highest at the fovea. The point where the optic nerve connects to the eye is called the blind spot. There are no rods or cones at this spot; consequently, there is no vision there.

There are about 120 million rods, but only 6 million cones. Rods and cones differ not only in location and number but also in function. The cones work most efficiently in medium to high levels of light and are responsible for the experience of color. Conversely, the rods work most effectively in low light. As a consequence, they are responsible for twilight and night vision. Rods do not discriminate among different wavelengths of light; therefore, the rods are not involved in color vision.

What are the three main physical characteristics of sound, and what psychological experience is produced by each?

Like light, sound may be represented as a wave-form of energy with three major physical characteristics: wave amplitude, frequency, and purity. Wave amplitude provides our experience of the loudness of a sound. Frequency determines pitch, and purity determines timbre.

What are the major structures of the human ear, and what are their roles in hearing?

Most of the structures of the ear (pinna, auditory canal, eardrum, hammer, anvil, and stirrup, and oval window) intensify and transmit the pressure of sound waves to the fluid in the cochlea, which then vibrates the basilar membrane. The basilar membrane stimulates tiny hair cells to transmit neural impulses along the auditory nerve to the temporal lobes of the cerebral cortex.

What are the stimuli and the receptors for the senses of gustation and olfaction?

The chemical senses are gustation (taste) and olfaction (smell). For both, the stimuli are chemical particles dissolved either in a liquid (for taste) or the air (for smell). The receptors for taste are cells in the taste buds located on the tongue. Taste appears to have five primary qualities: sweet, salty, sour, bitter, and umami. For smell, the sense receptors are hair cells that line the upper regions of the nasal cavity.

What are the characteristics of the cutaneous senses and the position senses?

The cutaneous senses are the senses of touch, pressure, warmth, and cold. Specific receptor cells for each of these so-called skin senses have not yet been identified, although they no doubt include free nerve endings and encapsulated nerve endings, which most likely work together. One of our position senses is the vestibular sense, which responds to the movement of small particles suspended in a fluid within our vestibular sacs and semicircular canals and informs us about orientation with regard to gravity or accelerated motion. The other position sense is the kinesthetic sense, which uses receptors in our tendons, muscles, and joints to inform us about the orientation of various parts of our bodies.

What is the pain sense?

The pain sense is a special sense. There are receptors for pain in the skin and throughout the body. Although most people experience pain as negative and seek to avoid it, pain serves an important function. It signals us that there is something wrong so that we can take steps to correct the problem. The brain plays a role in the experience of pain, but there is no specific area of the brain involved in pain sensation. Each person's experience of pain is unique and depends on a number of factors, including prior experiences, memories of those experiences, and attitudes about pain. In addition, each person's tolerance for pain may be partly genetic.

What stimulus factors influence which stimuli are attended to or selected for further processing?

Characteristics of the stimuli in our environments can determine which will be attended to. We are more likely to attend to a stimulus if it contrasts with others around it in terms of intensity, size, motion, novelty, or any other physical characteristic. The repetition of a stimulus also increases the likelihood that we will attend to it.

What personal factors can influence which stimuli are attended to or selected for further processing?

The selection of stimuli is partly based on characteristics of the perceiver. Such factors as motivation, expectation (or mental set), and past experience often determine which stimuli become selected for further processing. When characteristics of the perceiver are influential, we say that information is processed from the "top down" rather than from the "bottom up."

What are the characteristics of stimuli that guide our bottom-up organization of information presented by our senses?

How we organize or group objects and events in our experience depends in part on the characteristics of the available stimuli themselves, such as proximity (occurring together in space or time), similarity (the extent to which stimuli share physical characteristics), continuity (the extent to which stimuli appear to end as they began), and closure (filling in gaps in our perceptual world in a sensible way). When these factors influence organization, we have bottom-up processing, moving from stimulus input up to higher cognitive processing (organizing, storing, and remembering).

How does top-down processing influence how incoming sensory messages are organized or grouped together?

These factors originate in our cognitive (largely memory) systems and are referred to as personal factors. The personal factors that affect perceptual organization are the same as those that influence attention: motivation, mental set, and past experience. Simply put, we perceive stimuli as belonging together because we want to perceive them together, we expect them to be together, or we have experienced them being grouped together in the past.

What are the cues that allow us to perceive depth and distance?

We are able to perceive three-dimensionality and distance, even though we sense the environment on two-dimensional retinas at the back of our eyes, because of the many cues with which we are provided. Some have to do with the visual system. Retinal disparity refers to the fact that each eye gets a slightly different view of three-dimensional objects. Convergence occurs when we look at something near our eyes and they move in toward each other. Retinal disparity and convergence are called binocular cues because they require both eyes. Accommodation, a monocular cue requiring only one eye, occurs when our lenses change shape to focus images as objects move toward or away from us.

Cues for depth and distance also come from the environment, and include such phenomenon as linear perspective (parallel lines seem to come together in the distance), relative size (everything else being equal, the smaller the stimulus, the farther away we judge it to be), interposition (near objects partially obscure our view of more distant objects), texture gradients (details of texture that we can see clearly up close are difficult to determine at a distance), patterns of shading, and motion parallax (as we move toward stationary objects, those close to us seem to move past us more rapidly than do objects in the distance). Depth and distance perception have been found to be susceptible to cultural influences.

What are the perceptual constancies?

Perceptual constancies are mechanisms that help us organize and interpret the stimulus input we receive from our senses. The perceptual constancies allow us to recognize a familiar object for what it is, regardless of the image it forms on our retinas. Size constancy is the tendency to see objects as being of constant size regardless of the size of the retinal image. Shape constancy refers to our perception that objects maintain their shape even though the retinal image they cast may change (as when they are viewed from different angles). Brightness constancy means that the apparent brightness of familiar objects is perceived as being the same regardless of the actual amount or type of light under which they are viewed. Finally, color constancy allows us to see the color of objects as stable despite being illuminated with different-colored lights.

Key Terms

Information processing (p. 49)
Sensation (p. 49)
Transducer (p. 49)
Perception (p. 49)
Sensory threshold (p. 50)
Difference threshold (p. 50)
Sensory adaptation (p. 51)
Dark adaptation (p. 51)
White light (p. 53)
Cornea (p. 53)
Pupil (p. 53)
Iris (p. 53)
Lens (p. 54)
Ciliary muscles (p. 54)
Accommodation (p. 54)
Aqueous humor (p. 54)
Vitreous humor (p. 54)
Retina (p. 54)
Rods (p. 54)
Cones (p. 54)
Optic nerve (p. 54)
Fovea (p. 55)
Blind spot (p. 55)
Decibel scale (p. 57)
Timbre (p. 58)

Pinna (p. 59)
Cochlea (p. 59)
Gustation (p. 61)
Olfaction (p. 61)
Taste buds (p. 61)
Pheromones (p. 62)
Cutaneous senses (p. 62)
Vestibular sense (p. 63)
Kinesthetic sense (p. 63)
Contrast (p. 64)
Mental set (p. 66)
Bottom-up processing (p. 66)
Top-down processing (p. 67)
Figure-ground relationship (p. 67)
Closure (p. 68)
Proximity (p. 69)
Similarity (p. 69)
Continuity (p. 69)
Retinal disparity (p. 71)
Convergence (p. 71)
Size constancy (p. 75)
Shape constancy (p. 75)
Brightness constancy (p. 75)
Color constancy (p. 75)

Learning

CHAPTER 15

Source: Monkey Business Images/Shutterstock

Chapter Outline

Questions You Will Be Able to Answer

After reading Chapter 4, you should be able to answer the following questions:

- How do psychologists define learning?
- What are the steps involved in demonstrating the classical conditioning of the salivation response in dogs to the tone of a bell?
- What are generalization and discrimination, and how are they demonstrated in classical conditioning?
- How did Watson and Rayner classically condition fear in "Little Albert"?
- How can classical conditioning be used in the treatment of phobias?
- How does one demonstrate operant conditioning?
- What are the distinguishing characteristics between reinforcement and reinforcers, between primary and secondary reinforcers, and between positive and negative reinforcers?
- How do psychologists define punishment, and under what circumstances is it an effective means of behavior control?
- What are latent learning and cognitive maps?
- What is the essence of "social learning theory"?

Preview

Directly or indirectly, learning has an impact on every aspect of our being. Learning affects how we perceive the world, how we interact with it as we grow and develop, how we form social relationships, and how we change during the course of psychotherapy. Who we are as unique individuals is a reflection of the interaction of our biological/genetic constitution and our learning experiences. Indeed, the human organism is poorly suited to survive without learning. If we are to survive, much less prosper, we must profit from our experience.

We begin by considering how psychologists define learning. Learning surely produces changes in an organism's psychological functions (affect, behavior, and/or cognition), but we will see that some such changes can be attributed to processes other than learning. Then we focus on a simple form of learning, classical conditioning. (Although learning and conditioning are technically not synonymous, they can be used interchangeably. We follow common usage here by referring to the most basic and fundamental types of learning as "conditioning.") The basic processes of classical conditioning are straightforward. So that we can fully understand those processes, we will spend most of our discussion talking about dogs learning to salivate when bells ring. Don't worry. Before we are through, we will see how important salivating dogs are to our everyday human experience.

We then turn our attention to operant conditioning. In operant conditioning, what matters most are the consequences of an organism's behaviors. The basic premise of operant conditioning is that behaviors are shaped by the consequences they have produced in the past. In this case, learning is a matter of increasing the rate of those responses that produce positive consequences and decreasing the rate of those behaviors that produce negative consequences. A great deal of human behavior can be explained in terms of operant conditioning.

As we did with classical conditioning, we will take a close look at a laboratory demonstration of operant conditioning. Because the concept of reinforcement is so central in operant conditioning, it is sensible to focus on some of the principles of reinforcement—and punishment.

This chapter ends with a brief discussion of some approaches to basic learning procedures that are cognitive in nature. Classical conditioning and operant conditioning both focus on the behavior of organisms and changes in those behaviors. By definition, cognitive approaches consider relatively permanent changes that take place within an organism and may or may not be reflected in that organism's behavior. We conclude the chapter with a discussion of social learning theory, which includes information on how we learn by observing others.

What Is Learning?

There is little doubt that learning is a critically important psychological process, but how shall we define it? Psychologists say that **learning** is a relatively permanent change in behavior that occurs as a result of practice or experience. This is a standard definition, and it raises some important points that we should explore.

When psychologists say that learning is *demonstrated by* a change in behavior, they mean that learning (like many other psychological processes) cannot be observed directly. In a literal sense, there is no way that anyone can directly observe or measure what you have learned. Therefore, we have to make a distinction between "learning," which is an internal process that is not observable, and "performance," which is overt, observable behavior. All we can measure is your performance. To see if you have learned something, we ask you to perform, to do something, and then make inferences about your learning on the basis of your performance. Unfortunately, there may be times when performance does not adequately reflect underlying learning. For example, you may learn a great deal while

Learning—a relatively permanent change in behavior that occurs as a result of practice or experience.

studying for a test. However, you may perform poorly on that test because you are ill or overly anxious. Note that this example can work both ways. Occasionally a student who barely studies and who learns little may do well on a multiple-choice test simply with the good luck of guessing well.

A second aspect of our definition that takes a bit of explaining is that learned changes in behavior are *relatively permanent*. They are not fleeting, short-lived, or cyclical changes such as those due to fatigue or brief shifts in motivation. Consider, for example, the change in keyboarding behavior that occurs, even for a skilled typist, between 8 and 10 each morning. There is likely to be a significant improvement in behavior that we ought not to attribute to learning, but to "warm-up." That same person might not function as well at the end of the day—a change in behavior better attributed to fatigue than to forgetting. These are important changes in behavior, but they are not due to learning. Learned changes are relatively permanent.

As college students (and professors), we tend to think of learning as being a good thing. However, people learn all sorts of behaviors that are ineffective or downright dangerous. Hardly anyone can claim that they truly enjoyed the first cigarette they ever smoked, but (sadly) many people have learned the habit and, having done so, find it difficult to stop.

Another idea in our definition reminds us that there are other changes in behavior that do not result from learning. Learned changes in behavior result from *practice* or *experience*. Some behavioral changes may be due to maturation. The fact that birds fly, salamanders swim, or humans walk has more to do with genes and physical development than with learning. In addition, some changes in our behaviors are due to automatic physiological processes, such as sensory adaptation, and are not learned. When we enter a darkened theater, we don't "learn" to see in the dark. Our vision improves, and our behaviors change as our eyes adapt to the change in lighting.

One final point about learning: We often fall into the habit of thinking that learning is a good thing. Clearly, this is not always true. We can learn maladaptive, ineffective habits just as readily as we learn good, adaptive ones. Few people claim to have enjoyed the first cigarette that he or she smoked. Yet many people have learned the habit—hardly an adaptive one. Learning is reflected in a change in behavior, be it for better or worse.

When we put these ideas together, we have our definition: Learning is demonstrated by (inferred from) a relatively permanent change in behavior that occurs as the result of practice or experience.

STUDY CHECK

How do psychologists define learning?

THINKING CRITICALLY

How could you demonstrate that a given behavior—say a chick's pecking at pieces of grain—was learned or inherited?

Classical Conditioning: The Basics

When people think about learning, they typically think about such things as memorizing the Bill of Rights, studying for an exam, or learning to drive a car. However, our study of learning begins over a hundred years ago in the laboratory of a Russian physiologist who taught dogs to salivate in response to tones. How salivating dogs could be relevant to college students may be difficult to imagine, but be patient; the relevance will soon become apparent.

TABLE 4.1 Basic Classical Conditioning Terms

Terms	Definitions
Reflex	An unlearned, automatic response that occurs in the presence of a specific stimulus (e.g., salivation to food).
Orienting reflex	A simple, unlearned response of attending to a new or unusual stimulus. For example, a tone elicits a response from a dog, but not salivation.
Unconditioned stimulus (UCS)	A stimulus that elicits a response with no prior learning (e.g., food produces salivation without learning).
Unconditioned response (UCR)	The unlearned response made to the UCS.
Neutral stimulus (NS)	A stimulus (e.g., a tone) that does not elicit the UCR.
Conditioned stimulus (CS)	After being paired with the UCS, the NS becomes associated with the food and is now the CS.
Conditioned response (CR)	The learned response (e.g., salivation) made to the CS. The CR is weaker than the UCR.

Late in the nineteenth century, Ivan Pavlov was studying processes of digestion—work for which he would be awarded a Nobel Prize in 1904. Pavlov focused on the salivation reflex in dogs. He knew that he could get his dogs to salivate by forcing food powder into their mouths. He measured the number of drops of saliva produced each time food was introduced. Salivation is a **reflex**—an unlearned, automatic response that occurs in the presence of a specific stimulus. Every time Pavlov presented the food powder, his dogs salivated.

Pavlov then followed up on an observation made by one of his laboratory assistants (Domjan, 2005). His dogs sometimes began salivating before food was put in their mouths. They would salivate at the sight of the food or even at the sight of the laboratory assistant who usually delivered the food. With this observation, Pavlov went off on a tangent that he pursued for the rest of his life. What he studied is now called classical conditioning (or sometimes Pavlovian conditioning). **Classical conditioning** is a learning process in which a neutral stimulus is paired with a stimulus that elicits an unconditioned (unlearned) response. After conditioning, the neutral stimulus alone elicits a new, conditioned (learned) response, much like the original unconditioned response. As an abstract summary statement, that may not make much sense, but as we go through the process step by step, you will realize that the process is straightforward and simple. Some key terms relating to classical conditioning are summarized in **Table 4.1**.

To demonstrate classical conditioning, we first need a stimulus that reliably or consistently produces a predictable response. The relationship between this stimulus and the response it elicits is usually an unlearned, reflexive one. Given this stimulus, the same response always follows. Here is where the food powder comes in. If we present the food powder to a dog, the salivation response follows. We call the stimulus an unconditioned stimulus (UCS). An **unconditioned stimulus** is a stimulus that reliably elicits a response with no prior learning. The **unconditioned response** (UCR) is the unlearned response to an unconditioned stimulus. A UCS (food powder) produces a UCR (salivation) with no prior learning. It happens naturally with no learning involved.

Now we need a neutral stimulus that, when presented, produces a minimal response, or a response of no particular interest. For this neutral stimulus, Pavlov chose a tone. At first, when a tone is sounded, a dog *will* respond. It will, among other things, perk up its ears and try to orient toward the source of the sound. We call this response an **orienting reflex**, a simple, unlearned response of attending to a new or unusual stimulus. Imagine students sitting in class while repairs are going on in the hallway. From time to time the

Reflex—an unlearned, automatic response that occurs in the presence of a specific stimulus.

Classical conditioning—a learning process in which a neutral stimulus is paired with a stimulus that elicits an unconditioned response. After conditioning, the neutral stimulus alone elicits a new, conditioned response, much like the original unconditioned response.

Unconditioned stimulus—a stimulus that reliably elicits a response with no prior learning.

Unconditioned response—the unlearned response to the unconditioned stimulus.

Orienting reflex—a simple, unlearned response of attending to a new or unusual stimulus.

sound of a pounding hammer snatches everyone's attention as they reflexively orient toward the noise.

Pavlov found that after hearing the tone for a while, the dog would get used to it and ignore it. Essentially, the dog learns not to orient toward the tone. (And students in the classroom soon get used to the hammering in the hallway and no longer orient toward it.) We're ready to go. We have two stimuli: a tone that produces a minimal response and food powder (UCS) that reliably produces salivation (UCR).

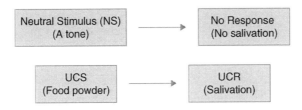

Once we get our stimuli and responses straight, the rest is easy. The two stimuli are paired. That is, they are presented at about the same time—the tone first, then the food. The salivation then occurs automatically in response to the food. We have a neutral stimulus, then a UCS, followed by the UCR (or tone-food-salivation).

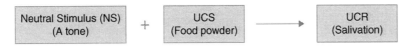

Each pairing of the two stimuli may be considered a conditioning *trial*. If we repeat this procedure several times—for several trials—conditioning will take place. There will be a relatively permanent change in behavior as a result of this experience. After a number of trials, when we present the tone alone, the dog will salivate, something it did not do before. Now the dog salivates not just in response to the food powder, but to the tone as well. The tone is no longer "neutral." It produces a response, so we call the tone a conditioned stimulus (CS). A **conditioned stimulus** is a stimulus that comes to elicit a learned response after being paired with an unconditioned stimulus. To keep the salivation response that it elicits separate from the salivation in response to the food powder, we call it a **conditioned response** (CR), which is the learned response made to a conditioned stimulus. Thus, anytime you see the term "conditioned," you will know that you are dealing with the learned component of classical conditioning.

Conditioned stimulus—a stimulus that comes to elicit a learned response after being paired with an unconditioned stimulus.

Conditioned response—the learned response made to a conditioned stimulus.

Let's review:

1. We start with two stimuli: the neutral stimulus (soon to be the CS), which elicits no UCR, and the UCS, which elicits the UCR.
2. We repeatedly present the CS and UCS together.
3. As a result, when we present the CS alone, it now elicits a CR.
4. Or, we can say, Pavlovian conditioning is basically "ding-poof-slobber."

Note that the same stimulus—say a bell's tone—can be either a neutral stimulus (before learning occurs) or a conditioned stimulus (when it elicits a learned response). Similarly, the same type of response (salivation, for example) can be either an unconditioned response (if it is elicited without learning) or a conditioned response (if it is elicited as the result of learning). If you have a pet, you have no doubt seen this process in action. You may have noted a range of excited, anticipatory behaviors every time your pet hears you open the cabinet where its food is kept. The open door (CS) has been paired with the food inside (UCS), which produces the same sort of reaction (CR) that was originally reserved for the food (UCR).

Assume we have a well-conditioned dog producing a strong CR. If we now go through a series of trials during which the CS is presented but is not paired with the UCS, we will discover that the CR will weaken. As we continue to present the CS without the UCS, the CR will become progressively weaker. Eventually, the dog will stop salivating to the CS. This is called **extinction**—the process in which the strength of a CR decreases with repeated presentations of the CS alone.

Let's make it clear that classical conditioning is not something that occurs only in dogs and cats. You demonstrate a classically conditioned salivation response whenever you see pictures or smell the aromas of your favorite foods (particularly if you're hungry). If you respond with anxiety at the sight of your instructor entering the classroom with exam papers, you are displaying a classically conditioned response.

Extinction—the process in which the strength of a conditioned response (CR) decreases with repeated presentations of the conditioned stimulus (CS) alone.

STUDY CHECK

What are the steps involved in demonstrating the classical conditioning of the salivation response in dogs to the tone of a bell?

THINKING CRITICALLY

Unconditioned responses are those that reliably and naturally occur in the presence of some stimulus *without* any previous learning. How many unconditioned responses in humans can you list?

Generalization and Discrimination

During the course of conditioning, assume that we consistently use a tone of a given pitch as the conditioned stimulus. After repeated pairings of this tone with food powder, a dog salivates when the tone is presented alone. What will happen if we present a tone that the dog has not heard before? The dog will salivate in response to the new tone also. This response will probably not be as strong as the original CR (there may not be as much saliva). How strong it will be depends on how similar the new tone is to the original CS. The more similar the new tone is to the original, the more saliva will be produced. This is **stimulus generalization**—a process by which a conditioned response is elicited by stimuli similar to the original CS.

Stimulus generalization—a process by which a conditioned response is elicited by stimuli similar to the original conditioned stimulus (CS).

Thus, an unconditioned stimulus need not be paired with all possible conditioned stimuli. If you choose a mid-range tone as a CS, a conditioned response automatically generalizes to other, similar tones. If a dog is conditioned to salivate to a tone of middle pitch, it will also salivate to higher and lower tones through generalization. The CR gets weaker and weaker as the new CS differs more and more from the original CS tone. This phenomenon is called the *generalization gradient*.

Discrimination learning is a process by which an organism learns to discriminate between different stimuli, emitting the CR in the presence of some stimuli and not others. In a sense, generalizing a response from one stimulus to others is the opposite of coming to discriminate among them. To produce discrimination learning, we would present a dog with many tones, but would pair the UCS food powder with only one of them—the CS we want the dog to salivate to. We might, for example, pair food powder with a tone of middle C. A lower tone, say, A, would also be presented to the dog but would not be followed by food powder. At first the dog would salivate some in response to the lower tone (stimulus generalization), but eventually, our dog would learn to discriminate and stop salivating to the tone of A.

Discrimination learning—a process by which an organism learns to discriminate between different stimuli, emitting the conditioned response (CR) in the presence of some stimuli and not others.

STUDY CHECK

What are generalization and discrimination, and how are they demonstrated in classical conditioning?

THINKING CRITICALLY

What examples of generalization and discrimination can you think of that occur in everyday life? Can you identify a voice on the telephone? Can you tell one brand of spaghetti sauce from another? How might these be examples of classical conditioning?

Classical Conditioning in Everyday Life

It is time to leave our discussion of dogs, salivation, and Pavlov's laboratory and turn our attention to the practical application of classical conditioning. There are examples of classically conditioned human behaviors everywhere. Many of our physiological reactions have been classically conditioned to stimuli in our environments. The sights or aromas of certain foods can cause a CR of salivation or of hunger pangs. The sight, sound, or mention of some (often food-related) stimuli may produce a rumbling nausea in the pit of the stomach. Certain stimuli can make us sleepy. And in each case, the response is not naturally occurring but has been learned, or classically conditioned.

One of the most significant aspects of classical conditioning is its role in the development of emotional responses to stimuli in our environment. There are few stimuli that naturally, or instinctively, produce an emotional response. Yet think of all the things that directly influence how we feel.

For example, very young children seldom seem to be afraid of spiders, snakes, or airplane rides. (Some children actually seem to enjoy them.) Yet how many adults do you know who are afraid of these things? Many stimuli in our environments evoke fear. There are stimuli that produce feelings of pleasure, calm, and relaxation. What scares you? What makes you feel relaxed? Why? Might you feel upset in a certain store because you once had an unpleasant experience there? Might you anticipate a trip to the beach with great pleasure because of a very enjoyable vacation you had there as a child? Do you shudder at the sight of a police car or smile at the thought of a payroll envelope? In each case, we are talking about classical conditioning. (Not all of our learned emotional reactions are acquired through classical conditioning alone. As we will see, there are other possibilities.)

The Case of Little Albert

In 1920, psychologist John B. Watson and his student assistant, Rosalie Rayner, published a summary research article about a series of experiments they had performed with "Little Albert" (Not his real name, we are unsure of Albert's true identity). Albert's experiences have become well known. Although Watson and Rayner's summary of their own work tended to oversimplify matters (Samuelson, 1980), the story of Little Albert provides a good model for the classical conditioning of emotional responses—in this case, fear.

Eleven-month-old Albert was given many toys to play with. Among other things, he was allowed to play with a live white rat. Albert showed no sign of fearing it. At this point, the rat was a neutral stimulus (NS) with respect to fear. Then conditioning began. One day, as Albert reached for the rat, one of the experimenters (Rayner) made a sudden loud noise by striking a metal bar

Not unlike Pavlov's dogs, sometimes we salivate at the very sight of attractive-looking foods.

with a hammer. The loud noise frightened Albert. Two months earlier, Watson and Rayner had established that a sudden loud noise would frighten Albert—at least he behaved in a way that seemed to indicate fear.

After repeated pairings of the rat and the loud noise, Albert's reaction to the rat underwent a relatively permanent change. Albert would at first start to reach toward the rat, but then would recoil and cry out, often trying to bury his head in his blanket. He was making emotional responses to a previously neutral stimulus (NS) that did not elicit those responses before it was paired with a sudden loud noise. This sounds like classical conditioning: The rat is the CS, and the sudden loud noise is the UCS that elicits the UCR of an emotional fear response. After repeated pairings of the rat and the loud noise (CS and UCS), the rat elicits the same sort of fear response (or CR).

Watson and Rayner then demonstrated that Albert's fear of the white rat generalized to all sorts of stimuli: a dog (in fact, a brown spotted dog, not a white one), a ball of cotton, even a Santa Claus mask with a white beard and mustache. Through classical conditioning, Watson and Rayner demonstrated that an emotional response to several stimuli could be learned.

Several issues have been raised concerning Watson and Rayner's demonstration of learned fear—not the least of which is the unethical treatment of Albert. It is unlikely that anyone would even attempt such a project today. Watson (1919) previously had argued that emotional experiences of early childhood can affect an individual for a lifetime, yet he purposely frightened a young child (and without the advised consent of the boy's mother). Watson and Rayner were convinced that they could reverse Little Albert's fear, but as fate would have it, they never got the chance. Albert's mother removed him from the hospital before they had a chance to undo the conditioning, and it was never determined if Albert's fear of white rats persisted beyond the confines of Watson's study (DeAngelis, 2010).

Treating Phobias

Classical conditioning surely is relevant to our everyday lives. It continues to intrigue psychologists searching to understand the underlying processes involved. Psychologists also are interested in finding new ways to apply conditioning in the real world. In this section, we briefly explore an example of such an application.

There are many things in this world that are life-threatening and downright frightening. Being afraid of some stimuli is often a wise, rational, and adaptive reaction. Occasionally, however, people experience distressing fears of stimuli that are *not* threatening in any real or rational sense. Some people are intensely afraid of heights, spiders, the dark, riding on elevators, or flying. Psychologists say that these people are suffering from a *phobic disorder*—an intense, irrational fear of an object or event that leads a person to avoid contact with it (We shall explore phobic disorders more in Chapter 12). There are many explanations of how phobic disorders or phobias occur, but one possibility is classical conditioning. This accounting for phobias suggests that a previously neutral stimulus (a spider, for example) is associated with a fear-inducing event (e.g., a painful spider bite). Through a process of association, the previously neutral stimulus (the CS) comes to elicit a fear response that, through generalization, also may be elicited by all sorts of spiders and bugs.

An effective way to treat such fears and phobias is to make use of the principles of classical conditioning. Mary Cover Jones (1924) made one of the earliest attempts to apply classical conditioning to the elimination of a fear. Jones worked with a young boy named Peter who had a fear of rabbits. Jones began pairing a pleasing food with the presence of the rabbit. The food by itself did not elicit fear, but rather feelings of pleasure. By pairing the food with the fear-producing rabbit, Jones was able to condition the boy to substitute the feelings of pleasure for the feelings of fear that had been associated with the rabbit. Over 30 years later, the application of classical conditioning to the treatment of fears was elaborated by Joseph Wolpe (1958, 1997). Wolpe's technique is called **systematic desensitization**, which is a technique with the goal of gradually teaching a patient to associate positive feelings of relaxation with a previously feared stimulus.

Systematic desensitization—a technique with the goal of gradually teaching a patient to associate positive feelings of relaxation with a previously feared stimulus.

In its standard form, systematic desensitization occurs in three stages. First, the therapist instructs or trains the client to relax. As you might know from your own experience, this is not always easy to do at first, but after a few hours of training, the client learns how to enter a relaxed state quickly. The second stage is to construct an "anxiety hierarchy"—a list of stimuli that gradually decrease in their ability to elicit anxiety. The most-feared stimulus is placed at the top of the list (for example, giving a formal speech to a large group, being called on in class, talking to a small group of strangers, being introduced to two or more people, talking with friends, talking to a friend on the phone, etc.). The third stage involves conditioning.

The client relaxes completely and thinks about the stimulus that is lowest on the anxiety hierarchy. The client is then to think about the next highest stimulus, and the next, and so on, all the while remaining as relaxed as possible. As they move up the list toward the anxiety-producing stimuli at the top, the therapist constantly monitors the client's level of tension or relaxation. When anxiety seems to be overcoming relaxation, the client is told to stop thinking about that item on the hierarchy and to think about an item lower on the list.

Systematic desensitization is more than the forgetting of a previously conditioned fear response. A new response (relaxation) is being acquired to "replace" an old one (fear). This process is called *counter-conditioning*. The logic is that a person cannot be relaxed and anxious at the same time. These are incompatible responses. If one pairs a stimulus with the feelings of being relaxed, classical conditioning produces a reaction of calm, not the response of tension and anxiety. For many people, this technique can be effective. It works best for fears or anxieties associated with specific, easily identifiable stimuli; it is less successful for a diffuse, generalized fear, for which it is difficult to generate anxiety hierarchies.

STUDY CHECK

How did Watson and Rayner classically condition fear in "Little Albert"?
How can classical conditioning be used in the treatment of phobias?

THINKING CRITICALLY

Consider those stimuli that frighten you. Is your fear an unlearned, natural reaction, or is it conditioned? If it is learned, how might it be "unlearned?"

Operant Conditioning: The Basics

Most of the early research on operant conditioning was done by Harvard psychologist B. F. Skinner, although he really did not discover it. The techniques of operant conditioning had been in use for hundreds of years before Skinner was born. What Skinner did was bring that earlier work—most of it casual, some of it scientific—into the laboratory. There he studied the process of operant conditioning with a unique vigor that helped the rest of us realize the significance of the process.

Skinner used the term "operant" to refer to a behavior or behaviors an organism uses to operate on its environment in order to produce certain effects. Operant behaviors are controlled by their consequences: They will maintain or increase their rate if they are reinforced; they will decrease their rate if they are not reinforced or if they are punished (Staddon & Ceruti, 2003). **Operant conditioning** is a learning process that changes the rate, or probability, of responses on the basis of the consequences that result from those responses. Note that Skinner is careful not to claim here that the future governs what happens in the present, but rather that past experiences influence present ones. Skinner put it this way: "...behavior is shaped by its consequences, but only by consequences that

Operant conditioning—a learning process that changes the rate, or probability, of responses on the basis of the consequences that result from those responses.

lie in the past. We do what we do because of what has happened, not what will happen" (Skinner, 1989).

Examples of operant conditioning are all around us. You don't need any special apparatus to observe the principle. Imagine a father rushing through a supermarket with his toddler seated in a shopping cart. The youngster is screaming at the top of his lungs, "I want a candy bar! I want a candy bar!" Father is doing a good (and an appropriate) job of ignoring this unruly behavior until he spies a neighbor coming down the next aisle. The neighbor has her three children with her, all of whom are acting like perfect angels. What's a parent to do? He races by the checkout lanes, grabs a candy bar, and gives it to his child. He has reinforced the child's tantrum by giving the child the candy. Does one have to be an expert in psychology to predict what is likely to happen on the next visit to the store? Screaming "worked" this time, so it will be tried again. Reinforced behaviors tend to recur.

To demonstrate operant conditioning in the laboratory, Skinner built a special apparatus that he called an *operant chamber*. Although Skinner never used the term and said he didn't like it, some psychologists continue to call this device a "Skinner box." The box is empty except for a small lever that protrudes from one wall and a small cup that holds a piece of rat food. Food pellets are dispensed, one at a time, through a tube into the food cup when the lever is pressed all the way down.

Now that we have our chamber, we need a learner. If we put a hungry rat into the chamber and do nothing else, the rat will occasionally press the lever. There is, after all, little else for it to do in there. Rats naturally explore their environments and tend to manipulate objects in them. The rate at which the rat freely presses the lever is called its *base rate* of responding. A rat will typically press the lever at a base rate of 8 to 10 times an hour.

So, how do we get our friend the rat to start pressing the lever at a higher rate? We train the rat by *shaping through successive approximations*. First, we activate the food dispenser whenever the rat faces in the right direction (i.e., the side of the chamber with the lever). Next, we activate it when the rat approaches the lever. Finally, we activate the dispenser so that a food pellet is delivered every time the lever is pressed. We will now observe that the rate of lever pressing increases. The rat may reach the point of pressing the lever at a rate of 500 to 600 times an hour. Learning has taken place. There has been a relatively permanent change in behavior as a result of experience.

When we give the rat a food pellet (reinforce) after every lever press, we are using what is called *continuous reinforcement*. Continuous reinforcement is good for training behavior but not for maintaining high rates over time; eventually, the rat gets full of rat pellets. To maintain higher rates of behavior, we would use a *partial schedule of reinforcement*. For example, we might reinforce every other lever press, eventually requiring more and more nonreinforced lever presses between reinforced lever presses.

As with classical conditioning, extinction can also occur with operant conditioning. If we wanted to extinguish the lever pressing we have conditioned in our rat, we would simply stop providing reinforcement for the lever press. Eventually, the rat will stop pressing the lever because it no longer is associated with the delivery of food. Interestingly, it takes longer to extinguish a behavior maintained on a partial schedule of reinforcement because it takes longer for the animal to learn that the lever press is no longer associated with food.

Here is a subtlety: Has the rat learned to press the lever? In any sense, can we say that we have taught the rat a lever-pressing response? No. The rat "knew" how to press the lever and did so long before we introduced the food pellets as a reward for its behavior. The change in behavior that took place was a change in the *rate* of the response, not in the nature of the response.

STUDY CHECK

How does one demonstrate operant conditioning?

THINKING CRITICALLY

What are the similarities and the differences between classical and operant conditioning?

Reinforcement

Clearly, reinforcement is a crucial concept in operant conditioning. At this point, it is useful to make a distinction between *reinforcement* and a *reinforcer*. Reinforcement refers to the *process* of increasing the rate or probability of a response. Any time you see the term "reinforcement," you know that someone is talking about a way to increase the probability of a behavior. A reinforcer refers to the actual stimulus used in the process of reinforcement that increases the probability or rate of a response. Terms relating to operant conditioning are summarized in **Table 4.2**.

Skinner and his students have long argued that we should define reinforcers only in terms of their effect on behavior. Reinforcers are stimuli. If a stimulus presented after a response increases the rate of that response, then that stimulus is a reinforcer regardless of its nature or its "quality." For example, imagine the following scenario: A parent spanks his 4-year-old child each time the child pulls the cat's tail. The parent then notices that instead of pulling the tail less, the child is actually pulling the cat's tail more often. If the operant behavior we are trying to influence is pulling of the cat's tail, then the spanking is serving as a reinforcer because the frequency of the operant behavior has increased. This is despite the fact that the parent sees the spanking as negative. The intent was to punish the tail-pulling behavior. Perhaps the child is being reinforced by the attention from the parent attached to the spanking! In short, identifying which stimuli will function as reinforcers may be difficult to do ahead of time. We need to observe the effect of a stimulus on the level of a behavior before we can really know if that stimulus is a reinforcer. The intent of the person trying to do the reinforcing is simply not relevant.

So, reinforcers are defined in terms of their effects on behavior—events that increase the rate of the behaviors that they follow are said to be reinforcing. When psychologists distinguish between primary and secondary reinforcers, the issue is the extent to which those reinforcers are natural and unlearned or acquire their reinforcing capability through learning or experience.

A **primary reinforcer** is a reinforcer whose properties are unlearned and do not require previous experience to be effective. In some way, they are related to the organism's survival and are usually physiological or biological in nature. Food for a hungry organism or water for a thirsty one are common examples. Providing a warm place by the fire to a cold, wet dog involves primary reinforcement. A **secondary reinforcer** is a reinforcer whose properties are learned and may be referred to as a conditioned, acquired, or learned

Reinforcement—the *process* of increasing the rate or probability of a response.

Reinforcer—the actual stimulus used in the process of reinforcement that increases the probability or rate of a response.

Primary reinforcer—a reinforcer whose properties are unlearned and do not require previous experience to be effective.

Secondary reinforcer—a reinforcer whose properties are learned and may be referred to as a conditioned, acquired, or learned reinforcer.

TABLE 4.2 Basic Operant Conditioning Terms

Terms	Definitions
Reinforcement	The process of increasing the rate or probability of a response. Any time you see the term "reinforcement," you know that you are trying to *increase* the probability of a behavior.
Reinforcer	The actual stimulus used in the process of reinforcement that increases the probability or rate of a response.
Primary reinforcer	A reinforcer that is unlearned and does not require previous experience to be effective.
Secondary reinforcer	A conditioned, acquired, or learned reinforcer.
Punishment	When a stimulus delivered to an organism *decreases* the rate, or probability, of the response that preceded it.

In some circumstances, a simple piece of cloth with writing on it, or a small metal trophy can be very reinforcing indeed.

Positive reinforcement—delivering a reinforcer *after* a behavior that is intended to increase or maintain the strength of a response.

Negative reinforcement—delivering an aversive (i.e., something the organism doesn't like) stimulus *before* a response is made, with the intention of increasing or maintaining a response that removes it.

reinforcer. There is nothing about secondary reinforcers that implies that they are inherently reinforcing in any biological sense, yet they increase response rates.

In fact, most of the reinforcers that you and I work for are of this sort. Money, praise, high grades, and promotions are good examples. Money in itself is not worth much. But previous experiences have convinced most of us of the reinforcing nature of money, largely because it can be traded for something we need (such as food) or value (such as a new car). Thus, money can serve to increase the rate of a variety of responses.

Another important distinction is between positive and negative reinforcement. Positive reinforcement involves delivering a reinforcer *after* a behavior; it is intended to increase or maintain the strength of a response. The pellet of food delivered after a rat presses a lever is a positive reinforcer because it strengthens or maintains the lever-pressing behavior it follows. Negative reinforcement involves delivering an aversive (i.e., something the organism doesn't like) stimulus *before* a response is made; it is intended to increase or maintain a response that removes it. Thus, it is the removal of the aversive stimulus that is reinforcing. For example, you could turn on a loud, unpleasant noise (aversive stimulus) and then turn it off each time a rat presses a lever. The rat will learn to press the lever to turn off the noise. The distinction between positive and negative reinforcement is illustrated in **Figure 4.1**.

Perhaps because operant conditioning can be so effective, some students and parents find the process disturbing, especially in terms of parenting. They argue, "Why, this isn't psychology; you're just bribing the child to behave." There are at least two reasons why we need not be overly concerned. First, bribery involves contracting to reward (reinforce) someone for doing something that both parties view as inappropriate. People are bribed to steal, cheat, lie, change votes, or otherwise engage in behaviors they know are wrong. Operant conditioning, on the other hand, reinforces behaviors judged in the first place to be appropriate. Second, as Skinner argued for many years, the long-term hope is that the child (in our example) will come to appreciate that having trash removed, walking the dog, or having a clean room is a valued end in itself and can be its own reward. The hope is that the use of reinforcers will no longer be needed as appropriate behaviors become reinforced by more subtle, intrinsic factors.

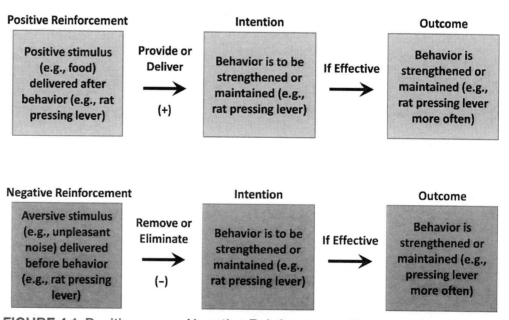

FIGURE 4.1 Positive versus Negative Reinforcement Illustrated

PSYCHOLOGY IN ACTION

The Training and Use of Service Dogs

While out and about, you may have seen people with dogs that have a special vest with the words "Service Dog" emblazoned on it. Dogs in a service role are specially trained animals that help a person with physical and/or mental disabilities better navigate and adjust to the world around him or her. Service dogs have a long history of helping people with disabilities. For example, "guide dogs" (also known as seeing-eye dogs) have a long history of helping people with poor or no vision navigate the world. Some of the first uses of guide dogs were to help veterans blinded during World War I combat. Since then, the role of service dogs has been expanded to include service to people with hearing impairments, physical disabilities (e.g., paralysis), mental illness (e.g., post-traumatic stress disorder or PTSD), as well as a host of other disabilities. Some service dogs are trained to recognize the onset of specific symptoms of a disorder. For example, I (Bordens) have a friend with a service dog trained to detect the onset of seizures resulting from exposure to a toxic agent while serving in the military in Iraq. Other service dogs can be trained to do specific tasks. They can, for example, be trained to open doors, help a person get dressed, or turn lights on and off for a physically disabled person. For people with PTSD, service dogs help reduce the symptoms of the disorder and help a person better adjust to the world. In the discussion that follows, we explore how service dogs are trained and how they help individuals with PTSD.

Training of a service dog, whether for a person with a physical or mental disability, starts with the selection of the right breed of dog. In short, not all breeds are equally suitable for the role of a service dog. Potential service dogs must have the temperament and willingness to learn necessary for a service role. They also must be sociable, friendly, and loyal. In some cases, service dogs in training go through socialization training experiences. For example, in one training program, dogs trained to help combat veterans with PTSD are socialized by having multiple people (often other veterans) pet and handle the dog (Warrior Canine Connection, 2018). After a dog has been selected and socialized, specific training can begin. Training a service dog involves training for some basic behaviors (e.g., sitting, staying, heeling, and ignoring distractions) and for specific tasks (e.g., opening a door, retrieving an object on command). Training for these tasks involves the very same principles discussed in this chapter: positive reinforcement, successive approximations, discrimination learning, and secondary reinforcement. You may have trained your pet using these principles. Let's see how this works.

Many training guides recommend that the first step in training a service dog is to "clicker train" the dog. This makes use of the principle of secondary reinforcement. Clicker training is accomplished by training the dog to associate a food treat (a primary reinforcer) with the sound of a toy clicker. The dog is given a treat followed immediately by the clicker. After a number of pairings of the treat with the sound of the clicker, the sound of the clicker takes on the reinforcing properties of the food and can be used to reinforce the dog's behavior. Clicker training is recommended because the clicker provides instant reinforcement and makes the training process easier (Anything Pawsable, 2018). It is important to note that clicker training is not required to train a dog; you could simply use the treat itself.

Next, let's see how you could train a basic skill (sitting) using operant conditioning techniques. Teaching a dog (whether your pet or a service dog) to sit is relatively easy. Now, sitting is a natural behavior for any dog. However, dogs generally will not sit on command (you can use a verbal command such as "sit" or a hand command), which is something you want the dog to do. So, you have to teach the dog to sit on command using a variant of conditioning using successive approximations. While in front of the dog, say the word "sit," then take a treat and hold it above its nose. Slowly move the treat over the dog's head and gently push down on its hindquarters. Once the dog is in the sitting position, give the dog the treat. Repeat this process several times until the dog learns to perform the entire sitting sequence on command. Eventually, you can eliminate the treat completely! Teaching a dog this simple behavior involves several operant conditioning processes: positive reinforcement (the treat), discrimination learning (learning to associate the word "sit" only with sitting down by associating the command with the treat), and training through successive approximations. Other simple behaviors (e.g., staying, heeling) can be achieved in the same way. More complex behaviors, like turning on or off a light, involve the same process and training in sequences of behavior.

Training a service dog yourself requires a great deal of work, time, and patience. This is why many people choose to have service dogs trained by professionals. Once a service dog has been trained and put into service, the dog can make life for a person much easier. For example, a person using a manual wheelchair can have his or her service dog help with mobility in the chair, relieving the physical strain and discomfort associated with using a manual chair (Hubert, Tousignant, Routhier, Corriveau, & Champagne, 2013). There is also mounting evidence that service dogs can significantly reduce the severity of symptoms associated with PTSD among combat veterans. Veterans with PTSD-trained service dogs report reductions in PTSD symptoms such as hypervigilance, sleep disturbances, nightmares, and trauma-related thoughts (Yarborough, Stumbo, Yarborough, Owen-Smith, & Green, 2018). Research not relying on self-reports of well-being also show the benefits of having a service dog. In one study, for example, PTSD veterans with a service dog were compared with those on a waiting list who did not currently have a service dog. The results showed that those with a service dog reported higher levels of well-being than those on the waiting list (O'Haire & Rodriguez, 2018). Other research shows that service dogs can also affect physiological as well as psychological indicators of well-being among PTSD sufferers (Rodriguez, Bryce, Granger, & O'Haire, 2018).

Punishment

Punishment—when a stimulus delivered to an organism *decreases* the rate, or probability, of the response that preceded it.

Punishment occurs when a stimulus delivered to an organism *decreases* the rate, or probability, of the response that preceded it. Punishment is usually hurtful or painful, either physically (e.g., a spanking) or psychologically (e.g., ridicule). It is (usually) a painful, unpleasant stimulus presented to an organism *after* some response is made.

Determining ahead of time which stimuli will be punishing is as difficult to do as determining ahead of time which stimuli will serve as reinforcers. Once again, intentions are irrelevant. We'll know for sure that something is a punisher only after observing its effect on behavior. We may think we are punishing Jon by sending him to his room when he begins to throw a temper tantrum. It may be that "in his room" is exactly where Jon would like to be. We very well may have reinforced Jon's temper tantrum behaviors simply by attending to them. The only way to know for certain is to note the effect on behavior. If Jon's tantrum-throwing behaviors become less frequent, sending him to his room may indeed have been a punishing thing to do.

Commonly, punishment is a matter of presenting a painful, unpleasant stimulus (e.g., a slap on the hand) following an inappropriate response. On other occasions, punishment involves removing a valued, pleasant stimulus (e.g., "No TV for a week!") following an inappropriate response. Another example of this approach is the use of "time out" sessions, which work well with children in groups. If one child begins acting inappropriately (say, by yelling and bullying others), that child is taken aside and placed away from the other children in a quiet setting for a prescribed period of time.

Is punishment an effective means of controlling behavior? Does it really work? Yes, it can. Punishment can be an impressive

Sometimes, punishment can be more psychologically painful than physically hurtful. It also may involve the removal of valued opportunities.

modifier of behavior. A rat has learned to press a lever in order to get food. Now you decide that you no longer want the rat to press the lever. You pass an electric current through the lever so that each time the rat touches the lever, it receives a strong shock. What will happen? Actually, several things may happen, but—if your shock is strong enough—there is one thing of which we can be sure: The rat will stop pressing the lever. If punishment is effective, why do psychologists so often argue against its use, particularly the punishment of children for their misbehavior? There are potential problems connected with the use of punishment when it is used correctly, and often it is not. Let's review some of what we know about the use of punishment in general, and then we'll see about spanking.

1. *To be effective, punishment should be delivered immediately after the response.* The logic is clear. Priscilla is caught in mid-afternoon throwing flour all over the kitchen. Father counts to ten in an attempt to control his temper (a good reaction) and then says, "Just wait until your mother gets home" (not so good). For the next three hours, Priscilla's behavior is angelic. By the time mother gets home, what gets punished, Priscilla's flour-tossing or the appropriate behaviors that followed?

2. *For punishment to be effective, it needs to be administered consistently.* If one chooses to punish a certain behavior, it should be punished whenever it occurs, and often that is difficult to do. Threatening punishment ("If you do that one more time . . .," "I'm warning you . . .," "You'd better stop right now, mister") but not delivering on the threat simply reinforces a child to ignore the caregiver.

3. *Punishment may decrease (suppress) overall behavior levels.* Although an effectively punished response may end, so may other responses as well. For example, that rat who has been shocked for pressing the bar will not only stop pressing the bar but will also cower in the corner of the operant chamber, doing very little of anything.

4. *When responses are punished, alternatives should be introduced.* Think about your rat for a minute. The poor thing knows what to do when it is hungry: Press the lever. Indeed, you reinforced the rat for making that response. Now it gets shocked for doing that very thing. Without an alternative response to make in order to get food, the rat is in a conflict that has no solution. There is no way out. The result may be fear, anxiety, and even aggression. In other words, punishment does not convey any information about what to do; it only communicates what not to do. Rubbing your puppy's nose in a "mess" it just made on the living room carpet doesn't give the dog much of a sense of what it is supposed to do the next time it feels a need to relieve itself; taking it outside will.

Now let's consider the use of the physical punishment of children—spanking—as a separate case. There are fewer issues related to child-rearing that can get so many people emotionally engaged than whether hitting or spanking a child is always, never, or occasionally warranted (Kazdin & Benjet, 2003). If nothing else, corporal punishment is common in the United States, where 74 percent of parents of children younger than 17 years of age and 94 percent of parents of 3- and 4-year-olds use spanking as a discipline technique (e.g., Benjet & Kazdin, 2003).

Spanking is a form of punishment that is (a) physically noninjurious, (b) intended to modify behavior, and (c) administered with an opened hand to the extremities or buttocks (Friedman & Schonberg, 1996, p. 853). Clearly, no one can be in favor of child abuse: striking a child with a fist or an object so as to cause bleeding, bruising, scarring, broken bones, and the like. What about spanking? Does it work? We have to be very careful here, but yes, spanking does work in the sense that it can be an effective means to get a child to stop engaging in a given behavior (Gershoff, 2002; Kazdin & Benjet, 2003).

Are there negative consequences of using spanking as a disciplinary measure? Yes, there are several. Spanking diminishes the quality of parent-child relationships, may result (in the long term) in poorer mental health, and may lead to an increase in criminal or antisocial behaviors (Gershoff, 2002). It seems to convey the message that hitting when frustrated is an acceptable response, that it is okay for larger people to hit smaller people, and that can lead to bullying (Simons & Wurtele, 2010).

Spanking—a form of punishment that is (a) physically noninjurious, (b) intended to modify behavior, and (c) administered with an opened hand to the extremities or buttocks.

So what is a parent to do? A reasonable strategy would be to search for other—non-physical—means of providing discipline. Psychologists have no problem with the idea that some behaviors (e.g., dangerous ones) are worthy of punishment. Perhaps as much as anything else, parents who consistently punish their children with spanking and hitting are showing a lack of creativity for finding less physical means for delivering punishment.

STUDY CHECK

How do psychologists define punishment, and under what circumstances is it an effective means of behavior control?

THINKING CRITICALLY

Imagine that as a matter of principle, you have decided not to spank or hit your child. What other things could you do to punish inappropriate or dangerous behaviors?

FOCUS ON DIVERSITY

Ethnic and Racial Differences in Parenting

In 2014, a former star running back for the Minnesota Vikings, Adrian Peterson, was charged with felony reckless or negligent injury to a child. After a fight between his children, Peterson used a "switch" (a narrow tree branch) to "discipline" his four-year-old son. The beating that Peterson meted out was so harsh that it resulted in severe injuries to the child's back, buttocks, ankles, legs, scrotum, and hands (defensive wounds). Peterson's explanation was that he was only using a discipline technique his parents used on him, resulting in building his character. Although Peterson's example is an extreme one, crossing the line from punishment to child abuse, it represents a category of punishment still used and endorsed by many parents: corporal punishment (specifically, spanking). In one study, for example, around 73 percent of participants agreed or strongly agreed that spanking is necessary in disciplining children (Friedson, 2016). Many studies have documented the negative effects that corporal punishment has on children. Although corporal punishment often leads to immediate compliance by the child, it is also associated with elevated levels of aggression, antisocial behavior, and delinquency in children (Gershoff, 2002). It is also associated with more externalizing of negative behavior (e.g., aggression and rule breaking), lower levels of cognitive functioning (MacKenzie, Nicklas, Waldfogel, & Brooks-Gunn, 2012), and child depression (Wang & Kenny, 2014).

Are there ethnic, racial, and demographic differences in attitudes toward and the use of corporal punishment? Indeed, there are. A Pew Research Center survey (2015) revealed that African American parents were more likely to report using corporal punishment (spanking) at some time (64 percent) than were white (42 percent) or Hispanic (41 percent) parents. Moreover, African American parents were more likely to report using corporal punishment "often or sometimes" (32 percent) than were white (14 percent) or Hispanic (19 percent) parents. These findings parallel findings from other studies (e.g., Wang & Kenny, 2014). We should note that using corporal punishment is also related to a parent's level of education. The Pew survey found, for example, that using corporal punishment often or sometimes was more frequent among parents with a high school or less education (22 percent) than for parents with some college (19 percent), college education (15 percent), or a post-graduate education (8 percent). Additionally, parents with lower socioeconomic status (SES) are more likely to approve of spanking than higher-SES parents (Friedson, 2016).

Why do African American parents use corporal punishment more than parents from other racial or ethnic groups? One possibility is that the socialization goals of parents of different racial or ethnic groups may differ. *Socialization* is the process whereby a child learns the attitudes, morals, and behaviors deemed appropriate by a given culture. It is fair to say that *most* parents have the goal of positively socializing their children, regardless of the parenting style used. There is some evidence that parents from different racial or ethnic backgrounds have somewhat different socialization goals. In one study (Harding, Hughes, & Way, 2017), for example, researchers had parents sort cards with different socialization goals (one goal on each card) according to importance. The results showed that more African American mothers

(77.55 percent) indicated that "deference" (listening to and respecting adults) was important than did mothers who were white (6.66 percent), Chinese (58.14 percent), or Latino (62.5 percent). On the other hand, white mothers (95.55 percent) more frequently placed importance on academic engagement (e.g., working hard in school) compared with African American (79.35 percent), Chinese (53.28 percent), and Latino (62.5 percent) mothers. These, and other, differences show that mothers from different racial or ethnic groups do have different goals when socializing their children. African American mothers believe that corporal punishment will be effective in socializing their children. They also see corporal punishment as being normative (expected) for their racial group (Taylor, Hamvas, & Paris, 2011).

What could be the origin of the more positive view of corporal punishment among African American parents? An interesting perspective comes from Stacey Patton (2017). According to Patton, "whupping" (like the beating meted out by Adrian Peterson) was not part of African culture before Africans were brought to America in the slave trade. Patton states that Africans learned to use corporal punishment from their white slave masters who came from a European culture. In that European culture, children were brutalized for centuries. According to Patton, a goal of African slaves was to socialize their children to be cooperative field workers and show deference to their white masters. All of this had to be done quickly and efficiently. Consequently, corporal punishment became a preferred method to socialize children into the slave mentality and culture (Patton, 2017). This method of socialization was supported by institutions within the African American slave culture: "With sanctioning from the black church, black parents enacted the master's lash to instill obedience" (Patton, 2017, para. 10). According to her analysis, Patton points out that acceptance and use of corporal punishment in the modern African American community is a by-product of centuries of slavery and subsequent oppression during the Jim Crow era in the United States. Although we do not have empirical data to support this position, it is a compelling hypothesis.

Cognitive Approaches to Learning

Cognitive approaches to learning focus on changes that occur within an organism's system of cognitions—its mental representations of itself and its world. Cognitive learning involves acquiring knowledge or understanding that may or may not be reflected in actual behavior. The implication is that there may be less than a perfect correspondence between what has been learned and how one performs. In this section, we'll briefly review the work of two theorists who stressed cognitive approaches to learning: Edward Tolman and Albert Bandura.

Latent Learning and Cognitive Maps

The brain of a rat isn't very large, and its cerebral cortex is small indeed. Can a rat use that brain to "think"—to form and manipulate cognitions? Can they figure things out? They can form simple associations. They can learn to associate a light with a shock and a lever-press response with a food pellet, and they can modify their behaviors on the basis of these associations. Can they do more?

Consider a classic experiment performed over 85 years ago by Tolman and Honzik (1930). Even then, it was established that a rat could learn to run through a complicated maze of alleyways and dead ends to get to a goal box, where it would find a food reward. Tolman and Honzik wanted to understand just what the rats were learning when they negotiated such a maze. They used three groups of rats with the same maze.

One group of hungry rats was given a series of exposures to the maze (trials). Each time the rats ran from the starting point to the goal box, they were given a food reinforcer for their efforts. Over the course of 16 days, the rats in this group demonstrated a steady improvement in maze-running. Their rate of errors dropped from about nine per trial to just two. A second group of rats was also given an opportunity to explore the maze for 16 days. However, they were not given a food reinforcer for making it to the end of the maze. When they got to the goal box, they were simply removed from the maze. The average number of errors made by the rats in this group also dropped over the course of the experiment (from about nine errors per trial to about six). The fact that the rats in this group did improve their maze-running skills suggests that simply being removed from the maze provided some measure of reinforcement. Even so, after 16 days, this group was still having much

If it were not for our ability to form cognitive maps, we soon would be disoriented in complex, busy environments, such as a shopping mall. We need to "know" where we parked our car and where the store we want to visit is located.

more difficulty in their maze-running than was the group receiving a food reinforcer.

Now for the critical group. A third group of rats was allowed to explore the maze on their own for ten days. The rats were not given a food reinforcer upon reaching the goal box but were simply removed from the maze, as were the rats in the second group. But, beginning on day 11, a food reinforcer was introduced when they reached the goal box; the food was provided on days 11 through 16. Introducing the food reward had a very significant effect on the rats' behaviors. Throughout the first ten days in the maze—without food—the rats showed only a slight improvement. Soon after the food was introduced, however, the rats' maze-running improved markedly. In fact, on days 13 through 16, they made fewer errors than did the rats that received food all along!

What do you make of this experiment? Why did the third group of rats do so much better after the food reward was introduced? Did they learn something about the pattern of the maze *before* they received reinforcement for getting to the goal box? Did they "figure out" the maze early on but fail to rush to the goal box until there was a good reason to do so? Tolman thought they did. He argued that the food rewarded a change in the rats' performance, but that the actual learning had taken place earlier. This sort of learning is called latent learning. **Latent learning** is a form of learning that is hidden and not shown in behavior until it is reinforced.

Latent learning—a form of learning that is hidden and not shown in behavior until it is reinforced.

Cognitive map—a mental picture or representation of the physical environment, noting significant landmarks when possible.

During those first ten days in the maze, the rats developed a cognitive map of the maze. A **cognitive map** is a mental picture or representation of the physical environment, noting significant landmarks when possible. The rats knew about the maze, but until food was provided at the goal box, there was no reason, or purpose, for getting there in a hurry.

What Tolman and Honzik's rats did is impressive. But cognitive maps acquired by small birds that live in the Alps are even more so. These birds spend most of the summer and early fall hiding seeds in the ground (about four or five at a time). During the winter, they find their hidden supplies of seeds with remarkable accuracy. Have they formed cognitive maps of their seed placements? Apparently so. Making their judgments on the basis of nearby landmarks, these Clark's nutcrackers can remember the location of at least 2,500 hiding places (Vander Wall, 1982).

You can find examples from your own experiences that approximate latent learning and the formation of cognitive maps. You may take the same route home from campus every day. If one day an accident blocks your path, won't you be able to use your knowledge of other routes (a cognitive map) to get where you are going? When you park your car in a large parking lot, what do you do as you walk away from your car? Don't you look around, trying to develop a mental image, a cognitive representation, of the parking lot and some of its features? You are to meet a friend in a new classroom building on campus. You arrive early, so you stroll around the building for a few minutes. Isn't it likely that this apparently aimless behavior will be useful if you have to locate a room in that building for class at some later time? If you know that the entrance to the Banana Republic store is on the ground floor, just before the food court, and just after Kohl's in your neighborhood shopping center, might we not argue that you have formed a cognitive map? Absolutely!

> **STUDY CHECK**
>
> What are latent learning and cognitive maps?

Social Learning Theory

Albert Bandura's approach to learning is social and cognitive; **social learning theory** considers learning that takes place through the observation and imitation of models (Bandura, 2001a, 2001b). What makes social learning theory social is that we often learn from others. What makes it cognitive is that what is learned by observation, or modeling, is changes in cognition that may never be expressed as behavior nor be directly reinforced.

Social learning theory— considers learning that takes place through the observation and imitation of models.

The classic study of observational learning was reported in 1963 by Bandura, Ross, and Ross. Ninety-six preschoolers were randomly assigned to one of four experimental conditions. One group of children observed an adult model act aggressively toward a large inflated plastic "Bobo" doll. The adult model vigorously attacked the doll. Children in the second group saw the same aggressive behaviors directed toward the doll, but in a movie. The third group watched a cartoon version of the same aggressive behaviors, this time performed by a cat. Children in the fourth group constituted the control group and did not watch anyone or anything interact with Bobo dolls, either live or on film.

Then each child, tested individually, was given new and interesting toys to play with for a brief time. The child was soon led to another room containing fewer, older, and less-interesting toys, including a small version of the Bobo doll. Each child was left alone in the room while researchers, hidden from view, watched the child's behavior.

The children who had seen the aggressive behaviors of the model, live, on film, or in a cartoon, were much more aggressive in their play than were the children who did not have the observational experience. Children in the first three experimental conditions even attacked the Bobo doll the very same way the model had.

According to social learning theory, the children had learned simply by observing. As with latent learning, the learning was separated from performance. The children had no opportunity to imitate (to perform) what they had learned until they had a Bobo doll of their own. The learning that took place during observation was internal, or cognitive.

Later studies have shown that reinforcement and punishment can play a major role in observational learning. For example, a twist was added to an experiment that replicated the one just described. The difference was that after attacking the doll, the adult models were either rewarded or punished for their behavior. Children who observed the model being punished after attacking the doll engaged in very little aggressive behavior toward their own dolls. Those who saw the model reinforced for attacking the doll acted aggressively, imitating the model's behaviors in considerable detail.

The application of these data can be very straightforward. For example, Bandura's research shows that children learn many potential behaviors just by watching TV. Research confirms the idea that children learn aggressive behavior from watching violent television programs (Anderson & Bushman, 2002; Carnagey, Anderson, & Bartholow, 2007; Landhuis et al., 2007). There is a consistent relationship between the amount of violent television a child watches and the level of aggressive behavior he or she displays. The same conclusion has been reached about playing violent video games and subsequent levels of aggression—in both boys and girls (Anderson, et al. 2010).

Learning through observation and imitation is a common form of human learning. Television provides many examples, particularly if you watch PBS, or the Food Network, or HGTV. All day long there are people (role models) trying to teach us how to paint landscapes, build desks and cabinets, do aerobic exercises, improve our golf games, prepare a low-cost meal, or remodel the basement. The basic message is, "Watch me; see how I do it. Then try it yourself."

THINKING CRITICALLY

Some behaviors may be more difficult to learn through imitation than others. Which behaviors might be particularly difficult to learn just by exposure to role models?

Chapter Summary

How do psychologists define learning?
Learning is demonstrated by a relatively permanent change in behavior that occurs as the result of practice or experience. We can use the same definition for "conditioning" in that it is a simple, basic form of learning.

What are the steps involved in demonstrating the classical conditioning of the salivation response in dogs to the tone of a bell?
In classical, or Pavlovian, conditioning, a neutral stimulus that originally does not elicit a response of interest is paired with a stimulus that reliably does elicit a given response. As a result, the once-neutral stimulus comes to elicit a response that is similar to the original reflexive response. For example, the unconditioned stimulus, or UCS, of food powder reliably elicits a reflexive, unconditioned response, or UCR, of salivation. The association between the UCS and UCR is unlearned. The conditioned stimulus, or CS (e.g., the tone of a bell), is the previously neutral stimulus, which, after being paired with the UCS, comes to elicit a learned response that resembles the UCR. The learned response is the CR (also salivation). Extinction is the process in which the strength of a CR decreases with repeated presentations of the CS alone.

What are generalization and discrimination, and how are they demonstrated in classical conditioning?
In generalization, a response (the CR) conditioned to a specific stimulus (the CS) will also be elicited by other, similar stimuli. The more the new stimuli are similar to the original CS, the greater the resultant CR. As new stimuli become less and less similar to the original CS, the CR becomes progressively weaker. In many ways, discrimination is the opposite of generalization. Discrimination is a matter of learning to make a CR in response to a specific CS (paired with the UCS) while learning NOT to make the CR in response to other stimuli, which are not paired with the UCS.

How did Watson and Rayner classically condition fear in "Little Albert"?
Classical conditioning has its most noticeable effect on emotion or mood. Most of the stimuli to which we respond emotionally have probably been classically conditioned to elicit those responses. In the Watson and Rayner "Little Albert" demonstration, a sudden loud noise (the UCS) was paired with the presentation of the neutral stimulus, a white rat. As a result of such pairings, 11-month-old Albert came to display a learned fear response (a CR) to the originally neutral rat (now the CS). The classically conditioned fear generalized to other, similar stimuli. The demonstration has been used to explain learned emotional reactions to events in our environments.

How can classical conditioning be used in the treatment of phobias?
Phobic disorders are those in which someone experiences an irrational and intense fear of something that is not truly dangerous. Wolpe and others have found that the disorder can be treated using systematic desensitization, which involves training a person to relax and stay relaxed while thinking about a hierarchy of stimuli that are more and more likely to elicit anxiety or fear. If relaxation can be conditioned to thoughts of anxiety-producing stimuli, the sense of calm and relaxation will come to replace the competing response of anxiety.

How does one demonstrate operant conditioning?
Skinner constructed a special apparatus he called an operant chamber. The chamber allowed him to control an organism's environment during learning. A typical chamber for a rat has a bar or a lever and a food cup to deliver reinforcement. A hungry animal is placed in the chamber and is reinforced (with a pellet of food) for the appropriate operant behavior (depressing the bar or lever). Learning occurs as an organism learns to associate a behavior with its consequence. In operant conditioning, it is produced by reinforcing a response so that its rate increases.

What are the distinguishing characteristics between reinforcement and reinforcers, between primary and secondary reinforcers, and between positive and negative reinforcers?
Reinforcement refers to the process of strengthening a response. A reinforcer is any stimulus that increases or

maintains the rate of a response, regardless of the nature of the stimulus. A primary reinforcer is a stimulus that is in some way biologically important or related to an organism's survival, such as food for a hungry organism or warm shelter for a cold one. No previous learning is required for a primary reinforcer to strengthen or maintain behavior. A secondary reinforcer increases or maintains response rates only because of an earlier learning experience. These reinforcers have no direct biological significance for an organism. They take on reinforcing qualities having been previously associated with something else. Examples include praise, money, and letter grades.

A positive reinforcer is a stimulus that increases or maintains the rate of the response it follows. Food for hungry organisms, water for thirsty ones, and high grades for well-motivated students are examples. A negative reinforcer is an aversive stimulus present before an operant behavior occurs. When that behavior is produced, the aversive stimulus is removed. Behavior occurring before the removal of a negative reinforcer will be strengthened or maintained. Thus, it is the removal of an aversive stimulus that is reinforcing.

How do psychologists define punishment, and under what circumstances is it an effective means of behavior control?

Punishment is the process of decreasing the strength of a behavior by delivering a painful, unpleasant, or aversive stimulus after a behavior has occurred. Punishment can either involve administering a punisher after an undesired behavior has occurred, or withdrawing a stimulus that an organism desires. For example, a child can be spanked for aggressive behavior in the former case, or have television privileges suspended in the latter case. Punishment can be effective in suppressing a response when it is strong enough and is delivered immediately after the response to be punished. Inconsistent use of punishment reduces the effectiveness of punishment for the immediate behavior and desensitizes the organism to the effects of future punishment. The punishment of one response should be paired with the reinforcement of another, more appropriate response. There are several drawbacks to using physical punishment (spanking) with children: It leads only to a temporary suppression of behavior; physical punishment provides children with aggressive role models and a lesson that the way to deal with frustration and anger is through aggression.

What are latent learning and cognitive maps?

According to E. L. Tolman, latent learning is the acquisition of information (an internal, mental, cognitive process) that may not be demonstrated in performance until later, if at all. Latent learning demonstrates the distinction between learning and performance. Rats can learn their way around a maze, but not demonstrate that they know the pathways of the maze until they are reinforced with food. We cannot say whether Billy can play the piano until we make it worth his while to show us. A cognitive map is a mental picture, or representation, of one's physical environment, noting significant landmarks when possible. The formation of a cognitive map can be viewed as a type of latent learning. When one acquires a cognitive map, one develops a cognitive representation (or picture) of one's surroundings—an appreciation of general location and placement of key objects.

What is the essence of "social learning theory"?

Bandura's social learning theory emphasizes the role of the observation of others (models) and imitation in the acquisition of cognitions and behaviors. We often learn by imitating models. A commonly cited example of social learning is the acquisition of aggressive behaviors based on the viewing of violent television (and other media) programs. Behaviors of a model are most likely to be imitated if the model's behaviors are seen to be reinforced. If a model's behaviors are seen to be punished, they are less likely to be imitated.

Key Terms

Learning (p. 80)
Reflex (p. 82)
Classical conditioning (p. 82)
Unconditioned stimulus (p. 82)
Unconditioned response (p. 82)
Orienting reflex (p. 82)
Conditioned stimulus (p. 83)
Conditioned response (p. 83)
Extinction (p. 84)
Stimulus generalization (p. 84)
Discrimination learning (p. 84)
Systematic desensitization (p. 86)
Operant conditioning (p. 87)

Reinforcement (p. 89)
Reinforcer (p. 89)
Primary reinforcer (p. 89)
Secondary reinforcer (p. 89)
Positive reinforcement (p. 90)
Negative reinforcement (p. 90)
Punishment (p. 92)
Spanking (p. 93)
Latent learning (p. 96)
Cognitive map (p. 96)
Social learning theory (p. 97)

Memory

Source: Peshkova/Shutterstock.

Questions You Will Be Able to Answer

After reading Chapter 5, you should be able to answer the following questions:

- How can memory be characterized as a stage of information processing?
- What do psychologists mean by "sensory memory"?
- What are the basic features of short-term, or working, memory?
- What are the capacity and duration of long-term memory?
- How does information get encoded into long-term memory?
- What are the varieties of long-term memory?
- What does research on repressed and eyewitness memories tell us about the accuracy of long-term memories?
- What factors can affect the accuracy of an eyewitness?
- How can encoding processes be used to improve retrieval?
- How do overlearning and practice (study) schedules affect retrieval?
- What does it mean to say that retrieval is a practicable skill?

Preview

Memory is so central to our everyday existence that it is nearly impossible to imagine life without it. As students of psychology, we care about memory in an academic, study-learn-test sense, but the importance of memory goes well beyond classroom exams. All of those things that define us as individuals—our feelings, beliefs, aspirations, attitudes, and experiences—are stored in our memories.

As usual, we'll begin by formulating a working definition of memory. It will soon become clear that human memory is complex, multi-faceted, creative, and elusive. We will consider how information and personal experiences get into memory and how they are stored there. We will explore the possibility that there are several types of memory and see what these varieties of memory might be.

Once we have our foundation set, we turn to the practical matter of accounting for why we forget things. Our focus will be on factors that affect the retrieval of information from memory. Whether we are talking about a simple well-learned habit, a precise definition, a personal experience, or a telephone number, if retrieval fails at a critical time that information will be of no use to us. What can be done to increase the likelihood that memory retrieval will succeed? In truth, the list is not a very long one. Indeed, we will see that most of the important means of improving memory have to do with how information gets placed into memory in the first place. Throughout this discussion, we will assume that the to-be-remembered information is actually stored in memory. That is, we focus on problems of *retrieval*, not *retention*.

How Can We Best Describe Human Memory?

One approach to human memory is to think about it as a final step in a series of psychological activities that process information. The processing of information begins when sensory receptors are stimulated. The process of perception then selects and organizes the information provided to us by our senses. With memory, a record of that information is formed.

Although we often give a single label to what we commonly call "memory," it is not a single structure or process. Instead, memory is a set of systems involved in the acquisition, storage, and retrieval of information that can hold information for periods of time ranging from fractions of a second to a lifetime. These systems have storage capacities that range from the very limited to the vast; from a few simple sounds to complex events and the details of an entire human life.

Using memory is a cognitive activity that involves three inter-related processes (see **Figure 5.1**). The first step is **encoding**, the process of putting information into memory, or forming cognitive representations of information. Encoding is an active process involving a decision (perhaps unconscious) as to which details of an experience to place into memory. **Storage** is the process of keeping information and experiences in memory. In order to use stored information, it must be gotten out again. **Retrieval** is the process of getting information out of memory. So if memory involves the inter-related processes of encoding, storing, and retrieving information, how shall we describe those "systems" in which these processes operate?

Memory—a set of systems involved in the acquisition, storage, and retrieval of information that can hold information for periods of time ranging from fractions of a second to a lifetime.

Encoding—the process of putting information into memory, or forming cognitive representations of information.

Storage—the process of keeping information and experiences in memory.

Retrieval—the process of getting information out of memory.

FIGURE 5.1 The Three Inter-related Processes Involved in Memory

There is some disagreement among psychologists as to how to best characterize the different levels or storehouses that constitute human memory. The most popular model of memory, the information processing model, states that memory consists of three storage systems: sensory memory, short-term memory, and long-term memory. Let's look at each in turn.

STUDY CHECK

How can memory be characterized as a stage of information processing?

THINKING CRITICALLY

Sometimes we can remember events or experiences vividly and nearly without effort. At other times (like taking an exam) we cannot seem to remember what we want to when we want to. What might account for these differences?

Sensory Memory

Sensory memory is a storage system that stores large amounts of information for very short periods (only a few seconds, or less). The concept of such a very brief memory is a strange one (we usually don't think about remembering something for only a fraction of a second), but it has a place in the processing of information.

Remember: Information that gets stored in memory must first have entered through our senses. Simply put, before you can recall what a lecturer says, you must first hear the lecture. To remember a picture from this book, the image of the picture must first stimulate your visual system. You can't remember the aroma of fried onions if you've never smelled them. Each of your senses most likely has some form of sensory memory. However, the best understood are *visual sensory memory* (also called iconic memory) and *auditory sensory memory* (also called echoic memory).

The basic idea of a sensory memory is that information does not pass immediately through our sensory systems; instead, it is held for a brief time. Even after a stimulus leaves our environment and is no longer present, it has left its imprint, having formed a sensory memory.

The capacity of sensory memory seems, at least in theory, to be very large. At one time it was believed that we are able to keep as much in sensory memory as our sense receptors can respond to. Such claims may give sensory memory more credit than it is due. Sensory memory can hold much more information than we can attend to, but there *are* limits on its capacity.

Sensory memory is typically viewed as being a rather mechanical or physical type of storage. Information is *not* encoded in sensory memory; you have to take it pretty much as your receptors deliver it. It is as if stimuli from the environment make an impression on our sensory systems, reverberate momentarily, and then rapidly fade or are replaced by new stimuli.

Here are two demonstrations of sensory memory. You can demonstrate visual sensory memory in the following way. In a reasonably dark area, stand about 20 feet from a friend who is pointing a flashlight at you. Have your friend swing the flashlight around in a small circle, making about one revolution per second. What do you see? Your *experience* is that of a circle of light. At any one instant, you are seeing where the light is, and you are experiencing from your sensory memory where the light has just been. If your friend moves the light slowly, you may see a "tail" of light following it, but you will no longer see a full circle because the image of the light's position will have fallen from sensory memory.

Has this ever happened to you? Someone asks you a simple question, to which you reply something like, "Huh? What'd you say?" Then, before the person even gets a chance

Sensory memory—a storage system that stores large amounts of information for very short periods.

to repeat the question, you answer it (which, in turn, may provoke a response like, "Why didn't you answer me in the first place?"). Perhaps you did not hear the entire question you were asked, but while it was still echoing in your auditory sensory memory, you listened to it again and formed your answer.

STUDY CHECK

What do psychologists mean by "sensory memory"?

THINKING CRITICALLY

Perhaps sensory memory is pertinent only to the psychology laboratory. Can you think of any examples of sensory memory from your own experience?

Short-Term Memory (STM)

Information can get into sensory memory with relative ease. Once it gets there, where does it go next? Most of it fades rapidly or is quickly replaced with new stimuli. But with a little effort, we can process material from our sensory memories more fully by moving it to short-term memory. **Short-term memory (STM)** is a level, or store, in human memory with a limited capacity and, without the benefit of rehearsal, a brief duration. As noted, information can enter STM from sensory memory. It can also be pulled back into STM from long-term memory.

Short-term memory is referred to as *working memory* by researcher Alan D. Baddeley (1998, 2001), who sees this memory as something like a workbench or desktop on which we pull together and use the information to which we pay attention. Thus, short-term memory holds information in our consciousness, or awareness, ever so briefly while we "work with it."

Figure 5.2 is a diagram of the model of memory we are building. At the left are stimuli from the environment activating our senses and moving directly to our sensory memory. In the middle is short-term memory. We see that information from sensory memory or from long-term memory can be moved into STM. To get material into short-term memory requires that we attend to it.

Once attended to, information will remain accessible in short-term memory for about 20–30 seconds. That doesn't sound very long, but in many cases, 20–30 seconds is all we need. Consider this scenario. Having studied for hours, you decide to reward yourself with a pizza. Never having called Pizza City before, you look the number up on your phone and find the number: 555-5897. You repeat the number to yourself: 555-5897. You open your phone app and dial the number without error. Buzzz-buzzz-buzzz-buzzz. Darn, the line's busy! Well, you'll call back in a minute.

Just as you hang up, the doorbell rings. It's the paper carrier. You owe $13.60 for the past two weeks' deliveries. Discovering that you don't have enough cash on hand to pay for the paper and a pizza, you write a check. "Let's see, what is today's date? Oh yeah, September 9th. How much did you say I owed you? Oh yes, $13.60, and a dollar and a half for a tip, comes to $15.10. This is check number 1079; I'd better write that down."

The paper carrier leaves, and you return to your studying. Then you recall that you were going to order a pizza. Only five or six

Short-term memory (STM) — a level, or store, in human memory with a limited capacity and, without the benefit of rehearsal, a brief duration.

Most of the time when we look up a telephone number, we only need to (or want to) remember that number long enough to get it dialed successfully. That is, all we want to do is attend to it in order to get it into short-term memory.

Source: Zadorozhna Natalia/Shutterstock.

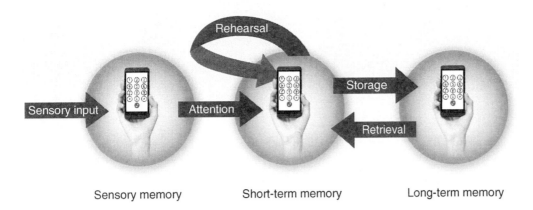

Rehearsal

Sensory input → Attention → Storage

Retrieval

Sensory memory   Short-term memory   Long-term memory

FIGURE 5.2 Memory Processes

The information-processing model of memory assumes that information (such as a seven-digit phone number) passes from sensory memory to short-term memory to long-term memory. Information might also pass from long-term memory to short-term memory. Each of the stages involves information encoding, storage, and retrieval.
Source: ImageFlow/Shutterstock.

minutes have passed since you got a busy signal from Pizza City. As you go to dial, you cannot remember the telephone number. The number, once attended to, was active in your short-term memory. When you were kept from rehearsing it, and particularly when other numbers entered as interfering information, that original telephone number was soon inaccessible.

We can increase the duration of short-term memory by rehearsing the information stored there. **Maintenance rehearsal** (or rote rehearsal) is rehearsal we use to keep material active in short-term memory that amounts to little more than the simple repetition of the information already in STM. To get material into STM (encoding), we have to attend to it. By repeating that material (as we might if we wanted to remember a telephone number until we could dial it), we are re-attending to it with each repetition.

The duration of STM is long enough for us to use it in many everyday activities. Usually, all we want to do with a telephone number is remember it long enough to dial it. Few people feel the need to make a permanent record of every telephone number they dial. Another example of STM in action is in the processing of language. As you read one of our longer sentences, such as this one, it helps to have a short-term storage place to keep the beginning of the sentence in mind until you finally get to the end of the sentence, so that you can figure out the basic idea of the sentence before deciding whether anything in the sentence is worth remembering!

Now, how much information can we hold in STM for that 20 to 30 seconds duration? The answer is "not much"—about five to nine "chunks" of information. A **chunk** is the representation in memory of a meaningful unit of information. Thus, the claim is that we can store about six or seven meaningful pieces of information in STM (Cowan, 2001, 2005; McElree, 2001).

We can easily attend to, encode, and store five or six numbers in STM. Holding the numbers 15295670913 in short-term memory would be a challenge. Eleven randomly presented numbers exceed the capacity of STM for most of us. What if you were asked to remember the numbers as a telephone number? You would chunk them in the manner shown in **Figure 5.3**, and they would be easier to remember. In fact, you can easily store larger strings of numbers or letters in short-term memory if you recode them into meaningful chunks. For example, you could store 50 letters in short-term memory if you chunk them as the "days of the week."

Maintenance rehearsal (or rote rehearsal)—rehearsal we use to keep material active in short-term memory that amounts to little more than the simple repetition of the information already in our STM.

Chunk—the representation in memory of a meaningful unit of information.

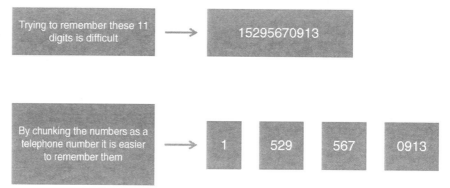

FIGURE 5.3 Remembering a Long String of Numbers Using Chunking

At best, short-term memory works rather like a leaky bucket. From the vast storehouse of information available in sensory memory, we scoop up some (not much, at that) by paying attention to it and holding it for a while until we either use it, hang onto it with maintenance rehearsal, move it along to long-term storage, or lose it.

STUDY CHECK

What are the basic features of short-term, or working, memory?

THINKING CRITICALLY

In what circumstances would more effective chunking of information improve your memory?

Long-Term Memory

Long-term memory (LTM)—memory for large amounts of information that is held for long periods of time.

Long-term memory (LTM) is memory for large amounts of information that is held for long periods of time. LTM is memory as we usually think of it. Our own experience tells us that the capacity of long-term memory is huge—virtually limitless. At times we even impress ourselves with the amount of material we have stashed away in LTM. How much can be stored in human memory may never be measured, but we can rest assured that there is no way we will ever learn so much that there won't be room for more. (Getting that information out again when we want it is another matter, which we'll get to shortly.)

On an experiential basis, we can again impress ourselves with the duration of some of our memories. Assuming you remain free from disease or injury, you're likely never to forget some information, such as your own name or the words to the "Happy Birthday" song. As an adult, you can recall many experiences from high school. Perhaps you have some fond memories from grade school. How about memories of preschool events? Is there an age before which lasting memories are not possible, or, as some argue, do we carry memories of our own births or prenatal experiences? "The earliest scientifically documented childhood memories recalled by adults happened to them when they were around 2 years of age" (Howe, 2003, p. 63). Those people who might tell you that they can remember their own birth, and vividly recall the day they were brought home from the hospital's nursery, are no doubt mistaken, even though they can tell a good story.

Simple repetition (maintenance rehearsal) is used to keep material active in short-term memory. This type of rehearsal is also one way to move information from STM to LTM. However, simply attending to information—the essence of repetition—is an inefficient means of encoding information into long-term memory.

To encode information into long-term memory, we need to use rehearsal that differs from maintenance rehearsal. **Elaborative rehearsal** is rehearsal used to transfer information from short-term to long-term memory. It involves organizing, forming images of, attaching meaning to, or relating information to something already in long-term memory. Elaborative rehearsal is not an either/or process. Information can be elaborated to greater or lesser degrees. When we do no more than attend to an item, as in maintenance rehearsal, our processing is fairly minimal, or shallow, and that item is likely to remain in memory for a relatively short time. The more we rehearse an item elaboratively, the easier it will be to remember.

Elaborative rehearsal—rehearsal used to transfer information from short-term to long-term memory. It involves organizing, forming images of, attaching meaning to, or relating information to something already in long-term memory.

> **STUDY CHECK**
>
> What are the capacity and duration of long-term memory?
> How does information get encoded into long-term memory?

> **THINKING CRITICALLY**
>
> Can you think of any way(s) in which we can determine if the failure to remember something is because it is there, but we cannot retrieve it versus it is simply no longer in LTM?

Are There Different Types of Long-Term Memory?

From experience, we know that we can retrieve what we have stored in LTM in various forms. We can remember the definitions of words. We can visualize people and events from the past. We can recall the melodies of songs. We can recollect how our bodies moved when we first tried to roller-skate.

Are there different long-term memory storage systems that encode and store information differently? Apparently, there are. The most commonly used scheme breaks down long-term memory into three rather distinct types: *semantic*, *episodic* (together making up declarative memory), and *procedural* (or nondeclarative) (Thompson, 2005).

Semantic memory is where we store all our vocabulary, simple concepts, and rules (including the rules for using language) (Tulving, 1972, 2003). Within semantic memory, we store our knowledge of the world. Our semantic memories are filled with facts, both important and trivial. Can you answer these questions?

Semantic memory—memory where we store all our vocabulary, simple concepts, and rules.

> *Who opened the first psychology laboratory in Leipzig in 1879?*
> *How many stripes are there on the American flag?*
> *Is "Colorless green ideas sleep furiously" a well-formed, grammatically correct sentence?*
> *What do dogs eat?*

If you can, you found the answers in your long-term semantic memory.

Information in semantic memory is stored in an organized fashion. Psychologists are not yet sure how to characterize the complex structure of semantic memory, but they have put forth several ideas. At the very least, some concepts elicit others. If we ask you to say the first thing that comes to mind when you hear the word "hot," aren't you likely to say "cold"? When people are asked to recall a list of randomly presented words from various categories (e.g., pieces of furniture, fruits, sports, and colors), they do so by category, for example, recalling furniture and naming "sofa," "chair," "table," etc., then fruits, naming, "apple," "pear," "apricot," "grape," then sports and colors. Psychologists call this process *category clustering* (Bousfield, 1953).

Semantic long-term memory is also abstract. For example, although we may know how many stripes are on the American flag and what dogs generally eat, we may have difficulty remembering how, why, or when we acquired that information. Information in semantic memory is not necessarily tied in any way to our memories of our own life experiences.

Episodic memory—storage system where we store the memories of our life events and experiences.

Episodic memory is a storage system where we store the memories of our life events and experiences. Episodic memory is time-related and stores experiences in chronological order (Eichenbaum & Fortin, 2003; Tulving, 2003). Episodic memory registers, or catalogues, all of our life's events. That is, episodic memories are of specific, not abstract, events. An eyewitness account of a crime is drawn from episodic memory. The answers to these questions all draw upon episodic memory:

> *What did you have for lunch yesterday?*
> *Did you sleep well last night?*
> *How did you spend last summer's vacation?*
> *What did your dog eat yesterday?*
> *What was your fifth birthday like?*

Some researchers claim that there is a separate category of episodic memory called *autobiographical memory*. Autobiographical memory contains memories of significant life events. A memory of what you ate for lunch last Monday may be in your episodic memory, but your memory of your first day in college is probably in autobiographical memory, as well. Children develop autobiographical memory between three and three and a half years of age, at around the time they begin to talk to themselves and others about the events of their lives (Howe, 2003).

There is an altogether different type of long-term memory called procedural memory.

Procedural memory—a storage system where we store motor responses and chains of motor responses that we have learned well.

Procedural memory is a storage system where we store motor responses and chains of motor responses that we have learned well, such as how to ride a bicycle, type, shave, or apply makeup. Simply stated, procedural memory stores the basic procedures of our lives. What we have stored here is retrieved and put into use with little or no effort. At one time in your life, handwriting was difficult, as you strained to form letters and words correctly. But by now, your writing skills, or procedures, are so ingrained that you can retrieve the processes involved almost without thinking. In fact, if you try to explicitly remember and describe each aspect of a procedural memory, you will find the task difficult. For example, try to explain step-by-step how to tie a shoe. John Anderson (1987) calls the information in this subsystem procedural knowledge, or "knowing how." The other types of LTM hold what Anderson calls declarative knowledge, or "knowing that."

STUDY CHECK

What are the varieties of long-term memory?

THINKING CRITICALLY

If elaborative rehearsal is required to process information into long-term memory, why do we seem to remember so many things for which we have no recollection that we elaborated on them at all?

How Accurate Are Long-Term Memories?

When we try to remember a fact we learned in school many years ago, it is often easy to determine the accuracy of our recall. On classroom tests, we are either right or wrong. Determining the accuracy of our memories for past experiences is difficult at best and is sometimes impossible. Do we *really* remember all the details of that family vacation when we were six years old, or are we recalling bits and pieces of what happened along with fragments of what we've been told and then adding other details to reconstruct a likely story? Most of the time, the accuracy of one's recall of experiences from the distant past is of little or no consequence. In some situations, the accuracy of one's memory can be of critical importance.

Retrieval from memory involves an active construction process, and memories based on such a process may be inaccurate because information is either left out or added. The construction process involves storing patterns of features in which each feature represents a different aspect of what is experienced. Furthermore, the stored features are widely scattered over different parts of the brain. That is, no single part of the brain houses a complete memory. Retrieval of information is rather like putting together a jigsaw puzzle. Features stored in various parts of the brain are reactivated, and they, in turn, reactivate other features. This process continues until a memory is reconstructed (Schacter et al., 1998; Thompson, 2005).

The accuracy of long-term memory retrieval is a particularly important issue when witnesses are asked to testify in courts of law about what they remember about a given event.

Sometimes the reconstruction process results in inaccurate reports of what truly did happen. That is, memories are not fixed, nor are they necessarily accurate representations of what was experienced. Can people be fooled into believing that they remember things that never happened? Indeed, "There is ample evidence that people can be led to believe that they experienced things that never happened. In some instances, these beliefs are wrapped in a fair amount of sensory detail and give the impression of being genuine recollections" (Loftus, 2004, p. 147). In one experiment, Loftus and her colleagues had people evaluate advertisements for Disneyland (Braun, Ellis, & Loftus, 2002). One advertisement showed Bugs Bunny in the Magic Kingdom. The ad's text referred to meeting Bugs Bunny as being the perfect ending to a perfect day. Participants were then asked about their childhood experiences at Disneyland. Initially, about 16 percent of those who saw the Bugs Bunny advertisement claimed to have met him at Disneyland. The more often participants saw the Bugs Bunny advertisement, the greater the percentage that remembered him at Disneyland. The details were often very rich even though these were "constructed" memories. Bugs Bunny is a Warner Brothers character and has never appeared at Disney.

One example of the importance of accuracy in the retrieval of information from long-term storage involves what is called *repressed memory*. Repression is said to have occurred when extremely unpleasant or traumatic events are pushed deep into the unconscious corners of memory, from which retrieval is, at best, very difficult. A repressed memory is one that is so disturbing to a person that it is pushed deep into the unconscious and is no longer readily available for retrieval.

In recent years the idea of repression, or "motivated forgetting," has created quite a stir. Repressed memories have been linked to psychological symptoms, including eating disorders, anxiety, and depression. One theory is that a repressed memory of childhood sexual abuse (CSA) is at the root of these disorders, and the only way to deal with an individual's symptoms is to recover the repressed memory (or memories) and deal with it.

Without questioning the enormity of the problem of child abuse or challenging reports of its prevalence, Elizabeth Loftus (1993a, 1993b, 2003) has challenged the authenticity of the repressed memories of some adults who "remember" events that may never have happened in the first place. Loftus has never said that child abuse is not a real phenomenon. It may be, however, that some people genuinely come to believe that they were abused as children in order to help make sense of the difficulties they are now having as adults (Goodman et al., 2003; McNally, 2003a, 2003b).

What is the bottom line on repressed and recovered memories? There is research showing that memories can be implanted (Laney & Loftus, 2008). However, this does not mean that all recovered memories are false memories. The problem lies in the ability to distinguish between those recovered memories that are actual memories of real events and those that are false memories resulting from suggestive techniques. One study does provide some evidence that repressed memories of abuse that actually occurred are as accurate (74.7 percent) as memories of the event that were not repressed (74.6 percent) (Dalenberg, 1996). Of course this does not tell us how many repressed memories are valid, only that those that were verified appear to be accurate. The problem of repressed memory recovery presents a challenge not only to psychology but also to the legal system, which must deal with cases relying on recovered memories.

The accuracy of long-term memory is also critical in eyewitness testimony. Eyewitnesses are called on to accurately recall the details of a crime as well as identify the suspect. Unfortunately, eyewitnesses are not as accurate as we think they are. The challenges posed to eyewitnesses occur at each phase of the memory process: encoding, storage, and retrieval. When you encode information, you select information to be placed into memory. For any event, it is likely that not all details of an event are equally attended to and encoded. Only details that are salient to the individual are encoded. For example, if you saw a person with a gun holding up a bank, you might encode information about the gun, the robber's clothing, his height, and his weight—particularly if he were very heavy or very thin. Other information (e.g., the color of the robber's shoes) may not be encoded. As you might expect, you will probably focus on the weapon the most. This is known as the *weapon focus effect* (Loftus, Loftus, & Messo, 1987). Our attention is most likely drawn to the weapon because it is threatening to us (i.e., it becomes a salient detail) and not because it is an unusual object (Hope & Wright, 2007). In addition to the presence of a weapon, there are other factors affecting eyewitness accuracy. **Table 5.1** summarizes those factors that experts in the field agree can influence the accuracy of an eyewitness (Kassin, Tubb, Hosch, & Memon, 2001).

TABLE 5.1 Statements and Observations About Eyewitness Testimony on which Experts in the Field Agree

1. An eyewitness's testimony about an event can be affected by how the questions put to that witness are worded.

2. Police instructions can affect an eyewitness's willingness to make an identification.

3. Eyewitness testimony about an event often reflects not only what the witness actually saw, but information he or she obtained later.

4. An eyewitness's perception and memory for an event may be affected by his or her attitudes and expectations.

5. Hypnosis increases suggestibility to leading and misleading questions.

6. An eyewitness's confidence is not a good predictor of his or her identification accuracy.

7. The presence of a weapon impairs the eyewitness's ability to accurately identify the perpetrator's face.

8. The rate of memory loss for an event is greatest right after the event and then levels off over time.

9. The less time an eyewitness has to observe an event, the less accurately he or she will remember it.

10. Eyewitnesses sometimes identify as a culprit someone they have seen in another situation or context.

STUDY CHECK

What does research on repressed and eyewitness memories tell us about the accuracy of long-term memories?
What factors can affect the accuracy of an eyewitness?

THINKING CRITICALLY

In our discussion of perception (Chapter 3), we noted that we often perceive what we expect to, or want to, or have perceived in the past. How might selective perception limit the accuracy of long-term memory?

FOCUS ON DIVERSITY

Gender Differences in Memory

In 1974, Maccoby and Jacklin attempted to find out whether there were gender differences in basic memory processes. They found that females had higher levels of verbal abilities than males. However, they did not find many significant differences between males and females in those basic memory processes. This early finding did not stop researchers from looking for gender differences in memory. What did they find?

Researchers have uncovered differences between females and males in episodic and autobiographical memory. In one interesting study, Wang (2013) sent men and women a text three times a week asking them to record what had happened to them during the last 30 minutes. Then, at the end of the week, the participants received another text message with a surprise memory test over the events (the encoding test). Wang also had participants come to the lab a week later for another memory test (the recall test). Wang found that for both encoding and recall, women recalled more accurate details of events than men. At recall, women remembered more socially oriented details than men. Wang concluded that women do better than men in episodic memory in terms of both encoding and delayed recall. Other studies show the same pattern of gender differences (Herlitz, Nilsson, & Bäckman, 1997; Herlitz & Yonker, 2002).

There are also gender differences in autobiographical memory, a specific type of episodic memory. For example, Azriel Grysman (2017) emailed female and male participants a survey asking them to record a specific event that happened to them within the past 24 hours. A few weeks later, they received another survey again asking them to describe the event. Grysman found that women provided more details specific to the events reported than men, both immediately and after the delay of several weeks. Another difference between men and women is that women reported more emotional details (both positive and negative) than men (Davis, 1999; Seidlitz & Diener, 1998). Women also remember more memories of childhood and can access them faster than men (Davis, 1999), and they also remember earlier memories from childhood than men (Kingo, Berntsen, & Krøjgaard, 2013). Women also report more vivid memories than their spouses for events related to their first date, last vacation, and a recent argument (Fujita, Diener, & Sandvik, 1991), and they tend to produce richer, more evaluative descriptions of autobiographical events compared with men. However, men tend to produce descriptions that contain more facts compared with women (Schulkind, Schoppel, & Scheiderer, 2012). Interestingly, these differences may relate to differences in brain activity between men and women during autobiographical memory recall (Manns, Varga, Trimper, & Bauer, 2018; St. Jacques, Conway, & Cabeza, 2011).

Another area of episodic memory in which women and men show some differences is eyewitness memory. Women's memory for a violent crime is better than men's (Lindholm & Christianson, 1998). Women also tend to provide more accurate descriptions of those involved in a violent robbery, especially of the victim. However, men are more accurate than women describing the robbery itself and are more confident than women in their memories (Areh, 2011). Lindholm and Christianson suggest that women's advantage might be due to their more elaborate cognitive categories for encoding information about people. They speculated that this may be due to different socialization experiences for men and women. Males and females may be socialized to attend to, and consequently remember, different kinds of information. It appears that females attend to and recall information about people better than males. Males, on the other hand, may be socialized to attend to more features of the event itself, resulting in the better memory for event details.

The final gender difference in memory we shall explore is for working memory (short-term memory). Whether there is a gender difference in working memory depends, in part, on the nature of the task (Robert & Savoie, 2006). In one experiment, women and men performed either a visual or verbal working memory task under conditions of distraction or no distraction (Harness, Jacot, Scherf, White, & Warnick, 2008). Harness et al. found that males performed better than females only when there was distraction. They also found that females did better than males on the visual task. There was no difference in the verbal working memory task.

In another interesting study (Verde et al., 2015), male and female pilots and non-pilots were compared on two working memory tasks relevant to piloting an aircraft (visual-spatial memory and reaching memory). Verde et al. found that male non-pilots performed better on the visual-spatial working memory task compared with female non-pilots. There was no difference between males and females on the reaching task. However, experience is an important factor. Female and male pilots performed equally well on both tasks. It seems, then, that working memory skills can be learned.

Females are also better than men at recognizing emotional working memory stimuli (positive and negative facial expressions). On the other hand, males do better than females on a working memory task applying the application of rules (Saylik, Raman, & Szameitat, 2018). Working memory differences may relate to differences in the neural networks used by the brain in working memory tasks. Although women and men show highly consistent patterns of neural activity on working memory tasks, there are some differences. For example, during a working memory task, women show more activity than men in areas of the limbic system (amygdala and hippocampus) and areas of the frontal lobes. Men show more activity in the parietal areas of the brain (Hill, Laird, & Robinson, 2014).

Improving Memory Retrieval

Encoding, storage, and retrieval are inter-related memory processes. The issue is simple: If you do not encode information properly, you will have difficulty retrieving it. You may not recall a stranger's name simply because you never knew it in the first place. You have had countless encounters with pennies. Can you draw a picture of a penny, locating all its features? Can you recognize an accurate drawing of a penny (**Figure 5.4**)? In fact, few of us can, and even fewer can recall all its essential features. Nearly 90 percent fail to note that the word Liberty appears right behind Lincoln's shoulder (Nickerson & Adams, 1979). These retrieval failures do not result from a lack of experience but from a lack of proper encoding. Few of us have ever sat down to study (encode) exactly what a penny looks like.

Here's an example to which nearly all students can relate—the difference between recall and recognition. **Recall** is a memory process where one produces information to which he or she has been previously exposed. For example, if you were presented with a list of 15 words to learn and were then asked to write down as many of the words as possible, in any order, you would be using recall. We merely specify the information wanted and say, "Go into your long-term memory, locate that information, get it out, and write it down." **Recognition** is a memory process where we ask someone to identify material previously experienced. A good example of a recognition task occurs when an eyewitness must try to pick a suspect out of a lineup. The witness was exposed to the perpetrator at the scene of the crime. An image of the perpetrator's face was encoded into memory. During a lineup, the witness is asked if he or she recognizes anyone in the lineup.

When recall and recognition memory are compared, recognition turns out to be a more sensitive measure of memory than recall. In other words, we can often recognize things we cannot recall. For example, have you ever seen someone you know walking toward you, and you recognize the person (perhaps an acquaintance from high school), but you just cannot recall the person's name? In virtually every case, retrieval by recognition is superior to retrieval by recall. Most students would rather take a multiple-choice exam, in which they only have to *recognize* the correct response from among a few alternatives, than a fill-in-the-blank test (or essay test), which requires *recall*.

Recall—a memory process where one produces information to which he or she has been previously exposed.

Recognition—a memory process where we ask someone to identify material previously experienced.

FIGURE 5.4 Fifteen Drawings of the Head of a Penny (Nickerson & Adams, 1979)

Consider these questions, each of which is after the same information.

1. The physiologist best associated with the discovery of classical conditioning was _____.

2. The physiologist best associated with the discovery of classical conditioning was a) Thorndike b) Helmholtz c) Pavlov d) Skinner.

For the first question, recall is required; the second only requires that you recognize Pavlov's name. Reinforcing the notion that encoding and retrieval are related are the data that tell us that students who expect and study for a fill-in-the-blank test of recall will do better on that test than will students who expect and study for a test of recognition. Test scores are best when the measure of retrieval matches the strategy of encoding. There are other ways in which we can see the relationship among encoding, storage, and retrieval, which is where we go next.

Information Encoding Affects Retrieval

Retrieval is most successful when the situation, or *context*, in which retrieval occurs matches the context that was present at encoding. When cues present at encoding are also present at retrieval, retrieval is enhanced. Not only do we encode and store particular items of information, but we also note and store the context in which those items occur. This is known as *encoding specificity*.

Here's a hypothetical experiment that demonstrates this point (based on Tulving & Thompson, 1973). Students learn a list of 24 common words. Half the students are given cue words to help them remember each item on the list. For the stimulus word "wood," the cue word is "tree"; for cheese, the cue is "green," and so on for each of the 24 words. The other students receive no such cues during their learning (i.e., encoding). Later, students are asked to recall as many words as they can. What happens is that giving the cue at recall helps those students who had seen it during learning but *decreases* the recall for those who had not seen it during learning. If learning takes place without a cue, recall will be better without it.

A psychology professor has a hypothesis. She believes she can determine the learning ability of students by noting where they sit in the classroom. The best, brightest students choose seats farthest from the door. Poorer students sit by the door, apparently interested in getting easily into and out of the room. (There may be some truth to this, but I am not serious: This is just an example of a hypothesis.) To make her point, she does an experiment. Students seated away from the door are asked to learn a list of words. They can listen to the list, read aloud, only once. A second list of words is needed for the students seated by the door—they've already heard the first list. The list the "smart students" hear contains words such as *university, registrar, automobile, environmental, and psychology*. As predicted, they have little problem recalling this list even after just one presentation. The students huddled by the door get the second list: *insidious, tachistoscope, sophistry, flotsam, and episcotister*, and the like. Needless to say, the professor's hypothesis will be confirmed.

This obviously is not a fair experiment. Those students sitting by the door will yell foul. The second list of words is clearly more difficult to learn and recall than the first list. The words on the first list are more familiar, and they are easier to pronounce. However, the major difference between these lists is meaningfulness. **Meaningfulness** is the extent to which information elicits existing associations already in memory. The *university, registrar, automobile* list is easy to remember because each word in it is meaningful. Each word makes us think of many other things or produces many associations. These items are easy to elaborate. Words like "episcotister" are more difficult because they evoke few, if any, associations.

An important observation: Meaningfulness is not a characteristic or feature built into materials to be learned. Meaningfulness resides in the learner. "Episcotister" may be a meaningless collection of letters for many, but for others it is a word rich in meaning, a word with which they can easily form many associations. What is or is not meaningful is a function of one's individual experiences. (An episcotister, by the way, is a type of apparatus used in psychology. To make this word truly meaningful for you, you might want to check the Internet on "episcotisters.")

It follows, then, that one of your tasks as a learner is to do whatever you can to make the material you are learning as meaningful as possible. You need to seek out and form associations between what you are learning and what you already know. You need to elaboratively rehearse what you are encoding so that you can retrieve it later. You need to ask questions about what you are studying. What does this mean? What does it make me think of? Does this remind me of something I already know? How can I make this more meaningful? Perhaps you now see the reason for including "STUDY CHECK" questions within each chapter.

So retrieval is enhanced when we elaborate on the material we are learning—when we organize it and make it meaningful during the encoding process. Now we'll look at a few encoding techniques. A **mnemonic device** is an encoding technique that aids retrieval by helping to organize and add meaningfulness to new material.

Research by Bower and Clark (1969), for example, shows us another way to improve the retrieval of information. **Narrative chaining** is a technique that helps improve the retrieval of otherwise unorganized material by weaving that material into a meaningful story. A group of college students learned a list of 10 simple nouns in a specific order. This is not a terribly difficult task, and the students had little trouble with it. Then they were given another list of 10 nouns to learn, and then another, and another until they had learned 12 lists. These students were given no instructions other than to remember each list of words in order.

A second group of students learned the same 12 lists. But they were asked to make up stories that used each of the words on the list in order. After each list was presented, both groups were asked to recall the list of words they had just heard. At this point, there was no difference in the recall scores for the two groups. Then came a surprise. After all 12 lists had been recalled, the students were tested again on their recall for each of the lists. Students were given a word from one of the 12 lists and were asked to recall the other nine words from that list. Now the difference in recall between the two groups of students was striking (see **Figure 5.5**). Students who used a narrative-chaining technique recalled 93 percent of the words (on average), whereas those who did not organize the words

Meaningfulness—the extent to which information elicits existing associations already in memory.

Mnemonic device—an encoding technique that aids retrieval by helping to organize and add meaningfulness to new material.

Narrative chaining—a technique that helps improve retrieval of otherwise unorganized material by weaving that material into a meaningful story.

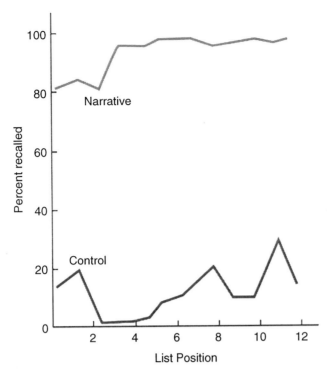

FIGURE 5.5 Percent Correct Recall for Words from 12 Lists Learned under Two Study Conditions (after Bower & Clark, 1969)

recalled only 13 percent. The message is clear and consistent with what we've learned so far: Organizing unrelated words into sensible stories helps us remember them.

Forming mental images can also improve memory. It is the contention of psychologist Allan Paivio that visual images provide a unique way of encoding meaningful information; that is, we are at an advantage if we can encode not only what a stimulus means, but also what it looks like (Paivio, 1986). Imagery helps us retrieve words such as "horse," "rainbow," and "computer" more readily than words such as "treason," "session," or "effort"—even when the frequency and meaningfulness of the words are equated.

Another imagery-related mnemonic device may be the oldest. It is attributed to the Greek poet Simonides and is called the *method of loci*. The idea here is to get in your mind a well-known location (*loci* are locations)—say, the floor plan of your house or apartment. Visually place the material you are trying to recall in various places throughout your house in a sensible order. When the time comes for you to retrieve the material, mentally walk through your chosen locations, recalling the information you have stored at each place.

Assume that you want to learn the meanings of a large number of Spanish words. You could use simple rote repetition, but this technique is tedious and inefficient. Richard Atkinson (1975) suggested the key word method to help memory. The **key word method** is a method of study that works by imagining a connection that visually ties a word to a key word. The Spanish word for "horse," for example, is *caballo*, which is pronounced *cab-eye-yo*. To remember this association, you might choose eye as the key word and picture a horse with a very large eye. The Spanish word for "duck" is *pato*. Here your key word might be pot, and you could picture a duck wearing a pot on its head (**Figure 5.6**) or sitting in a large pot on the stove. Atkinson's learning method may sound strange, but research suggests that it works (Pressley, Levin, & Delaney, 1982).

Mnemonic devices don't have to be formal techniques with special names, nor do they have to involve imagery. You used a mnemonic trick to learn how many days are in each month when you learned the ditty, "Thirty days hath September, April, June, and November. All the rest have . . .". Some students originally learned the colors of the rainbow in order (that's red, orange, yellow, green, blue, indigo, and violet) by remembering the name "ROY G. BIV," which I grant you is not terribly meaningful, but it does help.

Key word method—a method of study that works by imagining a connection that visually ties a word to a key word.

FIGURE 5.6 The Key-Word Method

Nursing and medical school students have long used a similar device for learning the 12 pairs of cranial nerves in order (that would be the olfactory, optic, oculomotor, trochlear, trigeminal, abducens, facial, acoustic, glossopharyngeal, vagus, spinal accessory, and the hypoglossal). What all those students remember (even after they can no longer associate the correct name with the letter) is, "On Old Olympian Towering Tops, a Finn and German Viewed Some Hops." No doubt you have used several mnemonic devices to organize and make material meaningful. In each case, the message is that retrieval will be enhanced whenever we can organize otherwise-unrelated material in a meaningful way.

STUDY CHECK

How can encoding processes be used to improve retrieval?

THINKING CRITICALLY

How can you use the techniques just listed to help remember the material in this chapter?

Scheduling Practice

Retrieval, no matter how it is measured, depends on how one goes about encoding, rehearsing, or practicing information in the first place. Retrieval also is a function of the amount of practice and how that practice is spaced or distributed. One of the reasons some students do not do as well on exams as they would like is that they simply do not have (or make) enough time to study the material covered on those exams. Another reason is that some students do not schedule wisely what time they do have.

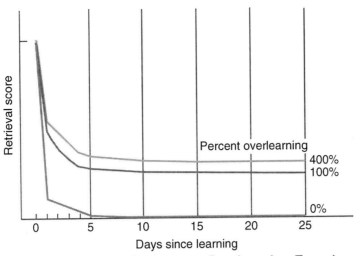

FIGURE 5.7 Hypothetical Results from an Overlearning Experiment

Once we decide to learn something, we read, practice, and study the material (elaborate it) until we know it. We study until we are satisfied that we have encoded and stored the information in our memories, and then we quit. In other words, we often fail to engage in overlearning, the process of practicing or rehearsing material over and above what is needed to learn it. Consider this example, and see if you can extend this evidence to your own study habits.

A student comes to the laboratory to learn a list of nonsense syllables such as dax, wuj, pib, lep, and zuw. There are 15 such items on the list, and they have to be presented repeatedly before the student can recall all of the items correctly. Having correctly recalled the items, the student is dismissed with instructions to return two weeks later for a test of his recall of the same syllables. Not surprisingly, he does not fare very well on this retrieval task.

What do you think would have happened if we had continued to present the list of syllables at the time of learning, well beyond the point at which it was first learned? Let's say the list was learned in 12 trials. We may have the student practice the list for six additional presentations (50 percent overlearning—practice that is 50 percent more than it took to learn in the first place). What if we required an additional 12 trials of practice (100 percent overlearning), or even an additional 48 trials of practice (400 percent overlearning)?

The effects of overlearning are well documented and very predictable. The recall data for this imaginary experiment might look like those in **Figure 5.7**. Note three things about these data:

1. If we measure retrieval at various times after learning, forgetting is rather impressive and quite sudden.
2. Overlearning improves retrieval and has its greatest effects with longer retention intervals.
3. There is a "diminishing returns" effect present here; that is, 50 percent overlearning is much more useful than no overlearning; 100 percent overlearning is somewhat better than 50 percent; and 400 percent is better than 100 percent, but not by very much. For any learning task, or individual, there is probably an optimal amount of overlearning.

The scheduling of learning time is also an important factor in determining the likelihood of retrieval, and it is to this issue we turn next.

Some of the oldest data in psychology tell us that retrieval will be improved if practice (encoding) is spread out over time with rest intervals spaced in between. The data in **Figure 5.8** are fairly standard. In fact, this experiment, first performed in 1946, provides such reliable results that it is commonly used as a student project in psychology classes. The task is to write the letters of the alphabet, upside down and from right to left. (If you think that sounds easy, give it a try.)

Overlearning—the process of practicing or rehearsing material over and above what is needed to learn it.

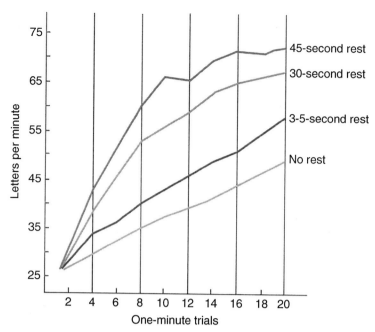

FIGURE 5.8 Improvement in Performance as a Function of the Distribution of Practice Time

Participants are given the opportunity to practice the task under four different conditions. The *massed-practice group* works with no break at all between trials. The three *distributed-practice groups* receive the same amount of practice but get rest intervals interspersed between each one-minute trial. One group gets a three- to five-second rest between trials, a second group receives a 30-second rest, and a third group gets a 45-second rest between trials.

As can be seen in Figure 5.8, participants in all four groups begin at about the same (poor) level of performance. After 20 minutes of practice, the performance of all groups shows improvement, but by far, the massed practice (no rest) group does the poorest, and the 45-second rest group does the best.

The conclusion from years of research is that, almost without exception, distributed practice is superior to massed practice (Cepeda et al., 2006; Rohrer & Pashler, 2007). There are exceptions, however. Some tasks may suffer from having rest intervals inserted in practice time. In general, whenever you must keep track of many things at the same time, you should mass your practice until you have finished what you are working on. If, for example, you are working on a complex math problem, you should work it through until you find a solution, whether it's time for a break or not. And, of course, you should not break up your practice in such a way as to disrupt the meaningfulness of the material you are studying. Meaningfulness is a powerful factor in memory retrieval.

What we're talking about here surely applies to the scheduling of study time. The message is always the same: Short (and meaningful) study periods with rest periods interspersed are more efficient than study periods massed together. There may be times when cramming is better than not studying at all, but as a general strategy, cramming is simply inefficient, is usually very tiring, and often leads to lower grades (Thacher, 2008).

STUDY CHECK

How do overlearning and practice (study) schedules affect retrieval?

On Practicing Retrieval

One final point on improving memory retrieval: *Retrieval of information from long-term memory is enhanced when one practices retrieval.* In other words, retrieval is a practicable skill. This observation turns out to be true for the retrieval of all sorts of information by all sorts of organisms, but it is particularly relevant in the context of retrieving information in the classroom (Roediger & Karpicke, 2006a; Roediger & Karpicke, 2006b).

Here is one way to think about this: What do classroom quizzes, tests, and exams really measure? Teachers often claim that they are measuring what you—as a student—have learned about a prescribed body of knowledge. In fact, what a classroom test measures is not what you have learned as much as what you can remember (retrieve) at the time of the test! Now, of course, what you can retrieve on a test is surely a function of what you have learned, or studied, and we already have seen that there are several steps you can take to enhance your learning of classroom materials (elaborating the material, making it meaningful, organizing it, employing mnemonic techniques, overlearning, and distributing your practice).

The point being made here is that it is powerfully advantageous to practice your retrieval of material. How do you that? Testing. Test yourself before your instructor gives you a test that will impact your grade. Once you have understood a section of your test, pause and try to imagine how you might be tested on that information. If your instructor goes on and on in class about some particular point, you might guess that the point will show up on the next test. How will your instructor ask you about that material? Two leading researchers in this area, Henry Roediger and Jeffrey Karpicke put it this way, "A powerful way of improving one's memory for material is to be tested on that material. Tests enhance later retention more than additional study of the material [overlearning], even when tests are given without feedback" (2006a, p. 181).

PSYCHOLOGY IN ACTION

Hypnosis and Memory Improvement

From almost the beginning of human history, people have been trying to come up with ways to improve memory. We discussed a few of these in this chapter (mnemonic devices). Another method that has been applied to this problem is hypnosis. Among the many, often false, beliefs about how human memory works is the belief that hypnosis can improve memory. In one survey, for example, 55 percent of respondents indicated that hypnosis can improve memory (Simons & Chabris, 2011). Can hypnosis actually improve your memory? In the sense of, "Can you hypnotize me to remember psychology material better for the test next Friday?" the answer is almost certainly no. Someone might be able to convince you under hypnosis (i.e., suggest to you) that you had better remember your psychology and, thus, motivate you to remember. But there is no evidence that hypnotic suggestion can directly improve your ability to learn and remember new material. In fact, people who are most susceptible to hypnosis actually show poorer academic performance than those who are not (West, 2003). Although it may not improve your memory directly, hypnosis might help your memory through relaxation, but so can a good old midday nap (Schichl, Ziberi, Lahl, & Pietrowsky, 2011).

There are those who believe that when under hypnosis, one can return to childhood and remember events that ordinarily cannot be remembered. This is called *age regression*. But is it true that hypnosis can take you back in time (regression) and make you remember what it was like when you were a child? Here, we have a clear-cut answer, and the answer is no. So-called age-regression hypnotic sessions have simply not proven to be valid (e.g., Nash, 1987; Spanos, Menary, Gabora, DuBreuil, & Dewhirst, 1991). Often there is no way to verify the validity of memories "recovered" during age or past-life regression. It is entirely possible that a person who is age-regressed with hypnosis will produce false memories or pseudomemories. Under hypnosis, a person is in a highly suggestible state and may be susceptible to having facts or events that never occurred implanted in their memories. The research on pseudomemories is inconclusive. Some studies show that hypnosis does not lead to high levels of pseudomemory creation (Lynn, Milano, & Weekes, 1992), whereas other studies do show an increase, especially among those who are highly susceptible to hypnosis (Barnier & McConkey, 1992; Sheehan, Statham, & Jamison, 1991).

One highly controversial use of hypnosis is to refresh and enhance the memory of eyewitnesses. It is important for an eyewitness that recall and identification of a suspect be accurate. After all, a person's freedom may hinge on what an eyewitness remembers. Research shows that using hypnosis to refresh an eyewitness's memory might not be such a good idea. It may lead to inaccurate memories, false memories, and suggestibility to misleading questions (Kebbell & Wagstaff, 1998). For example, in one study, participants watched a video of a victim whose pocket was picked. Participants then tried to identify the suspect in a line-up and recall what they saw. These tasks were done either under hypnosis or not under hypnosis. The results showed that hypnotized participants performed worse than non-hypnotized participants on both tasks (Sanders & Simmons, 1983). Another study showed that there was no particular benefit to using hypnosis to enhance an eyewitness's memory of a bank robbery (Yuille & McEwan, 1985). At least in this study, memory was not degraded, nor were hypnotized participants more susceptible to misleading information. On the other hand, McConkey and Kinoshita (1988) found that hypnosis led to better recall for pictures. However, they suggest that this might be due to hypnotized participants being more motivated to do well than non-hypnotized participants. There may be nothing special about the state of hypnosis, then, beyond motivating witnesses to do better. And consider this: merely closing one's eyes (a common practice in hypnosis) can lead to better recall (Perfect et al., 2008)! One danger involved in using hypnosis to help eyewitnesses remember better has nothing to do with enhancing the witnesses' memory. Jurors may place more weight on hypnotically elicited testimony than non-elicited testimony. One study found that simulated jurors were more likely to convict a defendant based on hypnotically elicited than non-hypnotically elicited eyewitness testimony (Wagstaff, Vella, & Perfect, 1992).

Chapter Summary

How can memory be characterized as a stage of information processing?
Memory is a set of systems involved in the encoding, storage, and retrieval of information. Memory is composed of systems that can hold information for periods ranging from fractions of a second to a lifetime. The storage capacities of memory systems range from very limited to vast. The information processing view of memory

sees it as the end product of sensation, perception, and learning. In this view, encoding refers to the active process of deciding what should be placed into memory and forming cognitive representations for encoded information. Storage refers to the process of keeping information in memory after cognitive representations have been formed. Retrieval is the process of getting information out of memory.

What do psychologists mean by "sensory memory"?
Memory is a set of systems involved in the encoding, storage, and retrieval of information. Sensory memory is a memory storage system that stores large amounts of information for very short periods of time (usually, only a few seconds or less).

What are the basic features of short-term, or working, memory?
Short-term memory is a storage system in which information can be held for several seconds before it fades or is replaced. Encoding information into this memory requires that we attend to it. Information may enter short-term storage from sensory memory or be retrieved from long-term memory. We keep material in STM by re-attending to it, a process called maintenance rehearsal. The capacity of short-term memory is approximately five to nine "chunks of information," where a chunk is an imprecise measure of a unit of meaningful material. Organizing information into meaningful clusters, units, or chunks can expand the apparent capacity of STM.

What are the capacity and duration of long-term memory?
Long-term memory (LTM) is a storage system that houses large amounts of information for long, virtually limitless, periods of time. Barring illness or injury, memories of a lifetime are stored in long-term memory. There seems to be no end to the amount of information that can be stored in long-term memory.

How does information get encoded into long-term memory?
Although rote (maintenance) rehearsal can move information into LTM, elaborative rehearsal is much more efficient. This type of rehearsal requires one to think about what is being encoded to organize it, make it meaningful, and relate it to something already stored in long-term memory.

What are the varieties of long-term memory?
Semantic memory is the subsystem of LTM in which we store vocabularies, simple concepts, facts, and rules for language use. Information is stored in semantic memory in an organized fashion. Episodic memories record life events and experiences. They are tied to specific times and places. There may be a separate category of episodic memory known as autobiographical memory, which stores particularly important life events. Procedural memory is where we keep recollections of learned responses. Procedural memories involve knowing how to perform some skill (for example, riding a bicycle or hitting a golf ball).

What does research on repressed and eyewitness memories tell us about the accuracy of long-term memories?
Unlike the popular view of memory working like the video recorder on a cell phone, recording information exactly for later playback, memory is a constructive process. Features of information are stored, and recall involves a reconstruction of those features. According to this view, stored features are scattered in different areas of the brain. When we want to remember something, a feature is activated that sets off a chain reaction in other related features. Recall can be influenced by several events other than the to-be-recalled event itself.

Repressed memories are events presumed to be in one's long-term memory (retained) but that cannot be retrieved because doing so would be anxiety-producing. Some psychologists have challenged the reality of some repressed memories, as when adults remember incidents of sexual abuse from when they were children. It may be that our recall of events long past has been influenced by events that have occurred since.

What factors can affect the accuracy of an eyewitness?
Eyewitnesses are called on to provide accurate descriptions of a crime and identify suspects. However, a number of factors can affect the accuracy of eyewitness accounts and identifications. The challenges posed to eyewitnesses occur at each phase of the memory process: encoding, storage, and retrieval. Eyewitnesses encode salient details into memory the best. These may include information about the gun, the robber's clothing, his height, and his weight. Not all details will be remembered equally. The weapon focus effect shows us that eyewitnesses pay a lot of attention to a weapon at the expense of other details. Those other details will not be remembered as well as the weapon. Experts in the field agree that several factors can affect the accuracy of an eyewitness. These include how a witness is questioned, when a witness is interviewed, and information the witness is exposed to after the event.

How can encoding processes be used to improve retrieval?
The ability to retrieve information stored in LTM is partially determined by how one is asked to do so. Recall involves asking someone to produce information to which he or she has been previously exposed. Recognition is a measure of memory in which the information to be retrieved is presented and a person is asked if it can be identified as familiar. Retrieval measured by recognition is generally superior to retrieval measured by recall. We can often recognize things that we cannot recall. Retrieval is maximized when encoding expectations match the means of measuring retrieval.

Indeed, retrieval depends heavily on encoding. For example, the greater the extent to which the cues or context available at retrieval match the cues or context available at encoding, the better retrieval will be.

Meaningfulness reflects the extent to which material is associated with information already stored in memory. In general, the more meaningful the material, the easier it will be to learn and to retrieve. Meaningfulness resides in the individual and not in the material to be learned.

Narrative chaining is a mnemonic technique that involves making up a story that meaningfully weaves together otherwise unorganized words or information. Forming mental images, or pictures in one's mind, of information to be remembered is also helpful. The method of loci is an imagery method in which one "places" pieces of information at various locations (loci) in a familiar setting and then retrieves those pieces of information while mentally traveling through the setting.

How do overlearning and practice (study) schedules affect retrieval?

Overlearning is the rehearsal or practice of material above and beyond that necessary for immediate recall. Within limits, the more one engages in overlearning, the greater the likelihood of accurate retrieval. Retrieval also is affected by how one schedules study (or encoding) sessions.

In massed practice, study or rehearsal continues without any intervening rest intervals. Distributed practice uses shorter segments of rehearsal interspersed with rest intervals. In nearly every case, distributed practice is found to be superior to massed practice.

What does it mean to say that retrieval is a practicable skill?

Although retrieval certainly can be enhanced by using the proper means of encoding information, it also is true that practicing the process of retrieving information from long-term memory will enhance the retrieval of that information later on. One efficient means of practicing retrieval amounts to engaging in self-testing of the to-be-retrieved material.

Key Terms

Memory (p. 102)
Encoding (p. 102)
Storage (p. 102)
Retrieval (p. 102)
Sensory memory (p. 103)
Short-term memory (STM) (p. 104)
Maintenance rehearsal (p. 105)
Chunk (p. 105)
Long-term memory (LTM) (p. 106)
Elaborative rehearsal (p. 107)

Semantic memory (p. 107)
Episodic memory (p. 108)
Procedural memory (p. 108)
Recall (p. 112)
Recognition (p. 112)
Meaningfulness (p. 114)
Mnemonic device (p. 114)
Narrative chaining (p. 114)
Key word method (p. 115)
Overlearning (p. 117)

Consciousness

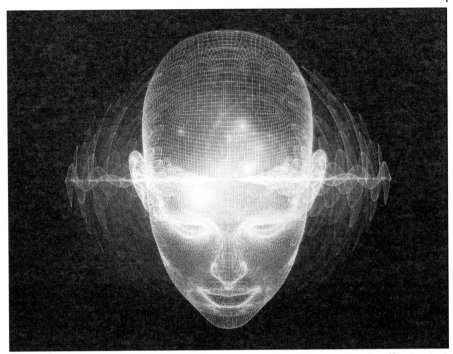

Source: agsandrew/Shutterstock

Questions You Will Be Able to Answer

After reading Chapter 6, you should be able to answer the following questions:

- What are the characteristics of normal, waking consciousness?
- What is meant by "levels of consciousness," and how did Freud characterize such levels?
- How are the conscious and unconscious minds related?
- What are the different stages of sleep and how are they measured?
- What is the difference between REM and NREM sleep?
- How do Freud and Hobson characterize the content of dreams?
- What is hypnosis, who can be hypnotized, and for what purposes may hypnosis be valuable?
- What is meditation, and what are its benefits?
- What are the effects of psychoactive drugs on consciousness?

Preview

Many of the early psychologists (Wilhelm Wundt and William James, for example) *defined* psychology as the science of consciousness. However, dealing with consciousness scientifically proved to be a very tricky business. After years of struggling with a science of consciousness, psychologists abandoned it altogether and turned their attention to observable behaviors. But consciousness would not go away, and over the last 40 years, the study of consciousness re-emerged, resuming its place in mainstream psychology.

This chapter begins with a focus on "normal waking consciousness"—and that distortion of consciousness called sleep. We can still rely on William James' characterization of consciousness as a point of departure for our discussion. We will rely on another famous person from psychology's early days, Sigmund Freud, to begin our consideration of the levels or degrees of consciousness.

Sleep is an alteration of consciousness that happens to everyone. We will see how scientists describe sleep and look at the phenomenon of rapid-eye-movement sleep, during which dreams occur. Next, we shall consider dreaming and explore how psychologists have characterized the nature and content of our dreams.

Consciousness normally changes throughout the day when we are awake and varies throughout the night as we sleep. These changes in consciousness are quite natural, automatic, and involuntary. We do not really decide when we will go to sleep, when we will dream, or when we will spontaneously awaken. For the second half of this chapter, we direct our attention to altered states of consciousness that require some effort to attain. We consider three processes that alter consciousness: hypnosis, meditation, and the use of psychoactive drugs.

Toward a Definition

"Consciousness" is a commonly used term. It is one of those wonderful concepts that everyone appears to understand and no one seems able to define precisely. Consciousness seems to be something that people have and rocks do not. Dogs and cats may have some sort of consciousness, but the issue gets terribly muddy if one considers plants.

Consciousness does seem to take on different meanings, forms, or types (Anthony, 2002; Baars, 2003). Philosophers say things such as, "The notion of consciousness is notoriously obscure" (Armstrong, 1981, p. 55), while neuroscientists look for ways in which "some active neuronal processes in your head correlate with consciousness, while others do not" (Crick & Koch, 1998, p. 97), or "ways in which physical processes in the brain give rise to subjective experience" (Chalmers, 1995, p. 63).

Although historically it has been difficult to define consciousness, we offer the following, which we believe captures the essence of the phenomenon. **Consciousness** is the subjective awareness of the environment and of one's own mental processes. Normal consciousness, then, shows two aspects: (a) a perceptual consciousness or an awareness of the world around us, and (b) an introspective consciousness or awareness of those thoughts, feelings, and perceptions that are active in our own minds—a sort of awareness of one's self (Blakemore, 2001). With this as a working definition, we ask how best to characterize consciousness.

Consciousness—the subjective awareness of the environment and of one's own mental processes.

Normal Waking Consciousness

We probably have no better description of consciousness than that provided by William James over a hundred years ago (1890, 1892, 1904). According to James, there are four aspects of normal, waking consciousness. Keep these four factors in mind—in your own consciousness—as we work through this chapter.

1. *Consciousness is always changing*. Consciousness does not hold still. It cannot be held before the mind for study. "No state once gone can recur and be identical with what was before," James wrote (1892, p. 152).

2. *Consciousness is a very personal experience*. Consciousness does not exist without someone to have it. My consciousness and yours are separate and different. The only consciousness that I can experience with certainty is mine. You may try to tell me about yours, but I will never be able to fully appreciate the state of mind that is your consciousness.

3. *Consciousness is continuous*. Our awareness of our environment and of our own mental processes cannot be broken into pieces. There are no gaps in our awareness. We cannot tell where one thought begins and another leaves off. James wrote, "Consciousness, then, does not appear to itself chopped up in bits. Such words as 'chain' or 'train' do not describe it fitly as it presents itself in the first instance. It is nothing jointed; it flows. A 'river' or 'stream' is most naturally described. In talking of it hereafter, let us call it the stream of thought, of consciousness" (James, 1890, p. 243).

4. *Consciousness is selective*. Awareness is often a matter of making choices, of selectively attending to some aspect of experience while ignoring others. "We find it [consciousness] always doing one thing, choosing one out of several of the materials so presented to its notice, emphasizing and accentuating that and suppressing as far as possible all the rest" (James, 1890, p. 139). Here we clearly see the interdependence of the processes of perception and consciousness.

You can appreciate why studying human consciousness scientifically, or experimentally, has been a challenge. An even more slippery notion is that consciousness is not an either/or proposition; it functions to different degrees, or levels.

STUDY CHECK

What are the characteristics of normal, waking consciousness?

THINKING CRITICALLY

In what ways might we compare the consciousness of a human with that of an ape, a dog, a bat, a spider, a dandelion, or a rock?

Levels of Consciousness

The observation that levels of consciousness may vary throughout the day seems intuitively obvious. At times we are wide-awake, paying full attention to nearly everything around us, processing all sorts of information. At other times, our minds "wander" and we find ourselves without focus—not paying attention, not processing much information of any sort from anywhere. And, of course, when we are asleep, there are times when we are seemingly unaware of anything that is happening either in the environment or in our own minds.

It also seems obvious that the higher the level of our consciousness, the better able we are to process (i.e., interpret, understand, recall, or react to) information. Is it not more likely that you will remember something said in class if your consciousness is focused—if you are truly attentive, wide-awake, and straining your attention to understand what is being said? Are you not more likely to trip over something on the sidewalk if you are daydreaming about your weekend plans rather than remaining fully conscious of the environment around you?

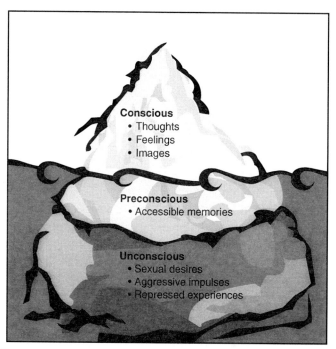

FIGURE 6.1 Freud's View on the Levels of Consciousness

According to Sigmund Freud, there are three levels of consciousness. The conscious level contains thoughts, images, and feelings that we are aware of. The preconscious level contains memories that we can retrieve at will. And the unconscious level contains repressed motives and memories that would evoke intense feelings of anxiety if we became aware of them.

Now we come to an interesting question: Is it even possible to process information without being aware of it? Can we process information unconsciously? The idea of an unconscious aspect of mind has a long history in philosophy and psychology (Blakemore, 2001; Dijksterhuis & Nordgren, 2006; Fazio & Olson, 2003; Merikle & Daneman, 1998).

Sigmund Freud was trained in medicine and can rightfully be called the father of *psychiatry*, that field of medicine that studies, diagnoses, and treats mental disorders. Early in his medical career, Freud became intrigued by what were then called "nervous disorders." He was struck by how little was known about disorders wherein a person's psychological experiences and mental life seemed to produce pain and suffering for which there was no medical explanation. Freud proposed an elaborate theory of personality and put his ideas about human nature into practice by developing new techniques for treating mental disorders. A central aspect of both his theory and therapy was Freud's view of consciousness.

Freud's vision of consciousness is often depicted as an iceberg nearly totally submerged in the sea (**Figure 6.1**). What does it imply? Freud wrote that only a very small portion of a person's mental life was readily available to awareness at any given time. For Freud, the **conscious** is a level of consciousness housing ideas, memories, feelings, or motives of which we are actively aware. At the moment, we hope you are conscious of the words you are reading, what they mean, and how you can relate them to your own experience. The **preconscious** is a level of consciousness containing aspects of our experience of which we are not conscious at any moment but that can easily be brought to awareness. Right now you may not be thinking about what you had for dinner last night or what you might have for dinner tonight, but with just a little effort these matters—now in your preconscious—can be brought into your conscious awareness.

The **unconscious** is the level of consciousness containing cognitions, feelings, or motives that are not available at the conscious or the preconscious level. At this level are ideas, desires, and memories of which we are not aware and cannot easily become aware.

Conscious—a level of consciousness housing ideas, memories, feelings, or motives of which we are actively aware.

Preconscious—a level of consciousness containing aspects of our experience of which we are not conscious at any moment but that can easily be brought to awareness.

Unconscious—the level of consciousness containing cognitions, feelings, or motives that are not available at the conscious or the preconscious level.

This is a strange notion: There are thoughts and feelings stored in our minds of which we are completely unaware. Freud theorized that the unconscious level of mind can and does influence us. Much of the content of our unconscious mind is there, Freud reasoned, because thinking about or dwelling on these issues would cause anxiety and distress. A husband, for instance, who constantly forgets his wedding anniversary and occasionally cannot even remember his wife's name when he tries to introduce her, may be having some unconscious conflict or doubts about being married in the first place. (There are, of course, other explanations!) Unconscious mental content passing (we might say "erupting," "slipping," or "bursting") through the preconscious can show itself in dreams, humor, and slips of the tongue. It could be significant that following a lively discussion of some issue, Dan says to Heather, "That's one of the breast discussions I've had about that," when he meant to say, "That's one of the best discussions . . ." As we will see in Chapter 13, many Freudian techniques of psychotherapy are aimed at helping the patient learn about and deal with the contents of his or her unconscious mind.

Demonstrating levels of consciousness as Freud proposed them has proven difficult in controlled laboratory research. Nonetheless, Freud's ideas about levels of consciousness have gained wide acceptance in psychology, particularly among clinical psychologists.

One can easily come to believe that the conscious and the unconscious minds are separate things, operating independently. Although some researchers believe this to be the case, there is evidence suggesting that there is a dynamic interplay between conscious and unconscious processes (Kiefer, 2012). In a review of the literature in this area, Kiefer demonstrated two important things about the relationship between conscious and unconscious processes. First, there is evidence that unconscious processes can affect higher cognitive functions known as *executive cognitive functions* (ECFs). ECFs include things like your ability to plan, make complex decisions and direct attention to important aspects of a problem. Kiefer points out that research shows that unconscious processes can affect spatial reasoning and other executive cognitive functions. Second, conscious processes also can affect unconscious processes. For example, Kiefer cites research showing that ECFs can influence unconscious semantic priming.

STUDY CHECK

What is meant by "levels of consciousness," and how did Freud characterize such levels?
How are the conscious and unconscious minds related?

THINKING CRITICALLY

Personal experience may lead one to report that his or her level or degree of consciousness shifts and changes throughout the day, but self-reports of mental states tend to be unreliable. How might we operationally define "levels of consciousness" in someone else without taking his or her word for it?

Sleep

Sleep is a state of consciousness that reduces our alertness, awareness, and perception of events occurring around us. Sleep is more an altered state of awareness than a total loss of consciousness. After all, we remain aware enough of the extent of the bed not to fall off (very often). Parents who are able to "sleep through anything" awaken quickly at the muffled cry of their child in a room down the hall.

We seldom are aware or conscious of our own sleeping, even though we may spend more than 200,000 hours of our lifetime asleep. Just as the level or degree of our awareness

Sleep—a state of consciousness that reduces our alertness, awareness, and perception of events occurring around us.

There are four stages of sleep, from very light (Stage 1) to deep sleep (Stage 4). There also are periods of rapid eye movement or "REM" sleep and "non-REM" sleep.

Electroencephalograph (EEG)—an instrument that measures and records the electrical activity of the brain.

Electromyogram (EMG)—an instrument that measures a muscle's activity, tone, or state of relaxation.

varies, so does our sleep vary in its level or quality throughout the night, and from night to night.

The Stages of a "Good Night's Sleep"

How do we know when someone is asleep? Self-reports are notoriously unreliable. A person who claims that he or she "didn't sleep a wink last night" may have slept soundly for many hours (Espie, 2002).

Our best indicators of sleep are measurements of brain activity and muscle tone. The electroencephalograph (EEG) is an instrument that measures and records the electrical activity of the brain. It does so by means of small electrodes pasted onto the scalp. Each electrode is measuring the summation of the action potentials of hundreds of the neurons that lie below it. The process is slightly messy, but it is in no way painful. The electromyogram (EMG) is an instrument that measures a muscle's activity, tone, or state of relaxation.

When you are awake and alert, your EEG pattern shows fast, small, irregular patterns called *gamma waves* and *beta waves*. Gamma waves occur more than 30 times per second, while beta waves occur between 12 and 30 times per second. You have fast eye movements as you look around at objects and events in your environment, and your breathing may be fast and shallow or slow and deep, depending on your level of physical activity.

When you are in a calm, relaxed state with your eyes closed but not yet asleep, your EEG pattern shows a rhythmic cycle of brain-wave activity called *alpha waves*. In this pre-sleep stage, your brain produces smooth EEG waves cycling eight to twelve times per second. If, as you lie still, you start worrying about an event of the day or trying to solve a problem, the alpha waves become disrupted and are replaced by an apparently random pattern of heightened electrical activity typical of that found in wakefulness.

As you enter sleep, your brain waves change. The transition between the waking state and the sleep state is not sudden or abrupt. The onset of sleep is more like someone gradually turning down the brightness of a light than shutting it off at a switch. Once asleep, EEG tracings of the activity of the brains of sleeping subjects reveal that sleep can be divided into four stages. As you review these stages, you can refer to the EEG patterns for each stage of sleep shown in **Figure 6.2**.

Stage 1 Sleep: This is a very light sleep. Sometimes it is referred to as *descending stage 1 sleep* because it represents a descent from wakefulness into sleep. The smooth cyclical alpha pattern disappears and is replaced by the slower theta waves (4 to 7 cycles per second). The amplitude (magnitude) of the electrical activity becomes more regular. Breathing becomes more regular, heart rate slows, and blood pressure decreases. Some slow, rolling eye movements (SEMs) may occur, or the eyes may be still. If aroused from sleep, individuals report being in a light sleep or just "drifting off" to sleep. This stage does not last long—generally less than ten minutes. Then one starts to slide into stage 2 sleep.

Stage 2 Sleep: In this stage, the EEG pattern is similar to Stage 1—low amplitude, with no noticeable wavelike pattern. The difference is that now there are *sleep spindles* in the EEG record—brief bursts of electrical activity (12 to 14 cycles per second) that occur with regularity (every 15 seconds or so). In addition to sleep spindles, we also see *K-complexes* in the EEG record. A K-complex is indicated by a large, sharp waveform made up of a single positive wave followed by a single negative wave. Both sleep spindles and K-complex patterns may be signs of the brain's efforts to turn off incoming sensory messages from the environment.

Stage 3 Sleep: With this stage, one is getting into deep sleep. There is an overall reduction in the brain's electrical activity. *Delta wave* activity now appears in the EEG. Delta waves are high, slow waves (from 0.5 to 4 cycles per second). In this stage, delta waves constitute between 20 percent and 50 percent of the EEG pattern. Heart rate and breathing become slower, and temperature lowers. It is going to be difficult to wake the sleeper now.

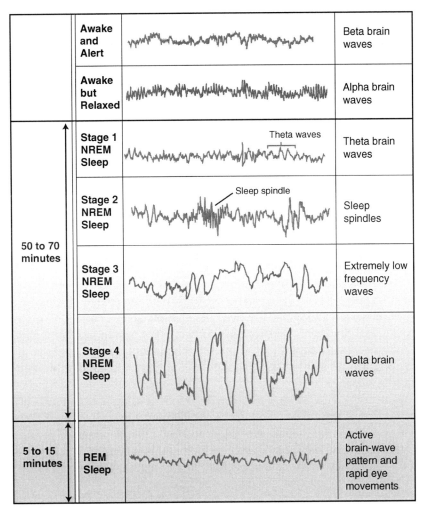

	Awake and Alert	(brain wave pattern)	Beta brain waves
	Awake but Relaxed	(brain wave pattern)	Alpha brain waves
50 to 70 minutes	Stage 1 NREM Sleep	Theta waves (brain wave pattern)	Theta brain waves
	Stage 2 NREM Sleep	Sleep spindle (brain wave pattern)	Sleep spindles
	Stage 3 NREM Sleep	(brain wave pattern)	Extremely low frequency waves
	Stage 4 NREM Sleep	(brain wave pattern)	Delta brain waves
5 to 15 minutes	REM Sleep	(brain wave pattern)	Active brain-wave pattern and rapid eye movements

FIGURE 6.2 The Stages of Sleep

Studies of participants in sleep laboratories have found that the stages of sleep are associated with distinctive patterns of brainwave activity. As we drift into deeper stages of sleep, our brain waves decrease in frequency and increase in amplitude. When we are in rapid eye movement (REM) sleep, our brainwave patterns resemble the patterns of our waking state. Sometimes this is called paradoxical sleep.

Stage 4 Sleep: Now the person is in deep sleep. The EEG record is nearly filled with slow, recurring delta waves. This differs from Stage 3 sleep, where delta waves made up only a portion of brain-wave activity. Readings from an electromyogram show that muscles are almost totally relaxed. About 15 percent of a night's sleep will be spent in this stage. During this stage, the pituitary gland releases growth hormone, and the immune system is most active. Infants spend a great deal of time in this "restorative stage" of sleep—and adults will increase their Stage 4 sleep time after periods of unusual exertion and physical activity.

REM and NREM Sleep

In the early 1950s, Nathaniel Kleitman and Eugene Aserinsky made a remarkable observation. They discovered that sometimes during sleep a person's eyes move rapidly under his or her closed eyelids. These eye movements are called *rapid eye movements* and are said to occur during "REM sleep." **REM sleep** is a stage of sleep characterized by rapid eye movements and clear, vivid dreams. Sometimes rapid eye movements are totally absent—periods called non-REM, or NREM sleep (Aserinsky & Kleitman, 1953).

REM sleep—a stage of sleep characterized by rapid eye movements and clear, vivid dreams.

NREM sleep—a type of sleep characterized by fragmented thoughts rather than vivid dreams.

Atonia—muscular immobility observed in REM sleep.

NREM sleep is a type of sleep characterized by fragmented thoughts rather than vivid dreams. NREM sleep is the type of sleep seen in stages 1 through 4.

The last segment of Figure 6.2 is a typical REM sleep EEG tracing. Note how similar this part of the figure is to the EEG for wakefulness. Indeed, there are areas of the visual cortex (in the occipital lobe) and elsewhere in the brain where neural activity is greater during REM sleep than at any time during the waking day. Paradoxically, REM sleep produces **atonia**, a muscular immobility caused by the total relaxation of the muscles. Atonia may be the body's way of preventing the dreamer from reacting to the action of the dreams. For most persons, atonia is occasionally interrupted by slight muscle twitches. Some individuals might thrash about wildly during REM sleep. This is a condition called *REM sleep disorder*. Research shows that REM sleep disorder can be more than a minor irritation. It may be the initial, early, indication of the development of several disorders classified as "neurodegenerative"—disorders such as Parkinson's disease and various forms of dementia. Additionally, disturbances in REM sleep are associated with post-traumatic stress disorder and major depression, although each is associated with a different neurobiological underpinning (Ebdlahad et al., 2013).

During REM sleep there is often an excitement of the sex organs, males having a penile erection, females having a discharge of vaginal fluids (although this latter finding is not as common). Breathing usually becomes shallow and rapid. Blood pressure levels may skyrocket and the heart rate increases, all while the person lies "peacefully" asleep. Scientists have long suspected that the marked increase in physiological activity during REM sleep is related to heart attacks, strokes, and other cardiovascular problems that can develop during sleep.

If awakened during REM sleep, a person reports a vivid, story-like dream about 85 percent of the time. At first, scientists believed that the rapid eye movements during REM sleep were being made as the dreamer literally viewed, or scanned, images produced by the dream. As a result of this belief and the speed of the eye movements, scientists concluded that dreams lasted only a few seconds. We now know that dreams last far longer and that a dreamer's rapid eye movements are unrelated to the content of dreams.

Periods of REM sleep occur throughout the night and normally last from a few minutes to half an hour, and account for about 25 percent of the sleep of adult humans. About 90 to 120 minutes each night is spent in REM sleep. A person's first REM episode (first dream) will typically occur about 90 minutes after entering Stage 1 sleep, followed by another episode about an hour later. As the person reaches the fifth, sixth, and seventh hours of sleep the number of REM periods increases dramatically. As one goes through a night's sleep, he or she tends to have longer REM episodes and more vivid dreams. Remember, of course, that these are averages and "typical" patterns, and not necessarily those followed by every sleeper every night.

Dreaming

If, indeed, everyone dreams every night, as research indicates, is it not reasonable to ask what function dreams have? *Why* do we dream every night? *Why* do we dream what we dream? The meaning of dreams has interested people at least as far back as the time of the ancient Greek philosophers. For example, Aristotle believed that dreams were simply the contents of daily sensory experiences that manifested themselves during sleep. Aristotle did not attach much significance to dreams because he viewed them as leftovers from the day's sensory experiences.

One of the more influential views of the nature of dreams was that of Sigmund Freud (1900) in his book, *Interpretation of Dreams*. Recall that Freud emphasized the role of the unconscious in our everyday lives. Freud saw dreams as a way to uncover the mischief that was going on in the unconscious. In fact, he saw dreams as a sort of "royal road to the unconscious."

Freud's theory of dreams focused on the importance of the meaning of dreams. He suggested that many dreams serve a wish-fulfillment purpose. That is, the content of a dream

Behavioral Approaches to Treating Insomnia

Getting a good night's sleep is something that many of us take for granted. Just about everyone has experienced a night where we have difficulty falling asleep. We know that the feeling of not getting enough sleep is not terribly pleasant. For most people, disruptions of sleep are temporary. However, for millions of others, problems falling asleep or staying asleep are more enduring and may even be chronic. *Insomnia* is a sleep disorder involving difficulty falling or staying asleep. Insomnia can be brought on as a result of a stimulant (e.g., coffee) taken too close to bedtime or by stressful life events or illness. Chronic, debilitating insomnia affects nearly 30 million Americans, women more commonly than men, and the elderly about one and one-half times as often as younger adults (Espie, 2002). Estimates of Americans who suffer less chronic, but still debilitating bouts of insomnia approach 16 million (Pawaskar et al., 2008). Once a pattern of insomnia has been established, it can be very hard to break.

In pursuit of a good night's sleep, a person with insomnia might turn to drugs. Prescription medications are available to treat insomnia (e.g., *Ambien*). There are also many over-the-counter, nonprescription drugs available. These can be effective in the short run. However, the long-term use of these drugs can be a problem. Often, one develops a tolerance to sleep medications, requiring a higher and higher dose to get the desired effect. In some cases, the drug may lose its effectiveness completely. When sleep medications are withdrawn, a rebound effect might occur, making it more difficult to fall asleep than before the drugs were used. Some sufferers turn to alcohol to help them fall asleep. Although alcohol might help a person fall asleep, the quality of sleep obtained is degraded. Alcohol (as well as some other sleep medications) tends to disrupt REM sleep. So the person may fall asleep but awake the next morning feeling unrested. Given these effects, drugs and alcohol may not be the best way to approach the treatment of insomnia.

Fortunately, there are alternatives to sleep medications. Many cases of insomnia relate to learning and the development of poor sleep habits. For example, after a poor night's sleep or two, a person might begin to dwell on not being able to sleep, which may lead to anxiety at bedtime. The person, in short, learns to associate the bedroom with anxiety and negative feelings, which are incompatible with the relaxation that is needed to fall asleep. Research shows that good and poor sleepers differ on several behavioral dimensions (Libman, Creti, Amsel, Brender, & Fichten, 1997). When good sleepers do wake up in the middle of the night, they are able to fall back to sleep quickly. Poor sleepers tend to engage in counterproductive activities, such as tossing and turning, looking at the clock, or worrying about personal problems.

Because so many cases of insomnia relate to cognitive, affective, and behavioral problems, a person suffering from insomnia may find success with techniques that target unproductive sleep-related thoughts and behaviors. The following summarizes several behavioral techniques that are used to fall asleep (Pawlicki & Heitkemper, 1985):

- Do not drink alcohol or caffeine within 4 to 6 hours of bedtime.
- Avoid the use of nicotine before bedtime—or at any time during the night, should you get up.
- Exercise during the day but not just before bedtime.
- Establish a regular bedtime and a regular time for getting up each morning.
- Avoid sleeping pills; as helpful as they may be at first, they can make matters worse in the long run.
- Do your best to minimize light, noise, and extreme temperatures where you sleep.
- Eat a light snack before bedtime, but avoid anything approaching a large meal.
- Don't use your bed for studying, reading, or watching television. At bedtime, turn off electronics, such as tablets and cell phones.
- If you feel that you have to nap during the day, do so sparingly. One good nap now and then is all right. A series of several short naps is ultimately disruptive.
- Should you awaken during the night and find that you are unable to get back to sleep, get out of bed. Go to another room. Your bed is for sleeping, not for worrying. Similarly, don't let yourself fall asleep someplace else. Return to your bed when—and only when—you are sleepy.

Cognitive-behavioral techniques can be helpful in treating insomnia. Bootzin and Rider (1997) compared several behavioral techniques, including stimulus control instructions (use one's bedroom only for sleep, get up and leave the bed if one doesn't fall asleep in a reasonable time, wake at a regular time, do not take naps), relaxation training, biofeedback, and cognitive therapy. They found that stimulus-control techniques had the strongest effect in treating insomnia. Such techniques were also found to be effective in helping persons with insomnia fall asleep after they had quit using sleep-aiding medications (Riedel et al., 1998). Traditional cognitive-behavioral therapy for insomnia typically involves direct interaction between the therapist and the client. An alternative is to deliver cognitive-behavioral therapy via computer or smartphone, often via the Internet (Voinescu, Szentagotai, & David, 2013). Highly structured approaches to computer-aided cognitive-behavioral therapy (CCBT) can be effective in reducing the symptoms of insomnia (Voinescu et al., 2013). For example, in one study using a CCBT technique called Sleep Healthy Using the Internet (SHUTi), participants assigned to the group receiving CCBT therapy showed a significant reduction in the severity of their insomnia (compared with control participants) and maintained improvement over a 6-month period (Ritterband et al., 2009).

is related to something you need or want. So, if you are thirsty when you go to bed and you dream of drinking water, your wish for water has been fulfilled in the dream. Freud also suggested that all dreams are related to (but not simply a replay of) events in the few days preceding the dream.

In his theory of dreams, Freud made a distinction between two types of dream content. **Manifest content** is the content of a dream of which the dreamer was aware. For example, if you were to awake and remember a dream of being chased by a motorcycle-riding bear in a clown suit, that is the manifest content. For Freud, the manifest content was important but only as a pathway to the latent content. The **latent content** is the "true," underlying meaning of the dream that resides in a person's unconscious mind. Arriving at the (largely symbolic) latent content was quite an art because latent content shows itself in a highly disguised form. So the bear riding the motorcycle could be a dramatization of some unconscious thought (e.g., a desire to get away from your parents). Unlocking latent content was made even more difficult because, as Freud noted, something vivid in the manifest content may relate to something insignificant in the latent content and vice versa. That is, maybe a bear and a motorcycle chase are unimportant, compared to the clown suit which, perhaps, signals the embarrassment that you feel about the way your mother dresses in public.

Although Freud's theory on dreams was comprehensive and well-articulated, not everyone agreed with it. For example, Carl Jung (a fellow psychoanalytic theorist) believed that dreams were more transparent and their symbols more closely related to universal human concerns (Hobson, 1988). Despite these differences, the psychoanalytic theory dominated most of the thinking on dreams in the twentieth century.

Alan Hobson and his colleagues proposed another quite different theory of dreams (e.g., Hobson, 1995). According to the **activation-synthesis theory**, dreams are activated by physiological mechanisms in the brainstem, probably in the pons, and given meaning through a synthesis process. Dream activation produces and sends impulses up through higher levels of the brain. These impulses do not come from the outside environment; instead, they are produced in the brainstem. Once these impulses reach the cerebral cortex, they are synthesized by being related to existing memories, interpreted, and made meaningful. Although the exact nature of synthesis is mysterious, it appears as if the brain is trying to make sense of what are likely to be random patterns of neural activity. The involvement of memories (mostly recent ones) in the synthesis process provides the "plot" or "story" for the dream. Hobson (1988) maintains that dreams are "rather transparent and unedited" (p. 214). Hobson's position is in sharp contrast to Freud's view of dreams as being highly disguised and distorted.

Which position is "correct" is still open to debate. Some psychologists and psychiatrists adhere to Freud's theory of dreams, claiming that they find it useful in understanding a patient's problems or needs. However, like almost all of Freud's theoretical concepts, his theory of dreams has little empirical support. Conversely, the activation-synthesis theory is based on years of research on both animals and humans. What is most important, however, is that both approaches say that our dreams have meaning and the content of our dreams is important to us. The major difference lies in the characterization of a dream as being highly distorted (psychoanalysis) or transparent (activation-synthesis).

Manifest content—the content of a dream of which the dreamer was aware.

Latent content—the "true," underlying meaning of the dream that resides in a person's unconscious mind.

Activation-synthesis theory—a theory of dreaming stating that dreams are activated by physiological mechanisms in the brainstem, probably in the pons, and given meaning through a synthesis process.

<table>
<tr><td>

STUDY CHECK

What are the different stages of sleep, and how are they measured?
What is the difference between REM and NREM sleep?
How do Freud and Hobson characterize the content of dreams?

</td></tr>
</table>

<table>
<tr><td>

THINKING CRITICALLY

Everyone sleeps and everyone dreams (at least everyone experiences REM sleep).
What ideas can you generate to explain why everyone seems to have a need to
sleep and dream?

</td></tr>
</table>

Hypnosis

Hypnosis is a state of consciousness that typically requires the voluntary cooperation of the person being hypnotized. **Hypnosis** is a state of consciousness characterized by (a) a marked increase in suggestibility, (b) a focusing of attention, (c) an exaggerated use of imagination, (d) an unwillingness or inability to act on one's own, and (e) an unquestioning acceptance of distortions of reality (Hilgard & Hilgard, 1975; Raz & Shapiro, 2002). Being hypnotized is not like going to sleep. Few characteristics of sleep are to be found in the hypnotized subject. EEG patterns, for example, are significantly different.

Hypnosis has been used for various purposes and with varying degrees of success. As you may know, it has been used as entertainment, as a routine in which members of an audience are hypnotized—usually to do silly things. It has been used to access memories of events not in immediate awareness. It has been touted as a treatment for a wide range of physical and psychological disorders. In this section, we will examine hypnosis and the research concerning its effectiveness for various purposes.

Can everyone be hypnotized? No, probably not. Susceptibility to hypnosis varies: "Some people respond to almost all suggestions; others respond to none; most show moderate levels of response" (Kirsch & Braffman, 2001, p. 58). Contrary to popular belief, a person cannot be hypnotized against his or her will. Some hypnotists claim that they can hypnotize anyone under the right conditions, which is why we hedged and said "probably" not.

Although not everyone can be easily hypnotized, some people are excellent subjects, can readily be put into deep hypnotic states, and can learn to hypnotize themselves (Hilgard, 1975, 1978). A few traits are correlated with one's ability to be hypnotized. The most important factor seems to be the ability to engage easily in daydreaming and fantasy, to be able to "set ordinary reality aside for a while" (Wilkes, 1986, p. 25), and become totally "engaged" or absorbed in a particular task (Barnier & McConkey, 2004). In fact, it turns out that being susceptible to hypnosis is not extraordinary. Some people simply are more open to imaginative suggestibility (Kirsch & Braffman, 2001). Other factors that may identify a good candidate for hypnosis include a degree of passivity or willingness to cooperate (at least during the hypnotic session), and a proneness to fantasy (Barber, 2000).

Can I be made to do things under hypnosis that I would not ordinarily do? Next to being unknowingly hypnotized, the greatest fear associated with hypnosis is that it will somehow force a person to do things that he or she would not ordinarily do. For entertainment, stage hypnotists often hypnotize audience members and have them do silly things (e.g., running about the

> **Hypnosis**—a state of consciousness characterized by (a) a marked increase in suggestibility, (b) a focusing of attention, (c) an exaggerated use of imagination, (d) an unwillingness or inability to act on one's own, and (e) an unquestioning acceptance of distortions of reality.

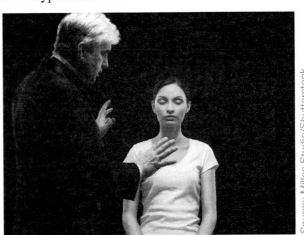

Hypnosis is used for various purposes and with varying degrees of success.

stage, clucking like a chicken). Is this due to the hypnosis? Maybe yes, maybe no. Under the right circumstances, you might do those same things without being hypnotized. It is unlikely you would do under hypnosis anything that you would not do otherwise. However, under certain (unusual) circumstances, people can do outrageous—and dangerous—things, which is why hypnosis should be used with great caution.

Does hypnosis really represent a truly altered state of consciousness? The issue is in dispute. Some believe that hypnosis is really no more than a heightened level of suggestibility (Barber, 2000; Kirsch, 2000), whereas others believe it to be a special state, separate from the compliance of a willing subject. When hypnotized people are left alone, they usually maintain the condition induced by their hypnosis. Those who are not hypnotized, but simply complying with a hypnotist, revert quickly to normal behaviors when left alone (Hilgard, 1975). The EEG recordings of the brain activity of hypnotized individuals reveal few, if any, alterations from normal consciousness, but newer brain-imaging techniques (PET scans and fMRIs, for instance) show significant changes (Raz & Shapiro, 2002).

Can hypnosis be used to alleviate physical pain? Yes. It will not (it cannot) cure the underlying cause, but it can be used to control the feeling of pain (Keefe, Abernethy, & Campbell, 2004; Montgomery & DuHamel, 2000). Hypnosis can be used to create hallucinations (perceptual experiences that occur without sensory input) in the hypnotized subject. Hallucinations are said to be positive when a person perceives something that is not there and negative when a person fails to perceive something that is there. Pain reduction uses negative hallucinations. If a person is a good candidate for it, hypnosis has a significant chance of blocking a portion of perceived pain from conscious awareness (Liossi & Hatira, 2003; Weisberg, 2008).

Hypnosis has received attention as a means of controlling pain in older adults. Pain in older adults is a common phenomenon, often related to chronic illnesses, depression, social isolation, and sleep problems (Chodosh et al., 2001). Hypnosis holds allure as a pain management tool because of its noninvasive nature and the possibility of treating pain without the side effects of medications. Using hypnosis to manage pain in older adults has met with considerable success and is becoming more and more common (Cuellar, 2005; Gay, Philippot, & Luminet, 2002).

Is it true that one can remember things under hypnosis that could not otherwise be remembered? Probably not. This question may be the most hotly contested issue related to hypnosis. In the sense of, "Can you hypnotize me to remember psychology material better for the test next Friday?" the answer is almost certainly no. Someone might be able to convince you under hypnosis (i.e., suggest to you) that you had better remember your psychology and thus motivate you to remember. But there is no evidence that hypnotic suggestion can directly improve your ability to learn and remember new material. In the more restrictive sense of, "I don't remember all the details of the accident and the trauma that followed. Can hypnosis help me recall those events more clearly?" the answer is less certain. Distortions of memory can easily occur in normal states. In hypnotic states, a person is by definition in a suggestive state and susceptible to distortions in recall furnished or prompted by the hypnotist (even assuming that the hypnotist has no reason to cause such distortions). To the extent that hypnosis can reduce feelings of anxiety and tension, it may help in the recollection of anxiety-producing memories. The evidence on this issue is neither clear nor convincing in either direction.

What of the related questions, "Can hypnosis take me back in time and make me remember what it was like when I was only three or four years old?" or "Can hypnosis help me recall experiences from past lives?" Here, we do have a clear-cut answer, and the answer is no. So-called age-regression hypnotic sessions have simply not proven to be valid (e.g., Nash, 1987; Spanos et al., 1991). Often there is no way to verify the validity of memories "recovered" during age or past-life regression.

The use of hypnosis to refresh the memory of a witness in a legal proceeding presents a particular concern: the potential for hypnosis to lead to the creation of *pseudomemories*, or false memories. Under hypnosis, a person is in a highly suggestible state and may be susceptible to having facts or events that never occurred implanted. The research on pseudomemories is inconclusive. Some studies show that hypnosis does not lead to high levels of pseudomemory creation (Weekes, Lynn, Green, & Brentar, 1992); whereas, other studies do show an increase, especially among those who are highly susceptible to hypnosis (Sheehan, Green, & Truesdale, 1992).

STUDY CHECK

What is hypnosis, who can be hypnotized, and for what purposes may hypnosis be valuable?

THINKING CRITICALLY

Why would anyone want to alter his or her normal state of consciousness? Are some reasons for doing so more valid than others?

Meditation

Meditation is a self-induced state of consciousness characterized by a focusing of attention and relaxation. It is often associated with Eastern cultures, where it has been practiced for centuries. Meditation became popular in North America in the 1960s and psychologists began to study it seriously during this time.

One form of meditation requires mental focusing or concentration. An example of this variety is *transcendental meditation (TM)*. In TM, a meditator begins by assuming a comfortable position and becoming calm and relaxed. The meditator then focuses his or her attention on one particular stimulus. This focus could be on some bodily function, such as breathing, or some softly spoken or chanted word, or *mantra*, such as "ooom," "one," or "calm." The meditator blocks other external or internal stimuli from consciousness. The challenge is to stay relaxed, peaceful and calm. *Mindfulness meditation* takes a nearly opposite approach of attending to whatever ideas, thoughts or feelings enter consciousness. It is a matter of becoming aware and accepting of whatever is going on in one's own mind at the moment (Baer et al., 2006; Johnson et al., 2010).

Once a person is in a meditative state, measurable physiological changes occur that allow psychologists to claim meditation to be an altered state of consciousness. The most noticeable is a predominance of alpha waves in the EEG record. Such waves characterize a relaxed state of the sort experienced just before one enters into sleep. Breathing slows and becomes deeper, oxygen intake is reduced, and the heart rate and blood pressure may decrease (Cahn & Polich, 2006; Davidson et al., 2003; Schneider et al., 2005).

Although it is true that individuals enter meditative states of consciousness, it is not clear whether these individuals benefit from the practice. One of the major claims for meditation is that it is a simple, very effective, even superior way to enter into a state of relaxation. The reduction of somatic (bodily) arousal is taken to be one of the main advantages of meditation. The claim is that by meditating, one can slow bodily processes and enter into a state of physical as well as psychological calm.

Another claim made for meditation is that those who practice it are better able to cope with stress, pressure, or threatening situations. Some advocates of meditation claim its benefits reach far beyond relaxation and somatic arousal reduction. Many psychologists are skeptical of the claims that meditation can raise one's

Meditation—a self-induced state of consciousness characterized by a focusing of attention and relaxation.

Source: Luna Vandoorne/Shutterstock.

Meditation is a self-induced state of consciousness characterized by a focusing of attention and relaxation.

consciousness to transcendental heights of new awareness and thus make one a better person, largely because these claims are not able to be verified in the laboratory. But is there any support for these claims? Evidence is mounting that meditation practices can—and often do—provide significant, measurable benefits. In one experiment, N. Broome, Orme-Johnson, and Schmidt-Wilk (2005) randomly assigned employees of a company to a TM training group, a progressive muscle relaxation (PMR) training group or a control group and measured stress at several points. N. Broome et al. found that TM was more effective in reducing stress after six weeks than PMR. They also found that TM training led to greater reductions in blood pressure than did PMR. These results are consistent with those of Butler and others (2008) and Menezes et al., (2013) who found that regular meditation improved the ability to control stress and one's affective state—even including severe depression. Another study (Zeiden et al., 2010) reports that mindfulness meditation—even after just four brief training sessions—reduced fatigue and anxiety while also improving working memory.

STUDY CHECK

What is meditation, and what are its benefits?

THINKING CRITICALLY

Assume that you agree with the argument that total mental and somatic relaxation is a good thing. How might you attain such a state?

Altering Consciousness with Drugs

In this final section of the chapter, we will discuss some of the chemicals that alter consciousness by inducing changes in perception, mood, or behavior. **Psychoactive drugs** are chemicals that alter psychological processes.

Drugs have been used for centuries to alter consciousness. At least initially, psychoactive drugs are taken to achieve a state of consciousness the user considers to be positive, pleasant, or even euphoric. No reasonable person would take a drug because he or she expected to have an unpleasant or bad experience. Nonetheless, the use of drugs that alter mood, perception, and behaviors has seriously negative outcomes in many cases. A few definitions (presented in **Table 6.1**) are required to advance our discussion of these outcomes.

Psychoactive drugs—chemicals that alter psychological processes.

TABLE 6.1 Definition of Terms Relating to Psychoactive Drugs

Terms	Definition
Dependence	A state in which the use of a drug is required to maintain bodily functioning (called physical dependence), or continued use of drug is believed to be necessary to maintain psychological functioning at some level (called psychological dependence).
Tolerance	A condition in which the use of a drug leads to a state in which more and more of it is needed to produce the same effect.
Withdrawal	A powerfully negative response, either physical or psychological (including reactions such as headaches, vomiting, and cramps), that results when one stops taking a drug.
Addiction	An extreme dependency, physical or psychological, in which signs of tolerance and painful withdrawal are usually found (American Psychiatric Association, 2000). Addiction also implies seeking a short-term gain (for example, a pleasurable feeling) at the expense of long-term negative consequences.

An important distinction we should make is that between drug use and drug abuse. **Drug abuse** is a condition involving (a) a lack of control, as evidenced by daily impairment and continued use, even knowing that one's condition will deteriorate; (b) a disruption of interpersonal relationships or difficulties at work that can be traced to drug usage; and (c) indications that maladaptive drug use has continued for at least one month (American Psychiatric Association, 2000). In other words, although drug use may not have negative consequences, drug abuse will. In truth, no clear line divides drug use and drug abuse. For that matter, no clear lines divide drug use, drug dependency, and drug addiction (Byrne, Jones, & Williams, 2004). Instead, a continuum runs from total abstinence through heavy social use to abuse and addiction (Robinson & Berridge, 2003).

The U.S. Centers for Disease Control and Prevention (2018a) reported that there were 63,632 drug overdose deaths in 2016. Another estimate is that 88,000 alcohol-related deaths occur annually in the United States (National Institute on Alcohol and Alcoholism, 2018). Drug and alcohol abuse costs American taxpayers more than $294 billion annually. Ominously, the age-adjusted rate of drug overdose deaths in the United States increased by 21.5 percent between 2015 and 2016 (Centers for Disease Control and Prevention, 2018a). And drug and alcohol abuse are not limited to the United States. Globally, there were 3.3 million alcohol-related deaths in 2012 (National Institute on Alcohol and Alcoholism, 2018). These statistics make it clear that drug and alcohol abuse are serious problems worldwide. Consequently, it is a good idea that we understand something about how drugs and alcohol affect behavior.

There are many psychoactive drugs. Some are summarized in **Table 6.2**. We will focus on the more common ones in the next sections.

Drug abuse—a condition involving (a) a lack of control, as evidenced by daily impairment and continued use, even knowing that one's condition will deteriorate; (b) a disruption of interpersonal relationships or difficulties at work that can be traced to drug usage; and (c) indications that maladaptive drug use has continued for at least one month.

TABLE 6.2 Examples of Common Psychoactive Drugs

Drug Type	Example	Comments
Stimulants	Caffeine	Found in coffee, tea, colas, and chocolate; increases CNS activity and metabolism; disrupts sleep
	Nicotine	Activates excitatory synapses; leads to tolerance and addiction
	Cocaine	Produces short-lived "high"; raises blood pressure and heart rate; masks fatigue; blocks reuptake; highly addictive
	Amphetamines	Release excess neurotransmitters; act slower than cocaine; mask fatigue
Depressants	Alcohol	Decreases nervous system activity; impairs decision making; reduces inhibitions; leads to dependency and addiction
	Opiates	Analgesics; produce feelings of calm and ease; lead to addiction
	Heroin	Produces "rush" of euphoria; reduces pain; highly addictive
	Barbiturates	Slows nervous system activity; can move from calm to sleep to coma to death; cause addiction
Hallucinogens	LSD	Produces hallucinations, usually visual; increases serotonin levels; raises levels of emotionality
Others	Marijuana	Alters mood; slight depressant; in high doses, causes cognitive deficits and chromosomal abnormalities when taken at early age; may lead to other drug use/abuse
	Ecstasy	Produces euphoria and lessening of inhibitions; can have hallucinogenic properties; may cause confusion, depression, anxiety and paranoia

Stimulants

Stimulants—drugs that stimulate or activate an organism, producing a heightened sense of arousal and an elevation of mood.

Stimulants—are drugs that stimulate or activate an organism, producing a heightened sense of arousal and an elevation of mood. Most of the time, these drugs also activate neural reactions, but at this level, we have to maintain a healthy respect for the complexity of the brain and the various ways stimulants interact with its parts. For example, one stimulant administered directly to one part of a cat's reticular formation can awaken and arouse a sleeping cat, but if that same stimulant is administered to a different area of a cat's reticular formation, the cat will go to sleep.

Caffeine is one of the most widely used stimulants. It is found in many foods and drinks (soft drinks, coffee, tea, and chocolate), as well as in several varieties of painkillers. In moderate amounts, it seems to have no serious or life-threatening effects. At some point, a mild dependence may develop. Caffeine temporarily increases cellular metabolism (the process of converting food into energy), which then results in a burst of newfound energy. It also blocks the effects of some inhibitory neurotransmitters in the brain. Caffeine disrupts sleep, making it more difficult to fall and to stay asleep.

Nicotine is a popular stimulant found in cigarettes. Nicotine is absorbed into the lungs and reaches the brain very quickly—in a matter of seconds. Nicotine stimulates central nervous system activity, but it also relaxes muscle tone slightly, which may explain why smokers claim a cigarette relaxes them. Nicotine produces its effects by activating excitatory synapses in both the central and peripheral nervous systems. Most smokers (but not all) develop a tolerance to nicotine, requiring more and more to reach a desired state of stimulation. Nicotine is addictive, despite earlier claims to the contrary (Maxhom, 2000).

Cocaine is a stimulant derived from leaves of the coca shrub (native to the Andes region of South America). The allure of cocaine is the rush of pleasure and energy it produces when it first enters the bloodstream. If it is snorted in powder form, cocaine enters through the nose's mucous membranes. If it is smoked in its base form, cocaine enters through the lungs. Cocaine can also be injected directly into the bloodstream in liquid form. The length of a cocaine high varies depending on the method of ingestion, but 15 to 20 minutes is an average.

Cocaine use elevates the blood pressure, increases the heart rate, and blocks the reuptake of two important neurotransmitters: norepinephrine and dopamine. As a result, for a time, excess amounts of these two neurotransmitters are available in the nervous system. Norepinephrine acts in the central and the peripheral nervous systems to provide arousal and the sense of extra energy. Dopamine acts in the brain to produce feelings of pleasure and euphoria. Cocaine affects dopamine receptors in areas of the brain associated with reward. With extended cocaine use, the user loses the ability to feel pleasurable feelings without the cocaine (National Institute on Drug Abuse, 2007).

Some of the effects of cocaine use are permanent, and others are long-lasting, even though the high lasts only a few minutes. Not only is the rush produced by cocaine short-lived, but a letdown approaching depression follows. As users well know, one way to combat letdown and depression is to take more of the drug, a vicious cycle that leads to dependency and addiction.

Amphetamines are synthetically manufactured stimulants that usually come in the form of capsules or pills. In addition to blocking reuptake, amphetamines release excess dopamine and norepinephrine into the nervous system. The action of amphetamines is considerably slower and less widespread than that of cocaine. Once an amphetamine takes effect, it gives users a feeling of being alert, awake, aroused, filled with energy, and ready to go. These results are relatively short-lived. The drug does not create alertness so much as it masks fatigue, which ultimately overcomes the user when the drug wears off.

Methamphetamine (or "meth," "chalk," or "ice," among other street names) is chemically related to amphetamine, but its effects on the central nervous system are faster. Methamphetamine is easy to make, requiring no sophisticated apparatus, and is usually manufactured in small illegal "labs." The powdery substance can be taken orally, snorted, injected intravenously, or smoked. The latter two methods create an intense sensation called a "rush" or a "flash" that lasts only a few minutes but is described as extremely pleasurable. Users usually become addicted very quickly. Methamphetamine releases high levels of dopamine, which enhance mood and body movement. At the same time, "meth" damages or destroys cells that produce dopamine (and serotonin), causing symptoms like those of Parkinson's disease.

Depressants

Depressants are drugs that reduce awareness of external stimuli, slow bodily functioning, and decrease levels of overt behavior. Predictably, a person's reaction to depressants depends largely on how much is taken. In small doses, they may produce relaxation, a sense of freedom from anxiety, and a loss of stifling inhibitions. In greater amounts, they can result in sedation, sleep, coma, or death.

Alcohol is the most common of all depressants.

Alcohol is the most common of all depressants, and its use started many thousands of years ago—perhaps as long ago as 8000 B.C. (Monastersky, 2003). As noted previously, alcohol abuse is a serious health problem. Alcohol dependence has been associated with a wide range of negative outcomes including early death, heart disease, liver disease, psychological problems and cancer (Cargiulo, 2007). Long-term alcohol abuse is associated with *alcoholic dementia* where the formation of new memories is affected, although the exact clinical picture is under debate (Moriyama, Mimura, Kato, & Kashima, 2006).

Alcohol is associated with a wide range of behavioral changes and impairments. It is related, for example, with increased levels of aggression. Alcohol does this by depressing inhibitory brain centers making a person more likely to act out. As more alcohol is consumed, a person often becomes more irritable and easily angered causing hostility and aggressiveness to increase. Alcohol also impairs judgment and motor skills. The latter effect contributes to significant impairments in driving ability that cut across gender, age, driving skill, and alcohol tolerance levels (Martin et al., 2013). Alcohol also impairs the formation of memories. It does this by affecting the functioning of the brain mechanisms associated with memory. Interestingly, the effects of alcohol on the brain depend on the amount of alcohol consumed (Ryabinin, 1998). At lower doses, the primary effect of alcohol on memory is to reduce activity in the hippocampus. At moderate doses, a number of neurotransmitter functions are affected. Finally, at high doses, disruption occurs in a wider range of structures and functions in the brain (Ryabinin, 1998).

Opiates, such as morphine and codeine, are called *analgesics* because they can be used to reduce or eliminate pain. In fact, opiates were first used for this purpose. In small doses, they create feelings of well-being, ease, relaxation, and a trance-like state. Like cocaine, opiates affect dopamine systems in areas of the brain associated with reward and positive feelings (National Institute on Drug Abuse, 2007). Unlike alcohol, opiates seem to have little effect on motor behavior. However, they produce dependence and addiction, and withdrawal causes extreme pain and depression.

Heroin is an opiate, originally (in the 1890s) derived from morphine but considered less addictive—a notion soon proven wrong. Strong dependency and addiction occur rapidly. In 2015, approximately 948,000 Americans reported using heroin. Recent data show an increase in heroin use from 2007 to 2016 (National Institute on Drug Abuse, 2018c). In 2015 around 591,000 Americans had a "substance abuse disorder" relating to heroin (American Society of Addiction Medicine, 2016). Heroin is a highly addictive drug, with many users becoming addicted after only a few uses. As with other drugs, heroin may owe its addictive properties to its effect on the reward circuitry in the brain. Methadone, a drug used in some heroin treatment programs for long-term users, shares many of heroin's chemical properties and effects but is slower to reach the brain, tends not to produce heroin's "rush," and is somewhat less addictive.

Barbiturates are synthetically produced sedatives of which there are over 2,500 varieties. All barbiturates slow nervous system activity—in small amounts producing a sense of calm and tranquility, in higher doses producing sleep or coma. This tranquilizing effect is

Depressants—drugs that reduce awareness of external stimuli, slow bodily functioning, and decrease levels of overt behavior.

achieved by either blocking receptor sites of excitatory synapses or enhancing the effects of inhibitory neurotransmitters. Barbiturates also depress the cells and organs outside the central nervous system, slowing muscular responses and reducing respiration and heart rates. All barbiturates produce dependency if used regularly. Some are addictive, producing strong withdrawal symptoms when discontinued.

Hallucinogens

Hallucinogens—drugs that have unpredictable effects on consciousness. One obvious reaction to these drugs is the formation of hallucinations.

Hallucinogens are drugs that have unpredictable effects on consciousness. One obvious reaction to these drugs is the formation of hallucinations. That is, users often report seeing things when there is nothing there, or seeing things that are there in ways others do not. Drug-induced hallucinations are not only visual, but hallucinations of hearing, smell, taste, and touch are much less common. There are nearly a hundred different types of hallucinogens, and many have been used for centuries. In many cultures, these drugs are used in religious practices to induce trance-like states intended to help the user communicate with the supernatural.

LSD (lysergic acid diethylamide), a potent and popular hallucinogen, was introduced in the United States in the 1940s. LSD raises levels of emotionality and can produce major changes in perception—usually vivid, visual hallucinations. LSD acts on serotonin receptor sites, much like a neurotransmitter. Small doses can produce major behavioral effects.

LSD usually does not alter mood as much as it exaggerates a user's present mood. From the start, LSD's mood-magnifying capability has been recognized as what makes the drug so dangerous. The person drawn to experiment with LSD is often seeking escape from an unpleasant situation. He or she may be depressed or feeling hopeless. LSD will most likely worsen this user's mood by exaggerating already unpleasant feelings. The result will not be relief and escape, but instead a "bad trip."

Marijuana

Marijuana is a difficult drug to categorize. It can act as a depressant. In small doses, its effects are similar to those of alcohol: decreased nervous system activity and depressed thought and action. In larger doses, marijuana often acts as a hallucinogen, producing hallucinations and/or alterations in mood.

Marijuana is produced from the cannabis, or hemp plant, the source of most of the rope manufactured for sailing ships in the eighteenth century. Grown by George Washington and other prominent colonists, hemp was an important cash crop in the American colonies. During World War II, the plants were grown in great numbers throughout the Midwest. The cannabis plant is hardy, and many of the remnants of those early farms still grow in Illinois and Indiana, where every summer, adventurers come in search of a profitable—albeit illegal—harvest. More marijuana is grown in the United States than anywhere else in the world. Use of the drug is widespread. It is the number-one cash crop in the state of Kentucky! Indeed, marijuana is the most commonly used illicit drug in the United States. The active ingredient in marijuana is *tetrahydrocannabinol*, or *THC*. However it works, marijuana has become more potent than in times past. Levels of THC found in marijuana increased dramatically between 1980 and 1997 (ElSohly et al., 2000).

Legalization of marijuana has become more widely accepted in recent years. In fact, ten U.S. states and the District of Columbia have legalized recreational marijuana use. Another 20 states allow medical use of marijuana. Despite these changes, legalization of marijuana remains controversial. One of the points made by opponents of legalization is that marijuana may be a gateway drug to other, more serious drugs (e.g., cocaine). According to the *gateway hypothesis*, the use of legal or less serious drugs like marijuana increases the likelihood that a person will eventually use other illegal drugs. Is there evidence for this gateway hypothesis? The answer is a qualified yes. Some studies show that marijuana increases the likelihood that a person will try other illegal drugs (Mayet, Legleye, Falissard, & Chau, 2012; Lessem et al., 2006). Mayet et al. found that the likelihood of using another drug increased significantly after marijuana use. They also found that this increase was markedly higher for heavy marijuana users than casual users. The gateway relationship is strongest for adolescents and tends to get weaker as people get older (Fergusson, Bodon, & Horwood, 2006). Other research suggests that social factors may operate along with early marijuana use to affect later drug use. Early marijuana use that takes place in a social context also contributes to later illegal drug use (Lessem et al., 2006). Additionally, the gateway relationship also appears to be mediated by social factors such as life stress and unemployment (Van Gundy & Rebellon, 2010).

Illegal drug use and addiction are personal as well as global problems.

There is some evidence that users of marijuana may rapidly develop a tolerance for it, but there is little evidence that it is addictive. Is marijuana dangerous? One would think certainly, if for no other reason than that it is usually smoked, and smoking is a danger to one's health. And smoking marijuana is more dangerous than cigarette smoking in terms of causing many respiratory problems. Strangely enough, there is evidence that smokers of marijuana—even heavy, long-term smokers—do *not* have an increased risk of developing lung cancer (Tashkin et al., 2006). In fact, the researchers reported that smokers of marijuana had a slightly *smaller* risk of developing lung cancer than did nonsmokers in the control group.

Marijuana also is dangerous in the sense that alcohol is dangerous. Marijuana use during adolescence is associated with poor short-term memory recall and increased impulsive behavior (Dougherty et al., 2013). Marijuana appears to impair short-term memory by altering brain functioning and requiring the brain to use compensatory mechanisms to make up for this alteration (Schweinsburg et al., 2010). Excessive use leads to impaired judgment, impaired reflexes, unrealistic moods, poor physical coordination, and hallucinations. Excessive use also is related to deficits in tasks requiring sustained attention and cognitive flexibility. It also appears that marijuana impairs the ability to drive a car. The *Denver Post* (2017) reported that since 2013, the number of fatal car accident victims testing positive for marijuana has nearly doubled.

Ecstasy

Ecstasy is a drug that is classified as a *psychedelic amphetamine*. Because of its euphoric effects, ecstasy has become a very popular drug, especially among young people. According to the National Survey on Drug Abuse and Health, over 17 million Americans used ecstasy in 2013 (DRUGABUSE.COM).

Ecstasy produces feelings of emotional openness and euphoria, fewer critical thoughts, and fewer inhibitions. Regular users may develop a tolerance for the drug, requiring higher and higher doses to obtain the desired effects.

As is the case with most drugs, ecstasy has a downside. On the physical side, ecstasy use has been associated with symptoms such as nausea, blurred vision, rapid eye movement, faintness, and chills or sweating. It can cause a dangerous increase in body temperature that can lead to kidney failure. On the psychological side, ecstasy use can produce confusion, sleep problems, depression, severe anxiety, and paranoia. These adverse reactions may be immediate or may occur weeks after taking the drug. Additionally, increases in depression, sleep disturbances, and impulsiveness persist even after a person stops using ecstasy (Taurah, Chandler, & Sanders, 2014). Ecstasy leads to significant impairments in a number of areas of memory (Murphy et al., 2012). Ecstasy appears to impair memory by damaging parts of the brain associated with thought and memory—probably the serotonin systems in the brain (Reneman et al., 2001; Schilt et al., 2007)—and by reducing activity in the hippocampus (Becker et al., 2013).

THINKING CRITICALLY

Given the obvious and inherent danger of psychoactive drugs, why do millions of people use these drugs, sometimes regularly, and sometimes to the point of addiction?

FOCUS ON DIVERSITY

Demographic Differences in Illegal Drug Use

We have seen how illegal drug use and addiction are global problems affecting millions of people. Are their demographic differences in illegal drug use and abuse? Yes, there are. The rates of illicit drug use among persons 12 and older for a number of racial/ethnic groups are shown in **Figure 6.3**. As you can see, the rate of illegal drug use is lowest among Asian Americans and highest among those reporting two or more racial identities. Although higher, the rate of illegal drug use among blacks is not that much different from the rate for whites. Hispanics show lower rates of illegal drug use than both blacks and whites. When we look at gender, we find that males aged 12 and older (11.5 percent) are more likely than females (7.3 percent) to use illegal drugs (U.S. Department of Health and Human Services, 2013). Moreover, males are more likely (9.7 percent) than females (5.6 percent)

to use several different drugs, including marijuana (U.S. Department of Health and Human Services, 2013).

It is important to note that when we consider demographic differences like these, we should not view groups as homogeneous. Within a demographic group, there can be differences among subgroups. For example, in one study, researchers compared native-born and immigrant Hispanic populations. The results showed that native-born Hispanics show higher rates of drug and alcohol abuse than immigrant Hispanics (Villalobos & Bridges, 2018). The same can be said for Native Americans. Tragesser, Beauvais, Burnside, and Jumper-Thurman, (2010) compared 7th- to 12th-grade Oklahoma and non-Oklahoma Native Americans on their drug use. They found that the Oklahoma youths showed lower levels of drug use

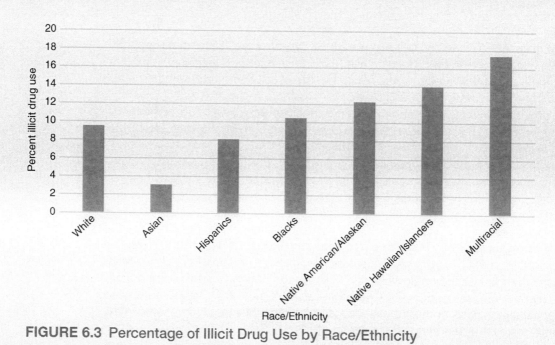

FIGURE 6.3 Percentage of Illicit Drug Use by Race/Ethnicity

Source: U.S. Department of Health and Human Services (2013).

than the non-Oklahoma youths. Looking at possible factors contributing to this difference, Tragesser et al. found that among Oklahoma youth, there was more family concern about drug use, less peer pressure to do drugs, an older age of first use, a greater perception that drugs are harmful, and greater exposure to anti-drug programs. So, within a demographic group, different social and cultural experiences can lead to different drug use outcomes.

When we think of illegal drug use, what frequently comes to mind are drugs like marijuana, cocaine, and heroin. However, as we have seen, abuse of prescription drugs is also a problem. Women are more sensitive than men to pain and appear to be more likely than men to take non-prescribed opiates for pain. However, men are more likely than women to die from an overdose of non-prescribed opiates (National Institute on Drug Abuse, 2018b). In the United States, whites are far more likely to die from an opioid overdose (33,450 per year) than are blacks (4,374) or Hispanics (3,440; Kaiser Foundation, 2016). The same is true for benzodiazepine (e.g., *Valium*) abuse (Cook et al., 2018).

Why do individuals from different ethnicities differ with respect to drug abuse? Daniel Becker and Carlos Grilo (2007) looked at a number of possible predictors (e.g., age, history of child abuse, impulsivity) of drug abuse among white, black, and Latino adolescents hospitalized for drug and alcohol abuse. Although they found that most of the predictors were relevant for all three ethnic groups, they did find some differences. For whites, age, impulsivity, a predisposition toward delinquency, and a history of child abuse were significant predictors of drug abuse. For Latinos, a predisposition toward delinquency and child abuse were significant predictors. For blacks, age and depression were significant predictors. These findings suggest that different experiences among different ethnic groups can account for at least some of the observed ethnic differences in drug abuse.

Another demographic variable relating to illegal drug use is sexual orientation. Research in this area shows that gay, lesbian, and bisexual individuals show higher rates of illegal drug use than heterosexuals (Newcomb, Birkett, Corliss, & Mustanski, 2014; Rosario et al., 2014). They are also more likely than heterosexuals to abuse prescription drugs (Goldbach, Mereish, & Burgess, 2017). Even students who have not yet settled on a same-sex orientation (i.e., "questioning" individuals) show a higher rate of illegal prescription drug use than heterosexual individuals (Shadick, Dagirmanjian, Trub, & Dawson, 2016). This pattern of drug use also emerges when we look at the transgender orientation. Transgender adolescents show higher levels of illegal drug use than their non-transgender counterparts (De Pedro, Gilreath, Jackson, & Esqueda, 2017).

To illustrate, Newcomb et al. (2014) compared a sample of "sexual minority" (i.e., gay, lesbian, and bisexual) high school students with a sample of heterosexual high school students and found that sexual minority students had higher rates of illegal drug use than heterosexual students. They also found that bisexual students had a higher rate of illegal drug use than gay or lesbian students. This was especially true for male bisexual students, who showed higher rates of illegal drug use than female bisexual students. Interestingly, lesbian students reported the highest rates of heroin and methamphetamine use.

Why is there this disparity in drug use among different sexual orientations? One explanation put forth is that sexual minority individuals face far more stress, prejudice, and discrimination than heterosexual individuals. Overall, sexual minority adolescents experience more harassment and bullying than their heterosexual peers, which is related to higher rates of drug abuse (Reisner, Greytak, Parsons, & Ybarra, 2015). According to one view, bullying, harassment, and a general lack of social support are related to elevated levels of stress. The higher levels of stress then manifest themselves in higher levels of drug use and a host of other physical and mental issues (e.g., depression, higher risk of suicide; Rosario et al., 2014).

Chapter Summary

What are the characteristics of normal, waking consciousness?
Consciousness is the awareness or perception of the world around us and of our own mental processes. William James described the four aspects of normal waking consciousness, claiming that: (1) It is always changing (it cannot be held in mind to be studied). (2) Consciousness is a personal experience (one person's consciousness is different from every other person's). (3) Consciousness is continuous (it cannot be broken down into separate pieces). (4) Consciousness is selective (allowing one to selectively attend to some things while ignoring others).

What is meant by "levels of consciousness," and how did Freud characterize such levels?
Levels of consciousness refer to the notion that we experience different degrees of awareness of self and the environment (e.g., wide-awake and attentive, mind wandering,

sleepy). We perform at optimal levels when we are at the highest level of consciousness. At the unconscious level, we may be able to process information without being aware of the fact we have done so. Sometimes bits and pieces of experience enter our consciousness, without our paying attention to them.

Freud believed that consciousness occurred on three levels: conscious, preconscious, and unconscious. He also argued that consciousness was much like an iceberg, with only a small portion (the conscious mind) above the surface. The conscious mind was said to represent the ideas, memories, feelings, and motives of which we are actively aware. Just below the waterline is the preconscious. In the preconscious are mental processes of which we are not immediately aware but which we can access quite easily (e.g., what we did yesterday). Deep under the water is the unconscious, containing ideas, desires, memories, and so forth of which we are not aware and cannot easily become aware. Recent evidence suggests that the unconscious processing of complex information is often used to help make decisions and solve problems. In fact, the unconscious processing of information actually may lead to improved decision-making and problem solving.

How are the conscious and unconscious minds related?

Although some researchers believe that the conscious and unconscious minds are separate, there is evidence suggesting that there is a dynamic interplay between conscious and unconscious processes. There is evidence that unconscious processes can affect higher cognitive functions known as executive cognitive functions (ECFs). Also, conscious processes also can affect unconscious processes. For example, Kiefer (2012) cites research showing that ECFs can influence unconscious semantic priming.

What are the different stages of sleep, and how are they measured?

The stages of sleep are measured using an EEG, a device that measures electrical activity in the brain. In the period preceding sleep, while you are calm and relaxed, your brain produces alpha waves (8 to 12 cycles per second). Sleep has four stages, each with a distinct EEG pattern. In Stage 1 sleep, theta waves (3 to 7 cycles per second) replace alpha waves, heart rate slows, breathing becomes more regular, and blood pressure decreases. The eyes move slowly or remain still. A person awakened during Stage 1 sleep reports being in a light sleep or drifting off to sleep. During Stage 2 sleep, the EEG shows sleep spindles. Sleep spindles are brief, high amplitude bursts of electrical activity (12 to 14 cycles per second) that appear about every 15 seconds. During Stage 2, a person enters deeper sleep, but he or she still can be easily awakened. During Stage 3 sleep, high and slow delta waves (.5 to 4 cycles per second) comprise between 20 and 50 percent of the EEG pattern. A person's normal bodily functions

slow during Stage 3 sleep, and it is difficult to wake a person at this stage. In Stage 4 sleep, the EEG shows a pattern comprised almost entirely of delta waves. Stage 4 sleep accounts for about 15 percent of a night's sleep.

What is the difference between REM and NREM sleep?

REM sleep refers to periods during which the sleeping person's eyes can be seen moving rapidly under his or her eyelids. Rapid Eye Movement (REM) sleep is the period during which vivid, story-like dreams occur. The eye movements are not associated with "watching" a dream but are a by-product of brain activation. NREM sleep (or non-REM sleep) describes periods of sleep without these rapid eye movements. Persons awakened during NREM sleep report fewer and more fragmented dreams. Periods of REM sleep occur throughout the night and usually last between a few minutes and half an hour. The length of REM periods and the vividness of dreams increase as sleep progresses. REM sleep accounts for about 25 percent of the sleep of adults. Every person experiences REM sleep and dreams, but not everyone can remember dreams in the morning. Yet, during a normal night's sleep, each of us has several dreams. Unless we make a conscious effort to remember a dream, we are unlikely to do so. During REM sleep, muscles are totally relaxed (a condition called atonia), sex organs are aroused, blood pressure increases markedly, and breathing becomes shallow and irregular.

How do Freud and Hobson characterize the content of dreams?

According to Freud, dreams originate in the unconscious and provide some keys to the unresolved conflicts that explain behaviors. Freud called the elements the dreamer was aware of and could recall manifest content. Using psychoanalysis, Freud and his disciples could decode dreams to reveal their hidden symbolic meanings. Freud called these hidden meanings latent content. More recently, Hobson developed the activation-synthesis theory. He did not attach any special hidden meanings to dreams. Instead, he suggested that dreams were caused by incidental activation of the visual system by lower brain centers and attempts of higher brain centers to synthesize (give meaning to) this near random neuronal activity.

What is hypnosis, who can be hypnotized, and for what purposes may hypnosis be valuable?

Hypnosis is an induced state of consciousness under which a person is susceptible to suggestion. Only the willing can be hypnotized, and susceptibility to hypnosis varies from person to person. A person may be a better subject for hypnosis if he or she possesses a vivid imagination, a passive nature, or a willingness to cooperate.

Hypnosis has been successfully used to help people manage pain. Although hypnosis is not a cure, it can help control pain. Hypnosis cannot improve memory for learned information (for example, for a test), nor can it make people recall long-forgotten childhood memories or past lives. However, hypnosis has been used to ease the anxiety surrounding the recall of emotionally traumatic events.

What is meditation, and what are its benefits?
Meditation is a self-induced state of consciousness characterized by an extreme focusing of attention and relaxation. There are several types of meditation. The practice of transcendental meditation generally includes assuming a comfortable position, relaxing, and directing attention to a particular stimulus (like breathing) or to a softly spoken word called a mantra. Mindfulness meditation is more a matter of opening one's consciousness to whatever passes through it. Proponents of meditation claim that it is an easy way to relax. There is mounting evidence that meditation can provide significant benefits, including an improved ability to cope with stress and to develop more positive affective states. Meditation may also reduce fatigue and anxiety while improving working memory.

What are the effects of psychoactive drugs on consciousness?
Psychoactive drugs are substances that influence psychological functioning. Caffeine, found in coffee, tea, colas, and chocolate, is characterized as a stimulant drug. It produces a heightened sense of arousal and an elevation of mood. Withdrawal effects are common after lengthy use of caffeine. Nicotine is a stimulant, commonly found in tobacco products. Even the tobacco companies admit that nicotine is an addictive drug. Cocaine is a highly addictive stimulant that produces a short-lived euphoria, or "high." The amphetamines (plural because there are several varieties) are synthetically produced stimulants once thought to mimic, but to be safer than, cocaine. They act on the body more slowly than cocaine does, but they still produce a sense of alertness and arousal that is relatively short-lived. Amphetamines seem to mask fatigue more than they create additional energy. Methamphetamine is a synthetic drug related to amphetamine but with greater potency and likelihood of inducing addiction.

Alcohol is a depressant. It reduces awareness and slows bodily functions. The most popular of the depressants, alcohol contributes to nearly 100,000 deaths each year in the United States. Whether a person becomes dependent upon alcohol seems to depend on both genetic and sociocultural factors. Opiates (such as codeine and morphine) are called analgesics because of their pain-killing capabilities. They are addictive. Heroin is a very addictive opiate to which users quickly develop tolerance. Heroin users need ever-increasing amounts of the drug to maintain the same level of pleasure, and withdrawal symptoms are extreme. Barbiturates are synthetic sedatives of which there are many varieties. In small doses, barbiturates create a sense of calm and relaxation by slowing nervous system activity. In higher doses, they produce sleep, and in sufficient doses, they can even be fatal.

Hallucinogens (such as LSD) are drugs that alter mood and perceptions. They get their name from their ability to induce hallucinations (perceptual experiences without the benefit of sensory input). In short, users of hallucinogens have experiences unrelated to what is going on in their environment. Hallucinogens may intensify already unpleasant moods. The active ingredient in marijuana is the chemical compound THC. Smoking marijuana may be more dangerous to the respiratory system than is the smoking of regular cigarettes, but research also tells us that it does not increase the risk of developing lung cancer. Long-term marijuana use has been associated with impaired judgment, unrealistic mood, impaired coordination, and hallucinations. Early marijuana use has been associated with later use and abuse of other psychoactive drugs. Ecstasy is a drug with the qualities of amphetamines and hallucinogens that produces feelings of emotional openness, reduces critical thoughts, and decreases inhibitions. Ecstasy creates feelings of euphoria. The drug has short- and long-term negative physical side effects (e.g., nausea, blurred vision, rapid eye movement, faintness, and chills or sweating) and negative psychological side effects (e.g., confusion, sleep problems, depression, and severe anxiety).

Key Terms

Consciousness (p. 124)
Conscious (p. 126)
Preconscious (p. 126)
Unconscious (p. 126)
Sleep (p. 127)
Electroencephalograph (EEG) (p. 128)
Electromyogram (EMG) (p. 128)
REM sleep (p. 129)
NREM sleep (p. 130)
Atonia (p. 130)

Manifest content (p. 132)
Latent content (p. 132)
Activation-synthesis theory (p. 132)
Hypnosis (p. 133)
Meditation (p. 135)
Psychoactive drugs (p. 136)
Drug abuse (p. 137)
Stimulants (p. 138)
Depressants (p. 139)
Hallucinogens (p. 140)

Thinking, Language, and Intelligence

CHAPTER 7

Source: mavo/Shutterstock

Chapter Outline

Preview

Some Thoughts on Thinking

Problem Solving

Psychology in Action: Paths to Effective and Ineffective Problem Solving

Language

Just What Is Intelligence?

Focus on Diversity: Group Differences in Measured Intelligence

Questions You Will Be Able to Answer

After reading Chapter 7, you should be able to answer the following questions:

- What is meant by "thinking," and to what extent does it involve concepts, reasoning, and problem-solving?
- What is a problem, and how do well-defined and ill-defined problems differ?
- What are the defining characteristics of language?
- How are the rules and structures of language reflected in the use of phonemes, morphemes, and syntax?
- What is the study of pragmatics, and what does it tell us about language use?
- How do the theoretical and operational definitions of intelligence differ?
- What are the models of intelligence offered by Gardner and Sternberg?
- What is emotional intelligence?
- What is a psychological test, and by what criteria is the quality or value of a test judged?
- How was IQ calculated when it was first introduced, and how is it calculated today?
- What are the *Stanford-Binet Intelligence Scales* and the *Wechsler Adult Intelligence Scale*?
- What does it mean to be "intellectually gifted" or an "individual with an intellectual disability," and what are some of the causes of the latter?

Preview

We have already discussed three cognitive processes: perception (the selection and organization of stimuli delivered by our senses), learning (demonstrated by relatively permanent changes in behavior that occur as the result of practice or experience), and memory (the encoding, storing, and retrieval of information). The cognitive processes reviewed in this chapter are referred to as "higher" because they build upon the processes of perception, learning, and memory. They are not tied to direct experience. Instead, they use and manipulate cognitions that have already been processed.

We begin with "thinking," a term that includes forming concepts, reasoning and making decisions. Then, we examine the processes of solving problems and using language. We focus on problem solving because it requires that we have the right set of concepts to consider, that we can reason logically, and that we make sound decisions.

Then we consider language. Arguably, the use of language sets humans apart from other species. Other species may have complex means of communicating, but only humans have language—at least as we shall define it.

The second half of this chapter deals with intelligence. Defining intelligence is difficult. Most likely intelligence is not a singular, unitary talent, or process: People can be intelligent or act intelligently in a variety of ways. When doing research on intelligence, psychologists tend to define it operationally—recall that an operational definition specifies how a concept is measured. Therefore, we will look at some ways to measure intelligence. We will examine group differences in measured intelligence, and finally, we will consider individual differences in measured intelligence, looking at giftedness and intellectual disability.

Some Thoughts on Thinking

Thinking—cognitive processes that build on existing cognitions, perceptions, ideas, experiences, and memories.

Thinking is a term that refers to cognitive processes that build on existing cognitions—perceptions, ideas, experiences, and memories. Thinking uses concepts: The answer to "What is the reciprocal of 25?" requires thinking about what a reciprocal is. Thinking involves reasoning: "I don't like chemistry, and I am earning Cs and Ds in it. I do like psychology and haven't earned anything but As in my psychology classes. Maybe I ought to switch majors." Thinking involves problem solving: "I missed class on Wednesday; how can I get the notes?" Thinking reflects the ability of the human system of cognition to go beyond and manipulate information that is readily available in the environment (Markman & Genter, 2001).

John Locke was a philosopher who helped lay the foundation for the emergence of psychology. Locke (1690) suggested that our minds contain *ideas* and that those ideas come from our experience (a notion psychologists agree with). In today's terminology, however, Locke's *ideas* are called concepts. **Concepts** are mental categories or classes into which we place the events and objects we experience. Concepts are what we use when we think. Concepts are crucial to the survival of thinking beings: "Is the plant edible or poisonous? Is the person friend or foe? Was the sound made by a predator or by the wind? All organisms assign objects and events in the environment to separate classes or categories. This allows them to respond differently, for example, to nutrients and poisons, and to predators and prey. Any species lacking this ability would quickly become extinct" (Ashby & Maddox, 2005, p. 150).

Concepts—mental categories or classes into which we place the events and objects we experience.

Think about chairs. Really. Take a moment and think about them. As you do, pay attention to what you are doing. Images come to mind. You may imagine armchairs, dining-room chairs, rocking chairs, high chairs, chairs in the classroom, easy chairs, overstuffed chairs, broken chairs, and so on. As you thought about chairs, did one chair—some standard, definitional chair—come to mind? Are there defining characteristics of chairs? Most have four legs, although beanbag chairs have none. Most chairs are used for sitting, although people also stand on chairs to reach high places. Most chairs have backs, but if the back gets too low, you have a stool, not a chair. Most chairs are made for one person; if they get too wide, they become benches, loveseats, or sofas.

In fact, most concepts in our memories are "fuzzy" (Labov, 1973). What is the difference between a river and a stream? Somehow we know, but because these concepts are not exact, they are difficult to distinguish. Fuzzy concepts are precisely why we say things such as, "Technically, a tomato is a fruit, not a vegetable." Or, "Actually, a spider really is not an insect." One way to deal with this complication is to follow the lead of Eleanor Rosch (1973). She argued that we think about concepts in terms of **prototypes**—members of a category that typify or represent the category to which they belong.

Rosch suggests that, within our concept of chair, are certain examples that are more typical—more "chair-ish"—than others. The same principle applies to birds. A robin may be a prototypic bird. Crows are less prototypic. Vultures are even less so, and that penguins even *are* birds may be difficult to remember because they seem so different from the prototype. Concepts, then, are the mental representations of our experience. They are what we talk about when we communicate. They are what we manipulate when we think and when we solve problems.

Reasoning is the process of reaching conclusions that are based on either a set of general (cognitive) principles or an assortment of acquired facts and observations. There are two major categories of reasoning, *inductive* and *deductive*, but some instances of reasoning do not fall neatly into either category.

When fictional detectives or real-life crime scene investigators pull together many pieces of evidence to determine who committed a crime—and when and how it was committed—they are reasoning inductively. **Inductive reasoning** leads to a likely general conclusion based on separate, specific facts and observations. Indeed, reasoning inductively is not easy. Errors can enter the process in many ways: Are the facts and observations accurate in the first place? Are they relevant? Do these facts also support a different, but just as logical, conclusion? We will treat reasoning as a subset of problem-solving in the next section.

Many of the same barriers to effective inductive reasoning also apply to deductive reasoning. **Deductive reasoning** leads to specific conclusions about events based on a small number of general principles (concepts again). In a way, deductive reasoning is inductive reasoning in reverse. You have a few general concepts that cover life on campus. Eighteen to 28-year-olds who walk around campus, sit in classrooms and carry textbooks are likely to be students. Indeed, these general principles of college life have grown from personal experience as well as from reading and hearing about college students. So when you see 24-year-old Bob walking across campus and into a psychology class, with textbooks under his arm, you deduce that Bob is a college student. And well he may be. Can you imagine possibilities for this scenario in which Bob is *not* a college student? Again, we will treat deductive reasoning as a special case of problem-solving, where the problem takes the form, "Given what you know about the world, how can you explain this particular event or observation?"

Source: Timothy Yue/Shutterstock.

We might think of a robin as a prototypic member of the general concept of "birds." Penguins are less prototypical, and sometimes it is easy to forget that penguins really are birds.

Prototypes—members of a category that typify or represent the category to which they belong.

Reasoning—the process of reaching conclusions that are based on either a set of general (cognitive) principles or an assortment of acquired facts and observations.

Inductive reasoning—reasoning leading to a likely general conclusion based on separate, specific facts and observations.

Deductive reasoning—reasoning leading to specific conclusions about events based on a small number of general principles.

STUDY CHECK

What is meant by "thinking," and to what extent does it involve concepts, reasoning, and problem solving?

Chapter 7 Thinking, Language, and Intelligence   **149**

Problem Solving

In their 1954 text, *Experimental Psychology*, Woodworth and Schlosberg began their chapter on problem-solving with this observation: "If the experimentalist could show us how to think clearly, and how to solve our problems successfully and expeditiously, his social contribution would be very great" (p. 814). Their hope has yet to be fulfilled. Our daily lives are filled with problems of various sorts. Some are simple, straightforward, and even trivial; others are complex and crucial. Here we focus on cognitive, or intellectual, problems—those that require the manipulation of cognitions for their solution. The first thing to do is define what a problem is, and then we can consider how to go about solving one.

Sometimes our goals are obvious, our situation is clear, and the way from where we are to where we want to be is also obvious. In such cases, we do not have a problem, do we? Suppose you're hungry for breakfast and you have eggs, bacon, bread, and butter. You also have a stove, pans, and a spatula and know how to cook. Further assume you like to eat eggs, bacon, and buttered toast. With little hesitation, you will engage in the appropriate behaviors and reach your goal. More plainly, you will cook and eat.

Problem—a discrepancy between one's present state and one's perceived goal state and no readily apparent way to get from one to the other.

A **problem** exists when there is a discrepancy between one's present state and one's perceived goal state and no readily apparent way to get from one to the other. When the path to attaining your goal is not clear, a problem exists, and you need to engage in problem-solving behaviors—as might be the case if halfway through making breakfast you were to discover you had no butter or margarine.

A problem has three major components: (a) an *initial state*—the situation as it exists, or is perceived to exist, at the moment; (b) a *goal state*—the situation as the problem-solver would like it to be; and (c) possible routes or *strategies* for getting from initial state to goal state.

Psychologists also distinguish between well-defined and ill-defined problems. *Well-defined* problems are those in which both the initial state and the goal state are clear. We know what the current situation is and what the goal is, and we may even know some of the possible ways to go about getting from one to the other. "What English word can be made from the letters *teralbay*?" We see that this question presents a problem. We understand what the question is asking, have some ideas about how we might go about answering it, and will surely know when we have succeeded. "How do you get home from campus if you discover that your car won't start?" Again, we know our initial state (on campus with a car that won't start), and we will know when we have reached our goal (we're at home), but we have to find a different way to get there.

Most problems we face are *ill-defined*. In such cases, we have neither a clear idea of what we are starting with nor a clearly identified solution. "What should my college major be?" Many high school seniors (and a few college seniors) do not even know what their options are. They have few ideas about how to investigate college majors. And once they have selected a major, they are not at all sure that their choice was the best one—which may explain why so many college students change their majors so often. Ill-defined problems usually involve several variables that are difficult to define (much less control), so psychologists usually study problems that are reasonably well defined.

> **STUDY CHECK**
>
> What is a problem, and how do well-defined and ill-defined problems differ?

List five or six problems you faced yesterday and determine whether each is well-defined or ill-defined.

PSYCHOLOGY IN ACTION

Paths to Effective and Ineffective Problem Solving

In everyday life, we are often faced with a myriad of problems to solve. Which college should I attend? Should I buy a car or SUV? How can I get my car unstuck from the mud? Early in the process of problem solving, you have to correctly represent the elements of the problem, assess what you have at hand to solve the problem, and set a clear goal. Once you have an adequate representation of the initial state of a problem and have a clear idea of what an acceptable goal state might be, you still have to figure out how to get to that goal. Not surprisingly, problem solvers use strategies. In this context, a *problem-solving strategy* is a systematic plan for generating possible solutions that can be tested to see if they are correct. Cognitive strategies permit the problem-solver to exercise some control over the task at hand. They allow solvers to choose the skills and knowledge they bring to bear on any particular problem at any time (Sternberg, 2011). We will consider two problem-solving strategies: algorithms and heuristics.

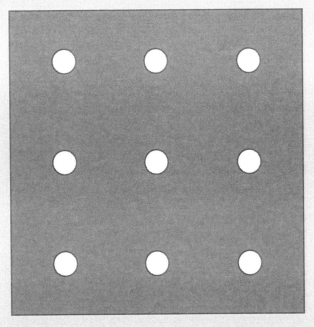

An *algorithm* is a strategy that, if correctly applied, guarantees a solution to the problem eventually. An algorithm explores and evaluates all possible solutions in a systematic way until the correct one is found. For example, imagine that you go to your local supercenter to buy some marshmallows. You know that the store has them, but you are not sure where to find them. Using an algorithm would involve going up and down every aisle until you happened upon the marshmallows. Of course, this strategy is ultimately successful. However, it is very time consuming. Maybe there is a better way to find those marshmallows.

You might try applying a heuristic solution. A *heuristic* is an informal, rule-of-thumb strategy involving the generation and testing of hypotheses. This strategy is more efficient than an algorithm, but there is no guarantee of success. Let's go back to the marshmallow problem. Rather than wandering around the entire store, you could narrow your search by hypothesizing that the marshmallows are most likely to be in one of two aisles: the candy aisle or the baking aisle. You then proceed first to the candy aisle only to find no marshmallows. Next you go to the baking aisle, and alas, there they are. Here you met with success. However, what would have happened had some genius department manager decided to put the marshmallows in the camping section along with the other ingredients to make S'mores around a campfire? You might have left the store empty-handed!

Even if you adopt an effective strategy to solve a problem, there is still no guarantee of success. There are several things that can get in the way of successful problem solving. Recall from Chapter 3 the idea of a mental set. A mental set is a set of preconceived ideas or expectations that can affect perception. A mental set can also affect how you perceive and approach solving a problem. A classic example of this can be demonstrated using the accompanying figure. Without lifting your pencil or pen, connect the nine dots inside the square. Most people struggle with the problem because they bring to it the notion that they must stay within the square when connecting the dots. Try the task again without that mental set. You will probably be able to connect all nine dots.

Another impediment to effective problem solving is functional fixedness. *Functional fixedness* occurs when you fail to see a novel use for a familiar, common object. Think about this problem: You are to tie together two strings hanging from the ceiling that are several feet apart. The problem is that they are too far apart for you to reach both at the same time. On a table in front of you are several objects, including a pair of pliers. Ah, you think, "I will use the pliers to grab one of the strings and then the other." Unfortunately, you find that the strings are too far apart for that to work. None of the other objects seems to be of much help either. You might, at this point, give up in frustration. However, you could solve the problem if you used the pliers in a manner other than as a grabbing tool. What would happen if you tied the pliers to one of the strings and used it as a pendulum to swing the string toward you? You could now solve the problem! You can overcome functional fixedness by using the *generic-parts technique* (GPT; McCaffrey, 2012). The GPT involves asking yourself two questions about a common object. First, can the object be broken down into component parts? Second, can those component parts be used in new ways to solve a problem? McCaffrey found that individuals trained in GPT were better able to overcome functional fixedness than those who were not.

Yet another impediment to effective problem solving is applying inappropriate heuristics. The *availability heuristic* is the assumption that things that come to mind easily are more common (or occur more frequently) than things that do not come to mind as easily. Let's say that we are briefly shown a list of 40 names. On this list are 19 names of famous women (e.g., Amelia Earhart, Michelle Obama) and 21 not-so-famous men. Later, you are asked to recall how many men's and women's names were on the list. Most likely you will overestimate the number of women's names because they more easily come to mind than the men's names. Another heuristic that can get in the way of problem solving is the *representativeness heuristic*, which is the assumption that beliefs about a representative member of a group will hold for all members of that group. For example, let's say that you know that a group of men comprises 70 percent basketball players and 30 percent doctors. I tell you that one of the men selected is tall and agile. Are you more likely to say that the person is a basketball player than a doctor? Probably so, but you might be wrong. Some doctors might be tall and agile. Finally, there is the *confirmation bias*—the notion that we tend to select from among several options the one that best fits with what we have suspected to be true for some time. In other words, we tend to seek and accept information that is consistent with what we already believe—even if that information is patently false (Aronson, Wilson, & Akert, 2005; Reich, 2004). For example, a person who strongly opposes gun rights may avoid reading articles, viewing news broadcasts, and visiting websites that present pro-gun views. That person may find him- or herself at a disadvantage in a debate with a friend with a more well-rounded perspective on gun rights.

Language

Language sets humans apart from other animal species. The philosopher Suzanne Langer put it this way:

> Language is, without a doubt, the most momentous and at the same time the most mysterious product of the human mind. Between the most clear animal call of love or warning or anger, and a man's least, trivial word, there lies a whole day of Creation or in a modern phrase, a whole chapter of evolution. (1951, p. 94)

Let's Talk: What Is Language?

Language—a large collection of arbitrary symbols that have a common, shared significance for a language-using community and that follow certain rules of combination.

How shall we characterize this mysterious product of the human mind—this higher cognitive process—called language? Here is a classic definition: Language is a large collection of arbitrary symbols that have a common, shared significance for a language-using community and that follow certain rules of combination (Morris, 1946).

Before we examine this definition, we need to make a distinction between *communication* and *language*. Communication is the act of passing information from one point to another. Language, on the other hand, is a specific means of communication. You may find yourself arguing with someone who insists that animals (e.g., chimpanzees, dolphins, bees) use language. They do not. They do have elaborate communication systems. For example, chimpanzees use vocalizations and gestures to communicate messages. However, this and other animal communication systems do not qualify as a language. You will see why as we discuss the definition of language further and examine language's properties in greater detail.

Language consists of a large number of *symbols* that can be combined in an infinite number of ways to produce an infinite number of utterances. The symbols that constitute language are commonly referred to as words—labels we have assigned to concepts, or our mental representations. When we use the word *chair* as a symbol, we don't use it to label just one specific instance of a chair. We use the word as a symbol to represent our concept of chairs. As symbols, words need not stand for real things in the real world. We have words to describe objects or events that cannot be perceived, such as *ghost* or, for that matter, *mind*. With language, we can communicate about owls and pussycats in teacups and a four-dimensional, time-warped hyperspace. Words stand for cognitions, or concepts, and we have a great number of them.

Language use is a social process, a means of communicating our understanding of events to others. One property of all true languages is **arbitrary symbolic reference**, which means that there need be no resemblance between a word and its referent. In other words, there is no requirement for using the particular symbol for a given object. You call what you are reading a *book* (or a *textbook*, to use a more specific symbol). As speakers of English, we agreed to use the symbol book to describe what you are reading. But we didn't have to. We could have agreed to call it a *relm*, or a *poge*. The symbols of a language are arbitrary, but—once established by common use or tradition—they become part of the language and must be learned and applied consistently by each new user of the language. Arbitrary symbolic reference is unique to human language. Animal communication systems do not have this quality.

Notice also that the arbitrary reference for symbols in one's language can change over time. Think how the symbols "gay" or "cool" or "web" have changed in terms of what they reference today compared to just 50 years ago. Consider the new symbols that have entered the language because of new technologies, such as *blog* or *iPad*, or *app*. Or consider how the meanings of symbols can change. A symbol that once referred to a canned meat product now refers to unsolicited junk email (*spam*), and we talk about *burning* digital music or data to a *CD*.

To be part of a language, at least in a practical sense, symbols need to have shared significance for a language-using community. That is, people have to agree on both the symbols and their meanings. You and I might decide to call what you are now reading a *relm*, but we would be in a tiny language-using community.

The final part of our definition tells us that the symbols of a language must follow certain *rules of combination*. Language is structured or rule-governed, which makes it a special form of communication. For one thing, rules dictate how we can and cannot string symbols together in language. In English we say, "The small boy slept late." We do not say, "Slept boy late small the." We *could* say it, but it would not communicate anything.

Using language is a remarkably creative, generative process. The ability of language users to express an infinite number of ideas with a finite number of symbols is called *productivity*. Nearly every time we use language, we use it in ways that are different from how we have used it before. Still, as native speakers, we are able to apply the underlying rules of language to these new situations without much difficulty. Like arbitrary symbolic reference, productivity is unique to human language. No known animal communication system has this quality. Yet another characteristic of language is *displacement*, the ability to communicate about the "not here" and the "not now." We can use language to talk about yesterday's lunch and tomorrow's class schedule. We can talk about things that are not here, never were, and never will be. Language is the only form of communication that allows us to do so.

Finally, note that *language* and *speech* are not synonymous terms. Speech is just one way in which language is expressed as behavior. There are others, including writing, coding (as in Morse code), or signing (as in American Sign Language).

Arbitrary symbolic reference—the idea that there need be no resemblance between a word and its referent.

STUDY CHECK

What are the defining characteristics of language?

Other than language as we use it every day, can you think of any other system of unitary symbols with a common shared significance for some user community that follows rules of combination? Would mathematics qualify? How about music? What are the similarities and differences?

Describing the Structure of Language

Psycholinguistics is a hybrid discipline of psychology and linguistics. When psycholinguists analyze a language, they usually do so at three levels. The first level involves the sounds that are used when we express language as speech. The second level deals with the meaning of words and sentences, and the third level involves the rules used for combining words and phrases to generate sentences. At each of these three levels, we can see structure and rules at work.

Phonemes—meaningless language sounds that result in a meaningful utterance when put together in the proper order.

The individual speech sounds of a language are called **phonemes**. They are the sounds we make when we talk to one another. Phonemes by themselves have no meaning, but when we put them together in the proper order, they result in a meaningful utterance. For example, the word *cat* consists of three phonemes: an initial consonant sound (a "k" sound here), the vowel sound of "a" and the consonant sound, "t." *Rules* govern how phonemes are to be combined to form words and phrases. If we were to interchange the consonant sounds in *cat*, for example, we would have a different utterance, *tack*, with an altogether different meaning. Language usage, therefore, requires knowing which speech sounds are part of that language and understanding how they may be combined to form larger language units. There are approximately 45 phonemes in English. (And because those 45 sounds are represented by only 26 letters in our alphabet, it is little wonder that many of us have trouble spelling.)

Semantics—the study of meaning in language.

Morphemes—the smallest units of meaning in a spoken language; a collection of phonemes that means something.

Describing a language's phonemes—noting which sounds are relevant and which combinations are possible—is only a small part of a language's complete description. The study of meaning is called **semantics**. Those who study semantics examine morphemes in detail. **Morphemes** are the smallest units of meaning in a spoken language—a collection of phonemes that means something (in sign language a *grapheme* is its equivalent). In many cases, a morpheme is a word. For example, *write* is a morpheme and a word; it has meaning, and it is not divisible into smaller, meaningful units. Such a morpheme is a *free morpheme* because it can stand alone. Others, known as *bound morphemes*, are not words and cannot stand alone. Prefixes (for example, *re-* and *un-*) and suffixes (for example, *-ing* and *-ed*) are bound morphemes because they must be attached to another morpheme to be used properly. Many words are a combination of free and bound morphemes. *Rewrite* consists of two morphemes, *write* (a free morpheme) and *re* (a bound morpheme), which in this context means roughly, "write it again." *Tablecloth* is a word composed of two morphemes, *table* and *cloth* (both free morphemes).

The use of morphemes is governed by rules. For example, we cannot go around making nouns plural in any way we please. The plural of *ox* is *oxen*, not *oxes*. The plural of *mouse* is *mice*, not *mouses*, *mousen*, or *meese*. If you want to write something over again, you have to *rewrite* it, not *write-re* it. Note (again) how morphemes are verbal labels for concepts (mental representations). Asking you to rewrite something would make no sense if we did not share the concepts of "writing" and "doing things over again."

Syntax—the rules that govern how sentences are formed or structured in a language.

Grammar—the formal expression of the syntax of a language.

There is one aspect of our language that obviously uses rules: the generation of sentences—stringing words (or morphemes) together to create meaningful utterances. **Syntax** describes the rules that govern how sentences are formed or structured in a language. The formal expression of the syntax of a language is **grammar**.

Understanding the syntax of one's language involves a peculiar sort of knowledge, or cognitive process. We all know the rules of English in the sense that we can use them. But few of us could explain or describe those rules to someone else. For example, try to write out the rule in the English language for pluralization. It might take you a while. We say that people have a *competence*, a cognitive skill that governs language use. That skill allows us to judge the extent to which an utterance is meaningful and well formed. We know that "The dog looks terrifying" fits the rules of English and that "The dog looks barking" does not. And, somehow, we recognize that "The dog looks watermelon" is downright absurd. At the same time, we recognize that "Colorless green ideas sleep furiously" *does* fit the rules of English, even though it does not make sense (Chomsky, 1957). It may be a silly thing to say, but we realize that it is a grammatically correct thing to say.

We also know that these two utterances communicate the same message, even though they look (and sound) quite different from one another:

The student read the textbook.
The textbook was read by the student.

In either case, we know who is doing what. Another intuition that demonstrates our competence with the rules of language lies in our ability to detect ambiguity. Look at these two sentences:

They are cooking apples.
They are cooking apples.

The two sentences above appear identical. But upon reflection, we realize that they may be communicating different (ambiguous) ideas. In one case, we may be talking about what some people are cooking (apples, as opposed to spaghetti). In another interpretation, we may be identifying a variety of apple (those best-suited for cooking, as opposed to those best-suited for eating raw). In yet another case, we may be describing what is being done to the apples (cooking them, as opposed to eating them). This is not an isolated example of ambiguity in language. There are many. Consider the ambiguity of the following statements: "The shooting of the marines was terrible," or "Flying airplanes can be dangerous."

Our awareness of proper syntax tells us immediately that the utterance "the puppies are playing in the yard" is acceptable, but that "yard the playing in puppies are" is not. Note that we know that the second utterance is unacceptable even if we are not able to specify why it is wrong or which grammatical rules have been violated.

Language Use as a Social Process

The main purpose of language is communication. Language helps us share our thoughts, feelings, intentions, and experiences with others. In this context, when a child acquires language it is not done to learn the language for its own sake. Instead, the child learns language to communicate with others. Thus, using language is a social behavior. **Pragmatics** is the study of how language is related to the social context in which it occurs. Our understanding of sarcasm (as in, "Well, this certainly is a beautiful day!" when in fact it is rainy, cold, and miserable), or simile (as in, "Life is like a sewer . . ."), or metaphor (as in, "His slam dunk to start the second half was the knockout blow"), or cliché (as in, "It rained cats and dogs") depends on many things, including an appreciation of the context of the utterance and the intention of the speaker. The rules of conversation (turn-taking) are also part of the pragmatics of speech. That is, we have learned that it is most efficient to listen while others speak, and to speak while they listen. When someone violates this understanding, it is difficult to have a conversation.

Pragmatics—the study of how language is related to the social context in which it occurs.

It is our knowledge of a language's pragmatics that informs us that the statement "It's raining cats and dogs" is not to be taken literally.

Pragmatics involve making language decisions based on the social situation at hand. Think about how you modify your language usage when you talk to your best friend, a preschool child, a college professor, or a driver who cuts you off at an intersection. Contemporary concerns about "political correctness" seem relevant here, don't they? In most contexts, words such as *pig*, *Uncle Tom*, *boy*, and *girl* are reasonable and proper; in other contexts, they can evoke angry responses. Cultural differences also play a role in pragmatics. For example, in some Native American cultures, periods of silence—even lengthy periods of silence—during conversation are common and acceptable. Someone unfamiliar with this pragmatic reality, however, might become anxious or upset when long pauses disrupt the flow of their conversation (Brislin, 1993). Translations from one language and culture to another can cause huge changes in meaning. Two favorite examples (from Berkowitz, 1994) involve the translation of English advertising slogans into Asian languages. "Finger-Lickin' Good" in Chinese translates into "Eat Your Fingers Off" and "Come alive with the Pepsi Generation" in Taiwanese means "Pepsi will bring your ancestors back from the dead."

STUDY CHECK

How are the rules and structures of language reflected in the use of phonemes, morphemes, and syntax?
What is the study of pragmatics, and what does it tell us about language use?

THINKING CRITICALLY

In what ways do specific languages (e.g., English, French, Swahili, etc.) differ from each other?

Just What Is Intelligence?

Intelligence is a troublesome concept in psychology. We all know what we mean when we use the word, but we have a terrible time trying to define it concisely. Consider the varying concepts of intelligence in the following:

- Is John's failure in school due to his lack of intelligence, or to some other factor—his motivation, perhaps?
- Locking your keys in the car was not a very intelligent thing to do.
- A student with any intelligence can see the difference between positive and negative reinforcement.

Intelligence—the capacity of an individual to understand the world around him or her and his or her resourcefulness to cope with its challenges.

In this section, we will develop a working definition of intelligence. To guide us throughout this discussion, let us first accept two definitions of intelligence: one academic and theoretical, the other practical and operational. For our theoretical definition of **intelligence**, we will use a definition offered by David Wechsler (1975, p. 139): "The capacity of an individual to understand the world about him [or her] and his [or her] resourcefulness to cope with its challenges." This definition, and others like it, sounds sensible at first, but it does present some ambiguities. Just what does "capacity" mean in this context? What is meant by "understand the world"? What if the world never really challenges one's "resourcefulness"? Would such people be considered less intelligent? Although there are difficulties with Wechsler's definition, most psychologists today take a similar approach to intelligence, emphasizing adaptation, problem-solving, and finding ways to meet one's goals.

Defining a concept operationally can help us understand an abstract concept. Indeed, as E. G. Boring put it in 1923, "Intelligence is what the intelligence tests measure" (Hunt, 1995, p. 356). Before we get to tests of intelligence, let's spend a bit of time reviewing some of the ways in which psychologists have thought about and described intelligence.

In the past 25 years, theories about the nature of intelligence assume that intelligence is a multidimensional concept; that is, rather than talking about a singular intelligence, we should be talking about *intelligences*. Newer theories also view intelligence as an active processing of information, rather than a trait that one either has or doesn't have to some degree.

The model that best characterizes the notion of "multiple intelligences" belongs to Howard Gardner (1993, 2003a, 2003b). Gardner suggests that people can display intelligence in any one of several different ways. "I was claiming that all human beings possess not just a single intelligence (often called 'g' for general intelligence). Rather, as a species, we human beings are better described as having a set of relatively autonomous intelligences" (Gardner, 2003a, p. 4).

Contemporary views of intelligence see it expressed in many forms beyond the academic sense with which we usually associate the term. Intelligence and giftedness can be expressed in many ways—including artistic endeavors.

Just how many "intelligences" might we possess, and what might they be? First, Gardner acknowledges a scholastic/academic intelligence, made up of *mathematical/logical* and *verbal/linguistic abilities*. He characterizes the combination of these two intelligences as formulating the concept of "intelligence" used by both scholars and laypeople. Gardner maintains that scholastic/academic abilities are the strengths of a law professor. And if one is a law professor, these abilities are wonderful, useful strengths to have. There are, however, other ways to be intelligent. *Spatial intelligence* is demonstrated by the ability to know where you are, where you've been, and how to get to where you want to be. People with strong spatial intelligence are good at visualizing things, like how furniture will look in a room—without physically moving it around. This is an intelligence characteristic of successful architects, designers, surgeons—and those who blaze trails through the jungle. *Musical intelligence* is rather self-evident. It is the ability needed not only to produce, but also to appreciate pitch, rhythm, tone, and the subtleties of music. We often speak of musicians as having a "gift" or great "talent." Isn't that exactly what law professors have—a talent or a gift—but for more academic pursuits? *Body-kinesthetic intelligence* is reflected in the ability to control one's body and to handle objects, as found in skilled athletes, dancers, and craftspeople. *Interpersonal intelligence* is exemplified by the ability to get along with others and to "read other people" (Rosnow et al., 1995). You would expect successful teachers, therapists, politicians, and salespeople to display this sort of intelligence. *Intrapersonal intelligence* amounts to a keen self-awareness, and is required for people to understand themselves, to realize their strengths and weaknesses, and to look their best.

Gardner anticipated that, over time, he would add to his list of the seven intelligences. In fact, in 1999 he added *naturalistic intelligence* to his list. People with this intellectual strength are particularly in tune with their natural environment and the patterns that it presents. This would be a handy intelligence for anyone who lived off the land, or for someone who was a naturalist or biologist. Gardner also thought about adding a ninth intelligence, which he calls *existential intelligence*, reflecting the ability to deal easily with matters mystical, or even religious (see also, Halama & Strizene, 2004). He calls this "the intelligence of big questions," but he is not yet comfortable with it as a freestanding variety of intelligence, leaving his list at "eight and a half" (Gardner, 2003a, p. 7).

Obviously, a person can find success in life with any one (or more) of these multiple intelligences, but which intelligences are most-highly valued depends on the demands of one's culture. Highly technological societies, such as ours, value the first two types of intelligence. In cultures where one must climb tall trees or hunt wild game for food, body/kinesthetic skills are valued—as they are in the American subculture we call "professional athletics." Interpersonal skills are valuable in cultures that emphasize family and group activities over individual accomplishment. Again, context matters.

Robert Sternberg is a cognitive psychologist who also views intelligence as multifaceted (1997, 1999, 2004, 2007). He focuses on how one *uses* intellectual abilities, rather than trying to describe a particular set of skills or talents. Where Gardner emphasizes the separateness of his varieties of intelligence, Sternberg sees intelligent behavior as a reflection of three different processes, or components, working together. What matters most for Sternberg is how people achieve success in their lives, given the socio-cultural context in which they live.

Sternberg's *Triarchic Theory of Intelligence* has three components:

1. *Analytic*: This involves analyzing, comparing, judging, processing information, evaluating ideas, and the like. College students need this sort of intelligence when they are asked to do such things as compare and contrast two theories of color vision. "What is the problem here?" "How shall I get started?" "What will I need to see this through?" "How will I know when I have succeeded?"

2. *Practical*: This involves the sort of thinking required to solve real problems in the real world. You are at the library late at night and discover that your car won't start. What will you do? You will rely on those skills that Sternberg would say exemplify practical intelligence—knowing which friend is most likely to come to your aid, or having the phone number of a "road-side assistance" service available.

3. *Creative*: This component of intelligence comes into use when we face new problems or challenges; when old solutions no longer work, and a creative one is needed. "How can I generate a mnemonic device to help me remember all these different approaches to intelligence?"

Sternberg is quick to point out that his first component of intelligence is much easier to measure with standard psychological tests than are the other two. From this theoretical perspective, people are intelligent to the extent to which they understand their strengths and weaknesses, work to apply their strengths whenever they can, and continue to try to improve their weaknesses.

Finally, let us look at the work of John Mayer and Peter Salovey (1995, 1997), who introduced the term "emotional intelligence" into psychology's vocabulary. The concept was an immediate hit with the general public. It was discussed on television talk shows and in news magazines. Daniel Goleman's 1995 book on the topic, *Emotional Intelligence*, became a bestseller. **Emotional intelligence** is characterized by four sets of skills: "1) *managing* emotions so as to attain specific goals, 2) *understanding* emotions, emotional language, and the signals conveyed by emotions, 3) *using* emotions to facilitate thinking, and 4) *perceiving* emotions accurately in oneself and others" (Mayer, Salovey, & Caruso, 2008, p. 507). What is interesting about this concept is that emotional intelligence (EQ) seems to be unrelated to standard measures of general intelligence (IQ) (e.g., Lam & Kirby, 2002), but does predict both academic and social success (Mayer, Roberts, & Barsdale, 2008).

Some people are successful in life, particularly in social situations, not because they are so "smart" in a cognitive, academic sense, but because they are good at controlling their own feelings and are sensitive to the feelings of others (Salovey & Grewal, 2005). Consider the following situation. As you drive down a four-lane highway, you notice a construction sign indicating that the left lane is closed ahead. You move to the right lane. Whizzing by you and the other drivers who have responded to the warning sign is a driver in a red car who zips down the left lane until the very last minute, jogging over to the right just before hitting the barricades. Is this driver aggressive, rude, obnoxious, and worthy of scorn and rage? Or did he or she simply not attend to the warning sign? Perhaps the driver was responding to an emergency. Being able to weigh such alternatives and monitor one's own response accordingly is a sign of emotional intelligence.

Emotional intelligence—intelligence characterized by four sets of skills: (1) *managing* emotions so as to attain specific goals; (2) *understanding* emotions, emotional language, and the signals conveyed by emotions; (3) *using* emotions to facilitate thinking; and (4) *perceiving* emotions accurately in oneself and others.

STUDY CHECK

How do the theoretical and operational definitions of intelligence differ?
What are the models of intelligence offered by Gardner and Sternberg?
What is emotional intelligence?

Psychological Tests of Intelligence

Just as there are several ways to define intelligence, there several ways to measure it. Most involve psychological tests. Although the focus of our discussion here is intelligence, we must recognize that psychological tests have been devised to measure the full range of human traits and abilities. For that reason, we start with a few words about tests in general.

A **psychological test** is an objective, standardized measure of a sample of behavior, used as an aid in the understanding and prediction of behavior. A psychological test measures behavior, because that is all we can measure. We cannot directly measure feelings, aptitudes, abilities, or intelligence. We can make inferences about such things on the basis of our measures of behavior, but we cannot measure them directly.

The quality of a psychological test depends on the extent to which it has three characteristics: *reliability*, *validity*, and *adequate norms*. A test's *reliability* refers to its ability to produce the same or highly similar results across similar testing situations. Suppose someone gives you a test and, on the basis of your responses, claims that you have an IQ just below average—94, let's say. Three weeks later, you retake the same test and are told that your IQ is now 127, nearly in the top 3 percent of the population. We have not yet discussed IQ scores, but we can agree that a person's IQ as a measure of intelligence should not change by 33 points in a matter of three weeks and that this test likely lacks reliability.

When people worry about the usefulness of a test, their concern is usually with validity. Measures of *validity* tell us the extent to which a test actually measures what it claims to be measuring. In other words, validity is the extent to which there is agreement between a test score and the quality or trait that the test is believed to measure (Kaplan & Saccuzzo, 2001).

There is one more issue to address: the adequacy of test norms. Suppose that you have filled out a long questionnaire designed to measure the extent to which you are outgoing. You know that the test is a reliable and valid instrument. You are told that you scored a 50 on the test. So what? What does *that* mean? It does not mean that you answered 50 percent of the items correctly—on this test there are no correct or incorrect answers. The point is this: If you do not have a basis of comparison, one test score by itself is meaningless. You have to be able to compare your score with the scores of other people like you who have also taken the test. Results of a test taken by a large group of people whose scores are used to make comparisons are called **test norms**. By using test norms in our example above, you may discover that a score of 50 is average—or that it reflects a very high or very low level of extroversion.

Alfred Binet (1857–1911) may not have authored the first intelligence test (that distinction goes to Sir Francis Galton [1822–1911]), but Binet's was the first effort to stand the test of time. The fifth-edition revision of his test was published in the spring of 2003 (Roid, 2003). Binet was the leading psychologist in France early in the twentieth century. Of great concern in those days were children in the Paris school system who seemed unable to profit from the educational experiences they were being given. Binet and his collaborator, Theodore Simon, wanted to identify students who should be placed in special (remedial) classes, where their education could proceed more efficiently than it had in the standard classroom.

Binet theorized that *mental age* (how well children performed on academic tasks) was more important than *chronological age* (how old the children were) as a means for evaluating students' classroom success. He reasoned that no matter how long it had been since a child's birth, if that child could answer questions and perform as well as an average 8-year-old, then that child had a mental age of 8 years. If the child performed as an average 10-year-old, that child had a mental age of 10 years.

> **Psychological test**—an objective, standardized measure of a sample of behavior; used as an aid in the understanding and prediction of behavior.

> **Test norms**—results of a test taken by a large group of people whose scores are used to make comparisons.

In 1912, William Stern furthered Binet's theory by introducing the concept of the intelligence quotient, or IQ. Stern recognized that having the intellectual abilities of an 8-year-old is unremarkable for a child of 8, but for a child of 6, it is quite remarkable, indeed. In addition, there might be cause for concern if a 10-year-old child has the mental age of an 8-year-old. Stern used a simple formula to evaluate a child's intelligence based on his or her age. As you know, a quotient is the result derived when you divide one number by another. **IQ (Intelligence Quotient)** was determined by dividing the person's mental age (MA) by his or her actual, chronological age (CA). This quotient was then multiplied by 100. For example, if an 8-year-old girl had a mental age of 8, she would be average, and her IQ would equal 100:

IQ (Intelligence Quotient)—a measure of intelligence determined by dividing the person's mental age (MA) by his or her actual, chronological age (CA) and multiplying the result by 100.

$$IQ = \frac{MA}{CA} \times 100 = \frac{8}{8} \times 100 = 1 \times 100 = 100$$

If the 8-year-old were above average, with the intellectual abilities of an average 10-year-old, her IQ would be 125 (10/8 x 100, or 1.25 x 100). If she were below average, say with the mental abilities of an average 6-year-old, her computed IQ would be 75.

It did not take long for psychologists to find fault with the traditional IQ, and they developed the deviation IQ that is now used. The **deviation IQ** uses established group norms and allows for comparing intelligence scores across age groups. Because it is a term ingrained in our vocabulary, we will continue to use the term "IQ" for a measure of general intelligence—even though psychologists use group norms and no longer calculate MAs or compute quotients. **Figure 7.1** presents the idealized distribution of scores on the *Stanford-Binet Intelligence Scales*, reflecting scores of a huge sample of the population. Note that the average IQ score is 100 *by definition*. Also note that about two-thirds of the population has an IQ score between 85 and 115, and that scores above 130 or below 70 are quite rare.

Deviation IQ—a measure of intelligence using established group norms that allows for comparing intelligence scores across age groups.

David Wechsler published his first intelligence test in 1939. Unlike the Stanford-Binet that existed at the time, it was designed for use with adult populations, and it attempted to reduce the heavy reliance on verbal skills that characterized Binet's tests. With a revision in 1955, the test became known as the *Wechsler Adult Intelligence Scale (WAIS)*. It was revised again in 2008 and is known as the *WAIS-IV*. It is appropriate for persons between 16 and 74 years of age.

A natural extension of the WAIS was the *Wechsler Intelligence Scale for Children (WISC)*. With updated norms and several new items, the *WISC-V* appeared in 2014. It is

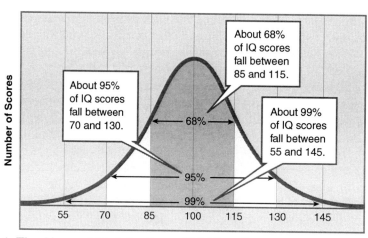

FIGURE 7.1 The Normal Distribution of IQ Test Scores

Scores on standardized tests, such as the Wechsler intelligence scales, form what is known as a normal distribution (also called a "bell-shaped curve"). Given that the mean of the Wechsler and Stanford-Binet scales is set at 100 and the standard deviation is 15, we can determine the percentage of individuals who fall above or below particular IQ scores and the percentage who fall between any two IQ scores.

appropriate for children ages 6 to 16 (there is some overlap with the *WAIS-IV*). A third test in the series is for younger children, between the ages of 4 and 6. It is called the *Wechsler Preschool and Primary Scale of Intelligence,* or *WPPSI*. It was published in 1967 and last revised in 2012, as the *WPPSI-IV*.

The *WAIS-IV* consists of 14 subtests organized into four categories: verbal comprehension scale, perceptual reasoning scale, working memory scale, and processing speed scale. **Table 7.1** shows the four subscales and the tests that comprise each. Some of the

TABLE 7.1 The Subsets of the Wechsler Adult Intelligence Scale, Fourth Edition, WAIS-IV

Subscale	Description
VERBAL COMPREHENSION	
Vocabulary	Person must provide an acceptable definition for a series of words
Similarities	Person must indicate the way(s) in which two things are alike; for example, "In what way are a horse and a cow alike?"
Information	Person must answer questions about a variety of topics dealing with one's culture; for example, "Who wrote *Huckleberry Finn*?" or "How many members are there in the U.S. Congress?"
Comprehension	Test of judgment, common sense, and practical knowledge; for example, "Why do we bury the dead?" or "Why do we have prisons?"
PERCEPTUAL REASONING	
Block design	Using blocks, person must copy a pattern provided on a card
Matrix reasoning	Person is presented with non-verbal, figure stimuli and is to describe a pattern or relationship between the stimuli
Visual puzzles	Person must determine which three pieces among many go together to form a particular puzzle
Picture completion*	Person must identify or name the missing part or object in a drawing; for example, a truck with only three wheels
Figure weights*	Person must determine which of a number of objects balances a balance scale
WORKING MEMORY	
Digit span	Person is to repeat a series of digits, given at the rate of one per second, both forward and backward
Arithmetic	Simple math problems must be answered without paper and pencil; for example, "How far will a bird travel in 90 minutes at the rate of 10 miles per hour?"
Letter-number sequencing	Letters and numbers in scrambled order, person is to re-order them correctly; for sequencing example, "Given Z, 3, B, 1, 2, A" the correct response would be, "1, 2, 3, A, B, Z"
PROCESSING SPEED	
Symbol search	Person is given a geometric figure and must locate that figure from among five figures in a search group of figures as quickly as possible
Coding	Each nine-digit "key" is paired with a simple symbol; given a random series of digits, the person must provide the paired symbol within a time limit
Cancellation*	Person must draw a line through designated geometric form within an array of forms

*Supplemental test

tests within each subscale are "core" tests, whereas others are "supplemental" tests (designated with an * in Table 7.1). The supplemental tests may be added if more detailed information is needed about a person's cognitive abilities.

Items on each subtest are scored (some of the performance items have time limits that affect scoring). As is now the case with the Stanford-Binet, each subtest score is compared to a score provided by the test's norms. How an individual's score compares to the scores of people in the norm group (others of the same sex and age who have already taken the test) determines the standard score for each Wechsler subtest. In addition to one overall score (essentially, the IQ score), the Wechsler tests provide separate verbal and performance scores, which can tell us something about a person's particular strengths and weaknesses.

STUDY CHECK

What is a psychological test, and by what criteria is the quality or value of a test judged?

How was IQ calculated when it was first introduced, and how is it calculated today?

What are the *Stanford-Binet Intelligence Scales* and the *Wechsler Adult Intelligence Scale*?

THINKING CRITICALLY

What reasons or justifications can you generate for administering an IQ test to a 25-year-old adult? That is, what purpose(s) might be served by such testing?

FOCUS ON DIVERSITY

Group Differences in Measured Intelligence

Recognizing that there are individual differences in IQ, can we make any general statements about group differences in IQ? For example, as a group, who are smarter, women or men? Do we become more or less intelligent with age? Are there differences in intelligence among ethnic groups? Simple answers to such questions are often misleading and, if interpreted incorrectly, can be harmful to some groups of people.

Reported average differences in IQ test scores are often misleading. Let us imagine that two large groups of people are tested: 1,000 *Alphas* and 1,000 *Thetas*. On average, the IQ score for *Alphas* is 95, and for *Thetas*, it is 110. An appropriate statistical analysis tells us that the difference of 15 points is too large to attribute to chance. Are *Thetas* smarter than *Alphas*? Yes, on average, they are—that is exactly what has been discovered.

Now look at **Figure 7.2**, which shows two curves that represent the IQ scores from the study. We can see the difference in the averages of the two groups. However, there are several *Thetas* whose IQs are below

that of the average *Alpha*. And there are several *Alphas* with IQs above that of the average *Theta*. We may draw conclusions about average IQs, but making definitive statements about individual *Thetas* and *Alphas* is just not possible.

In addition, being able to demonstrate a significant difference between the average IQs of the two groups in itself tells us nothing about *why* those differences exist. Are *Thetas* genetically superior to *Alphas*? Maybe, maybe not. Have *Alphas* had equal access to the sorts of experiences that IQ tests ask about? Maybe, maybe not. Are the tests biased to provide *Thetas* with an advantage? Maybe, maybe not. Learning that two groups of people have different average IQ scores usually raises more questions than it answers.

Here is a question to which we have a reasonably definitive answer: Is there a difference between the IQs of males and females? The answer is no. Very few studies report any differences between men and women on tests of general intelligence, or IQ. With a few exceptions, what differences have been found seem to be

---

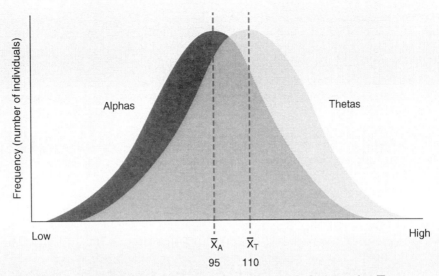

FIGURE 7.2 Hypothetical Distributions of IQ Scores for Two Groups (*Alphas* and *Thetas*)

The average IQ for *Thetas* is higher than that for *Alphas*, but there is considerable overlap between the two distributions. That is, some *Alphas* have IQs higher than the average for *Thetas* (110), and some *Thetas* have IQs lower than the average for *Alphas* (95).

getting smaller (Halpern et al., 2007; Hyde et al., 2008; Jackson & Rushton, 2006).

When we look beyond global measures of IQ, there are some signs of gender differences on specific intellectual skills (which offset each other on general IQ tests). For example, males score significantly higher than females on tests of spatial relations—particularly on tests that require one to visualize how a three-dimensional object would look when rotated in space (Halpern et al., 2007). What is curious about this ability is that males do better than females on such tasks from an early age, widening the gap in the school years, even though this ability is only marginally related to academic coursework.

You know a great deal more now than you did when you were 12. You knew more when you were 12 than you did when you were 10. Many 12-year-olds think they know more than their parents do. What we know about and how much we know change with age, but neither provides a measure of intelligence. IQ scores are computed so that, by definition, they remain consistent with age. The IQ of the average 12-year-old is 100, the same as the IQ of the average 30-year-old and the average 60-year-old, regardless of which test is used. But what happens to the IQ of an individual as he or she ages? If Kim's IQ is 112 at age 4, will it still be 112 at age 14, or 40?

Infant and preschool IQ tests have proven to be poor predictors of IQ at an older age. The IQ scores of children younger than 7 simply do not correlate well with IQs measured later. This does not mean that testing young children is without purpose. Having even a rough idea of the intellectual abilities of young children is often useful, particularly if there is concern about intellectual disability or belief that the child might be exceptional.

Researcher Timothy Salthouse and his colleagues have compiled some very compelling data on cognitive skills and aging. Across many studies, four tests were used: (a) a *vocabulary test* (select best synonym), (b) a *speed test* (classify pairs of patterns as same or different as rapidly as possible), (c) a *reasoning test* (identify the geometric pattern that best fits in the larger pattern from which a piece is missing), and (d) a *memory test* (recall a list of words after each of three auditory presentations). Scores on the *vocabulary test* were high with increased age, until about the mid-50s; after that, they declined slightly or remained stable. For the other three tests, there were large, consistent, and steady declines in the scores from age 20 until age 80. These age-related effects are apparent before the age of 50. Remarkably, within age groups, variability in the test scores was not that great. The steep declines in speed, reasoning, and memory test scores were not a reflection of some people doing very badly, most doing okay, and a few doing well; the declines were across the board (Salthouse, 2004; Salthouse & Ferrer-Caja, 2003).

That there are significant differences between the IQ test scores of African Americans and Caucasian Americans is not a new discovery. It was one conclusion drawn from the testing of Army recruits during World War I. Since then, many studies have reconfirmed the fact that—on average—Caucasians score about 15 points higher on general intelligence (IQ) tests than do African Americans (Hunt & Carlson, 2007; Lynn, 2006). The nagging question, of course, is why? Why do these differences appear?

The proposed answers have been controversial and point to several possibilities: (a) The tests are biased and unfair. Current IQ tests may reflect mainstream life and the experiences of Caucasian Americans to a greater extent than they reflect the experiences of most African Americans or Hispanics. (b) Differences in IQ scores can be attributed to environmental factors, such as available economic or educational opportunities, or the extent to which one is exposed to a wide range of stimuli. (c) There are genetic factors that place some groups at a disadvantage. (d) There are cultural differences in motivation and attitudes about test performance.

Where do psychologists stand on the issue of racial/ethnic differences in IQ? They stand in a position of considerable uncertainty. For one thing, even the very concept of race has been challenged as a meaningful descriptor of people (Nguyen & Ryan, 2008; Sternberg, Grigorenko, & Kidd, 2005). Sternberg et al. argue that because race is a social construction, the argument over race and intelligence may have social value but not scientific value. And the argument over the causes of any racial differences may someday become moot. Among other things, the gap between African Americans and Caucasians on intelligence tests has been closing (Dickens & Flynn, 2006; Williams & Ceci, 1997). The narrowing of the gap is related more to gains by African Americans than to declines by Caucasians.

Extremes of Intelligence

When we look at the IQ scores earned by large, random samples of people, we find that they are distributed in a predictable pattern. The most frequently occurring score is the average score, 100. Most other earned scores are close to this average. In fact, about 95 percent of all IQ scores fall between 70 and 130 (see Figure 7.1). We end this chapter by considering those individuals who score at the extremes. People in these two "tails" of the IQ distribution are at opposite ends of a spectrum, but they do share certain attributes, including a certain sense of "differentness." Children and adolescents who are either intellectually gifted or intellectually disabled "have in common a desire, reinforced by well-meaning adults and peers, to 'be like everyone else,' that is, to be more like the norm" (Robinson, Zigler, & Gallagher, 2000 p. 1413).

There are several ways in which a person can be gifted. As we have seen, many contemporary theories of intelligence speak of intelligences. In all cases, however, there is the expectation that a gifted individual can do something better, with more precision, more impact than can most of us. People can be gifted (we often say "talented") in as many human endeavors as one can imagine. There are gifted musicians, athletes, glassblowers, ballet dancers, public speakers, nurturers, and racecar drivers. Such people are said to be "gifted" because they excel at their task, whatever it might be. But here we are talking about intelligence, in particular, intelligence of an academic sort—the sort measured by IQ tests. The intellectually gifted are people of exceptionally high IQ, with scores of 130 or above. Some reserve the label "gifted" for those with IQs above 135. In either case, we are dealing with a very small portion of the population: fewer than 3 percent.

How can we describe intellectually gifted individuals? Actually, there have been few large-scale attempts to understand the cognitive processing of people at the very upper end of the IQ distribution (Winner, 2000). A lot of what we do know about the mentally gifted comes from a study begun by Lewis M. Terman in the early 1920s. Terman supervised the testing of more than 250,000 children throughout California. His research group at Stanford University focused on those who earned the highest

From childhood to adolescence to adulthood to old age, a person's measured IQ is not likely to change very much. What may very well change as we age is the nature of our intelligence, that is, what we know, not how much we know.

scores, 1,528 in all, each with an IQ above 135. Lewis Terman died in 1956, but the study of those gifted individuals who were between the ages of 8 and 12 in 1922 continued. Since their inclusion in the study, and at regular intervals, they continued to be retested, surveyed, and interviewed by psychologists and others (Friedman et al., 1995).

Most of Terman's results fly in the face of the classic stereotype of the bright child as a skinny, anxious, clumsy, sickly kid who wears thick glasses (Sears & Barbee, 1977). In fact, if there is any overall conclusion to draw from the Terman-Stanford study, it may be that, in general, gifted children experience advantages in virtually everything. They are taller, faster, better coordinated, have better eyesight, fewer emotional problems, and tend to stay married longer than average. These findings have been confirmed by other researchers, studying different samples of subjects (Deary et al., 2007; Gottfredson, 2004; Gottfredson & Deary, 2004; Winner, 1996, 2000). Many obvious things are also true: The mentally gifted received more education; found better, higher-paying jobs; and had brighter children than did people of average intelligence. However, if we have learned anything by now, it is that we shouldn't overgeneralize. Not all of Terman's children (occasionally referred to as *Termites*) grew up to be rich and famous or live happily ever after. Many did, but not all.

Intellectual disability is as a disorder involving deficits of intellectual and adaptive functioning as well as deficits in conceptual, social, and practical domains with an onset during the developmental period. You will notice that we have used the term *intellectual disability* instead of *mental retardation*. These days, the term *intellectually disabled* has replaced the narrow term *mentally retarded* (Schalock, Luckasson, & Shogren, 2007). Although intelligence, as measured by IQ tests, has been used to confirm suspected cases of intellectual disability, the modern definition includes other dimensions. In fact, there are three criteria for diagnosing intellectual disability: intellectual functioning, adaptive functioning, and onset (American Psychiatric Association, 2013). *Developmental disability* is a related category of disorders. Developmental disability is a set of disorders characterized by difficulties in areas including but not limited to learning, behavior, and self-care (National Health Interview Survey, 2017).

Intellectual disability—a disorder involving deficits of intellectual and adaptive functioning as well as deficits in conceptual, social, and practical domains with an onset during the developmental period.

The IQ cutoff for intellectual disability is usually taken to be 70, with IQs between 70 and 85 considered "borderline." These scores are *suggested* limits. Given what we know about IQ tests, it is silly to claim after one administration of a test that a person with an IQ of 69 is intellectually disabled, while someone with an IQ of 71 is not. A diagnosis of intellectual disability is not (or should not be) made on the basis of IQ score alone. According to the American Association on Intellectual and Developmental Disabilities (2018), the symptoms of the below-average intellectual functioning must show up before age 18.

The number of people with intellectual disability is very large. Approximately 6.5 million Americans have some form of intellectual disability. Around 545,000 of these individuals are between the ages of 6 and 21 (National Down Syndrome Society, 2018). Most of these individuals have a mild form of intellectual disability. According to the National Health Interview Survey (2017), the incidence of developmental disability is on the rise. Between 2014 and 2016, the incidence increased from 5.76 percent to 6.99 percent. Fortunately, however, the incidence of intellectual disability did not increase during the same time period.

The extent to which normal levels of intelligence are inherited is open to debate. Some types of intellectual disability, however, are genetic in origin (Plomin & McGuffin, 2003). One of the best examples is the intellectual disability accompanying *Down syndrome*, first described in 1866. No one knows exactly why it happens, but occasionally a fetus develops with 47 chromosomes, instead of the usual 46 that combine to create 23 pairs. It is known that Down syndrome is more likely to occur as the age of either parent increases. The physical signs are well known: small, round skull; flattened face; large tongue; short, broad nose; broad hands; and short, stubby fingers. Children with Down syndrome experience delayed behavioral development.

Fragile X syndrome is a variety of intellectual disability with a genetic basis that was discovered in the late 1960s (Bregman et al., 1987; Kaufman & Reiss, 1999). Although it can occur in females, it is found primarily in males. Males with fragile X syndrome usually have long faces, big ears, and, as adults, large testes. Individuals with this form of intellectual disability have difficulty processing sequences of events, which means that they have problems with language. A curiosity is that males with Down syndrome show a gradual but steady decrease in IQ scores with age; males with fragile X syndrome show their most noticeable declines during puberty.

Most cases of intellectual disability do not have obvious causes. About one-half to three-quarters of intellectual disability cases do not have known biological or genetic causes.

As strange—and as frustrating—as it may be, there are still many more questions about how best to accommodate exceptional children with intellectual deficits than there are answers. For example, is mainstreaming, placing mildly intellectually disabled and borderline children in regular classroom settings, a beneficial practice? Is it any better than segregating exceptional children in special schools or special classrooms? As yet, there is simply no clear-cut evidence one way or the other.

There is greater hope in the area of prevention. As we all continue to appreciate the influences of the prenatal environment on the development of cognitive abilities, mothers and fathers can be better educated about how their behaviors affect the development of their unborn children.

STUDY CHECK

What does it mean to be "intellectually gifted" or an "individual with an intellectual disability," and what are some of the causes of the latter?

THINKING CRITICALLY

Imagine that you were a teacher of a 6th-grade class. How do you think you would deal with having two students with IQ scores of 140 or higher? How would you deal with having two students with IQ scores of, say, 60?

Chapter Summary

What is meant by "thinking," and to what extent does it involve concepts, reasoning, and problem solving?
Thinking is a general term that refers to the use of perceptions, ideas, and memories—cognitive processes not tied to direct experience. Thinking also involves the manipulation of concepts—the mental representations of categories or classes of events and of objects. Thinking is often taken to be synonymous with problem-solving and reasoning. Reasoning is a matter of coming to conclusions that are based either on a set of general principles (deductive reasoning) or on a set of specific acquired facts and observations (inductive reasoning).

What is a problem, and how do well-defined and ill-defined problems differ?
A problem has three components: (a) an initial state—the situation as it exists, (b) a goal state—the situation as the problem-solver would like it to be, and (c) routes or strategies for getting from the initial state to the goal state. Whether a problem is well defined or ill-defined is a matter of the extent to which the elements of the initial state and goal state are well-delineated and clearly understood by the problem-solver. An example of a well-defined problem might be that which you face when a familiar route home from campus is blocked. An example of an ill-defined

problem might be that which you face when you have to write a term paper on the topic of your choice.

What are the defining characteristics of language?
Language is a complex and creative cognitive skill used for communication. A language consists of a large number of arbitrary symbols (usually words) that are combined in accordance with certain rules to stand for, or label, our conceptualization of objects and events that have meaning for users of that language. The use of language is a generative process that, among other things, allows us to communicate about the "not here" and the "not now."

How are the rules and structures of language reflected in the use of phonemes, morphemes, and syntax?
A phoneme is the smallest unit of sound in the spoken form of a language (i.e., a speech sound). How phonemes can be combined in a language follows strict rules. Morphemes are the smallest units of meaning in a language, including words, prefixes, and suffixes. How morphemes are ordered, or structured, in language affects their meaning. Syntax refers to the rules that govern the way morphemes are ordered, or structured, to produce sentences. Language speakers are competent in the use of these rules, even though they may not be able to state them explicitly. We can determine intuitively (without being able to explain why) when utterances are syntactically correct and when they are not. We can tell when two sentences that take different forms are communicating the same idea or message. We can identify ambiguous sentences and can often remove that ambiguity, but only when we are aware of a larger context in which the utterance occurred.

What is the study of pragmatics, and what does it tell us about language use?
Pragmatics is the study of how the social situation, or context, in which language is used influences the meaning of what is being said. An appreciation of that context allows us to recognize the use of sarcasm, simile, metaphor, and the like.

How do the theoretical and operational definitions of intelligence differ?
Theoretically, intelligence is said to be the capacity of an individual to understand the world and use resourcefulness to cope with its challenges. Operationally, intelligence can be defined as that which intelligence tests measure.

What are the models of intelligence offered by Gardner and Sternberg?
Gardner proposes a theory of multiple intelligences—different, autonomous ways in which a person may be intelligent, including mathematical/logical, verbal/linguistic, spatial, musical, body-kinesthetic, interpersonal, intrapersonal, and naturalistic abilities. Sternberg focuses on how one uses intelligence and argues for an organized set of three cognitive processes, working together, and present in individuals to varying degrees. His three components are: (a) analytic—involving analyzing, comparing, judging, and evaluating ideas; (b) practical—involving what it takes to solve real problems in the real world; and (c) creative—involving the discovery of new or different solutions to problems.

What is emotional intelligence?
Emotional intelligence is characterized by four sets of skills: (1) managing emotions so as to attain specific goals; (2) understanding emotions, emotional language, and the signals conveyed by emotions; (3) using emotions to facilitate thinking; and (4) perceiving emotions accurately in oneself and others.

What is a psychological test, and by what criteria is the quality or value of a test judged?
A psychological test is an objective, standardized measure of a sample of behavior. To be a "good," quality test, an instrument must demonstrate: (a) reliability—that it measures something consistently, (b) validity—that it measures what it says it's measuring, and (c) adequate norms that can be used to assign meaning to an individual score.

How was IQ calculated when it was first introduced, and how is it calculated today?
The IQ, or intelligence quotient, was originally determined by dividing an individual's mental age (MA), as determined by testing, by that individual's chronological age (CA), and multiplying the result by 100. The formula is IQ = MA/CA x 100. IQ scores are now determined by comparing the test score of an individual with the scores earned by large norm groups of other people of the same age. By definition, if a person earns the same test score as the average of the norm group, his or her IQ is 100.

What are the *Stanford-Binet Intelligence Scales* and the *Wechsler Adult Intelligence Scale*?
First published in 1905, the *Stanford-Binet* is the oldest test of general intelligence. Its most recent revision yields an overall score ("g"), as well as scores for a number of abilities assumed to underlie general intelligence. The test is individually administered, and it consists of subtests, each assessing a specific cognitive task. Scores on the test compare the performance of an individual to that of others of the same age level.

The three Wechsler scales are individually administered tests of general intelligence, each appropriate for a specific age group. The *Wechsler Adult Intelligence Scale (WAIS)* is used for persons between 16 and 74 years of age. The WAIS consists of verbal and performance subtests of varied content. Hence, three scores can be determined: an overall score, a score on the verbal subtests, and a score on the performance subtests. Scores on the Wechsler tests are standard scores, comparing one's abilities to those of others of the same age.

What does it mean to be "intellectually gifted" or an "individual with an intellectual disability," and what are some of the causes of the latter?
Giftedness can mean several things, in addition to overall intellectual ability as measured by IQ tests (usually an IQ over 130 or 135). Other abilities in which individuals may be gifted include psychomotor skills, the visual and performing arts, leadership, creativity, and abilities in specific academic areas. The Terman-Stanford research tells us that people who are mentally gifted experience other physical, educational, social, and economic advantages.

Intellectual disability is indicated by below-average intellectual functioning (IQ scores of less than 70), originating before the age of 18, and associated with impairment in adaptive behavior (as well as academic behaviors). In addition to genetic causes (as in Down syndrome and fragile X syndrome), most of the known causes of intellectual disability involve the health of the parents at conception, and the care of the mother and fetus during pregnancy and delivery. Drug use, lack of oxygen, and poor nutrition have been implicated in intellectual disability. In other words, many causes of intellectual disability appear to be preventable.

Key Terms

Thinking (p. 148)
Concepts (p. 148)
Prototypes (p. 149)
Reasoning (p. 149)
Inductive reasoning (p. 149)
Deductive reasoning (p. 149)
Problem (p. 150)
Language (p. 152)
Arbitrary symbolic reference (p. 153)
Phonemes (p. 154)
Semantics (p. 154)

Morphemes (p. 154)
Syntax (p. 154)
Grammar (p. 154)
Pragmatics (p. 155)
Intelligence (p. 156)
Emotional intelligence (p. 158)
Psychological test (p. 159)
Test norms (p. 159)
IQ (Intelligence Quotient) (p. 160)
Deviation IQ (p. 160)
Intellectual disability (p. 165)

Motivation and Emotion

Source: fizkes/Shutterstock

Questions You Will Be Able to Answer

After reading Chapter 8, you should be able to answer the following questions:

- How do psychologists define motivation, and how have they used the concepts of instincts, needs, and drives to account for motivated behaviors?
- How can incentives, homeostasis, arousal, and cognitive dissonance be useful in explaining motivated behaviors?
- What are the needs for achievement, power, affiliation, and intimacy?
- What do psychologists mean when they talk about emotion?
- What has become of attempts to identify and classify basic emotions?
- How do the autonomic nervous system and the brain affect emotional reactions?
- What are some of the factors involved in the communication of an emotional state from one organism to another?

Preview

In this chapter, we address some important theoretical and practical issues. For the first time, our focus will be on questions that begin with **why**. "Why did she *do* that (as opposed to her doing nothing)?" "Why did she do *that* (as opposed to her doing something else)?" "Why does she *keep doing* that (as opposed to her stopping)?" As you can see, the study of motivation gets us involved with attempts to explain the causes of certain behaviors.

We begin with a definition of motivation and then explore several different approaches to understanding motivation—different "theories of motivation," if you will. As is so often the case, you will see that no one approach tells us all we would like to know about motivation, but each adds something to our appreciation of motivated behavior. This section will summarize instincts, needs and drives, incentives, homeostasis, arousal, and cognitive dissonance as concepts that can explain why we do what we do and keep on doing it. Then we will look at some motives that have no clear biological basis. They are called "psychologically based motives," and include the needs for achievement, power, and affiliation.

Since its emergence in the late 1800s, psychology has included the study of emotions as part of its subject matter. Psychologists have learned a great deal about emotional reactions, but answers to some very fundamental questions have remained elusive. We wish that psychologists could tell us just what emotions are and where they come from. We want to know how to increase the number and intensity of pleasant emotions and decrease our experience of unpleasant ones. Some emotional reactions do seem quite unpleasant: fear, shame, jealousy, and rage. Just the same, we would not want to give up our ability to experience emotions. To do so would be to surrender the likes of love, joy, satisfaction, and ecstasy. Life without the color of emotion would be flat and drab.

We will begin this discussion as we have begun others, by trying to generate an acceptable working definition. With a definition in hand, we will look at some attempts to organize or classify the various emotions. This exercise will bring up the notion of basic emotions, what they might be, and if they even exist. We then turn to the physiological bases of emotions. Emotional reactions require the central nervous system, to be sure, but it is the autonomic nervous systems that are most intimately involved. Finally, we will discuss the outward display of emotion. This will take us first to a consideration of how internal emotional states are communicated from one organism to another.

Explaining What Motivates Us

Arousal—an organism's level of activation or excitement.

Motivation—the process that arouses, directs, and maintains behavior.

Motivation involves two sub-processes. The first is arousal—an organism's level of activation or excitement. Here we are using the word "motivation" to describe a force that initiates behaviors, gets an organism going, energized enough to do something and keep doing it. The second sub-process provides direction, or focus, to the organism's behaviors. More than being aroused and active, a motivated organism's behavior is in some way purposeful or goal-directed. Thus, motivation is the process that arouses, directs, and maintains behavior.

From its earliest days, psychology has tried to find some systematic theory to summarize and organize what various motivational states have in common. Psychologists have struggled to find one general theory that could be used to account for why organisms tend to do what they do. Here we will review some of these theories in a somewhat chronological order.

Instincts

During the 1880s, psychologists often explained behaviors in terms of **instincts**—unlearned, complex patterns of behavior that occur in the presence of certain stimuli. Why do birds build nests? A nest-building instinct. When conditions are right, birds build nests. It is what birds do. Why do salmon swim upstream to mate? Instinct. Swimming upstream at mating season is part of what it means to be a salmon. These behaviors can be modified by experience, but the force behind them is unlearned or instinctive. It is simply part of their nature to engage in these behaviors.

Explaining why and how birds build their nests—in very much the same sort of way every time—can be handled rather easily by attributing the behavior to instinct.

Instincts may be useful for explaining the behaviors of birds and salmon, but what about people? William James (1890) reasoned that because they are more complex, humans had to have more instincts than do "lower" animals. William McDougall (1908) championed the instinctual explanation of human behavior. He said that human behaviors were motivated by 11 basic instincts: repulsion, curiosity, flight, reproduction, gregariousness, acquisitiveness, parenting, construction, self-assertion, self-abasement, and pugnacity. Soon, McDougall had to extend his list to include 18 instincts. As different behaviors required explanation, new instincts were devised to explain them.

Instincts—unlearned, complex patterns of behavior that occur in the presence of certain stimuli.

As lists of human instincts got longer and longer, trying to account for more and more behaviors, the problem with this approach became obvious. Particularly for humans, explaining behavior patterns by alluding to instinct only re-labeled them and did not explain anything at all. Still, those psychologists who argued for instincts did introduce, and draw attention to, an idea very much with us today: We may engage in some behaviors for reasons that are basically biological, or physiological, and more inherited than learned.

Needs and Drives

An approach that provided an alternative to explaining behavior in terms of instincts was one that attempted to explain the whys of behavior in terms of needs and drives. We will look at two such theories.

Clark Hull's ideas about motivation were dominant in the 1940s and 1950s (Hull, 1943). In Hull's system, a **need** is defined as a lack or shortage of some biological essential that is required for survival. A need arises from deprivation. When an organism is kept from food, it develops a need for food. Needs give rise to drives. A **drive** is a state of tension, arousal, or activation. If an organism is in a drive state, it is aroused and directed to engage in some behavior to satisfy the drive by reducing the underlying need. Needs produce tensions (drives) that the organism seeks to reduce; hence, this approach is referred to in terms of drive reduction.

Need—a lack or shortage of some biological essential that is required for survival.

Drive—a state of tension, arousal, or activation.

Whereas instincts are tied to specific patterns of behavior, needs and drives are not. They can be used to explain why we do what we do and still allow for the influence of experience and the environment. Going without food may give rise to a need, which in turn gives rise to a drive, but how that drive is expressed in behavior is influenced by an organism's experiences and learning history. For example, someone from a hunting culture would probably go out and hunt for his or her food. In Western culture, a person might head for the drive-through window at a fast-food restaurant.

A problem with a drive-reduction approach centers on the biological nature of needs. To claim that needs result only from biological deprivations seems overly restrictive. It may be that not all of the drives that activate a person's behavior are based on biological needs. Humans often engage in behaviors to satisfy learned drives. A drive derived from an organism's learning experience is called a **secondary drive**, as opposed to a **primary drive**, which is based on unlearned, physiological needs. In fact, most of the drives that arouse and direct your behavior have little to do with biology. You may feel you need a

Secondary drive—a drive derived from an organism's learning experience.

Primary drive—a drive based on unlearned, physiological needs.

It is difficult to argue for a "need to put one's life in danger by climbing ice cliffs." The behavior hardly seems to be one that reduces tension.

new car this year. Your brother may convince himself that he needs a new set of golf clubs, and you'll both work very hard to save the money to buy what you need. You may say you are "driven," but it's difficult to imagine how your new car or your brother's golf clubs could be satisfying some sort of biological need. A lot of advertising is directed at trying to convince people that certain products and services are needed, even though, in fact, they will have very little impact on survival.

A related complication is that organisms often continue behaving even after their biological needs appear to be met. Drives are states of arousal or tension, and the claim is that we behave as we do in order to reduce tension or arousal. Yet we know that skydivers jump out of airplanes, mountain climbers risk life and limb to scale sheer cliffs of stone, monkeys play with mechanical puzzles even when solving those puzzles leads to no other reward, and children explore the pots and pans in kitchen cabinets even when repeatedly told not to. These actions do not appear to be reducing tension, do they? Perhaps these organisms are trying to satisfy a curiosity drive, or an exploration drive, or a manipulation drive. But then we run the risk of trying to explain why people behave as they do by generating longer and longer lists of drives—the same problem that comes up when we try to explain behavior in terms of instinct.

So what do these complications mean? It seems that people often *do* behave in ways that reduce drives and thereby satisfy needs. How drives are satisfied, or needs are reduced, may reflect each organism's learning history. The concept of drive reduction is a useful one and is still very much with us in psychology, but it cannot be accepted as a complete explanation for motivated behaviors.

Abraham Maslow believed that the needs that motivate human action are few and are arranged hierarchically (Maslow, 1943, 1970). **Figure 8.1** summarizes this hierarchy of needs.

Maslow's approach is basically a stage theory. It proposes that what motivates us first are *physiological needs*, including the basic needs related to survival—food, water, and shelter. Until these needs are met, there is no reason to suspect that an individual will be concerned with anything else. Once physiological needs are under control, a person is still motivated, but now by *safety needs*—the need to feel secure, protected from dangers that might arise in the future. We are now motivated to see to it that the cupboard has food for later, we won't freeze this winter, and there's enough money saved to protect against sudden calamity. The hierarchical nature of this theory is already clear. We are not going to worry about what we'll be eating tomorrow if there's not enough to eat today, but if today's needs are taken care of, we can then focus on the future.

Once safety needs are met, concern shifts to *love and belongingness*, a need for someone else to care about us. If these needs are satisfied, then our concern shifts to *esteem*. Our aim is to be recognized for our achievements and efforts. These needs are not physiological, but social. Our behaviors are motivated by our awareness of others and a concern for their approval. A person moves on to higher stages in the hierarchy only if needs at lower stages are met. Ultimately, we may reach the highest stage in Maslow's hierarchy: the need for *self-actualization*. We self-actualize when we become the best we can be, taking the fullest advantage of our potential. We are self-actualizing when we try to be as creative or productive as possible. Self-actualization may be described as "the tendency of an organism to grow from a simple entity to a complex one, to move from dependence toward independence, from fixity and rigidity to a process of change and freedom of expression" (Pervin & John, 2001, p. 177).

It should be clear to you, as it was to Maslow, that many people never make it to the self-actualization stage in the hierarchy of needs. There are millions of people in this

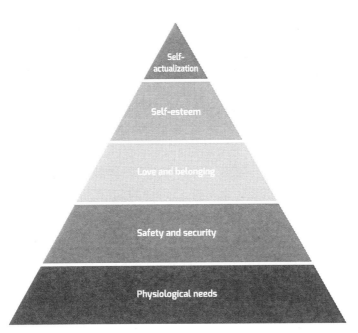

FIGURE 8.1 Maslow's Hierarchy of Needs

Abraham Maslow assumed that our needs are arranged in a hierarchy, with our most powerful needs at the bottom. We will be weakly motivated by higher needs until our lower needs are met.

Source: Pyty/Shutterstock.

world who have great difficulty dealing with the very lowest stages and who never have the time, energy, or opportunity to be concerned with such issues as belongingness or self-esteem, much less self-actualization.

As a comprehensive theory of human motivation, Maslow's hierarchy has some problems. The truth of the matter is that there is little research support for Maslow's approach to ranking needs in a hierarchy. Perhaps the biggest stumbling block is the idea that anyone can assign ranks to needs and put them in a neat order, regardless of what that order may be. Some people are motivated in ways that violate the ordered-stage approach. Individuals will, for example, freely give up satisfying basic survival needs for the sake of "higher" principles (as in hunger strikes). For the sake of love, people may abandon their own needs for safety and security.

STUDY CHECK

How do psychologists define *motivation*, and how have they used the concepts of instincts, needs, and drives to account for motivated behaviors?

THINKING CRITICALLY

When they are hungry, chickens—even very young chickens—peck at the ground as if searching for grain. How might you determine whether this behavior pattern is instinctive or learned?

Culture, Needs, and Job Performance

In many ways, Maslow's arrangement of needs in a hierarchical fashion reflects the values of Western culture, particularly those that focus on the notion of the individual working hard to overcome obstacles and to achieve. One can hardly expect people to be motivated to grow and achieve success if they are concerned about their very survival on a day-to-day basis. When people's needs for safety, belonging, and esteem are fulfilled, they don't just die, unmotivated to do anything else.

In the past decades, businesses have become increasingly global in nature. Because of this, it is important to consider how different motives, such as Maslow's hierarchy of needs, might relate to worker performance in different cultural contexts (Mirabela & Madela, 2013). Mirabela and Madela suggest, for example, that worker concerns for physiological and safety needs may be most relevant in countries where uncertainty exists in the economy (e.g., Greece). On the other hand, belongingness may be more important in more "feminine" cultures (e.g., Sweden), and esteem may be more important in more "masculine" cultures (e.g., Hungary). They also argue that theories of motivation like Maslow's may only be relevant in the cultural context within which they were developed.

How might we apply Maslow's hierarchy of needs to the workplace? Let's say that Samantha is a mid-level manager in a bank, and her manager wants to motivate her to be more productive. She makes more than enough money to pay for food and pay the rent (physiological and safety needs are met). Samantha's manager might try to figure out if Samantha's social needs are being met. Is she connected with other co-workers and customers? If her social needs on the job are being met, then the manager might try to motivate Samantha by satisfying her esteem needs, perhaps by developing an employee recognition program (e.g., "Employee of the Month").

When considering the relationship between worker needs and job motivation, it is important to understand that not all needs relate to one's job motivation. For example, Maslow's need for self-actualization may have nothing to do with one's motivation as an auto worker. When assessing the relationship between needs and job motivation, we must consider the salience of the needs with respect to the job (Sahoo, Sahoo, & Das, 2011). A salient need is one that is closely associated with one's job. Sahoo et al. studied the relationship between need salience and job motivation in four studies of workers in India. They found that only salient needs correlated significantly with job motivation. Nonsalient needs were not related to job motivation. Across

cultures, workers may not be strongly motivated by individualistic needs such as the need for self-esteem or self-actualization, but different needs, salient to the job itself, may motivate workers.

Beyond Maslow's theory, research shows cultural differences in what motivates workers to perform their jobs well. For example, Jain, Normand, and Kanungo (1979) compared English-speaking and French-speaking hospital workers in Canada. Participants filled out a questionnaire measuring several job motivating factors. Jain et al. found that both groups of workers placed high levels of importance on having an interesting job. However, English-speaking workers attached more importance to having an interesting job than their French-speaking counterparts. They also attached more importance to job autonomy and achievement than the French-speaking workers. On the other hand, French-speaking workers placed more importance on job security, earnings, and good working conditions than English-speaking workers.

Some cultures place a great deal of emphasis on individualism (e.g., Western cultures such as Canada and the United States), whereas others place emphasis on collectivism (e.g., Korea, Japan). Researchers on cross-cultural differences in job motivation and satisfaction distinguish between two types of efficacy related to job satisfaction and consequent productivity. One is *perceived collective efficacy*, which is essentially a shared belief among group members in their collective ability to perform tasks successfully (Bandura, 1997). The other is *personal self-efficacy*, which is a belief in one's personal abilities to perform his or her job (Klassen, Usher, & Bong, 2010). Klassen et al. compared North American (U.S., Canadian) and South Korean teachers on the extent to which these factors relate to job satisfaction and performance. They found that collective efficacy was significantly related to job satisfaction for the Korean teachers but not for the North American teachers. Interestingly, American teachers rated collective teaching strategies higher than Canadian teachers. Klassen et al. (p. 480) concluded that "In cultures that value the group over and above the individual, being a collectivist appears to influence satisfaction from work." They suggest that this mindset may come from collectivist cultures placing greater emphasis on avoiding conflict and promoting group harmony than individualist cultures. Findings such as these suggest that it is important to take cultural context into account when considering how motivational factors relate to the behavior of individuals in the workplace (Klassen et al., 2010).

Incentives

One alternative to a drive-reduction approach to motivation focuses on the end state, or goal, of behavior, not needs or drives within the organism. In this view, external stimuli serve as motivating agents, or incentives, for behavior. Incentives are external events that are said to pull our behavior from without, as opposed to drives, which are internal events that push our behavior from within. We are pushed by drives, pulled by incentives.

When a mountain climber says she climbs a mountain "because it is there," she is indicating that she is being motivated by an incentive. After enjoying a large meal, we may order a piece of cherry cheesecake, surely not because we need it in any physiological sense, but because it's there on the dessert cart and looks so good (and because previous experience tells us that it is likely to taste good as well).

Some parents want to know how to motivate their children to clean up their rooms. We can interpret this case in terms of establishing goals or incentives. What the parents really want is a clean room, and they would like to have the child do the cleaning. What those parents want to know is how they can get their child to value, work for, and be reinforced by a clean room. If they want the child to be motivated to clean the room, the child needs to learn the value or incentive of having a clean room. How to teach a child that a clean room is a thing to be valued is another story, involving other incentives the child does value.

If you think this sounds like our discussion of operant conditioning, you are right. Remember, the basic tenet of operant conditioning is that behaviors are controlled by their consequences. We tend to do (are motivated to do) what leads to reinforcement (positive incentives), and we tend not to do what leads to punishment or failure of reinforcement (negative incentives).

Some of our behaviors may be explained in terms of incentives. We reach out for and consume a hot fudge sundae not because we need it in any way, or are driven to, but because we are pulled to—it just looks so good, and past experience tells us that it is going to taste so good. This is the "incentive" approach to motivation.

Incentives—external stimuli that serve as motivating agents for behavior.

Balance or Equilibrium

A concept that has proven useful in understanding motivation is balance or equilibrium. The idea is that we are motivated to reach and maintain a state of balance. But what are we motivated to balance? Sometimes maintaining balance involves physiological processes that need to be kept at some level, or within a restricted range of activity. Sometimes equilibrium is required among our thoughts or cognitions. There are three approaches to motivation that emphasize maintaining a state of equilibrium, or optimal level of functioning: homeostasis, arousal, and cognitive dissonance.

One of the first references to a need for equilibrium can be found in the work of Walter Cannon (1932). Cannon referred to homeostasis—a state of balance within our internal physiological reactions. The idea is that each of our physiological processes has a balanced set point of operation. An organism's set point is a level of activity that is "normal or most suitable." When anything upsets this balance, we become motivated, driven to do what we can to return to our set point, that optimal homeostatic level of activity. If we drift only slightly from our set point, our physiological mechanisms return us to homeostasis without our awareness. If automatic processes are unsuccessful, we may have to take action, motivated by the drive to maintain homeostasis.

Everyone has normal, set levels for body temperature, blood pressure, heart rate, metabolism (the rate at which energy is used by bodily functions), and so on. If any of these processes deviate from their set point, we become motivated to do something to return us to our state of balance. Cannon's concept of homeostasis was devised to explain physiological processes, but the ideas of balance and optimal level of operation have been applied to psychological processes as well.

Homeostasis—a state of balance within our internal physiological reactions.

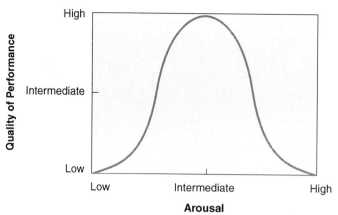

FIGURE 8.2 The Yerkes-Dodson Law

The graph depicts the relationship between arousal level and task performance for a moderately difficult task. Note that the best performance occurs at a moderate level of arousal. Performance declines when arousal is below or above that level.

Arousal, as we noted earlier, is defined as an overall level of activation or excitement. A person's level of arousal may change from day to day and within the same day. After a good night's sleep and a brisk morning shower, your arousal level may be high. (It also may be high as your instructor moves through class handing out exams.) Late at night, after a busy day at school, your level of arousal may be quite low. Your arousal level is at its lowest when you are in the deepest stages of sleep.

Arousal theories of motivation claim that there is an optimal level of arousal (an "arousal set point") that organisms are motivated to maintain. Drive-reduction theories, remember, argue that we are motivated to reduce tension or arousal by satisfying the needs that give rise to drives. Arousal theories argue that sometimes we seek out ways to increase arousal in order to maintain our optimal arousal level. If you find yourself bored and in a rut, the idea of going to an action-adventure movie may seem like a good one. On the other hand, if you have had a very busy, hectic day, just staying at home doing nothing may sound appealing.

This approach is like Cannon's idea of homeostasis but in slightly more general terms. It suggests that for any situation there is a "best," or most efficient, level of arousal. To do well on an exam, for example, requires that a student have a certain level of arousal. If a student is tired, bored, or just doesn't care, we can expect a poor performance. If, on the other hand, a student is so worried, so uptight and anxious that she or he can barely function, we also can expect a poor exam score. The relation between arousal and the efficiency of performance is depicted in **Figure 8.2**.

An interesting twist on the theory of arousal is that, for some reason, optimal levels of arousal vary widely from person to person. Some people seem to need and seek particularly high levels of arousal and excitement in their lives. Psychologists call such people "sensation seekers." They enjoy skydiving or mountain climbing and look forward to the challenge of driving in heavy city traffic. Some evidence suggests that there may be a genetic basis for individual differences in sensation-seeking, or risk-taking (Ebstein et al., 1996).

Now let's consider the point of view that we are motivated to maintain a state of balance among ideas or beliefs (our cognitions), what Leon Festinger (1957) called a state of consonance among our cognitions.

You believe yourself to be a pretty good student. You study hard for an exam in biology and think you are prepared. You judge the exam to be a fairly easy one. But when you get your exam paper back, you discover you failed the test! Now that's hard to accept. You believe that you studied adequately and that the test wasn't difficult. But now you also know you failed the test. Here are cognitions that do not fit together. "I am a good student and studied, but I failed the exam!" These cognitions do not fit together; they are not balanced. You are experiencing **cognitive dissonance**—a state of tension or discomfort that

Cognitive dissonance—a state of tension or discomfort that exists when we hold and are aware of inconsistent cognitions.

exists when we hold and are aware of inconsistent cognitions. When this occurs, we are motivated to bring about a change in our system of cognitions. You may come to believe you are not such a good student after all. You may come to believe that your exam was unfairly graded. Or you may come to believe you are a poor judge of an exam's difficulty. This theory doesn't predict *what* will happen, but it does predict that cognitive dissonance will produce motivation to return to a balanced state of cognitive consonance.

Almost all smokers experience cognitive dissonance. They *know* that smoking is a dangerous habit, yet they continue to smoke. Some reduce their dissonance by convincing themselves that, although smoking is bad for a person's health in general, it really isn't that bad for them in particular, at least not when compared to perceived "benefits." Another dissonance reducer is convincing one's self that if they stopped smoking, they would gain weight—which is seldom true (White, McKee, & O'Malley, 2007).

Putting It Together: Applying Motivational Concepts

You had a great time. You and your friends spent the day backpacking in the mountains. The signs of spring were everywhere, and you enjoyed every minute. After a full day in the fresh mountain air, no one was terribly choosy about what to have for dinner. Everyone enjoyed large servings of beef stew and baked beans from the can. You even found room for dessert: toasted marshmallows and chocolate squeezed between two graham crackers.

As your friends settle around the campfire and darkness just begins to overtake the campsite, you excuse yourself. You need to walk off some of that dinner, so you head off to stroll down a narrow trail. As you meander down the trail, you feel totally relaxed. When you are about 200 yards from the campsite, you think you hear a strange noise in the woods off to your left. Looking back down the trail, you notice that you can barely see the campfire's glow through the trees and underbrush, even though the leaves are not yet fully formed. Well, maybe you had better not venture too much farther, perhaps just over that ridge, and then—suddenly—from behind a dense thicket, a large growling black bear appears! It takes one look at you, bares its teeth, and lets out a mighty roar! What will you do now?

In this situation, and in many similar, but less dramatic ones, we can be sure of one thing: Your reaction will involve both motivational and emotional states. You will certainly become emotional. Encountering a bear in the woods is not something that one does with reason and intellect alone. You will be motivated to do something; getting away from that bear seems reasonable. (We'll return to this meeting-a-bear-in-the-woods story shortly, when we discuss emotion.)

For now, and granting that this example is somewhat far-fetched and we'll oversimplify a bit, let's apply the approaches we have been discussing to explain your behavior. Let's say that, seeing the bear, you throw your arms straight up in the air, scream at the top of your lungs, and race back to camp as fast as you can. Your friends, still sitting around the campfire, can see and hear you coming. How might they explain your behaviors?

1. "Clearly, it's a matter of instinct. Humans have a powerful and useful instinct for avoiding large animals in the wild. In this instance, running away is just an unlearned, natural, instinctive reaction to a specific stimulus."

2. "No, I think the fear that arose upon seeing the bear created a tension—a drive—that needed to be relieved. There were several options available, but in your need to reduce your fear, you chose to run away."

3. "Why do you folks keep relying on all this internal instinct-need-drive nonsense? Previous learning, even if it was secondhand, taught you that bears in the wild are incentives to be avoided. They are negative goals. You ran back here to reach the goal of safety with us, your friends."

4. "I see your reaction as an attempt to maintain a state of equilibrium or balance. Seeing that bear was certainly an emotional experience that increased many physiological functions. Your running away was just one way to try to return those physiological functions to their normal, homeostatic levels."

5. "Why get so complicated with physiological functions? Why not just say that your overall arousal level was much higher than normal—higher than you wanted it to be—so you ran away from the bear simply to lower your level of arousal?"

6. "The same argument can be made for your cognitions—and cognitive dissonance reduction. You know that you like being safe and free of pain. You believe that bears in the woods can be very hurtful, and there's one in front of you. These two ideas are in conflict. You will do something. In this case, you chose to run away. If you believed that a bear in the woods would be afraid of you and of no potential harm, then there wouldn't have been any dissonance, and you wouldn't have run away."

STUDY CHECK

How can incentives, homeostasis, arousal, and cognitive dissonance be useful in explaining motivated behaviors?

THINKING CRITICALLY

You hear a teacher moan, "Teaching would be so much easier if my students were motivated to learn." What do you suppose that teacher is moaning about? How would you advise this teacher to motivate his or her students?

PSYCHOLOGY IN ACTION

The Hunger Motive and Eating Disorders

Our need for food is as obvious as our need for water. If we don't eat, we die. How do we know that we are hungry? When we skip a meal, we may feel a rumble in our stomachs. Are these rumblings a reliable cue for hunger? Over a century ago, researchers found that a subject's feelings of hunger correlated closely with stomach contractions (Cannon & Washburn, 1912). However, the role of stomach contractions in hunger is not quite so simple. People and animals with no stomachs and people and animals with intact stomachs eat the same amounts of food. It turns out that cues from our stomachs don't seem to be very important in *producing* our hunger drive. Researchers have identified two structures that are involved in the hunger drive: the hypothalamus and the liver. Theories of hunger that focus on the hypothalamus are *dual-center theories* because two regions in the hypothalamus are involved in food intake. The ventromedial hypothalamus is a "no-eat" center that lets us know when we've had enough, and the lateral hypothalamus is an "eat" center that gives rise to feelings of hunger (van den Pol, 1999).

We know from our own experiences that eating behaviors are influenced by factors beyond our physiology. We often respond to external cues such as how a food smells, tastes, or looks. We may not want any dessert after a large meal until the waitress shows us a piece of chocolate cake that looks so delicious. Eating that cake has nothing to do with internal physiological conditions. Sometimes we eat because the clock tells us it is "lunchtime" or "dinnertime." Other times we eat simply because others we are with are eating. This is called *socially facilitated eating*, which is not limited to humans.

Few of us eat properly all the time. Sometimes we overstuff ourselves to the point of bursting. Other times we eat less than we need. However, for most of us, this represents a normal fluctuation in our eating patterns. For some people, disruptions in eating become pathological. A person who refuses to maintain a normal weight is said to be suffering from an *eating disorder*. The two most common eating disorders are *anorexia nervosa* and *bulimia nervosa*. Although they both involve disruptions in normal eating patterns, they are separate disorders. However, a person can display symptoms of both at the same time. At least 30 million Americans of both genders and all ages suffer from eating disorders. A vast majority of these are women (National Association of Anorexia Nervosa and Associated Disorders, 2018). An alarming trend is the significant increase in eating disorders in children (Rosen, 2010). The American Academy of Pediatrics reports an increasing rate of eating disorders in boys, younger children, and children of color (Rosen, 2010).

Anorexia nervosa is characterized by an inability (or refusal) to maintain a normal body weight. It is essentially a condition of self-starvation, accompanied by a fear of becoming fat and a feeling of being overweight in spite of having a weight that is less than minimally normal for adults or less than minimally expected for children and adolescents (American Psychiatric Association, 2013). The anorexic person stays abnormally thin by eating far less, being more physically active, or both. Eating disorders have a mortality rate of nearly 20 percent. The mortality rate for anorexia is the highest for any psychological disorder. Around 5 to 10 percent of anorexics will die within 10 years, and 18 to 20 percent will die after 20 years. The good news is that the mortality rate drops to 2 to 3 percent with treatment (Mirasol Recovery Centers, 2018). Individuals aged 15 to 24 with anorexia have a risk of dying that is 10 times higher than that of same-aged peers without anorexia. Male anorexics are more likely to die from anorexia than females because the disorder is often diagnosed later in males (National Eating Disorders Association, 2018).

Bulimia nervosa (or simply, bulimia) is characterized by episodes of binge eating followed by purging. Purging usually involves self-induced vomiting or the use of laxatives to rapidly rid the body of just-eaten food (American Psychiatric Association, 2013). Binge-eating episodes are often well planned, anticipated with pleasure, and involve rapidly eating large amounts of high-calorie, sweet-tasting food. The person with bulimia is very likely to be female, upper class, and concerned about weight (Mulholland & Mintz, 2001). More than half of individuals with bulimia also have a mood disorder (e.g., depression) or an anxiety disorder (National Association of Anorexia Nervosa and Associated Disorders, 2018). Unlike a person with anorexia nervosa, a bulimic patient may maintain a normal body weight.

Eating disorders have several interacting causes. One possible cause is the value that Western cultures place on thinness. We are constantly being bombarded with messages that communicate the same theme: "To be thin is good; to be fat is bad." Many young girls idolize super-thin fashion models, dancers, and entertainers. Very few young women can hope to match the body of a super-thin supermodel. So, do these media portrayals relate to symptoms of eating disorders? There is evidence that media portrayals have a modest effect on eating disorder symptoms (Hausenblas et al., 2013). Another cause is how a person views his or her body. For example, anorexics see themselves as fat even though they are just the opposite. Also, anorexics show a greater tendency to interpret information about their bodies negatively than non-anorexics (Brockmeyer et al., 2018). Personality factors that correlate with eating disorders include strong needs for achievement and approval, and self-oriented perfectionism (Castro-Fornieles et al., 2007). There also may be physiological and genetic links. Anorexics show lower levels of serotonin and tryptophan (a precursor of serotonin) in the brain than normal-weight individuals (Gauthier et al., 2014). There is a small but significant genetic component to eating disorders. Relatives of patients with eating disorders are four to five times more likely to develop an eating disorder than are people in the general population (Kaye, Fudge, & Paulus, 2009).

Treatment for anorexia nervosa usually involves medical interventions aimed at restoring body weight and nutrition. Hospitalization may be required. Interestingly, no effective drug treatments have been found for anorexia nervosa (Barlow & Durand, 2009). Nearly all forms of psychotherapy have been tried, and all are far more likely to be successful when the patient's family is involved. When compared with individual-focused therapy, family-based treatment is significantly more effective when assessed at 6 months and 12 months after treatment (Lock et al., 2010). The outlook for bulimia nervosa is usually much better than that for anorexia, but even so, about a third of patients still have the disorder five years after initial treatment (Fairburn, Cooper, Doll, Norman, & O'Connor, 2000).

Psychologically Based Motives

As much as we might like to think otherwise, those early theorists who directed psychology's attention toward biological or physiological processes were on the right track. A good deal of our behavior *is* motivated by internal, physiological mechanisms. Without attention to these basic, physiological needs—and the drives they give rise to—we could die.

Indeed, you may be able to analyze many of your own behaviors in terms of physiologically based needs and drives. That you had breakfast this morning soon after you got up may have reflected your response to a hunger drive. That you got dressed may have been your attempt to do what you could to control your body temperature, which also may have influenced your choice of clothes. Some (biologically based) sexual motivation may also have affected what you chose to wear today. On the other hand, many of our behaviors are aroused, maintained, and directed (which is to say motivated) by forces that are not clearly biological in origin.

The hypothesis that people are motivated to varying degrees by a need to achieve was introduced to psychology in 1938 by Henry Murray. The **need to achieve (nAch)** is the acquired need to meet or exceed a standard of excellence in one's behaviors. Finding ways to measure this need to achieve and determining its implications has been the focus of David McClelland and his associates (McClelland, 1985; McClelland et al., 1953).

There are short paper-and-pencil tests for the purpose, but nAch is usually assessed by means of the *Thematic Apperception Test* (TAT). This is a test in which people are asked to tell short stories about a series of rather ambiguous pictures depicting people in various settings. The stories are interpreted and scored according to a series of objective criteria that note references to attempting difficult tasks, succeeding, being rewarded for one's efforts, setting short- and long-term goals, and so on. There are no right or wrong responses. Judgments are made about the references to achievement a person projects into the pictures as he or she tells stories about them.

One of the first things McClelland and his colleagues found was that there are consistent differences in measured levels of the need to achieve. A reliable finding about people with high needs for achievement is that, when given a choice, they attempt tasks in which success is not guaranteed (otherwise, there is no challenge) but in which there still is a reasonable chance of success. Both young children and college students who were high in nAch were observed playing a ring-toss game in which the object was to score points by tossing a small ring over a peg from a distance. The farther away from the peg one stood, the more points one could score if successful. In both studies, students with high nAch scores stood at a moderate distance from the peg. They didn't stand so close as to guarantee success, but they didn't choose to stand so far away that they would almost certainly fail. People with low achievement motivation scores tended to go to either extreme—very close, earning few points for their successes or so far away that they rarely succeeded.

People with high achievement needs are not always interested in their own success or in achievement at the expense of others. Particularly in collectivist societies, people may work very hard to achieve goals that are available only to the group of which they are a part.

McClelland would argue that you are reading this text at this moment because you are motivated by a need to achieve. You want to do well on your next exam. You want to get a good grade in this course, and you have decided that to do so you need to study the assigned text material. Some students, however, may read assignments not because they are motivated by a need to achieve, but because they are motivated by a fear of failure. In such a case, the incentive is negative (avoid an F) rather than positive (earn an A). Individuals motivated by a fear of failure tend to take few risks. They choose either tasks in which they are bound to do well or those that are virtually impossible (if the task is impossible they don't have to take responsibility and blame themselves for failures).

It seems that the need to achieve is learned, usually in early childhood. Children who show high levels of achievement motivation are those who have been encouraged in a positive way to excel ("Leslie, that grade of B is very good. You must feel proud!" versus "What! Only a B?"). Children with high needs to achieve are generally encouraged to work things out for themselves, perhaps with parental support and encouragement ("Here, Eli, see if you can do this" as opposed to "Here, dummy, let me do it; you'll never get it right!"). McClelland is convinced that achievement motivation can be acquired by almost anyone of any age, and he has developed training programs to increase achievement motivation levels.

Some people are motivated not only to excel, but also to be in control, to be in charge of both the situation and other people. In such

Someone motivated by a need to achieve (nAch) has an acquired need to meet or exceed some standard of excellence.

cases, psychologists speak of a **need for power**. Power needs are also measured by the interpretation of stories generated with the Thematic Apperception Test. Please note that a high need for power is, in itself, neither good nor bad. What matters, in an evaluative sense, is the end to which one uses power.

People with high power needs like to be admired. They prefer situations in which they can control the fates of others, usually by manipulating access to information. They present an attitude of "If you want to get this job done, you'll have to come to me to find out how to do it." People with low power needs tend to avoid situations in which others would have to depend on them and tend to be somewhat submissive in interpersonal relationships. Although the situation is changing, men have been more commonly found in positions of power than have women. At the same time, there are no reliable differences between men and women in measured needs for power.

Another psychologically based motivator is the **need for affiliation**—a need to be with others, to work with others toward some end, and to form friendships and associations. Individuals with a high affiliation need express a stronger desire to be with friends than those with a low need for affiliation. For example, college men with a high need for affiliation tend to pick living arrangements that enhance the likelihood of meeting others. As a result, men with high affiliation needs have more housemates and are more willing to share a room than those with low affiliation needs. There are some gender differences in the need for affiliation. Teenage girls, for example, express a greater desire to spend time with girlfriends; teenage boys tend to have less of a need to spend time with their peers.

One interesting implication of having a high need for affiliation is that it is often at odds with a need for power. Logic suggests that, if you are simultaneously motivated to be in control and to be with others in a truly supportive way, conflicts may arise. It is more difficult to exercise power over people whose friendship you value than it is to exercise power or control over people whose friendship is of little concern to you. It remains the case, however, that there are circumstances in which we find people who are high on both power and affiliation needs. These are often politicians who enjoy the exercise of power but who also value being public figures and being surrounded by aides and advisors. Affiliation and achievement needs are also somewhat independent. Success can be earned either with others (high affiliation) or on one's own (low affiliation).

Although psychologists are quite confident that achievement and power motives are learned and culturally determined, they are less confident about the sources of affiliation motivation. There is a reasonable argument that the need to affiliate and be with others is at least partly biologically based. We are social animals for whom social isolation is difficult, especially when we are young. On the other hand, some of the degree to which we value affiliation can be attributed to our learning experiences.

Merely affiliating with others does not always satisfy our social needs. Individuals also may have a **need for intimacy**, or a need to form and maintain close affectionate relationships. Intimacy in a relationship involves sharing and disclosing personal information, also known as self-disclosure. Individuals with a high need for intimacy tend to be warm and affectionate, and to express concern for others. There is evidence that women are more likely to show a higher need for intimacy than men (McAdams, 1989).

What happens when our needs for affiliation and intimacy are not met? In this situation, a psychological state called loneliness results. **Loneliness** is a subjective, psychological state that arises when there is a discrepancy between relationships we would like to have and those we actually have (Peplau & Perlman, 1982). Being alone does not constitute loneliness. There are people who prefer to be alone and are probably low on the needs for affiliation and intimacy. For some people, loneliness is only temporary. For others, loneliness is a chronic way of life, with few, if any, close relationships. In many cases, lonely individuals lack the social skills necessary to form intimate relationships. A lonely person may have negative expectations for social interactions. They enter social settings (for example, a party) apprehensive and expecting failure. They then act in ways that fulfill this expectation.

Need for power—a need to be in control, to be in charge of both the situation and other people.

Need for affiliation—a need to be with others, to work with others toward some end, and to form friendships and associations.

Need for intimacy—a need to form and maintain close, affectionate relationships.

Loneliness—a subjective, psychological state that arises when there is a discrepancy between relationships we would like to have and those we actually have.

STUDY CHECK

What are the needs for achievement, power, affiliation, and intimacy?

THINKING CRITICALLY

What motivated you to take this class? How do you feel about it now?

Defining and Classifying Emotions

In this section, we consider two inter-related issues: defining emotion and classifying primary emotions. The simple goal for this section is to describe human emotions as best we can. Try to recall the last time you experienced an emotion of some significance—perhaps the fear of going to the dentist, the joy of receiving an A on a classroom exam, the sadness at the death of a friend, or the anger at being unable to register for a class you wanted to take. You should be able to identify four components to your emotional reaction:

1. You experience a subjective feeling, or affect, which you may label fear, joy, sadness, anger, or the like.
2. You have a cognitive reaction; you recognize, or "know," what has happened.
3. You have an internal, physiological reaction, involving glands, hormones, and internal organs.
4. You engage in an overt behavioral reaction. You tremble as you approach the dentist's office. You run down the hallway, a broad smile on your face, waving your exam over your head. You cry at the news of your friend's death. You shake your fist and yell at the registrar when you find you can't enroll in the class of your choice.

Note that when an overt behavioral component is added to emotions, we can see how emotions and motivation are related. Emotions are motivators. To be motivated is to be aroused to action. Emotional experiences also arouse behaviors. Theorist Richard Lazarus put it this way: "Without some version of a motivational principle, emotion makes little sense, inasmuch as what is important or unimportant to us determines what we define as harmful or beneficial, hence emotional" (1991, p. 352).

There has been considerable debate in psychology (and beyond) concerning how best to define emotion (Solomon, 2003). As one researcher puts it, ". . . there is no consensus on a definition of the term emotion, and theorists and researchers use it in ways that imply different processes, meanings, and functions" (Izard, 2007, p. 260). For now, however, we need a working definition, and we will say that an **emotion** is an experience that includes a subjective feeling, a cognitive interpretation, a physiological reaction, and a behavioral expression. With this definition in mind, we turn to the related issue of how to classify emotions.

Although cognitions, physiology, and overt behavior are involved in an emotion, there is little doubt that what makes emotion special, if not unique, is the "subjective feeling" component of emotionality. Perhaps it would help if we had a scheme or plan that described and classified various emotional reactions or feelings in a systematic way.

As it turns out, there are several ways to classify emotional responses. Carroll Izard (1993, 2009) proposed a classification scheme calling for six primary emotions. Izard's six primary emotions are joy, interest, sadness, anger, disgust, and fear. Izard calls these emotions "primary" because he believes that they cannot be dissected into simpler, more basic emotions and because each is thought to have its own underlying physiological basis. Other emotions are some combination of any two or more of these six.

Emotion—an experience that includes a subjective feeling, a cognitive interpretation, a physiological reaction, and a behavioral expression.

Psychologists continue to propose theories to account for the nature of emotional reactions, but there is little agreement among them (Barrett, 2006; Barrett & Wager, 2006; Russell, 2003). Whether there are six or eight or nine primary emotions (or more or fewer) and how they might be combined to form other emotions depends on one's theoretical perspective.

The only issue on which there appears to be something of a consensus is that emotions represent a *valenced state*, meaning that emotions can be classified as being either positive (relief, joy, or happiness, and the like) or negative (fear, anger, or shame, and the like) (Russell, Bachorowski, & Fernández-Dols, 2003). Unfortunately, there isn't even complete agreement on how best to distinguish between positive and negative emotions. Fear, for example, seems like a reasonable candidate for a list of negative emotions. Yet it is clear that fear can be useful and serve to guide a person's behavior in positive or adaptive ways. After all, to be without fear in the real world can be very dangerous.

So where does this leave us? As sensible as it may sound to try to construct a system of basic, primary, emotions—particularly if such a system had a physiological or evolutionary foundation—such an attempt will prove difficult at best. One problem is that there is little agreement on just what basic or primary *means* when we are talking about emotions (Barrett, 2006). "Thus, the question 'Which are the basic emotions?' is not only one that probably cannot be answered, it is a misdirected question, as though we asked, 'Which are the basic people?' and hoped to get a reply that would explain human diversity" (Ortony & Turner, 1990, p. 329).

If there is one conclusion regarding emotion with which all theorists agree, it is that part of being emotional is a physiological, visceral response. To put it plainly, being emotional is a gut-level reaction. To be emotional involves more than our thinking, reasoning cerebral cortex. We turn next to a discussion of the physiological aspects of emotion.

STUDY CHECK

What do psychologists mean when they talk about emotion?
What has become of attempts to identify and classify basic emotions?

THINKING CRITICALLY

Given that psychologists cannot agree on "basic" emotions, or even if there is such a thing, what would you propose as a list of basic emotional responses?

The Physiology of Emotion

Do you remember our story about meeting a bear while walking in the woods? It suggested that after backpacking in the mountains and enjoying a large meal, you took a quiet stroll down a path, only to have a huge bear appear from behind some bushes. One question we asked was, "What will you do now?" If nothing else, your reaction would be an emotional one. You will experience affect (call it "fear," if not "panic"). You will have a cognitive reaction (realizing you've just encountered a bear and wishing that you hadn't). You will engage in some overt behavior (perhaps freezing in your tracks or racing back to the campfire). A significant part of your reaction in this situation (or one like it) will be physiological, or "gut-level." Responding to a bear in the wild is not something people would do in a purely intellectual sort of way. When we are emotional, we respond with our viscera.

Our biological reaction to emotional situations takes place at several levels. Of primary interest is the autonomic nervous system, or ANS. The brain has a role to play in emotion, but first we'll consider the autonomic response.

The autonomic nervous system (ANS) consists of two parts that serve the same organs but have nearly opposite effects. The *parasympathetic division* is actively involved in maintaining a relaxed, calm, and unemotional state. As you strolled down the path into the woods, the parasympathetic division of your ANS actively directed your digestive processes to do the best they could with the meal you had just eaten. Blood was diverted from the extremities to the stomach and intestines. Saliva flowed freely. With your stomach full, and with blood diverted to it, you felt somewhat drowsy as your brain responded to the lower levels of blood supply. Your breathing was slow, deep, and steady, as was your heart rate. Again, all of these activities were under the control of the parasympathetic division of your autonomic nervous system.

Suddenly, there's that bear! As with any emotional response, the *sympathetic division* of your ANS now takes over. Automatically, many physiological changes take place— changes that are usually quite adaptive.

1. The pupils of your eyes dilate, letting in as much of what light is available, increasing your visual sensitivity.
2. Your heart rate and blood pressure are elevated (energy needs to be mobilized as fast as possible).
3. Blood is diverted away from the digestive tract toward the limbs and brain, and digestion stops. You've got a bear to deal with; digestion can wait until later. Let's get the blood supply out there to the arms and legs where it can do some good (with what is called the fight-or-flight response).
4. Respiration increases, becoming deeper and more rapid; you'll need all the oxygen you can get.
5. Moisture is brought to the surface of the skin in the form of perspiration; as it evaporates, the body is cooled, thus conserving energy.
6. Blood sugar levels increase, making more energy readily available.
7. Blood will clot more readily than usual—for obvious, but it is hoped, unnecessary reasons.

The sympathetic system makes some of these changes directly (for example, stopping salivation and stimulating the cardiac muscle). Others are made indirectly through the release of hormones into the bloodstream, mostly from the adrenal glands. Because part of the physiological aspect of emotion is hormonal, it takes a few seconds for the effect to be experienced. If you were, in fact, confronted by a bear in the woods, you would probably not have the presence of mind to notice, but the reactions of sweaty palms, gasping breaths, and "butterflies in your stomach" take a few seconds to develop.

Is the autonomic and endocrine system reaction the same for every emotion that we experience? That's a very difficult question. There may be slight differences. There appears to be a small difference in the hormones produced during rage and fear reactions. There may be differences in the biological bases of emotions that prepare us for defense or for retreat—fight or flight. Consistent differences in physiological reactions for the various emotional states are, at best, very slight. This issue has been controversial in psychology for many years and is likely to remain so (Barrett & Wager, 2006).

When we become emotional, our sympathetic nervous system does not just spring into action on its own. Autonomic nervous system activity is related to, and coordinated by, central nervous system activity.

The brain structure most intimately involved in emotionality is the limbic system. The limbic system is a "lower" center in the brain, consisting of a number of small structures (the amygdala may be the most important for emotionality). These centers are "lower" in the sense of being well below the cerebral cortex and in the sense of being present (and important) in the brains of "lower" animals, such as rats and cats. As it happens, positive emotions (your team just won a big game) are associated with activity in the *left side* of the amygdala, while unpleasant emotional reactions (your team lost that game) are associated with increased activity in the *right side* of the amygdala (Zalla et al., 2000).

The limbic system is most involved in emotional responses that call for defensive or attacking responses—those emotions stimulated by threat. Electrical stimulation or destruction of portions of the limbic system reliably produce a variety of changes in emotional reaction.

The role of the cerebral cortex in emotionality is poorly understood. It seems to be largely inhibitory. That is, the limbic system seems to act as the source for extreme and rather poorly directed emotional reactions. The cortex interprets impulses from these lower centers and other information available to it and modifies and directs the emotional reaction accordingly. This is another way of saying that the involvement of the cerebral cortex in emotionality is in the cognitive aspect of an emotion. It is the cerebral cortex that is involved in the interpretation and memory of emotional events. When you get back to camp, having just been frightened by a bear, you will use your cortex to tell the emotional details of your story. Emotional reactions tend to be processed in the right hemisphere of the brain; the left hemisphere is usually unemotional (Damasio et al., 2000; LeDoux, 1995). Beyond that, research indicates that no specific, particular parts of the cerebral cortex are associated with any specific emotional reaction (Barrett & Wager, 2006).

To review: Along with the autonomic nervous system, the limbic system and the hypothalamus are centers of emotion. These centers are coordinated by higher centers in the cerebral cortex, which, among other things, provides the cognitive interpretation of emotional responses.

STUDY CHECK

How do the autonomic nervous system and the brain affect emotional reactions?

THINKING CRITICALLY

What are the physiological bases of discovering that you just aced an exam that you had been worried about?

Expressing Emotion

An aspect of emotion that has long intrigued psychologists is how inner emotional states are communicated to others. Charles Darwin was one of the first to popularize the idea that facial expressions provide indicators of an organism's emotional state. More than a hundred years later, psychologists are discovering evidence that suggests that Darwin might have been correct, but only in restricted ways (Barrett, 2006). For example, it is not likely that emotional expressions are "broadcast" for the benefit of anyone who sees them. At least some are directed at specific observers. Nor is it likely that receivers of emotional expressions can interpret such messages simply and reflexively (Russell, Bachorowski, & Fernández-Dols, 2003). In many circumstances, it is very useful for one organism to let another know how it is feeling. As one wild animal approaches a second, the second had better have a good idea about the emotional state of the first. Is it angry? Does it come in peace? Is it just curious, or is it looking for dinner? Is it sad, looking for comfort, or is it sexually aroused, looking for a mate? An inability to make such determinations quickly can be disastrous. Animals need to know the emotional state of others if they are to survive for long.

Non-human animals have many instinctive and ritualistic patterns of behavior they can use to communicate aggressiveness, interest in courtship, submission, and other emotional states. Humans also express their emotional states in a variety of ways, including verbal communication. Surely, if you are happy, sad, angry, or jealous, you can try to tell us

As one lion approaches another, each needs to have a pretty good idea of the emotional state of the other.

how you feel. In fact, the ability to communicate with language often puts humans at an advantage in this regard. Research tells us that emotional states can be reflected in *how* we speak, even if our message is not related to emotion at all (Bachorowski & Owren, 1995; Juslin & Laukka, 2003). Even without verbal language, there is a school of thought that suggests that the human animal uses body language to communicate its emotional condition. Someone sitting quietly, slumped slightly forward with head down may be viewed as feeling sad, even from a distance. We similarly interpret postural cues and gestures as being associated with fear, anger, happiness, and so on. Such expressions often result from learning and may be modified by cultural influences.

Darwin recognized facial expression as a cue to emotion in animals, especially mammals. Might facial expression provide the key to underlying emotions in humans, too? Are there facial expressions of emotional states that are universal among the human species, just as there appear to be among non-humans? A growing body of evidence supports the hypothesis that facial expressions of emotional states are innate responses, only slightly sensitive to cultural influence, but the relation between facial expression and underlying emotion is far from simple.

Paul Ekman and his colleagues have conducted several studies trying to find a reliable relationship between emotional state and facial expression across cultures (Ekman, 1992, 1993). In one large study college students were shown six pictures of people's faces. In each picture, a different emotion was displayed: happiness, disgust, surprise, sadness, anger, or fear. When students from the United States, Argentina, Japan, Brazil, and Chile were asked to identify the emotion experienced by the people in the photographs, their agreement was remarkable. One problem with this study is that all of the participants did have many shared experiences, even though they were from basically different cultures. They were all college students and had many experiences in common (perhaps they had seen the same movies or watched the same TV shows). Even though Ekman's subjects came from different countries, their agreement could be explained in terms of the similarities of their experiences rather than some innate tendency to express emotions through facial expression. A conservative conclusion at this time is that some facial expressions—e.g., for happiness—can be readily identified across cultures, but others—e.g., disgust—are difficult to interpret cross-culturally (Elfenbein & Ambady, 2002).

Another study of facial expression (Ekman et al., 1983) has shown that simply moving one's facial muscles into the positions associated with emotional expression can cause distinctive physiological changes associated with an emotional state. As bizarre as it sounds, the idea is that if you raise your eyebrows, open your eyes widely, and raise the corners of your mouth, you will produce an internal physiological change not unlike that which occurs when you are happy, and you will smile as a result.

STUDY CHECK

What are some of the factors involved in the communication of an emotional state from one organism to another?

THINKING CRITICALLY

Actors communicate feelings or emotions that their characters are experiencing. What methods might actors use to accomplish this task?

Chapter Summary

How do psychologists define motivation, and how have they used the concepts of instincts, needs, and drives to account for motivated behaviors?

Motivation is the process that arouses, directs, and maintains an organism's behaviors. Instincts are complex patterns of unlearned behavior that occur in the presence of certain stimuli. The concept of instinct theories has not been a satisfactory approach for explaining human behaviors. Needs are shortages of some biological necessity. Deprivation leads to a need, which gives rise to a drive, which arouses and directs an organism's behavior. Many drives are more learned than biological and are called secondary drives. Maslow devised a system that places needs in a hierarchy, from physiological survival needs to a need to self-actualize.

How can incentives, homeostasis, arousal, and cognitive dissonance be useful in explaining motivated behaviors?

Focusing on incentives explains behaviors in terms of goals and outcomes rather than internal driving forces. Incentives may be thought of as goals—external stimuli that attract (positive goals) or repel (negative goals). The thrust of balance or equilibrium theories is that organisms are motivated to reach and maintain a state of balance—a set point level of activity or arousal. Homeostasis, for example, is a drive to maintain a state of equilibrium among internal physiological conditions, such as blood pressure, metabolism, and heart rate. Other theorists argue for a general drive to maintain a balanced state of arousal, with an optimal level of arousal being best suited for any given task or situation. Festinger claimed that we are motivated to maintain consonance, or balance, among cognitive states, thereby reducing, if not eliminating, cognitive dissonance.

What are the needs for achievement, power, affiliation, and intimacy?

Achievement motivation, or need to achieve (nAch), is a need to attempt and succeed at tasks so as to meet or exceed a standard of excellence. These needs are usually assessed through the interpretation of stories generated in response to the Thematic Apperception Test, or TAT, in which one looks for themes of striving and achievement. The need for power is the need to be in charge, to be in control of a situation, often by controlling the flow of information. Affiliation needs involve being motivated to be with others, to form friendships and interpersonal relationships. The need for intimacy is the need for close, affectionate relationships. Individuals with a high need for intimacy tend to be warm and affectionate and to express concern for others. Although psychologists believe that achievement and power needs are learned and socially influenced, they are not so sure about affiliation and intimacy needs. There may be a biological basis for these latter two needs.

What do psychologists mean when they talk about emotion?

There are four possible components of an emotional reaction: (a) the experience of a subjective feeling, or affective component; (b) a cognitive appraisal or interpretation; (c) an internal, visceral, physiological reaction; and (d) an overt behavioral response.

What has become of attempts to identify and classify basic emotions?

Several attempts have been made to categorize emotional reactions. Izard calls for six primary emotions: joy, interest, sadness, anger, disgust, and fear. Each of the primary emotions is believed to have its own underlying physiological basis. All other emotions would be combinations of the six primary emotions. There does appear to be some consensus that emotions represent valenced states, being either positive or negative, but even then it is not clear just what positive and negative means in regard to emotion. Fear, for example, seems like a candidate for a list of negative emotions. Yet, fear can be useful and serve to guide a person's behavior in positive or adaptive ways. After all, to be without fear in the real world can be very dangerous. Inconsistencies among theories lead some psychologists to wonder if the attempt to classify basic emotions is misguided. It is difficult—and may be impossible—to determine how many primary or basic emotions exist.

How do the autonomic nervous system and the brain affect emotional reactions?

Among the changes that take place when we become emotional are those produced by the sympathetic division of the autonomic nervous system. Occurring to varying degrees, these reactions include dilation of the pupils, increased heart rate and blood pressure, cessation of digestive processes, deeper and more rapid breathing, increased perspiration, and elevated blood sugar levels. Most of these reactions require a few seconds to take effect.

Two brain structures closely involved in emotional reactions are the limbic system (primarily the amygdala) and the cerebral cortex. The limbic system is most involved in defensive or attacking responses. The role of the cerebral cortex in emotion is not well understood. However, the cerebral cortex appears to play mainly an inhibitory role in emotionality. The cerebral cortex interprets impulses from the limbic system and then modifies and directs the emotional reaction. Thus, the most prominent role of the cortex in emotion is cognitive in nature, giving meaning to emotional experiences.

What are some of the factors involved in the communication of an emotional state from one organism to another?

From the time of Charles Darwin, who theorized that facial expressions provide information about internal states, a great deal of attention has focused on the role of facial expressions in the communication of emotions. Expressing emotions via facial expressions has adaptive value. It allows one to communicate a wide range of emotions that can be interpreted by others. Recent research has made it clear that communicating emotion by facial expression is more complex than Darwin realized, and it involves a specific sender and receiver of such messages. Paul Ekman and his colleagues claim to have identified facial expressions that appear to be universal. They include happiness, disgust, surprise, sadness, anger, and fear. Subjects from five countries were able to identify the emotion that went with each face shown in a photograph with remarkable accuracy. Again, further research indicates that some emotional states (happiness, for example) are more easily interpreted from facial expression than are others (such as fear and disgust). In addition to facial expressions, organisms—especially humans—communicate how they feel through postural cues and, of course, can verbally express their emotions should they so choose.

Key Terms

Arousal (p. 170)
Motivation (p. 170)
Instincts (p. 171)
Need (p. 171)
Drive (p. 171)
Secondary drive (p. 171)
Primary drive (p. 171)
Incentives (p. 175)

Homeostasis (p. 175)
Cognitive dissonance (p. 176)
Need to achieve (nAch) (p. 180)
Need for power (p. 181)
Need for affiliation (p. 181)
Need for intimacy (p. 181)
Loneliness (p. 181)
Emotion (p. 182)

Human Sexuality and Relationships

Source: Michael Traitov/Shutterstock.

Questions You Will Be Able to Answer

After reading Chapter 9, you should be able to answer the following questions:

- What is the definition of human sexuality?
- How do the concepts of sex and gender differ?
- What factors relate to sexual motivation?
- How are different sexual orientations defined?
- What do we know about the same-sex and heterosexual orientations?
- What have scientists found concerning the origins of the same-sex orientation?
- What is known about the transgender identity?
- What are the origins of the transgender identity?
- What are the needs for affiliation and intimacy, and how do they relate to relationship formation?
- What factors contribute to interpersonal attraction?
- What have social psychologists discovered about love relationships?

Preview

In this chapter we shall explore two major topics: human sexuality and relationships. In Chapter 8 we covered a number of topics relating to motivation and emotion. In many ways the topics in this chapter extend that discussion. Scientists, in general, and social scientists, in particular, have researched what motivates sexual behavior and explored how and why humans form interpersonal relationships. We shall explore some of this research in the sections that follow.

We will start this journey by covering topics relating to human sexuality. First, we shall define some basic concepts relating to the topics that follow, including sex, gender, gender identity, and gender roles. A clear understanding of these terms is important for you to understand the range and dynamics of human sexual orientation and expression.

Next, we will explore the biological and psychological components of sexual motivation. You will see that it is not possible to understand the complexities of human sexual motivation just by considering biological factors. As is the case for much human motivation and behavior, sexual motivation also relates to a variety of social and psychological factors. You will also learn how men and women differ with respect to sexual motivation and how we think about our sexuality.

The next major topic in this chapter reviews the varieties of human sexuality. Although we cannot hope to cover the complexity of this topic in a single section of a single chapter, we hope to provide you with some basic information to help you understand the variety of ways we express our sexuality. We shall define and cover heterosexual orientation, same-sex orientation, and transgender identity. You will learn about the difference between an "orientation" and a "preference" with respect to heterosexual and same-sex orientations. We will extend the discussion of sexual orientations with an exploration of the transgender identity. In this section of the chapter we shall provide a definition for this identity. Then, we will introduce information on the prejudice and discrimination faced by transgender individuals and how that prejudice may result in higher suicide rates among transgender persons. We will close the section with information on the roots of transgender identity, a topic that is highly controversial.

The third section of this chapter will cover interpersonal attraction and relationship formation. We start by defining the needs for affiliation and intimacy, two motives that foster relationship formation. You will see how some people have difficulty forming relationships and may, as a consequence, experience loneliness.

Social psychologists have studied the factors that affect interpersonal attraction for decades. We will explore three of these factors: physical proximity, similarity, and physical attractiveness. You will see how being physically close to others increases the likelihood that you will form a relationship with those people. In this context, we will also discuss how the Internet has made it possible for us to form relationships over long distances that share many of the qualities of more traditional relationships.

Social psychologists also have studied love relationships. One theory of love is the triangular theory. This theory states that love consists of three components, representing three legs of a triangle: passion, intimacy, and commitment. We will look at different types of love, including romantic love, consummate love, unrequited love, and secret love.

Before we can love someone, we have to find that person. Social psychologists have studied human mate selection. A good amount of this research relates to the evolutionary perspective in psychology. Evolutionary psychology attempts to apply principles of evolution to human behavior, seeing parallels between human mate selection and animal mate selection. We will cover research looking at gender differences in mate selection, focusing on how males and females differ in the characteristics they look for in a potential mate.

Human Sexuality

Sexuality is one of those topics that everyone thinks he or she knows about and can define easily. After all, it seems to dominate just about every aspect of Western culture. We are exposed to sexuality in our entertainment (e.g., movies, television, Internet), education (e.g., "health" classes), and in our casual conversation with family and friends. However, like many concepts in psychology, sexuality is not as easy to define scientifically and concisely.

There seem to be as many definitions of sexuality as there are scholarly publications. We shall use a definition offered by Craig Hill (2008). Hill defines **human sexuality** as "all [of the] emotional, cognitive, behavioral, and physical experiences of humans related to their sexuality" (p. 4).

The emotional component includes all of our feelings, desires, and moods surrounding sexuality. The cognitive component encompasses our sexual thoughts, expectations, judgments, and plans relating to sexuality. Behavioral experiences are all of our overt sexual behaviors, actions, and activities relating to sexuality. Finally, the physical component includes all sexual sensations and physical reactions to sexual stimuli (e.g., increased blood flow and heart rate, warmth).

We also need to distinguish between the terms sex and gender. **Sex** refers to one's biological status with respect to sexuality. Male humans are born with an XY chromosomal configuration, whereas females are born with an XX configuration. These configurations determine the hormonal environment present during prenatal development and influence the direction of the development of sexual characteristics. With an XY configuration, an embryo will develop male sexual characteristics. With an XX configuration, an embryo will develop female sexual characteristics. These configurations will also affect sexual development later in life. On the other hand, **gender** refers to the social and sociocultural characteristics associated with one's sex (Crooks & Baur, 2014). An important concept related to our discussion of sexual orientation below is gender identity. **Gender identity** is a person's subjective experience of his or her gender. It involves acceptance of the idea that one belongs to the category of male or female. Finally, a **gender role** consists of the cultural expectations for males and females. Stereotypical gender roles exist for males (e.g., independent, strong) and females (e.g., dependent, weak).

> **Human sexuality**—all of the emotional, cognitive, behavioral, and physical experiences of humans related to their sexuality.

> **Sex**—one's biological status with respect to sexuality.

> **Gender**—the social and sociocultural characteristics associated with one's sex.

> **Gender identity**—a person's subjective experience of his or her gender.

> **Gender role**—the cultural expectations for males and females.

STUDY CHECK

What is the definition of human sexuality?
How do the concepts of sex and gender differ?

THINKING CRITICALLY

You are trying to explain human sexuality and different sexualities to a friend. What would you tell your friend and why?

Sexual Motivation

Sex is a powerful motivator for behavior, both animal and human. Sexual motivation varies considerably, not only among individuals but also among species. Sexuality involves a complex interplay of physiological, cognitive, and affective processes. *Sexual motivation* relates to several underlying factors including physiological, cognitive and affective factors. We explore these underlying factors next.

On the physiological level, the sex drive is unique in many ways. For one thing, *individual* survival does not depend on its satisfaction. If we do not drink, we die; if we do not regulate our body temperatures, we die; if we do not eat, we die. If we do not have

Sexuality involves a complex interplay of physiological, cognitive, and affective processes, and is shaped by society, religion, family, and personal experiences.

sex—well, we don't die. The survival of a *species*, on the other hand, *does* depend on the sex drive. Survival of a species requires that an adequate number of its members respond successfully to a sex drive, even though an individual member can get along without doing so.

Most physiologically based drives, including thirst and hunger, provide mechanisms that ultimately replenish or maintain the body's energy. When it is satisfied, the sex drive depletes the body's energy. Third, the sex drive is not present—in the usual sense—at birth, but appears only after puberty. The other physiological drives are present and even most critical early in life.

A unique quality of the sex drive is the extent to which internal and external forces have differing degrees of influence on sexual behaviors, depending on the species involved. Internal, physiological states are much more important in "lower" species than in humans. For example, sex for rats is simple and straightforward. If adequate testosterone (the male sex hormone) is present, and if the opportunity presents itself, a male rat will engage in sexual behaviors. If adequate levels of estrogen (a female sex hormone) are present, and if the opportunity arises, the female rat will engage in sexual behaviors. For rats, learning or experience has little to do with sexual behaviors—instead; these behaviors are tied closely to physiology, to hormone levels.

There is virtually no difference between the mating behaviors of sexually experienced rats and virgin rats. Furthermore, if the sex glands of rats are removed, sexual behaviors cease. Removal of the sex glands from experienced male cats and dogs ("higher" species than rats) produces a gradual reduction in sexual behaviors. However, an experienced male primate ("higher" still) may persist in sexual behaviors for the rest of his life, even after the sex glands have been surgically removed. (The same seems true for most human males, but the data are sketchy.)

Biology alone cannot adequately account for human sexual behaviors. Hormones may provide humans with an arousing force toward sexual behaviors, but hormones may be neither necessary nor sufficient to account for them. It is obvious, for example, that physiological mechanisms cannot account for what a person does when sexually aroused, or with whom he or she does it.

Sexual behaviors are shaped by society, religion, family, and personal experience. Particularly in Western societies where sexual behaviors are so influenced by learning experiences one could easily come to believe that sexual drives are acquired through learning and practice alone. (Satisfying the sex drive may also involve considerable unlearning of many of the prohibitions acquired in childhood and adolescence.) Sex manuals of the "how-to" variety sell well, and sex therapy has become a standard practice for many clinical psychologists helping people to cope with the pressures that external factors put on their "natural" sexual motivation.

Finally, are there cultural differences in sexual motivation? One study (Tang, Bensman, & Hatfield, 2014) explored how various aspects of sexual motivation related to culture (North American and Chinese) and gender. One finding was that Chinese men were more likely to use sex to please their partner than Chinese women. However, American men and women did not differ on this factor. Americans were more likely than Chinese to report using sex to please their partner and reduce stress.

STUDY CHECK

What factors relate to sexual motivation?

THINKING CRITICALLY

If you had to give an informational speech in a class on the topic of sexual motivation, what arguments would you make for the relative contributions of biology, learning, and culture to sexual motives?

FOCUS ON DIVERSITY

Gender Differences in Sexual Motivation

With regard to sexuality, men and women differ in a few important ways. Having reviewed the research data, UCLA psychologist Letitia Peplau (2003) lists four male–female differences regarding human sexuality.

One area in which men and women differ in sexual motivation is sexual interest. Compared with women, men are more interested in sex, fantasize more about sex, and want sex more often (Baumeister, 2000; Baumeister, Catanese, & Vohs, 2001). Men also have sex more frequently than women (Petersen & Hyde, 2010) and masturbate more frequently than women. Peplau takes these measures as indicative of men's greater sexual desire. Additionally, research from the University of Western Australia tells us that men lose their sexual desires very slowly—if at all. As many as one in five men over the age of 100 say that sex is important to them. Among men age 75 to 95, 40 percent wish they were having more sex (Hyde et al., 2010). Men also are more likely to report using sex to please their partners than women (Tang et al., 2014).

Women and men also differ with respect to the importance of sexuality in relationships. Women are more likely than men to require commitment and a relationship before engaging in sexual behaviors. Men are more likely to see sexuality simply in terms of intercourse and physical pleasure (Regan & Berscheid, 1999). Women's sexual fantasies usually involve a familiar partner, affection, and commitment, but men's sexual fantasies involve strangers and multiple partners. Also, men are more likely than women to use sex to maintain a relationship (Tang et al., 2014).

Overall, men are more physically aggressive than women. For example, men are commonly more assertive, even coercive, and more prone to be the ones who initiate physical sexual contact (Felson, 2002; Impett & Peplau, 2003). They are also more likely to use sexual aggression than women. "Although women use many strategies to persuade men to have sex, physical force and violence are seldom part of their repertoire" (Peplau, 2003, p. 38). Men are almost exclusively the perpetrators of sexual assault against women, men, and children (National Intimate Partner and Sexual Violence Survey, 2017). According to the National Intimate Partner and Sexual Violence Survey, estimates of female victims of rape (completed or not completed) being assaulted by only a male perpetrator range between 91.1 and 100 percent.

Men and women differ in their sexual attitudes. Men tend to have more permissive attitudes about sex than women (Petersen & Hyde, 2010). Women's beliefs and attitudes about sexual issues can be changed by societal and environmental influences to a greater degree than men's (Baumeister, 2000). The sexual activities of women are significantly more variable than those of men, being more frequent when in an intimate relationship and dropping to near zero following a break-up. It is worth noting, however, that gender differences in sexual attitudes are fewer than one might think (Petersen & Hyde, 2010). According to Petersen and Hyde, where gender differences exist, they are a product of an interaction between biological factors, social power differences, and pressure to behave in a manner consistent with existing gender roles.

Women and men also differ in their attitudes toward and use of pornography. Men have more positive attitudes toward pornography than women (Carroll et al., 2008). Men are significantly more likely to view pornography than women. One concern researchers have expressed is that there might be a relationship between pornography use and sexual violence. Although the causes of rape are complex (Groth, 1979; Malamuth, 1986), some researchers and observers have focused on pornography as a factor that contributes to the social climate in which sexual violence against women is tolerated. Exposure to sexually violent materials does relate to increased sexual violence (Malamuth & Check, 1980). However, mild, nonviolent forms of erotica, such as pictures from *Playboy* magazine or scenes of sex between consenting couples, may inhibit sexual violence against women (Donnerstein, Donnerstein, & Evans, 1975). Men who watch pornography frequently tend to have lower relationship quality and derive less satisfaction from sex than men who view it less frequently (Szymanski & Steward-Richardson, 2014).

The Varieties of Human Sexuality

Sexual orientation—one's pattern of emotional, sexual, and romantic attraction of those of a particular gender.

Heterosexual orientation—individuals mostly attracted to members of the opposite sex.

Same-sex orientation—individuals mostly attracted to members of the same sex.

Bisexual orientation—individuals attracted to both members of the same and opposite sex.

Transgender identity—individuals whose appearance and/or behaviors do not conform to traditional, accepted gender roles.

Transsexual—individual whose gender identity is opposite from his or her biological sex and is likely to seek medical intervention to change their sex.

Complicating the picture of human sexuality is the fact that it is a diverse concept, including a wide range of different modes of sexual orientations and expressions. **Sexual orientation** refers to one's pattern of emotional, sexual, and romantic attraction of those of a particular gender (WebMD, 2018).

Individuals with a **heterosexual orientation** are mostly attracted to members of the opposite sex. Individuals with a **same-sex orientation** (formerly referred to as a homosexual orientation [see our discussion below]) are mostly attracted to members of the same sex. Others with a **bisexual orientation** show attraction to both members of the same and opposite sex. **Transgender identity** refers to individuals whose appearance and/or behaviors do not conform to traditional, accepted gender roles (Crooks & Baur, 2014). Finally, **transsexual** refers to individuals whose gender identity is opposite from his or her biological sex (Crooks & Baur, 2014) and are likely to seek medical intervention (hormone therapy or surgery) to change their sex (Dargie, Blair, Pukall, & Coyle, 2014).

In terms of the demographics of different sexual orientations, it is difficult to get accurate numbers. This is due to the varying definitions of the terms used to label the categories of sexual orientation. According to a 2017 Gallup poll, 4.5 percent of U.S. adults self-identify as lesbian, gay, bisexual or transgender (LGBT), up from 3.4 percent in 2012. The increase from 2012 is due to a significant increase in millennials identifying as LGBT (Gallup, 2017). Interestingly, as shown in **Figure 9.1**, non-whites are more likely than whites to self-identify as LGBT. According to the 2017 Gallup poll, women are slightly more likely to self-identify as LGBT than men (5.1 percent vs. 3.9 percent). Younger individuals (18–29 years) are more likely than older individuals to self-report being LGBT (Gallup, 2017). Finally, a higher percentage of individuals self-reporting as LGBT can be found among less educated and lower income respondents (Gallup, 2017).

The Same-Sex and Heterosexual Orientations

As noted earlier, a same-sex orientation involves sexual attraction and arousal toward members of the same sex. It is important to understand that scientists consider the same-sex orientation to be an *orientation* and not a sexual *preference*. Like handedness or language, one does not choose sexual orientation voluntarily.

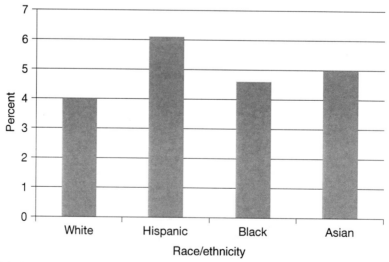

FIGURE 9.1 Percentage of U.S. Adults Identifying as LGBT (Gallup, 2017)

Additionally, there is a trend toward not using the term "homosexual" to refer to persons of a same-sex orientation. This is because of the negative stereotypes associated with the term (Peters, 2014). In fact, the Gay and Lesbian Alliance Against Defamation (GLADD) identify "homosexual" on its list of terms to avoid (GLADD, 2015).

The term homosexuality focuses only on the sexual nature of a relationship while ignoring the affective preferences and identity issues (Kelly, 1995). In fact, some have distinguished between sexual orientation, which refers to the pattern of an individual's sexual attraction, and *affectional orientation*, which refers to the pattern of a person's emotional or romantic attraction (Unitarian Universalist Association, 1996–2015).

Researchers now use the term, as we shall, same-sex orientation. Also, males and females with a same-sex orientation may be referred to as *gay* or *lesbian*, respectively. Finally, keep in mind that sexuality is rarely an either/or proposition. Instead, scientists studying sexual orientation conceptualize it as existing on a 7-point continuum, with individuals with an exclusive heterosexual orientation on one end and individuals with an exclusive same-sex orientation on the other (Kinsey, Pomeroy, & Martin, 1948).

Psychologists have no generally accepted theory about why a person displays a same-sex orientation.

Individuals with same-sex and heterosexual orientations do not differ significantly in terms of expression of sexuality. Most individuals with a same-sex orientation have experienced heterosexual sex. They simply find same-sex relationships more satisfying.

There are, however, some differences among heterosexuals, gays, and lesbians in terms of relationship satisfaction. Compared to married heterosexual partners, lesbian couples report more intimacy, more autonomy, and more equality in their relationships (Kurdek, 1998). Additionally, partners in lesbian couples report a higher level of relationship quality than partners in either gay or heterosexual relationships (Kurdek, 2008). As a relationship progresses, partners in gay and lesbian couples show little change in reported relationship quality, whereas partners in heterosexual relationships show a decline in relationship quality that eventually levels off (Kurdek, 2008).

Generally, same-sex orientation couples are more at ease and more comfortable with their sexual relationship than most heterosexual couples. When therapy is needed, the issues are much the same, focusing on developing clear communication, exploring personal values, expectations within the relationship, and matters related to developing as individuals as well as partners (Glick, Berman, Clarkin, & Rait, 2000). Comparative studies have produced some insights: "Relative to partners from married heterosexual couples, partners from gay and lesbian couples tend to assign household labor more fairly, resolve conflict more constructively, experience similar levels of satisfaction, and perceive less support from family members but more support from friends" (Kurdek, 2005, p. 251).

One major problem associated with a same-sex or bisexual orientation is an elevated risk of suicide attempts and actual suicide compared to the heterosexual orientation (Haas et al., 2011). According to Haas et al., individuals in a same-sex relationship are 3–4 times more likely to attempt and actually commit suicide than those in heterosexual relationships.

The elevated rate of suicide attempts among individuals with a same-sex or bisexual orientation appears to be related to a higher incidence of psychological issues, most notably depression and anxiety (Haas et al., 2011). Haas et al. point out that the elevated levels of depression, anxiety, and suicide

Lesbian couples tend to report greater satisfaction in their relationships than gay or heterosexual couples.

among same-sex orientation persons can, at least in part, be traced to individual and institutional prejudice and discrimination experienced by same-sex orientation individuals and bisexuals.

Factors Relating to the Same-Sex Orientation

Psychologists have no generally accepted theory about why a person displays a particular sexual orientation. Still, it is safe to assume that a same-sex orientation results from an interaction of genetic, hormonal, and environmental factors. There is ample evidence that the same-sex orientation has something of a genetic basis, and tends to "run in families" (Pool, 1993; Whitman, Diamond, & Martin, 1993). For example, a study of Australian male twins found that between 42–60 percent of the variability in several measures of same-sex orientation is related to genetic factors (Kirk, Bailey, & Martin, 2000). Research suggests that the genetic basis for same-sex orientation may lie more in the part of one's genetic code that is sensitive to environmental influences (i.e., epigenetics) (Rice, Friberg, & Gavrilets, 2012).

There are no differences in the sex hormone levels of adult heterosexuals and adults with a same-sex orientation (Gladue, 1994; Tuiten et al., 2000). Providing gay males and lesbians with extra sex hormones may increase overall sex drive, but it has virtually no effect on sexual orientation.

One hypothesis is that the prenatal (before birth) hormonal environment may affect sexual orientation in adulthood (Auyeung et al., 2009; Ellis & Ames, 1987; Money, 1987). There is evidence that lesbians are exposed to higher levels of male sex hormones prenatally than heterosexual women (Breedlove, 2017). However, heterosexual and gay men appear not to be exposed to different levels of male sex hormones. It may be that gay men may show a greater response to male hormones prior to birth rather than being exposed to more of them (Breedlove, 2017). It is important to note that most women who were exposed prenatally to higher-than-normal levels of male hormones do not eventually show a same-sex orientation (Pasterski, 2017).

Although there is some evidence to support the hypothesis that the brains of individuals with a same-sex orientation and heterosexuals differ, it is by no means conclusive. Research in this area is plagued by methodological problems, reliance on post-mortem studies, and failure to replicate results (Gallo, & Robinson, 2000).

A vast majority of the research on the origins of the same-sex orientation focuses on biological factors. There is relatively little research looking at social and environmental factors (Felson, 2011). In fact, there is evidence that attempts by parents to socialize sex-consistent behaviors in children may fail (Pasterski, 2017). For example, Pasterski reports that when parents attempted to steer female children who were exposed to higher-than-normal levels of male hormones toward play with girl's toys, their children resisted such attempts. Similarly, Pasterski states that girls exposed to higher-than-normal levels of male hormones prenatally "showed reduced imitation of female models and reduced responsiveness to information that particular objects were for girls" (p. 1616).

One thing, however, is clear: sexual orientation cannot be attributed to any one early childhood experience. Still, some evidence does point to childhood experiences. For example, Bearman and Bruckner (2001) suggest that socialization experiences may also explain at least some of how people express different sexual orientations. In one study, Felson (2011) found that a person's religious upbringing relates to the expression of a same-sex attraction. Individuals raised in a Jewish or a secular environment were more likely to show a same-sex attraction than those raised in a more conservative Protestant environment. Finally, Felson reported that how frequently a person attended religious services as an adolescent was not significantly related to same-sex attraction.

What might we conclude today about how a person comes to be heterosexual, or a person with a same-sex orientation? Consistent with so many other complex behavior patterns, the ultimate explanation may be biopsychosocial. As one researcher put it:

> With a larger data base . . . we may be able to construct a biosocial model in which different events—genetic, hormonal, and environmental—occurring at critical times are weighted for

their impact on the development of sexual orientation. Associated with this model would be the idea that not all men and women arrive at their sexual orientation following the same path (Gladue, 1994, p. 153).

STUDY CHECK

How are different sexual orientations defined?
What do we know about the same-sex and heterosexual orientations?
What have scientists found concerning the origins of the same-sex orientation?

THINKING CRITICALLY

What arguments would you make to convince a person who believes strongly that persons with a same-sex orientation are "born with their orientations"?

The Transgender Identity

On April 24, 2015, Bruce Jenner gave an interview in which he discussed his transition from being a male to being a female. His process of transition began months before. Bruce Jenner, at the time, was a well-known reality TV star and author. However, his main claim to fame was his record-setting performance in the decathlon of the 1976 Olympics. After winning the gold medal, Jenner's picture appeared on the Wheaties cereal box. From that point on, Jenner enjoyed fame and fortune as a male. However, in his interview with ABC news correspondent Diane Sawyer, Jenner stated, "For all intents and purposes, I'm a woman."

He went on to say: "People look at me differently. They see you as this macho male, but my heart and my soul and everything that I do in life—it is part of me. That female side is part of me. That's who I am." Jenner clearly stated that although he was outwardly a male, he always identified more strongly with the female gender. Consequently, Jenner underwent the process of transitioning from a male to a female. This process culminated in May 2015; Jenner underwent surgery to "feminize his face" but did not have surgery to change his sex organs. Subsequently, Bruce Jenner declared that he was Caitlyn Jenner and appeared in his new female identity on the cover of *Vogue* magazine in July 2015.

A transgender sexual identity involves a person having a gender identity that differs from one's actual gender. So, for example, a biological male who identifies more strongly with being a female would be expressing a transgender identity. An individual who transitions from a male to a female is termed a male-to-female (MtF) or *transwoman* transgender person. A biological female who more strongly identifies with the male gender and transitions to a male is termed a female-to-male transgender person (FtM) or *transman*.

According to Dargie et al. (2014), a transgender person rejects the culturally defined categories of male and female. Rejection of the male/female dichotomy then allows the transgender person to live a more authentic life (Dargie et al., 2014). We can contrast the transgender identity with individuals who show consistency between their biological sex and their gender identities. Researchers refer to individuals who show this consistency as *cisgendered* individuals (Schilt & Westbrook, 2009).

The transgender identity is very complex, and individuals with this identity express their sexual identities differently. Although most transgender individuals show strong identifications with the gender they transition toward, many still show attachment to the gender assigned at birth (Dargie et al. 2014). So, for example, an MtF transgender person is likely to show strong gender identification with the female gender role, but still feel some connection to the male gender role. According to Dargie et al., this shows that there is a degree of fluidity in how transgender individuals define themselves. They point

Source: JStone/Shutterstock

Bruce Jenner transitioned to Caitlyn Jenner, a MtF transwoman person, and appeared with a new identity in 2015.

out that the complexity and fluidity of transgender identity must be taken into account by health care professionals when dealing with transgender individuals.

For Caitlyn Jenner, the transition from male to female was gradual, involving a *process* of transition. For many transgender individuals, this process takes time and many adjustments. In one study, transitioning adolescents and caregivers described difficulties at the beginning of the process because of a lack of knowledge and the language needed to adequately describe the emotions involved with the transition (Schimmel-Bristow et al., 2018). During the transition process, the participants reported both positive and negative experiences relating to reactions of family, friends, school administrators, and providers. Schimmel-Bristow et al. reported that many transitioning adolescents and caregivers sought information from the Internet during the process.

Although many transitioning individuals go through a relatively gradual process of transition, a new trend is emerging. Parents are reporting that their adolescent children are experiencing a rapid onset of a transgender identity with no prior history or indication of gender confusion. This is referred to as *rapid-onset gender dysphoria* (Littman, 2018). Although there is not much research to date, one study found that rapid-onset transitioning is associated with the transitioning individual having one or more peers coming out as transgender and a marked increase in social media use (Marchiano, 2017).

The sexual orientations of transgender women and men span the entire spectrum of orientations. In one study, for example, 32.7 percent of transgender women reported being lesbian, 29.2 percent bisexual, and 18.1 percent straight or heterosexual. The remaining transgender women were distributed across a range of other orientations (Budge, Adelson, & Howard, 2013). In contrast, the largest percentage (37.6 percent) of transgender men identified themselves as "queer" (a catchall term used to refer to individuals who do not define themselves according to normative male/female gender identities). Other transgender men identified themselves as straight/heterosexual (20 percent) or bisexual (19.2 percent). The remainders were distributed across a range of other identities (Budge et al. 2013).

For many transgender individuals, the transition period can be difficult. A sizeable percentage of transgender women (51.4 percent) and transgender men (48.3 percent) experience depression and anxiety (40.4 percent and 47.5 percent, respectively). These percentages are significantly higher than those found in the general population (Budge et al. 2013).

These high rates of depression and anxiety are related to a lack of social support during the transition period and adopting "avoidant" coping strategies. Avoidant strategies involve suppressing emotional responses using, for example, avoidant behaviors (Budge et al. 2013). Another factor contributing to depression in transgender women is gender abuse, or harassment concerning the individual's gender status (Nuttbrock et al., 2010).

The higher rate of depression among transgender individuals relates to an increase in suicide attempts. And, once a transgender person attempts suicide, the likelihood of another suicide attempt increases ten-fold (Mustanski & Liu, 2013). Overall, transgender women and men have an attempted suicide rate that is higher (42 percent and 46 percent, respectively) than the general population (Haas, Rodgers, & Herman, 2014). This problem is most pronounced among transgender youths (Haas, et al., 2014).

A harsh reality of expressing a transgender identity is being the target of prejudice and discrimination. For example, in a national survey exploring discrimination against transgender individuals (Grant et al. 2011), respondents reported experiencing a wide range of discrimination. As shown in **Figure 9.2**, transgender individuals reported discrimination in the areas of housing (19 percent), employment (90 percent), public accommodations such as hotels and restaurants (53 percent), and health care (41 percent). One potential consequence of transgender prejudice is attempted or actual suicide. One study of suicide attempts among transgender individuals found that those who experienced gender-based prejudice were four times more likely to attempt suicide than those who had not experienced such prejudice (Goldblum et al. 2012).

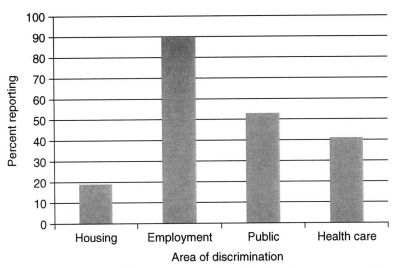

FIGURE 9.2 Percentage of Transgendered Individuals Reporting Various Forms of Discrimination

Origins of the Transgender Identity

The most widely accepted explanation for transgender identity suggests that the root of transitioning one's gender relates to a person having a gender identity that differs from the gender identity assigned at birth. For example, when a man feels more at home with the idea of being female, this provides the motivation to transition from male to female. Caitlyn Jenner's statement to Diane Sawyer exemplifies this idea. She said that she was living a lie as a man and that she always felt that she was more female than male. According to the dominant view of the transgender identity, the conflict that Jenner experienced between her biological sex and her female gender identity motivated her transition. There is emerging evidence that there may be differences in brain anatomy between transgender individuals and heterosexuals. One study, for example, found more white matter in the connections between the right parietal lobes and right frontal lobes in the brains of transgender individuals, but not in the brains of heterosexuals and those with a same-sex orientation (Burke, Manzouri, & Savic, 2017). According to Burke et al., these connections are in the part of the brain associated with the perception of the self and one's body. What about the cases of rapid-onset transgender transitioning? There does not seem to be this process of reflection on one's gender identity. In these cases, a different process may be operating that involves social contagion (Littman, 2018). According to Littman, social contagion is the spread of behaviors and emotions through a population. She points out that for adolescents, members of an adolescent peer group can mutually influence each other to develop a new set of emotions and behavior with respect to gender identity. Peer social contagion has been observed among adolescent peer groups in other conditions, such as depression, suicide, and eating disorders.

STUDY CHECK

What is known about the transgender identity?
What are the origins of the transgender identity?

THINKING CRITICALLY

If you were in a debate about the roots of the transgender identity, which possible cause would you defend (and why)?

The matching principles suggest that many people tend to become involved with a partner who is similar in terms of physical attractiveness or social status.

Source: Yuliia Popova/Shutterstock

Interpersonal Attraction and Relationships

In Hill's (2008) ideas about human sexuality, he states that an important component of human sexuality is emotion. One way to approach the emotional component of sexuality is to explore the emotion we attach to sexuality via the relationships we form with others.

Humans are gregarious, social beings, and as such, we are motivated to form relationships with others. As noted in Chapter 8, social psychologists have defined two powerful social motives that impel us toward forming these relationships. The first need is the *need for affiliation*, which is a need to establish and maintain relationships with others (Wong & Csikzentmihalyi, 1991).

The relationships we form with friends, for example, provide us with emotional support, attention, and the opportunity to evaluate the appropriateness of our opinions and behavior through the process of social comparison. People vary in their level of the need for affiliation. An individual with a high need for affiliation will be motivated to form many relationships. An individual with a low need for affiliation will form few, if any, relationships. The need for affiliation is the fundamental factor underlying our interpersonal relationships.

You can probably guess that as humans our need to form relationships goes beyond simply forming friendships and extends to more intimate, deep relationships. This is why social psychologists define the second social motive as the *need for intimacy*, which is a need to form close and affectionate relationships (McAdams, 1982, 1989).

Intimate relationships (for example, with friends or lovers) involve sharing and disclosing personal information. Individuals with a high need for intimacy tend to be warm and affectionate and to show concern about other people. Intimacy is an essential component of many different interpersonal relationships (Laurenceau, Barrett, & Pietromonaco, 1998).

What happens when our needs for affiliation and intimacy are not met adequately? As noted in Chapter 8, a person may experience *loneliness*. It is important to understand that loneliness is a *psychological* state that is unrelated to the number of relationships a person has. A person who has a strong need for intimacy may have many acquaintances, but without intimate relationships, he or she may still experience loneliness. Loneliness can be temporary (e.g., after the breakup of a relationship) or long-lasting. Loneliness can lead to conditions such as depression, low-quality sleep, and heart disease among the elderly.

Social anxiety—a condition resulting when a person expects negative encounters with others.

One condition that also can lead to loneliness is social anxiety. Social anxiety (sometimes referred to as social phobia) occurs when a person expects negative encounters with others (Leary, 1983a, 1983b). Socially anxious people dwell on the negative aspects of a social interaction, anticipate negative interactions, and think that other people will not like them very much. Ultimately, this causes a person to avoid social encounters with others and lack meaningful relationships.

STUDY CHECK

What are the needs for affiliation and intimacy, and how do they relate to relationship formation?

If you found yourself feeling lonely in your life, what do you think you could do to reduce your loneliness?

The Factors that Affect Interpersonal Attraction and Relationship Formation

In the previous section we established that most people have a strong need to form and maintain relationships with others. Of course, there are people who prefer a more solitary life. However, for most of us it is important to have interpersonal relationships. In this section we will explore some of the factors that increase interpersonal attraction.

Physical Proximity

Think for a moment about the person you consider to be your "best friend." How did you first meet that person? It is more likely that you met via happenstance rather than providence. That is, you probably lived on the same street as your friend or worked together, or were in the same classes in school. Often, the people we become friends with are those who we find ourselves in close physical contact with. Social psychologists refer to this as the **physical proximity effect**.

One reason physical proximity is such a powerful determinant of attraction is the *mere exposure effect*. This effect occurs when repeated exposure to a neutral stimulus enhances one's positive feeling toward that stimulus. We have all experienced this. One example is when you download a new album and it takes you a while to really like it. When you first listen to it you may be unsure about it. However, as you listen to it more and more it starts to "grow on you" and you start liking it more. Of course, if you started out hating the album it is less likely that you will come to like it after listening to it. In fact, you may come to hate it even more! Since it was first identified in 1968 by Robert Zajonc, there have been over 200 studies of the mere exposure effect (Bornstein, 1989). These studies used a wide range of stimuli and, in virtually every instance, repeated exposure to a stimulus produced liking.

In addition to merely exposing us to others, proximity also increases the chances that we will interact with them. That is, proximity also promotes liking, because it gives us an opportunity to find out about each other. Physical proximity and the nature of the interaction combine to determine liking (Schiffenbauer & Schavio, 1976). If we discover that the other person has similar interests and attitudes, we are encouraged to pursue the interaction.

For decades, social psychologists talked about proximity in physical terms. That is being *physically* close to others. In recent years the Internet has become an important tool that helps people to form relationships, even over great distances. In effect, the Internet reduces *psychological distance* between people, even though *physical distance* may be great. Research tells us that people are, in fact, using the Internet as a way to form relationships. In one study, 88.3 percent of males and 69.3 percent of females reported using the Internet to form "casual or friendly" relationships with others. The study also found that 11.8 percent of men and 30.8 percent of women used the Internet to form intimate relationships (McCown, Fischer, Page, & Homant, 2001).

How do these Internet relationships stack up against more traditional, face-to-face relationships? For the most part, Internet and traditional relationships are very similar. For example, like traditional relationships, Internet relationships are important in people's lives and are stable over time (McKenna, Green, & Gleason, 2002). However, there are some differences. Traditional relationships were more interdependent, involved more commitment, and had greater breadth and depth than Internet relationships (Chan & Cheng, 2004).

Physical proximity effect—the idea that we become friends with those whom we find ourselves in close physical contact with.

Similarity

Once again, think about your best friend. What is his or her personality like? What attitudes does he or she hold? What are his or her interests? If you think carefully about your best friend, you will probably find that you and your friend are quite alike.

This illustrates the impact of similarity in relationship formation. In most cases, the people with whom we have relationships are highly similar to us. In fact, social psychologists have found that we tend to match ourselves to our friends and intimate partners on factors such as personality, attitudes, religion, race and even physical attractiveness. This effect is called the **matching principle**, which means that we tend to become involved with a partner with whom we are usually closely matched in terms of physical attributes or social status (Schoen & Wooldredge, 1989).

Why does similarity promote attraction? Attitude similarity promotes attraction in part because similar others support the "correctness" of our beliefs, which we like. Similarity allows us to compare our beliefs to those of others through a process called *social comparison*. Social comparison allows us to test the validity of our beliefs by comparing them to those of our friends and acquaintances (Hill, 1987). When we find that other people believe the same things that we do, we can be more confident that our attitudes are valid. It is rewarding to know that someone we like thinks in the same way that we do; it shows how smart we both are. Similarity may also promote attraction because we believe we can predict how a similar person will behave (Hatfield, Walster, & Traupmann, 1978).

Physical Attractiveness

One of the strongest factors affecting attraction, especially in the early stages of a relationship, is physical attractiveness. Generally, we are more attracted to attractive others than less attractive others. Physical attractiveness affects how we think and feel about others. We tend to hold physically attractive people in higher regard than less attractive people. We also tend to like physically attractive people more than less attractive people. Physical attractiveness also affects how we interact with others. Both men and women try to intensify an interaction with an unseen other person when they believe that the other person is attractive rather than unattractive (Garcia, Stinson, Ickes, Bissonette, & Briggs, 1991).

Physical attractiveness also affects how we perceive and treat others. Social psychologists have identified a **physical attractiveness bias** whereby physically attractive people are thought to have a wide range of positive attributes (Zebrowitz, Collins, & Dutta, 1998). For example, we are likely to believe that physically attractive people, compared to unattractive people, are generally happier, smarter, and more competent. The cultural stereotype we hold seems to suggest that what is beautiful is good (Dion, Berscheid, & Walster, 1972).

Unfortunately, there is a downside to the attractiveness bias. There also exists an unattractiveness bias. Unattractive individuals may experience discrimination because of their appearance. Noor and Evans (2003) found that a person with a less attractive face was perceived to be more neurotic, less open, less agreeable, and less attractive than a person with a more attractive face. Weight is another factor that affects perceived attractiveness, with overweight people being perceived as less attractive than normal weight people. Weight can affect how we treat others. In one study, overweight college students were less likely than other students to get financial help from home (Crandall, 1991).

Where does the attractiveness/unattractiveness bias come from? Undoubtedly, much of the bias is learned. From childhood forward, Western culture bombards us with the message that physically attractive people are preferred. Think about magazine and television advertisements for clothing and cosmetics. The models used in these advertisements are usually very attractive. Stereotypic body images are also portrayed in children's literature and movies (Herbozo, Tantleff-Dunn, Gokee-Larose, & Thompson, 2004). Just think, for example, about the Disney film *The Little Mermaid*, in which the mermaid Ariel is depicted as a slim, beautiful, young woman and the sea witch (the villain) is depicted as an obese, unattractive woman.

Matching principle—the idea that we tend to become involved with a partner with whom we are usually closely matched in terms of physical attributes or social status.

Physical attractiveness bias— physically attractive people are thought to have a wide range of positive attributes.

Despite all of the evidence that the attractiveness bias is learned, there is also evidence that the bias may be inborn. In one study, researchers found that infants as young as 2-months of age showed a preference for attractive over unattractive faces (Langlois, Roggman, Casey, Riesner-Danner, & Jenkins, 1987). Most likely, the best explanation is a combination of the learning and biological explanations. We appear to be born with a bias in the direction of attractiveness which is reinforced and enhanced via the learning process.

STUDY CHECK

What factors contribute to interpersonal attraction?

THINKING CRITICALLY

If you were given the assignment to try to counter the attractiveness bias in children, how would you go about reducing the bias?

PSYCHOLOGY IN ACTION

How Do We Select Our Mates?

We have seen in this chapter that there are several factors leading us to be attracted to others. How do we take the next step beyond liking others to forming a long-lasting love relationship? In other words, how do we select our mates? *Evolutionary psychology* is a subfield of both psychology and biology that uses the principles of evolution to explain human behavior. According to this approach, humans select mates for the same reasons that animals select mates: to propagate the species. But why is one member of a species attracted to another member of that species? We have seen how physical attractiveness is an important factor in interpersonal attraction. What makes a potential mate attractive to us? One factor is symmetry, which evolutionary psychologists describe as being reflective of underlying genetic quality. Lack of symmetry is thought to be caused by various stresses, such as poor maternal nutrition, late maternal age, attacks by predators, or disease, and may therefore reflect bad health or poor genetic quality. Thus, the preference for symmetry in potential mates, whether human or animal, may be instinctive (Watson & Thornhill, 1994). Indeed, even small differences matter. Twins with lower levels of symmetry are reliably rated as less attractive than their slightly more symmetrical counterparts (Mealey, Bridgstock, & Townsend, 1999). Gangestad and Thornhill (1998) have argued that physical appearance marked by high symmetry reveals to potential mates that the individual has

good genes and is therefore, for both men and women, a highly desirable choice.

David Buss, a prominent evolutionary social psychologist, suggested that to find and retain a reproductively valuable mate, humans engage in love acts—behaviors with near-term goals, such as display of resources the other sex finds enticing. The ultimate purpose of these acts is to increase reproductive success (Buss, 1988a, 1988b). Human sexual behavior thus can be viewed in much the same way as the sexual behavior of other animal species.

Research shows that men and women view desirable characteristics in a potential mate somewhat differently. Men tend to seek women who are young and attractive (Schwarz & Hassebrauck, 2012). Women, on the other hand, tend to select partners on the basis of attributes such as social status and industriousness (Ben Hamida, Mineka, & Bailey, 1998). This difference appears across a range of cultures. One study by Shackelford, Schmitt, and Buss (2005) had males and females evaluate several characteristics that could define a potential mate. The participants were drawn from 37 cultures (including African, Asian, and European). Their results confirmed that, across cultures, women valued social status more than men, and men valued physical attractiveness more than women.

Although this gender difference exists, we should not make too much of it. In fact, men and women show more similarities than differences in the characteristics valued in a potential mate. A recent meta-analysis showed, for example, that physical attractiveness and good earning potential are desirable characteristics for both men and women (Eastwick, Luchies, Finkel, & Hunt, 2014). However, men value physical attractiveness more than women and are less willing to compromise on this characteristic than women. For example, although women want an attractive partner for casual sex, they also want a male who is older and more interpersonally responsive. Men desire attractiveness and will compromise on everything else. In fact, a woman's attractiveness seems to overcome a male potential partner's common sense as well (Regan, 1998).

Finally, students often ask about any differences between heterosexual and same-sex-orientation mate preferences. The available research suggests that mate-selection preferences between these groups may not differ all that much (Over & Phillips, 1997). For example, a study of personal advertisements placed by heterosexual and same-sex-orientation males and females was conducted by Kenrick, Keefe, Bryan, Barr, and Brown (1995). Kenrick et al. found that mate-selection patterns for heterosexual and same-sex-orientation men were highly similar and showed similar patterns of change with age. Both groups of men preferred younger mates, and this preference grew stronger with age. This finding was replicated in a similar study of personal ads conducted by Burrows (2013).

Burrows (2013) found that gay men advertised for partners who were on average 13 years younger than themselves (heterosexuals advertised for someone 14 years younger). In another study examining personal ads, Russock (2011) found that heterosexual females more frequently sought resources from a potential mate than their same-sex-orientation counterparts. However, same-sex-orientation females were more interested in a physically attractive potential mate than heterosexual females. Finally, same-sex-orientation females were the least likely to offer information about physical attractiveness to potential mates (Russock, 2011).

Love Relationships

The *Beatles* in their 1967 song famously said, "All you need is love." The sentiment expressed by the *Beatles* supports the importance that humans have attached to love relationships. For thousands of years poets, singers, and novelists have extolled love relationships. But what exactly do we mean by the word "love?" It is a word we use a lot but understand little. Most of us know what love is but cannot define it. Social psychologists have attempted not only to define love but also to study it scientifically. In the sections that follow, we shall explore this important, yet elusive, concept.

The Triangular Theory of Love

Triangular theory of love—theory stating that love consists of three interrelated components: passion, intimacy, and commitment.

One important theory of love is the triangular theory of love which states that love consists of three interrelated components: passion, intimacy, and commitment (Sternberg, 1986, 1988). According to this theory, each component of love is represented by a leg of a triangle (see **Figure 9.3**).

Passion is the emotional component of love and dominates in the early stages of a love relationship. It is manifested in the aching one gets in his or her stomach and an intense desire to be with one's partner.

Intimacy involves self-disclosure, or the willingness to share important intimate details of your life with your partner. Intimacy also involves showing concern for your partner and being able to count on your partner when times get tough.

Finally, *commitment* is the cognitive component of love involving a decision to maintain the love relationship over time.

How do the three components of love change over the course of a relationship? Passion tends to dominate a love relationship early on. Keep in mind, however, that this may not be true for love relationships in all cultures. In Western culture it is true that passion often comes first (although it need not), but in other cultures passion may come later, if at all.

Because passion is difficult to sustain over time, it tends to burn hot, but burn fast. Consequently, in long-term relationships, passion tends to decline over time (Acker & Davis, 1992). Intimacy, on the other hand, tends to increase over time. Interestingly, passion and

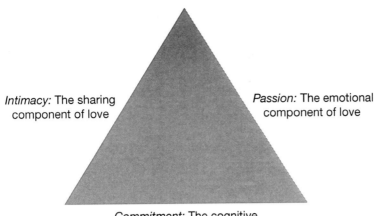

Intimacy: The sharing
component of love

Passion: The emotional
component of love

Commitment: The cognitive
component of love

FIGURE 9.3 Triangular Theory of Love

intimacy appear to be related. Research shows that as intimacy increases, passion often increases as well (Baumeister & Bratslavsky, 1999). Commitment also increases over time in a long-term relationship. In fact, it may come to dominate in later stages of a long-term love relationship.

The Varieties of Love

Sternberg's theory states that different types of love represent differing amounts of the three components. Perhaps the most important type of love, especially in Western cultures is romantic love. This is the type of love portrayed in books and movies. **Romantic love** involves high levels of passion and intimacy but low levels of commitment. When we state that we are "in love" with another, it is most likely romantic love to which we refer.

Romantic love appears to be experienced by members of a wide range of cultures (Jankowiak & Fischer, 1992). However, the way romantic love is experienced and expressed appears to differ across cultures. In one study, for example, Albanian students were found to be less romantic than American students. Additionally, American students were more likely to express romantic love verbally and Albanian students behaviorally (Hoxha & Hatala, 2012).

Another type of love is consummate love, with high levels of passion, intimacy, and commitment. Couples experiencing this type of love "have it all." They are able to maintain their passion and intimacy along with a commitment to a lifetime together. **Table 9.1** shows other types of love defined by Sternberg and how each relates to the three components of love.

Romantic love—a type of love with high levels of passion and intimacy but low levels of commitment.

Consummate love—a type of love with high levels of passion, intimacy, and commitment.

TABLE 9.1 Triangular Theory and Different Types of Love

Kind of Love	Love Component		
	Intimacy	Passion	Commitment
Non-love	No	No	No
Liking	Yes	No	No
Infatuated love	No	Yes	No
Empty love	No	No	Yes
Romantic love	Yes	Yes	No
Companionate love	Yes	No	Yes
Fatuous love	No	Yes	Yes
Consummate love	Yes	Yes	Yes

Beyond Sternberg's types of love, there are other types of love defined by social psychologists. *Unrequited love* occurs when we fall in love, but that love is not returned by the other person. Almost all of us have had some experience with unrequited love. In one study, 98 percent of the subjects had been rejected by someone they loved intensely (Baumeister, Wotman, & Stillwell, 1993).

Unrequited love is painful to both parties involved because both parties are likely to feel victimized in the relationship. Additionally, men are more likely to experience unrequited love than women (Aron, Aron, & Allen, 1998). Finally, unrequited love is often difficult for those involved to handle. This may be because western culture provides ample models for other types of love (e.g., romantic love) via books and movies. However, there are few cultural lessons on how to handle unrequited love. In most popular portrayals, unrequited love often involves a crazed rejected lover going after the rejecting partner (for example, the movie *Fatal Attraction*).

Another type of love is secret love. In *secret love*, the love partners may be deeply in love, but they cannot express it in public. For example, two married people may be madly in love but must keep that love secret (for obvious reasons). If unrequited love is the most disturbing type of love, secret love may be the most exciting.

Secret love relationships make lasting impressions on the people involved. In one study, for example, people who had been involved in secret love thought about the love relationship for a longer period of time than those who were involved in open love relationships (Wegner, Lane, & Dimitri, 1994). Interestingly, secrecy actually seems to increase the attraction between the parties involved. This may be because those involved in secret love experience strong emotions and think about one another all the time. Of course, the downside of secret love is that it is often destructive to existing love relationships (Wegner et al., 1994) and may have consequential effects that affect career, reputation, finances, and psychological functioning

---

STUDY CHECK

What have social psychologists discovered about love relationships?

THINKING CRITICALLY

Think about your own love relationships. Where do you think they fit with the triangular theory of love? Have you ever experienced unrequited love? If so, how did you react?

Chapter Summary

What is the definition of human sexuality?
Human sexuality is all of the emotional, cognitive, behavioral, and physical experiences of humans related to their sexuality (Hill, 2008). The emotional component includes all of our feelings, desires, and moods surrounding sexuality. The cognitive component encompasses our sexual thoughts, expectations, judgment, and plans relating to sexuality. Behavioral experiences are all of our overt sexual behaviors, actions, and activities relating to sexuality.

The physical component includes all sexual sensations and physical reactions to sexual stimuli.

How do the concepts of sex and gender differ?
"Sex" is a term that refers to one's biological status as a female or male. Females have an XX chromosome pattern and males an XY pattern. These different patterns result in different body hormonal environments relating to sexual characteristics. "Gender" refers to the social and

sociocultural characteristics associated with one's sex. Gender identity is a person's subjective experience of his or her gender. A gender role consists of the cultural expectations for males and females.

What factors relate to sexual motivation?

Sexual motivation relates to several underlying factors including physiological, cognitive and affective factors. On the physiological level, the sex drive is unique because individual survival does not depend on its satisfaction. However, the survival of a species does depend on the sex drive. Biology alone cannot account for human sexual motivation and behavior. Especially in Western culture sexual behaviors are influenced by learning experiences. One example is that culture influences how sexual motives are defined and expressed.

How are different sexual orientations defined?

Individuals with a heterosexual orientation are mostly attracted to members of the opposite sex. Individuals with a same-sex orientation are mostly attracted to members of the same sex. Others with a bisexual orientation show attraction to both members of the same and opposite sex. Another category of sexual orientation is transgender. Transgender identity refers to individuals whose appearance and/or behaviors do not conform to traditional, accepted gender roles. Transsexual refers to individuals whose gender identity is opposite from his or her biological sex.

What do we know about the same-sex and heterosexual orientations?

Same-sex orientation is an orientation and not a sexual preference because one does not choose sexual orientation voluntarily. There is a movement away from using the general term "homosexual" toward the same-sex orientation. Individuals with same-sex and heterosexual orientations do not differ significantly in terms of expression of sexuality.

Research shows some differences in the relationships of individuals with a same-sex orientation and those who are heterosexual. For example, compared to married heterosexual partners, lesbian couples report more intimacy, more autonomy, and more equality in their relationships. Same-sex orientation couples are more at ease and more comfortable with their sexual relationship than most heterosexual couples. When therapy is needed, the issues are much the same: focusing on developing clear communication, exploring personal values, expectations within the relationship, and matters related to developing as individuals as well as partners.

What have scientists found concerning the origins of the same-sex orientation?

There is no generally accepted theory about why a person displays a particular sexual orientation. Same-sex orientation likely results from an interaction of genetic, hormonal, and environmental factors. There is evidence for a genetic component. However, the genetic basis for the same-sex orientation may lie more in epigenetic factors than one's underlying genetic code. There is also some evidence that there are differences between the brains of individuals with a same-sex orientation and heterosexuals. There is also evidence that different socialization experiences in childhood can account for some of the differences.

What is known about the transgender identity?

A transgender identity involves a person having a gender identity that differs from one's actual gender. A person can transition from male to female (MtF or transwoman) or female to male (FtM or transman). Research shows that a transgender person rejects the culturally defined categories of male and female which may allow the transgender person to live a more authentic life. Although most transgender individuals show strong identifications with the gender they transition toward, many still show attachment to the gender assigned at birth. Transgender individuals face prejudice and discrimination in a number of areas which may contribute to higher rates of suicide attempts and actual suicides.

What are the origins of the transgender identity?

There is a degree of controversy over the origins of the transgender identity. The most widely accepted explanation for the transgender identity is that a transgender person has a gender identity that differs from the gender identity assigned at birth. There is emerging evidence that there may be differences in brain anatomy between transgender individuals and heterosexuals. Another recent observation is rapid-onset transitioning involving adolescents transitioning with no prior history of questioning their gender identity. Rapid-onset transitioning relates to peer social contagion.

What are the needs for affiliation and intimacy, and how do they relate to relationship formation?

The need for affiliation is a need to establish and maintain relationships with others. Individuals with a high need for affiliation are motivated to form many relationships with others. Those with a low need will have fewer relationships. The need for intimacy is the need to form close, affectionate relationships with others and goes beyond the need for affiliation. Individuals with a high need for intimacy tend to be warm and affectionate, showing concern about other people. If a person's relationships do not adequately meet these needs, a person may experience loneliness. Loneliness is a psychological state unrelated to the number of relationships a person has. Social anxiety is one condition that can lead to loneliness.

What factors contribute to interpersonal attraction?

We are likely to be attracted to individuals to whom we are physically close. That is, you are more likely to become friends with someone who lives close to you than far away.

The Internet, however, allows people to form relationships over long distances. Relationships formed via the Internet share many characteristics with more traditional relationships, but there are some differences.

We are also attracted to people who are similar to us with respect to a number of characteristics (e.g., personality, attitudes, and attractiveness). Additionally, we are more likely to be attracted to a physically attractive person than a less attractive person. There is a physical attractiveness bias which involves attributing positive characteristics to physically attractive individuals. A downside of this bias is that unattractive people are often seen in a negative light. The physical attractiveness bias is related to inborn and learning factors.

What have social psychologists discovered about love relationships?

An important theory of love is the triangular theory which suggests that love comprises three components: passion, intimacy, and commitment. Different types of love are defined with the three factors. For example, romantic love involves high levels of passion and intimacy, but lower levels of commitment. Unrequited love is love that is not returned and can be very disturbing to both parties involved. Secret love is love that cannot be made public. It is very exciting, but it can be destructive to existing love relationships and have a variety of negative consequences.

Key Terms

Human sexuality (p. 191)
Sex (p. 191)
Gender (p. 191)
Gender identity (p. 191)
Gender role (p. 191)
Sexual orientation (p. 194)
Heterosexual orientation (p. 194)
Same-sex orientation (p. 194)
Bisexual orientation (p. 194)

Transgender identity (p. 194)
Transsexual (p. 194)
Social anxiety (p. 200)
Physical proximity effect (p. 201)
Matching principle (p. 202)
Physical attractiveness bias (p. 202)
Triangular theory of love (p. 204)
Romantic love (p. 205)
Consummate love (p. 205)

Personality

Chapter Outline

Source: Rawpixel.com/Shutterstock.

Questions You Will Be Able to Answer

After reading Chapter 10, you should be able to answer the following questions:

- What is meant by "theories of personality"?
- What are the main features of the Freudian psychoanalytic approach to personality?
- What are the contributions of the neo-Freudian approaches to personality?
- How can we evaluate the psychoanalytic approach to personality?
- What is the behavioral/learning approach to personality, and what are some of its strengths and weaknesses?
- What is the basic thrust of the approaches to personality that are classified as cognitive or humanistic?

- What are trait theories of personality?
- What is the Five-Factor Model of personality?
- To what extent is behavioral observation a useful technique for assessing personality?
- How might interviews be helpful in assessing personality?
- What are the MMPI-2 and projective tests of personality?

Preview

Personality is a term that we use regularly but without giving much thought to exactly what we mean when we use it. Personality often appears to exist in greater or lesser degrees, as in, "She is so bubbly and outgoing! She's just Miss Personality." It also seems that someone's personality can be evaluated as being great or awful or somewhere in between, as in, "True, he doesn't look like much, but he sure has a great personality." We like to think that we are reasonably accurate in our assessments of the personalities of others—and the truth is, we probably are.

The major task of this chapter is to describe some of the theories of personality. First we will focus on a working definition for both "theory" and "personality." We organize our discussion of personality theories into five sections, each summarizing a major approach to the study of personality.

Because it is the oldest and arguably the most elegant of the theories of personality, we begin with that of Sigmund Freud. One reflection of the value of Freud's theory is that it attracted the attention and the interest of so many others. Some of them developed theories of their own. We then consider how behavioral psychologists and learning theorists have dealt with the notion of human personality. The contrast with Freud's approach is immediately clear. Some psychologists have claimed that if we want to understand human personality, our first focus should be cognitive. We consider these approaches next.

Of the five approaches discussed in this section, students often find the humanistic theories of Rogers and Maslow most to their liking—partly because they allow for the possibility that people can take charge of their own lives and that they are not ruled by inner drives or rewards from the environment. Whereas most theoretical approaches to personality at least address the issue of explaining why people think, act, and feel as they do, the so-called trait theories have no such interest. Their goal is description: How shall we best describe the human personality?

Not all psychologists who claim personality as one of their areas of interest are actively involved in trying to devise a grand theory to describe or explain human nature. Many are involved in research on intriguing aspects of the complex concept we call personality. For example, we will explore the extent to which personality really is a useful concept when trying to explain someone's behavior. The basic question, first raised decades ago, is whether a person's behaviors are determined by the situation presented by the environment, or by those internal dispositions called personality traits. Here is a debate that once raged, but that now may be considered resolved. Finally, we address ways in which psychologists measure or assess an individual's personality.

Introducing Personality "Theories"

A *theory* is a series of assumptions or beliefs; in our particular topic, these assumptions are about people and their personalities. Theories are designed both to describe and to explain. The beliefs that constitute a theory are based on observations and are logically related to one another. A theory should lead—through reason—to specific, testable hypotheses. In short, a **theory** is an organized collection of testable ideas used to describe and explain a particular subject matter.

What then is personality? Few terms have been as difficult to define. Actually, each of the theoretical approaches we will study in this chapter generates its own definition of personality. But just to get us started, we will say that **personality** includes those affects, behaviors, and cognitions of people that characterize them in a number of situations over time. (Here again is our ABC mnemonic.) Personality also includes those dimensions we can use to judge people to be different from one another. So with personality theories, we look for ways that allow us to describe how people remain the same over time and circumstances and to describe differences that we know exist among people. Note that personality is something a person brings to his or her interactions with the environment. Somehow, personality originates within the individual (Burger, 2000), but personality also reflects the influences of one's culture or social context (McAdams & Pals, 2006).

Personality psychology faces three inter-related goals or missions. The theoretical mission of psychologists who specialize in understanding personality is "to account for individuals' characteristic patterns of thought, emotion, and behavior together with the psychological mechanisms—hidden or not—behind those patterns" (Funder, 2001, p. 198). The empirical mission of personality psychologists is to gather and analyze observations on how personalities, environmental situations, and behaviors are inter-related. The third mission of personality psychology is "institutional"—to bring together the contributions of many of psychology's sub-fields to better understand the whole person.

> **STUDY CHECK**
>
> What is meant by "theories of personality"?

> **THINKING CRITICALLY**
>
> In what ways do psychologists tend to view personality differently from the way it is used in everyday conversation?

Freud's Psychoanalytic Approach

We begin our discussion of personality with the psychoanalytic approach associated with Sigmund Freud (1856–1939) and his students. We begin with Freud because he was the first to present a unified theory of personality. His theory of personality has been one of the most influential and, at the same time, most controversial in all of science. There are many facets to Freud's theory, but two basic premises characterize the **psychoanalytic approach**: a reliance on innate drives as explanatory concepts for human behavior, and an acceptance of the power of unconscious forces to mold and shape behavior. In addition—more than anyone else—Freud emphasized the importance of early childhood experiences. He argued that the most important aspects of anyone's personality were pretty well in place by the age of seven.

Central to Freudian personality theory is the notion that information, feelings, wants, drives, desires, and the like can be found at various levels of awareness or consciousness. Mental events of which we are actively aware at the moment are *conscious*. Aspects of our mental life of which we are not conscious at any moment but that can be easily brought to awareness are stored at a *preconscious level*. When you shift your awareness to think about what you might do this evening, those plans were probably already there, in your preconscious mind.

Cognitions, feelings, and motives that are *not* available either at the conscious or preconscious level are said to be in the *unconscious*. Here we keep ideas, memories, and desires of

Theory—an organized collection of testable ideas used to describe and explain a particular subject matter.

Personality—the affects, behaviors, and cognitions of people that characterize them in a number of situations over time.

Psychoanalytic approach—a personality theory relying on innate drives as explanatory concepts for human behavior and an acceptance of the power of unconscious forces to mold and shape behavior.

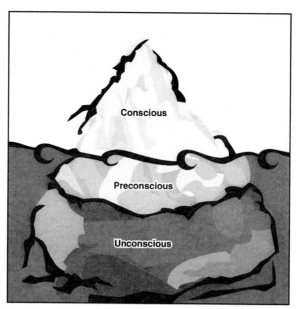

FIGURE 10.1 In the theories of Sigmund Freud, the mind is likened to an iceberg, where only a small portion of one's mental life is available in normal waking consciousness; more is available with some effort of retrieval at the preconscious level; and most is stored away in an unconscious level from which intentionally retrieval occurs only with great effort.

which we are not aware and cannot easily become aware. The significance of this unconscious level of the mind is that even though thoughts and feelings are stored there so that we are completely unaware of them, the contents of the unconscious mind can still influence us. Unconscious content, passing through the preconscious, may show itself in slips of the tongue, humor, anxiety-based symptoms, and dreams. Freud believed that unconscious forces could explain behaviors that otherwise seemed irrational and beyond description. He also maintained that most of our mental life takes place on the unconscious level. A common representation of Freud's levels of consciousness, and one that Freud used himself, is an iceberg (see **Figure 10.1**). In this representation, the conscious is the small part of the iceberg visible above the surface (like an iceberg, the smallest part). Just below the surface is the preconscious, and deep below the water is the unconscious (which makes up the largest portion of the iceberg).

According to Freudian theory, our behaviors, thoughts, and feelings are largely governed by innate biological drives, referred to as *instincts* in this context. These are inborn impulses or forces that rule our personalities. There may be many separate drives or instincts, but they can be grouped into two categories.

On the one hand are life instincts (Eros), or impulses for survival, including those that motivate sex, hunger, and thirst. Each instinct has its own energy that compels us into action (drives us). Freud called the psychic energy through which the sexual instincts operate libido. Opposed to life instincts are death instincts (Thanatos). These are impulses of destruction. Directed inward, they give rise to feelings of depression or suicide; directed outward, they result in aggression. (For Freud, seeing aggression as reflective of an inborn instinct was the only way he could account for the prevalence and universality of violence and aggression.) In large measure, life (according to Freud) is an attempt to resolve conflicts between these two natural but opposed sets of instincts.

Freud believed that the mind operates on three interacting levels of awareness: conscious, preconscious, and unconscious. He also proposed that personality consists of three separate, interacting structures or subsystems: the id, ego, and superego (see **Figure 10.2**). Each of these structures, or subsystems, has its own job to do and its own principles to follow.

The id is the totally inborn portion of personality. It resides in the unconscious level of the mind, and it is through the id that basic instincts are expressed. The driving force of

Life instincts (Eros)—impulses for survival, including those that motivate sex, hunger, and thirst.

Libido—the psychic energy through which the sexual instincts operate.

Death instincts (Thanatos)—the impulses of destruction.

Id—the totally inborn portion of personality. It resides in the unconscious level of the mind, and it is through the id that basic instincts are expressed.

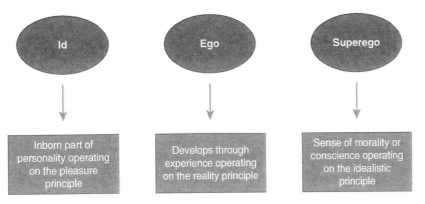

FIGURE 10.2 The Three Parts of the Personality

the id is libido, or sexual energy, although it may be more fair to say "sensual" rather than "sexual" so as not to imply that Freud was always talking about adult sexual intercourse. The id operates on the **pleasure principle**, indicating that the major function of the id is to find immediate gratification and satisfaction for basic pleasurable impulses. Although the other divisions of personality develop later, our id remains with us always and is the basic energy source in our lives.

The **ego** is the part of the personality that develops through one's experience with reality. In many ways, it is our "self"—at least the self of which we are consciously aware at any time. One of the ego's main jobs is to find satisfaction for the id, but in ways that are reasonable and rational. The ego operates on the **reality principle**, which is the reasonable and rational way to satisfy the impulses of the id. The ego may delay gratification of some libidinal impulse or find an acceptable outlet for some need. Freud said that "the ego stands for reason and good sense while the id stands for untamed passions" (Freud, 1933).

The last of the structures of personality to develop is the **superego**, the part of the personality involving one's sense of morality or conscience. It reflects our internalization of society's rules. The superego operates on principles driven by idealism. One problem with the superego is that it, like the id, has no contact with reality and therefore often places unrealistic demands on the individual. For example, a person's superego may have that person believe that he or she should always be kind and generous and never harbor unpleasant or negative thoughts about someone else, no matter what. The superego demands that we do what it deems right and proper, no matter what the circumstances. Failure to do so may lead to guilt and shame. Again, it falls to the ego to try to maintain a realistic balance between the conscience of the superego and the libido of the id.

Although the dynamic processes underlying personality may appear complicated, the concepts underlying these processes are not as complicated as they sound. Suppose a bank teller discovers an extra $50 in his cash drawer at the end of the day. He certainly could use an extra $50. "Go ahead. Nobody will miss it. The bank can afford a few dollars here and there. Think of the fun you can have with an extra $50," is the basic message from the id. "The odds are that you'll get caught if you take this money. If you are caught, you may lose your job; then you'll have a tough time finding another one," reasons the ego. "You shouldn't even think about taking that money. Shame on you! It's not yours. It belongs to someone else and should be reported," the superego protests. Clearly, the interaction of the components of personality isn't always this simple and straightforward, but this example illustrates the general idea.

Given that we have reviewed only a few major ideas from a very complex approach to personality, can we make any value judgments about its contribution? Psychologists have debated the relative merits of Freud's works for decades, and the debate continues, with efforts to generate more empirical research (Funder, 2001). On the positive side, Freud and other theorists with a psychoanalytic orientation must be credited for focusing our attention on the importance of the childhood years and for suggesting that some (even biologically determined) impulses may affect our behaviors even though they are beyond our immediate awareness. Although Freud may have overstated the matter, drawing our attention

Pleasure principle—the idea that the major function of the id is to find immediate gratification and satisfaction for basic pleasurable impulses.

Ego—the part of the personality that develops through one's experience with reality. In many ways, it is our "self."

Reality principle—the reasonable and rational way to satisfy the impulses of the id.

Superego—the part of the personality involving one's sense of morality or conscience.

Freud's personality structures of id, ego, and superego are not as abstract as many believe at first. A cashier at the end of the day finds an extra $50 in her drawer. The conflict among id ("Go ahead; take it; no one will know") and superego ("No, that's not your money") may put pressure on the ego ("Is this the sort of risk you want to take for $50") may be very real indeed.

to the impact of sexuality and sexual impulses as influences on personality and human behavior is also a significant contribution. Freud's concept that the unconscious may influence our pattern of responding to the world has generated considerable research and has found general acceptance (Westen, 1998).

On the other hand, many psychologists have been critical of Freud's theory. Some who followed Freud tended to downplay innate biological drives and take a more social approach to personality development. One of the major criticisms of the psychoanalytic approach is that so many of its insights cannot be tested. Freud thought of himself as a scientist, but he tested none of his ideas about human nature experimentally. Some seem beyond testing. Just what is libidinal energy? How can it be measured? How would we recognize it if we saw it? Concepts such as id, ego, and superego may sound sensible enough, but how can we prove or (more importantly) disprove their existence? A very heavy reliance on instincts, especially with sexual and aggressive overtones, as explanatory concepts, goes beyond where most psychologists are willing to venture.

STUDY CHECK

What are the main features of the Freudian psychoanalytic approach to personality?

THINKING CRITICALLY

How could it possibly be that a theory of human personality written over 100 years ago could still be at all relevant?

The Psychoanalytic Approach after Freud

Sigmund Freud was a prolific writer and a persuasive communicator. His ideas were challenging, and they attracted many followers. Freud founded a psychoanalytic society in Vienna with a circle of colleagues and friends who shared his ideas. However, some colleagues did not agree with all aspects of his theory. Among other things, several of them were bothered by the very strong emphasis on biological instincts and libido and what they perceived as a lack of concern for social influences. Some of these analysts proposed theories of their own. These analysts became known as *neo-Freudians*. Because they had their own ideas, they had to part from Freud; he would not tolerate disagreement with any aspect of his theory from those within his inner circle.

The theories proposed by the neo-Freudians are complex and comprehensive. Each consists of logically inter-related assumptions, and it is not possible to do justice to any theory of personality in a short paragraph or two. However, we can sketch the basic idea(s) behind the theories of a few neo-Freudians.

Alfred Adler (1870–1937). As the psychoanalytic movement began to take shape, Adler was one of Freud's closest friends. However, Adler left Freud's inner circle and, in 1911, founded his own version of the psychoanalytic approach to personality. Two things seemed most to offend Adler: (1) the negativity of Freud's views (for example, the death instinct) and (2) the idea of sexual libido as the prime impulse in life.

Adler argued that we are a product of the social influences on our personality. We are motivated not so much by drives and instincts as we are by goals and incentives. For

Adler, the future and one's hope for what it held were often more important than one's past. In Adler's theory, the goal in life is the achievement of success or superiority. This goal is fashioned in childhood when, because we are then weak and vulnerable, we develop an **inferiority complex**— the feeling that we are less able than others to solve life's problems and get along in the world. Although we may seem inferior as children, with the help of social support and our own creativity, we can overcome and succeed. Simply striving for superiority—to be the best—was viewed by Adler as a healthy reaction to early feelings of inferiority only when it was balanced with a sort of "social interest" or "community feeling," or a genuine desire to help and serve others.

Albert Bandura was presented with the National Medal of Science by President Obama on May 19, 2016.

Inferiority complex—the feeling that we are less able than others to solve life's problems and get along in the world.

Carl Jung (1875–1961). Carl Jung left Freud's inner circle in 1913. Freud had chosen Jung to be his successor, but shortly after he did so, the two men disagreed about the role of sexuality and the nature of the unconscious—two central themes in psychoanalysis. Jung was more mystical in his approach to personality and, like Adler, was more positive about a person's ability to control his or her own destiny. He believed the major goal in life is to unify all of the aspects of our personality, conscious and unconscious, introverted (inwardly directed) and extroverted (outwardly directed). Libido was energy for Jung, but not sexual energy. It was energy for personal growth and development.

Jung readily accepted the idea of an unconscious mind and expanded on it, arguing for two types of unconscious: the *personal unconscious*, which is very much like Freud's notion, and the *collective unconscious*, which contains those very basic ideas that go beyond an individual's own personal experiences. Jung believed that the collective unconscious contained concepts common to all of humanity and inherited from all past generations. The contents of our collective unconscious include what Jung called *archetypes*—universal forms and patterns of thought. These are basic "ideas" that transcend all of history. Jung's archetypes include themes that recur in myths: motherhood, opposites, good, evil, masculinity, femininity, and the circle as a symbol of journeys that come full circle, returning to their point of origin, or of the complete, whole self.

Karen Horney (1885–1952). Trained as a psychoanalyst in Germany, Karen Horney (pronounced "horn-eye") came to the United States in 1934. She accepted a few Freudian concepts but changed most of them significantly. Horney believed that the idea of levels of consciousness made sense, but she argued that the prime impulses that drive or motivate behavior are not biological and inborn, nor are they sexual and aggressive.

A major concept for Horney was *basic anxiety*, which grows out of childhood when the child feels alone and isolated in a hostile world. If parents properly nurture their children, children overcome basic anxiety. If parents are overly punishing, inconsistent, or indifferent, however, children may develop *basic hostility* and may feel hostile and aggressive toward their parents. However, young children cannot express hostility toward their parents openly, so the hostility gets pushed down into the unconscious, building even more anxiety.

Horney did emphasize early childhood experiences, but from a perspective of social interaction and personal growth. Horney claimed that there are three distinct ways in which people interact with each other. In some cases, people *move away from others*, seeking self-sufficiency and independence. The idea here is, "If I am on my own and uninvolved, you won't be able to hurt me." On the other hand, some *move toward others* and are compliant and dependent. This style of interaction shields against anxiety in the sense: "If I always do what you want me to do, you won't be upset with me." Horney's third interpersonal style involves *moving against others*. In this third case, the effort is to be in control, gain power, and dominate: "If I am in control, you'll have to do what I want you to." Horney's ideal state is a balance among these three styles, but she argued that many people have one style that predominates in their dealings with others.

Horney also disagreed with Freud regarding the biological basis of differences between men and women. Freud's theories have been challenged many times for their male bias (Fisher & Greenberg, 1977; Jordan et al., 1991). Karen Horney was one of the first to do so.

STUDY CHECK

What are the contributions of the neo-Freudian approaches to personality? How can we evaluate the psychoanalytic approach to personality?

THINKING CRITICALLY

How might psychoanalytically oriented psychologists account for the success or failure of students in a beginning psychology class?

The Behavioral/Learning Approach

Many American psychologists in the early twentieth century did not think much of the psychoanalytic approach. Right from the beginning, American psychology was oriented toward the laboratory and theories of learning. Explaining personality in terms of learning and observable behaviors seemed a reasonable course of action.

John B. Watson (1878–1958) and his followers in behaviorism argued that psychology should turn away from the study of consciousness and the mind because the contents of mental life were beyond the scope of science. They argued that psychologists should study observable behavior. Yet here were Freud and the other psychoanalysts arguing that *unconscious* forces are determiners of behavior. "Nonsense," the behaviorist would say. "We don't even know what we mean by consciousness, and here you want to talk about levels of unconscious influence!"

Watson emphasized the role of the environment in shaping behaviors. Behaviorists did not accept the Freudian notion of inborn traits, whether they were called drives, id, libido, or anything else. What mattered was learning. A personality theory was not needed. An adequate theory of learning would include all the details about personality that one would ever need.

Who we are is determined by our learning experiences, and early experiences do count heavily—on this point Watson and Freud would have agreed. Even our fears are conditioned (remember Watson's "Little Albert" study?). So convinced was Watson that instincts and innate impulses had little to do with the development of behavior that he could write, albeit somewhat tongue in cheek, "Give me a dozen healthy infants, well-formed, and my own specified world to bring them up in, and I'll guarantee to take any one at random and train him to become any type of specialist I might select—doctor, lawyer, artist, merchant, chief, and yes, even beggarman and thief, regardless of his talents, penchants, tendencies, abilities, vocations, and race of his ancestors" (Watson, 1925, p. 104).

B.F. Skinner (1904–1990) avoided any reference to internal variables to explain behavior, which is the essence of what we normally think of as personality. Skinner believed that psychology should focus on observable stimuli, observable responses, and the relationships among them. He argued—as did Watson—that one should not go meddling about in the mind of the organism. Behavior is shaped by its consequences. Some behaviors result in reinforcement and, thus, tend to be repeated. Other behaviors are not reinforced and, thus, tend not to be repeated. Consistency in behavior simply reflects the consistency of the organism's reinforcement history. A pivotal question, from a Skinnerian point of view, is: How will external conditions be manipulated to produce the sorts of consequences that we want?

John Dollard (1900–1980) and *Neal Miller* (1909–2002) also tried to see if they could use the principles of learning theory to explain personality and how it developed. What matters for a person's personality, they argued, was the system of habits developed in response to cues in the environment. Behavior was motivated by primary drives (upon whose satisfaction survival depended) and learned drives, which developed through experience. For example, pushing an anxiety-producing event into the unconscious is simply a matter of learned forgetfulness; forgetting about some anxiety-producing experience is reinforcing and, consequently, tends to be repeated.

Albert Bandura (b. 1925) is one learning theorist more than willing to consider the internal cognitive processes of the learner. He claims that many aspects of personality are learned, but often through observation and social influence (Bandura, 1999, 2001a). For Bandura, learning is more than forming connections between stimuli, responses, and resulting reinforcers; it involves a cognitive rearrangement and representation of the world. In simpler terms, this approach argues, for example, that you may learn to behave honestly through the observation of others. If you observe your parents being honest and see their behaviors being reinforced, you may acquire similar responses.

Theorists who take a behavior-learning approach to personality argue that who we are in this world is a reflection of our learning and our experiences. Although many women in our society acquire what is often referred to as "gender-approach" careers, others acquire a different set of expectations.

Source: goodluz/Shutterstock.

Many critics of the behavioral-learning approach to personality argue that Watson, Skinner, and others dehumanize personality and that even the social learning theory of Bandura is too deterministic. The impression is that everything a person does, thinks, or feels is in some way determined by his or her environment or learning history. This leaves nothing—or very little—for the *person*, for personality, to contribute. Behavioral-learning approaches to personality often are not theories at all, at least not very comprehensive theories. To their credit, learning theorists demand that theoretical terms be carefully defined and that hypotheses be verified experimentally. It is also the case that many ideas reflected in this approach to personality theory have been successfully applied in behavior therapy.

STUDY CHECK

What is the behavioral/learning approach to personality, and what are some of its strengths and weaknesses?

THINKING CRITICALLY

Which aspects of your own personality do you believe reflect your learning experiences?

The Cognitive Approach

According to the cognitive approach to human personality, many of the basic cognitive processes humans use (for example, memory and accessing information) intersect with patterns of thought and perception normally thought to be involved in personality.

George Kelly (1905–1967) proposed an early cognitive theory of personality. According to Kelly (1955), each person has a set of *personal constructs* that direct his or her thoughts and perceptions. These personal constructs are a part of one's long-term memory, and they exert a directive influence over how information is stored and processed in other memory stores. As it happens, Kelly's work was being done just as the "cognitive revolution" in psychology was beginning, and Kelly never really made a connection between his notion of personal constructs and the developing ideas about human cognitive functioning.

Walter Mischel (1930–2018), a student of Kelly, provided links between personal constructs and human cognition. Mischel (1973, 1999, Mischel, Shoda, & Smith, 2004) proposed a model of personality that includes the following four "person variables":

1. *Cognitive and behavioral construction competencies*: Included in this set of competencies are personal abilities such as intelligence, social skills, and creativity. These competencies would be part of one's procedural memory, or memory involving how to do things.
2. *Encoding strategies and personal constructs*: Included here are cognitions we use to make sense out of the world. They include beliefs about one's self (for example, "I am a friendly person").
3. *Subjective stimulus values*: Here a person houses his or her expectations about achieving goals, as well as the weight placed on possible outcomes for goal achievement (for example, rewards).
4. *Self-regulatory systems and plans*: This dimension includes strategies for self-reinforcement and how those strategies control cognitions.

The cognitive approach to personality fits in well with what is known about human cognition. Kelly's and Mischel's approach to personality has withstood the test of time. In fact, since Mischel first proposed his theory, it has undergone only one change: the addition of a fifth, affective, factor. Other cognitive systems have also been proposed that incorporate the time-honored cognitive concepts. There has been a blending of trait and cognitive theories of personality that has provided a rich new area for research into personality.

The Humanistic Approach

To some degree, the humanistic approach to personality contrasts with both the psychoanalytic and behavioral approaches. It claims that people have the ability to shape their own destinies, to chart and follow their own courses of action, and that biological, instinctive, or environmental influences can be overcome or minimized. The humanistic view may be thought of as more optimistic than either the Freudian approach (with its death instincts and innate impulses) or the learning approach (with its emphasis on control exerted by forces of the environment). It tends to focus more on the "here and now" than on early childhood experiences as molders of personality. The humanistic point of view emphasizes the wholeness or completeness of personality, rather than focusing on its structural parts. What matters most is how people perceive themselves and others.

Carl Rogers' (1902–1986) approach to personality is referred to as "person-centered." Like Freud, Rogers developed his views of human nature through the observation of clients in a clinical setting. (Rogers preferred the term *client* to *patient* and the term *person-centered* to *client-centered* to describe his approach.) Rogers believed that the most powerful of human drives is the one to become fully functioning.

Fully functioning—a person strives to become all that he or she can be.

To be **fully functioning** implies that the person is striving to become all that he or she can be. To be fully functioning is to experience "optimal psychological adjustment, optimal psychological maturity, complete congruence, complete openness to experience..." (Rogers, 1959, p. 235). People who realize this drive are described as living in the present, getting the most from each experience, not moping around over opportunities lost or anticipating events to come. As long as we act only to please others, we are not fully functioning. To be fully functioning involves openness to one's own feelings and desires, awareness of one's inner self, and a positive self-regard.

Helping children become fully functioning requires that we offer what Rogers calls *unconditional positive regard*. Some of the things children do bring rewards, but other things do not. How we (or children) behave can influence how we are regarded by those we care about. If we behave in an appropriate manner, others regard us positively. If we behave inappropriately, others may regard us negatively. Thus, we tend to receive only conditional positive regard. If we do what is expected or desired, then we get rewarded. As a result, we try to act in ways that bring rewards and avoid punishment; we try to act in ways that please others. Feelings of self-worth are thus dependent on the actions of others who then either reward us, do not reward us, or even punish us. Rogers also argued that we should separate the child's behaviors from the child's self. That means that we may punish a child for doing a bad thing, but never for being a bad child (for example, "I love you very much, but what you have done is dangerous, and I told you not to, and therefore you will be punished"). Helping people achieve positive self-regard is one of the major goals of Carl Rogers' person-centered therapy.

Note that what matters here is not so much what *is*, but what is *felt* or *perceived*. One's true self (whatever it may be) is less important than one's image of oneself. How the world is experienced is what matters. You may be an excellent piano player, but if you feel you are a poor piano player, that perception or self-regard is what matters most.

Abraham Maslow's (1908–1970) basic criticism of the psychology he had studied was that it was altogether too pessimistic and negative. A person was seen as battered about by either a hostile environment or by depraved instincts, many of which propelled the person on a course of self-destruction.

There must be more to living than this, thought Maslow. He preferred to attend to the positive side of human nature. Maslow felt that people's needs are not low and negative but are positive or, at worst, neutral. Our major goal in life is to realize those needs and put them into practice—or to self-actualize.

Let's look, Maslow argued, at the very best among us. Let's focus our attention on characteristics of those who have realized their fullest positive potential and have become self-actualized. Compare this point of view with Freud's, who drew many of his ideas about personality from interactions with his patients, people who hardly could be categorized as self-actualizers. In his search for such individuals, Maslow could not find many. Most were historical figures, such as Thomas Jefferson and Eleanor Roosevelt.

Like the others, the humanistic approach has a number of strengths. For one, it reminds us of the wholeness of personality and of the danger in analyzing something as complex as personality in small, artificial segments. The humanistic approach is more positive and optimistic, stressing personal growth and development. As we will see in our discussion of psychotherapy, the humanistic approach has had a significant impact on many therapists and counselors.

Humanistic theories also have drawbacks. A major problem with this approach is much like the basic problem with Freud's theory: It seems to make sense, but how does one go about testing any of the observations and statements made by proponents of the approach? Many of the key terms are defined in general, fuzzy ways. What *is* self-image? How do we really know when someone is *growing*? How can anyone really document the advantages of unconditional positive regard? In many ways, what we have here is a blueprint for living, a vision for the nature of personality, not a scientific theory. There also are critics who claim that the notions of striving to be fully functioning or self-actualized are both naïve and far from universal.

STUDY CHECK

What is the basic thrust of the approaches to personality that are classified as cognitive or humanistic?

THINKING CRITICALLY

Of our ABCs—affect, behavior, and cognition—which do you think is most important? In other words, which of these three do you think plays the largest role in your life?

Chapter 10 Personality **219**

The Trait Approach

Trait theories of personality have a markedly different flavor than any of the approaches we have looked at thus far. Trait theories have two important aspects. First, the trait approach is an empirical one, relying on research using carefully constructed tests. Second, the trait approach focuses on individual differences in personality and not on measuring which traits are dominant in a given individual. We may define a personality **trait** as "any distinguishable, relatively enduring way in which one individual differs from others" (Guilford, 1959, p. 5).

Traits are descriptive dimensions. That is, any trait (e.g., friendliness) is not a simple either/or proposition. Friendliness falls on a continuum, and it can range from extremely unfriendly to extremely friendly, with many possibilities in between. Traits need to be measurable so we can assess the extent to which people may differ on those traits. We will briefly summarize three trait theories: one a classic, the others contemporary.

A classic trait theory is *Raymond Cattell's* (1905–1998) empirical approach, which relies on psychological tests, questionnaires, and surveys. Talking about personality traits without talking about how they are measured made little sense to him. Cattell used a technique called *factor analysis*—a correlation procedure that identifies groups of highly related variables that may be assumed to measure the same underlying factor (here, a personality trait). The logic is that, if you know that some people are outgoing, you do not need to test them to see if they are sociable or extroverted, because these traits are all highly correlated, and such information would be redundant.

Cattell argued for two major types of personality traits (1973, 1979). *Surface traits* are clusters of behaviors that go together, like those that make up curiosity, trustworthiness, or kindliness. These traits are easily observed and can be found in many settings. More important than surface traits are the fewer number of underlying traits from which surface traits develop. These are called *source traits*. A person's pattern of source traits determines which surface traits get expressed in behavior. Source traits are not as easy to measure as surface traits because they are not directly observable. Some of Cattell's 16 source traits are as follows: Reserved (detached, aloof), Outgoing (participating), Trusting (accepting), Suspicious (circumspect), Conservative (disinclined to change), Experimenting (open to change), Relaxed (tranquil, composed), and Tense (frustrated, driven).

For many years psychologists have struggled to identify the most reasonable set of personality traits. Cattell found many surface traits and a smaller number of source traits. Other trait theorists have proposed different traits as most descriptive of human personality. Whose theory is correct? Which set of traits is more reasonable? Is there any set of personality traits that is acceptable?

It may surprise you to learn that personality psychologists are coming to a consensus concerning which traits have the most research support as descriptors of personality. One such model suggests that there are five core traits making up personality. This model, or approach, is referred to as the **Five-Factor Model** (McAdams & Pals, 2006; Caspi, Roberts & Shiner, 2005; John, Nauman, & Soto, 2008; McCrae & Costa, 2008). What are the dimensions of personality that are referred to as the "Big Five"?

Although there is support for the Five-Factor Model, there is disagreement on how to describe these five. The following is a compilation from several sources (listed previously). Please note that there is no particular ranking involved in this list. That is, Dimension I is not to be taken as more important or more common than Dimension IV.

1. Dimension I is called *Extroversion/Introversion* and embodies such things as assurance, talkativeness, openness, self-confidence, and assertiveness, on the one hand, and silence and passivity on the other. The extrovert seeks stimulation, particularly from social situations, and is a generally happy person (Lucas & Fujita, 2000). Persons ranked high on extroversion tend to experience more positive emotions than negative ones (Clark & Watson, 2008).
2. Dimension II is *Agreeableness* (sometimes *Friendliness*), with altruism, trust, caring, and providing emotional support at one end, and hostility, indifference, selfishness, and distrust on the other.

Trait—any distinguishable, relatively enduring way in which one individual differs from others.

Five-Factor Model—a trait model of personality suggesting that there are five core traits making up personality.

3. Dimension III is called *Consciousness* and amounts to a "will to achieve." It includes self-control, dependability, planning, thoroughness, and persistence, paired with carelessness, impulsivity, negligence, and unreliability. As you might imagine, this dimension correlates well with positive life outcomes such as occupational outcomes (Roberts et al., 2007).

4. Dimension IV is an emotionality dimension, usually called *Neuroticism* (or *Stability-Instability*). In many ways, this is the extent to which one is emotionally stable and able to handle most of the stress that he or she encounters or, at the other extreme, is anxious, depressed, or in some way psychologically disordered. It includes such things as nervousness and moodiness.

Which dimension of the Five-Factor Model would characterize the young woman in the forefront of this photo?

5. Dimension V is *Openness to Experience and Culture*. (In this context, "culture" refers to aspects of experience such as art, dance, literature, music, and the like.) This factor includes such characteristics as curiosity, imagination, and creativity. Persons rated low on this dimension are quite focused, with narrow interests and little desire to try different things, such as travel. This is the one trait of these five that has been consistently correlated with measures of intelligence (DeYoung et al., 2010).

The recurrent finding that all personality traits can be reduced to just five, with these names (or names like these), is remarkable. Each of these five traits represents a dimension of possible habits and individual responses that a person may bring to bear in any given situation.

These five traits have emerged from more than 50 years of research in many cultures. They have emerged regardless of the individuals being assessed, and "the Big Five have appeared now in at least five languages, leading one to suspect that something quite fundamental is involved here" (Digman, 1990, p. 433).

Another trait approach that expands on the Five-Factor Model is the *HEXACO model*. The HEXACO model (Ashton & Lee, 2001) includes six personality traits: Honesty (H), Emotionality (E), Extroversion (X), Agreeableness (A), Conscientiousness (C), and Openness to Experience (O). As you can see, there is considerable overlap between the HEXACO and Five-Factor Models. The major addition in the HEXACO model is the Honesty-Humility dimension. At first glance, it might appear that this dimension would be essentially the same as the Conscientiousness dimension in the Five-Factor Model. However, Ashton and Lee point out that there is, in fact, little overlap. Across a number of studies in several cultures, the Honesty trait includes characteristics such as truthfulness, trustworthiness, and sincerity (Ashton & Lee, 2001).

Clearly, trait approaches to personality are different from the others, even in their basic intent. Trait theories do have a few obvious advantages. They provide us not only with descriptive terms but also with the means of measuring the important dimensions of personality. They give us an idea of how measured traits are related to one another. On the other hand, debate continues concerning the number of traits that are important in personality and in predicting behavior. Even with the so-called Big Five traits—the most widely accepted trait theory—there is some disagreement over whether the five traits are completely independent and whether personality really can be reduced down to five traits (Paunonen & Jackson, 2000). This idea is supported by the addition of a sixth trait (Honesty) in the HEXACO model. There is support for the HEXACO model and the unique contribution of the Honesty dimension to specific behaviors (Lee, Ashton, Morrison, Cordery, & Patrick, 2008). For example, Lee et al. found that honesty related strongly to ethical occupational decisions beyond the other dimensions of the model.

So, as might have been predicted, when we try to evaluate approaches or theories of personality, there are no real winners or losers. Each approach has its shortcomings, but each adds something to our appreciation of the complex concept of human personality.

STUDY CHECK

What are trait theories of personality?
What is the Five-Factor Model of personality?

THINKING CRITICALLY

How might each of the "Big Five" dimensions of personality show up in the observable behaviors of college students? Where do you think that you fall on these five traits?

FOCUS ON DIVERSITY

Are There Cultural Differences in Personality?

The theories and approaches to personality we have covered in this chapter come from thinking rooted in Western thought and research. Theories such as Freud's, Jung's, and trait approaches all were developed within a Western cultural context. Although these theories gained some degree or another of acceptance in Western cultures, in other cultures, such acceptance was not the case. For example, Freudian theory and therapy techniques never gained wide acceptance in Indian culture (Kanwal, 2015).

Beyond the applicability of Western personality theories, another valid question is whether there are similarities and differences in personality across cultures. In this area, research tells us that there are some similarities and differences in personality across cultures. For example, one study (Ion et al., 2017) investigated the HEXACO model across several cultures. Ion et al. looked at the HEXACO traits among individuals from India, Indonesia, Oman, Romania, and Thailand. Ion et al. found that the HEXACO best fit participants from the Indonesian and Romanian cultures and least fit participants from the Thai and Indian cultures. These results show that there may be variance across cultures for the personality traits included in the HEXACO model.

In another study, Costello, Wood, and Tov (2018) compared individuals from the United States and Singapore on traits comprising the HEXACO model. In this study, Costello et al. had participants describe a situation that exemplified a trait from the model. They then categorized the "action scenarios" as representative of the conscientiousness or other HEXACO traits. Another group of participants then evaluated 150 of these action scenarios. Other participants rated the degree to which a number of personality traits applied to them. Costello et al. found differences between the two cultures that are typically found in this type of research. Participants from Singapore rated themselves lower on traits associated with conscientiousness and extroversion than American participants. When they looked at how participants responded to the action scenarios, they found that members of the two cultures were more similar than different. One difference was on items related to conscientiousness. For example, more Americans agreed that they would clean their messy room before going on a trip to a greater extent than Singaporeans.

In addition to looking at similarities and differences in personality across diverse cultures, researchers have also looked at similarities and differences across subcultures within a larger cultural group. For example, Fetvadjiev et al. (2018) looked at the personalities of black and white South Africans. They found that there were far more similarities than differences between these two groups. One difference found was on a negative social-relational personality factor. This factor includes things such as getting into arguments with others or saying something that hurts another person. Whites were higher on this dimension than blacks. Another interesting difference was in how blacks and whites perceived the variability of their behavior across situations. In this case, blacks saw their behaviors as more variable than whites. Locke, Sadler, and McDonald (2018) compared Canadians with a European heritage with Canadians of Asian heritage. They looked at how these groups responded to situations involving interactions with parents, friends, siblings, and professors. Participants were asked to indicate how desirable or appropriate it would be to express a particular trait in the four different situations. Locke et al. also found more similarities than differences between the two groups. One difference observed was that the European Canadians showed greater consistency in one of the four areas: comparing behavior with parents and peers. These two studies reinforce the ideas that people from subcultures with a culture are more alike than they are different, but there are some differences.

The final area we shall explore is the relationship between personality and negative behaviors. First, let's look at the relationship between personality and intimate partner violence (IPV) across cultures. Catalá-Miñana, Walker, Bowen, and Lila (2014) compared English and Spanish IPV offenders. Catalá-Miñana et al. found personality and behavioral differences between the two groups. The English offenders scored higher than the Spanish offenders on a number of personality disorder dimensions: antisocial personality characteristics, borderline personality characteristics, dysthymia (depressive symptoms), and alcohol dependence. Spanish offenders scored higher on the dimensions of social desirability (wanting to present oneself in a positive way), histrionic characteristics (overly dramatic), narcissism (excessive self-love), compulsive characteristics, and delusional disorder characteristics. Additionally, the English offenders were more likely to use higher levels of physical and psychological violence against their partners than the Spanish offenders.

Another study looked at dishonesty on job applications from members of a wide range of cultures, specifically lying on personality tests (Fell & König, 2016). Fell and König obtained data from 43 countries on the Five-Factor Model personality dimensions and faking on the dimensions comprising the model. Countries were grouped according to how they are characterized by the Global Leadership & Organizational Behavior Effectiveness (GLOBE) Project (2016). The GLOBE Project characterizes cultures along nine dimensions: uncertainty avoidance, future orientation, power distance, institutional collectivism, gender egalitarianism, humane orientation, in-group collectivism, performance orientation, and assertiveness. Among Fell and König's results were that members of cultures that place a premium on uncertainty avoidance and a future orientation (e.g., Denmark, Sweden, and Finland) were most likely to fake on items relating to agreeableness, extroversion, and emotional stability. Members of a culture emphasizing a humane orientation (e.g., sub-Saharan Africa) were less likely to fake on agreeableness, conscientiousness, and emotional stability.

Personality Assessment or Measurement

As we know, personality is a difficult concept to define. Common to most definitions is the idea that there are characteristics of an individual (called "dispositions" or "traits") that remain fairly consistent over time and over many (if not all) situations. It would be useful to be able to reliably and validly measure those personal characteristics. Let's consider a few of the assessment techniques used to discover the nature of someone's personality.

Behavioral Observations

As we form impressions of the personalities of friends and acquaintances, we usually do so by relying on **behavioral observation**, which is a type of personality measurement that involves drawing conclusions about someone's personality on the basis of observations of his or her behaviors. We judge Dan to be bright because he was the only one who knew the answer to a question in class. We feel that Heather is submissive because she seems to do whatever her husband demands.

Behavioral observation—personality measurement that involves drawing conclusions about someone's personality on the basis of observations of his or her behaviors.

As helpful as our observations may be, there might be problems with the casual, unstructured observations you and I normally make. Because we have observed only a small number of behaviors in a limited range of settings, we may be over-generalizing when we assume that those same behaviors will show up in new or different situations. Dan may never again know the answer to a question in class. Heather could have given in to her husband only because we were there. That is, the behaviors that we observe may not be typical at all.

Nonetheless, behavioral observation can be an excellent source of information, particularly when the observations being made are purposeful, careful, and structured, and when steps are taken to make the observations reliable and valid and to ensure our sample is representative. Among other things, the accuracy of observations is related to the degree of acquaintance between the observer and the person being observed.

Consider an example: A child is reportedly having trouble at school, behaving aggressively and being disruptive. One thing a psychologist may do is visit the school and observe the child's behaviors in the natural setting of the classroom. It could be that the child does behave aggressively and engage in fighting behavior, but only when the teacher is in the room. In other circumstances, the child is pleasant and passive. It may be that the child's aggressive behaviors reflect a ploy to get the teacher's attention.

Observational techniques can be supplemented with a rating scale (for example, a scale ranging from 1 to 10). Rating scales provide many advantages over casual observation. For one thing, they focus the attention of the observer on a set of specified behaviors to be observed. Rating scales also yield a more objective measure of behavior. Using rating scales, behaviors can be observed by several raters. If several raters are involved in the observation of the same behaviors (say, children at play in a nursery school), you can check on the reliability of the observations. If all five of your observers agree that Timothy engaged in hitting behavior on the average of six times per hour, the consistency of that assessment adds to its usefulness.

STUDY CHECK

To what extent is behavioral observation a useful technique for assessing personality?

THINKING CRITICALLY

Consider your best friend. On the basis of your observations, which four or five traits best describe your friend's personality? Which traits might your friend think are most important for describing your personality?

Interviews

We can learn some things about people just by watching them. We also can learn about aspects of personality by simply asking people about themselves. The interview is "one of the oldest and most widely used, although not always the most accurate, of the methods of personality assessment" (Aiken, 1984, p. 296). Its popularity is largely due to its simplicity and flexibility.

An interview measures what people say about themselves, rather than what they do. Interview results are usually impressionistic and not easily quantifiable (although some interview techniques are clearly more structured and objective than others). The interview is more a technique for discovering generalities than uncovering specifics.

A major advantage of the interview is its flexibility. The interviewer may decide to drop a certain line of questioning if it is producing no useful information in order to pursue some other area of interest. Studies conducted more than 30 years ago demonstrated very clearly that interviews had very little reliability and even less validity (Tenopyr, 1981). The technique was nearly abandoned as a means of assessing personality. It turns out, however, that the low marks that interviewing received only held for free-form, rambling, unstructured interviews. Structured interviews, on the other hand, involve a specific set of questions to be asked in a prescribed order. The structured interview, then, becomes more like a psychological test to the extent that it is objective and standardized and asks about a particular sample of behavior. Analyses of structured interviews show that their reliability and validity can be very high (Campion, Palmer, & Campion, 1997, 1998).

Psychological Tests

Observational and interview techniques barely qualify as psychological tests. A *psychological test* is defined as an objective, standardized measure of a sample of behavior. Here we

Interview—measurement of what people say about themselves, rather than what they do.

will focus on one of the most-often-used paper-and-pencil personality tests, the **Minnesota Multiphasic Personality Inventory**, or **MMPI-2** for short. The test is called multiphasic because it measures several personality dimensions with the same set of items.

The MMPI-2 (the "2" indicating a 1990 second edition of the test) was designed to aid in the diagnosis of persons with mental disorders and, hence, is not a personality test in the sense of identifying personality traits. The test is a popular test largely because it repeatedly has been shown to be a reliable and valid measure of a set of personality characteristics (Wood et al., 2002). A new version of the MMPI-2 was introduced in 2008 called the MMPI-2-RF (*RF* stands for *restructured form*) (Ben-Porath & Tellegen, 2008). This version does not replace the MMPI-2. Rather, it has restructured "clinical scales" that help clinicians better identify specific psychological problems.

The MMPI-2 consists of 567 true/false items that ask about feelings, attitudes, physical symptoms, and past experiences. It is a *criterion-referenced test*, which means that items on the test are referenced to one of the criterion groups—either normal persons or patients with a diagnosis of a particular mental disorder. Some of the items appear sensible. "I feel like people are plotting against me" seems like the sort of item someone with paranoia would call "true," whereas normal persons would tend to respond "false." Many items, however, are not as obvious. "I like to visit zoos" is not an MMPI-2 item, but it might have been if individuals of one diagnostic group responded to the item differently from other people. What the item appears to be measuring is irrelevant. What matters is whether people of different groups respond differently to the item. A psychologist would not make even a tentative diagnosis of a psychological disorder on the basis of a person's response to just a few items. What matters is not just the simple scores or even the pattern of scores on any set of items, but the interpretation of those scores by a trained, experienced psychologist. It also is true that any testing results would only be one of the factors involved in coming up with a diagnostic impression of an individual.

We should also mention that most personality tests are designed to measure just one trait and, thus, are not multiphasic. One example is the *Taylor Manifest Anxiety Scale*. Taylor began with a large pool of items—many of them from the MMPI—and then asked psychologists to choose those items they thought would best measure anxiety. The 50 items most commonly chosen as signs of anxiety make up this test, which has gained wide acceptance. Another test, the *Endler Multidimensional Anxiety Scale*, not only assesses anxiety levels but also claims to distinguish between anxiety and depression (Endler et al., 1992).

A **projective test** asks a person to respond to ambiguous stimuli. The stimuli can be any number of things, and there are no clearly right or wrong answers. Projective procedures are unstructured and open-ended. Because there is, in fact, so little content in the stimulus being presented, the idea is that the person will *project* some of his or her own self (or personality) into the response. In many ways, projective techniques are more like aids to interviewing than they are psychological tests.

Some projective techniques are very simple. The *word association technique*, introduced by Galton in 1879, is a projective procedure. "I will say a word, and I want you to say the first thing that pops into your head. Do not think about your response; just say the first thing that comes to mind." There are no right answers. The hope is that the psychologist can gain some insight into the problems of a patient by using this technique.

Of the projective techniques, none is as well known as the *Rorschach inkblot test*. This technique was introduced in 1921 by Hermann Rorschach, (1884–1922). There are 10 cards in the Rorschach test: Five are black on white, two are red and gray, and three are multicolored. People are asked to tell what they see in the cards or what the inkblot represents.

The scoring of Rorschach test responses has been controversial. Standard scoring procedures require attending to many

Minnesota Multiphasic Personality Inventory (MMPI-2)—a personality test that measures several personality dimensions with the same set of items.

Projective test—a personality test that asks a person to respond to ambiguous stimuli. The stimuli can be any number of things, and there are no clearly right or wrong answers.

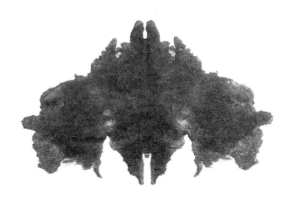

A sample Rorschach-like inkblot. The subject is asked what the inkblot represents and what she or he sees in it.

Source: xpixel/Shutterstock.

factors: what the person says (content), where the person focuses attention (location), mention of detail versus global features, reacting to color or open spaces, and the total number of distinct responses. Many psychologists have questioned the use of the Rorschach as a diagnostic instrument. Much of what it suggests to an examiner may be gained more directly. For example, Rorschach responses that include many references to sadness, death, and dying are indicative of a depressed person. One wonders if inkblots are really needed to discover such depression. As a psychological test, the Rorschach seems neither reliable nor valid (Hamel, Gallagher, & Soares, 2001; Wood et al., 2010). Once a very popular tool, there is evidence that its use is on the decline (Piotrowski, Belter, & Keller, 1998). It is used primarily as an aid to assessment.

The Thematic Apperception Test, or *TAT*, was devised in 1938. This test is a series of ambiguous pictures about which a person is asked to tell a story. The person is asked to describe what is going on, what led up to the situation, and what the outcome is likely to be. It is designed to provide a mechanism to discover a person's hidden needs, desires, and emotions—which will be projected into his or her stories. The test is called a "thematic" test because scoring depends on the interpretation of the themes of the stories. Although scoring schemes are available, scoring and interpretation are usually subjective and impressionistic. It is likely the TAT is popular for the same reason that the Rorschach is: Psychologists are used to it, are comfortable with the insights it provides, and are willing to accept any source of information in order to make a reasonable assessment or diagnosis.

PSYCHOLOGY IN ACTION

Predicting Criminality from Personality

Although crime in the United States is generally down, certain cities are experiencing high levels of violent crime. For example, in 2017, Chicago, Illinois, had 650 murders. Although down from the year before, it is still a very high number. By September 2018 there were 550 murders. What do we know about the relationship between personality and crime? Some of the most notorious criminals in history have been described in terms of their personality characteristics. For example, Ted Bundy was one of the most prolific serial killers of the twentieth century. Just before his execution in 1989, Bundy confessed to 30 murders across the United States. Bundy was often described with adjectives such as *articulate*, *charming*, and *intelligent*. Wouldn't it be nice if we could predict who was going to commit murder and stop that person before the crime takes place? Could we screen people for certain personality characteristics and cut crime? Although such an outcome is not really possible, we might still be able to see if there is a connection between personality and crime.

We will start our discussion by looking at the relationship between the General Factor of Personality (GFP) and criminal behavior. The GFP is a global measure of personality based on several established personality measures (Musek, 2007). The GFP can be viewed as a reflection of socially desirable personality characteristics (van der Linden, Dunkel, Beaver, & Louwen, 2015). van der Linden et al. had male criminal offenders complete several measures of personality from which the GFP can be extracted. They also analyzed FBI information on the nature of the offenders' crimes along with other information on their criminal behavior. van der Linden et al. found that more violent offenders had lower GFP scores. The same pattern emerged when the researchers looked at crime committed while incarcerated and for those who committed more than one crime (recidivists). Inmates who were classified as violent had lower GFP scores. In other words, violent offenders/inmates had less socially desirable personalities than nonviolent offenders/inmates. In another study, Dargis and Koenigs (2018) were able to distinguish between different personality types among six groups of criminal offenders with distinct behavioral, cognitive, and affective profiles. For example, nonviolent criminals with higher IQs and reading scores scored in the average range on most of the measures of personality (e.g., positive affect, negative affect, and constraint (avoidance of risk)). Another group of more violent criminals scored high on positive affect and psychopathy (psychopathic traits such as lying and lack of empathy/callousness). These criminals were also more likely than others to be substance abusers.

Singh and Rani (2017) measured a number of personality traits among criminals and noncriminals in India. Singh and Rani found that criminals scored higher than noncriminals on the personality dimensions of extroversion, neuroticism, and psychoticism. They were also more likely to try to lie on the measures than noncriminals.

With another sample of Indian criminals and noncriminals, Sinha (2016) found that criminals scored higher than noncriminals on measures of intelligence, impulsiveness, suspicion, self-sufficiency, spontaneity, and self-concept and scored lower on emotional stability.

The research we just reviewed makes a pretty good case that there is a relationship between personality and criminal behavior. Does this mean that we can reliably predict who will become a criminal based on their personality? As you might guess, the answer to this question is no. Just because a person has a set of personality characteristics that we know is predictive of criminality does not mean that the person is destined to become a criminal. Such an assumption completely ignores the power of the situation to influence behavior. Kurt Lewin (1936), one of the founders of social psychology, tells us that behavior is best accounted for by the interaction of the situation and the individual's characteristics. He proposed a simple formula to describe this relationship: Behavior = f (social situation × individual characteristics). Lewin arrived at this observation based on his own experience. Lewin was a soldier in the German army during World War I. He noticed that as he came nearer to the battlefield, his view of the world changed. Where he once might have seen beautiful flowers and forests, he now saw boulders to hide behind and gullies from which he could ambush the enemy. Lewin came to believe that a person's perception of the world is influenced by what he or she has to do in that situation. He termed the combination of individual needs and situational factors the *psychological field* in which the individual lives (Pratkanis & Aronson, 1992).

A similar analysis was provided by Walter Mischel (1968) decades later. Mischel challenged the long-held belief that there was consistency in personality across situations. That is, he proposed that whether a personality trait led to behavior depended on the situation. Think about your own behavior and your own personality. Let's say that you see yourself as easygoing. Now ask yourself: Are you always easygoing and easy to get along with? Are there some situations in which you would be easygoing but others in which you might fight to have your way? Are there some situations in which you tend to be social and outgoing, yet different situations in which you prefer to be alone and not mix in? Such was the thrust of Mischel's challenge: Personality characteristics appear to be consistent only when they are viewed in similar or consistent situations.

STUDY CHECK

How might interviews be helpful in assessing personality?
What are the MMPI-2 and projective tests of personality?

THINKING CRITICALLY

What might you conclude about a person who looked at all of the inkblots in the Rorschach Test and said, "I'm sorry, but these just look like inkblots to me."?

Chapter Summary

What is meant by "theories of personality"?
A theory is an organized collection of testable ideas used to explain a given subject matter, such as personality. Personality includes affects, behaviors, and cognitions that characterize an individual in a number of situations over time. Personality also includes those dimensions that we can use to judge people to be different from one another. Personality resides within a person and includes characteristics that he or she brings to interactions with the environment.

What are the main features of the Freudian psychoanalytic approach to personality?
Freud's theory of personality has been one of the most influential and most controversial. There are two basic premises to Freud's theory: a reliance on innate drives to explain human behavior and an acceptance of the role of the unconscious in motivating behavior. Freud proposed that at any given time we are aware, or conscious, of only a few things. With a little effort, some ideas or memories

can be accessed from our preconscious, whereas others, those in our unconscious mind, may be accessed only with great difficulty. Freud believed that unconscious motives could explain behaviors that seem irrational, and that most of our mental lives take place on the level of the unconscious. Freud believed that human behavior was guided by innate biological drives called instincts. The life instincts, or Eros, are related to survival and include motives for hunger, thirst, and sex. The death instincts, or Thanatos, are related to destruction, such as depression and aggression. The libido is the psychic energy through which the instincts operate.

The structures of personality, according to Freud, are the instinctive id, operating on the pleasure principle and seeking immediate gratification; the ego, or sense of self that operates on the reality principle, mediating needs in the context of the real world; and the superego, or sense of morality or conscience, which operates on an idealistic principle, attempting to direct one to do what is right and proper.

What are the contributions of the neo-Freudian approaches to personality?

Adler, Jung, and Horney each parted with Freud on theoretical grounds, while remaining basically psychoanalytic in their respective approaches to personality. For Adler, social influences and inferiority complexes mattered much more than did innate drives. Jung was less biological and more positive; he expanded on Freud's view of the unconscious mind, adding the notion of a collective unconscious. Horney rejected the notion of instinctual impulses and instead discussed the concept of basic anxiety and how one reacts to it as the sculptor of one's personality.

How can we evaluate the psychoanalytic approach to personality?

The strengths of the psychoanalytic approach include the fact that Freud and other psychoanalytic theorists rightly focused attention on the importance of the childhood years, the role of the unconscious, and biological factors in shaping an individual's behaviors. The greatest weakness of the approach may be that many of its central concepts cannot be empirically tested.

What is the behavioral/learning approach to personality, and what are some of its strengths and weaknesses?

Many psychologists have argued that personality can be explained using learning principles and observable behavior. Watson emphasized behavior and argued that psychology should abandon mental concepts. Skinner emphasized the notion of operant conditioning and how one's behaviors are shaped by their consequences. Dollard and Miller tried to explain personality development in terms of learning and habit formation. Bandura stressed the role of observation and social learning

in the formation of personality. This approach has been criticized for dehumanizing personality and being too deterministic. Also, the various learning approaches to personality are not comprehensive theories. On the positive side, the approach demands that terms be carefully defined and verified experimentally.

What is the basic thrust of the approaches to personality that are classified as cognitive or humanistic?

According to the cognitive approach, basic information-processing strategies such as memory and attention intersect with patterns of thought and perception normally thought to be involved in personality. An early cognitive theory proposed by Kelly suggested that personal constructs, which are a part of long-term memory, direct an individual's thoughts and perceptions. Mischel's approach to personality more clearly links personality constructs with cognitive psychology. According to Mischel, there are four "person variables" that make up personality: cognitive and behavioral competencies, encoding strategies and personal constructs, subjective stimulus values, and self-regulatory systems and plans.

The humanistic theories of Rogers and Maslow are alike in many ways, emphasizing the integrity of the self and the power of personal development. Both theorists challenge the negativity and biological bias of psychoanalytic theory, as well as the determinism of behaviorism. On the positive side, this approach reminds us of the wholeness of personality and the inherent dangers in trying to break down a complex concept like personality into artificial segments. Another strength of the approach is its focus on personal growth and striving. The approach has had a positive impact on psychotherapy techniques. On the negative side, the central concepts of the approach are difficult to test in any scientific way.

What are trait theories of personality?

A personality trait is a characteristic and distinctive way in which an individual may differ from others. Trait theories are attempts to discover and organize that set of traits that could be used to describe the characteristics of an individual and also to characterize ways in which any individual may differ from others.

What is the Five-Factor Model of personality?

Research in personality trait theory suggests that, from all of those traits that have been proposed, five emerge most regularly, although there is as yet no agreement on what to call these dimensions. One version calls them (1) Extroversion-Introversion; (2) Agreeableness or Friendliness; (3) Conscientiousness or Will; (4) Neuroticism, or Stability-Instability; and (5) Openness to Experience and Culture. The trait approach has provided a powerful way of describing and measuring personality dimensions. There is still debate over the number of traits that are involved in personality and whether the so-called "Big Five" traits are independent of one another and can adequately represent personality. The HEXACO model is an update to the five-factor model and adds an honesty dimension to those proposed in the five-factor model.

To what extent is behavioral observation a useful technique for assessing personality?

Behavioral observation involves drawing inferences about an individual's personality based on observations of his or her overt behaviors. Behavioral observation can be an important tool for assessing personality, particularly when the observations are made in a purposeful, careful, and structured way; if steps are taken to ensure reliability and validity of observations; and if the sample of individuals observed is representative.

How might interviews be helpful in assessing personality?

Interviews simply ask people about their own behaviors and personality traits. The major advantages of the interview are its ease and flexibility of administration. The procedure allows the interviewer to pursue avenues of interest and abandon lines of questioning that are not useful. Unfortunately, unstructured interviews lack validity. Structured interviews (which give up flexibility) show as much reliability and validity as many psychological tests.

What are the MMPI-2 and projective tests of personality?

Multiphasic instruments attempt to measure several characteristics or traits using one set of items. The Minnesota Multiphasic Personality Inventory, or MMPI (revised as the MMPI-2), was developed as an aid to diagnosis. It includes 567 true-false items that discriminate among persons of differing diagnostic categories.

With a projective technique, the assumption is that, in responding to an ambiguous stimulus, a person will project aspects of his or her personality into test responses. Projective techniques include word association tests, the Rorschach test, and the TAT. The Rorschach test includes ten cards showing inkblot patterns. A person is asked what he or she sees on the card or what the inkblot represents. Scoring the test involves attending to what the person says, where the person focuses attention, mentions of detail, and how many direct responses are made. The TAT is a projective technique introduced by Henry Murray in 1938. The test consists of a series of ambiguous pictures. The individual taking the test is required to tell a story to go with each picture, describing what is going on in the picture and the likely outcome. Scoring centers on the themes of the stories told by the examinee. Although the projective techniques continue to be used in clinical practice, there is scant evidence that any of them have any useful degree of reliability or validity.

Key Terms

Theory (p. 211)
Personality (p. 211)
Psychoanalytic approach (p. 211)
Life instincts (Eros) (p. 212)
Libido (p. 212)
Death instincts (Thanatos) (p. 212)
Id (p. 212)
Pleasure principle (p. 213)
Ego (p. 213)
Reality principle (p. 213)

Superego (p. 213)
Inferiority complex (p. 215)
Fully functioning (p. 218)
Trait (p. 220)
Five-Factor Model (p. 220)
Behavioral observation (p. 223)
Interview (p. 224)
Minnesota Multiphasic Personality
    Inventory (MMPI-2) (p. 225)
Projective test (p. 225)

Stress and Health Psychology

Source: Master 1305/Shutterstock.

Chapter Outline

Questions You Will Be Able to Answer

After reading Chapter 11, you should be able to answer the following questions:

- What do the terms stress and stressor mean?
- What is "frustration," and in what way can it act as a stressor?
- What are "motivational conflicts," and in what ways can they act as stressors?
- In what ways can life events act as stressors?
- How do people differ in their reactions to stress?
- What are problem-focused and emotion-focused strategies for effective coping with stress?
- What are the three inappropriate, ineffective reactions to stress?
- What is the relationship, if any, between the Type A behavior pattern and physical health?
- What are some of the components of an unhealthy lifestyle?
- Why are health psychologists so concerned about smoking, and how are they attempting to reduce the number of smokers?
- What are the causes of AIDS, and what roles can health psychologists play in its prevention and treatment?

Preview

Stress is a consequence of living. Every college student is familiar with stress. This chapter covers what psychologists have learned about stress, both its causes and our reactions to it. Our study of stress is divided into two main sections. First, we'll explore the common sources of stress in our lives. You realize, of course, that there are a nearly infinite number of events and situations that cause stress. We will focus on three major categories of events that tend to produce stress: frustration, conflict, and life events. Second, we will examine the complex patterns of responses that people make when they experience stress. We shall see that some reactions to stress can be positive and healthy, while others are maladaptive.

Health psychology is the study of psychological or behavioral factors that affect physical health and illness. Stress is surely one of those factors. As researchers, health psychologists seek to understand the relationships between psychological functioning and physical health. As practitioners, health psychologists help patients cope with physical diseases and illnesses, and they help people try to prevent health problems before they occur.

Here, we examine two major thrusts of health psychology: research and practice. We'll look at the relationships between psychological variables and physical health, where researchers still ask the basic questions: What is it about psychological functioning that influences a person's physical health? Is it stress? Are there personality traits that predict illness, disease, and bad health? Then we will consider how psychologists are joining the fight against illness and disease. In this regard, we focus on two important health problems: smoking and HIV/AIDS.

A Few Examples with Which to Work

Stress is such a common phenomenon that one could argue it is unavoidable. Being "stressed out" seems to be a universal condition—particularly among college students. In that spirit, a list of potentially stressful events could be endless. To guide our study, here is a list of a few (fictitious) examples to which we shall refer throughout this chapter:

- It's Friday, and you have a chance to get away for the weekend. Unfortunately, you have two big exams scheduled for Monday and need the weekend to study.
- Latisha is almost done typing a term paper on her computer when suddenly the power goes out. Having failed to save her work as she went along, she'll have to redo it all.
- Cindy and Jerry have known each other since grade school. They dated throughout high school and college. Next week, family and friends will join in the celebration of their marriage.
- Amal wants to make the basketball team, but the coach informs him that despite his best efforts, he is just too short to make the team.
- Marian is excited about going to Germany in a student-exchange program, but she also is very nervous about getting along in a new country.
- After 11 years on the road as a salesman, Javon is being promoted to district sales manager—an office job with a substantial raise in pay.
- Jake cut back his smoking to one pack a day and was considering starting an exercise program. Now he is in a coronary intensive care unit, having just suffered a heart attack.
- Three-year-old Emma keeps asking her mother for a cookie. Mother steadfastly refuses because it's almost dinner time. Emma returns to her room and promptly pulls an arm off her favorite doll.

- You are late for class, driving down a two-lane road, when someone pulls out in front of you and drives ten miles per hour below the speed limit.
- Shirley wants to be a concert pianist, but her music teacher tells her she does not have the talent or discipline to reach that goal.

Stressors: The Causes of Stress

Although each of us is familiar with stress and how it feels, psychologists have struggled with how to characterize stress for nearly 60 years (Rice, 1999). A generally acceptable definition is to say that stress is a complex set of reactions made by an individual under pressure to adapt. In other words, stress is a *response* that people make to real or perceived threats to their sense of well-being. Stress is something that happens inside people. There are physiological reactions and unpleasant feelings (for example, distress and anxiety) associated with stress. A curious aspect of this response that we call stress is that it often involves such unpleasant affect (emotions or feelings, remember) that it, in turn, acts as a motivating stimulus. If nothing else, when we experience stress we are motivated to do something to reduce it, if not get rid of it altogether.

There are many circumstances or events that can produce stress. A source of stress is called a stressor. We'll consider three types of stressors: frustration, conflict, and life events. As we go along, we'll provide examples as a reminder that stress is not necessarily a reaction to an overwhelming or catastrophic event, such as the death of a loved one or a natural disaster. Once we understand where stress comes from, we can consider techniques people use to cope with it.

Frustration-Induced Stress

Motivated behaviors are goal-directed. Whether by internal drives or external incentives, we are pushed or pulled toward positive goals and away from negative goals. For example, you are hungry and go to the cafeteria for a bite to eat. When you get there, you find it closed. Now here is a fact: Organisms do not always reach all of their goals. Have you always gotten everything you've ever wanted? Have you always been able to avoid unpleasantness, pain, or sorrow? Do you know anyone who has?

Sometimes we are prohibited from ever reaching a particular goal. At other times our progress may be slower or more difficult than we would like. In either case, we are frustrated. Frustration is the reaction to blocking or thwarting of goal-directed behavior—blocking that may be total and permanent or partial and temporary.

Stress that results from frustration is a normal, commonplace reaction. Frustration is a stressor, and the stress it produces is part of life. In no way does it imply weakness, pathology, or illness. What matters is how people react to the stressors in their lives.

To someone who is frustrated, the source of the resulting stress may be of little consequence. However, in order to respond adaptively to stress brought on by frustration, it may be helpful to recognize the source of the blocking—the particular stressor—keeping us from our goals. There are two basic types of frustration: environmental and personal.

Environmental frustration implies that the blocking or thwarting of one's goal-directed behavior is caused by something or somebody in the environment. (Note that we talk about the source of frustration, not whose fault it is or who is to blame.) Remember our example of Latisha, who lost her term paper when the power went out? This would be environmental frustration. Latisha wanted to finish her paper. Her goal-directed behavior led her to use her computer. Something in her environment—a momentary power outage—kept her from reaching her goal. And remember Emma? She wanted a cookie, but her mother said, "No, it is dinner time." Emma was also being frustrated by her environment, but in a slightly different way. She wanted a cookie, and her mother blocked that motivated behavior. This type of environmental frustration, in which the source of the blocking is another person, is sometimes called "social frustration."

Stress—a complex set of reactions made by an individual under pressure to adapt.

Stressor—a source of stress.

Frustration—the reaction to blocking or thwarting of goal-directed behavior—blocking that may be total and permanent or partial and temporary.

Occasionally we become frustrated not because something in our environment blocks our progress, but because of an internal or personal reason. This is *personal frustration*. Amal fails to make the basketball team simply because he is too short. Shirley, who wants to be a concert pianist, may be frustrated in her attempt to do so simply because she doesn't have sufficient talent. Shirley's frustration and resulting stress are not her fault (fault and blame are just not relevant, remember), but if she persists in this goal-directed behavior, she will be frustrated. Some of us are learning that simply getting older can be stressful. When someone now has difficulty doing things that at one time were easy to do, the result may be stress. That stress is frustration-induced, and this type of frustration is personal.

STUDY CHECK

What do the terms stress and stressor mean?
What is "frustration," and in what way can it act as a stressor?

THINKING CRITICALLY

It is likely that you have experienced some sort of frustration every day. What are some examples of potentially frustrating events that occurred to you yesterday?

Conflict-Induced Stress

Sometimes we are unable to satisfy a particular drive or motive because it is in conflict with other motives that are influencing us at the same time. That is, stress may result from conflicts within our motivational system. With *motivational conflicts*, there is the implication of a decision or choice to be made. Sometimes the choice is relatively easy, and the resulting stress will be slight; sometimes decision-making is difficult, and the resulting stress will be greater. When discussing conflicts, we talk about positive goals or incentives that one wishes to approach, and negative goals or incentives one wishes to avoid. There are four major types of stress-inducing motivational conflicts.

Conflicts are necessarily unpleasant, stress-producing situations, even when the goals involved are positive. In an **approach-approach conflict**, an organism is caught between two (or more) alternatives, and each of them is positive, or potentially reinforcing. If alternative A is chosen, a desired goal will be reached. If B is chosen, a different desirable goal will be attained. This *is* a conflict because both goals/alternatives are not available at the same time. It has to be one or the other. Example A of **Figure 11.1** illustrates this type of conflict.

Once an approach-approach conflict is resolved, the person does end up with something positive, no matter which alternative is chosen. If Carla enters an ice cream shop with only enough money to buy one scoop of ice cream, she may experience a conflict when faced with all the flavors from which she can choose. Typical of conflict, we will probably see some swaying back and forth among alternatives. We can assume that this conflict will be resolved with a choice, and Carla will at least walk out of the store with an ice cream cone of some flavor she likes. Her life might have been easier (at least less stressful) if the store had just one flavor and she did not have to make a choice.

Sometimes the choices we have to make are much more serious than those involving ice cream flavors. What will be your college major? On the one hand, you would like to go to medical school and be a surgeon (a positive incentive or goal). On the other hand, you would like to study composition and conducting at a school of music (also a positive goal). At the moment, you cannot do both. The courses you would take as a pre-med student are

Approach-approach conflict—a conflict in which an organism is caught between two (or more) alternatives, and each of them is positive, or potentially reinforcing.

Types of Conflict

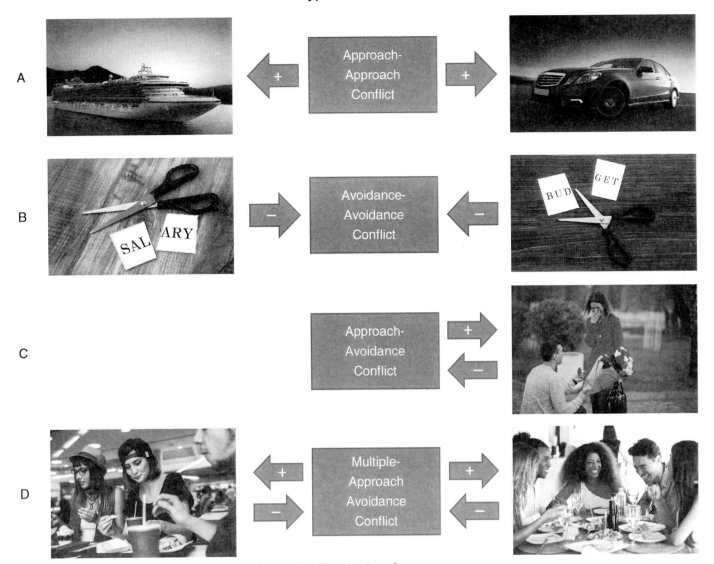

FIGURE 11.1 Four Different Types of Conflict Producing Stress

Sources: Shutterstock: A. (left) NAN728, (right) Maksim Toome; B. (left and right) takasu; C. Wedding Stock Photo; D. (left) zeljkodan, (right) Monkey Business Images.

different from those you would take if you were to follow music as a career path. Both are constructive, desirable alternatives, but at the time of registration you have to make a choice, one that may have long-lasting repercussions. The consequences of such a conflict qualify it as a stressor. Example A of Figure 11.1 shows another example of an approach-approach conflict. Should you spend your limited money on a new car or a cruise?

Perhaps the most stress-inducing of all motivational conflicts is the **avoidance-avoidance conflict**. In this type of conflict, a person is faced with several alternatives, and each of them is negative or in some way punishing. To be in an avoidance-avoidance conflict is, in a way, to be boxed in so that, no matter what you do, the result will be punishing or unpleasant. An avoidance-avoidance conflict is illustrated in Example B of Figure 11.1.

This sort of conflict is not at all unusual in the workplace. Imagine that you are a supervisor in charge of a reasonably large department. Your department has been doing well and is making a profit, but management directs you to cut your operating budget 20 percent by next month. There are ways you can reduce expenses—limit travel, cut down on supplies, reduce pay, eliminate expense accounts—but each involves an action you'd rather

Avoidance-avoidance conflict—a conflict in which a person is faced with several alternatives, and each of them is negative or in some way punishing.

not take. If you do nothing at all, you may lose your job. The result may be stress, and the stressor is an avoidance-avoidance conflict.

With an **approach-avoidance conflict**, a person is in the position of considering only one goal. What makes this situation a conflict is that the person would very much like to reach that goal, but at the same time would very much like not to. It's a matter of "Yes, I'd love to . . . Well, I'd rather not . . . Maybe I would . . . No, I wouldn't . . . yes . . . no." Consider the possibility of entering into a relationship with someone you think of as special. On the one hand, such a relationship might turn out to be wonderful and rewarding. On the other hand, it might put you in the position of being rejected. Example C of Figure 11.1 shows an approach-avoidance conflict.

Typical of conflict, we will find vacillation between alternatives—motivated to approach and, at the same time, motivated to avoid. Like Marian in our opening examples, you might find yourself in an approach-avoidance conflict if you want to interact with people who are culturally different, perhaps to show that you are open-minded. At the same time, you may be reluctant to initiate such an interaction for fear that your behaviors will be inappropriate or misinterpreted.

A **multiple approach-avoidance conflict** may be the most common of the conflicts experienced by adults. This type of conflict arises when an individual is faced with a number of alternatives, each one of which is in some way both positive and negative. A multiple approach-avoidance conflict is illustrated in Example D of Figure 11.1.

Perhaps you and some friends are out shopping. You realize that it's getting late and that you all are hungry. Where will you go to lunch? You may have a multiple approach-avoidance conflict here. "We could go to Bob's Diner, where the food is cheap and the service is fast, but the food is terrible. We could go to Cafe Olé, where the food is better, but service is a little slower, and the food is more expensive. Or, we could go to Woo's, where the service is elegant and the food is superb, but the price is very high." Granted this is not an earth-shaking dilemma, but in each case, there is a plus and a minus to be considered in making the choice. The more difficult the choice, the greater the induced stress.

Think of your own decision-making processes when you decided to go to college. First, there was the multiple approach-avoidance conflict of whether to go at all. "I could forget about it, just stay here; get a good job; lay back and be happy, but all my friends are going, and college graduates do make more money than high school graduates." The conflicts continue when one considers all of the pluses and minuses of where to go to college. The choices, with their strong and weak points, can be maddening. Stay at home and go to school nearby? Stay in state for lower tuition, but move away from home? Get away from it all to someplace you have always wanted to live?

Life is filled with such conflicts, and some of them can cause extreme stress. They may encompass questions of the "What will I do with the rest of my life?" sort. "Should I stay at home with the children (+ and –), or should I have a career (+ and –)?" "Should I get married or stay single, or is there another way (+ and – in each case)?" "Should I work for company A (+ and –), or should I work for company B (+ and –)?" Clearly, such lists could go on and on. Reflect back on the conflicts you have faced just during the past few weeks. You should be able to categorize each of them into one of the four types listed here.

STUDY CHECK

What are "motivational conflicts," and in what ways can they act as stressors?

THINKING CRITICALLY

What are some of the more common motivational conflicts that college students face at the beginning of the term?

Life Events as Stressors

Frustration and conflict are potent sources of stress and often are simply unavoidable consequences of being a motivated organism. Psychologists also have considered sources of stress that do not fit our descriptions of either conflict or frustration. One useful approach is to look at events and changes that occur in one's life as potential sources of stress.

In 1967, Thomas Holmes and Richard Rahe published the first version of their *Social Readjustment Rating Scale*, or *SRRS* (Holmes & Holmes, 1970). The basic idea behind this scale is that stress results whenever life situations change. The scale provides a list of life events that might be potentially stressful. The original list of such events was drawn from the reports of patients suffering from moderate to high levels of stress in their lives. Marriage was arbitrarily assigned a value of 50 stress points, or life-change units. With "marriage = 50" as their guide, the patients rated a number of other life changes in terms of the amount of stress they might provide. The death of a spouse got the highest rating (100 units), followed by items such as divorce (73 units), pregnancy (40 units), trouble with the boss (23 units), changing to a new school (20 units), and minor violations of the law (11 units). In a rather direct way, the SRRS gives us a way to measure the stress in our lives.

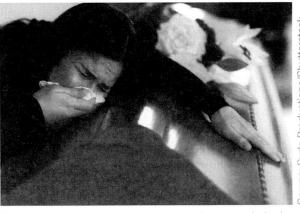

The death of someone close to us can be excruciatingly painful. The SRRS rated the death of a spouse at the top of its list in terms of experienced, stressful events.

There is a positive correlation between scores on the SRRS and the incidence of physical illness and disease (Adler & Matthews, 1994; Thorenstein & Brown, 2009). People with SRRS scores between 200 and 299 have a 50-50 chance of developing symptoms of physical illness within the subsequent two years, whereas 80 percent of those with scores above 300 develop symptoms within the same time period. Several studies that have looked at correlations between SRRS scores and health problems have found the correlations to be positive. The logic is that stress predisposes one to physical illness (Krantz & McCeney, 2002). But correlations do not tell us about cause and effect, as you recall. And, some of the SRRS items are worded to include mention of a physical illness or are health-related. It is not much of a surprise, then, to find that scores on this scale are related to levels of physical illness.

Socioeconomic status, or **SES**, is a measure that reflects income, educational level, and occupation. Sensibly, there is a negative correlation between socioeconomic level and experienced stress (Bradley & Corwyn, 2002; Gallo et al., 2013; Miller, Chen, & Cole, 2009). SES is related to stress in at least two ways: (a) Persons of higher socioeconomic status are less likely than are persons of low SES to encounter negative life events, such as unemployment, poor housing, frequent household moves, and less access to quality health care, and (b) Persons of low SES necessarily have fewer resources to deal with stressful life events when they do occur (Adler & Rehkopf, 2008).

Socioeconomic status (SES)—a measure that reflects income, educational level, and occupation.

It doesn't take a lot of imagination to think of other life situations that are likely to be stress inducing. For example, being a working mother is a stressor, and to a much greater extent than being a working father (Chandola, Brunner, & Marmot, 2006; Light, 1997). And isn't it logical that being a single parent or being a college student with children can be stressful? Certainly, being diagnosed with a serious, life-threatening disease is a stress-producing life event (Anderson, 1997).

Richard Lazarus (1981, 2000) has argued that psychologists ought to focus more attention on those causes of stress that are less dramatic than major life changes such as the death of a family member, moving, or marriage. What often matters most are life's little hassles—the traffic that goes too slowly, the toothpaste tube that splits, ants at a picnic, the cost of a pizza compared to what it was just a few years ago. This argument claims that big crises or major life-change events are too large to have a direct impact on us. What causes us to feel stressed are the ways in which events produce little, irritating changes, hassles in our lives. Being retired may mean a lack of access to friendly conversation at coffee-break time. A spouse who returns to work may make life more difficult; the other

Source: Dragon Images/Shutterstock.

Moving into a new home is an exciting and surely positive life event, but no matter how positive it may be, the process is bound to be stressful.

spouse may have to cook dinner for the first time. Thus, stress is not so much a reaction to an event itself but to the hassles it creates. Also, large traumatic events are rare (one hopes), and "thus their cumulative effect on health and well-being may not be as great as that of minor yet frequent stressors, such as work deadlines and family arguments" (Almeida, 2005, p. 64).

One final note about life-induced stressors: The events in our lives that we characterize as stressors do not have to be negative or unpleasant. Many events that we look forward to and consider changes for the better can bring with them the hassles associated with stress (Folkman & Moskowitz, 2000; Somerfield & McCrae, 2000). For example, everybody is happy about Cindy and Jerry getting married—no doubt a pleasant, positive life event. At the same time—as anyone who has ever gone through the process will attest—weddings and the preparations for them are stressors. They may produce new conflicts. If Aunt Sarah is invited, does that mean that Aunt Louise must be invited as well? Cindy and Jerry are planning an outdoor reception. What if it rains? And there's Javon, the experienced salesman, now a sales manager. Javon may have become used to being on the road and setting his own hours. Now that he has a promotion ("good news"), his daily routine may be drastically altered by his being confined to an office, which may produce new stress.

STUDY CHECK

In what ways can life events act as stressors?

THINKING CRITICALLY

What stressors did you experience last week? Sort them out into the categories we listed in this section.

Responses to Stressors

As with so many other things, there are large individual differences in how people respond to stressors. What constitutes a stressor and what someone may do when he or she experiences stress can vary considerably from person to person. Some people fall apart at weddings; others find them only mildly stressful. For some people, simple choices are difficult to make; for others, choices are not enough, and they seek challenges. The variability in stress we see among different people can usually be found within any one person at different times. For example, on one day, being caught in slow-moving traffic might drive you up the wall. In the very same situation a few days later, you find you couldn't care less. So we need to remember that reactions to stressors vary from time to time and from person to person.

Some people seem so generally resistant to the negative aspects of stress that they have been said to have *hardy personalities* (Ford-Gilboe & Cohen, 2000; Kobasa, 1979, 1987; Neubauer, 1992). Hardiness in this context is related to three things: a) challenge (being able to see difficulties as opportunity for change and growth, not as a threat to status); b) control (being in charge of what is happening and believing that a person is the master of his or her fate); and c) commitment (being engaged and involved with life and its circumstances, not just watching life go by from the sidelines).

Here is another observation about how people deal with stress: Some responses are more effective or adaptive than others. Stress often follows as a natural consequence of being alive and motivated in the real world. What is unfortunate is that people occasionally develop ineffective or maladaptive strategies for dealing with stressors, meaning that, in the long run, they will not be successful in reducing stress.

STUDY CHECK

How do people differ in their reactions to stress?

THINKING CRITICALLY

Who do you know personally that might qualify as a "hardy personality"? What do you suppose makes such folks "hardy"?

Effective Strategies for Coping with Stress

In the long run, the most effective way to deal with stress is to make relatively permanent changes in our behaviors as a result of the experience of stress. Learning is defined as a relatively permanent change in behavior that occurs as the result of practice or experience. Responding to a stressor with learning makes particularly good sense for frustration-induced stress. In a frustrating situation, the pathway to our goal is being blocked. An adaptive way to handle such a stressor is to learn a new way to reach our goal or to learn to modify our goal.

In fact, much of our everyday learning is motivated by frustration-induced stress. You've had to learn many new responses as a way of coping with frustration. Having been frustrated once (or twice) by locking yourself out of your house or car, you learn to hide another set of keys in a location where you can easily find them. Having been caught at home in a blizzard (or a tropical storm) with no cookies in the house, you have learned to bake them yourself. You may have learned as a child to get what you wanted from your parents by smiling sweetly and asking politely. In each of these cases, what motivated the learning of new responses or the establishment of new goals was the stress resulting from frustration.

Learning that is motivated by stress can also teach us the value of escape and avoidance. You now know how to avoid getting into many motivational conflicts. You may have learned that a sensible thing to do once you are in a conflict is to escape from the situation altogether or to make major changes in what is motivating you. This is one way in which stress can be seen as a positive force in our lives. If we were never challenged, if we never set difficult goals, if we never faced stressful situations, we would miss out on many opportunities for personal growth. The stress that we experience surely is unpleasant at the time, but it may produce positive consequences (Carver & Scheier, 1999; Cramer, 2000; Folkman & Moskowitz, 2000; 2004).

To say that we should respond to stressful situations by learning new, effective behaviors is sensible enough, but are there any *specific* measures that we can take to help alleviate the unpleasantness of stress in our lives? Indeed, there are many. Here, we review eight such strategies, which we have summarized in **Table 11.1**.

Know the Stressor. Remember that stress is a reaction to any one of several types of stressors. If you are experiencing stress in your life, the first thing to do is ask, "Where is this stress coming from?" Are you having difficulty resolving a motivational conflict?

TABLE 11.1 Effective Strategies for Coping with Stress

Strategy	Description
Know the Stressor	Understanding the nature of the stressor so that you can direct your efforts effectively.
Minimize the Stressor	Determining what you can do about the stressor and taking control of the situation.
Rethink the Situation	Reassess the severity if the stressor using *cognitive reappraisal* involving rethinking the stressor to put it in best possible light.
Inoculate Against Future Stressors	Anticipating and preparing for stress and recognizing that stress has occurred before, will occur again, and that present situation will pass.
Take Your Time with Important Decisions	Taking the time to think through possible courses of action. Tough decisions are often made more difficult by a rushed decision.
Learn Techniques of Relaxation	Learning techniques that will allow you to relax in the face of stress (e.g., meditation, hypnosis, and biofeedback)
Engage in Physical Exercise	Research shows that exercise can reduce stress. Exercise should be enjoyable and not overly strenuous.
Seek Social Support	Social support from friends and relatives or from others, such as physicians, clergy, therapists, or counselors, can be very helpful in coping with stress.

What positive or negative goals are involved? Is your goal-directed behavior being blocked? If so, what is the source of your frustration? What recent changes or events in your life are unusually upsetting or problematic? A successful strategy for coping with stress will require change and effort on your part, and the first thing to do is to make sure your efforts are well directed.

Efforts for coping with stress can be categorized as either emotion-focused or problem-focused (Lazarus & Folkman, 1984). The difference is self-evident. With an **emotion-focused strategy**, you deal with how you feel and with finding ways to change how you feel. This is often one's first reaction to stressors. "I feel miserable and stressed out; how can I feel better?" Real progress, however, usually requires that you use a problem-focused strategy. With a **problem-focused strategy** you look beyond how you feel at the moment to find the underlying situation causing your present feelings. "Where did this stress come from, and how can I make it go away?"

Minimize the Stressor. Once a stressor has been identified, the next logical question is, "Can I do anything about it? Do I have to stay in this situation, or can I bring about a change?" If an interpersonal relationship has become a constant, nagging, painful source of stress, might this be the time to at least think about breaking it off? If the stress you experience at work has become overwhelming, might this be a good time to consider a different job? The issue is one of taking control, of trying to turn a challenge into an opportunity.

Granted, this sounds very cut and dried, even easy. What makes the process difficult is that there usually is affect involved, often very strong emotional reactions. What we are describing here is largely a cognitive, "problem-solving" approach. If it is going to be at all successful, negative emotions are going to have to be set aside—at least for the time being. Remember: A tendency to take control of potentially stressful situations is one of the characteristics of people with the so-called hardy personality, who usually manage to avoid many of the negative consequences of stress. Even people with terminal illnesses fare much better if they take control, find out everything there is to know about their

Emotion-focused strategy—a coping strategy in which you deal with how you feel and with finding ways to change how you feel.

Problem-focused strategy—a coping strategy in which you look beyond how you feel at the moment to find the underlying situation causing your present feelings.

illness, seek second or third opinions, and make the most of what time they have left (van der Pompe, Antoni, & Heijnen, 1998).

Rethink the Situation. We should assess whether the stressors in our lives are real or (even partially) imagined threats to our well-being. Making this determination is part of what is called a *cognitive reappraisal* of one's situation (Folkman & Moskowitz, 2000). In the context of stress management, cognitive reappraisal means rethinking a situation to put it in the best possible light.

Is that coworker really trying to do you out of a promotion? Do you really care if you are invited to the party? Must you earn an A on the next test in order to pass the course? Are things really as bad as they seem? Lazarus (1993) sees this as realizing that "people should try to change the noxious things that can be changed, accept those that cannot, and have the wisdom to know the difference"—a paraphrase of an ancient Hebrew prayer.

Meichenbaum (1977) argues that we can deal with a lot of stress simply by talking to ourselves, replacing negative statements (such as, "Oh boy, I'm really in trouble now. I'm sure to be called on, and I'll embarrass myself in front of the whole class") with coping statements (such as, "I'll just do the best I can. I'm as prepared as anybody in here, and in a little while, this will all be over"). This cognitive approach does take a bit of practice, but it can be very effective.

Inoculate Against Future Stressors. This strategy involves accepting and internalizing much of what we have been saying about the universality of stress and stressors. It is a matter of convincing yourself that stress has occurred before, will occur again, and that this, too, will pass. It is a matter of anticipation and preparation—truly coming to accept the reality that "worrying about this won't make it any better," or "no matter how bad things look, I'll be able to figure out some plan to deal with it." We know that surgery patients recover faster and with fewer post-surgical complications if they are fully informed before their surgery of what they can expect, how they are likely to feel, and what they can do to aid in their own recovery. People in high-stress jobs (emergency-room personnel, for example) can be trained to anticipate the occurrence of stressors and develop skills to deal with these stressors even before they occur. This "stress-exposure training" or SET, as it is called, can both reduce the perception of stress and increase performance on the job (Salas & Cannon-Bowers, 2001).

Inoculating yourself against future stressors often amounts to trying to develop a sense of optimism in the belief that generally good things, as opposed to bad things, will happen to you (Cohen & Pressman, 2006). People with this sort of optimistic outlook "routinely maintain higher levels of subjective well-being during times of stress than do people who are less optimistic" (Scheier & Carver, 1993, p. 27).

Take Your Time with Important Decisions. Stress often accompanies the process of making tough decisions. You are frustrated. A goal-directed behavior is being blocked. You have to decide if you will pursue a different course of action. Which course of action? Would it be wiser to change your goal? Do you want to do this (+ and −) or do you want to do that (+ and −)? We can make matters worse by rushing a decision "just to have it over with," even granting that occasionally we are faced with deadlines by which final decisions must be made. We can add to an already-stressful situation by racing to conclusions before we have all the facts, or before we have explored all the costs and benefits associated with the alternatives we are contemplating. For example, if you can't make up your mind about a new car you're thinking about buying, why not rent one for a few days to see if you would be happy with it in the long run?

The strategies listed above are suggestions for dealing with the stressor that has caused stress in one's life. As noted above, as problem-focused strategies, these are the only effective, long-term ways to deal with stressors. In the short-term, however, there are some things you can do to combat the unpleasant feelings or effects that accompany stress (that is, emotion-focused strategies). We'll look at three.

Learn Techniques of Relaxation. Learning effective ways to relax may not be as easy as it sounds, but the logic is simple: Feeling stressed and being relaxed are not compatible.

Effective, emotion-focused strategies for dealing with the stress that comes to our lives include learning to relax, perhaps by meditation, and engaging in physical exercise (without overdoing it).

Sources: (*left*) Alter-ego/Shutterstock; (*right*) fizkes/Shutterstock.

If you can become relaxed, the experience (feelings) of stress will be diminished. Hypnosis may help. Meditation may help. So may relaxation training.

A variety of operant conditioning called biofeedback can provide relief from the tension associated with stress. **Biofeedback** is "the process of providing information to an individual about his [her] bodily processes in some form which he [she] might be able to use to modify those processes" (Hill, 1985, p. 201). A person's heart rate, let's say, is constantly monitored, and the rate is fed back to the person, perhaps in the form of an audible tone. As heart rate increases, the pitch of the tone becomes higher. As heart rate decreases, the tone gets lower. Once the learner knows what his or her heart rate (or blood pressure, or muscle tension, and so on) is doing, a certain degree of control over that response is possible. The reinforcement involved here is simply the newly gained knowledge that a desired change is being made. As a result of being reinforced, the stress-fighting responses increase in their frequency (Linden & Moseley. 2006). Biofeedback techniques *can* produce remarkably helpful reactions, including the reduction of blood pressure, insomnia, and irregular heart rhythms (McClay & Spira, 2009; Stokes & Lappin, 2010, Wheat & Larkin, 2010).

Engage in Physical Exercise. There is a good deal of evidence that physical exercise (aerobic exercise in particular) is a useful agent in the battle against stress (Anshel, 1996; Miller, Chen, & Cole, 2009). Physical exercise is helpful once stress is experienced, but it is difficult to say if exercise combats stress directly or does so indirectly by improving physical health, stamina, self-esteem, and self-confidence. In that regard, exercise can be part of a program to inoculate against stress in the first place. And, of course, one must be careful. Deciding that tomorrow you'll start running five miles a day, rain or shine, may be a decision that in itself will create more stress than it will reduce. Exercise should not be overly strenuous, should be enjoyable, and should help you feel better about yourself.

Seek Social Support. Finally, there is the advantage of social support for persons who are experiencing stress. Stress is a common phenomenon. Perhaps no one else knows precisely how you feel, or has experienced exactly the same situation in which you find yourself, but all of us have known stress, and we are all aware of the types of situations that give rise to it. Social support from friends and relatives or from others, such as physicians, clergy, therapists, or counselors, can be very helpful (Adler & Matthews, 1994). If at all possible, one should not face stress alone.

Now that we've reviewed some of the steps that can be taken to help alleviate the unpleasantness of stress, let's consider some reactions stress can produce that are not as adaptive.

Biofeedback—the process of providing information to an individual about his or her bodily processes in some form that he or she might be able to use to modify those processes.

STUDY CHECK

What are problem-focused and emotion-focused strategies for effective coping with stress?

THINKING CRITICALLY

No doubt you have used several of the strategies described in this section when you have experienced stress. Which have proven most useful? Are there any that you have not tried?

FOCUS ON DIVERSITY

Are There Group Differences in the Perception of and Coping with Stress?

As we have seen, stress can be a highly disturbing condition that most of us have experienced at one time or another. The sources of stress are many, and there are effective and ineffective ways of coping with stress. From your own experience, you probably know that not everyone experiences stress and copes with stress the same way. Your best friend might be resilient and shrug off most stressors and cope with others easily. Your sister, on the other hand, might melt down at the first hint of stress and not cope very well. Certainly, there are individual differences in perceiving and coping with stress. But are there group differences in how stress is perceived and addressed? Here we will look at whether there are gender, racial, and ethnic differences in how stress is handled.

Some researchers argue that the amount of stress one experiences and the means of coping with stress are not different for men and women (Baum & Grunberg, 1991; Lazarus, 1993). Others (Taylor et al., 2000), however, argue that there are significant differences between how males and females deal with stress. Whereas males are more likely to display the so-called "fight-or-flight" response to stress, females (and not just human females at that) are more likely to respond with what Taylor and her colleagues call a "tend-and-befriend" response. A father at home alone with a sick and crying child is likely to scurry around to find someone else to look after the baby. A mother in the same situation is more likely to simply call her older sister or her mother, seeking advice.

When you are exposed to a stressor, there are several physiological changes that occur in your body. These changes involve the brain, endocrine system, and a number of other organs in your body (Ježová, Juránková, Mosnárová, Kriška, & Skultétyovi, I. 1996).

Of course, this physical response to stress will vary across individuals and situations. There is clear evidence that there are gender differences in how rats respond physiologically to stress. Systems involved in the stress response (hormones and nervous system activity) are more pronounced in female than male rats. However, it is not clear whether the gender differences observed in rats are true for humans as well (Ježová et al., 1996). According to Ježová et al., gender differences in humans are observed, but not in all circumstances. Ježová et al. report a study in which male and female humans were exposed to mild levels of heat (via a sauna) while their physiological responses were recorded. They found an increase in some stress-related hormones (ACTH and prolactin) in females but not males. Another stress hormone (cortisol) did not differ between males and females. They concluded that the physiological response to mild levels of a stressor was more pronounced in women than men.

So, men and women differ to some extent in their physical responses to some stressors. How about psychological reactions? In a study of college students, Brougham, Zail, Mendoza, and Miller (2009) found that female college students experienced higher levels of stress than male students. A second study (Anshel, Sutarso, & Jubenville, 2009) looked at differences between male and female athletes in response to sports-related stressors. Anshel et al. found that women reported a more intense reaction to coaching-related stress than men. Female athletes may get more upset than male athletes when their coaches get angry with them. However, males and females did not differ in their responses to performance-related sources of stress. Matud (2004) compared how women and men responded to chronic (long-term) and minor daily (shorter-term) stressors. Matud found that women had a more intense reaction to both types of stressors than men. Women tended to rate their stressors more negatively than men. However, women did not experience more stressors over a two-year period than did men. This difference was also found in a second study by Matud, Bethencourt, and Ibáñez (2015) on Spanish adult men and women: women had more intense psychological reactions to stress than men.

There are also some racial and ethnic differences in responses to stress. One study looked at ethnic and racial differences in responses to Hurricane Andrew, which devastated areas of Florida in 1992 (Perilla, Norris, & Lavizzo, 2002). Perilla et al. specifically looked at post-traumatic stress disorder (PTSD) responses six months after the storm hit. Their results showed that Latinos showed the highest rate of PTSD (38 percent), followed by African Americans (29 percent), and Caucasians (15 percent). Perilla et al. suggest that these differences may be accounted for by the fact that members of the different groups may differ in their exposure to the hazards posed by the hurricane. They point out that minority populations are more likely to live in areas of the state that are less safe than Caucasian populations. They also suggest that members of different cultural groups may respond differently to stressors because of their different socialization experiences.

So far we have seen that there are gender, racial, and ethnic differences in how people respond to stress. Are there also differences in how people cope with stress? It turns out that there are. Compared with men, women college students use more emotion-focused coping strategies (Brougham et al., 2009). This finding was supported by Matud (2004), who found that women are more likely than men to adopt emotional and avoidance coping styles (Matud, 2004). Matud found that men were more likely to use rational and detached coping styles. Generally, women are more likely than men to adopt emotion-focused than problem-focused coping strategies (Larson & Pleck, 1998). In a study of coping styles of male and female medical school students, Madhyastha, Latha, and Kamath (2014) found that female students relied more heavily on social support to cope with stress than male students. They found that female students were more likely than male students to seek both problem-focused and emotion-focused support from social support sources. On the other hand, the male students were more likely than female students to use humor to cope with school-related stress. Male students were also more likely to rely on self-blame, an ineffective coping strategy. Matheny, Ashby, and Cupp (2005) report that female college students used more effective coping strategies than their male counterparts. They found that male college students were more likely to become ill in response to school-related stress than female college students.

In terms of ethnic differences in coping styles, Sinha, Willson, and Watson (2000) found that Indian college students are more likely to adopt an emotion-focused coping style than Canadian college students. Sinha and Watson (2007) report that Canadian college students adopting an avoidance strategy (avoiding stress) are more likely to show psychological symptoms (e.g., anxiety) than Indian college students adopting the same strategy. O'Connor and Shimizu (2002) compared British and Japanese individuals on their coping strategies. The main difference they found was that the Japanese individuals used emotion-focused coping to a greater extent than British individuals. No difference was found between the groups with respect to using problem-focused coping. They also found that having a sense of control over stressful situations was a significant predictor of effective coping for the British but not the Japanese individuals. The greater emphasis on personal control and responsibility in Western cultures might account for this difference. In another study, Asian students were found to be more likely to rely on religion-based coping than European students (Chai, Krägeloh, Shepherd, & Billington, 2012). Chai et al. also found that Asian students used self-distraction as a coping mechanism to a greater extent than European students.

Ineffective Strategies for Coping with Stress

Coping effectively with stress is a matter of bringing about change. If you do not change, you fixate and accept the same stress from the same stressor. Fixation is seldom an adequate reaction to stress. The adage, "If at first you don't succeed, try, try again" is sound advice. But again and again and again? At some point, we must give up a particular course of action to try something else.

In a way, procrastination is a form of fixation, isn't it? A term paper is due in two weeks and you can't seem to start, deciding to "put it off until this weekend." The weekend brings no progress either, and the stress of dealing with the paper is momentarily postponed. The catch is that you are going to pay a price. Eventually, you have to do the paper. Then, with very little time before the deadline, you will probably experience stress more than ever before. A long-term study of procrastination in college students found that procrastinators experienced less stress and less illness early in the term, but as the term progressed, they reported greater stress, more illness, and more serious illnesses. And, procrastinators earned significantly lower grades. As the authors of this study put it, "Procrastination thus appears to be a self-defeating behavior pattern marked by short-term benefits and long-term costs" (Tice & Baumeister, 1997, p. 454). In addition to not changing one's behavior or one's goals, there are two other reactions to stressors that are clearly maladaptive: aggression and anxiety.

There are many causes of aggression, and one source of aggressive behaviors is stress—in particular, the stress that results from frustration. A student expecting a grade of A on a paper receives a grade of C–, returns to her room, and throws her hairbrush at the mirror, shattering it. A driver in a hurry to get to campus rams the rear bumper of the car ahead, judging it to be going far too slowly. Remember Emma, who was frustrated because she couldn't have a cookie and then tore the arm off her doll? At one time, it was proposed that frustration was the *only* cause of aggression, the so-called **frustration-aggression hypothesis** (Dollard et al., 1939). This point of view claimed that frustration could produce a number of reactions, including aggression, but that aggression was always caused by frustration. We now recognize that there are other sources of aggression (it may be an innate or instinctive response, or it may be a response learned through reinforcement or modeling). It is true, however, that frustration remains a prime candidate as the cause of aggression. Although it usually doesn't do much good in the long run, a flash of aggressive behavior often follows stress.

> **Frustration-aggression hypothesis**—the hypothesis stating that frustration is the *only* cause of aggression.

You are in the parking lot trying to get home from class, and your car won't start. Over and over you crank the ignition. Continuing to turn the key without success is a good example of fixation—it's not doing you any good, but you keep at it, perhaps until you run down the battery. Still frustrated, you swing open the door, get out, kick the front left fender, throw up the hood, and glower at the engine. You're mad! Now, having released a bit of tension, you might feel better for a few seconds, but being angry and kicking at the car, or yelling at someone who offers to assist, won't help you solve your problem.

Another negative consequence of stress is **anxiety**—a general feeling of tension, apprehension, and dread that involves predictable physiological changes. Anxiety is a very difficult concept to define precisely, but everyone seems to know what you are talking about when you refer to anxiety. Like stress, anxiety is a reaction we all have experienced. Often it is a reaction that accompanies stress. We can think of anxiety as an unpleasant emotional component of the stress response. As much as anything else, we want to rid ourselves of stress in order to minimize our anxiety.

> **Anxiety**—a general feeling of tension, apprehension, and dread that involves predictable physiological changes.

Sometimes, the amount of stress and anxiety in a person's life becomes more than he or she can cope with effectively. Feelings of anxiety start to interfere with normal adaptations to the environment and other people. Such feelings may become the focus of one's attention. More anxiety follows, and then more distress, and more discomfort, and more pain. For many people—tens of millions of people in the United States and Canada—the anxiety that accompanies stress is so discomforting and so maladaptive we say that they are suffering from a psychological disorder.

STUDY CHECK

What are the three inappropriate, ineffective reactions to stress?

THINKING CRITICALLY

At some time or another, most of us have reacted to stress by fixating, becoming aggressive, or feeling anxious. When you have any of these reactions, how can you respond to them? That is, how can you make these ineffective strategies more effective?

Psychological Factors That Influence Physical Health

Is there a relationship between a person's personality and that person's physical health? Can individual psychological evaluations predict physical as well as psychological disorders? Is there a disease-prone personality? Are some lifestyles unhealthy? "Why do some people get sick and some stay well?" (Adler & Matthews, 1994, p. 229; Schneiderman, 2004). A tentative answer to these questions is yes. There is a positive correlation between some personality variables and physical health.

The Type A Personality

Type A behavior pattern (TABP)—a behavior pattern involving a person being competitive, achievement-oriented, and impatient; the individual typically works at many tasks at the same time, is easily aroused, and is often hostile or angry.

Although researchers had been exploring the link between psychology and physical health for years, they first caught the attention of the public with a series of studies examining the association between coronary heart disease (CHD) and the Type A behavior pattern (TABP). As originally defined, a Type A person is a competitive, achievement-oriented, impatient individual who typically works at many tasks at the same time, is easily aroused, and is often hostile or angry (Friedman & Rosenman, 1959). The symptoms of coronary heart disease include chest pains and heart attacks, and it is caused by a buildup of substances (cholesterol, for example) blocking the supply of blood to the heart. People who show none of the characteristics of the TABP and who are relaxed and easygoing are said to have a *Type B behavior pattern*.

From the early 1960s to the early 1980s, several studies reported a positive relationship between CHD and behaviors typical of the Type A personality (Jenkins, 1976; Rosenman et al., 1975; Wood, 1986). The National Institutes of Health declared the Type A behavior pattern an independent risk factor for heart disease (National Institutes of Health, 1981). The Type A personality pattern was implicated in hypertension (chronic high blood pressure) even when no other signs of coronary heart disease were present (Irvine et al., 1991). It all seemed clear. Find people with the Type A behavior pattern, intervene to change their behaviors, and watch the incidence of coronary heart disease decline. But, as we have said repeatedly, complex problems seldom have simple solutions.

Data began to surface that did *not* show a clear relationship between TABP and coronary heart disease (Hollis et al., 1990). Perhaps Type A people were not more at risk for heart disease than anyone else. Perhaps studies that failed to find a relation between TABP and CHD were flawed. As it happens, both of these hypotheses appear to be valid. For one thing, the Type A behavioral pattern is complex and difficult to assess. It is likely that simple paper-and-pencil inventories—which had been used in many studies—fail to identify a large number of people with the TABP.

It also may be that the TABP as originally defined is too global a pattern of behaviors (Adler & Matthews, 1994). Perhaps there is a set of behaviors within the general definition of Type A behaviors that does predict coronary heart disease. The best bet seems to be that the "active ingredients" of TABP that are most predictive of CHD are anger, impatience, and hostility. Of particular interest is something called "cynical hostility"—being suspicious, moody, distrusting, and quick to get upset and criticize others (Bunde & Suls, 2006; Miller, Chen, & Cole, 2009). A large-scale study by the Committee on Health and Behavior of the National Institute of Medicine (2001) concluded that "Strong links have been identified between the trait of hostility and the incidence of and mortality from heart disease" (p. 5), a finding consistent with a nine-year study that found that men high in hostility had more than twice the risk of dying of a cardiovascular incident than did men low in hostility (Everson et al., 1997).

More work still needs to be done. Better techniques of diagnosing Type A behavior patterns are needed, as is research on the mechanisms that underlie whatever relationships there may be between TABP and coronary heart disease. As an example,

Hostility and impatience with hypertension can be a major risk factor for coronary heart disease.

consider a study of 2,394 men aged 50 to 64 who were assessed for CHD. They also were assessed on three measures of Type A personality, as well as other CHD risk factors. After nine years, there was no increased risk of coronary heart disease associated with *any* of the measures of TABP. The researchers did conclude that: a) If a man is likely to have a heart attack, he will have it sooner rather than later if he has a Type A personality, and b) Being Type A increases exposure to potential triggers of heart problems (such as alcohol and/or cigarette smoke) rather than directly producing cardiovascular problems (Gallacher et al., 2003). Then, just one month later, a report of a major study was issued that clearly *did* associate hostility and impatience with hypertension—a major risk factor for CHD (Yan et al., 2003). More research is also needed on which changes in Type A persons would be likely to reduce their chances of heart disease. After all, most of the traits of the TABP are the same ones many Americans value and try to imitate in their quest to "get ahead."

STUDY CHECK

What is the relationship, if any, between the Type A behavior pattern and physical health?

THINKING CRITICALLY

Do you have a Type A or a Type B personality?

Why People Die: The Unhealthy Lifestyle

Death is unavoidable, and people die for many reasons. On the other hand, many deaths are premature and preventable. Let us review a few statistics.

In 2015, in the United States, 2,712,630 deaths occurred (Centers for Disease Control and Prevention, 2015). **Figure 11.2** shows the top 10 causes of death in the United States in 2015. As you can see, by far, heart disease and cancer are the top-two causes of death.

Many health psychologists wonder how many deaths in the United States can be traced to psychological or behavioral factors. We are aware of a few potentially unhealthy behaviors from the research on the Type A behavior pattern: hostility, anger, and time-urgency as risk factors for cardiovascular disease (which, includes both heart disease and stroke). As stated previously, we also know that obesity rates are increasing and that obesity has negative consequences for personal health (Centers for Disease Control and Prevention, 2010). What other risk factors contribute to an "unhealthy lifestyle"?

Risk factors for coronary heart disease include cigarette smoking, obesity, a sedentary lifestyle, family history, and such psychosocial factors as depression, anxiety, lack of social support, and work-related stress (Frasure-Smith & Lespérance, 2005; Grundy, 1999; Hemingway & Marmot, 1999; Miller, Chen, & Cole, 2009). Obviously, many of these factors interact and make matters worse. For example, cigarette smoking, alcohol consumption, and depression work together to interrupt normal sleep patterns, and together they pose a much greater risk of coronary heart disease than any single factor by itself (Kiecolt-Glaser et al., 2002). Persons who live an unhealthy lifestyle also increase their risk of cancer. Poor diet, stress, lack of exercise, excessive exposure to ultraviolet rays, lack of social support, and

The truth is, it is very easy to list the components of an "unhealthy lifestyle." Doing something to reduce or eliminate such components is not so easy.

Source: suparat wanpen/Shutterstock.

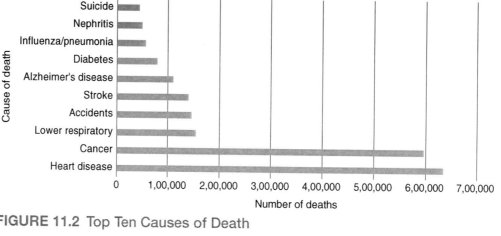

FIGURE 11.2 Top Ten Causes of Death

tobacco use are risk factors for cancer (Glanz, 1997; Glanz et al., 1999; Lerman, Rimer, & Glynn, 1997; McKenna et al., 1999). In the case of cancer, positive behaviors that can reduce one's risk include taking steps to ensure early diagnosis (getting PAP smears for cervical cancer, mammograms for breast cancer, PSA blood tests for prostate cancer, and the like) (Schneiderman et al., 2001). One's educational level also matters. "Despite increased attention and substantial dollars directed to groups with low socioeconomic status, within race and gender groups, *the educational gap in life expectancy is rising*" (Meara, Richards, & Cutler, 2008, p. 350 [emphasis added]).

Globally, 56.9 million people died in 2016. Of these deaths, 15.9 million were caused by heart disease and stroke, the top-two killers worldwide (World Health Organization, 2018a). Other causes of death in 2016 were chronic pulmonary disease (3 million), lower respiratory diseases (3 million), lung cancer (1.7 million), diabetes (1.6 million), and tuberculosis (1.3 million). It might surprise you to learn that diarrhea accounted for 1.4 million deaths and was the ninth most frequent cause of death. Alzheimer's and other dementia diseases were the fifth leading causes of death. Happily, AIDS is no longer in the top-10 causes of death, most likely due to better prevention and treatment.

An unhealthy lifestyle (see **Table 11.2**) may involve behaviors that are fatal—failing to wear safety belts or recklessness at work or at play, for instance. By their nature, accidents are haphazard, unpredictable, and unforeseen, but, caution, safety training, and awareness can reduce accidents. Health psychologists promote such things as smoke-free spaces, safe workplaces, exercise programs at work, and air bags in cars. At the same time, many health psychologists work with individuals who want to change behaviors and develop a healthier lifestyle.

Remember that many causes of death—even death at a young age—are largely determined by biology (infections, for example) and not directly susceptible to changes in lifestyle. A woman with high cholesterol can change her diet and exercise rigorously and still, after six months, not change her cholesterol level. On the other hand, you may know a 93-year-old who eats saturated fats daily—butter, fried foods, sausage, and ice cream are the bulk of his diet. Yet he has no cholesterol build-up and the blood pressure of a healthy teenager. Sometimes, it is just in the genes.

For the remainder of this chapter, we will examine two areas where psychologists have been particularly active: helping people stop smoking and helping people prevent or cope with HIV and AIDS.

A major premise of health psychology is that many health problems have more to do with behaviors and choices than with bacteria and viruses. Cigarette smoking and overeating are behaviors that lead directly to negative health consequences. Engaging in risky behaviors with motorcycle stunts and tricks on the street can led to all sorts of problems (and doing so without a helmet or protective clothing is even worse).

TABLE 11.2 Unhealthy Lifestyles and Early Death

Factors Contributing to the Unhealthy Lifestyle
Obesity and a sedentary lifestyle.
Cigarette smoking, alcohol consumption, and depression work together to contribute to early death, more so than any one alone.
Poor education relating to lower socioeconomic status.
Risky behaviors like not wearing seat belts, engaging in risky work or risky leisure activities.
A biological predisposition or sensitivity to certain factors (e.g., high cholesterol, sensitivity to toxins).

STUDY CHECK

What are some of the components of an unhealthy lifestyle?

THINKING CRITICALLY

Everyone knows that smoking, eating too much, and not exercising are strongly associated with health problems. Why do people behave in ways they know to be unhealthy?

PSYCHOLOGY IN ACTION

Can Optimism Cure What Ails You?

In 1964, Norman Cousins was diagnosed with anky-losing spondylitis, a degenerative disease of the connective tissue in his spine. His doctor's prognosis was grim: Cousins had a 1 in 500 chance of survival. Cousins took control of the situation. He researched what drugs were available for his condition. He left the hospital and got himself a hotel room. He also got himself a cache of comedy films and a projector. While watching Marx Brothers movies and laughing himself silly, Cousins started to feel better. The pain that was wracking his body subsided enough that he could get a good night's sleep. He also discovered that blood tests showed that the inflammation in his body dropped when he watched the funny movies. After a few weeks of this laughter therapy, Cousins felt good enough to go back to work. Had Cousins laughed his way back to health? Is such a thing really possible? Can laughter actually affect one's physical well-being?

There is research showing that it may be, on some level, possible! Laughter and a good mood appear to help hospitalized patients cope with their illnesses (Taylor & Gollwitzer, 1995). Humor may also help reduce anxiety surrounding surgery and post-operative pain. In one study, Yun, Kim, and Jung (2015) investigated whether a nurse clown could affect children who were surgical patients. Children and their parents were assigned to one of two groups. In one group, a nurse dressed as a clown was trained to engage in several positive behaviors and interacted with children and one parent. In the other group, children were not exposed to the clown nurse and received standard pre-operative treatment. Yum et al. measured the level of anxiety the children and parent were experiencing, blood pressure (a physiological measure of anxiety), and level of post-operative pain. Yum et al. found that there were no significant differences between the two groups on any of the pre-operative measures. However, there were differences on the post-operative measures. Children and parents exposed to the clown nurse showed less psychological and physiological anxiety than the control children and parents. Additionally, children exposed to the clown nurse experienced less post-operative pain than the control children. So, in this study, humor in the form of the clown nurse helped reduce the stress and pain associated with the negative experience of surgery. In another study, medical clowning reduced the amount of crying among children having blood drawn and reduced the amount of pain experienced (Meiri, Ankri, Hamad-Saied, Konopnicki, & Pillar, 2016).

Laughter can also affect your immune system. In one study (Kyung Hee, Hye Sook, & Eun Young, 2015), women who just delivered babies were tested for levels of a protein associated with immune system functioning before and after birth. Some women were exposed to a 60-minute laugh therapy session twice a week for two weeks after birth. Other women (control group) did not receive the laugh therapy. The results showed that the women in both groups experienced a reduction in the immune system protein from pre- to post-birth analysis. However, the women in the control group showed a sharper decline than those in the laugh therapy group. The post-birth protein level for women in the laugh therapy group was higher ($M = 486.84$ mg/dL) than women in the control group ($M = 312.39$ mg/dL). Although the findings on the effects of laughter on the immune system are encouraging, we should not overstate these effects. A review of the research by Bennett and Lengacher (2009) found only tentative support for the relationship. Clearly, more research is needed.

At this point, if you are not feeling up to par, you might be tempted to laugh yourself into a state of hysterics and hyperventilation. But how much laughter is beneficial? If a little bit is good, wouldn't a whole lot be better? Maybe not. One study suggests that there may be an optimal level of laughter that is most beneficial to one's health (Hasan & Hasan, 2009). Hasan and Hasan had respondents from two cultural groups (India and Canada) complete a questionnaire asking about various aspects of their health, well-being, and how much they laugh. Hasan and Hasan found that among both groups, a moderate level of laughter was associated with the best health outcomes. Too little or too much laughter was not as good. So, if you want to improve your health by laughing, don't laugh too hard!

Laughter is not the only good medicine for what ails you. The attitude and coping style you bring to a health situation also matter. An optimistic coping style helps individuals recover more rapidly and more effectively from coronary bypass surgery, for example. Optimistic coronary bypass patients had fewer problems after surgery than pessimistic patients (Tindle et al., 2012).

Following their surgery, the optimists reported more positive family, sexual, recreational, and health-related activities than the pessimistic patients. Optimistic patients with traumatic brain injuries (TBIs) also do better than their less optimistic counterparts (Ramanathan, Wardecker, Slocomb, & Hillary, 2011). Ramanathan et al. found that people who scored higher on a measure of dispositional optimism showed less distress after TBI than those scoring lower. They also found that the relationship between dispositional optimism and cognitive ability after TBI was mediated by distress. This means that more optimistic TBI patients do better cognitively because they experience less psychological distress after their head injuries.

Optimism can also help military personnel adjust to life after traumatic experiences. In one study, optimism was a strong predictor of positive physical and psychological health among returning Vietnam War prisoners (Segovia, Moore, Linnville, & Hoyt, 2015). It is well known that combat is related to post-traumatic stress disorder (PTSD) among veterans. Optimism can help soldiers cope with the negative effects of combat. In one study, optimistic Iraq War combat veterans showed fewer symptoms of PTSD than did less optimistic veterans. Optimistic combat veterans also showed fewer symptoms of depression and less work impairment than did less optimistic veterans (Thomas, Britt, Odle-Dusseau, & Bliese, 2011).

Why would optimism contribute to better health outcomes after a traumatic event such as bypass surgery or TBI? One explanation is that optimistic individuals are more likely to see positive outcomes from adversity, and optimism allows a person to apply more flexible coping strategies than pessimism (Prati & Pietrantoni, 2009). Additionally, optimistic people react to threatening events by developing *positive illusions*, which are beliefs that include unrealistically optimistic notions about their ability to handle the threat and create a positive outcome (Taylor, 1989). Positive illusions are adaptive in the sense that ill people who are optimistic will be persistent and creative in their attempts to cope with the psychological and physical threat of disease. The tendency to display positive illusions has been shown in individuals who have tested positive for the HIV virus but have not yet displayed any symptoms (Taylor, Kemeny, Aspinwall, & Schneider, 1992). These individuals often expressed the belief that they had developed immunity to the virus and that they could "flush" the virus from their systems. They acted on this belief by paying close attention to nutrition and physical fitness.

Promoting Healthy Behaviors

In the second half of this chapter we have reviewed many statistics. Our motivation in doing so is not to have you memorize a large number of large numbers. Rather, we want you to appreciate the enormity of health-related issues that are rooted in people's choices and behaviors. Some personality characteristics affect physical health. The specific traits involved and exactly how they operate are being debated and researched right now. However, we do know that certain behaviors put people at greater risk for physical disease and death. One role of the health psychologist is to help change these potentially dangerous behaviors (Schneiderman et al., 2001).

Helping People to Stop Smoking

Few efforts to change behavior have received as much attention as those meant to discourage people from smoking. The main reason is that smoking is so deadly. The Centers for Disease Control and Prevention (2018d) tells us that in 2016 an estimated 15.5 percent of all adults (37.8 million people) smoked cigarettes in the United States. The good news is that this number is down from just a decade earlier. Cigarette smoking remains the leading preventable cause of death in the United States, accounting for 1 in 5 deaths (480,000 people) each year. More than 16 million Americans are now living with a smoking-related disease. Additionally, tobacco use is associated with 7 million deaths per year worldwide, a majority of whom live in lower to middle-income households (World Health Organization, 2018b). Smoking "is regarded as one of the leading causes of premature death" (Hatsukami, Stead, & Gupta, 2008, p. 2027; Lichtenstein, Zhu, & Tedeschi, 2010). The American Cancer Society (2005, p. 1) reports that "Cigarettes kill more Americans than alcohol, car accidents, suicide, AIDS, homicide, and illegal drugs combined." Smoking provides an increased risk for colon and rectal cancers (Slattery et al., 2003), multiple sclerosis (Riise, Nortveldt, & Ascherio, 2003), and prostate cancer, particularly in its aggressive forms (Plaskon et al., 2003).

Studies of "secondhand smoke" tell us that the children of smokers face increased risk for lung cancer even if they have never smoked. According to the Centers for Disease Control and Prevention (2018e), among adult nonsmokers in the United States, approximately 34,000 deaths from heart disease occurred each year during 2005–2009. The Centers for Disease Control and Prevention estimates that secondhand smoke accounted for around 7,300 lung cancer deaths in the same span of years. Moreover, children of mothers who smoked during their pregnancy are significantly more likely to have attention deficit hyperactivity disorder than children of non-smoking mothers (Thapar, Fowler, & Rice, 2003). Children of low socioeconomic status mothers who smoked during pregnancy also showed poorer neurological development than offspring of mothers who did not smoke (Wehby, Prater, McCarthy, Castilla, & Murray, 2011). Fortunately, quitting smoking at any point during pregnancy or postpartum is beneficial for both the mother's and the baby's health (Fiore, Jaen, & Baker, 2008), and with the aid of smoking cessation counseling *and* psychotherapy, attempts to give up smoking during pregnancy can be very successful (Cinciripini et. al., 2010).

Programs to persuade smokers to quit have shown some promise, but quitting is extremely difficult. In fact, it appears to be easier to kick the heroin or cocaine habit than to quit smoking (Grinspoon, 1997). Nearly 70 percent of smokers say they want to quit, and over 40 percent say that they have attempted to quit at least once in the past year (Dunston, 2003). Only five percent of smokers manage to quit on their first try, and almost 80 percent relapse within a year, but after repeated attempts nearly 50 percent of smokers eventually do quit. A person who finally does give up smoking permanently has quit, on the average, five times before. When smokers who are about to try quitting are asked about what concerns them, they report worrying about being around others who are smoking, socializing in general, or drinking coffee or alcohol. Actually, in one study, none of these factors was found to be associated with relapse. Only negative affect (depression and anxiety) was

(Shiffman et al., 2007). Similarly, many smokers worry about the possibility of significant weight gain if they were to give up their habit, but "heavy smokers tend to have greater body weight than do light smokers or nonsmokers" (Chiolero et al., 2008, p. 801).

Psychologists have had some success helping to design programs to get people not to smoke in the first place. These anti-smoking programs have been effective with teenagers in particular (Farrelly et al., 2005; Henriksen et al., 2004; Pierce, White, & Gilpin, 2005). Even campaigns focused on adult smokers seem to have a greater effect on adolescents (White et al., 2003). With increasing data suggesting that just watching others smoke in movies promotes teenage smoking, efforts were made to reduce if not eliminate smoking in motion pictures (Dal Cin et al. 2007; Heatherton & Sargent, 2009). As more facilities declare themselves "smoke-free environments," the more difficult it is for people to begin or continue smoking.

STUDY CHECK

Why are health psychologists so concerned about smoking, and how are they attempting to reduce the number of smokers?

THINKING CRITICALLY

Assume that you are on a committee of your local school system charged with developing a program to keep youngsters between the ages of 10 and 12 from starting to smoke. List some of the factors that will be important determiners of this program's success.

Coping with STDs, HIV, and AIDS

Sexually transmitted disease (STD)—a contagious disease usually passed on through sexual contact.

A **sexually transmitted disease (STD)** is a contagious disease usually passed on through sexual contact. STDs provide an excellent example of a health problem directly associated with psychosocial causes. Sexually transmitted diseases (such as chlamydia, gonorrhea, syphilis, and genital herpes) affect tens of millions of people. In 2017, chlamydia was the most frequently reported STD (over 1.7 million cases), followed by gonorrhea (555,608 cases) and syphilis (30,644 cases) (Centers for Disease Control and Prevention, 2018g).

As unpleasant, even painful, as all of the sexually transmitted diseases can be, none has attracted as much attention as *acquired immune deficiency syndrome, or AIDS*. AIDS is caused by the *human immunodeficiency virus or HIV*. HIV is one of the "slow viruses," meaning that there may be a long interval between the initial infection and the onset of serious symptoms. There are large individual differences in the pace at which the virus has its effects. A faster progression of symptoms is associated with an accumulation of stressful life events, depression, and lack of social support (Leserman et al., 2000). HIV attacks the body's immune system, which normally fights off infections. When the immune system becomes sufficiently weakened, an HIV-infected person is said to have AIDS. Someone with AIDS simply does not have the bodily resources to defend against other infections—infections that otherwise might not be life threatening. In other words, patients do not die of AIDS directly, but from other diseases or infections (for example, cancer or pneumonia) against which the body cannot defend.

AIDS was virtually unknown in the United States before 1981. The U.S. government has estimated that 1.1 million people in the United States are living with HIV—and nearly one in seven are not aware that they are infected. In 2015, there were approximately 38,000 new infections with the HIV virus (HIV.gov, 2018). Among the new infections, the largest number of cases is for gay black men (10,223 cases) (Centers for Disease Control and Prevention, 2018b). The United Nations and its World Health Organization claim that the number of people living with HIV/AIDS world-wide in 2017 was approximately 36.9 million persons, and that AIDS-related deaths totaled approximately 940,000 (World Health Organization, 2018c). The good news is that the number of AIDS deaths is down dramatically from 2008.

HIV almost always enters the body through sexual contact or by the use of contaminated needles in intravenous (IV) drug use. Men who have sex with men contribute most to new HIV infections (63 percent) yearly (Centers for Disease Control and Prevention, 2013). Infections for African Americans are higher than other racial groups, and the Centers for Disease Control and Prevention reports that the infection rate for black women remains 20 times higher than that of white women, and five times that of Hispanic females. About one infant in three born to an HIV-positive mother will also be infected. In infected persons, concentrations of the virus are highest in the blood and in the semen and/or vaginal fluids.

At the moment, there is no cure for AIDS, but symptoms can be controlled with proper medication and medical care. Some drugs, when taken together in a potent mix called "Anti-Retroviral Therapy," (ART), seem able to at least increase the life span and quality of life for many diagnosed patients (Centers for Disease Control and Prevention, 2014). It is important that treatment begins as soon as possible after diagnosis. The longer a patient waits, the more damage is done to the immune system, putting the individual at risk for infection to set in (HIV.gov, 2017). Not surprisingly, given the power of ART drugs, their side effects can be significant, ranging from nausea and diarrhea to inflammation of the pancreas and painful nerve damage. Another potential problem with the use of ART is that although research continues to confirm its effectiveness as a treatment option for those with HIV/AIDS, it does *not* reduce the chances of transmitting the disease through unprotected sexual behaviors. The concern is that those using the anti-retroviral therapy will continue (or even increase) their unsafe sexual practices.

There also has been some encouraging news about the chances of preventing HIV infection. There is a vaginal gel that blocks the transmission of HIV (Cohen, 2010). The evidence comes from a large-scale study of nearly 900 South African women (Abdool Karim, et al., 2010). The gel, called *Tenofovir*, significantly reduced HIV transmission for the women who used it rather than a placebo. Soon after publication of research on *Tenofovir* came word that sexually active gay men who took an anti-AIDS pill—called *Truvada*—were well protected against contracting HIV (Grant et al., 2010). The pill was 90 percent effective for those men who took it faithfully every day. A potential problem at the moment is that *Truvada* is very expensive—costing around $1,600 for 30 pills.

Although interventions are often successful at achieving changes in knowledge and motivation, they tend to be less successful in achieving actual behavioral change. Even early changes in motivation decay with time. The most lasting techniques for behavioral change "engage audiences in particular activities, such as role-playing condom use" and use expert intervention facilitators rather than lay community members (Albarracín, Durantini, & Earl, 2006, p. 73).

AIDS is a physical disease, but it has unprecedented psychological complications. Patients diagnosed with HIV who have not yet developed AIDS tend to be more depressed and disturbed than those who have the full-blown and fatal symptoms of the disease. As you might expect, AIDS patients experience significant stress, depression, anger, anxiety, and denial. Individual and group-based interventions can significantly reduce the distress associated with a diagnosis of HIV infection. Of particular benefit are interventions that increase the patient's social support network. Such interventions improve the quality of life of HIV/AIDS patients and may even extend survival periods.

STUDY CHECK

What are the causes of AIDS, and what roles can health psychologists play in its prevention and treatment?

┌─ **THINKING CRITICALLY** ─────────────────────────────────┐
│   │
│ AIDS can be prevented if people were to abstain from risky behaviors. Are you for │
│ or against programs that promote sexual abstinence?   │
│   │
└──┘

Chapter Summary

What do the terms stress and stressor mean?
Stress is defined as a complex set of reactions made by a person under pressure to adapt. Stress is a response that an individual makes to real or perceived threats to his or her well-being that give rise to physiological reactions and unpleasant feelings like distress and anxiety. Feelings of stress are aroused when an individual is exposed to a stressor. There are three types of stressors: frustration, conflict, and life events. Although in some cases stress is aroused because of some major event (for example, the death of a loved one), it need not be. In some cases consistent but relatively minor events can arouse stress.

What is "frustration," and in what way can it act as a stressor?
Frustration is the reaction to the blocking or thwarting of goal-directed behaviors. If someone or something in one's environment blocks goal-directed behaviors, environmental frustration is the result. If the source of the frustration is a personal characteristic, we have personal frustration.

What are "motivational conflicts," and in what ways can they act as stressors?
Motivational conflicts are stressors. They are situations in which we find ourselves faced with difficult choices to make with regard to our motivated behaviors. In an approach-approach conflict, one is faced with two or more attractive (positive) goals and must choose between or among them. In an avoidance-avoidance conflict, a choice must be made between unpleasant (negative) alternatives. In an approach-avoidance conflict, there is one goal under consideration; in some ways that goal is positive, in others it is negative (it attracts and repels at the same time). In a multiple approach-avoidance conflict, a person faces a number of alternatives, each of which has its strengths and its weaknesses, and a choice must be made between or among them.

In what ways can life events act as stressors?
Many psychologists argue that life events, particularly changes in one's life situation, can act as stressors. The Social Readjustment Rating Scale (SRRS) is one example of an instrument that measures the amount of stress by having a person indicate recent life-change events. High scores on such scales are associated with an above-average incidence of physical illness. Some psychologists claim that the little hassles of life can be more stressful than large-scale life events. Life-change events do not have to be negative or unpleasant events to act as stressors. Socioeconomic status (SES) relates to stress in at least two ways. First, individuals in higher SES brackets are less likely than lower SES individuals to encounter negative life events that can arouse stress. Second, low SES individuals have fewer resources to deal with life events that arouse stress.

How do people differ in their reactions to stress?
People may respond differently to the same stressor. What some find merely challenging, others may find overwhelmingly stressful. Reaction to stressors varies over time: Events that do not seem stressful today may be very stressful tomorrow. Some people are particularly resistant to stressors and have been called "hardy personalities." Such people tend to see difficulties as opportunities, have a sense of being in control of their lives, and are fully engaged in and committed to life.

What are problem-focused and emotion-focused strategies for effective coping with stress?
In general, the most effective means of dealing with stress is to deal with the stressors that caused it by learning new behaviors that help cope with those stressors. There are two approaches to dealing with stress. One is problem-focused and includes such things as identifying the specific stressor causing stress, removing or minimizing the stressor, reappraising the situation, inoculating against future stressors, and taking one's time in making difficult decisions. Battling the feelings associated with stress—with what are called emotion-focused approaches—includes learning relaxation techniques, engaging in physical exercise, and seeking social support.

What are the three inappropriate, ineffective reactions to stress?
Maladaptive reactions to stressors are those that interfere with attempts to change behaviors as a result of experiencing stress. Fixation describes a pattern of behaviors in which a person tries repeatedly to deal with stressors, is unsuccessful, but does not try anything new or different. Aggression often results from stress, particularly frustration. Although aggression may yield a momentary release of tension, it usually does not remove the original stressor. Anxiety is yet another maladaptive response to stress. This general feeling of apprehension and dread is often the aspect of experienced stress that motivates us to do something about it.

What is the relationship, if any, between the Type A behavior pattern and physical health?

There appears to be a relationship between some personality variables and physical health; that is, some psychological traits put a person at risk for disease. Beginning in the 1950s, evidence accumulated showing a strong positive relationship between a Type A behavior pattern, or TABP (a person who is competitive, achievement-oriented, impatient, easily aroused, often angry or hostile, and who tends to have many projects going at once) and coronary heart disease. The picture, it now seems, is a little less clear, as psychologists seek to identify the "active ingredients" of the TABP. The main personality variables associated with heart disease seem to be anger, hostility, and time-urgency (impatience). These three risk factors are surely also risk factors for the development of hypertension.

What are some of the components of an unhealthy lifestyle?

People die for many reasons. Heart disease and cancer account for more than half the deaths in the United States in any given year. Some causes of death are unavoidable; however, many result from risky behaviors. Psychosocial contributors to premature death include behaviors that are simply unhealthy. These unhealthy behaviors include such lifestyle issues as eating too much, exercising too little, smoking, and experiencing stress. Many health psychologists dedicate themselves to helping their clients reduce unhealthy behaviors and live longer, better lives.

Why are health psychologists so concerned about smoking, and how are they attempting to reduce the number of smokers?

Of the leading causes of death in this country, most could be reduced by behavioral change. Smoking accounts for nearly 480,000 deaths each year in the United States, nearly five million deaths worldwide. Smoking is a major risk factor for cardiovascular disease, cancers, and multiple sclerosis. Smoke-free environments, and designing programs to get people not to smoke in the first place are a focus of attention.

What are the causes of AIDS, and what roles can health psychologists play in its prevention and treatment?

AIDS is caused by the human immunodeficiency virus (HIV), which enters the body through sexual contact or through the use of contaminated needles. About one in three infants born to an HIV-positive mother will contract the disease. Eventually, HIV attacks the body's immune system, making the body susceptible to a wide range of diseases. Ordinary diseases become life-threatening. There are drugs and potent mixtures of drugs (like those available in (Anti-Retroviral Therapy) that can control the symptoms of AIDS and prolong life, although the side effects of such treatments are often unpleasant at best. There also are encouraging signs that HIV infection can be controlled in women with a drug called *Tenofovir*, and in men with an anti-AIDS drug called *Truvada*.

Health psychologists are involved in helping people change their risky sexual behaviors or their IV drug use. Awareness and understanding of the disease have increased markedly, but many at-risk people have made few changes in their sexual practices. More successful programs are those that are multifaceted, doing more than just presenting facts and figures about the prevalence of HIV/AIDS. These programs motivate participants to practice safe sex. Psychologists also help AIDS sufferers (and their friends and families) deal with the emotional aspects of the disease. Psychological interventions—particularly those that provide social support—can improve the quality of life, and even the length of life, of HIV-infected patients.

Key Terms

Stress (p. 233)
Stressor (p. 233)
Frustration (p. 233)
Approach-approach conflict (p. 234)
Avoidance-avoidance conflict (p. 235)
Approach-avoidance conflict (p. 236)
Multiple approach-avoidance conflict (p. 236)
Socioeconomic status (SES) (p. 237)

Emotion-focused strategy (p. 240)
Problem-focused strategy (p. 240)
Biofeedback (p. 242)
Frustration-aggression hypothesis (p. 245)
Anxiety (p. 245)
Type A behavior pattern (TABP) (p. 246)
Sexually transmitted disease (STD) (p. 252)

Psychological Disorders

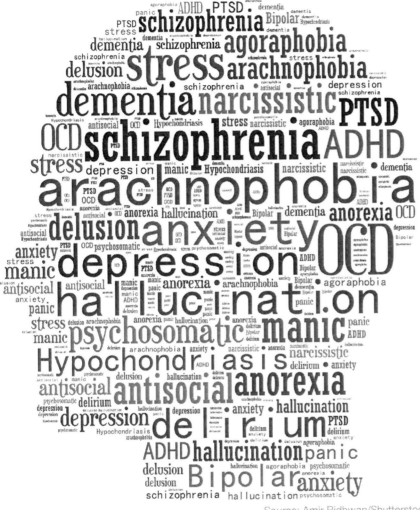

Source: Amir Ridhwan/Shutterstock.

Chapter Outline

Questions You Will Be Able to Answer

After reading Chapter 12, you should be able to answer the following questions:

- How do psychologists define the concept of "abnormality"?
- How are psychological disorders classified?
- How do "psychological disorders" and "insanity" differ?
- What are generalized anxiety disorder, panic disorder, and specific phobia?

- What is obsessive-compulsive disorder?
- What is posttraumatic stress disorder?
- What are the defining characteristics of autism spectrum disorder?
- What are the major characteristics of the dissociative disorders?
- What characterizes personality disorders?
- What is depressive disorder?
- What is the essence of the "diathesis-stress model"?
- What is bipolar disorder?
- What is schizophrenia, and what are the differences between positive and negative symptoms of the disorder?

Preview

Mental illness is something that most folks simply do not want to talk about. Many would rather not even think about the commonality of psychological disorders. Few of us like hearing that in a given year about 30 percent of the adult population will experience a diagnosable mental illness. Indeed, about half of all Americans will have a psychological disorder "sometime in their life, with the first onset usually in childhood or adolescence" (Kessler et al., 2005, p. 593). People who will share the gory details of their abdominal surgery at the dinner table may hesitate to mention that stress in their lives is growing to unbearable levels.

Psychological disorders *are* common. Some are very dramatic; a few may be devastating. But most can be treated successfully, even cured, if we talk openly about our psychological problems and seek help for them. This chapter provides an overview, a sketch of the psychological disorders.

Let us begin, as we have in previous chapters, with the definitions of a few basic terms. Then we will review some of the anxiety disorders. These all-too-common disorders share one characteristic: anxiety. They include such disorders as generalized anxiety disorder, panic disorder, specific phobia, obsessive-compulsive disorder, and posttraumatic stress disorder.

We will take a brief look at one of the more devastating of the neurodevelopmental disorders, autism spectrum disorder. Once rare, this disorder has become more common in recent times.

Dissociative disorders and personality disorders will also be discussed. Other disorders primarily involve disturbances of mood, such as depressive disorders and bipolar disorder.

We will end our introduction to psychological disorders with a discussion of schizophrenia, arguably the most devastating disorder of all. Schizophrenia is an attack on all that makes us human; it has an impact on affect, cognition, and behavior. It is a disorder that involves a gross impairment of functioning (difficulty dealing with the demands of everyday life), and a gross impairment in reality testing (a loss of contact with the real world as the rest of us know it).

What *Is* Abnormal?

Abnormal—maladaptive cognitions, affects, and/or behaviors that are at odds with social expectations and result in distress or discomfort.

We all have a basic idea of what is meant by such terms as abnormal, mental illness, or psychological disorder. The more we think about psychological abnormality, however, the more difficult it becomes to define. The concept of abnormal as it is used in psychology is not a simple one. We will use this definition: **Abnormal** refers to maladaptive cognitions, affects, and/or behaviors that are at odds with social expectations and result in distress or discomfort. That is lengthy, but to be complete, our definition should include all of these aspects. Let's consider each in turn.

The reactions of people with psychological disorders are maladaptive. This is a critical part of our definition. Thoughts, feelings, and behaviors are such that the person does not function as well as he or she could without the disorder. To be "different" or "strange" does not mean that someone has a psychological disorder. There must be some impairment, breakdown, or self-defeating interference with one's growth and functioning (Barlow & Durand, 2009).

Another observation reflected in our definition is that abnormality can show itself in a number of ways. A person with a disorder may experience abnormal affect, engage in abnormal behaviors, have abnormal cognitions, or any combination of these. Here again is our ABCs mnemonic.

Any definition of psychological abnormality should acknowledge social and/or cultural expectations. What may be abnormal and disordered in one culture may be viewed as quite normal or commonplace in another. In some cultures, loud crying and wailing at the funeral of a total stranger is considered strange or deviant; in others, it is common and expected. In some cultures, to claim you have been communicating with dead ancestors would be taken as a sign of mental disturbance; in others, it would be treated as a great gift. Even within any one culture, behaviors that are appropriate, or at least tolerated in one situation, say a party, may be judged as inappropriate in another context, say, a religious service.

A final point: Psychological disorders involve distress or discomfort. People we consider abnormal are suffering or are the source of suffering in others. Psychological disorders cause emotional distress, and individuals with such disorders are often the source of distress and discomfort to others—friends and family who care and worry about them. The behaviors, thoughts, or feelings associated with a psychological disorder are not what the individual wants to experience. They are beyond the individual's control, and that in itself is distressing (Widiger & Sankis, 2000).

Complex as it is, there is a reason for each point in our definition of abnormal: maladaptive behaviors or mental processes, at odds with social expectations, and that result in distress or discomfort.

Classifying Psychological Disorders

One way of dealing with the broad concept of psychological abnormality is to consider each psychological disorder separately in terms of how that disorder is diagnosed, where **diagnosis** is the act of recognizing a disorder on the basis of specified symptoms. Once individual disorders are identified, it is helpful to organize them in a systematic way.

In 1952, the American Psychiatric Association published a system for classifying psychological disorders, the *Diagnostic and Statistical Manual of Mental Disorders*, which became known as the *DSM*. Reflecting significant changes with each edition, the fourth edition, the *DSM-IV*, was published in 1994 and revised once again in the summer of 2000 as the *DSM-IV-TR* (or Text Revision). The most recent edition of the *DSM*, and the one currently in use, is the *DSM-5* (American Psychiatric Association, 2013).

The *DSM-5* is the system of classification most widely used in all mental health fields today. Indeed, the *DSM-5* is the major source of information for this chapter. The *DSM-5*

What is considered to be abnormal or deviant behavior has to be considered in terms of social context. Behaviors that are "normal" or "appropriate" at an off-campus party may be judged to be "abnormal" or at least "inappropriate" at a church service.

Diagnosis—the act of recognizing a disorder on the basis of specified symptoms.

Sources: Kzenon/Shutterstock; Zabotnova Inna/Shutterstock.com

classifies psychological disorders into 22 diagnostic categories. For each disorder, a set of *diagnostic criteria* defines what symptoms are necessary for a given diagnosis. In the following discussion, we cover a small sample of the disorders and a general description of symptoms contained in the *DSM-5*. The *DSM-5* avoids providing information on the causes (etiology) for psychological disorders.

It makes good sense to have a classification system for psychological disorders. The major advantage, of course, is communication. People cannot hold a reasonable conversation about a patient's problem if they disagree on the definition of the diagnosis appropriate for that patient. If everyone agrees on the *DSM-5*'s definition, then at least they're using the same terms in the same way. Still, classification schemes can cause difficulties. Assigning labels to people may be useful, but it can be dehumanizing. It may be difficult to remember that Sally is a complex, complicated human being with a range of feelings, thoughts, and behaviors, not just a "schizophrenic." Indeed, the *DSM-5* refers only to disordered behaviors, not to disordered people. That is, it refers to schizophrenic reactions, not individuals who are schizophrenic—to persons with anxiety, not anxious persons.

In this chapter, we will consider a variety of psychological disorders. As we do so, there are a few important points for you to keep in mind.

1. *"Abnormal" and "normal" are not two distinct categories.* They may be thought of as end points on some dimension we can use to describe people, but there is a large gray area between the two in which distinctions get fuzzy.

2. *Abnormal does not mean dangerous.* True, some people with mental disorders may cause harm to themselves or to others, but most people with psychological disorders are not dangerous at all. Even among persons who have been in jail for violent crimes, those with disorders have no more subsequent arrests than do persons without disorders. As David Holmes (2001, p. 546) puts it, ". . . we do not see headlines such as 'person with no history of mental illness commits murder,' although, in fact, that situation is more prevalent."

3. *Abnormal does not mean bad.* People with psychological disorders are not bad or weak people, in any evaluative sense. They may have done bad things, and bad things may have happened to them, but it is certainly not in the tradition of psychology to make moral judgments about good and bad.

4. *Most depictions of psychological disorders are made in terms of extreme and obvious cases.* Psychological disorders, like physical disorders, may occur in mild or moderate forms. No two people are exactly alike. Similarly, no two people, with the same diagnosis of a psychological disorder, will be alike in all regards.

A Note on "Insanity"

In common practice, the terms psychological disorder, mental disorder, and behavior disorder are used interchangeably. There is one term, however, with which we need to exercise particular care, and that is *insanity*. Insanity is not a psychological term. It is a legal term. It relates to problems with psychological functioning but in a restricted sense. Definitions of insanity vary from state to state, but a judgment of insanity usually requires evidence that a person did not know or fully understand the consequences of his or her actions at a given time, could not discern the difference between right and wrong, and was unable to exercise control over his or her actions at the time a crime was committed. The American public has long overestimated the use of an insanity defense in courts of law. The public's perception is that an "insanity plea" is "used too much"—in about 37 percent of all felony cases. In fact, it is used in less than 1 percent of all felony cases and is successful less than 20 percent of the time (Melton et al., 2007). And when the insanity defense *is* used successfully, defendants usually spend more time confined to a hospital than they would have been confined to jail (Gracheck, 2006).

Insanity—the legal concept that a person did not know or fully understand the consequences of his or her actions at a given time, could not discern the difference between right and wrong, and was unable to exercise control over his or her actions at the time a crime was committed.

Source: wavebreakmedia/Shutterstock.

Insanity is a legal term, not a psychological one.

A related issue, known as *competence*, has to do with a person's mental state at the time of trial. The central issues are whether a person is in enough control of his or her mental and intellectual functions to understand courtroom procedures and aid in his or her own defense. If not, a person may be ruled "not competent" to stand trial for his or her actions, whatever those actions may have been. Most likely, a person who is judged incompetent will be placed into a mental institution until he or she becomes competent to stand trial.

STUDY CHECK

How do psychologists define the concept of "abnormality"?
How are psychological disorders classified?
How do "psychological disorders" and "insanity" differ?

THINKING CRITICALLY

How might viewing psychologically disordered persons as weak or without the willpower to change influence how such persons would be treated or helped?

PSYCHOLOGY IN ACTION

How Do We Perceive People with Mental Illness?

The issue of mental illness becomes a major topic of debate especially after a mass murder such as a mass public shooting. News coverage can leave the public with negative perceptions of people with serious mental illness and lead them to assume that there is a strong relationship between mental illness and violence. Generally, however, the public's attitudes toward people with mental illness are positive and sympathetic (Borinstein, 1992). In a survey of attitudes about mental illness, Borinstein found that most respondents believed that anyone can become mentally ill (74 percent) and that most mentally ill people can get better with treatment (54 percent). However, they also believed that there was still a great deal of stigma attached to mental illness (65 percent). In another survey (TNS BMRB, 2015) respondents believed that having a mental illness is no different from having any other disease (78 percent), that mentally ill persons have the same rights to a job as anyone else (80 percent), and that mentally ill persons should not be excluded from their neighborhoods (83 percent). On the negative side, 24 percent of respondents in the Borinstein survey believed that mentally ill individuals are far more dangerous than others in the general population. Twenty-two percent believed that mental health facilities should be kept out of residential neighborhoods, and 21 percent believed that mentally ill people have the potential to commit violent acts even if they seem okay (Borinstein, 1992). These beliefs about the relationship between mental illness and violence are inconsistent with actual statistics about this relationship. Although mentally ill people can commit violent acts (as can people with no mental illness), the actual rate of violence among the mentally ill is only around 3 percent. Most of the violent acts committed by mentally ill people are not directed at strangers. Rather, they are directed at family members or friends with whom there had been prior conflict (Beeber, 2018).

Where does the perception come from that mentally ill people are violent? Like any attitude, it can come from personal experience, one's socialization experiences, or the media. Whenever there is a high-profile act of violence such as a school or other mass shooting, the issue of mental illness and violence comes to the forefront. Media coverage of these events usually gets around to the issue of the role of mental illness in such events. In fact, between 1997 and 2012, references to dangerous people with serious mental illness were more likely to be mentioned than the presence of a dangerous weapon as a cause for a mass shooting (McGinty, Webster, Jarlenski, & Barry, 2014). McGinty et al. also found that fewer than 10 percent of news stories about mass shootings presented any *facts* about mental illness. If specifics about mental illness were mentioned, schizophrenia (26 percent) and psychosis (29 percent) were most often mentioned. In another study, McGinty and her colleagues found an increasing trend from 1995 to 2014 of mentioning mental illness as a cause for mass shootings (McGinty, Kennedy-Hendricks, Choksy, & Barry, 2016).

Negative media coverage of mental illness can influence the public's perception of mental illness (Chan & Yanos, 2018). For example, Chan and Yanos had participants read a description of a violent event. For half of the participants, the description mentioned mental illness (perpetrator had a history of schizophrenia), and for the other half, it did not. Chan and Yanos then measured participants' memory for the description and attitudes toward mental illness. Chan and Yanos found that 43 percent of the participants in the mental illness condition attributed the violent event to mental illness, whereas only 2 percent in the control condition did so. For those in the mental illness condition, the mere mention of mental illness was enough to make mental illness a highly salient (important) piece of information. Interestingly, merely reading an article about a mass shooting, even if it makes no mention of mental illness, can increase negative attitudes toward the mentally ill (Wilson, Ballman, & Buczek, 2016). Wilson et al. had participants read a description of a mass shooting that contained no information about the perpetrator's mental status (factual article) or one that did mention that the perpetrator had a history of mental illness. Some participants read a description that contained a statement that even though the perpetrator had a history of mental illness, most individuals with mental illness are not violent (educational article). They found that participants were more likely to see a mentally ill person as dangerous in all of the conditions where mental illness was mentioned in the description of the event. The good news is that adding a statement educating people about the fact that most mentally ill people are nonviolent reduced this trend.

Other studies find that mental illness is weakly related to mass murder. In fact, mental illness is involved in only a small fraction of mass murders (Beeber, 2018). Beeber points out that recent data show that a majority of perpetrators of mass murders (70 percent) had no history of mental illness that could account for the murders. However, most news coverage still tends to portray the perpetrators as mentally ill (Taylor, 2018). If mental illness is not a strong predictor of mass murder,

just what is? How, for example, can we account for mass public shootings (a specific example of mass murder), which have been on the rise in the United States and worldwide?

Before we look at the characteristics of mass murderers, it is important to note that we are not saying that mental illness is *never* involved. As we shall see, mental illness does factor into some mass murders and school shootings. However, it is fair to say that most school shooters have multiple motivations (Taylor, 2018). Taylor analyzed news reports of mass murders that took place between 2007 and 2011 and developed a profile of the most dangerous mass murderers (defined in terms of the number of victims). She found that the following characteristics best describe these dangerous individuals: young, white, male, and those with a mental illness. Taylor also found that in most mass murders (51 percent), there was a triggering event such as the break-up of a relationship (22 percent) or loss of a job (5 percent). Among adolescent mass murderers, there are rarely any indications of heightened emotionality or other warning signs before a mass murder (Meloy, Hempel, Mohandie, Shiva, & Gray, 2001).

Although Taylor (2018) found that a majority (70 percent) of mass murderers were white, an analysis of the characteristics of mass public shootings between 1984 and 2015 shows a trend toward greater variability in the race of the shooter (Capellan & Gomez, 2017). From 1985 to 1999, 73.8 percent of shooters were white, 12.5 percent were black, and 4.5 percent were Latino. However, from 2000 to 2015, 55.7 percent of shooters were white, 25.6 percent were black, and 10 percent were Latino. Finally, Leary, Kowalski, Smith, and Phillips (2003) report that perpetrators of mass school shootings have a fascination with death/Satanism, have a fascination with guns and explosives, have a history of psychological issues (e.g., depression), and have been ostracized or rejected by their peers. Ostracism generates anger, which is related to antisocial behavior. Unfair ostracism leads to most anger and most antisocial behavior (Chow, Tiedens, & Govan, 2008).

Anxiety Disorders

Anxiety is a feeling of general apprehension or dread accompanied by predictable physiological changes: increased muscle tension; shallow, rapid breathing; cessation of digestion; increased perspiration; and drying of the mouth. Thus, anxiety involves two levels of reaction: subjective feelings (e.g., fear or dread) and physiological responses (e.g., rapid breathing). The major symptom of anxiety disorders is felt anxiety, often coupled with "avoidance behavior" or attempts to resist or avoid any situation that seems to produce anxiety.

Anxiety has been described as the most common human emotion (Barlow, 2002; Carter, 2002). Anxiety disorders are the most common of all the psychological disorders, affecting 19.1 million (13.3 percent) of the adult U. S. population, with nearly 30 percent of Americans likely to be diagnosed with an anxiety disorder in their lifetime (Kessler et al., 2005). A more recent survey of American adolescents (ages 13–18) found anxiety disorders to be the most commonly diagnosed (31.9 percent) (Merikangas et al., 2010). Anxiety disorders are two to three times more likely to be diagnosed in women than in men. Percentages of this sort do not convey the enormity of the problem. We are talking about millions of real people here. In this section, we consider five anxiety disorders: generalized anxiety disorder, panic disorder, specific phobia, obsessive-compulsive disorder, and posttraumatic stress disorder.

The major symptom of generalized anxiety disorder (GAD) is distressing, felt anxiety. This disorder is characterized by unrealistic, excessive, persistent worry. The *DSM-5* adds the criterion that people with this disorder find that the anxiety they experience causes substantial interference with their lives and that they need a significant dosage of medications to control their symptoms.

Generalized anxiety disorder (GAD)—a disorder involving distressing, felt anxiety. This disorder is characterized by unrealistic, excessive, persistent worry.

The experienced anxiety of this disorder may be very intense, but it is not brought on by anything specific; it just seems to come and go (or come and stay) without reason or warning. People with GAD are usually in a state of uneasiness and seldom have any clear insight or ideas about what is causing their anxiety. Those of us without any sort of anxiety disorder can be anxious from time to time, but when we are, we know why. The self-reports of persons with GAD show that their major concerns are an inability to relax, tension, difficulty concentrating, feeling frightened, and being afraid of losing control. More than half of those suffering from this disorder actively seek treatment for the discomfort it brings (Ruscio et al., 2008).

In the generalized anxiety disorder, the experience of anxiety may be characterized as chronic, implying that the anxiety is nearly always present, albeit sometimes more so than at other times. For a person suffering from panic disorder, the major symptom is more acute—an unpredictable, unprovoked onset of sudden, intense anxiety, or a "panic attack." These attacks may last for a few seconds or for hours. Attacks are associated with many physical symptoms—a pounding heart, labored breathing, sweating, trembling, chest pains, nausea, dizziness, and/or numbness and trembling in the hands and feet. There is no one particular stimulus to bring it on. The panic attack is unexpected. It just happens. Early in the disorder, nearly 85 percent of patients with panic attacks make visits to hospital emergency rooms, convinced that they are suffering some life-threatening emergency (Katerndahl & Realini, 1995). With panic disorder, there is a recurrent pattern of attacks and a building worry about future attacks.

Panic disorder—a disorder with the major symptoms of an unpredictable, unprovoked onset of sudden, intense anxiety, or a "panic attack."

Initial panic attacks are often associated with stress, particularly from the loss of an important relationship. The age of onset for panic disorder is usually between adolescence and the middle 20s (Craske & Barlow, 2001). A complication of panic disorder is that it can be accompanied by feelings of depression (Kessler et al., 1998). This may be why the rate of suicide and suicide attempts is so high for persons with a diagnosis of panic disorder (20 percent), which is higher than that for persons diagnosed with depression alone (15 percent).

The essential feature of a specific phobia is a persistent and excessive fear of some object, activity, or situation that leads a person to avoid that object, activity, or situation. Implied in this definition is the notion that the fear is intense enough to be disruptive. Also implied is the fact that there is no real or significant threat involved in the stimulus that gives rise to a phobia; that is, the fear is unreasonable, exaggerated, or inappropriate. Did you notice that the definition of this disorder uses the term fear, not anxiety? What is the difference? In nearly every regard, the two are exactly alike. The difference is that fear requires an object. One is not just "afraid." One is afraid *of* something. We may say that you are afraid of the dark, but we probably would not say that you are anxious of the dark.

Specific phobia—a disorder involving a persistent and excessive fear of some object, activity, or situation that leads a person to avoid that object, activity, or situation.

Many things in this world are life threatening or frightening. For example, if you drive your car down a steep hill and suddenly realize the brakes are not working, you will probably feel an intense reaction of fear. Such a reaction is not phobic because it is not irrational. Similarly, few of us enjoy the company of bees. That we don't like bees and would prefer they not be around us does not mean we have a phobic disorder. Key to a diagnosis is the intensity of response. People who have a phobic reaction to bees (called *mellissaphobia*) may refuse to leave the house in the summer for fear of encountering a bee and may become genuinely anxious at the buzzing sound of any insect, fearing it to be a bee. They may become uncomfortable reading a paragraph, such as this one, about bees.

Obsessive-Compulsive Disorder

Obsessive-compulsive disorder (OCD)—a disorder characterized by a pattern of recurrent obsessions and compulsions.

Obsessions—ideas or thoughts that involuntarily and constantly intrude into awareness.

Compulsions—constantly intruding, repetitive behaviors.

A major change from the *DSM-IV* to the *DSM-5* is the separation of obsessive-compulsive disorder (OCD) and related disorders from anxiety disorders and reclassification in its own category. **Obsessive-compulsive disorder (OCD)** is characterized by a pattern of recurrent obsessions and compulsions. **Obsessions** involve ideas or thoughts that involuntarily and constantly intrude into awareness. Generally speaking, obsessions are pointless or groundless thoughts, most commonly about cleanliness, violence, disease, danger, or doubt. Many of us have experienced mild, obsessive-like thoughts—for example, worrying during the first few days of a vacation if you really did turn off the stove back at home. To qualify as part of OCD, obsessions must be disruptive; they must interfere with normal functioning. They are also time-consuming and are the source of anxiety and distress.

Compulsions involve constantly intruding, repetitive behaviors. The most commonly reported compulsions are hand-washing, grooming, and counting or checking behaviors, such as checking repeatedly that the door is really locked. Have you ever checked an answer sheet to see that you've really answered all the questions on a test and then checked it again, and again, and again? To do so is compulsive. It serves no real purpose, and it provides no real sense of satisfaction, although it is done very conscientiously in an attempt to reduce anxiety or stress. People with OCD recognize that their behaviors serve no useful purpose; they know that they are unreasonable but cannot stop them.

A common symptom of obsessive-compulsive disorder (OCD) is "checking behavior." An example would be ritualistically locking a door not once or twice, but exactly 14 times before leaving.

An obsession or compulsion can exert an enormous influence on a person's life. Consider the case of a happily married accountant, the father of three. For reasons he cannot explain, he becomes obsessed with the fear of contracting AIDS. There is no reason for him to be concerned; his sexual activities are entirely monogamous; he has never used drugs; he has never had a blood transfusion. Still, he is overwhelmed with the idea that he will contract this deadly disease. Ritualized, compulsive behaviors are associated with his obsessive thoughts: He washes his hands vigorously at every opportunity and becomes anxious if he cannot change his clothes at least three times a day (all in an effort to avoid the dreaded AIDS virus).

Notice that we are using "compulsive" in an altogether different way when we refer to someone being a compulsive gambler, a compulsive eater, or a compulsive practical joker. What is different about the use of the term in such cases is that although the person engages in habitual patterns of behavior, he or she gains pleasure from doing so. The compulsive gambler enjoys gambling; the compulsive eater loves to eat. Such people may not enjoy the consequences of their actions in the long term, but they feel little discomfort about the behaviors themselves.

Posttraumatic Stress Disorder

Posttraumatic stress disorder (PTSD)—a disorder that involves distressing symptoms that arise sometime after the experience of a highly traumatic event.

Posttraumatic stress disorder is classified as a trauma-related and stressor-related disorder in the *DSM-5*. **Posttraumatic stress disorder (PTSD)** involves distressing symptoms that arise sometime after the experience of a highly traumatic event, where trauma is defined by the *DSM-5* as an event that meets two criteria: (a) the person has experienced, witnessed, or been confronted with an event that involves actual or threatened death or serious injury, and (b) the person's response involves intense fear, helplessness, or horror. The disorder was first recognized with the publication of the *DSM-III* in 1980 and was seen as a reasonable diagnosis for many mental health problems of veterans returning from the war in Vietnam. Ironically, the disorder affected only 1.2 percent of Vietnam veterans (compared to 3.7 percent of Korean War veterans and up to 10 percent of World War II veterans (McNally, 2003b)).

There are three clusters of symptoms that further define PTSD:

1. A re-experiencing of the traumatic event (e.g., flashbacks or nightmares),
2. An avoidance of any possible reminders of the event (including people who were there), and
3. An increased arousal or "hyper-alertness" (e.g., irritability, insomnia, difficulty concentrating).

The traumatic events that trigger this disorder are many, ranging from natural disasters (e.g., floods or hurricanes), to life-threatening situations (e.g., kidnapping, rape, assault, or combat), to the loss of property (e.g., the house burns down; the car is stolen).

It is important to keep in mind that, in response to traumatic stressors, only a minority of people develop PTSD symptoms (McNally, 2001). "Nearly half of U.S. adults experience at least one traumatic event in their lifetimes, yet only 10 percent of women and 5 percent of men develop posttraumatic stress disorder" (Ozer & Weiss, 2004, p. 169). Curiously, the course of PTSD does not show a predictable pattern of lessening symptoms. Indeed, over a four-year period following diagnosis, symptoms actually increase in number and severity (Port, Engdahl, & Frazier, 2001).

STUDY CHECK

What are generalized anxiety disorder, panic disorder, and specific phobia?
What is obsessive-compulsive disorder?
What is posttraumatic stress disorder?

THINKING CRITICALLY

When medical students study diseases, sometimes they develop the symptoms of the diseases they are studying. Do any of the disorders in this section sound like a problem you have had or are having?

A Neurodevelopmental Disorder: Autism Spectrum Disorder

There are several psychological disorders classified in the *DSM-5* as neurodevelopmental disorders (e.g., autism spectrum disorder and attention-deficit hyperactivity disorder). None, however, is quite as remarkable or as devastating as autism spectrum disorder (ASD), which is characterized by impaired social interaction, problems with communication, and unusual or severely limited activities and interests (American Psychiatric Association, 2013; Durand, 2004). In the *DSM-5*, autism is characterized by (1) deficits in social communication and social interaction and (2) restricted repetitive behaviors, interests, and activities (American Psychiatric Association, 2013). Formerly, Asperger's syndrome was a separate diagnostic category involving "milder" forms of autism. In the *DSM-5*, Asperger's syndrome is no longer a separate diagnostic category. Rather, it is included under autism spectrum disorders.

Autism spectrum disorder—a disorder characterized by impaired social interaction, problems with communication, and unusual or severely limited activities and interests.

Once thought to be a rare disorder, occurring in only 10 to 15 children of every 10,000, more recent data suggest the disorder occurs in 1 in every 500 births (with the disorder four times more common among boys than girls) (Shattuck, 2006). In 2018, the Centers for Disease Control and Prevention (2018c) reported that autism was diagnosed in one of every 59 children 8 years of age and older. They also reported that autism was more prevalent among whites than blacks. The diagnosis of autism is usually made within the first two-and-a-half years of life.

The lack of social interaction by autistic children is striking. Autistic children can seem oblivious to those around them (MacDonald et al., 2006). There are no apparent signs of attachment, even with primary caregivers, and little indication that they have any notion of what others may be thinking or feeling. They just do not seem to understand social cues, such as facial expressions and tone of voice. They often avoid eye contact. Children with autism have great difficulty communicating with others—about one-third never develop language skills (Chan et al., 2005).

Children with autism have a wide-range of challenges, including difficulties with communication and social interactions.

The behavioral differences in children with autism are easily recognized. Inattention, hyperactivity, and aggression are common in autistic children, and frequently cause significant impairment (Erickson et al., 2007). Behaviors are often repetitive and stereotyped, often just simple rocking and/or twisting about. They show an aversion to being hugged or held. Although they seldom attend to other people, they can become preoccupied with inanimate objects, and clearly prefer that their physical environment remain unchanged in every way—a phenomenon referred to as "insistence on sameness."

You will not be surprised to learn that there is as yet no known cause of autism, although there are some intriguing leads. To be sure, there is a genetic underpinning to the disorder, with probably several specific genes involved (Abrahams & Geschwind, 2008; Freitag, 2007; Wickelgren, 2005). Researchers are also focusing their attention on the causative influence of environmental toxins and pollutants (Edelson, 2007). Of particular interest—and controversy—is the possibility of mercury poisoning resulting from vaccinations and inoculations that virtually all children receive at the age of about 18 months. You can imagine the near panic that arose at the thought that simple immunizations could produce such a dramatic psychological disorder. Some parents refused to have their children vaccinated for fear that it would increase the chances of autism. Although the logic of the hypothesis may be reasonable, **no** research data have confirmed the hypothesis. In fact, recent studies (Price et al., 2010; Schedcter & Grether, 2008) have made it very clear that there is no evidence linking childhood vaccinations and autism. Finally, one study did find a relationship between the spacing of pregnancies and the odds of developing autism (Cheslack-Postava, DPhil, & Bearman, 2011). Simply put, the shorter the interval between pregnancies, the greater the risk of the second-born child developing autism, with the highest risk associated with pregnancies spaced less than one year apart.

There is no known cure for autism, although there are interventions that can bring about improvement in some symptoms. Highly structured and specifically focused therapy sessions can improve social and language skills in many autistic children. The focused use of *positive behavior support* (immediately and significantly rewarding appropriate behaviors) can bring about meaningful and lasting reductions of inappropriate behaviors. Therapy or counseling for the parents and siblings of a child with autism is useful in helping families cope (Lucyshyn et al., 2007; Myles, 2007).

What about adults with ASD? A psychologist who has been conducting research in this area writes, "This [ASD] spectrum includes affected individuals ranging from those with a severe learning disability and/or little to no language ability to intellectually highly able and linguistically competent individuals, who, nonetheless, struggle to function in their daily lives at a level commensurate with their intellectual ability and other competencies"

(Hill, 2014, p. 152). She and other psychologists suggest that "atypical" may be a more appropriate term than "maladaptive" for some of the behaviors that ASD individuals present and that comprehending the strengths and challenges of ASD workers can benefit the worker, the company, and society. Indeed, many large companies currently are recruiting individuals with ASD for the special skills that they may be able to offer.

STUDY CHECK

What are the defining characteristics of autism spectrum disorder?

THINKING CRITICALLY

What hypotheses can you think of for why the prevalence rates for childhood autism are so steadily on the increase?

Dissociative Disorders

To *dissociate* means to become separate from or to escape. The underlying theme of a dissociative disorder is that a person seeks to escape from some aspect of life or personality seen as the source of stress, discomfort, or anxiety. These disorders can be dramatic, and they have been the subject of novels, movies, and television shows. On the other hand, the symptoms of dissociative disorders can be so subtle that they are often overlooked. One research study was designed to find cases of dissociative disorder in a large sample of outpatients at an inner-city psychiatric institution. In addition to whatever disorder was responsible for their treatment at the facility, 29 percent were diagnosed to also have a dissociative disorder (Foote et al., 2006).

Dissociative amnesia is the inability to recall important personal information—an inability too extensive to be explained by ordinary forgetfulness. It is important to note that the amnesia (loss of memory) has a psychological rather than a physical origin. That is, no medical cause can be found for the memory loss in dissociative amnesia. What is forgotten is usually a traumatic incident and some or all of the experiences that led up to or followed the incident. The extent of forgetting associated with dissociative amnesia varies greatly. In some cases of *generalized amnesia*, a person may forget everything; in some cases of *selective amnesia*, a person may "lose" entire days and weeks at a time; in other cases, only specific details of a single incident resist being recalled. Dissociative amnesia is more common in wartime, when traumatic experiences occur more often.

The major symptom of dissociative identity disorder (DID) is the existence within the same person of two or more distinct personalities or personality traits. (Many psychologists still refer to dissociative identity disorder as "multiple personality disorder," as it was called before in the *DSM-IV*.) Up to 100 distinct personalities within the same person have been reported, but the average is about 15 (Ross, 1997). The disorder was once rare, but it has become more common for unknown reasons. From the 1920s to 1970, only a handful of cases were reported worldwide; since the 1970s, reported cases have increased astronomically, with thousands reported each year (Ross, 1997). An intriguing finding: the increase in the prevalence of DID has occurred only in North America. Dissociative identity disorder is seldom diagnosed in France, and it is very rare in Great Britain, Russia, and India. One study in 1990 failed to find even a single case of the disorder in Japan (Takahashi, 1990).

Two or more personalities in the same person are difficult to imagine. Perhaps a contrast would help. We all change our behaviors, and (in a way) our personalities, depending

Dissociative disorder—disorder in which a person seeks to escape from some aspect of life or personality seen as the source of stress, discomfort, or anxiety.

Dissociative amnesia—the inability to recall important personal information that is too extensive to be explained by ordinary forgetfulness.

Dissociative identity disorder (DID)—the existence within the same person of two or more distinct personalities or personality traits.

on the situation in which we find ourselves. We do not act, think, or feel exactly the same way at school as we do at work, at a party, or at a house of worship. We modify our affects, behaviors, and cognitions to fit the situation. But these changes do not qualify as an identity disorder. What are the differences?

The differences are significant. Someone with a dissociative identity disorder has changes in personality that are dramatic and extreme. They do not slightly alter their behavior; they have two or more distinct personalities, implying a change in underlying consciousness, not just in overt behaviors. Another difference is we change our behaviors in response to situational cues. Someone with DID can change in personalities without warning or provocation. The third major difference involves control. When we change our behaviors, we do so intentionally. Persons with a multiple personality disorder can seldom control or predict which of their personalities are dominant at any one time.

STUDY CHECK

What are the major characteristics of the dissociative disorders?

THINKING CRITICALLY

Having multiple personalities would be a convenient defense for a criminal. John's defense might be something like, "I didn't do it; this other, hidden, nasty personality did it." And John could be telling the truth. If you were suspicious, however, how could you determine if the multiple personalities were genuine or not?

Personality Disorders

Personality disorder—a disorder that involves a long-lasting pattern of perceiving, relating to, and thinking about the environment and oneself that is maladaptive and inflexible and causes either impaired functioning or distress.

With the exception of the neurodevelopmental disorders, the psychological disorders we have reviewed so far afflict persons who were normal and undisturbed at one time. In other words, the person did not always exhibit the symptoms of the disorder. This prior state of wellness is more difficult to find with personality disorders. A **personality disorder** involves a long-lasting pattern of perceiving, relating to, and thinking about the environment and oneself that are maladaptive and inflexible and cause either impaired functioning or distress. As we have seen, *personality* is defined by attitudes, behaviors, and traits that persist in many situations over long periods of time. With a personality disorder, the traits and habits that constitute one's personality are inflexible and damaging (Grinspoon, 1997). Recent research has begun to challenge the notion that the maladaptive dispositions of this disorder are necessarily stable and unchanging. Researchers in this area are arguing for changes in the description of the personality disorders, particularly with regard to their stability (Clark, 2009; Eaton, 2010; Krueger & Eaton, 2010).

The *DSM-5* categorizes personality disorders (PDs) into three clusters. Cluster A includes disorders in which the person can be characterized as odd or eccentric. People with disorders from this cluster are often difficult to get along with. The disorders in this cluster are paranoid personality disorder, schizoid personality disorder, and schizotypal personality disorder. Cluster B includes disorders in which the person seems overly dramatic, emotional, or erratic and where behaviors are impulsive. Disorders in this cluster are antisocial personality disorder, borderline personality disorder, histrionic personality disorder, and narcissistic personality disorder. Cluster C includes disorders that add anxiety or fearfulness to the standard criteria for personality disorder. Note that it is only for those personality disorders in Cluster C that we find any reports of fear, anxiety, or depression. Disorders in this cluster are avoidant personality disorder, dependent personality disorder, and obsessive-compulsive personality disorder.

Rather than deal with all of the personality disorders in detail, we will simply describe some of the major characteristics of disorders within each of the three main clusters. As we do so, keep in mind that personality disorders generally have long-standing symptoms that usually begin in childhood or adolescence.

Cluster A: Disorders of Odd or Eccentric Reactions

Paranoid personality disorder—an extreme sensitivity, envy, unjustified suspiciousness, and mistrust of others; the actions of other people are interpreted as deliberately demeaning or threatening. A person with this disorder shows a restricted range of emotional reactivity, is humorless, and rarely seeks help. Example: a person who continually, and without justification, accuses a spouse of infidelity and believes that every wrong number was really a call from the spouse's lover.

Schizoid personality disorder—an inability to form, and an indifference to, interpersonal relationships. A person with schizoid personality disorder appears cold and aloof and often engages in excessive daydreaming. Example: a person who lives, as she has for years, in a one-room flat in a poor part of town, venturing out only to pick up a social security check and a few necessities at the corner store.

Cluster B: Disorders of Dramatic, Emotional, or Erratic Reactions

Histrionic personality disorder—overly dramatic, reactive, and intensely expressed behaviors. A person with this disorder is emotionally lively, draws attention to himself or herself, and over-reacts to matters of little consequence. Example: a woman who spends an inordinate amount of time on her appearance, calls everyone darling, constantly asks for feedback about her looks, and describes most of her experiences as wonderful or outstanding even when such an experience is no more than finding a detergent on sale at the grocery store.

Antisocial personality disorder—characterized by an exceptional lack of regard for the rights and property of others. Someone with this disorder often engages in impulsive behaviors with little or no regard for the consequences of those behaviors. Diagnosis can be difficult because symptoms include deceit and the manipulation of others. A history of "getting into trouble" precedes diagnosis in many cases (Donnellan et al., 2005; Johansson, Kerr, & Andershed, 2005). Persons change residences, jobs, and relationships frequently. At best, they are irresponsible. At worst, their behaviors are criminal. Example: Having committed a series of holdups, a man is finally caught and sent to trial. Court records show a long history of run-ins with law enforcement. Upon being convicted, the man says, "Well, that's the way it goes. He shouldn't have been carrying that much money with him. A few more months in jail won't bother me much."

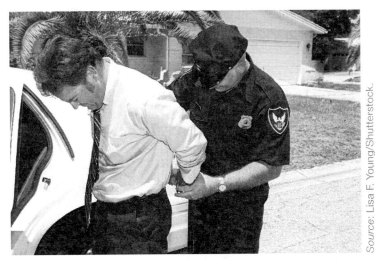

Unfortunately, psychologists often do not get to diagnose people with antisocial personality disorder until they have had a run-in with the law. And, by far, such diagnoses are much more common for males than for females.

Cluster C: Disorders Involving Anxiety and Fearfulness

Avoidant personality disorder—an over-sensitivity to the possibility of being rejected by others and an unwillingness to enter into relationships for fear of being rejected. A person with this disorder is devastated by disapproval but holds out a desire for social relationships. Example: a man with few close friends who almost never dates and talks only to women who are older and less attractive than he is; has worked for years at the same job, never seeking a job change or promotion, rarely speaks in public, and may attend meetings and public gatherings but without actively participating.

Dependent personality disorder—allowing others to dominate and assume responsibility for one's actions, this person has a poor self-image and lack of confidence. A person with this disorder sees himself or herself as stupid and helpless, thus defers to others. Example: a woman frequently abused by her husband; she has from time to time reported the abuse but refuses to take an active role in finding help or treatment, saying it is "her place" to do as he says and that if she does not please him, it is her fault.

Exactly how many people have personality disorders is difficult to determine because personality disorders are difficult to accurately diagnose. Most cases of personality disorder first come to the attention of mental health professionals on referral from the courts (or family members) or because of related problems such as child abuse or alcoholism. What we do find is that while the overall rate of PD may be between 10 percent and 20 percent, the rates of specific disorders are very low. The prognosis for the personality disorders is poor. The maladaptive patterns of behavior that characterize personality disorders have usually taken a lifetime to develop. As a result, changing them is very difficult.

STUDY CHECK

What characterizes personality disorders?

THINKING CRITICALLY

Antisocial personality disorder and substance abuse are often correlated. What arguments can you make for a cause-and-effect relationship and how would you test your hypothesis?

Depressive Disorders

Depressive disorder—a disorder involving a sad or depressed mood accompanied by physical and cognitive changes that make functioning difficult.

Major depressive disorder—depressive disorder defined as a period of at least two weeks during which the person experienced five or more of a list of specific symptoms nearly every day.

Persistent depressive disorder—a milder, but chronic form of depression, involving recurrent pessimism, low energy level, and low self-esteem.

The *DSM-5* defines a depressive disorder as one involving a sad or depressed mood accompanied by physical and cognitive changes that make functioning difficult (American Psychiatric Association, 2013). Major depressive disorder is described as a period of at least two weeks during which the person experienced five or more of the following symptoms nearly every day: (a) depressed or sad mood, (b) loss of pleasure or interest in normal activities, (c) weight loss or dramatic change in appetite, (d) either significantly more or less sleep than normal, (e) either physical slowness or agitation, (f) unusual fatigue or loss of energy, and (g) recurrent thoughts of death or suicide.

For 2016, it was estimated that 16.2 million adults experienced a major depressive episode, which represents 6.7 percent of the population (National Institute of Mental Health, 2016). The same report indicated that the prevalence was higher for adult women (8.5 percent) compared with men (4.8 percent). The diagnosis was most prevalent among people aged 18 to 25 (10.9 percent). Relapse and recurrence are common for those who have had a depressive episode.

Persistent depressive disorder (formerly known as dysthymia [diss-thigh´-me-a´]) is a milder, but chronic form of depression, involving recurrent pessimism, low energy level, and low self-esteem. Whereas major depression tends to occur in a series of extremely debilitating episodes, persistent depressive disorder is a more continuous sense of being depressed and sad. By definition, the depressed mood must last at least 2 years—and may last for 20 to 30 years.

Source: globalmoments/Shutterstock.

Simply being depressed is not, in and of itself, an indication of psychological disorder. Depressing things happen to all of us and feeling depressed in such a circumstance is not to be taken as "abnormal."

For both major depression and persistent depressive disorder, there need not be any event or situation that precipitates the person's depressed mood. That is, to feel overwhelmingly depressed upon hearing of the death of a close friend is not, in itself, enough to be regarded as a disorder of any sort. We all may feel periods of depression from time to time. With major depressive disorder, the depression is significant and is associated with many additional symptoms. With persistent depressive disorder, the depression is particularly long lasting.

The answer to the question, "What causes depression?" depends largely on how and where one looks. It seems most likely that depression is caused by several different but interrelated causes—both biological and psychological. There are clear indicators that major depressive disorder and bipolar disorder have a genetic basis. In fact, researchers have identified a variation of a certain brain chemistry gene that predicts which people are likely to develop depression following a traumatic or highly stressful life event (Caspi et al., 2003). This point gets us to the following model for the development of psychological disorders.

We may talk about a genetic basis for depression, but clearly, people do not inherit depression—they inherit genes. What the **diathesis-stress model** proposes is that individuals inherit multiple genes, which may give rise to the tendency or predisposition to express certain behaviors, but these behaviors are expressed only if activated by stress or trauma. *Diathesis* is a term that literally means "a condition that makes someone susceptible to developing a disorder." In our current discussion, the proposal would be that some people inherit predispositions to develop a depressive disorder when they encounter stress in their lives. Faced with the same or similar stress, someone else may have a diathesis to develop coronary heart disease or gastrointestinal problems, whereas someone else might respond to that stress with no disease or disorder at all. This interactive explanation is applicable to all sorts of disorders. A large body of research suggests that "stressful life events are strongly related to the onset of mood disorders" (Barlow & Durland, 2009).

Diathesis-stress model—a model proposing that individuals inherit multiple genes, which may give rise to the tendency or predisposition to express certain behaviors, but these behaviors are expressed only if activated by stress or trauma.

Bipolar Disorder

In **bipolar disorder**, episodes of depression are interspersed with episodes of mania. (This disorder is still commonly referred to as "manic depression.") **Mania** is characterized as an elevated mood with feelings of euphoria or irritability. In a manic state, a person shows an increase in activity, is more talkative than usual, and seems to get by with less sleep than usual. Mania is a condition of mood that cannot be maintained for long. It is too tiring to stay manic for an extended time. As is true for depression, mania seldom occurs as an isolated episode. Follow-up studies show that recurrences of manic reactions are common. People are rarely manic without periods of depression interspersed. In fact, episodes of depression are so common in bipolar disorder it is often misdiagnosed as major depression (Rosa et al., 2008). Nearly 6 million Americans are diagnosed with bipolar disorder every year (Kessler et al., 2005; Merikangas et al., 2007). For reasons that are not clear, the incidence of bipolar disorder has increased significantly in recent years (Clemente et al., 2015).

Bipolar disorder—episodes of depression are interspersed with episodes of mania.

Mania—a condition characterized as an elevated mood with feelings of euphoria or irritability.

The *DSM-5* defines two types of bipolar disorder. *Bipolar I disorder* involves the characteristic swing between mania and depression. However, there is no history of an incident of major depression in the person's past. In contrast, *bipolar II disorder* adds the requirement that the person must have experienced at least one instance of major depression *and* one hypomanic episode (abnormal and persistent elevation in mood) in his or her lifetime. A person with bipolar II disorder is likely to experience a serious disruption in social and occupational functioning (American Psychiatric Association, 2013).

Bipolar disorder is not common. A randomly selected person has less than a 0.5 percent chance of developing symptoms. The probability rises to 15 percent if a brother, a sister, or either parent had the disorder. For fraternal twins, this percentage is nearly 20 percent if the first twin has the disorder. However, if one of a pair of identical twins has bipolar mood disorder, the chance that the other twin will be diagnosed as having the disorder jumps to nearly 70 percent (Edvardsen et al., 2008; McGuffin et al., 2003). These increased probabilities are excellent evidence for a genetic, or inherited, predisposition to bipolar disorder.

┌─ STUDY CHECK ───┐

What is depressive disorder?
What is the essence of the "diathesis-stress model"?
What is bipolar disorder?
└───┘

┌─ THINKING CRITICALLY ───┐

Suppose someone you know becomes deeply depressed over the death of a loved
one. Is there a point in time when "normal" depression has lasted too long and has
become "abnormal" depression? Is it possible to establish "time limits" for grieving?
└───┘

Schizophrenia Spectrum Disorder

Schizophrenia—a disorder involving a distortion of reality; a retreat from other people; and disturbances in affect, behavior, and cognition.

Negative symptoms—symptoms of schizophrenia that involve a loss of or a decrease in normal functions.

Positive symptoms—symptoms of schizophrenia involving thoughts and perceptions (largely hallucinations and delusions) that are not present in normal people.

Hallucinations—false perceptions; perceiving that which is not there or failing to perceive that which is.

Delusions—false beliefs; ideas that are firmly held regardless of evidence to the contrary.

In the *DSM-5* schizophrenia is categorized under *schizophrenia spectrum and other psychotic disorders*. Schizophrenia is a diagnosis for what may be several different disorders, which have in common a distortion of reality, a retreat from other people, and disturbances in affect, behavior, and cognition (our ABCs again). The analogy with cancer is crude, but reasonable. If you hear that a friend has cancer that is certainly not good news. But, how bad the news is depends upon answers to a few questions, such as, "What sort of cancer is it?" "Is it a small spot of skin cancer on the tip of an ear, prostate cancer, breast cancer, pancreatic cancer, brain cancer?" "How aggressive, or fast-spreading, is the cancer?" So it is with schizophrenia, a term so general that it raises many follow-up questions. "Up to this point, investigators have not been able to identify a single factor that characterizes all patients with schizophrenia" (Walker et al., 2004, p. 402.). Nonetheless, we may say that schizophrenia is a disorder whose current definition includes hallucinations (false perceptions), delusions (false beliefs), disorganized speech, inappropriate or flattened affect (little or no emotional response at all), and bizarre behavior (Pogue-Geile & Yokley, 2010). "For a moderate to large percentage of schizophrenia patients (over 50 percent), the disorder is not chronic but, rather, is characterized by episodic periods of symptoms, often with continual or chronic malfunctioning, adjustment difficulties, and some impairment in functioning between episodes" (Jobe & Harrow, 2010, p. 221).

In earlier versions of the *DSM*, there were several different subtypes of schizophrenia defined (e.g., paranoid schizophrenia, catatonic schizophrenia). Research showed that these subtype classifications were unreliable. Consequently, the *DSM-5* no longer defines these different subtypes of schizophrenia. Instead, schizophrenia is classified into types on the basis of positive and negative symptoms.

Negative symptoms involve a loss of or a decrease in normal functions. These symptoms include emotional and social withdrawal; apathy; and reduced energy, motivation, and attention (Kring & Caponigra, 2010). Positive symptoms are thoughts and perceptions (largely hallucinations and delusions) that are not present in normal people. Hallucinations are false perceptions—perceiving that which is not there or failing to perceive that which is. Schizophrenic hallucinations are often auditory, taking the form of "hearing voices inside one's head." Delusions are false beliefs, ideas that are firmly held regardless of evidence to the contrary. The delusions of someone

Source: vchal/Shutterstock.

It is estimated that schizophrenia affects about 1 percent of the population worldwide.

with schizophrenia are inconsistent and unorganized. Positive symptoms of schizophrenia also may include disordered thinking and speech, bizarre behaviors, and inappropriate affect. Someone displaying these symptoms may say something like, "When you swallow in your throat like a key it comes out, but not a scissors, a robin too, it means spring" (Marengo & Harrow, 1987, p. 654), or the person may giggle and laugh or sob and cry for no apparent reason, or may stand perfectly still for hours at a time. Of those persons diagnosed with schizophrenia, about 75 percent show positive symptoms, whereas about 25 percent present negative symptoms (Barlow & Durand, 2009).

Schizophrenia can be found around the world at the same rate: about 1 percent of the population with diagnosis usually made in adolescents and young adults (Grace, 2010). People in developing countries tend to have a more acute (intense, but short-lived) course—and a better outcome—of the disorder than do people in industrialized nations. Schizophrenia occurs slightly more frequently in men than in women, and men are more likely to be disabled by the disorder and have a higher relapse rate (Aleman, Kahn, & Selten, 2003).

The prognosis for schizophrenia is not very encouraging, especially for those with negative symptoms. About 25 percent do recover fully from their first episode of the disorder and have no recurrences; in about 50 percent of the cases, there is a recurrent illness with periods of remission in between, and in the other 25 percent of cases there are no signs of recovery and there is a long-term deterioration in functioning. If treatment begins immediately after an initial episode, the prognosis is better, with as many as 83 percent recovering (Lieberman et al., 1993). We see this phenomenon with many physical ailments: The sooner treatment begins, the better the likelihood of recovery.

The usefulness of this negative-positive distinction is that there may be differences in both the causes and the most effective treatment plans for the two types. In brief, we find that the correlates of negative symptoms to include enlarged ventricles in the brain, a clearer genetic basis, more severe complications at birth, a lower educational level, poorer adjustment patterns before onset, and a poorer prognosis given the relative ineffectiveness of medications. Correlated with positive symptoms are excesses of the neurotransmitter dopamine, relatively normal brain configuration, severe disruptions in early family life, over-activity and aggressiveness in adolescence, and a relatively good response to treatment.

Finally, we need to be clear on two points. First, no matter how unsettling these symptoms may be, the average patient with schizophrenia does not present the picture of the crazed, wild lunatic that is often depicted in movies and on television. Day in and day out, the average patient is quite colorless, withdrawn, and of very little danger. Their "differentness" may be frightening, but people with schizophrenia are seldom more dangerous than anyone else. Second, when literally translated, schizophrenia means, "splitting of the mind," where the split of the mind of the patient is from the real world and social relationships as the rest of us experience them. The term has never been used to describe multiple or split personalities of the Jekyll and Hyde variety. Such disorders do occur, but they are of a totally different sort—the dissociative identity disorder we covered earlier.

STUDY CHECK

What is schizophrenia, and what are the differences between positive and negative symptoms of the disorder?

THINKING CRITICALLY

How would you react if you learned that one of your classmates was in treatment, diagnosed with schizophrenia?

Gender Differences in Alzheimer's Disease

Neurocognitive disorders involve disruptions in a person's cognitive abilities that are acquired rather than being a product of the developmental process (American Psychiatric Association, 2013). One high-profile disorder in this category *is neurocognitive disorder due to Alzheimer's disease*, more commonly called Alzheimer's disease. Alzheimer's disease (AD) involves a slow deterioration of intellectual functioning, which is the most common symptom associated with AD (Johnson, Davis, & Bosanquet, 2000). It is a degenerative disease, which means that the symptoms get worse over time, resulting in declines in daily living activities, reduced cognitive ability, personality change, and behavior change. A marked deterioration of short-term memory is the hallmark symptom of AD. A person with AD may be able to remember things from the past but may forget something that happened just a few minutes ago. Although we think of AD as a psychological disorder, it involves some dramatic changes in the brain: (1) a mass of a spaghetti-like jumble of abnormal protein fibers (tangles); (2) plaques (waste material), which are degenerated nerve fibers that wrap around a core of protein; (3) the presence of small cavities filled with fluid and debris; and (4) reduced size of some brain structures (Hanyu et al., 2010).

There is a gender difference in the rate of AD, with women showing a higher rate than men (9.37 percent and 8.31 percent, respectively). After age 80 this difference gets more pronounced. Women are also diagnosed with AD at a younger age ($M = 80.02$) than men ($M = 81.33$) (Beam et al., 2018). Almost two-thirds of people diagnosed with AD are women (Mielke, Vemuri, & Rocca, 2014).

Women with AD show worse performance than men with AD on a number of cognitive tasks (Heun & Kockler, 2002). For example, Pusswald et al. (2015) found a difference between male and female AD patients on a word-recall task. Women performed more poorly than men on both word-recall and word-recognition tasks. According to Pusswald et al., the gender difference observed could not be accounted for by differing levels of education or different living conditions between men and women. Additionally, women with mild AD are more likely than men to show symptoms of depression (Lee, Lee, & Kim, 2017).

Can the differences between men and women in AD symptoms be related to differential brain abnormalities? In one study, the brains of male and female AD patients were examined after they had died (Gallart-Palau et al., 2016). The researchers were specifically looking at possible differences in white-matter (WM) density between male and female AD patients. Degradation of

white matter in the brain is associated with neurocognitive impairment and later dementia. Gallart-Palau et al. did not find any differences in general levels of WM depletion between male and female AD patients' brains. However, they did find greater depletion in female patients' brains in areas of the temporal lobes. The temporal lobes are associated with memory functioning. WM depletion in these areas may account for memory loss among AD patients and the more severe cognitive impairment in female than male AD patients.

One interesting hypothesis about why more women than men are diagnosed with AD centers on brain reserve capacity (Mielke et al., 2014). According to this hypothesis, an individual with a larger brain would have more reserve capacity than an individual with a smaller brain and be able to cope better with any brain pathology. Generally, men have larger brains than women. Consequently, the male brain may be better able to deal with the brain pathology associated with AD. According to Mielke et al., there is some evidence supporting this idea. Women with AD show faster declines in brain volume than men, which could account for the higher prevalence of AD among women.

Hormone changes may also help explain the gender differences in AD. Sex hormones (estrogen and testosterone) play an important role in the prenatal (before-birth) and perinatal (after-birth) development of the male and female brain. They account for the development of structural and functional differences between the male and female brain (Mielke et al., 2014). It is important to understand that males and females have both male and female sex hormones. However, males have higher levels of male hormones, and females have higher levels of female hormones. Estrogen and progesterone are two female sex hormones that appear to have protective effects against AD-related brain pathology, specifically the plaques associated with AD (Vest & Pike, 2013). Research shows that in male AD patients' brains, there is a significant drop in testosterone (a male sex hormone), but not in estrogen, in men aged 60 to 79 (Rosario, Chang, Head, Stanczyk, & Pike, 2011). In women with AD, however, the levels of both male and female sex hormones are reduced compared with normal women. The reduced levels of female hormones (e.g., estrogen and progesterone) are believed to be related to the higher rates of AD among women than men (Mielke et al., 2014; Rosario et al., 2011). Additional evidence on the role of female sex hormones in AD is that AD is less common among women treated with hormone replacement therapy than those not treated with such therapy (Colucci et al., 2006).

Hormonal changes in women may also relate to another curious finding: the higher rates of AD among women with multiple pregnancies (Colucci et al., 2006). Colucci et al. found an unexpectedly higher rate of AD among women with three or more pregnancies compared with non-AD controls. What possible link could there be between pregnancy and AD? The answer appears to lie in a protein called *pregnancy zone protein* (PZP), which increases during pregnancy. PZP has been found in elevated levels in women with AD four years before the onset of the disease (Ijsselstijn et al., 2011). PZP appears to interact with the plaques that develop in the AD patient's brain (Nijholt et al., 2015). The fact that PZP can be detected in a woman's blood four years before the onset of symptoms has raised hope that a reliable early-warning test can be developed based on PZP levels.

Chapter Summary

How do psychologists define the concept of "abnormality"?

Within the context of psychological disorders, "abnormal" refers to maladaptive behaviors, cognitions, and/or affect at odds with social expectations, and result in distress or discomfort.

How are psychological disorders classified?

The *DSM-5* is a revision of the *DSM-IV-TR* edition of the *Diagnostic and Statistical Manual of Mental Disorders*, published by the American Psychological Association. It is the most widely used classification system for psychological disorders. The *DSM-5* spells out criteria for diagnosing disorders on the basis of observable symptoms. The advantage of classifying psychological disorders is that it provides one standard label and cluster of symptoms for each disorder that all mental health practitioners can use; as such, it is a basis for improved communication. It does have its limitations, however. Schemes of classification can confuse description with explanation; classifying and labeling persons as having psychological disorders may overlook the larger group or society of which that individual is a part.

How do "psychological disorders" and "insanity" differ?

Psychological disorder, mental disorder, and behavior disorder are concepts used to label abnormal mental and behavioral conditions. Insanity is a legal term. It relates to psychological problems but refers to an individual's state of mind at the time of a crime. The question of insanity centers on whether a person knew or fully understood the consequences of his or her actions, knew the difference between right and wrong, and could exercise control over his or her actions at the time of a crime.

What are generalized anxiety disorder, panic disorder, and specific phobia?

Anxiety disorders are the most common variety of psychological disorder. They are characterized by experienced, felt anxiety, usually coupled with attempts to avoid or escape from situations likely to bring on additional anxiety. The defining characteristic of generalized anxiety disorder is a high level of anxiety that cannot be attributed to any particular source. The anxiety is diffuse and chronic. The defining symptom of a panic disorder is a sudden, often unpredictable, attack of intense anxiety, called a panic attack. Such attacks may last for seconds or for hours. There is no particular stimulus that prompts the attack. A specific phobia is typified by an intense, persistent fear of some object, activity, or situation that is no real threat to the individual's well-being—in brief, an intense, irrational fear. Phobias imply attempts to avoid the phobic object.

What is obsessive-compulsive disorder?

Obsessive-compulsive disorder (OCD) is characterized by recurrent obsessions or compulsions. Obsessions are thoughts or ideas that involuntarily and constantly intrude into awareness. They often are pointless or groundless thoughts about cleanliness, violence, disease, danger, or doubt. Compulsions are constantly intruding repetitive behaviors. The most common are hand washing, grooming, and counting or checking behavior.

What is posttraumatic stress disorder?

Posttraumatic stress disorder, or PTSD, is a disorder in which the symptoms of anxiety, recurrent and disruptive dreams, and recollections of a highly traumatic event (e.g., rape, combat, or natural disaster) occur well after the danger of the event has passed.

What are the defining characteristics of autism spectrum disorder?

Autism spectrum disorder is one of the psychological disorders that is usually diagnosed within 30 months after birth. Its major symptoms include severely impaired social interactions. Children with autism seem oblivious to those around them, even their primary caregivers. There are difficulties in communication, with nearly one-third never developing speech or language skills. Behaviors are often repetitive and stereotyped. They insist on keeping their physical environments unchanged.

What are the major characteristics of the dissociative disorders?

Dissociative disorders are marked by a retreat or escape from (dissociation with) some aspect of one's experience or one's personality. It may be an inability to recall some life event (dissociative amnesia). In some cases, aspects of one's personality become so separated that the person suffers from dissociative identity disorder, where two or more personalities are found in the same individual. This disorder was once called multiple personality disorder and, for reasons unknown, has become increasingly common in the United States in recent years.

What characterizes personality disorders?

Personality disorders (PDs) are enduring patterns of perceiving, relating to, and thinking about the environment and oneself that are inflexible and maladaptive. They are lifelong patterns of maladjustment and are classified as belonging to one of three groups, or clusters. Cluster A includes those PDs involving odd or eccentric reactions, such as the paranoid and schizoid personality disorders. Cluster B includes disorders of dramatic, emotional, or erratic reactions, such as the narcissistic and histrionic personality disorders. Cluster C includes disorders involving fear and anxiety, such as the avoidant and dependent personality disorders.

What is depressive disorder?

In the depressive disorder, the prime symptom is a depressed or sad mood. Other symptoms can include loss of pleasure, weight or appetite changes, physical slowness or agitation, either significantly more or less sleep than usual, unusual fatigue, and/or thoughts of death or suicide; symptoms tend to be ongoing at least during a two-week period. Major depression affects about twice as many women as men. Persistent depressive disorder involves depression that may be a bit less devastating or debilitating but that is chronic (lasting for at least two years), involving recurrent feelings of pessimism, low energy levels, and low self-esteem.

What is the essence of the "diathesis-stress model"?

The diathesis-stress model is an attempt to account for the source of a disorder (such as depression) as an interaction of inherited, genetic predispositions and environmental stressors. The point being that neither by itself is likely to result in a particular disorder.

What is bipolar disorder?

In bipolar disorder, episodes of depression are interspersed with episodes of mania (e.g., heightened activity, talkativeness, reduced sleep). The *DSM-5* identifies two types of bipolar disorder. Bipolar I disorder involves the characteristic swing between mania and depression; however, there is no history of an incident of major depression in the person's past. Bipolar II disorder adds the requirement that the person must have experienced at least one instance of major depression *and* one hypomanic episode (abnormal and persistent elevation in mood) in his or her lifetime.

What is schizophrenia, and what are the differences between positive and negative symptoms of the disorder?

Schizophrenia is a label applied to disorders that involve varying degrees of impairment. It occurs in about 1 percent of the population worldwide, and, in general, is characterized by a distortion of reality, a retreat from others, and disturbances in affect, behavior, and cognition. About 25 percent of those diagnosed with the disorder recover fully from their first episode, while in 50 percent of cases symptoms are recurrent with periods of remission. In 25 percent of cases, there is no recovery and a deterioration of functioning.

There may be a difference between schizophrenia with positive symptoms and schizophrenia with negative symptoms. Negative symptoms involve a loss of normal functioning, social and emotional withdrawal, reduced energy and motivation, apathy, and poor attention. Positive symptoms are hallucinations (false perceptions) and delusions (false beliefs). Positive symptoms also include disordered thinking, bizarre behavior, and inappropriate affect.

Key Terms

Abnormal (p. 258)
Diagnosis (p. 259)
Insanity (p. 260)
Generalized anxiety disorder (GAD) (p. 263)
Panic disorder (p. 263)
Specific phobia (p. 263)
Obsessive-compulsive disorder (OCD) (p. 264)
Obsessions (p. 264)
Compulsions (p. 264)
Posttraumatic stress disorder (PTSD) (p. 264)
Autism spectrum disorder (p. 265)
Dissociative disorder (p. 267)
Dissociative amnesia (p. 267)

Dissociative identity disorder (DID) (p. 267)
Personality disorder (p. 268)
Depressive disorder (p. 270)
Major depressive disorder (p. 270)
Persistent depressive disorder (p. 270)
Diathesis-stress model (p. 271)
Bipolar disorder (p. 271)
Mania (p. 271)
Schizophrenia (p. 272)
Negative symptoms (p. 272)
Positive symptoms (p. 272)
Hallucinations (p. 272)
Delusions (p. 272)

Treatment and Therapy for Psychological Disorders

Source: Artur Szczybyl/Shutterstock

Chapter Outline

Questions You Will Be Able to Answer

After reading Chapter 13, you should be able to answer the following questions:

- What is psychosurgery, and what is a prefrontal lobotomy?
- What is ECT, and why is it still being used?
- What are the antipsychotic medications, and how effective are they?
- What medications are used to treat persons with depressive disorders?
- What are the antianxiety medications, and how effective are they?
- What is the essence of Freudian psychoanalysis, and how is the process different today from when it was practiced by Freud?
- What are the major features of client-centered therapy?
- What are some of the techniques that qualify as behavior therapies?
- What are the essential characteristics of the cognitive approaches to psychotherapy?
- What is "group therapy," and what are its potential benefits?
- Is psychotherapy an effective treatment for psychological disorders?

Preview

As we made clear in the previous chapter, psychological disorders present a major health challenge. Research data tells us that psychological disorders produce a loss of earnings in the United States amounting to more than *$193 billion a year* (National Alliance on Mental Illness, ND). What is to be done for the millions afflicted with psychological disorders? The care and treatment of such persons is the subject of this chapter.

We begin with a brief discussion of treatments that are outside the normal realm of psychologists, called *biomedical treatments*. We consider three different types: (a) surgical procedures to alleviate the symptoms of mental disorders, (b) electroconvulsive therapy (often called shock therapy) as a treatment for depression, and (c) the use of psychoactive drugs designed to treat psychotic symptoms, depression, or anxiety.

No matter what the specifics, psychotherapy's major goal is to help a person to think, feel, or act more effectively. Different types of therapy have different specific sub-goals. We will focus on five varieties of psychotherapy and will see that each approaches therapy from a different perspective. Given their historical significance, we begin by considering psychoanalytic approaches—first Freud's, then more contemporary versions. We then consider humanistic techniques—largely Rogers' client-centered therapy, behavioral techniques (of which there are many), cognitive therapies, and group approaches to psychotherapy. Finally, we consider how to evaluate the different forms of psychotherapy.

Biomedical Treatments

Psychologists are not medical doctors. As a result, psychologists cannot use medical treatments such as performing surgery and administering shock treatments. These treatments require a medical degree. Psychologists may recommend that a person consult with a physician about a medical treatment or refer a client to the care of a physician or psychiatrist (a person with a medical degree who specializes in mental disorders). In some states, licensed psychologists can prescribe medications for psychological disorders, but they still cannot perform psychosurgery or administer shock treatments.

Psychosurgery

Psychosurgery—surgical procedures, usually directed at the brain, used to affect psychological reactions.

Psychosurgery is the name given to surgical procedures, usually directed at the brain, used to affect psychological reactions. Psychosurgical techniques today are aimed at making rather minimal lesions in the brain. This was not the case in the early days of psychosurgery where the treatments involved more radical alterations of the brain, sometimes resulting in highly negative outcomes for patients.

The surgical destruction of the tissues that normally interconnect the two hemispheres of the brain's cerebral cortex is used as a last-chance effort to alleviate symptoms in extreme cases of epilepsy. Small surgical lesions in an area deep in the middle of the brain (called the limbic system) have been effective in reducing or eliminating violent behaviors. Of all of the types of psychosurgery, none has ever been used as commonly as a prefrontal lobotomy, or simply, lobotomy. This surgery severs the major neural connections between the prefrontal lobes (the area at the very front of the cerebral cortex) and lower brain centers.

Lobotomy—psychosurgery severing the major neural connections between the prefrontal lobes (the area at the very front of the cerebral cortex) and lower brain centers.

Cingulotomy is a treatment of last resort that involves cutting a bundle of nerve fibers connecting the very front of the frontal lobe with parts of the limbic system. As a treatment for severe obsessive-compulsive disorder (OCD) after all other interventions have proven unsuccessful, it has been used with notable success (Keller, 2012). Although not without controversy, cingulotomy continues to be a viable treatment option (Cosgrove, 2009). One review states, "Many patients are greatly improved after cingulotomy and the complications or side effects are few. Cingulotomy remains an important therapeutic option for disabling psychiatric disease and is probably underutilized." (Cosgrove & Rauch, 2003, p. 225).

The first lobotomy was performed in 1935 by Portuguese psychiatrist, Egas Moniz. For developing the procedure, Moniz was awarded the Nobel Prize in 1949. (Ironically, Moniz was then shot by one of his lobotomized patients in 1950. Rendered paraplegic, he was confined to a wheelchair for the rest of his life.) The logic behind a lobotomy is simple: The prefrontal lobes influence the more basic emotional centers low in the brain, and severely disturbed patients were thought to have difficulty exercising control over those lower parts of the brain. Thus, if these areas of the brain were separated surgically, the more depressed, agitated, or violent patients could be brought under control.

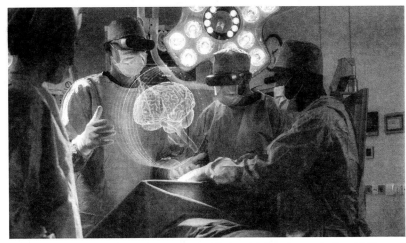

Psychosurgery today is much more sophisticated than it was in the 1940s and 1950s, when prefrontal lobotomies were performed.

Always a last resort, the operation was often successful. Stories of its impact on chronic mental patients circulated widely. The November 30, 1942, *Time* magazine called the surgical procedure "revolutionary," and claimed that "some 300 people in the United States have had their psychoses surgically removed." *Life* magazine, in a graphic photo essay titled "*Psychosurgery: Operation to Cure Sick Minds Turns Surgeon's Blade into an Instrument of Mental Therapy*," called results "spectacular," claiming that "about 30 percent of the lobotomized patients were able to return to everyday productive lives" (March 3, 1947, p. 93).

In the 1940s and 1950s, prefrontal lobotomies were performed with regularity. *Time* reported (September 15, 1952) that neurologist Walter Freeman alone was performing about one hundred lobotomies a week. It is difficult to estimate how many lobotomies were performed in these two decades, but certainly tens of thousands.

Everyone understood lobotomies could not be reversed. What took longer to realize was that they often brought terrible side effects. Between one and four percent of patients receiving prefrontal lobotomies died. Many who survived suffered seizures, memory loss, an inability to plan ahead, and a general listlessness and loss of affect. Many acted childishly or were difficult to manage within institutions. Such was the case of Rosemary Kennedy, the sister of late president John F. Kennedy. Rosemary had a history of mental illness; she eventually underwent a lobotomy in November 1941 at the age of 23. By all accounts, before the surgery, Rosemary was relatively normal, yet somewhat childish and rebellious. After the surgery, however, she had to be institutionalized and spent the rest of her life in one institution or another. By the late 1950s, lobotomies had become rare. Contrary to common belief, performing a prefrontal lobotomy is not illegal. The procedure is just no longer needed. Psychoactive drugs produce better results more safely and reliably and with fewer side effects.

STUDY CHECK

What is psychosurgery, and what is a prefrontal lobotomy?

THINKING CRITICALLY

Under what conditions might you grant permission for an irreversible surgical procedure on a loved one?

Electroconvulsive Therapy

Electroconvulsive therapy (ECT)—treatment that involves passing an electric current of between 70 and 150 volts across a patient's head for a fraction of a second.

As gruesome as psychosurgery may be, it is less objectionable to many people than electroconvulsive therapy (ECT), or shock treatments. Introduced in 1937, ECT involves passing an electric current of between 70 and 150 volts across a patient's head for a fraction of a second. Now, that sounds like enough to kill a person! However, the shock is delivered at low amperage (usually below 1 ampere) for a very short period of time (a second or less). Patients receive a fast-acting anesthetic and a muscle-relaxant drug before the shock is delivered to minimize muscular contractions. The electric shock induces a reaction in the brain not unlike an epileptic seizure; the entire process takes about five minutes. ECT patients cannot remember events just before the shock or the shock itself.

At first, ECT was used to calm agitated patients, but mental health professionals learned that ECT works better for patients with major depressive disorder and bipolar disorder that are resistant to other treatments. For these patients, ECT often alleviates the symptoms of depression and can help relieve other symptoms (Scott & Fraser, 2008; Weiss, Allan, & Greenaway, 2012). It is also effective for patients demonstrating manic symptoms (Fink, 1997). In one study, a group of bipolar patients received ECT after all available medications failed. All patients in the group responded well to the procedure (de Macedo-Soareset et al., 2005).

Virtually all patients (97 percent) give their consent to the procedure, and negative side effects are rare (Pagnin et al., 2004). The most commonly reported side effects are memory loss and general mental confusion. In nearly all cases, these effects disappear in a few days or weeks. Interestingly, after an electroconvulsive treatment, a patient is much more likely to have a short-lived memory loss for recent public events (knowledge of the world) than for autobiographical, personal memories (Lisanby et al., 2000).

Once they have the procedure, most ECT patients are not afraid of having an electrical shock sent through their brains. One patient began ECT treatments in 1996, and by 2005 had received 244 "maintenance" treatments. In the four years before her ECT, she had five admissions and spent 29 months in the hospital. After her depression abated she asked to continue maintenance ETC to stay depression-free (Wijkstra & Nolan, 2005). Gregory Nuttall and his colleagues reviewed the records of 2,279 patients who had received 17,394 ECT treatments and found no permanent injury, and that "none of the patients died during or immediately after ECT. There were 18 deaths within 30 days of the final treatment, none related to ECT" (2004, p. 237).

Administering a shock to just one side of the brain, called a *unilateral ECT*, appears to be a safer and equally effective procedure with fewer side effects. Unilateral ECT works better in the right hemisphere of the cerebral cortex (which is more strongly associated with emotional reactions) than in the left hemisphere (Lisanby et al., 2000).

Why ECT works is not fully understood (Fink, 2000, 2001). Although it must be used with extreme care, ECT is still used today, although relatively rarely (Lesage et al., 2016). Antidepressant medications have reduced the need for ECT, but drugs are not always successful and may take longer to become effective. Electroconvulsive therapy can work in a matter of days. Time is no small consideration for patients who are extremely depressed or suicidal.

STUDY CHECK

What is ECT, and why is it still being used?

THINKING CRITICALLY

What ethical considerations are involved in asking a person with a severe psychological disorder to give his or her consent to a procedure like ECT or psychosurgery?

Suicide and Suicide Prevention

Suicide is an increasing problem in the United States. Before we explore the issues of suicide and suicide prevention, let's look at some basic definitions. *Suicide* is defined as "death caused by self-directed injurious behavior with intent to die as a result of the behavior" (National Institute of Mental Health (NIMH), 2018, para. 2). A *suicide attempt* is a self-directed, non-fatal, potentially injurious behavior intended to cause death as a result of the behavior. A suicide attempt need not necessarily result in injury. *Suicide ideation* involves considering, thinking about, or planning suicide (NIMH, 2018).

In the United States in 2016, suicide was the 10th leading cause of death, resulting in about 45,000 deaths. It was the second leading cause of death among individuals between the ages of 10 and 34, and fourth among individuals between 35 and 54. There were over two times as many suicides (44,965) as homicides (19,362) in the United States in 2016 (Centers for Disease Control and Prevention, 2016). Between 1999 and 2016, the suicide rate increased from 10.5 to 28 percent. Males are far more likely (21.3 per 100,000) than females (6.1 in 100,000) to commit suicide (NIMH, 2018). However, females are four times more likely than males to attempt suicide. Suicide rates among Native Americans/Native Alaskans are the highest among several ethnic groups, followed by whites. Blacks, Hispanics, and Asians have lower rates than whites and Native Americans/Alaskans. The suicide rate among veterans is 22 times higher than among the non-veteran U.S. population (U.S. Department of Veterans Affairs, 2018). Finally, most suicides involve the use of a firearm (22,963), followed by suffocation (11,642), poisoning (6,698), and other methods (3,662).

What are the risk factors for suicide? Mental illness is strongly associated with suicide, especially depression (Mann et al., 2005). Other risk factors include a family history of suicide, substance or alcohol abuse, having a serious chronic medical illness, being male, having a history of trauma or abuse, prolonged stress, isolation, experiencing a recent loss, and agitation and sleep loss (National Alliance of Mental Illness, 2018). **Table 13.1** lists 12 warning signs for impending suicide.

Given the alarming statistics on the frequency of suicide, a reasonable question is whether there is anything that can be done to prevent suicide. Fortunately, there are several strategies that can be used to combat suicide. Psychotherapy is an obvious way to prevent suicide. Mann et al. (2005) reviewed the literature on suicide prevention and concluded that psychotherapy combined with antidepressant medication can be

TABLE 13.1 Twelve Warning Signs for Suicide

Feeling like a burden
Being isolated
Increased anxiety
Feeling trapped or in unbearable pain
Increased substance use
Looking for a way to access lethal means
Increased anger or rage
Extreme mood swings
Expressing hopelessness
Sleeping too little or too much
Talking or posting about wanting to die
Making plans for suicide

Source: Centers for Disease Control and Prevention (2018f).

an effective treatment for the depression underlying many suicides as well as suicidal ideation and suicide attempts. An unfortunate reality about suicide is that once a person attempts suicide, he or she is likely to make another attempt in the future. Cognitive therapy can be effective in reducing the likelihood of a subsequent suicide attempt (Mann et al.). Mann et al. suggest that other strategies are also desirable. These include screening for risk factors, restricting access to lethal weapons (e.g., firearms), training primary care physicians to recognize suicide risk factors, and gatekeeping.

A *gatekeeper* is a person who has regular contact with individuals at risk for suicide and can monitor the person for risk factors. Gatekeepers might be family members, friends, employers, co-workers, first responders, pharmacists, teachers, and so on (Mann et al., 2005). If a gatekeeper is to be effective, he or she should be trained to recognize risk factors for suicide. A review of the research conducted by Mo, Ko, and Xin (2018) found that training for school-based gatekeepers for adolescents was effective in increasing gatekeepers' knowledge, skills, and self-efficacy (the belief that one can be effective at a task). It is less clear whether training improves the actual identification of those at risk for suicide (Terpstra et al., 2018).

Another resource for dealing with suicide is a suicide hotline. A hotline is usually a telephone number that a person can call to get immediate help. Of course, in order for a hotline to be effective, the suicidal individual must use it. Unfortunately, many suicidal individuals resist seeking help. This is known as *help-negation* (Hedman-Robertson, 2018). Hedman-Robertson suggests that suicidal individuals may resist seeking help because they are isolated, are experiencing cognitive distortions, have poor problem-solving skills, or fear the stigma involved in seeking help. Hedman-Robertson conducted a study of the extent to which college students know about and use hotlines. Hedman-Robertson found that almost half of the participants reported that they saw materials posted concerning the National Suicide Prevention Lifeline. She also found that participants who had attempted suicide, had plans for suicide, or had suicide ideation indicated that they were willing to call the Lifeline. However, those who indicated that they knew that they had some of the warning signs for suicide were least likely to say they would use the Lifeline.

How effective are hotlines once a suicidal person calls? Gould, Kalafat, Harrismunfakh, and Kleinman (2007) evaluated the outcomes for adult suicidal individuals who called eight suicide hotlines. Gould et al. found that more than half of the callers had a suicide plan in place or had a suicide attempt in the past (57 percent). Additionally, 8.1 percent had taken steps to harm themselves before calling. They also found that calling a hotline improved the suicide status of the callers. Callers reported a drop in feelings of hopelessness and psychological pain by the completion of the call. A follow-up revealed that after a period of weeks, the callers felt less hopeless, less psychological pain, and less intention to harm themselves.

What can you do to help prevent suicide? First, if you are feeling suicidal or have suicidal ideation, please get help right away! A call to a suicide hotline would be a way to get you or a loved one immediate help. If someone you know seems to be at risk, you can encourage that person to get help. Offering to accompany a person to an appointment with his or her primary care physician or to meet with a mental health professional also can be a supportive approach. The Centers for Disease Control and Prevention (2018f) suggests the following five steps to help a person at risk for suicide: (1) Ask the person how he or she is feeling. (2) Keep the person safe. (3) Be there for the person. (4) Help the person connect to someone who can help: the National Suicide Prevention Lifeline number is 1-800-273-8255. (5) Follow up with the person.

Psychoactive Drug Therapy

Chemicals that alter a person's affect, behavior, or cognitions are called *psychoactive drugs*. Using chemicals to improve the condition of the psychologically disordered has been hailed as one of the more significant scientific achievements of the last half of the twentieth century. Three major types of medication are used as therapy: antipsychotic drugs, antidepressant drugs, and antianxiety drugs.

Antipsychotic drugs—drugs that alleviate or eliminate psychotic symptoms.

The **antipsychotic drugs** alleviate or eliminate psychotic symptoms. **Psychotic symptoms** signal loss of contact with reality, such as delusions and hallucinations, and a gross impairment of functioning. Inappropriate affect, or total loss of affect, is also a psychotic symptom. Antipsychotic medications are primarily designed to treat schizophrenia, but they also are used to treat other disorders, including substance abuse.

Psychotic symptoms—symptoms involving loss of contact with reality, such as delusions and hallucinations, and a gross impairment of functioning, inappropriate affect, or total loss of affect.

The breakthrough in the use of antipsychotic drugs came with the introduction of *chlorpromazine* in the early 1950s. A French neurosurgeon, Henri Laborit, was looking for a drug that would calm his patients before surgery so that they would recover better after surgery. A drug company gave Laborit *chlorpromazine*. It worked even better than anyone expected. Laborit convinced colleagues to try the drug on their more agitated patients, who were suffering from psychological disorders. The experiments met with great success, and by the late 1950s, the drug was widely used in North America and Europe. Not only did "Laborit's tranquilizer" produce a calm and relaxed state in his patients, but it also significantly reduced psychotic symptoms in other patients.

The drug revolution had begun. After the success of *chlorpromazine*, drug companies started the search in earnest for drugs to improve the plight of the mentally ill. Because its side effects tend to be severe, *chlorpromazine* is seldom used today to treat psychotic symptoms. However, many drugs have been developed that work in essentially the same way (e.g., *Haldol*, *Prolixin*). Because of their reduced side effects, second-generation antipsychotics are preferred (e.g., *Abilify*, *Latuda*, *Risperdal*, and *Zyprexa*) (Patel, Cherian, Gohil, & Atkinson, 2014). These drugs are most effective in treating the positive symptoms of schizophrenia: delusions, hallucinations, and bizarre behaviors.

A study by Jeffrey Lieberman and his colleagues reported on a large-scale comprehensive study of antipsychotic medications. The study involved 1,432 patients at 57 treatment sites and found that newer drugs—although seven-to-ten times more expensive—were no more effective than older, generic antipsychotics. The one exception was olanzapine (marketed as *Zyprexa*), but even with this medication, patients experienced dramatic weight gain, a higher risk of diabetes, and 64 percent of patients stopped taking the drug after 18 months (Lieberman et al., 2005). A follow-up study on the use of antipsychotic medications at 50 sites in 14 countries came to the same general conclusion: Medications can be very helpful (particularly for patients suffering their first episode of schizophrenia), but side effects often lead to the discontinuation of the drugs, and the newer, so-called "second-generation" antipsychotics are no more effective than the older medications (Kahn et al., 2008).

Nothing has had a more profound impact on the treatment of persons with severe psychological disorders than the introduction of psychoactive drugs.

Antipsychotic drugs can suppress the symptoms of schizophrenia, but the question is still worth asking: Are they in any sense curing the disorder? In the usual sense of the word *cure*, they are not. Symptom-free patients released from institutions soon stop using their medication. After the medication stops, the psychotic symptoms resume. One large review of 66 studies of 4,365 patients found that relapse was highly associated with sudden withdrawal from antipsychotic medication (Gilbert et al., 1995).

Antidepressant drugs elevate the mood of persons who are depressed. Examples of these drugs include *Prozac*, *Lexapro*, and *Zoloft*. Some antidepressant medications also may be useful in treating disorders other than depression (e.g., panic disorder and generalized anxiety disorder). An antidepressant drug that has little or no effect on one person may cause severe, unpleasant side effects in another and yet have markedly beneficial effects for a third person. Antidepressant drugs can elevate the mood of many depressed individuals, but these drugs will have no effect on people who are not depressed; that is, antidepressants do not produce a euphoric high in people who are already in a normal or good mood.

Antidepressant drugs—drugs that elevate the mood of persons who are depressed.

At the present time, there are many antidepressant drugs that appear to do the same thing. Although the net effect of each may be the same, each produces its effect in a slightly different way. Not everyone responds to the same drug in the same way. What works for one person may not work for another; prescriptions are often made simply on the basis of avoiding unpleasant side effects (Hanson et al., 2005; Zimmerman et al., 2005).

Antidepressant medications typically take two to four weeks to show any benefit. Their full effect may take six weeks, and they need to be taken long-term to prevent recurrence of the depression. Some antidepressant drugs also require patients to follow a strict diet and take the medications in the proper amounts on a fairly rigid schedule.

Unlike antipsychotics, when antidepressants are effective, they may actually *cure* depression rather than just suppress its symptoms. In other words, the changes in mood caused by the drugs may outlast use of the drug itself. Most treatment plans envision gradually reducing the antidepressant as the person breaks free of the depression. For persons with depression who do not respond to drugs presently available, electroconvulsive therapy may be effective. In addition, the pace of innovation in this area means new drugs are constantly being tested.

Antianxiety drugs—drugs (tranquilizers) that help reduce the felt aspect of anxiety.

The **antianxiety drugs** (tranquilizers) help reduce the felt aspect of anxiety. Some antianxiety drugs (e.g., *Miltown* or *Equanil*), are simply muscle relaxants. When muscular tension is reduced, a person usually reports feeling calm and at ease. Benzodiazepines (e.g., *Librium*, *Valium*, and *Xanax*) are the other major variety of antianxiety drugs. These are among the most commonly prescribed of all drugs (Cloos & Ferreira, 2009). They increase the effectiveness of a chemical that normally functions in the brain to reduce overall brain activity, which in turn inhibits all sorts of reactions. They help anxious people feel less anxious. Initially, the only negative side effects appear to be slight drowsiness, blurred vision, and slight impairment of coordination.

Unfortunately, the tranquilizing effect of antianxiety drugs is not long-lasting. Patients can fall into a pattern of relying on the medications to alleviate even the slightest fears and worries. A far more serious potential side effect is dependency and addiction. A major danger of antianxiety medications is the very fact that they are so effective. As long as a person can avoid the unpleasant feelings of anxiety simply by taking a pill, that person has little motivation to seek out and deal with the actual cause of the anxiety.

STUDY CHECK

What are the antipsychotic medications, and how effective are they?
What medications are used to treat persons with depressive disorders?
What are the antianxiety medications, and how effective are they?

THINKING CRITICALLY

What practical steps can be taken to help patients taking psychoactive drugs to continue to take them in spite of some very unpleasant side effects?

Psychotherapy Techniques

Decades ago, only 13 percent of the population sought psychotherapy at any time in their lives (Wang et al., 2005). As of 2018, around 17 percent of the U.S. population was currently receiving treatment for mental illness. Another 16 percent had treatment in the past but were no longer receiving treatment (Statista, 2018). Americans seek help from mental health professionals twice as often as they visit internists. Let's consider a few of the techniques or approaches that psychotherapists may employ. Please understand that summarizing a complex psychotherapeutic approach in a few short paragraphs can hardly do justice to the intricacies of these techniques. About all that we can do here is provide some sense or "flavor" of these psychotherapies while trying not to trivialize them.

Psychoanalytic Approaches

This approach begins our short list for two reasons: (a) nearly everyone has heard of Freud and psychoanalysis, and (b) it was the very first attempt to treat psychological disorders without any reliance on medications. In 1881, Sigmund Freud graduated from the University of Vienna Medical School. From the start, he was interested in what were then called *nervous disorders* (physical disorders or symptoms with no medical cause). Freud's method for treating these disorders was to have the patients talk about everything relevant to their lives in order to get at the underlying conflicts that were causing their symptoms. Freud's method became known as the "talking cure," better known as psychoanalysis.

Psychoanalysis is based on several assumptions, most of them having to do with conflict and the unconscious mind. For Freud, life is often a struggle to resolve conflicts between naturally opposing forces. The sexual, biological, aggressive strivings of the id are often in conflict with the superego, which is associated with being overly cautious and experiencing guilt. The strivings of the id also can be in conflict with the rational, reality-based ego, which may be called upon to mediate between the id and the superego. Anxiety-producing conflicts that go unresolved are repressed; that is, through the process of **repression,** they are forced out of awareness and into the unconscious mind. Conflicts and anxiety-producing traumas of childhood can be expected to produce symptoms of psychological disturbance later in life.

According to Freud, the way to rid oneself of anxiety is to enter the unconscious, identify the details of the repressed, anxiety-producing conflict, bring it out into the open, and then work to resolve it. The first step is to gain insight into the true nature of a patient's problems; only then can problem solving begin. Thus, the goals of Freudian psychoanalysis are insight and resolution of repressed conflict.

Psychoanalysis with Sigmund Freud was a time-consuming, often tedious process of aided self-examination. The major task for the patient was to talk openly and honestly about all aspects of his or her life, from early childhood memories to the dreams of the present. The main task of the therapist/analyst was to interpret what was being expressed by the patient, always on the lookout for clues to possible repressed conflict. Once identified, the patient and the analyst could work together to resolve the conflicts underlying the symptoms that brought the patient to analysis in the first place. Freudian psychoanalysis used several specific techniques to help uncover repressed conflicts.

Ever since Freud's early days of psychoanalysis, psychotherapy is rightfully thought of as "talk therapy," but listening plays an equally important role.

The technique of **free association** was a standard in psychoanalysis. Patients were to say aloud whatever came into their minds. Sometimes the analyst would provide a word to start a chain of freely flowing associations. To free associate the way Freud wanted was not easy. Many sessions were often required for patients to learn the technique. Patients were not to edit their associations but were to be completely honest and say whatever popped into their consciousness. Many people are uncomfortable, at least initially, sharing their private, innermost thoughts and desires with anyone, much less a stranger. Here is where the Freudian couch came in. To help his patients relax, Freud would have them lie down, be comfortable, and avoid eye contact with him. The job of the analyst through all of this was to try to interpret the apparently free-flowing verbal responses, always looking for expressions of unconscious desires and conflicts.

During the course of psychoanalysis, the analyst listens very carefully to what the patient says. The analyst also listens carefully for what the patient does not say. Freud believed that **resistance**—the unwillingness or inability to discuss freely some aspect of one's life—was a significant process in the analysis. Resistance can show itself in many ways, from simply avoiding the mention of some topic to joking about matters as being inconsequential, to disrupting a session when a particular topic comes up for discussion, to missing appointments altogether.

Say, for example, that over the last six months in psychoanalysis a patient has talked freely about a wide variety of subjects, including early childhood memories and all of her family members—all, that is, except her older brother. She has talked about all sorts of private experiences, some of them sexual, some of them pleasant, some unpleasant. But after six months of talking, she has not said one thing about her older brother. Her analyst, noting this possible resistance, suggests that during the next visit, he would like to hear about her older brother. Then, for the first time since analysis began, the patient misses her next appointment. She comes to the following appointment, but ten minutes late. The analyst may now suspect a problem with the relationship between the patient and her older brother, a problem that may have begun in childhood and been repressed ever since. Of

Repression—the process in which anxiety-producing unresolved conflicts are forced out of awareness and into the unconscious mind.

Free association—a technique in psychoanalysis where patients say aloud whatever comes into their minds.

Resistance—the unwillingness or inability to discuss freely some aspect of one's life during psychoanalysis.

course, there may be no problem at all, but for psychoanalysis to be successful, potential resistance needs to be broken down and investigated.

Analyzing patient dreams is an important aspect of psychoanalysis. Freud referred to dreams as the "royal road" to the unconscious level of the mind. Freud often trained his patients to recall and record their dreams in great detail. He analyzed dreams at two levels: *manifest content*, the dream as recalled and reported, and *latent content*, the dream as a symbolic representation of the contents of the unconscious. Latent content was usually analyzed to identify some sort of unconscious wish fulfillment. Symbolism hidden in the latent content of dreams has been one of the most controversial aspects of Freud's theories. Freud believed that true feelings, motives, and desires might be camouflaged in a dream. For example, someone who reports a dream about suffocating under a huge pile of pillows might be expressing feelings about parental over-protectiveness. Someone who dreams about driving into an endless tunnel and becoming lost might be expressing fears or concerns of a sexual nature. The analyst, Freud argued, was to interpret dreams in terms of whatever insights they could provide about the true nature of the patient's unconscious mind.

Source: Sergey Nivens/Shutterstock.

In order to get at the contents of his patients' unconscious minds, Freud would interpret their dreams, focusing not only on the content of those dreams as they were reported (manifest content), but also on what those dreams might symbolize (latent content).

Sigmund Freud died in 1939, but his approach to psychotherapy did not die with him. It has been modified (as Freud himself modified it over the years), but it remains true to the basic thrust of Freudian psychoanalysis.

Early in the twentieth century, Freudian psychoanalysis was the *only* form of psychotherapy, and through the 1940s and 1950s, it still was the therapy of choice. In recent years, psychoanalysis has become less common, but it remains a viable option for many therapists (Gabbard, Gunderson, & Fonagy 2002).

How has the Freudian system of therapy changed? Probably the most significant change since Freud's practice is the concern for shortening the length of analysis. Now psychotherapists talk about time-limited, or short-form, psychoanalytic therapy. Today's analysts take a more active role than did Freud, using interviews and discussions. Modern psychoanalysts tend to spend more time exploring the present, and a bit less on early childhood experiences. For example, a patient may come for analysis complaining about feelings of depression and anger to the point that the analyst believes there is a real and present danger that the patient might harm himself or herself or even commit suicide. The thrust of therapy is in the here and now, dealing with the patient's current anger and depression until the analyst is convinced the danger of self-harm has abated. Despite the modernization of psychoanalysis, it appears to have reached a crisis point (Richards, 2015). According to Richards, psychoanalysis has suffered on a number of fronts due to: a perception that it is unscientific, high costs (combined with limits on insurance coverage), an aging analyst population, fewer young analysts being trained, and ideological rigidity. If psychoanalysis is to survive, it may have to evolve (yet again).

STUDY CHECK

What is the essence of Freudian psychoanalysis, and how is the process different today from when it was practiced by Freud?

THINKING CRITICALLY

Do you remember your dreams? Are your dreams in any way symbolic of some content in your unconscious mind? Can you think of any one dream for which that might be the case?

Humanistic Approaches

There are many different types of humanistic psychotherapies. What they all have in common is a concern for self-examination, personal growth, and development. The goal of these therapies is not to uncover deep-seated conflicts, but to foster psychological growth and help a person take full advantage of life's opportunities. Based on the premise that people can take charge of themselves and their futures, that they can grow and change, therapy is directed at assisting with these processes.

Client-centered therapy, also called Rogerian therapy after its founder, Carl Rogers, best typifies the humanistic approach. As its name suggests, the client is the center of the therapeutic interaction. Given his medical training, Freud called the people he dealt with patients. Rogers never used the term patient, and before his death in 1987 began using the term *person-centered* rather than client-centered to describe his approach to therapy. In Rogers' view, therapy provides a special opportunity for a person to engage in self-discovery. That is to say, that a goal of client-centered therapy is to help the individual to grow and develop to the best of his or her potential.

What are the characteristics of client-centered therapy? Again, there are variants, but the following ideas characterize a client-centered approach. The focus is on the present, not the past or childhood. The focus is on affect or feelings, not beliefs or cognitions; that is, you are more likely to hear, "How do you feel about that?" than "What do you think about that?" The therapist will attempt to reflect, or mirror—not interpret—how a client is feeling (using statements such as, "You seem angry," or "Does that make you feel sad?"). This so-called *reflective listening*, assessing and reflecting the true nature of a client's feelings, is not easy to do. It requires that the therapist be an active listener and be empathic, and be able to understand and share the essence of another's feelings.

Most of the positive regard that we get in this world is conditional: If, then. If you behave as you should, then you will be well thought of. If you do what I ask, then I will give you a reward. In client-centered therapy, the therapist tries to express **unconditional positive regard**—the expression of being accepting and non-critical. "I will not be critical. If that is the way you feel, then that is the way you feel. Anything you say in here is okay, so long as you are being honest—not honest with me; that doesn't matter. Are you being honest with yourself?"

Unconditional positive regard—the expression of being accepting and non-critical in humanistic therapy.

STUDY CHECK

What are the major features of client-centered therapy?

THINKING CRITICALLY

Would you be a good, active listener? Give it a try, remembering that your job is to reflect and mirror what the speaker is saying while withholding your own opinions and assessments.

Behavioral Approaches

There is no one behavior therapy; it is a collection of several techniques. What unites these techniques is that they are "methods of psychotherapeutic change founded on principles of learning established in the psychological laboratory" (Wolpe, 1981, p. 159). The main assumption of behavior therapy is that maladaptive behaviors are learned, and thus they can be unlearned. There are many principles of learning and many psychological disorders to which such methods and principles can be applied. In this section, we list a few aspects of learning theory that have become part of behavior therapy.

Systematic desensitization, the application of classical conditioning to alleviate feelings of anxiety, particularly those associated with specific phobias, is one of the first applications of learning theory to meet with success. It was introduced by Joseph Wolpe (1958) in the late 1950s, although others had used similar procedures earlier. Systematic desensitization is basically a matter of teaching a person first to relax totally and then to remain relaxed as he or she thinks about or is exposed to ever-increasing levels of stimuli that produce anxiety. If the person can remain calm and relaxed, that response can be conditioned to replace the anxious or fearful response previously associated with a particular stimulus.

A form of behavior therapy called *exposure and response prevention* has shown promise as a treatment for obsessive-compulsive disorder (OCD), a disorder that is usually resistant to psychotherapy. In one clinic, patients are exposed for two hours, five days a week, for three weeks to whatever stimulus situation elicits obsessive thinking or compulsions. They are asked to vividly imagine the consequences they fear without engaging in their usual compulsive or obsessive routine; the procedure is also repeated in homework assignments. This is followed by a maintenance program of phone calls and clinic visits. For example, a patient who is obsessed with dirt and germs is told to sit on the floor and imagine that she has become ill because of insufficient washing and cleaning. For the first two weeks, she must not wash her hands (at all) and can take a shower for only ten minutes every other day. This program claims that 75 to 83 percent of the patients who complete the regimen show significant and lasting improvement (Foa, 1995).

It is sometimes difficult to imagine why someone would agree to aversion therapy. Imagine this scenario: A young man is virtually unable to say "no" to alcohol. Two or three times a week, he drinks so much he passes out in a stupor. There may be many ways to explore why this young man has a problem with alcohol, but it may be more important at first simply to find a way to get him to stop drinking. Aversion therapy may be the answer.

Aversion therapy is another example of learning applied to solving psychological problems. In aversion therapy, a stimulus that may be harmful but that produces a "pleasant" response is paired with an aversive, painful stimulus until the original stimulus is avoided. For example, every time you put a cigarette in your mouth, a painful shock is delivered to your lip. Every time you take a drink of alcohol, you get violently sick to your stomach from a nausea-producing drug. Every time a child molester is shown a picture of a young child, he gets an electric shock.

Techniques of aversion therapy do not sound like the sort of things anyone would agree to voluntarily. Many people do, however, volunteer for such treatments, for two reasons: First, aversion therapy is very effective at suppressing a specific behavior—at least for a while, and second, it is seen as the lesser of two evils. (Shocks and nausea-producing drugs are not much fun, but people see continuing their inappropriate, self-destructive, behaviors as even more dangerous in the long run.) Aversion therapy, in any form, is not commonly practiced, and when it is, it usually tends to suppress behaviors for only a relatively short time. During that time, other techniques may be used in an attempt to bring about a more lasting change in behavior. In other words, aversion therapy is seldom effective when used alone; it is usually used in conjunction with other therapy.

Contingency management and *contingency contracting* borrow from the learning principles of operant conditioning. The idea is to have a person appreciate the consequences of his or her behaviors. Appropriate behaviors lead to rewards and the chance to do valued things, whereas inappropriate behaviors do not lead to reinforcement and provide fewer opportunities.

In many cases, these procedures work well. As operant conditioning would predict, their effectiveness is a function of the extent to which the therapist has control over the situation. If the therapist can manage the control of rewards and punishments (called *contingency management*), he or she stands a good chance of modifying the client's behavior. For example, in an institutional setting, if a patient (e.g., a severely disturbed person with schizophrenia) engages in the appropriate response (leaving her room to go to dinner), then the patient gets something she really wants (a chance to watch TV for an extra hour). In an outpatient setting, the therapist tries to arrange the situation so that the client learns to reinforce his or her own behaviors when they are appropriate.

Contingency contracting amounts to establishing a contract with a client so that exhibiting certain behaviors (preparing dinner) results in certain rewards (watching TV). In many cases, contingency contracting involves establishing a token economy. What this means is that the person is first taught that some token—a checker, a poker chip, or just a check mark on a pad—can be saved. When enough tokens are accumulated, they are cashed in for something of value to the person. With contracting, the value of a token for a specific behavior is spelled out ahead of time. Because control over the environment of the learner is most complete in such circumstances, this technique is particularly effective in institutions and with young children.

STUDY CHECK

What are some of the techniques that qualify as behavior therapies?

THINKING CRITICALLY

For which psychological disorders do you think that behavior therapy is least likely to be effective?

Cognitive Approaches

Cognitive therapists believe that what matters most is a client's beliefs, thoughts, perceptions, and attitudes about himself or herself and the environment (Weinland, 1996). The major principle is that to change how a client feels and acts, therapy should first be directed at changing how that client thinks. The goal of treatment is not only to produce a change in the way the client thinks and behaves but also to teach the client how those changes were achieved. That is, the goal is not so much to provide a "cure" as it is to develop a strategy that the client can apply to a wide range of contexts and experiences (Hollon, Shelton, & Loosen, 1991). As with the other approaches to psychotherapy, cognitive therapy has several varieties.

Rational-emotive therapy (RET) is associated with Albert Ellis (1970, 1997). Its basic premise is that psychological problems arise when people try to interpret what happens in the world (a cognitive activity) on the basis of irrational beliefs. Ellis describes the therapy's assumptions in this way, "Rational-emotive therapy (RET) hypothesizes that people largely disturb themselves by thinking in a self-defeating, illogical, and unrealistic manner—especially by escalating their natural preferences and desires into absolutistic, dogmatic musts and commands on themselves, others, and their environmental conditions" (Ellis, 1987, p. 364).

When compared to person-centered techniques, rational-emotive therapy is quite directive. Ellis (1991) takes exception with techniques designed to help a person feel better without providing useful strategies by which the person can get better. In rational-emotive therapy, the therapist takes an active role in interpreting a client's system of beliefs and encourages active change. Therapists often act as role models and make homework assignments that help clients bring their expectations and perceptions

Cognitive therapist—a therapist who believes that what matters most is a client's beliefs, thoughts, perceptions, and attitudes about himself or herself and the environment.

Rational-emotive therapy (RET)—a therapy with the basic premise that psychological problems arise when people try to interpret what happens in the world (a cognitive activity) on the basis of irrational beliefs.

in line with reality. Ellis (1995) identifies some of the irrational beliefs that lead to psychological problems:

- That one must always do tasks well because of a great desire to perform tasks well
- That one must always have the approval of others due to a strong need for approval
- That one must be loved by everyone for everything done
- That it is better to avoid problems than face them
- That one must always maintain perfect self-control

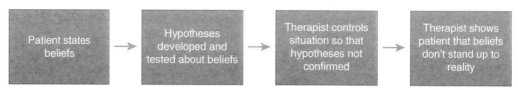

FIGURE 13.1 Steps in Cognitive Restructuring Therapy

Cognitive restructuring therapy—a cognitive therapy that is less confrontational and direct than rational emotive therapy.

Although similar in goals to RET, **cognitive restructuring therapy** is less confrontational and direct than RET. Cognitive restructuring theory is associated with Aaron Beck (1976, 1991, 1995). The steps involved in cognitive restructuring therapy are shown in **Figure 13.1**.

Beck's assumption is that considerable psychological distress stems from a few simple, but misguided, beliefs (cognitions). According to Beck, people with disorders (particularly those related to depression, for which cognitive restructuring was first designed) share certain characteristics:

- They tend to have very negative self-images. They do not value themselves or what they do.
- They tend to take a very negative view of life experiences.
- They over-generalize. For example, having failed one test, a person comes to believe that there is no way he or she can do college work, withdraws from school, and looks for a job, even though he or she believes that no one would offer a job to someone who is such a failure and a college dropout.
- They seek out experiences that reinforce their negative expectations. The student in the preceding example may apply for a job as a stockbroker or a law clerk. Lacking even minimal experience, he or she will not be offered either job and, thus, will confirm his or her own worthlessness.
- They tend to hold a rather dismal outlook for the future.
- They tend to avoid seeing the bright side of any experience.

In cognitive restructuring therapy, the patient is given opportunities to test or demonstrate his or her beliefs. The patient and therapist make up a list of hypotheses based on patient beliefs and assumptions and then test these hypotheses. The therapist tries to control the situation so that events do not confirm the patient's negative beliefs. Given the hypothesis "Nobody cares about me," the therapist need find only one person who cares to refute it. The therapist gradually leads the patient to the self-discovery that the negative hypotheses do not stand up to testing in the real world. Cognitive restructuring therapy has proven very successful in the treatment of depression, although it has been extended to cover a wide range of psychological disorders (Beck & Freeman, 1990).

Cognitive-behavior therapy (CBT)—a cognitive therapy that has a joint focus: Change the way that you have been behaving, and change the way you interpret and think about the situations in which behavior change is required.

Cognitive-behavior therapy combines the essential features of the two approaches that give it its name. **Cognitive-behavior therapy (CBT)** has a joint focus: Change the way that you have been behaving, and change the way you interpret and think about the situations in which behavior change is required. The notion is that "learning principles and cognitions interact to influence a person's behavior" (Kearney & Trull, 2012, p. 39).

CBT may include determining "problem ownership"—a matter of agreeing on who really has the problem. For example, Cathy is upset because some girls she would like to be friends with are not being very friendly in return. Cathy begins to believe that she is "unworthy" and not a nice person simply because she is scorned by this group. A cognitive-behavior therapist might ask Cathy, "Well, whose problem is this? You're a nice person; you are worthy, but if this snooty little group doesn't think so, that's their problem, not yours." Cathy is challenged not only to change the way she thinks about herself and this group of girls but also to change her behaviors regarding them. CBT can also be applied to family relationships. For example, Mom and Dad are upset that their 24-year-old son still lives at home, where he does illegal drugs with loud and obnoxious friends. In determining problem ownership, a cognitive-behavior therapist might ask these questions: Whose problem is this? Is this your home? Do you use illegal drugs? Your son is how old? Have you reported him to the police? Can you get him to come to talk with me?"

Cognitive-behavior therapy has proven to be as useful, if not more useful, than virtually any other treatment for depression—including therapy provided by anti-depressant medications. And the positive effects of CBT appear to have longer lasting effects than those provided by medications. The same beneficial effects for CBT also have been found in treatments for panic disorder and for cases of bulimia nervosa (Baker, McFall, & Shoham, 2008). Indeed, CBT seems to be the most popular approach to the nonmedical treatment of psychological disorders (Pilgram, 2011).

STUDY CHECK

What are the essential characteristics of the cognitive approaches to psychotherapy?

THINKING CRITICALLY

Do you hold any irrational, potentially defeating cognitions? What might they be?

Group therapy—a therapy technique in which several people are receiving therapy together.

Family therapy—a therapy technique focusing on the roles, interdependence, and communication skills of family members.

Group Approaches

Many patients profit from some type of group therapy, and many therapists use the technique. As the name implies, **group therapy** involves several people receiving therapy together. If nothing else, group therapy can be less expensive than individual psychotherapy: One therapist can interact with several people at once (Mackenzie, 1997). In standard group therapy, a therapist brings clients together and guides them while they share their feelings and experiences. Most groups are informal, and no particular form of psychotherapy is dominant.

Group therapy has several benefits for the participants, including the awareness that "I'm not the only one with problems." In addition, the sense of support that a participant can get from someone else with problems is sometimes even greater than that afforded by a therapist alone—a sort of "she really knows from experience the pain that I'm going through" logic. And getting involved in helping someone else with a problem is, in itself, therapeutic. Group therapy also teaches participants new, more effective, ways of "presenting" themselves to others (McRoberts, Burlingame, & Hoag, 1998). Group approaches are particularly well-suited for situations involving alcohol and substance abuse (Kearney & Trull, 2012).

A popular group approach is **family therapy**, which focuses on the roles, interdependence, and communication skills of

In some instances, group therapy can be very helpful. For one thing, it usually is less expensive than individual sessions with a therapist. It can give a patient the awareness that he or she is not the only person with a problem, and helping someone else who is having difficulties can, in itself, be therapeutic.

family members. Family therapy often starts after one member of a family enters psychotherapy. After discussing that person's problems for a while, other family members join the therapy sessions. Getting the family members involved in therapy benefits patients with a wide range of disorders, including alcoholism, phobias, depression, eating disorders, bipolar disorder, and schizophrenia (Eisler et al., 1997; Miklowitz et al., 2003; Schmidt & Asen, 2005).

Two related assumptions underlie a family therapy approach. Family therapists assume that each family member is a part of a system (the family unit), and his or her feelings, thoughts, and behaviors influence the other family members. As a result, a change (even a therapeutic one) in one member of the family system that does not involve the other members of the family unit will not last long. Unsupported changes are especially short-lived when the initial problem appears to be with a child or adolescent. We say "appears to be" because other family members have at least contributed to the troublesome symptoms of the child or adolescent. A therapist will have a difficult time bringing about significant and lasting change in a child whose parents refuse to become involved in therapy.

Family therapists recognize that some difficulties may arise from improper methods of family communication (Satir, 1967). Quite often, a family member develops false beliefs about the feelings and needs of other family members. The goal of therapy in such cases, then, is to meet with the family in a group setting to foster and encourage open expressions of feelings and desires. For example, it may be very helpful for an adolescent to learn that her parents are upset and anxious about work-related stress and family finances. The adolescent may have assumed all along that her parents yelled at her and at each other because of something *she* was doing. The parents may not have shared their concern over money with the adolescent for fear that it would upset her.

STUDY CHECK

What is "group therapy," and what are its potential benefits?

THINKING CRITICALLY

Imagine that you have a problem and have been invited by your therapist to join a group to talk about it. How would you feel about sharing your problems with others?

Evaluating Psychotherapy

Evaluating psychotherapy with carefully controlled experiments has proven difficult: Is psychotherapy effective? Compared to what? Is one variety of psychotherapy better than another? (Baker, McFall, & Shoham, 2008; Kazdin & Blasé, 2011).

Before reviewing the data, consider just a few of the problems encountered when doing research on the effectiveness of psychotherapy. First, little information is available on how people might have responded without treatment. In other words, there is seldom an adequate baseline, or control group, for comparison. Psychologists do know that sometimes there is a spontaneous remission of symptoms. Sometimes people just seem to "get better" without a therapist. To say that people get better on their own is seldom literally true—there are many factors that can contribute to improving one's mental health, even if one is not "officially" in psychotherapy. People may get better because a source of stress is removed—a nagging parent moves out of state, an aggravating boss gets transferred, or an interpersonal relationship begins that provides missing support.

Second, researchers do not agree on what is meant by recovery, or cure. These terms take on different meanings depending upon the goal of therapy. For some, recovery means the absence of observable symptoms for a specified period of time. For others, the goal of psychotherapy is different: the self-report of "feeling better," personal growth, a relatively permanent change in behavior, insight into deep-seated conflicts, or a restructuring of cognitions. In the same vein, who judges whether or not improvement, much less recovery, has occurred? Should the therapist or the client be the judge?

Despite these problems in designing studies to evaluate the outcome of psychotherapy, researchers have done quality studies. Most have focused on the effectiveness of just one technique, and the results generally have been very positive.

Psychotherapy is certainly effective when compared to doing nothing: "By about 1980 a consensus of sorts was reached that psychotherapy, as a generic treatment process, was demonstrably more effective than no treatment" (VandenBos, 1986, p. 111). Tested over nearly every possible kind of psychological disorder, and without distinguishing one type of treatment from another, psychotherapies produce significant effects. In general, after six months of therapeutic intervention, nearly three-quarters of those persons seeking help from psychotherapists show improvement, and no one type of treatment is significantly more effective than any other (Nathan, Stuart, & Dolan, 2000; Shadish et al., 2000). The authors of one review of research on effectiveness put it this way, "Copious evidence already exists for the proposition that psychotherapy in general is effective for clients in general" (Chambless & Ollendick, 2001, p. 699).

More treatment appears to be better than less treatment, and most improvement is made early on (Hansen, Lambert, & Forman, 2002). However, in one study, time-limited psychotherapy that actively involved family members in dealing with the problems of children was as effective as therapy that used an unlimited number of sessions (Smyrnios & Kirby, 1993; Sechrest & Walsh, 1997). Whether short-term or long-term intervention will be best is often a function of known variables, such as a client's awareness of his or her problems, willingness to change, and the extent to which the client lives in a supportive environment.

Research also confirms that the sooner therapy begins, the better the likely outcome (Wyatt & Henter, 1997). Some therapists are simply more effective than others, regardless of what type of therapy is practiced (Shaw et al., 1999; Trepka et al., 2004). A psychotherapist should be open, warm, and supportive. The qualities of the therapist are important, but so are the qualities of the patient. Regardless of disorder, some people are better patients than others. What makes a good patient? The brighter, the more insightful, and the more motivated to change the patient is, the more effective any therapy.

STUDY CHECK

Is psychotherapy an effective treatment for psychological disorders?

THINKING CRITICALLY

As a potential consumer of psychotherapy, which would matter more to you—the kind of therapy offered or the characteristics of the therapist?

Group Differences in the Therapy Process

As noted in this chapter, psychotherapy can be effective in helping people deal with mental illness. Before a person can benefit from therapy, regardless of type, the person must seek help. Once in therapy, the person must feel comfortable enough with his or her therapist to benefit from therapy. Unfortunately, a majority (57 percent) of people with serious mental illness do not receive treatment (National Institute of Mental Health, 2017). Globally, around 70 percent of mentally ill individuals receive no treatment for mental illness (Henderson, Evans-Lacko, & Thornicroft, 2013). Henderson et al. identify four reasons why a person does not seek treatment: lack of knowledge to identify mental illness symptoms, ignorance about how to get treatment, prejudice against individuals with mental illness, and expecting to be discriminated against because of mental illness.

One factor that relates to a person's receiving treatment for mental illness is his or her race or ethnicity. **Figure 13.2** shows the percentage of individuals from various racial/ethnic groups who received treatment for mental illness in the United States in 2016 (National Institute of Mental Health, 2017). As you can see, whites are most likely to receive treatment and Asians least likely. Gender also plays a role, with more females (48.9 percent) receiving treatment than males (33.9 percent) (National Institute of Mental Health, 2017). In one study of prison inmates (Drapalski, Youman, Stuewig, & Tangney, 2009), female inmates were more likely than male inmates to report symptoms of mental illness and seek treatment. There are also racial/ethnic differences in seeking help for mental illness. Luca, Blosnich, Hentschel, King, and Amen (2016) report that blacks and Latinos are less likely to seek help than non-Hispanic whites.

Why are there group differences in seeking help for mental illness? The gender difference may be accounted for by gender-role expectations. Generally, males are socialized to be more independent than women. Women tend to place more emphasis on social relationships than men. This could lead women to be more willing to seek help than men. With respect to ethnicity, the differences observed may relate to differing attitudes about seeking help among the members of different groups. For example, in one study (Jimenez, Bartels, Cardenas, & Alegría, 2013), attitudes toward mental illness were measured among black, white, Asian, and Latino participants. Jimenez et al. found that Asians expressed more shame or embarrassment about having a mental illness than whites. Jimenez et al. suggest that this is consistent with the emphasis placed on honor and saving face among Asian cultures. They found no difference between black and white participants. However, other research has found that blacks perceive greater stigma attached to mental illness than whites (Conner et al., 2010).

Next, let's explore whether there are differences in therapy outcomes for individuals from different demographic groups. Women appear to benefit from therapy more than men. In one study of patients with

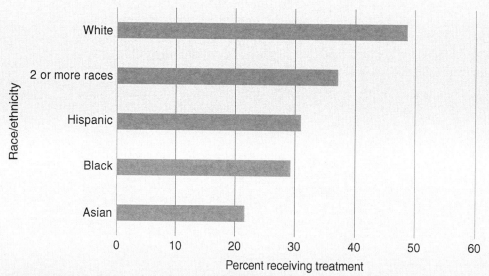

FIGURE 13.2 Percentage of Mentally Ill Individuals Receiving Treatment in the United States in 2016

Source: National Institute of Mental Health (2017).

coronary artery disease, women showed a greater reduction in vital exhaustion (a measure of fatigue, irritability, and feelings of demoralization) than men (Deter et al., 2018). These patients did not differ significantly in pretreatment levels of vital exhaustion. In another study, alcoholic women with depression or bipolar disorder benefitted from treatment more than men (Farren, Snee, & McElroy, 2011). Cottone, Drucker, and Javier (2002) assessed treatment outcomes for men and women with either an anxiety disorder or depression. Specifically, they looked at how long a client stayed in therapy (intake screening only, less than three months of therapy, more than three months of therapy, and completed therapy). Cottone et al. found that compared with men, women were more likely to advance in therapy and were more likely to complete therapy. However, there were no significant differences between male and female clients in the reduction of symptom severity. Research shows that women benefit more than men from the treatment of posttraumatic stress disorder. In this case, women show a greater reduction in stress-related symptoms than men (Békés, Beaulieu-Prévost, Guay, Belleville, & Marchand, 2016; Wade et al., 2016).

There are also race/ethnicity differences in treatment outcomes. In one study, whites with serious mental illness showed a greater reduction in symptoms than blacks when mental health services were received (Chinman, Rosenheck, & Lam, 2000). It should be noted that black patients started out with more severe symptoms than white patients. Eack and Newhill (2012) also found that black patients with serious mental illness showed less improvement than white patients. One reason why blacks may show less improvement than whites is that they are more likely to live in poverty and in high-stress conditions (Eack & Newhill, 2012).

Chapter Summary

What is psychosurgery, and what is a prefrontal lobotomy?

Psychosurgery is any surgical technique (usually directed at the brain) designed to bring about a change in a patient's affects, behaviors, or cognitions. Psychosurgical techniques are irreversible and treatments of last resort. There are few such operations performed these days, but exceptions include the split-brain procedure for epilepsy and the cingulotomy as a treatment for obsessive-compulsive disorder. A lobotomy was a commonly used psychosurgical technique for at least two decades. It involved severing the major connections between the prefrontal cortex and lower brain centers. The theory behind the surgery was that the prefrontal lobes influenced the more basic emotional centers in the lower brain. Often the surgery was successful in reducing a patient's violent emotions. It was used as a measure of last resort because of the potential for serious side effects. Prefrontal lobotomies are no longer performed because other, safer, reversible treatment options are available.

What is ECT, and why is it still being used?

ECT stands for electroconvulsive, or shock, therapy. In this treatment, a controlled brain seizure is produced with an electric current. Upon regaining consciousness, the patient has no memory of the procedure. Although there may be negative side effects, particularly with prolonged or repeated use, the technique is demonstrably safe and very useful for many patients as a means of reducing or even eliminating severe depression. Although it is not yet clear why ECT has the beneficial results that it does, it is commonly used because it is effective and carries little risk. ECT is particularly useful for those patients who do not respond to antidepressant medications.

What are the antipsychotic medications, and how effective are they?

Antipsychotic drugs are used to reduce or control psychotic symptoms—characterized by a loss of contact with reality and a gross impairment of functioning. These drugs are used primarily to treat schizophrenia. The first antipsychotic drug was chlorpromazine, first used as a drug to calm patients before surgery. It was found to be effective in treating some patients with mental disorders. The use of these drugs has steadily increased. Most of these drugs can act to relieve positive and negative psychotic symptoms of schizophrenia. Although these medications are effective, they can have very unpleasant side effects. Although they can reduce or eliminate symptoms, antipsychotic drugs cannot be said to cure a disorder like schizophrenia because symptoms return when a patient stops taking the drug.

What medications are used to treat persons with depressive disorders?

Antidepressant medications are designed to reduce the experience of depression. These drugs have some potentially serious side effects. Most antidepressant drugs require from 10 to 14 days to take effect and even longer to reach therapeutic levels. When they are effective, and after continued use, they may be slowly removed without the depressive symptoms returning.

What are the antianxiety medications, and how effective are they?

The antianxiety drugs include muscle relaxants and benzodiazepines. These drugs act on the central nervous system and relieve anxiety. Short-term side effects can include drowsiness, blurred vision, and slight impairment of coordination. The antianxiety drugs tend not to have a long-term effect. A person using these medications can come to over-rely on them because they are so effective, as a result becoming dependent and addicted. When antianxiety medications are effective, a person may be much less motivated to explore the causes of the anxiety that made the medications necessary in the first place.

What is the essence of Freudian psychoanalysis, and how is the process different today from when it was practiced by Freud?

Freudian psychoanalysis is aimed at uncovering repressed conflicts (often developed in childhood) so that they can be resolved. The process involves several specific techniques. The process involves free association, in which a patient is to share anything and everything that comes to mind, without editing; an examination of resistance, in which a patient seems unwilling or unable to discuss some aspect of his or her life; and dream interpretation, in which one analyzes both the manifest and latent content for insights into the nature of the patient's unconscious mind. Although the basic principles of psychoanalysis have remained unchanged since Freud's day, some changes have evolved. There is now more effort to shorten the time frame of analysis; there is less emphasis on childhood experiences and more concern with the here and now. Present-day analysis is also more involved with current feelings and interpersonal relationships than when it was practiced by Freud.

What are the major features of client-centered therapy?

Although there are different humanistic approaches, they share a focus on self-examination, personal growth, and development. These therapies focus on factors that foster psychological growth rather than uncovering deep-seated conflicts. A major premise is that the individual can take charge of himself or herself and grow and develop. Client-centered or person-centered therapy, associated with Carl Rogers, is based on the belief that people can control their lives and solve their own problems if they can be helped to understand the true nature of their feelings. It promotes self-discovery and personal growth. The therapist reflects the client's feelings, focuses on the here and now, and tries to be empathic, actively listening to and relating to the person's feelings. Throughout therapy, the therapist provides unconditional positive regard for the client.

What are some of the techniques that qualify as behavior therapies?

Behavior therapy is a collection of several techniques that have grown out of laboratory research on principles of learning. The main premise of behavior therapy is that maladaptive behaviors are learned, so they can be unlearned. Systematic desensitization applies principles of classical conditioning to the treatment of anxiety. In systematic desensitization, a person is taught to relax totally and then to remain relaxed as he or she thinks about or is exposed to anxiety-producing stimuli. The new relaxation response becomes classically conditioned to the stimulus, replacing the anxiety reaction. Exposure and response prevention is a treatment used for obsessive-compulsive disorder. Patients are exposed to the stimulus that evokes obsessive thinking and are then told to imagine the consequences of what they fear without engaging in their usual obsessive or compulsive routine. The procedure is repeated in homework assignments followed by a maintenance program of phone calls and clinic visits. During aversion therapy, one stimulus is paired with another aversive, painful stimulus until the original stimulus is avoided. Although unpleasant, individuals still opt for aversion therapy because it is very effective in suppressing behavior and it is seen as better than the original behavior.

Contingency management involves a health professional gaining control over the rewards and punishments that control a patient's behavior. Patients can be rewarded for productive behaviors and/or punished for unproductive behaviors. In contingency contracting, a contract is established with a patient, specifying those behaviors that will be rewarded and those that will be punished. When enough rewards are accumulated, they may be traded for something the patient wants.

What are the essential characteristics of the cognitive approaches to psychotherapy?

While not denying the importance of a person's behavior, cognitive therapists focus on an individual's thoughts, perceptions, and attitudes. The major premise of cognitive therapy is that if a therapist wants to change how a patient feels, then the therapist has to change how that patient thinks. In addition, the therapist must show the patient how those changes were achieved. Rational-emotive therapy (RET) works on the premise that people with problems are operating on irrational assumptions about the world and themselves. RET is directive in its attempts to change people's cognitions. Cognitive restructuring therapy is somewhat less directive but is based on the same idea as RET. The underlying premise is that people with psychological disorders have developed negative self-images and negative views (cognitions) about the future. The therapist provides opportunities for the patient to test those negative cognitions and discover that things are not as bad as they may seem. Cognitive-behavior therapy (CBT) explicitly combines cognitive and behavioral approaches. In order to make significant, long-lasting changes in a person's cognitions, the person may very well have to make changes in his or her behaviors.

What is "group therapy," and what are its potential benefits?

In group therapy, a number of clients are brought together at the same time under the guidance of a therapist. Group meetings are generally informal, and no particular form of psychotherapy is dominant. There are potential advantages to group therapy. Interpersonal issues may be better understood and dealt with in an interpersonal situation. Participants may learn that they are not the only ones in the world with a problem. Participants may come to appreciate that others face even more difficult problems of the same nature. Participants may benefit from providing support for someone else, and the dynamics of communication can be analyzed and changed in a group setting. Family therapy is a variety of group therapy based on the assumptions that family members can be seen as part of a system in which one member (and one member's problem) affects all of the others. Family therapists recognize that psychological problems often arise because of faulty communication, and they recognize the importance of communication among family members.

Is psychotherapy an effective treatment for psychological disorders?

Scientifically evaluating the effectiveness of psychotherapy has been difficult. It is challenging to set up a standard experimental procedure with adequate control groups or baselines against which to compare the outcomes of therapy. It is even more complicated to get consensus on what is meant by recovery—or even significant progress—because the goals of therapy vary from technique to technique. Nonetheless, in general, psychotherapy is effective. It is significantly better than leaving disorders untreated. More treatment tends to be better than less, and some therapists seem to be more effective than others, regardless of the techniques being used. As with physical disorders, the sooner mental disorders are properly diagnosed and treatment begins, the better.

Key Terms

Psychosurgery (p. 278)
Lobotomy (p. 278)
Electroconvulsive therapy (ECT) (p. 280)
Antipsychotic drugs (p. 282)
Psychotic symptoms (p. 282)
Antidepressant drugs (p. 283)
Antianxiety drugs (p. 284)
Repression (p. 285)
Free association (p. 285)

Resistance (p. 285)
Unconditional positive regard (p. 287)
Cognitive therapist (p. 289)
Rational-emotive therapy (RET) (p. 289)
Cognitive restructuring therapy (p. 290)
Cognitive-behavior therapy (CBT) (p. 290)
Group therapy (p. 291)
Family therapy (p. 291)

Social Psychology

Source: sirtravelalot/Shutterstock.

Questions You Will Be Able to Answer

After reading Chapter 14, you should be able to answer the following questions:

- What do psychologists mean by social cognition?
- How do social psychologists define an attitude?
- What are the components of an attitude, and how are they related?
- How is attitude change brought about by persuasion?
- What are prejudice, stereotypes, and discrimination, and how are they related?
- What is conformity, and how was it demonstrated by Solomon Asch?
- What is obedience and how was it demonstrated in the laboratory by Milgram?
- What are the factors that predict whether someone in need will be given assistance from bystanders?
- What are social loafing and social facilitation, and under what circumstances are they likely to occur?
- What are the factors known to influence decision-making within groups?
- What are group polarization and groupthink?

Preview

In this chapter, we consider the psychology of people as they really live, interacting with others as social organisms in a social world. Social psychology is the field of psychology concerned with how others influence the thoughts, feelings, and behaviors of the individual. Social psychologists focus on the person or the individual in a group setting and not on the group per se. Group study is more likely to be the focus of sociologists. Because we are social organisms, we are familiar, each in our own way, with many of the concerns of social psychology.

To claim that we are familiar with the concerns of social psychology has certain implications. On the one hand, it means that social psychology is perceived as relevant for all of us because it deals with everyday situations, both immediate (e.g., your personal relationships with friends and family) and more removed (e.g., conflicts in other parts of the world). On the other hand, it means that we are often willing to accept common sense and our own personal experience as the basis for our explanations of social behavior. Although common sense and personal experience may sometimes be valid and may suffice in our everyday lives, they are not acceptable for a scientific approach to understanding social behavior. Social psychology relies on experiments and other scientific methods as sources of knowledge about social behavior.

Over the last 50 years, much of social psychology has taken on a cognitive flavor. That is, social psychologists are attempting to understand social behavior by examining the underlying mental structures and processes (cognitions) reflected in such behavior. A premise of this approach, and this chapter, is that we do not view our social environment solely on the basis of the stimulus information it presents us. Instead, the argument goes, we have developed cognitive structures or processes (e.g., attitudes and schemas) that influence our interpretation of the world around us. Social psychologists have found that it is not only our conscious cognitive processes that affect social behavior, but there are also unconscious or implicit processes that play a role as well. "Discovering how people mentally organize and represent information about themselves and others has been a central task of social cognition research" (Berscheid, 1994, p. 84). Social cognition focuses largely on how we come to make sense of the social world in which we live, and how that information influences our social judgments, choices, attractions, and behaviors (Bordens & Horowitz, 2017; Worchel et al., 2000). First, we discuss the notion of building our own social realities, and then we cover two issues of social psychology with a distinctively cognitive flavor: (a) attitudes—their nature and change, and (b) prejudice, stereotyping, and discrimination.

For the rest of the chapter, there is a rather subtle shift to issues that involve the more direct influence of the social world on our everyday behaviors. The basic questions are simple ones: How do others influence our affects, cognitions, and behaviors? How do we, in turn, influence the affects, cognitions, and behaviors of others? In some cases, the answers are equally straightforward; in other instances, there may be some surprises.

We will begin with the processes of conformity and obedience. They are different processes, to be sure, but they have in common the intent—one way or another—to influence the behaviors of others. Next, we take up bystander apathy and intervention. The focus of research and theory in this field is on helping behaviors. Someone is in need. Other people are in the vicinity. Will they help? Will they turn away? Can psychologists predict which outcome is likely to occur? It is only a small cognitive step to the following issues: social loafing, social facilitation, and decision-making in groups. It is somewhat overly simplistic, but here the research centers on the advantages or disadvantages of working in a group setting, as opposed to working alone.

Social Cognition: Making Sense of the Social World

We now appreciate that a crucial element in understanding social behavior lies in discovering how individuals *think* about and evaluate what happens in their social environment. In other words, it is what you *make* of a situation that determines how you will behave. Social cognition describes the processes used to think about and evaluate social situations. We trust that you will recognize here two of the "Key Principles" that we introduced in Chapter 1: *Our experience of the world often matters more than what is in the world*, and *explanations in psychology often involve INTERACTIONS*.

Let us now see how this social cognition works. Imagine you are sitting in class one day and, all of a sudden, the fire alarm rings. What would you do? Would you automatically respond to this environmental signal for danger by getting up and running out of the room? Probably not. It is more likely you would look around you to see how *others* were reacting. You would take into account how your fellow students and professor were responding to the fire alarm. In other words, your evaluation of the situation would depend, in part, on how others (fellow students, your instructor) were reacting. This is the essence of social cognition. Based on your evaluation of the situation, you form a *behavioral intention* to act in a certain way (to sit there or to get up and leave).

Humans do not possess the ability to apply cold, hard logic when interpreting most social situations. Instead, our understanding of our social world is colored by our biases and expectations. Here is a classic example: Two sets of football fans watched a football game between Princeton and Dartmouth. During the game, Princeton's "All American" quarterback was injured on a play. Predictably, more Princeton students (55 percent) believed that the Dartmouth players were intentionally trying to hurt the quarterback, than did Dartmouth students (10 percent) (Hastroff & Cantril, 1954). This phenomenon is not rare, nor is it simply applicable to sports fans; it permeates how we perceive many situations. Opposing sides to a conflict often see the same event in very different ways. Most Americans view the terrorist attacks of September 11, 2001, as wanton acts of murder. However, these same events are seen as acts of bravery by others. For another example, people can read the same set of documents outlining the credentials of a judicial nominee and come to very different conclusions about that person's fitness to serve. Our ideology, attitudes, prejudices, and biases alter our perceptions of objective reality. In essence, each of us views the world through different (sometimes slightly different and sometimes vastly different) lenses.

Social psychologists focus their efforts on people as they really live, in small groups—be they families, work teams, study groups, or cheerleading squads.

Source: sirtravelalot/Shutterstock.

Social cognition—the processes used to think about and evaluate social situations.

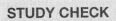

STUDY CHECK

What do psychologists mean by social cognition?

THINKING CRITICALLY

Can you identify from your own experience instances of when your actual overt behavior was more a reflection of what you thought *others* might do in the same situation?

Recognizing and Avoiding Biased Social Cognition

We like to think of ourselves as rational, unbiased thinkers and actors. This belief, however, is not totally accurate. There are several "flaws" built into our social cognition processes that can skew our view of others and the world around us. Based on these flaws, we form impressions of others that are inaccurate. We may stick with a course of action even though it would be better to change. We may like or dislike others for all the wrong reasons. We will review some of these flaws in how we process information about the social world with the hope that once you understand them, you will be in a position to avoid them and make more rational, valid inferences and decisions about your social world.

Before we look at our first bias in social cognition, it is important to understand that much of how we think about the social world and act in it is automatic. There are two modes of processing you can use in a given situation. *Controlled processing* involves conscious awareness, attention to the thinking process, and effort. Controlled processing involves knowing that we are thinking about something, being aware of choices we are making, and carefully considering alternatives. So, for example, if you were buying a new car, you would carefully consider what you are doing and reach a reasoned choice. You would not go to a car dealer and buy the first car you happened to bump into. The second mode of processing is automatic processing. *Automatic processing* is thinking that occurs primarily outside of consciousness. It is effortless in that it does not require us to use any of our conscious cognitive capacity. When we are in the automatic processing mode, which we are in quite a bit, we tend to be *cognitive misers*. Because we have a limited capacity for processing information, we only deal with limited amounts of information and use the easiest way to process the information we do pay attention to. Much of our cognitive and emotional lives is spent in the automatic mode. For example, if someone runs a red light and nearly kills you, your emotional reaction will be automatic. You don't have to think about raising your heart and respiration rates. When a cashier at a restaurant asks you how everything was, most likely you will say "fine" without giving your response much thought. Using automatic processing makes our lives easier, but it can lead to inaccurate views of the world and impressions of others.

The first "flaw" in social cognitive cognition we will explore is the *fundamental attribution error*. Attribution is the process of assigning causes for behavior, our own and that of others. We can attribute behavior to something inside the person (e.g., a personality characteristic or an attitude) or something situational that is outside the person (e.g., being stuck in traffic or the difficulty of a test you just took). The fundamental attribution error means that we first look to internal factors when making attributions and ignore situational factors. This is especially true when we are considering the negative behaviors of others. So, for example, while walking to class one day, you see a person trip and fall. Your first instinct might be to think the person is a klutz. You might be right, or you might be wrong. Let's turn things around. Let's say you trip and fall while walking to class. Most likely you will blame a hole in the sidewalk or that squirrel that ran in front of you. This tendency to attribute the negative behaviors of others internally and the same behaviors of ours externally is the *actor-observer bias*. You can avoid these first two biases by becoming more aware of and considering possible external causes for behavior. In other words, switch to controlled processing.

Another flaw is the *false consensus bias*, which is the tendency to believe that others share your own feelings and behavior (Harvey & Weary, 1984). We tend to think that others will find the same movies amusing as we do, share our political beliefs, and think the same foods are delicious. The false consensus bias is a way we can protect our self-esteem (how we feel about ourselves) by assuming that others agree with us and support us. The belief that others think and act as we do provides much-desired affirmation for ourselves and our views, which is highly rewarding for us. The overestimation of the trustworthiness of our own ideas can be a significant hindrance to rational thinking. If we operate under the false assumption that our beliefs are widely held, it serves as a justification for imposing our beliefs on others (Fiske & Taylor, 1991). It can also lead us down the path to unethical behavior. Many of our ethical practices and beliefs (e.g., in business) are rooted in what is agreed upon by others (Flynn & Wiltermuth, 2010). Flynn and Wiltermuth have found that ethical decisions are often guided by a false consensus bias where a person believes that there is greater agreement with his or her moral choices than actually exists. One way to break out of the false consensus bias is to pay attention to what others *actually* think and believe, rather than what you *believe* they think and do. Considering opposing points of view can help you better understand others and the way they think.

Belief perseverance is the tendency to maintain a belief or an impression of others even in the face of credible disconfirming evidence. For example, if you believe that the world is going to end tonight at 8:02 p.m. and still believe this when 8:03 p.m. rolls around, you are holding on to a disconfirmed belief. Don't laugh—social psychologists have found situations in which such beliefs persist despite disconfirmation (Festinger, Riecken, & Schachter, 1982). You have probably heard the old adage that "first impressions persist." The idea is that once you form an impression of someone, often quickly and based on limited information, it will stick to the person even if new information comes in. This happens because of belief perseverance. You can avoid belief perseverance by switching out of automatic processing mode and carefully considering new information while reassessing your pre-existing beliefs. You may find that your old belief does not look as appealing in the harsh light of the reality of new information.

A flaw related to belief perseverance is the sunk cost effect. The *sunk cost effect* is when you continue on a course of action because you have already invested resources in it, even though switching to a new course would be better. For example, imagine that you have put several thousand dollars into fixing up your old car. Now, it breaks down yet again! Wouldn't it be better to move on to a newer car rather than sink more money into the old car? Although this might be the most rational thing to do, you may not do so, thinking: "I have already invested this much in the old junker— might as well invest some more." Continuing to throw good money after bad is a manifestation of the sunk cost effect. The sunk cost effect rears its head in a number of business and economic situations. Rational economic theory suggests that decisions should be based on future potential rather than past sunk costs (Roth, Robbert, & Straus, 2015). In one study illustrating this effect, Garland (1990) had business students read a scenario involving a research and development project into which 10, 30, 50, 70, or 90 percent of a $10-million-dollar budget had already been invested. Garland found that participants were increasingly likely to invest all remaining funds as the amount already invested increased. This is despite the fact that there was no effect of the amount already invested on the perception that the project would be successful in the end. Roth et al. point out that the sunk cost effect transcends business and economic decisions and comes into play in a variety of different decisions. For example, there is evidence that the sunk cost effect surfaces when making decisions about committed relationships (Rego, Arantes, & Magalhães, 2018). Rego et al. had participants read a description of an unhappy relationship into which money and effort had or had not already been "sunk" into it. They found that participants were more likely to stay in a relationship into which money and effort had already been sunk. To avoid this flaw in reasoning, you should focus your analysis on future potential rather than past resources already invested. Once again, this will require controlled processing and careful consideration of future benefits.

The Nature of Attitudes

Since the 1920s, a central concern in social psychology has been the nature of attitudes, their formation, and their change. Today, the characterization of attitudes has gone beyond defining a core concern for social psychology.

An **attitude** is a relatively stable disposition used to evaluate an object or event. It is a cognitive summary of experience represented by such attributes as good-bad, pleasant-unpleasant, useful-useless, helpful-harmful (Ajzen, 2001; Ajzen & Fishbein, 2000). An attitude has consequences for influencing a person's feelings, beliefs, and behaviors toward that object or event.

The concept of *evaluation* in this definition refers to a dimension of attitudes that includes such notions as being for or against, or positive or negative. By *disposition* we mean a tendency, or a preparedness, to respond to the object of an attitude (actual responding is not necessary). Note that, by definition, attitudes have objects. We do not have attitudes in general; we have attitudes about objects or events.

We form attitudes about many of the events and objects in our environments. These attitudes reflect our evaluations. We like watching television, have heard that a certain brand is a good one (and is on sale), so we buy it.

Anything can be the object of an attitude, whether it is a person, an event, or an idea. You may have attitudes about this course, the car you drive, democracy, your father, the president, or the fast-food restaurant where you eat lunch. Some of our attitudes are more important than others, of course, but the fact that we have attitudes about so many things is precisely why the study of attitudes is so central in social psychology.

Attitude—a relatively stable disposition used to evaluate an object or event.

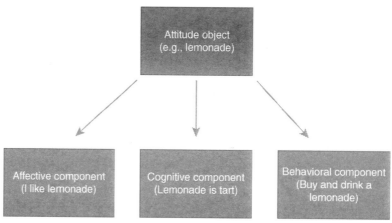

FIGURE 14.1 Three Components of an Attitude

Although many definitions of an attitude have been proposed over the years, most of them suggest that attitudes have three aspects or components. These components, illustrated in **Figure 14.1**, are affect, behavior, and cognition (which make up the ABCs of attitudes). When the term *attitude* is used in everyday conversation, it is likely that the reference is to the affective component, which consists of our feelings about the attitude object. For example, if you say that you really like lemonade but do not like iced tea, you are expressing your feelings, or your affect, about these beverages. This emotional aspect is what makes attitudes special and different from other cognitive schemas.

The behavioral component of an attitude consists of our response tendencies toward attitude objects. This component includes our behaviors and intentions to act, should the opportunity arise. Based on your attitude, you would probably order lemonade with your lunch, rather than iced tea. Keep in mind, however, that although our attitudes often relate to our behavior, sometimes they do not. For example, you may go see a horror movie even though you don't like horror movies because you want to be with your friends. In this case, your desire to be with your friends overrides your negative attitude toward horror movies. The cognitive component includes all of the information you have relating to an attitude object—both conscious (for explicit attitudes) and unconscious (for implicit attitudes). The cognitive component represents the information storage and organization component of an attitude, making an attitude similar to other information-processing cognitive schemas. You know that iced tea and lemonade are both beverages, you know how they are made, and you know that lemonade is sour. We form a positive attitude toward a beverage because we like the way it tastes (affective), because it is easy to buy (behavioral), and because we know it is good for us (cognitive).

Explicit attitude—type of attitude that works on a conscious level; we are aware of these attitudes and how they occasionally influence our behaviors.

Implicit attitude—type of attitude that operates below consciousness, at nearly "gut" level.

Social psychologists recognize that attitudes exist on two levels of consciousness. An **explicit attitude** works on a conscious level; we are aware of these attitudes and how they occasionally influence our behaviors. Another type of attitude does not operate on a conscious level. This type of attitude is an **implicit attitude**, which operates below consciousness, at nearly "gut" level. A special technique is needed to measure implicit attitudes. Instead of asking people about attitudes on a questionnaire (used to measure explicit attitudes), implicit attitudes are measured using the implicit association test (Greenwald, McGhee, & Schwartz, 1998). You can try the implicit association test for yourself at https://implicit.harvard.edu/implicit. It is important to understand that implicit and explicit attitudes are two different processes, not just different sides of the same coin (Wilson, Lindsey, & Schooler, 2000). Implicit and explicit attitudes affect behavior differently and under different circumstances.

Attitude Change via Persuasion

In Chapter 8 we discussed the idea of cognitive dissonance. Cognitive dissonance is one way that attitudes can be changed. If an attitude and behavior are inconsistent with one another, pressure will be felt to make a change, perhaps in one's attitude. Another mechanism for attitude change is persuasion. **Persuasion** is the application of rational and/or emotional arguments to deliberately convince others to change their attitudes or behavior (Bordens & Horowitz, 2017). The *Yale Communication Model* is the most widely accepted model of persuasion. According to this model, the ability to persuade someone to change an attitude depends on four factors: the source of the message (who delivers the message), the characteristics of the message (what is said), the nature of the audience (to whom the message is directed), and the channel of communication (how it is said) (Hovland, Janis, & Kelley, 1953). These factors operate to affect internal processes such as attention to, comprehension of, and acceptance of a persuasive message. Change is measured in a person's attitudes, opinions (defined as verbal expressions of attitudes), and overt behavior. In turn, we will explore how the source, message, and audience affect persuasion.

The most important characteristic affecting the ability of a communicator of a persuasive communication to persuade is credibility. **Credibility** is the believability of a source of a persuasive communication. Generally, the higher the credibility of a communicator, the more persuasive he or she will be. There are two components that make up credibility. One is *trustworthiness*, which is the motivation behind a communicator's attempt to persuade you. If the communicator has no vested interest in persuading you, then you perceive that source as highly trustworthy. On the other hand, if you come to the conclusion that the source has something to gain by persuading you, then you will see the communicator as less trustworthy. The second component is *expertise*, which involves the qualifications of the communicator to speak on the subject. A high-expertise communicator is perceived as one who has the education and background to speak on the topic.

How a message is structured affects persuasion. An important message characteristic is the nature of the appeal. Some persuasive appeals use emotion, most likely negative (e.g., fear), to persuade. *Fear appeals* have been used for issues such as not drinking and driving, not texting and driving, not doing drugs, and quitting smoking. There are four conditions that are necessary for a fear appeal to have its desired effect. First, the appeal must arouse a significant amount of fear. Second, the target of the appeal must believe that the dire consequences depicted in the appeal could happen to him or her. Third, the appeal must include instructions about how to avoid the dire consequences depicted in the appeal (drink only at home; use a designated driver; take a taxi and retrieve your car later). This condition is crucial. If it is not met, then the fear appeal will be ineffective, even if the first two conditions are met. Fourth, the target of the fear appeal must believe that he or she is capable of performing the recommended action to avoid the dire consequences. A *rational appeal* uses facts and figures to persuade. A rational message about stopping smoking might include statistics on how many people get lung cancer and die due to cigarette smoking.

The opinions held by the audience members play a part in persuasion. If a message is very different from the audience members' pre-existing opinions (known as high discrepancy), there is less persuasion than if the message is only moderately different from the pre-existing opinions. This is because the content of the highly discrepant message is likely to be rejected without serious consideration by the audience members. If there is too little discrepancy, not much persuasion will occur. In this case, the message may be nothing more than a restatement of the audience's opinion, and little or no persuasion will take place. Whether a given type of message is effective also depends on the audience. For example, rational appeals tend to work best on well-educated audiences who are better able to make sense of the facts and statistics presented. On the other hand, fear appeals work best with less-educated audiences.

A key assumption of the Yale Model is that we pay attention to a message, carefully consider its content, and then change or not change our attitudes. However, there are instances where we do not process messages carefully, yet we are still persuaded. For example, a juror might be persuaded by a DNA expert in a criminal trial, even though she may not understand much of his testimony. The **elaboration likelihood model** states that there are two routes to persuasion: the central route and the peripheral route (Petty & Cacioppo, 1986). *Central-route processing* is most likely to occur when an individual is motivated to process the content of a message and can understand the content of the message. In this case, the individual pays close attention to the quality of the message and creates a context for the message, based on pre-existing beliefs and ideas about the issue at hand. *Peripheral-route processing* is a matter of being persuaded by factors other than the content of the message. It is most likely to be used when the individual audience member is not motivated or is unable to understand the information contained in the message. Central- and peripheral-route processing are not mutually exclusive modes of processing. In many persuasion situations, both are used to process a message.

STUDY CHECK

How do social psychologists define an attitude?
What are the components of an attitude, and how are they related?
How is attitude change brought about by persuasion?

THINKING CRITICALLY

Reflect on your own collection of attitudes. Can you think of a time when your overt behaviors were inconsistent with how you really felt and what you really thought? If so, why did you behave in such a way?

Prejudice, Stereotypes, and Discrimination

Clearly, we all have many attitudes about a wide range of things, from the trivial to the profound. Of special interest to social psychologists are those attitudes that people direct toward members of groups other than their own. Unfortunately, history shows us that in many cases people hold negative attitudes toward members of groups perceived to be different from their own. Social psychologists call these *prejudicial attitudes*. Specifically, prejudice is a biased, often negative, attitude toward groups of people. Keep in mind that prejudice is an *attitude*—it does not require social power for a person to harbor prejudice. You may sometimes see someone on the news say that minorities cannot be prejudiced because they lack power over a majority group. This is simply not correct. Discrimination (see the following discussion) requires social power over a group, but prejudice does not.

Note that prejudice is usually thought of as a negative bias against a group of people (e.g., racial prejudice, gender prejudice). However, as the definition suggests, prejudice can also be a positive bias. For example, people often are positively prejudiced toward members of their own racial or religious groups and may give them preferential treatment simply because of their group membership.

Negative prejudicial attitudes, such as sexism and racism, have real and often significant consequences for those who are the targets of such prejudice. For example, groups of people may perform poorly on academic achievement tests simply because prevailing attitudes expect them to perform poorly. Obviously, being the target of prejudice can produce negative emotional consequences. Simply being the butt of prejudice-based jokes leads to negative feelings (Ryan & Kanjorski, 1998). In short, prejudice (even in its most seemingly benign forms) can have some serious negative consequences for its targets.

An important concept in the cognitive explanation of prejudice is the use of stereotypes. A stereotype is a rigid set of positive or negative beliefs about a group of people, especially members of a group we perceive to be different from us. A stereotype—perhaps based in part on reality or personal experience—leads to a rigid, overgeneralized image or schema of members of that group. For example, a person may have a stereotype of NASCAR drivers as being from the South. Whether this is true, in fact, matters little; what matters is that the person develops a rigid belief that this is the case. Stereotyping is a natural extension of our predisposition to categorize things. We categorize just about everything: A table is a piece of furniture;

Prejudice—a biased, often negative, attitude toward groups of people.

Stereotype—a rigid set of positive or negative beliefs about a group of people, especially members of a group we perceive to be different from us.

a dog is a mammal, a snake is not; a car is a means of transportation, and so on. We categorize based on the features we believe objects have. In much the same way, we categorize people into social categories, based on all kinds of features: skin color, gender, religion, occupation, nationality, and so on. We categorize people into in-groups (groups with which one identifies), and out-groups (groups whose members we perceive to be different from us). We are using a stereotype when we react by saying, "Oh, he's one of those," whatever "those" may be.

The predisposition to categorize people becomes a problem when the features or beliefs we hold about members of a group become rigid (we are unwilling to give them up, even in the face of contrary evidence) and overgeneralized (judging a person based on presumed group characteristics, rather than on individual characteristics). If a person believes that women are not able to do a certain job and assumes that all women, regardless of their individual talents, are incapable of doing that job, a stereotype exists because of an overgeneralization. We often develop expectations about how a person *should* behave based on stereotypes, and we often judge another person's behavior based on those stereotypes. For example, you may have a stereotype that older people tend to be out of shape and not fit to compete in certain extreme sporting events. Even though that stereotype is largely based on reality, on the fact that—compared to adults in their early twenties—older people are not as athletically able as they once were, the potential error, of course, is to over-generalize about all older persons. Many are superbly fit and able to compete in all sorts of athletic events. It would be just as inaccurate to stereotype all college professors as absentminded simply because some professors are forgetful.

Like attitudes in general, stereotypes exist on two levels. An **explicit stereotype** is one that we are consciously aware of and that is under conscious control. For example, if a real estate agent deliberately steers an African American couple toward houses in a certain neighborhood based on negative beliefs about African Americans and what they might like and not like, an explicit stereotype is at work. An **implicit stereotype** operates on an unconscious level and is activated automatically, without conscious thought (Bargh & Ferguson, 2000; Fazio & Olson, 2003). An implicit stereotype has a more subtle effect on behavior than does an explicit stereotype. For example, a white cab driver may be experiencing the influence of an implicit stereotype if he feels inexplicably uneasy about picking up a racial minority passenger at night.

Discrimination is the behavioral component of prejudice. Specifically, **discrimination** is biased, often negative, behavior directed at a member of a social group simply because of that person's group membership. If a person does not get a job simply because of her religion, gender, or age, then discrimination has occurred. It is important to note that *discrimination can occur with or without prejudice.* A property owner may not rent apartments to members of a certain ethnic group just because he harbors prejudicial attitudes against them. In this case, discriminatory behavior is clearly tied to underlying prejudicial attitudes. On the other hand, another property owner may not rent to members of that same ethnic group simply because not many of them live in that community or seek apartments to rent. This owner may have no prejudice against the ethnic group; instead, the discriminatory renting results from demographics, rather than prejudice.

In addition to the cognitive explanations for prejudice (e.g., categorization and stereotyping), there are social factors that underlie prejudice. Changes in social norms (those unwritten rules that guide social behaviors and social interactions) have led to a reduction in the overt expression of prejudice such as racism. Social psychologists call this overt form of racism *old-fashioned racism.* Research shows a definite trend indicating that old-fashioned racism is no longer socially acceptable. In fact, the trend is in the opposite direction. Data from the *General Social Survey* (1999), for example, shows that between the years 1972 and 1996, whites have increasingly shown positive attitudes toward blacks. Compared to 1972, whites in 1996 were more willing to accept a black president, support laws preventing housing discrimination, send their children to predominantly black schools, and support changing rules that exclude blacks from social clubs. And, of course, in 2008 Americans elected the first black president. Although this is good news, not all of the news is good. Comparisons of Americans from different generations show that the latest generation of Millennials is just as prejudiced

Explicit stereotype—a stereotype that we are consciously aware of and that is under conscious control.

Implicit stereotype—a stereotype that operates on an unconscious level and is activated automatically, without conscious thought.

Discrimination—biased, often negative, behavior directed at a member of a social group simply because of that person's group membership.

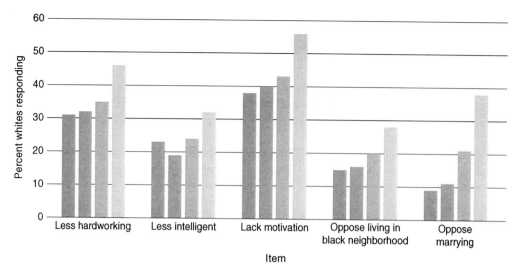

FIGURE 14.2 Results from General Social Survey (2012–2014) on White Prejudice toward Blacks

Millennials (born 1981–), Generation X (born 1965–1980), baby boomers (born 1946–1964), Silent Generation (born 1926–1945).

Source: Clement, 2015.

against blacks as Americans from previous generations on most measures (Clement, 2015). **Figure 14.2** shows results from the General Social Survey (2010–2014) provided by Clement on a number of measures of prejudice towards blacks. As you can see, other than the question about interracial marriage, Millennials show similar levels of prejudice as previous generations, except for the generation born between 1926 and 1945. Members of that latter generation are the most prejudiced on all measures. Evidently, there is still work to be done.

Unfortunately, prejudice still exists in the United States and the world. Despite the positive changes in racial attitudes and less old-fashioned racism, racism and other forms of prejudice still exist on a more subtle level. Social psychologists have noted that, even though overt expressions of prejudice are no longer prevalent, prejudicial attitudes and stereotypes still manifest themselves in less-obvious ways. This form of prejudice is called modern racism. **Modern racism** is racism that is not expressed openly but, rather, is manifested in an uncertainty in feelings and behaviors toward minorities. For example, a modern racist might freely and openly declare that racism is bad, but at the same time subscribe to ideas that "minorities are pushing too hard, too fast, and into places where they are not wanted" (McConahay, 1986, p. 93). A modern racist might declare that he or she is thrilled that Barack Obama can become president of the United States but would vote for nearly anyone who ran against him in a national election due to his race.

Modern racism—racism that is not expressed openly but, rather, is manifested in an uncertainty in feelings and behaviors toward minorities.

STUDY CHECK

What are prejudice, stereotypes, and discrimination, and how are they related?

THINKING CRITICALLY

Can you think of any example from your own experience that illustrates how making the distinction between in-groups and out-groups has led to or sustained prejudice and contributed to discrimination (or worse)?

FOCUS ON DIVERSITY

How Ideology Relates to Behavior

When we think about diversity, our attention is most likely drawn to things such as race, sex, ethnicity, and sexual orientation. But there is another aspect of diversity that is often overlooked: how people think about and view the world. *Ideology* is a set of doctrines or beliefs that are shared by the members of a social group or that form the basis of a political, economic, or other system (The Free Dictionary, ND). You can think of ideology as the lens through which you see the world, with the lenses for different ideologies being different. For example, if you were to view the world through a pair of sunglasses with green lenses, you would see the world with a given tint. If you changed the sunglasses to ones with amber lenses, the tint would change. In the same way, viewing the world through one ideological perspective will yield different social constructions of reality than viewing through another. Two common, and important, ideologies relating to the world of politics are liberalism and conservatism. *Liberalism* is an ideology emphasizing "an enthusiasm for freedom, toleration, individualism and reason, on the one hand, and a disapproval of power, authority and tradition, on the other" (Alexander, 2015, p. 984). *Conservatism* is an ideology that is more resistant to change than liberalism and roots change in what has worked in the past (Alexander, 2015).

Ideology comes into play in a variety of ways. For example, ideology contributes to *political polarization*. Political polarization occurs when people line up on different sides of an issue based on ideology. A good example is the abortion issue. People generally line up for or against abortion based on ideology, with most liberals supporting abortion rights and most conservatives opposing them. Political polarization has always existed, and between 1994 and 2014 it has increased (Pew Research Center, 2014). During this time period, polarization has increased from 10 to 21 percent. Pew also reported that there was also an increase in the degree to which Democrats and Republicans viewed the opposing party as a threat to the well-being of the United States. It appears that this polarization has only gotten worse following the 2016 presidential election. To make matters worse, people tend to believe that there is greater polarization than actually exists (Westfall, Van Boven, Chambers, & Judd, 2015). Believing that polarization is greater than it is in reality is important because the more polarization one perceives, the more likely it is that he or she will engage in political action (Westfall et al., 2015). Interestingly, when we are exposed to political polarization, it increases our own beliefs and emotions surrounding polarization. In other words, if a political figure you support takes a politically polarized point of view, you are likely to follow suit (Rogowski & Sutherland, 2016). Rogowski and Sutherland found that increased polarization was due to both increased warmth expressed toward one's preferred figure and decreased warmth toward an opposition figure. This effect was most pronounced for people with ideologically extreme positions.

Ideology also serves as a source of motivated social cognition. *Motivated social cognition* means that a person adopts a way of thinking (ideology) because it serves some psychological need and relates to a person's needs and motivations (Jost, Glaser, Kruglanski, & Sulloway, 2003). Research initially focused on conservative ideology and found that conservative thought was correlated with intolerance of ambiguity, anxiety about death, low openness to new experience, fear of threat and loss, and lowered self-esteem (among others) (Jost et al., 2003). However, later research revealed that whether a person shows ideological rigidity in thinking is domain specific (Conway et al., 2016). That is, whether your thinking is rigid depends on the issue. For example, a liberal person's thinking on gun control may be nuanced, but it may be rigid when it comes to climate change. Conversely, a conservative person's thinking may show the opposite pattern.

Whenever there is an opening on the U.S. Supreme Court, there is a battle, largely across ideological lines, over the president's nominee to fill the position. Most likely, a liberal president will nominate a liberal justice, and a conservative president will nominate a conservative justice. Senators often support or oppose the nominee based on ideology. Does it really matter all that much who sits on the Supreme Court? After all, in a vast majority of cases, the justices on the court agree. Although this is true for most cases, in some cases, the ideological leaning of a justice does matter. Most of these cases involve important social issues such as abortion, gun control, and same-sex marriage. In fact, research shows that for these ideologically related cases, one can predict with a high degree of accuracy how a justice will vote based on his or her ideology (Ringhand, 2007). Ringhand analyzed the voting patterns of the Supreme Court justices of the Rehnquist Court. Ringhand found a clear pattern of conservative justices (at the time, Thomas, Scalia, Rehnquist, O'Connor, and Kennedy) casting votes to invalidate a federal statute in a conservative direction and liberal justices (at the time, Ginsburg, Breyer, Souter, and Stevens) doing the same but in a liberal direction (Ringhand, 2007). Research also found that ideology was a strong predictor of how a senator voted on important abortion legislation in the 1980s, with ideologically conservative senators voting consistently against pro-abortion amendments (Chressanthis, Gilbert, & Grimes, 1991).

Ideology can influence how we perceive the attitudes, beliefs, and behaviors of others. Through our ideological lenses, we often see ourselves as rational and our positions as objectively correct. On the other hand, we tend to see those with views different from our own as biased, irrational, and flat-out wrong. This is a phenomenon called *naïve realism*. Naïve realism involves three related factors: (1) the belief that we see the world objectively; (2) the belief that other people who are rational will also see the world as we do; and (3) the belief that if others fail to see the world the way we do, they must be misinformed, are irrational, or harbor ulterior motives (Reeder, Pryor, Wohl, & Griswell, 2005). We tend to fall prey to a *bias blind spot*, which means that we are motivated to see ourselves as unbiased and objective.

Naïve realism is not strongly related to one's cognitive abilities. That is, it is not that only less intelligent people fall prey to naïve realism. West, Meserve, and Stanovich (2012) conducted a pair of studies testing the relationship between the level of sophisticated thinking and the bias blind spot. In their first study, West et al. measured the bias blind spot along with a number of measures of cognitive sophistication (e.g., open-minded thinking, SAT scores, ability to solve a complex cognitive problem). West et al. found that cognitive sophistication was not a strong correlate of the likelihood of showing the bias blind spot. In fact, they found that cognitively sophisticated thinkers were *more* likely to show the bias blind spot than less sophisticated thinkers.

One manifestation of ideology is that people tend to seek out news sources that agree with their ideological perspectives. This is known as *partisan selective exposure* to media. There is evidence that people tend to seek out news sources that agree with their perspectives (Rodriguez, Moskowitz, Salem, & Ditto, 2017). This trend toward partisan selective exposure to media has increased over time, more so for Republicans than Democrats. Another example of this selective exposure can be found on social media. One study,

for example, looked at the political Twitter accounts of members of the U.S. Congress to see what their followers were like (Hong & Kim, 2016). Hong and Kim found that the more ideologically extreme a member was, the more followers the member had. Hong and Kim suggest that this pattern provides evidence for the idea that people seek out ideological "echo chambers." You might expect that people who expose themselves to information beyond these echo chambers would become more flexible in their ideology. Unfortunately, you would be wrong! Bail et al. (2018) surveyed Democrats and Republicans who used Twitter at least three times a week. They identified how they felt about a number of social issues. Then, they had these individuals follow a Twitter bot exposing them to messages opposing their views. They resurveyed participants after a month to see if their positions on the social issues became more moderate. They found that both Republicans and Democrats became more extreme in their views. This effect was somewhat more pronounced for Republicans.

Our tendency to ascribe bad motives to our opponents on issues does not mean that we ignore or dismiss their views. It just means that we think they are wrong because they are irrational or biased. Is this because we only pay attention to information that agrees with our views and ignore information that does not? This is called the *congeniality hypothesis*. However, research shows that it is not so much that we ignore information that conflicts with our views but that we interpret it in a specific way (Eagly, Kulesa, Chen, & Chaiken, 2001). Eagly et al. examined a total of 70 experiments and found that people attend to information that disagrees with their strong views, but they examine it in a specific way. Individuals approach conflicting information with "skeptical and active scrutiny." On the other hand, information with which they agree is given less critical scrutiny. Our view of arguments that offend or challenge us is to figure out what is being said and devise counterarguments to that view. We know what the messages are saying, but we will not be convinced by them because that is not the purpose of our examination.

Conformity

Conformity—a direct form of social influence that occurs when we modify our behavior, under perceived pressure to do so, to make it consistent with the behavior of others.

One of the most direct forms of social influence occurs when we modify our behavior, under perceived pressure to do so, to make it consistent with the behavior of others, a process referred to as **conformity**. Although we often think of conformity in a negative way, it is natural and often desirable. Conformity helps make social behaviors efficient and, at least to a degree, predictable.

When he began his research on conformity, Solomon Asch believed that people were not terribly susceptible to social pressure in situations that are clear-cut and unambiguous. Asch thought an individual would behave independently of group pressure when there was little doubt that his or her own judgments were accurate. He developed an interesting technique for testing his hypothesis (Asch, 1951, 1956).

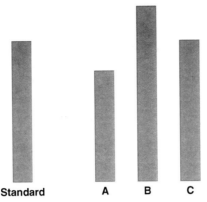

FIGURE 14.3 Example of an Asch-type task

Subjects in Asch's experiment had to say which line on the right (A, B, or C) matched the standard on the left.

A participant in Asch's experiments joined a group seated around a table. In the original study, the group consisted of seven people. Unknown to the participant, six of the people in the group were confederates of the experimenter; they were "in" on what was happening. The real participant was told that the study dealt with the ability to make perceptual judgments. The participant had to do nothing more than decide which of three lines was the same length as a standard line (see **Figure 14.3**). The experimenter showed each set of lines to the group and collected responses, one by one, from each member of the group. There were 18 sets of lines to judge, and the real participant was always the last one to respond.

Each judgment involved clearly unambiguous stimuli: The correct answer was obvious. On 12 of the 18 trials, however, the confederates gave a unanimous, but incorrect, answer ("critical trials"). What would the "real" participants do? How would they resolve this conflict? Their eyes were telling them what the right answer was, but the group was saying something else.

The results of his first study surprised even Asch. When confederates gave wrong answers, conformity occurred in 37 percent of the critical trials. That is, the participants responded with an incorrect answer, agreeing with the majority on more than one-third of the trials. Moreover, three-quarters of Asch's participants conformed to the group pressure at least once.

Why did Asch's participants conform? He interviewed his participants and found three pathways to conformity: distortions of perception, distortions of judgment, and distortions of action (see **Figure 14.4**). You will not be surprised to learn that there are predictable cultural differences in the conformity to group pressures. In those cultures characterized

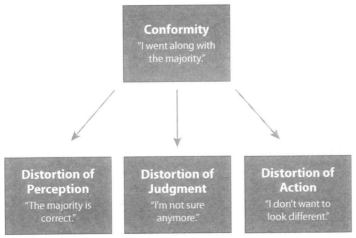

FIGURE 14.4 Reasons Why Participants Conformed in Asch's Experiment

as *collectivist*, in which the individual normally serves the group rather than self (largely Asian, and many Middle-Eastern cultures), conformity scores are much higher than in Western, *individualistic* cultures (e.g., Bond & Smith, 1996).

Conformity involves yielding to the perceived pressure of a group. In most cases, it is assumed, group members are peers, or at least similar to the conformer. When someone yields to the pressure of a perceived authority, the result is obedience. It is to this issue we turn next.

STUDY CHECK

What is conformity, and how was it demonstrated by Solomon Asch?

THINKING CRITICALLY

In what sorts of social situations does conformity tend to lead to negative outcomes, and in what situations might it lead to positive outcomes?

Obedience to Authority

Obedience—when we modify behavior in response to a command from someone in authority.

Obedience is when we modify behavior in response to a command from someone in authority. Like conformity, most obedience is beneficial. Life would be difficult if people did not obey traffic or other laws. However, some obedience is *destructive obedience*, which brings harm to others. History teaches us that acts of destructive obedience occur quite frequently. What interests social psychologists is the reasons people obey orders to harm others.

Adolph Eichmann, considered to be the "architect" of the Holocaust during World War II, was captured by Israeli agents in 1961. He was brought to Israel and placed on trial for crimes against humanity. Eichmann's principal defense was that he was only a mid-level officer, a simple administrator, who was "just following orders." It was his contention that he organized the trainloads of Jews sent to concentration camps and the gas chambers at the behest of individuals who had the power to inflict punishment if he did not obey their orders. Is "just following orders" a legitimate excuse? Remember, our predisposition is to attribute such behaviors internally. As a result, in the minds of many, Eichmann becomes an inhuman monster, not a human being caught up in a highly unusual social situation. Which is it? Was Eichmann an evil monster, or a victim of circumstances? Social psychologists now believe that obedience like Eichmann's can be accounted for by an interaction between an individual's personal characteristics and the power dynamics of the situation. When certain people are placed in a powerful social situation, destructive obedience can occur (Zimbardo, 2007).

The question of what leads to destructive obedience intrigued Yale University social psychologist Stanley Milgram (1933–1984). Milgram had been a student of Solomon Asch and was interested in the conditions that lead to conformity. The participants in Asch's studies took the experimental procedures seriously, but consequences of either conforming or maintaining independence were rather trivial. At worst, they might have experienced some discomfort as a result of voicing independent judgments. There were no external rewards or punishments for their behavior, and there was no one telling them how to respond. Milgram went beyond Asch's procedure to see if an ordinary person placed in an extraordinary situation would obey an authority figure and inflict pain on an innocent victim. Milgram's research, conducted in the early 1960s, has become among the most famous and controversial in all of psychology. His experiments pressured participants to comply with the demands of an authority figure. Those demands were both unreasonable and troubling (Milgram, 1963, 1965, 1974).

All of Milgram's studies involved the same procedure. Participants arrived at the laboratory to find they would be participating with a second person (a person working for the experimenter called a confederate). The experimenter explained that the research dealt with the effects of punishment on learning and that one participant would serve as a "teacher," while the other would act as a "learner." The roles were assigned by a rigged drawing in which the actual participant was always assigned the role of teacher, while the confederate was always the learner. The participant watched as the learner was taken into a room and wired to electrodes to be used for delivering punishment in the form of electric shocks.

After the teacher received a sample shock of 45 volts, just to see what the shocks felt like, the teacher received his instructions. He was to read to the learner a series of word pairs. The teacher was then to read the first word of one of the pairs, and the learner was to supply the second word. The teacher sat in front of a rather imposing electric "shock generator" that had 30 switches. From left to right, the switches increased by increments of 15 volts, ranging from 15 to 450 volts. Labels were printed under the switches, ranging from "Slight" to "Moderate" to "Extreme Intensity" to "Danger: Severe Shock." The label at the 450-volt end read: "XXX."

As the task proceeded, the learner periodically made errors according to a prearranged schedule. The teacher had been instructed to deliver an electric shock for every incorrect answer. With each error, the teacher was to move up the scale of shocks, giving the learner a more potent shock with each new mistake. (The learner, remember, was part of the act, and no one was actually receiving any shocks.)

When the teacher hesitated or questioned whether he should continue, the experimenter was ready with a verbal prod, "Please continue," or "The experiment requires that you continue." If the participant protested, the experimenter became more assertive and offered an alternative prod, such as, "You have no choice; you must go on."

Milgram was astonished by the results of his study, and the results still amaze us. Twenty-six of Milgram's 40 participants—65 percent—obeyed the demands of the experimenter and went all the way to the highest shock, closing all the switches. In fact, no participant stopped prior to the 300-volt level, the point at which the learner pounded on the wall in protest. One later variation of this study added vocal responses from the learner, who delivered an increasingly stronger series of demands to be let out of the experiment. The level of obedience in this study was still unbelievably high, as 25 of 40 participants—62.5 percent—continued to administer shocks to the 450-volt level. Milgram found that the level of obedience decreased as the distance between the "teacher" and "learner" decreased. Obedience dropped when the teacher and learner were in the same room (proximity). The lowest levels of obedience (30 percent) were observed when the teacher was required to physically force the learner's hand onto a shock plate device (touch proximity).

The behavior of Milgram's participants indicated that they were concerned about the learner. All participants claimed that they experienced genuine and extreme stress in this situation. Some fidgeted, some trembled, and many perspired profusely. Several giggled nervously. In short, the people caught up in this situation showed obvious signs of conflict and anxiety. Nonetheless, they continued to obey the orders of the experimenter, even though they had good reason to believe they might be harming the learner. A reanalysis of audiotapes made during Milgram's study was conducted in 2000 (Rochat, Maggioni, & Modigliana, 2000). This study suggested that participants were much more concerned about the learner than even Milgram may have believed. The researchers heard protests from teachers and defiant resistance to continuing, fairly early in the shock-generation process. Even by the 150-volt level of shock, nearly half of the teachers stopped to check with the experimenter to be reassured that they were doing the right thing.

Milgram's first study was performed with male participants, ranging in age from 20 to 50. A replication with adult women produced precisely the same results: 65 percent obeyed fully. Other variations of the procedure uncovered several factors that could reduce the amount of obedience. Putting the learner and teacher in the same room or having the experimenter deliver orders over the telephone, rather than in person, reduced levels of obedience markedly. When the shocks were to be delivered by a team made up of the participant and two confederates who refused to give the shocks, full-scale obedience dropped to only 10 percent. Obedience also was extremely low if there were conflicting authority figures, one urging the teacher to continue delivering shocks and the other urging the participant to stop. When given the choice, participants obeyed the authority figure who said to stop.

Although Milgram's first study on obedience was published more than 50 years ago, a few recent studies have replicated his results and provided a few additional insights. A re-analysis of Milgram's data by Dominic Packer of Ohio State University (2008) tells us that of those participants who were disobedient and stopped administering shocks, most did so when shock levels reached the 150-volt level—when the "learner" began to protest, with statements such as, "Stop, let me out! I don't want to do this anymore." It was at this point that some participants perceived the learner's right to terminate the experiment, as overriding the experimenter's orders to continue. Once past the 150-volt level, however, the learner's escalating expressions of pain had little effect. Those who continued felt that the responsibility for the learner's condition was then the experimenter's and not their own. A partial replication of Milgram's basic experimental design (shock levels never exceeded the 150-volt level) found (virtually) the same obedience/disobedience rates as reported by Milgram (Burger, 2009). This was true in the replication even though learners were repeatedly and explicitly told that they could leave the study at any time. In addition, participants were aware that the experimenter had given this same assurance to the confederate/learner. Finally, Milgram's research has been replicated using a virtual reality environment, with participants showing a highly similar level of obedience to Milgram's participants (Dambrun & Vatiné, 2010).

In reading about Milgram's research, it should have occurred to you that putting people in such a stressful situation could be considered ethically objectionable. Milgram, himself, was concerned with the welfare of his participants, and he took great care to debrief them fully after each session. He informed them that they had not really administered any shocks, and explained why deception had been used. It is, of course, standard practice in psychological experiments to conclude the session by disclosing the true purpose of the study and alleviating any anxiety that might have arisen.

Milgram reported that, after debriefing, the people in his studies were not upset at having been deceived. Their principal reaction was one of relief when they learned that no electric shock had been used. Milgram indicated that a follow-up study done a year later with some of the same participants showed no long-term adverse effects had been created by his procedure. Despite his precautions, Milgram was severely criticized for placing people in such an extremely stressful situation. One of the effects of his research was to establish in the scientific community a higher level of awareness of the need to protect the well-being of human research participants.

STUDY CHECK

What is obedience and how was it demonstrated in the laboratory by Milgram?

THINKING CRITICALLY

If you can find people who have not heard of Milgram's study, describe to them the procedures that were used, and ask them to estimate how many "teachers" they think would administer the highest level of shock. How do your results compare with Milgram's?

Bystander Intervention

On March 13, 1964, a New York City cocktail waitress, Kitty Genovese, was brutally murdered in front of her apartment building as she returned from work about 3:30 in the morning. Her assailant was Winston Moseley, a man whose only motivation that night was to kill a woman. What made this murder so noteworthy was that around 38 of Genovese's neighbors were aware of what was happening to her over the course of about an hour.

Although most of the "witnesses" did not actually *see* what was happening, they were aware of it. And, some did directly witness her being stabbed. It is astonishing to think that a young woman was brutally slain and nobody came to her aid. This tragic event stimulated public concern and sparked much commentary in the media. People wondered how all those witnesses could have shown such a lack of concern for another human being. *Apathy* and *alienation* were terms used to describe what had happened. The Kitty Genovese case was certainly not the first such incident of bystanders watching without intervening, nor was it the last. What makes it special—what gets it into psychology textbooks—is that the *New York Times* story of the Genovese murder caught the attention of Bibb Latané and John Darley, two social psychologists who, at the time, were at universities in New York City.

They were not satisfied that terms such as *bystander apathy* or *alienation* adequately explained what happened in the Genovese case. They were not willing to attribute people's failure to help to internal, dispositional, or personality factors. They were convinced that situational factors made such events possible. Latané and Darley pointed out that there were logical reasons to explain why people would not offer help in an emergency. Emergencies tend to happen quickly and without warning. Except for medical technicians, firefighters, and a few other select categories of individuals, people are not prepared to deal with emergencies when they arise. In fact, one good predictor of who will intervene in an emergency is that person's previous experience with a similar emergency situation (Cramer et al., 1988).

A Cognitive Model of Bystander Intervention

Latané and Darley (1968, 1970) suggested that a series of cognitive events must occur before a bystander can intervene in an emergency. First, the bystander must *notice* what is going on. A window-shopper who fails to see someone collapse on the opposite side of the street cannot be expected to rush over and offer assistance. Second, if a bystander does notice something happen, he or she must *label* the situation as an emergency (perhaps the person who collapsed is simply drunk or tired and not really having a stroke or a heart attack). Third, the bystander must make the *decision* that it is his or her (and not someone else's) responsibility to do something.

Even after these conditions are met—the bystander noticed something happening, labeled the situation as one calling for action, and assumed responsibility for helping—he or she must still decide what form of assistance to offer. Should he or she try to give first aid? Should he or she try to find the nearest telephone, or simply start shouting for help? As a final step, the person must decide how to *implement* the decision to act. What is the best first aid under these circumstances? Just where can help be found? Thus, intervening on behalf of someone else in a social situation involves a series of cognitive choices (see **Figure 14.5**).

A negative outcome at any of these steps will lead to a decision not to offer assistance. When one considers the cognitive events necessary for helping, it becomes apparent that the deck is stacked against the victim in an emergency when bystanders are present. Interestingly, bystanders need not be physically present for the bystander effect to occur. Just having someone imagine that there are bystanders present can suppress helping (Garcia et al., 2002). The bystander effect also can be found to occur in Internet chat rooms (Markay, 2000)! Perhaps we should be surprised that bystanders *ever* offer to help.

Social psychologists refer to the suppression of helping behaviors when bystanders are present at an emergency situation as the **bystander effect**. It has been found to be one of the most consistent and powerful phenomena discovered by social psychologists. Why does the bystander effect occur? We shall explore possible explanations next.

Bystander effect—the suppression of helping behaviors when bystanders are present at an emergency situation.

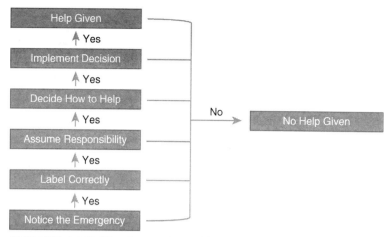

FIGURE 14.5 The Latané and Darley Model of Helping

Processes That Inhibit Helping Behaviors

Audience inhibition—the tendency to be hesitant about doing things in front of others, especially strangers.

Audience inhibition refers to the tendency to be hesitant about doing things in front of others, especially strangers. We tend to be concerned about how others will evaluate us. In public, no one wants to do anything that might appear to be improper, incompetent, or silly. The bystander who intervenes risks embarrassment if he or she blunders, and that risk increases as the number of people present increases. Those people who are sensitive to becoming embarrassed in public are most likely to be inhibited (Tice & Baumeister, 1985).

Emergencies tend to be ambiguous (e.g., Is the man who collapsed on the street ill, or is he drunk? Is the commotion in a neighboring apartment an assault, or a family quarrel that's a little out of hand?) When social reality is not clear, we often turn to others for clues. While getting information from others, a person will probably try to remain calm, cool, and collected, acting as if there is no emergency. Everyone else, of course, is doing the very same thing, showing no outward sign of concern. The result is that each person is led by the others to think that the situation is really not an emergency after all, a phenomenon called pluralistic ignorance (Miller & McFarland, 1987). **Pluralistic ignorance** is the belief on the part of the individual that only he or she is confused and does not know what to do in an emergency, whereas everyone else is standing around doing nothing for a good reason. The group becomes paralyzed by a type of conformity—conformity to the inaction of others.

Pluralistic ignorance—the belief on the part of the individual that only he or she is confused and does not know what to do in an emergency, whereas everyone else is standing around doing nothing for a good reason.

This process was demonstrated in a classic experiment by Latané and Darley (1968, 1970). Columbia University students reported to a campus building to participate in an interview. They were sent to a waiting room and asked to fill out some forms. As they did so, smoke began billowing out through a wall vent. After six minutes (at which time the procedure was ended if the "emergency" had not been reported), there was enough smoke in the room to interfere with breathing and prevent seeing across the room.

When participants were alone in the waiting room, 75 percent of them came out to report the smoke. When two passive confederates were in the room with the participant, only 10 percent responded. Those from the groups who failed to make a report came up with all sorts of explanations for the smoke: steam, vapors from the air conditioner, smog introduced to simulate an urban environment, even "truth gas." Participants who were unresponsive had been led by the inaction of others to conclude almost anything but the obvious—that something was very wrong. In the Kitty Genovese murder, it was clear that an emergency was in progress. After all, she did shout things such as, "Oh, my God, he stabbed me! Please help me! Please help me!" and "I'm dying! I'm dying!" Her cries left very little ambiguity about what was happening. Further, witnesses in the Genovese case were not in a face-to-face group that would allow social influence processes such as pluralistic ignorance to operate. Latané and Darley suggested that a third process is necessary to complete the explanation of bystander behavior.

A single bystander in an emergency situation has to bear the full responsibility of offering assistance, but a witness who is part of a group shares that responsibility with other onlookers. The greater the number of people present, the smaller is each individual's perceived obligation to intervene, a process referred to as **diffusion of responsibility**.

Incidentally, diffusion of responsibility comes in forms much less serious in their implications. Those of you with a few siblings can probably recall times at home when the telephone rang five or six times before anyone made a move to answer it, even though the entire family was home at the time. Some of you probably have been at parties where the doorbell went unanswered with everyone thinking that "someone else" would get it.

Diffusion of responsibility is generally considered to be one of the best explanations for the bystander effect. However, it need not always occur for the bystander effect to develop. In some cases, help can be suppressed if the bystanders assume that a *category relationship* exists between the parties involved in an incident (Levine, 1999). A **category relationship** means that parties involved in a social situation are perceived to belong together in some way (e.g., siblings, boyfriend-girlfriend). When a category relationship is assumed, people are less willing to intervene than when such a relationship is not assumed (Shotland & Straw, 1976).

Mark Levine (1999) maintains that what happened to Kitty Genovese can be accounted for (in part) by witnesses assuming that Genovese and her attacker had previously formed a category relationship. In fact, some of the witnesses expressed the sentiment that, "We thought it was a lover's quarrel." When a category relationship is believed to exist, a powerful social norm is activated: We don't stick our noses in the business of others.

We have made the case that the bystander effect is a powerful and pervasive social phenomenon. However, are there any circumstances in which the bystander effect does not occur, or where the presence of bystanders actually can facilitate helping? It turns out that the answer is "yes"—if the situation is potentially dangerous (Fischer et al., 2006). These researchers found the usual bystander effect (inhibition of helping when bystanders were present) in a low-danger helping situation. However, when help was dangerous (stopping a large, thug-like male from harming a woman), the presence of bystanders facilitated helping. Finally, the bystander effect is less likely to occur when a clearly defined social norm is violated, such as if someone litters in a public park in front of a group of bystanders (Chekroun & Brauer, 2001).

Diffusion of responsibility—a process in which the greater the number of people present, the smaller is each individual's perceived obligation to intervene.

Category relationship—exists when the parties involved in a social situation are perceived to belong together in some way (e.g., siblings, boyfriend-girlfriend).

> ### STUDY CHECK
> What are the factors that predict whether someone in need will be given assistance from bystanders?

> ### THINKING CRITICALLY
> To what extent have you observed the bystander effect on your campus? When there is a campus-wide election, what percentage of the student body actually votes? Is any of this preceding discussion relevant to that issue?

Social Loafing and Social Facilitation

A well-researched variety of social influence is **social loafing**—a tendency to work less (to decrease individual effort) as the size of the group in which one works becomes larger. In a classic study of the phenomenon, Latané, Williams, and Harkins (1979) had participants shout or clap as loudly as possible, either in groups or alone. If people were led to believe that their performance could not be identified, they invested less effort in the task as group size increased. Other studies have used different, more cognitive tasks, such as evaluating poetry. The results tend to be consistent: When people can hide in the crowd, their effort (and, hence, productivity) declines.

Social loafing—the tendency to work less (to decrease individual effort) as the size of the group in which one works becomes larger.

That the extent of social loafing is tied to an individual's anonymity in a group setting has been verified by several studies of problem solving or brainstorming (Levine & Moreland, 1990; Markay, 2000). Such studies consistently show that individual effort is greater in real, face-to-face groups than it is in "nominal groups" in which individuals work at their own computer stations, participating with others on some common task. Loafing is reduced to the extent that others in the group can monitor the inputs and behaviors of each individual.

Source: Andrei Kholmov/Shutterstock.

The notion of "social loafing" is not a new one in psychology. Social loafing refers to the tendency to decrease one's efforts when working on a task as the size of the group in which one is working expands.

Although social loafing is a widespread phenomenon, it is does not always occur when one works in a group. Social loafing is significantly less likely in those collectivist cultures—such as in many Asian countries—that place a high value on participation in group activities (Kerr & Tindale, 2004; Worchel et al., 1998). In individualist cultures, such as the United States and most Western countries, social loafing can be nearly eliminated if group members believe their effort is special and required for the group's success, or they believe their performance can be identified and evaluated individually. Loafing also reduces when individuals within the group find a task interesting or they get personally involved in the task at hand (Smith et al., 2001). Indeed, there are situations in which social influence actually facilitates behavior.

Well over 100 years ago, psychologist Norman Triplett observed that bicycle riders competing against other cyclists outperformed those racing against a clock. He then performed what is considered the first laboratory experiment in social psychology (Triplett, 1898). Triplett had children wind a fishing reel as rapidly as they could. They engaged in this task either alone or alongside another child doing the same thing. Just as he had noticed in his records of bicycle races, Triplett found that the children worked faster when another child was present. Such an effect occurs not only when working with co-actors (others engaged in the same task), but also when performing before an audience. For example, joggers, both male and female, pick up the pace and run faster when going past a person sitting on a park bench (Worringham & Messick, 1983). When the presence of others improves an individual's performance on some task, **social facilitation** has occurred.

Social facilitation—when the presence of others improves an individual's performance on some task.

Numerous studies of this phenomenon were performed early in the twentieth century, with a puzzling inconsistency in results. Sometimes social facilitation would occur, but on other occasions, the opposite would happen. Sometimes people performed more poorly in the presence of others than they did alone, a reaction that social psychologists call *social interference*. The inconsistency in these findings was so bewildering that most social psychologists eventually gave up investigating social facilitation. However, the research area was revived when Robert Zajonc (1965) suggested that the inconsistent findings were a result of different tasks being used in the experiments. He reasoned that the presence of others is a source of arousal, which should enhance performance on simple, well-learned tasks and inhibit performance on complex, not-well-learned tasks. By and large, subsequent research verified Zajonc's reasoning.

> **STUDY CHECK**
>
> What are social loafing and social facilitation, and under what circumstances are they likely to occur?

THINKING CRITICALLY

A teacher believes in the value of having small groups of students work together on some class projects. What can she do to prevent some students from engaging in social loafing and letting other students do most of the work?

Decision-Making in Groups

Many of the decisions we face in our daily lives are made within group settings. Committees, boards, family groups, and group projects for a class are only a few examples. There is logic in the belief that group efforts to solve problems should be superior to individual efforts. Having more people available should mean having more talent and knowledge available. It also seems logical that the cohesiveness of the group would contribute to a more productive effort (for some groups and some problems, this is exactly the case). But, we know better than to assume that just because a conclusion is logical, it is true.

Decades of research have shown us that groups can, and often do, outperform individuals. Here is a partial list of what we know about group decision-making:

- Groups outperform the average individual in the group mainly because groups recognize a correct answer to a problem faster, reject an incorrect answer, and have better memory systems than the average individual.

- Groups comprising high-quality members perform better than groups with low-quality members.

- As you increase the size of the group, you increase the resources available to the group. However, you also increase process loss (loss of productivity due to faulty group interaction). Additionally, in larger groups, you get even less member participation than in smaller groups. Whether you get an improvement in performance with increased size depends on the type of task the group is facing.

- When the problem a group must solve involves a great deal of interaction, interpersonal cohesiveness (how much members like each other) and task-based cohesiveness (mutual respect for skills and abilities) increase productivity. When a problem does not require much interaction, task-based cohesiveness increases productivity, but interpersonal cohesiveness does not.

Although it is generally true that groups outperform individuals, there are some liabilities attached to using groups to make decisions. In this section, we consider two aspects of group decision-making that can lead to low-quality decisions.

When he was an MIT graduate student in industrial management, James Stoner gave participants in his study a series of dilemmas to consider (Stoner, 1961). Participants were to decide how much risk a fictitious character in a dilemma should take. One dilemma, for example, involved a star quarterback who had to choose a late play in an important game with an archrival. One choice—a simple play, likely to succeed—would lead to a tie score, whereas another choice—a very risky play with only a slim hope of success—would lead to certain victory. Much to his surprise, Stoner found that the decisions rendered by the groups were much riskier than those formed by the individual group members prior to joining the group discussions. Stoner called this move away from conservative solutions a *risky shift*. For example, doctors, if asked individually, might claim that a patient's problem (whatever it might be) could be handled with medication and a change in diet. If these same doctors were to jointly discuss the patient's situation, they might conclude that a new and potentially dangerous (risky) surgical procedure was necessary.

Several hundred experimental studies later, psychologists now know that this effect also occurs in the opposite direction, a *cautious shift* (Levine & Moreland, 1990; Moscovici et al., 1985), and in situations that do not involve risk or caution (e.g., attitudes). In other

Source: nullplus/Shutterstock.

How fans perceive what happens during a football game is influenced by attitudes, biases, and expectations. Opposing sides can view the same event differently.

words, a risky shift is a general **group polarization effect** in which group participation makes an individual's reactions more extreme, or polarized. Group discussion usually leads to an enhancement of the group members' preexisting beliefs and attitudes. One explanation for group polarization is that open discussion gives group members an opportunity to hear persuasive arguments not previously considered, leading to a strengthening of their original attitudes (Isenberg, 1986). Another possibility is that, after comparing attitudinal positions with one another, some group members feel pressure to "catch up" with group members who have more extreme attitudes.

Irving Janis (1972, 1983) has described a related phenomenon of influence he calls **groupthink**, an excessive concern for reaching a consensus in group decision-making to the extent that critical evaluations are withheld. Janis maintains that this style of thinking emerges when group members are so interested in maintaining harmony within the group that differences of opinion or alternative courses of action are suppressed. Janis maintained that groupthink is most likely to occur in cohesive groups.

Janis (1972) identified eight common indicators of groupthink that lead to bad group decisions:

Group polarization effect—occurs when group participation makes an individual's reactions more extreme, or polarized.

Groupthink—an excessive concern for reaching a consensus in group decision-making to the extent that critical evaluations are withheld.

1. *An illusion of invulnerability*: Group members believe that nothing can harm them, which leads to excessive optimism.
2. *Rationalization*: Rather than realistically evaluating information, group members collectively rationalize away damaging information.
3. *Unquestioned belief in the groups' inherent morality*: The group sees itself on the side of what is right and just. This leads group members to ignore the moral implications and consequences of their actions.
4. *Stereotyped views of the enemy*: The "enemy" is characterized as too weak or stupid to put up any meaningful resistance to the group's planned course of action,
5. *Conformity pressures*: Direct pressure is placed on any group member who dissents from the group's consensus of action.
6. *Self-censorship*: Due to conformity pressure, individual group members remain silent because of the potential consequences.
7. *An illusion of unanimity*: Because of self-censorship, the group suffers the illusion that everyone agrees with the course of action being planned by the group.
8. *Emergence of self-appointed mindguards*: Self-appointed "mindguards" emerge to protect the group from damaging outside information. These people intercept potentially damaging information and don't pass it along to the group.

Janis analyzed the decision-making process involved in several key historical events—such as the bombing of Pearl Harbor military response, the Bay of Pigs invasion, and the Challenger explosion—in terms of groupthink. He found that such situations involved three common factors: a cohesive, decision-making group that was relatively isolated from outside judgments; a directive leader who supplied pressure to conform to his position; and an illusion of unanimity (see also, McCauley, 1989).

Generally, Janis' groupthink hypothesis has weathered the test of time. However, some research suggests that group cohesiveness may not be as crucial to the emergence of groupthink as Janis originally believed (Kerr & Tindale, 2004). Directive leadership and consensus seeking, which make groups more concerned with enhancing morale and reaching agreement than with attaining quality decisions, are important precursors of groupthink

(Tetlock, Peterson, McGuire, Chang, & Feld, 1992). Finally, Gerald Whyte (1989) has proposed that group polarization, risk-taking, and the potential for a fiasco occur when a group frames its decision in terms of potential failure. Whyte suggests that when a group frames possible outcomes in terms of potential failure, the group is more likely to make a risky decision. Working in an environment that favors risky decisions enhances the likelihood of a disastrous group decision. There also is good evidence that time pressure—or the perception of time pressure—increases the likelihood to seek consensus and solution, whether the solution is a good one or not (Kelly, Jackson, & Huston-Comeaux, 1997).

STUDY CHECK

What are the factors known to influence decision-making within groups?
What are group polarization and groupthink?

THINKING CRITICALLY

If psychologists have such a clear idea of why some decisions made by groups are—at best—overly risky, why do groups continue to make such errors?

Chapter Summary

What do psychologists mean by social cognition?
Social psychology is the field of psychology concerned with how others influence the thoughts, feelings, and behaviors of the individual. Social psychologists accept the premise that we do not view our social environment solely on the basis of the stimulus information that it presents to us, but that we have developed cognitive structures or processes (e.g., attitudes and schemas) that influence our interpretation of the world around us.

How do social psychologists define an attitude?
Social psychologists define an attitude as a relatively stable disposition used to evaluate an object or event.

What are the components of an attitude, and how are they related?
An attitude consists of feelings (affects), behaviors, and beliefs (cognitions). Although the affective and cognitive components of attitudes are often consistent with each other, they may be inconsistent with behavior, largely because behavior is influenced by so many situational variables. Because of the possible inconsistency of other attitude components and behaviors, some psychologists have argued that a significant component of an attitude is not actual, overt behavior, as such, but behavior intention. Additionally, attitudes operate on an unconscious level (implicit attitudes) and conscious level (explicit attitudes).

How is attitude change brought about by persuasion?
Persuasion is the process of changing attitudes through the use of rational and/or emotional arguments. The Yale Communication Model states that the source, message, audience, and channel of communication affect persuasion. The most important characteristic of the source is credibility, which is the believability of the source. It is made up of trustworthiness and expertise. The nature of the message affects persuasion. Fear appeals use emotion to persuade, whereas rational appeals use facts and figures. Messages that are moderately discrepant from a target's existing attitude are more effective than those that are high or low in discrepancy. The elaboration likelihood model states that there are two routes to persuasion. Messages processed along the central route are processed carefully. Those processed along the peripheral route are not.

What are prejudice, stereotypes, and discrimination, and how are they related?
Prejudice is an attitude about another person based solely on his or her membership in some group. Prejudices are usually negative. They lead to expectations of behaviors, based solely on group membership. Stereotypes are rigid beliefs about members of a group that lead to overgeneralized schemas or images of group members. It is a matter of over-categorization based on a small set of characteristics. Like attitudes, stereotypes may be explicit or implicit. Discrimination is the behavioral outcome of prejudice or stereotyping. It is a matter of actually acting toward someone based on his or her group membership. That is how these three concepts are related: Each uses group membership, rather than the characteristics of the individual, as a basis of action and reaction.

What is conformity, and how was it demonstrated by Solomon Asch?

Conformity is a social influence process in which behavior is modified in response to perceived pressure from others so that the behavior becomes consistent with that of others. Conformity is often thought of in negative terms, but conformity helps make social behavior efficient and predictable. In Asch's studies, people made judgments about unambiguous perceptual stimuli: the length of lines. During some trials, confederates gave judgments that were clearly incorrect, before the actual participant had a chance to respond. Although there were situations in which yielding to group pressure could be lessened, many of Asch's participants conformed.

What is obedience and how was it demonstrated in the laboratory by Milgram?

Obedience means complying with the demands of an authority figure, even if such compliance is against one's better judgment. Participants in Milgram's experiments were led to believe they were administering more and more potent shocks to another person in a learning task. When they hesitated to deliver shocks, an authority figure, the experimenter, prodded them to continue. All participants obeyed to some degree, and nearly two-thirds delivered what they thought was the most intense shock, even over the protests of the learner. Those who obeyed in Milgram's experiments were neither cruel nor inhumane. Rather, the experimenter created a powerful social situation that made it difficult to refuse the authority figure's orders. Milgram found that gender was not related to obedience rates. When Milgram moved the teacher and learner closer together (in the same room), obedience dropped. The lowest rate of obedience was observed when the teacher actually had to touch the learner to give him a shock.

What are the factors that predict whether someone in need will be given assistance from bystanders?

Darley and Latané proposed that a person must pass through a series of cognitive events before he or she will help someone in need. First, a bystander must notice the emergency. Second, the bystander must label the situation. Third, the bystander must assume responsibility for helping. Fourth, the bystander must decide how to help. Finally, the bystander must implement the decision to help. A negative decision at any point will result in no help being offered.

The likelihood that someone will intervene on behalf of another in an emergency is lessened as a function of how many others (bystanders) are present at the time. The greater the number of bystanders present, the less likely a person in need will receive help. This is known as the bystander effect. Several factors have been proposed to account for this phenomenon. Audience inhibition is the term used to describe the hesitancy to intervene in front of others, perhaps out of fear of embarrassing oneself. Pluralistic ignorance occurs when others lead someone to think (by their inactivity) that nothing is wrong in an ambiguous emergency situation. Diffusion of responsibility causes a member of a group to feel less obligated to intervene (less responsible) than if he or she were alone.

What are social loafing and social facilitation, and under what circumstances are they likely to occur?

Social loafing occurs when one is less likely to invest full effort and energy in the task at hand as a member of a group than he or she would if working alone (at least in Western, individualist cultures). Data suggest that as group size increases, social loafing increases. Being able to "hide" in a group and go unnoticed also increases the social loafing effect. On the other hand, when tasks are simple or well-rehearsed, performance may be enhanced, a process called social facilitation. When tasks are difficult, complex, or unrehearsed, the presence of others is likely to have a negative effect on performance.

What are the factors known to influence decision-making within groups?

Groups often outperform individuals because groups recognize a correct answer faster, reject an incorrect answer faster, and have better (or at least larger) memory systems than the average person. Groups with high-quality members perform better than groups with low-quality members. Increasing group size increases resources available to the group, but it also increases process loss. In larger groups, member participation is less even than in smaller groups. Interpersonal cohesiveness and task-based cohesiveness enhance group performance when a problem requires a great deal of interaction.

What are group polarization and groupthink?

Although there are advantages to problem-solving in a group setting, there are also liabilities. Group polarization (originally known as the risky shift) is the tendency for a group discussion to solidify and enhance pre-existing attitudes. Groupthink is an excessive concern for reaching a consensus at the expense of carefully considering alternative courses of action. Groupthink has been found to contribute to bad group decisions. Irving Janis identified eight symptoms of groupthink: An illusion of invulnerability, rationalization, an unquestioned belief in the group's morality, stereotyped views of the enemy, conformity pressures, self-censorship, an illusion of unanimity, and the emergence of self-appointed "mindguards."

Key Terms

Social psychology (p. 300)
Social cognition (p. 301)
Attitude (p. 303)
Explicit attitude (p. 304)
Implicit attitude (p. 304)
Persuasion (p. 305)
Credibility (p. 305)
Elaboration likelihood model (p. 305)
Prejudice (p. 306)
Stereotype (p. 306)
Explicit stereotype (p. 307)
Implicit stereotype (p. 307)
Discrimination (p. 307)

Modern racism (p. 308)
Conformity (p. 310)
Obedience (p. 312)
Bystander effect (p. 315)
Audience inhibition (p. 316)
Pluralistic ignorance (p. 316)
Diffusion of responsibility (p. 317)
Category relationship (p. 317)
Social loafing (p. 317)
Social facilitation (p. 318)
Group polarization effect (p. 320)
Groupthink (p. 320)

Development Throughout the Life Span

Source: Monkey Business Images/Shutterstock.

Questions You Will Be Able to Answer

After reading Chapter 15, you should be able to answer the following questions:

- What are the major events in prenatal development?
- What are the consequences of a pregnant mother's behaviors?
- What are the consequences of the father's behaviors for prenatal development?
- What are the basic features of Piaget's theory of cognitive development?
- What are the ages of, and characteristics of, Piaget's four stages of cognitive development?
- What is the information-processing approach to cognitive development, and how does it differ from Piaget's theory?
- What is gender identity, and when does it develop?
- What are the major—and conflicting—views of adolescence that have been put forward in psychology?
- What characterizes the onset of puberty?
- What are the consequences of reaching puberty before or after one's age-mates?

- What is meant by "identity formation" in adolescence, and what factors influence its development?
- How do psychologists characterize "early adulthood"?
- What factors tend to influence the choice of a mate?
- What are the consequences of young adults starting a family?
- What factors may be involved in making a decision about one's career?
- How is middle adulthood characterized?
- What are the major aspects of the last stage of human development, late adulthood?

Preview

From conception to death, human beings share many developmental events and experiences that unite us as one species. Still, each of us is unique and distinct from all others. Developmental psychologists are interested in both common patterns of development *and* the ways in which people differ throughout their lives. Growth and development begin before birth, so we will start with a discussion of prenatal development.

The focus of most discussions of the psychology of children is usually their cognitive development. Because it is such a classic and has inspired so many others, we will begin with the approach of Jean Piaget. We will look at the basics of his theory and each of his four stages of cognitive development. Next, we will explore an alternative view of cognitive development: the information-processing approach.

For more than 100 years, psychologists have struggled to determine how best to characterize that period of life called adolescence. Once we come to grips with just what it means to be an adolescent, we will address the issues of physical maturation and identity formation.

We will divide our discussion of adulthood into three sub-stages: early, middle, and late. Although there are no sharp dividing lines, each sub-stage does reflect a rather different set of challenges and adjustments, involving family, career, retirement and—ultimately—one's own mortality.

Prenatal Development

Human development begins at conception, when the father's sperm cell unites with the mother's ovum, or egg cell. At that time, all of the genes on the 23 chromosomes from each parent's cell pairs off within a single new cell, called the *zygote*. We have in that one action the transmission of all inherited characteristics. The period of development between conception and birth is called the **prenatal period**. From the one cell that defines conception until birth the newborn human will have grown to include about 200 billion cells (Shaffer & Kipp, 2007). The prenatal period includes three stages: the *stage of the zygote*, the *embryonic stage*, and the *stage of the fetus*.

The *stage of the zygote* begins at the moment of conception, when the sperm cell from the father unites with the ovum (or egg cell) of the mother, and lasts for just two weeks. In this time frame, the newly formed zygote travels down the fallopian tube toward the uterus. As it makes this journey, the zygote undergoes rapid cell growth, eventually forming a hollow ball of cells called the *blastocyst* and then implanting itself into the uterine wall. All remaining growth and development during the prenatal stage will take place in the uterus.

The time between two weeks after conception through week eight is called the *embryonic stage*. During this period, the embryo (as the developing organism is now called) develops at a rapid rate, and all of the organ systems of the body are laid in place. It is during the embryonic stage that the unborn child is most sensitive to environmental influences. If any prenatal problems occur, they are most likely to develop during this stage.

Prenatal period—the period of development between conception and birth.

Human Embryonic and Fetal Development

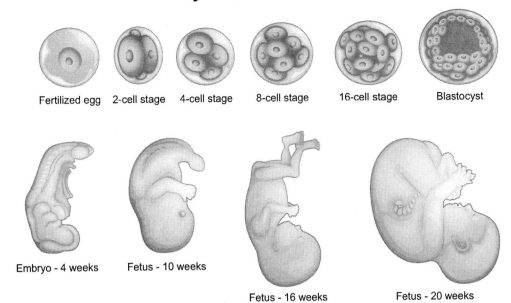

FIGURE 15.1 Prenatal Development

Human prenatal development is the process in which a fertilized egg becomes an embryo and develops as a fetus until birth. In the fetal stage, many organs are formed.

Source: BlueRingMedia/Shutterstock.com.

Two months after conception, the embryonic stage draws to a close. The 1-inch-long embryo now has enough of a primitive nervous system to respond to a light touch, exhibiting a simple reflex movement. The *stage of the fetus* has begun. Changes that occur during the fetal stage are shown in **Figure 15.1**. Now the most noticeable change, at least to the mother, is the significant increase in weight and movement of the fetus. Sometime in the seventh month, most fetuses reach the point of *viability*—the time when it could survive if it were born. However, if the fetus were to survive outside the mother, it would almost certainly do so only with medical intervention. After nearly 270 days, the fetus is ready to enter the world as a *newborn*.

In a vast majority of cases, the growth and development of the human organism from conception through birth progresses smoothly, according to the blueprint laid down in the genes. However, in the prenatal period, the human organism is not immune to influences from the environment. Most external influences on prenatal development have negative consequences.

The old expression, "You are what you eat" has some truth. In the same way, before we are born, we are what our mothers eat. Mothers who are malnourished have more miscarriages, stillbirths, and premature births. Newborns with low birth weight (four pounds or less) who survive have a much greater risk of cognitive deficits, even as they approach adolescence (Taylor et al., 2000). At a minimum, the newborn of a malnourished mother will also be malnourished.

There is ample evidence that smoking cigarettes has harmful effects on the smoker. Smoking during pregnancy is associated with low birth weight, premature birth, and stillbirths (Pollack, Lantz, & Frohna, 2000; Torpy, 2005). Infants born to smokers require more stimulation to arouse from sleep (Franco et al., 1999), show decrements in attention, are more irritable (Espy et al., 2011), and have a higher risk of hearing defects. Children whose mothers smoked a pack of cigarettes a day during pregnancy have a 75 percent increase in the risk for intellectual disability, even when other risk factors (e.g., maternal age, education, and alcohol use) are controlled (Drews & Murphy, 1996). As they get older, the children of mothers who smoked during pregnancy have more

Along with prenatal medical care, pregnant women can choose what is best for the yet unborn: to eat healthy food, and avoid alcohol, smoking, and drugs.

Fetal alcohol syndrome (FAS)—a condition occurring when mothers drink during pregnancy, resulting in smaller babies with retarded growth, poor coordination, poor muscle tone, intellectual disabilities, and other problems.

behavioral problems such as aggression and hyperactivity (Mick et al., 2002), and they perform less effectively on visual perceptual tasks (Fried & Watkinson, 2000) compared to children of nonsmokers. Researchers in Spain discovered that smoking in pregnancy can even cause genetic damage to the unborn fetus. One common type of chromosome damage linked to maternal smoking increases the risk of blood cancers (like leukemia) (de la Chica et al., 2005).

Alcohol is a drug that can seriously damage unborn children. Alcohol quickly and directly passes from the mother to the fetus. Alcohol then collects in organs that have high water content, most ominously in the gray matter of the brain. To make things worse, the fetus eliminates alcohol at half the rate of the mother. The bottom line is that alcohol gets into the fetus easily and stays in for a long time.

Heavy drinking (three drinks or more per day) or binge drinking during vulnerable periods of organ development significantly increases the chance of having a baby with birth defects. **Fetal alcohol syndrome (FAS)** occurs when mothers drink during pregnancy, resulting in smaller babies with retarded growth, poor coordination, poor muscle tone, intellectual retardation, and other problems. Lower alcohol consumption during critical periods of pregnancy can result in a range of negative outcomes less severe than full-blown FAS known as *fetal alcohol effects (FAE)*. For example, light alcohol consumption (as little as one drink per day) during early or mid-pregnancy is related to deficits in fine motor skills. Children whose mothers drank even small amounts of alcohol during pregnancy are at an increased risk for behavior problems later in life (Sood et al., 2001). Among other things, such children are more likely to be diagnosed with attention-deficit hyperactivity disorder (Mick et al., 2002) and are much more likely to have alcohol-related problems of their own, even at the age of 21 (Baer et al., 2003; Streissguth et al., 2004).

Mothers who use or abuse psychoactive drugs during pregnancy may seriously harm their unborn children. For example, 70 percent of newborns of mothers who used heroin during pregnancy showed symptoms of drug withdrawal (e.g., tremor, irritability, hyperactivity and respiratory problems) after birth (Weintraub et al., 1998). Deficits related to cocaine use during pregnancy can be found in preschool children (largely a slowing of language development), and in early grade school (largely behavior problems) (Delaney-Black et al., 2004; Estelles et al., 2005; Lewis et al., 2004).

As you were reading through this section on nourishment, alcohol, and drugs, did it sound at all sexist to you? Everything we have covered puts the focus on mothers—what *mothers* should and should not do. Eat a balanced diet. Don't drink. Don't do drugs. Don't smoke. Although most attention has been focused on mothers, fathers have not been totally ignored. Researchers have examined the role of fathers in the physical problems of their children (Lamb, 2004). The major impact of the father involves the condition of his sperm at conception. Psychologists now recognize that the age of the father is related to some cases of intellectual disability. Research also confirms that a father's age is a risk factor for schizophrenia in children. One study examined the medical records of over 50 thousand members of the Swedish army and found that advancing paternal age is associated with an increased risk of developing schizophrenia (Zammit et al., 2003). Research also supports the hypothesis that advanced *paternal* age is a significant risk factor for the development of autism (Reichenberg et al., 2006).

The Cognitive Development of Children

Cognitive development refers to age-related changes in learning, memory, perception, attention, thinking and problem-solving. From the moment a person is born, several changes are taking place in the basic psychological processes underlying cognition.

Jean Piaget (1952) proposed a comprehensive theory that describes the course of cognitive development from birth through adolescence. In 1919 he left his native Switzerland and went to France. There, although he was not trained as a psychologist, Piaget worked with Alfred Binet to help develop the first IQ test; he became fascinated with the *incorrect* answers children gave to items on the test. He noticed that children of about the same age gave very similar incorrect answers. His observations eventually led Piaget to conclude that cognitive development was represented by qualitative changes in the ways that children think.

Piaget claimed that intelligence has two aspects: structure (what is known) and function (how one comes to know it). A structure of cognitive knowledge is a **schema**—a mental representation that children construct in order to make sense of the world in which they live. Functions are the mechanisms that help children understand and adapt to their environments. They are the processes by which the child comes to discover the objects and events of his or her world and to create new or different schemas. One major cognitive function for Piaget is **adaptation**—developing the appropriate schemas so that one can manage the demands of the environment. How does a child get along in the world? By using the appropriate schemas. Where do these schemas come from? Adaptation.

Piaget's is a *stage theory*, maintaining that a child passes through four qualitatively different stages of cognitive development. Piaget further argued that these stages were universal across cultures and that movement through the stages was in one direction (from less complex to more complex thinking). Although Piaget allowed for no variation in the order of cognitive development, he did observe that there certainly were large individual differences in how rapidly children moved from one stage to the next. Let's take a brief look at Piaget's stages of cognitive development. Piaget's stages of development are summarized in **Table 15.1**.

In the **sensorimotor stage** (birth to two years), children learn about the world by sensing (*sensori-*) and by doing (*motor*). A child may come to appreciate, for example, that a quick pull on a dog's tail (a motor activity) reliably produces a loud yelp (a sensory experience), perhaps followed, in turn, by parental attention. One of the most useful schemas to develop in the sensorimotor stage is that of *causality*. Infants gradually come to realize that events may have knowable causes and that some behaviors cause predictable reactions. Pushing a bowl of oatmeal off the high chair causes a mess and gets Mommy's attention: if A, then B—a very practical insight.

Cognitive development—age-related changes in learning, memory, perception, attention, thinking, and problem solving.

Schema—a mental representation that children construct in order to make sense of the world in which they live.

Adaptation—in Piaget's theory, developing the appropriate schemas so that one can manage the demands of the environment.

Sensorimotor stage (birth to two years)—Piaget's first stage of development, in which children learn about the world by sensing (*sensori-*) and by doing (*motor*).

TABLE 15.1 Piaget's Stage of Cognitive Development

Stage	Description
Sensorimotor stage	Birth to two years; a child learns about the world by sensing (sensori-) and by doing (motor). Advances in understanding causality, development of object permanence, and imitation.
Preoperational stage	Two to seven years; a child's thinking is self-centered (*egocentric*). The child begins to use symbols in thinking but have difficulty with abstract concepts.
Concrete operations stage	Seven to eleven years; a child begins to form many new concepts, and shows that he or she can manipulate those concepts. The child can organize objects into categories, but the categories are concrete. Difficulty with abstract concepts and categories.
Formal operations stage	Twelve and older; involves the logical manipulation of abstract, symbolic concepts. The child can develop and mentally test hypotheses and work through problems mentally.

An important discovery that occurs near the end of this developmental stage is that objects exist even when they are not immediately in view. This is called *object permanence*. Early in this stage, an object that is out of sight is more than out of mind. It simply ceases to exist. By the end of the sensorimotor period, children have learned that objects can still exist even if they are not physically present and that their reappearance can be anticipated. Another useful skill acquired in the sensorimotor period is *imitation*. If it is within its range of abilities, a baby will imitate almost any behavior it sees. A cognitive strategy has developed, one that will be used for a lifetime: trying to imitate the behaviors of a model.

Throughout most of the **preoperational stage** (two to seven years), a child's thinking is self-centered (technically, *egocentric*). According to Piaget, the child has difficulty understanding life from someone else's perspective. In this usage, egocentrism was never meant to imply a selfish, emotional sort of reaction. It simply refers to a limitation on children's thinking when they are in the early years of preoperational thought. Imagine a 4-year-old child seated at a table upon which is placed a large paper maché mountain. In the child's view are several small plastic sheep "grazing" on the mountainside. At the other end of the table sits another child looking at the same mountain, but on this side there are no sheep. The children each assume that the other has exactly the same view, either with or without sheep.

In the preoperational stage, children begin to develop symbols, often in the form of words, to represent concepts. At this stage, children do not yet know how to manipulate symbols in a consistent, rule-governed way. It's not until the end of this period that they can play word games or understand why riddles about rabbits throwing clocks out of windows in order to "see time fly" are funny. It is similarly true that children at this stage have difficulty with many "abstract" concepts, such

Preoperational stage (two to seven years)—Piaget's second stage of development, in which a child's thinking is self-centered.

Source: Pazargic Liviu/Shutterstock.

Considering what you have just read, what is likely to happen in this scenario?

as religious beliefs. Still, they seem quite capable of playing "make believe," pretending to be mommies and daddies, for instance.

Children in the **concrete operations stage** (7 to 11 years) begin to form many new concepts and show that they can manipulate those concepts. For example, they can organize objects into categories of things: balls over here, blocks over there, plastic soldiers in a pile by the door, and so on. Each of these items is recognized as a toy, ultimately to be put away in the toy box and not in the closet, which is where clothes are supposed to go. It is in this period that rule-governed behavior begins. The concrete, observable objects of the child's world can be classified, ranked, ordered, or separated into more than one category, according to rules.

As its name suggests, in the concrete operations stage, children begin to use and manipulate (operate on) concepts and ideas. But manipulations are still very concrete—tied to real objects in the here and now. An 8-year-old can be expected to find her way to and from school, even if she throws in a side trip along the way. What she will have difficulty doing is telling you with any precision just how she gets from one place to another. Drawing a sensible map is difficult for her. If she stands on the corner of Maple Street and Sixth Avenue, she knows where to go next to get home. Dealing with the concrete reality, here and now, is easy. Dealing with such knowledge in abstract terms is tough.

The last of Piaget's stages is **formal operations stage** (12 and older) and involves the logical manipulation of abstract, symbolic concepts. The key to this stage is abstract, symbolic reasoning. By the age of 12, most children can develop and mentally test hypotheses—they can work through problems mentally.

In the stage of formal operations, youngsters can reason through hypothetical problems: "What if you were the only person in the world who liked rock music?" "If nobody had to go to school, what would happen?" Now they are able to deal with questions that are literally contrary to fact: "What if John F. Kennedy or Ronald Reagan were still president of the United States?"

There can be no doubting the significance of Piaget's influence. His observations and insights about intellectual development spanned decades. Considerable research has supported many of these insights. Finding evidence of Piaget's stages is one of the success stories of cross-cultural research. That evidence tells us that the stages just reviewed can be found in children around the world (Brislin, 1993; Segall et al., 1990). As Piaget predicted, there will be some individual differences, of course.

There are two major criticisms of Piaget's theory: First, the borderlines between his proposed stages are much less clear-cut than his theory suggests, and, secondly, Piaget underestimated the cognitive talents of preschool children (Bjorklund, 2000; Wellman & Gelman, 1992). As one example, the egocentrism said to characterize the child in the preoperational stage may not be as extreme as Piaget believed. In one study (Lempers et al., 1977), children were shown a picture pasted inside a box. They were asked to show the picture to someone else. In showing the picture, they turned it so that it would be right side up to the viewer. Every child over two years old indicated such an appreciation of someone else's point of view. More than that, research makes it clear

Source: Africa Studio/Shutterstock.

In the preoperational stage, children can play make-believe, and pretend to be a parent.

Source: Monkey Business Images/Shutterstock.

During Piaget's concrete operations stage, manipulating concepts and ideas are still concrete. These girls know the way to get home from school, but would have difficulty drawing a map to show you the route.

Source: Monkey Business Images/Shutterstock.

During Piaget's formal operations stage, abstract, symbolic reasoning occurs, and children can test hypotheses.

Concrete operations stage (7 to 11 years)—Piaget's third stage of development, in which children begin to form many new concepts and show that they can manipulate those concepts.

Formal operations stage (12 and older)—Piaget's fourth stage of development involving the logical manipulation of abstract, symbolic concepts.

that young children (18 months old) readily ascribe goals and intentions to the action of others. That is, preschoolers can observe someone else doing something and appreciate what it is they are trying to do (Meltzoff, 1995).

Although some of Piaget's observations and assumptions have come under attack, this is to be expected in science, particularly for so grand a theory. Nonetheless, Piaget made some important contributions. He focused attention on the social and emotional development of children and had considerable influence on the American educational system (Shaffer, 1999). He showed that children are not just passive receptacles during the development process but rather are active participants in their own cognitive development. One of the most important contributions of Jean Piaget is that he developed a theory of cognitive development in children that was so detailed, so thought-provoking, that it will continue to challenge researchers for years to come.

FOCUS ON DIVERSITY

Group Differences in Moral Reasoning

How children learn to reason and judge right and wrong is an aspect of cognitive development that has received considerable attention. Although Piaget (1932/1948) included the development of moral reasoning in his theory of cognitive development, the theory proposed by Lawrence Kohlberg (1981, 1985) dominates research in the area. Like Piaget's theory, Kohlberg's theory is a stage theory. The stages were developed based on male children's responses to a number of moral dilemmas. One dilemma, for example, went like this: Should a man steal a drug in order to save his wife's life after the pharmacist who invented the drug refuses to sell it to him? Why or why not? Based on the answers given, Kohlberg proposed three main stages of moral development: *preconventional*, *conventional*, and *postconventional morality*. A child at the level of preconventional morality would reason that the man should not steal the drug because "he'll get caught and be put in jail." At this level, the individual is mostly concerned with the rewards or punishments associated with behavior. At the level of conventional morality, the individual is most concerned with rule structures and accepted moral conventions. Moral behavior is guided by what is socially accepted or not accepted. So, a child might say that the man should not steal the drug because "you should always follow rules." At the postconventional level, moral behavior is guided by a person's inner sense of what is right or wrong. So, a person in this stage would say that the man should steal the drug because human life is more important than making a profit.

An inevitable criticism of Kohlberg's theory is that it was first developed based on judgments of only male children. It may be that male and female children do not reason morally in the same way. When girls were tested, some studies showed that girls showed less advanced moral development than boys. Carol Gilligan (1982) suggested that the moral reasoning of females is different from the moral reasoning of males, and that is why they showed less advanced moral development. According to Gilligan, males (at least in Western cultures) are concerned with rules, justice, and an individual's rights. As a result, they approach moral dilemmas differently than do females, who characteristically are more concerned with caring, personal responsibility, and interpersonal relationships (Gilligan, 1982).

Are there gender differences in moral reasoning as suggested by Gilligan? Research shows that sometimes there are, and sometimes there are not (Knox, Fagley, & Miller, 2004). Even when gender differences are found, they tend to be small (Darley & Schultz, 1990). With respect to reasoning via justice or caring, research shows that both females and males show concern for both aspects of moral reasoning (Smetana, Kilen, & Turiel, 1991). Also, the gender of the person making a moral judgment interacts with the gender of the person portrayed in a moral dilemma. If the main character and participant making a moral judgment are the same gender, higher levels of moral reasoning are used than if the main character and participant are of opposite sexes (McGillicuddy-DeLisi, Sullivan, & Hughes, 2003). So, if gender differences exist in moral reasoning, they are small and complex.

Culture also appears to relate to moral reasoning. Kohlberg's dilemmas and stages reflect mostly Western thought and culture. Western culture is geared toward individualism, or the idea that one is personally responsible for one's actions. Other cultures are more collective in nature. That is, they place more emphasis on what others think, and thinking is geared more toward the good of the group than the individual. Additionally, different cultures value different pathways to morality. For example, Indian culture relies heavily on the notion of karma yoga, or the path of unselfish action. In this view, the individual is driven more by spiritual growth than by personal gain. Mulla and Krishnan (2014) argue that Western notions of moral reasoning moving from a lower to a higher plane of reasoning may not be all that relevant in Indian culture.

So, are there actual differences between cultures in moral reasoning? Research suggests that there are. For example, Smith and Parekh (1996) compared blacks and whites in four age groups in South Africa. Participants judged Kohlberg's moral dilemmas, and the researchers analyzed their moral reasoning. Smith and Parekh found a significant difference only for participants in the oldest (19–28 years) age group. In this age group, whites showed higher levels of moral reasoning than blacks. In another study of blacks and whites in South Africa, Ferns and Thom (2001) also found that whites reasoned at a higher level than blacks. They also found that progression through Kohlberg's stages was more characteristic of the white participants than the black participants. The black participants progressed to a "law-and-order" (rule-based) orientation but not much further. Fern and Thom suggested the difference was related to blacks being socialized more toward collectivism than individualism, with the opposite being true for whites. Other research shows that Kohlberg's theory does not apply as well to collectivist as to individualistic cultures.

Interestingly, the rule-based orientation found for black South Africans has not been found in blacks from the United States (Jackson, Zhao, Witt, Fitzgerald, & Von Eye, 2009). Jackson et al. found that black American males (and white females) tended to show a strong caring orientation rather than a rule-based orientation. White males, on the other hand, took a more rule-based perspective indicative of conventional moral reasoning. The difference between South African and American black adolescents might be accounted for by the different social histories of the United States and South Africa. In apartheid South Africa, blacks were subjected to harsh rule up until the early 1990s and were expected to follow oppressive laws and rules or face harsh punishment. One can see how this could lead to a rule-based view of morality. American blacks, not experiencing this system, could develop a less rule-based moral system.

Another study investigated differences in prosocial moral reasoning between Spanish (Western culture) and Turkish (non-Western culture) adolescents (Kumru, Carlo, Mestre, & Samper, 2012). According to Kumru et al. prosocial moral reasoning "is the cognitive ability to make decisions about moral dilemmas in situations where one's own interests conflict with those of others and in contexts where formal rules are weak or absent" (p. 206). Kumru et al. found that adolescents from the two cultures showed differences in moral reasoning. Spanish adolescents scored higher on measures of internalized moral reasoning (a higher level of moral reasoning) than Turkish adolescents. Turkish adolescents showed a preference for moral reasoning focused on the needs of others. Kumru et al. suggest that these differences reflect a difference in the way children are socialized in Spain and Turkey. A study of generosity (used as an index of moral reasoning) showed that North American (U.S. and Canadian) and Chinese children showed higher levels of generosity (sharing resources) and egalitarianism (the belief in the equality of all people) than children from Turkey and South Africa (Cowell et al., 2017). Cowell et al. maintain that the differences found cannot be attributed to the individualism–collectivism dimension because members of both an individualistic (North American) and collectivist (Chinese) culture showed the highest level of generosity. Instead, they suggest that cultural differences rooted in the size of the economy and the history of market integration were important factors in the differences found.

The Information-Processing Approach

Piaget's theory is important on a number of levels. One is that it started developmental psychologists thinking about the cognitive development of children. An alternative view emerged that has a different perspective on cognitive development. Piaget's theory suggests that there are qualitative changes (changes in kind) in cognitive abilities with each stage of development. The information-processing approach looks at quantitative changes (changes in degree) in a number of information-processing systems, such as learning and memory.

Consistent with this view, we see that there are quantitative changes in learning with development. Newborns and young infants are capable of learning simple classically conditioned responses. A two-hour-old newborn is stroked on the forehead and seems not to respond. If we pair the stroking with a sugar solution delivered to the infant's lips, sugar solution (unconditioned stimulus) elicits the unconditioned response of turning the head and making sucking movements. After several pairings of the stroking of the forehead

Information-processing approach—a view of cognitive development suggesting quantitative changes (changes in degree) in a number of information-processing systems, such as learning and memory.

and the sugar solution, the baby turns its head and makes sucking movements when its forehead is touched (Blass, Ganchow, & Steiner, 1984). This is due to a simple classical conditioning process. Similarly, the newborn quickly learns to associate its mother's smell, voice, and heartbeat with the delivery of food (Moon & Fifer, 1990). As the infant gets older, he or she becomes capable of learning via operant conditioning. Eventually, the child learns via other mechanisms, such as imitation. Although very young infants can imitate simple behaviors, the sophistication of this type of learning increases with increasing development.

In order to benefit from what we learn, we must be able to store information in memory for later use. We see quantitative changes in memory systems as a child develops. There is evidence that infants as young as one to four days old can remember simple relationships over time (Friedman, 1972). For example, if an infant is shown the same stimulus over and over, the infant eventually stops looking at it. If a new stimulus is presented, the infant will look at it. If the old stimulus is presented again, the infant looks away. In order to make this discrimination between a new and old stimulus, the infant must have some memory of the original stimulus. By the time infants are two to three months old, they can remember an interesting event for several days (Shaffer, 2002). Over the course of infancy, memory gets better and better, mainly due to the rapid development of the frontal lobes of the brain associated with memory. Children's memories improve rapidly between the ages of 3 and 12 years of age. An important change is in the memory strategies used to remember information. For example, to learn a list of words, verbal rehearsal is an effective strategy (i.e., saying the words to yourself over and over). Flavell (1977) found that only 10 percent of kindergarteners used verbal rehearsal without being told to do so. By second grade, 60 percent are doing so. It is not that younger children cannot use verbal rehearsal; they can if they are told to. It is just they will not use it on their own. There are changes in how children rehearse with age. Younger children (five to eight years old) rehearse one item at a time. However, older children (12 years old) rehearse items in related clusters (Guttentag, Ornstein, & Siemens, 1987). The use of mental imagery (forming images to aid memory) is a sophisticated strategy that gets better with age. For example, Pressley and Levin (1980) found that first graders' memory was improved by imagery only if they were reminded to use the images when tested. On the other hand, sixth graders benefitted from imagery whether or not they were reminded to use images at retrieval.

STUDY CHECK

What are the basic features of Piaget's theory of cognitive development?
What are the ages of, and characteristics of, Piaget's four stages of cognitive development?
What is the information-processing approach to cognitive development, and how does it differ from Piaget's theory?

THINKING CRITICALLY

Can you relate any of the themes and characters of the PBS television series *Sesame Street* to the stages of cognitive development proposed by Piaget?

Developing Gender Identity

Cognitive theories of development deal with how (and when) children develop concepts or cognitions about themselves and the world in which they live. In this section we'll focus on the concept of *gender*—one's sense of maleness or femaleness, as opposed to one's sex, which is a biological term. Gender has been defined as "the socially ascribed characteristics of females and males, their roles and appropriate behaviors" (Amaro, 1995, p. 437), and "the meanings that societies and individuals ascribe to female and male categories" (Eagly, 1995, p. 145).

One of the first proclamations made upon the birth of a baby is, "It's a girl!" or "It's a boy!" Parents wrap little girls in pink, boys in blue, and dress an infant or small child in clothes that proclaim the child a boy or a girl. And, these labels matter!

As infants, boys develop a bit more slowly, have a little more muscle tissue, and are somewhat more active, but even these differences are slight. During the first year of life there are virtually no differences in temperament or "difficulty" between boys and girls. Many adults believe that there ought to be differences between little boys and little girls, and they may choose toys, clothing, and playmates based on what they believe is acceptable. However, when averaged over many studies, there are few areas in which parents consistently treat their sons and daughters differently (Lytton & Romney, 1991).

The only area in which North American parents show significant differentiation is in the encouragement of different sex-typed activities for girls and boys. For example, in one study, fathers were more likely to give dolls to 1-year-old girls than to boys of the same age. However, even at this age, children prefer certain toys; when offered dolls, boys are less likely to play with them. In the first few years of school, girls and boys place different values on activities and see themselves as good at different things. Girls tend to value reading and instrumental music, but boys tend to value math and sports (Eccles et al., 1993).

Children's peer groups are significant for both girls and boys (Maccoby, 1988, 1990). By the age of three or four, girls and boys gravitate toward playmates of the same sex, a pattern that is shown cross-culturally. Boys tend to dominate in mixed-sex interactions. In fact, by school age, boys prefer to play in groups, while girls prefer to either play alone or to play with only one other girl (Benenson & Heath, 2006). Boys tend to use direct commands to influence others, whereas girls tend to use polite suggestions, which work with other girls but not with boys (Serbin et al., 1984). Girls develop more intense friendships and are more distressed when those friendships end.

At what age do boys and girls begin to see each other as "different"? When do children develop *gender identity*, that sense of maleness or femaleness? Most children develop a sense of gender identity by two or three years old (Paludi & Gullo, 1986). By the age of four, most children demonstrate gender stereotypes, showing that they believe that certain toys, occupations, or activities go better with males and some go better with females. By the time they start school most children associate various personality traits with men and with women. This pattern crosses cultural lines (Williams & Best, 1990). Once gender identity is established, it remains invulnerable to change. By late childhood and early adolescence, peer pressure intensifies gender differences (McHale et al., 2001).

This leads us to an age-old question in psychology: Where do gender differences come from? Are they primarily a product of social forces, or are they more closely related to biological differences? In many respects, this question oversimplifies the origins of gender differences. Gender-related behavior and preferences are undoubtedly the result of a complex interaction between biological, cognitive, and social factors (Iervolino et al., 2005).

Although the basic idea that one is a girl or a boy may remain constant for most children, the manner in which gender identity is expressed may change with age. Developmental psychologists have identified a gender identity phenomenon called *pink frilly dress* involving female children showing a rigid adherence to gender identity early in childhood. This is expressed in the child wearing only frilly dresses (often pink) and refusing to wear anything else (Halim, Ruble, & Amodio, 2011). There are two interesting things about this rigidity. First, it is much more common among girls than boys. Second, rigidity changes with age, with 73 percent of girls exhibiting rigidity at ages 3 to 4 and 50 percent at ages 5 to 6 (Halim et al., 2014).

STUDY CHECK

What is gender identity, and when does it develop?

THINKING CRITICALLY

As more women become soldiers and firefighters, and more men become primary caregivers for their children, what will the long-term effects be on children's development of gender identity?

What It Means to Be an Adolescent

Adolescence—the period of transition from the dependence of childhood to the independence of adulthood. It is the period of development that begins at puberty (sexual maturity) and lasts through the teen years.

Adolescence is a period of transition from the dependence of childhood to the independence of adulthood. It is the period of development that begins at puberty (sexual maturity) and lasts through the teen years—essentially the second decade of life.

Adolescence can be viewed from several different perspectives. In biological terms, adolescence begins with puberty—sexual maturity and an ability to reproduce—and concludes with the end of physical growth—usually late in the teen years. A psychological perspective emphasizes the development of the cognitions, feelings, and behaviors that characterize adolescence. Such approaches stress the development of problem-solving skills and increased reliance on the use of symbols, logic, and abstract thinking. Psychological perspectives emphasize the importance of identity formation and the appreciation of self and self-worth. A social perspective looks at the role of adolescents in their societies and defines adolescence in terms of being "in between"—not yet an adult, but no longer a child. In this context, adolescence usually lasts from the early teen years through the highest educational level, when a person is thought to enter the adult world.

Actually, whether we accept a biological, psychological, or social perspective, we are usually talking about people who, in our culture, are between the ages of 12 and 20. An intriguing issue in the psychology of adolescence today is how to characterize this stage of development in a general way. Is it a time of personal growth, independence, and positive change? Or is adolescence a period of rebellion, turmoil, and negativism?

The view that adolescence can be best described in terms of turmoil, storm, and stress is actually the older of the two, attributed to G. Stanley Hall (who wrote the first textbook on adolescence in 1904) and to Anna Freud (who applied psychoanalytic theory to adolescents). This position claims that normal adolescence involves many difficulties of adjustment. "To be normal during the adolescent period is by itself abnormal" (Freud, 1958, p. 275). "Adolescents may be expected to be extremely moody and depressed one day and excitedly 'high' the next. Explosive conflict with family, friends, and authorities is thought of as commonplace" (Powers et al., 1989, p. 200). Actually, the teen years often *do* present pressures and conflicts that require difficult choices, and some teenagers do react to those pressures in maladaptive ways.

Adolescence requires making adjustments, but those adjustments are usually made in psychologically healthy ways (Steinberg & Morris, 2001). As adolescents struggle for independence and for means of self-expression, some engage in behaviors that may be considered risky or reckless. Such behaviors are often a reflection of the socialization process of the teenagers' culture. Nonetheless, the majority of teenagers weather the challenges of the period without developing significant social, emotional, or behavioral difficulties.

At least we can describe adolescence as a stage of development that presents the individual with a series of challenges. In the following sections, we will examine two of the challenges faced by an adolescent: puberty and identity formation.

STUDY CHECK

What are the major—and conflicting—views of adolescence that have been put forward in psychology?

THINKING CRITICALLY

Think about your own adolescence. To what extent were your teenage years fraught with "storm and stress"? (And we do know that some of you are still in your teenage years.)

Challenges of Puberty

The onset of adolescence is marked by two biological changes: the growth spurt and puberty. These changes are summarized in **Figure 15.2**. First, there is a marked increase in height and weight, known as a *growth spurt*, and second, there is sexual maturation. The growth spurt of adolescence usually occurs in girls at an earlier age than it does in boys. Girls begin their growth spurt as early as age nine or ten and then slow down at about age 15. Boys generally show increased rates of growth between the ages of 12 and 17. Males usually don't reach adult height until their early twenties; females generally attain maximum height by their late teens.

At least some of the challenge of early adolescence may be a direct result of the growth spurt. It is common to find increases in weight and height occurring so rapidly that they are accompanied by real, physical growing pains, particularly in the arms and legs. The spurt of adolescent growth seldom affects all parts of the body uniformly, especially in boys. Boys around the ages of 13 and 14 often appear incredibly clumsy and awkward as they try to coordinate their large hands and feet with the rest of their bodies. One of the most noticeable areas of growth in boys is that of the larynx and vocal cords. As the vocal cords lengthen, the pitch of the voice lowers. This transition is seldom a smooth one, and a teenage boy may suffer through weeks of a squeaking, cracking change of pitch in his voice.

Puberty occurs when a person becomes physically capable of sexual reproduction. With the onset of puberty, there is a marked increase in levels of sex hormones—androgens in males and estrogens in females. (Everyone has androgens and estrogens. Males simply have more androgens; females have more estrogens.) Boys seldom know when their puberty begins. For some time they have experienced penile erections and nocturnal emissions of seminal fluid. Puberty in males begins with the appearance of live sperm in the semen, and most males have no idea when that happens; that requires a laboratory test. In females, the onset of puberty is quite recognizable. It is indicated by the first menstrual period, called **menarche**.

Puberty—when a person becomes physically capable of sexual reproduction.

With puberty, adolescents are biologically ready to reproduce. Dealing with that readiness and making the adjustments that we associate with psychological maturity, however, do not come automatically with sexual maturity. Some boys and girls reach puberty before or after most of their peers and are referred to as early or late bloomers. Reaching puberty well before or after others of the same age may have some psychological effects, although few are long lasting.

Menarche—the first menstrual period.

Let's first get an idea of what early and late puberty means. The age range during which the major developments associated with puberty may be expected to occur is between 10 and 15 years of age for girls and between 11 and 16 for boys. This age range is quite large and is subject to change. In the United States 150 years ago, the average age of menarche was 16; now it's close to 12. However, the trend of menarche appearing at younger and younger ages is apparently leveling off (Shaffer, 2002). It may be that earlier maturation

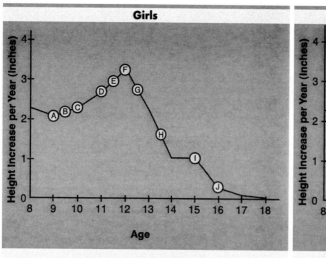
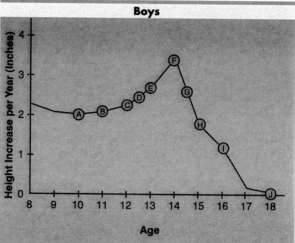

Girls

A. Ovaries increase production of estrogen and progesterone.

B. Vagina, uterus, and ovaries begin to increase in size.

C. Breasts begin to increase in size.

D. Growth of pubic hair begins.

E. Body fat increases, especially in hips and breasts.

F. Pubertal growth spurt peaks.

G. Menarche occurs.

H. First ovulation occurs.

I. Final pubic hair pattern is established.

J. Full breast growth is established.

Boys

A. Testes increase testosterone production.

B. Testes and scrotum begin to increase in size.

C. Growth of pubic hair begins.

D. Penis begins to increase in size.

E. Spermarche occurs.

F. Pubertal growth spurt peaks.

G. Muscular growth peaks.

H. Voice deepens.

I. Growth of facial hair begins.

J. Final pubic hair pattern is established.

FIGURE 15.2 The Adolescent Growth Spurt and Pubertal Change

The onset of puberty is associated with a rapid increase in height. The growth spurt of girls occurs earlier than that of boys. Note that the ages given for the timing of particular physical changes during puberty are based on averages. Individual pubertal changes may vary from these averages without falling outside the range of normal development.

is related to the quality of family relationships. Families that are characterized by stress, conflict, and a lack of closeness among its members tend to see their children reaching puberty at younger ages (Kim & Smith, 1998).

What are the advantages and disadvantages of early maturation? A girl who enters puberty early will probably be taller, stronger, faster, and more athletic than other girls (and many boys) in her class at school. She is more likely to be approached for dates, have earlier sexual encounters, and marry at a younger age than her peers. She may have self-image and self-esteem problems and be more susceptible to emotional problems, especially if she puts on weight and shows marked breast development (Ge, Conger, & Elder, 1996).

Because of the premium put on physical activity in boys, the early-maturing boy is at a greater advantage than the early-maturing girl. He will have more dating and sexual experiences than his peers, which probably will raise his status among his peers. He'll have a better body image and higher self-esteem. Also, physically mature adolescents are *expected* by parents, teachers, and friends to show higher levels of social and emotional maturity (Jaffe, 1998). This presents the physically mature adolescent with quite a challenge, because physical development usually progresses more quickly than social and emotional development. Indeed, early-maturing boys (often influenced by others who are older than they) are at greater risk for all sorts of problems, including delinquency and drug and alcohol use (Dick et al., 2000; Patton et al., 2004; Williams & Dunlap, 1999). The early-maturing male will experience more sexual arousal early on and will become sexually active sooner than age-mates who reach puberty later (Ostovich & Sabini, 2005), and is at a higher risk for the development of testicular cancer (Golub et al., 2008).

For teens of both sexes, being a late bloomer is more negative in its impact (at the time) than is being an early bloomer. Late-maturing boys may carry a sense of inadequacy and poor self-esteem into adulthood. Late maturity for girls has virtually no long-term negative consequences. Some feel, at least in retrospect, that being a late bloomer was an advantage because it allowed them to develop other, broadening interests, rather than becoming "boy-crazy" like so many of their peers in early adolescence.

STUDY CHECK

What characterizes the onset of puberty?
What are the consequences of reaching puberty before or after one's age-mates?

THINKING CRITICALLY

The timing of puberty seems to have a greater effect on boys than on girls. Why do you suppose this is so?

Challenges of Identity Formation

Adolescents around the world give the impression of being great experimenters. They experiment with hairstyles, music, religions, drugs, sexual outlets, fad diets, part-time jobs, part-time relationships, and part-time philosophies of life. It often appears that most of a teenager's commitments are made on a part-time basis. Teens are busy trying things out, doing things their own way, off on a grand search for Truth.

Identity crisis—the struggle to define and integrate the sense of who one is, what one is to do in life, and what one's attitudes, beliefs, and values should be.

This perception of adolescents as experimenters is not without foundation. It is consistent with the view that one of the major tasks of adolescence is the resolution of an **identity crisis**—the struggle to define and integrate the sense of who one is, what one is to do in life, and what one's attitudes, beliefs, and values should be. The concept of identity formation is associated with psychologist Erik Erikson (1963), in whose view the search for identity is a stage of psychosocial development that occurs during the adolescent years. During adolescence we come to grips with questions like "Who am I?" "What am I going to do with my life?" "What is the point of it all?" Needless to say, these are not trivial questions (Habermas & Black, 2000).

For many young people, resolving their identity crisis is a relatively simple and straightforward process. In such cases, the adolescent years bring very little confusion or conflict in terms of attitudes, beliefs, or values. Many teenagers are able and willing to accept the system of values and the sense of self they began to develop in childhood. For some teenagers, however, the conflict of identity formation is quite real. They have a sense of needing to give up the values of parents and teachers in favor of new ones—their own. Physical growth, physiological changes, increased sexuality, and the perception of societal

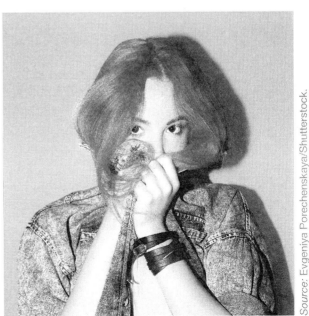

Adolescence is a time of experimenting and challenging, as teens struggle to determine who they are in the world.

Source: Evgeniya Porechenskaya/Shutterstock.

pressures to decide what they want to be when they "grow up" may lead to what Erikson calls *role confusion*, the state in which wanting to be independent, to be one's own self, does not fit in with the values of the past, of childhood. As a result, the teenager experiments with various possibilities in an attempt to see what works best, often to the obvious dissatisfaction of bewildered parents. It seems that most of the process of forging a new and independent sense of self takes place rather late in adolescence. Most of the conflicts between parents and teenagers over independence occur early in adolescence and then gradually decline (Smetana & Gaines, 1999). Further, there is evidence that black adolescents are more likely to develop a sense of self-esteem and identity adjustment than are white adolescents and that developing a sense of ethnic identity is one of the contributing factors to this observation (Gray-Little & Hafdahl, 2000).

A slightly different perspective on identity formation comes from the work of James Marcia (1980). According to Marcia, identity development begins in infancy but becomes a dominant theme in adolescence. At this point the teenager works to develop a plan for movement into adulthood. Marcia has identified four ways that identity issues can be resolved during adolescence: identity achievement, foreclosure, identity diffusion, and moratorium. *Identity achievers* have reached a decision-making period during which they have settled on a career and ideological path that they have chosen for themselves. A person in *identity foreclosure* is also set on a career and ideological path. However, that path was chosen by someone else—most likely the parents. *Identity diffusers* are individuals who have not yet set a career or ideological path, even if they have gone through a decision-making process. Finally, those in *moratorium* are in a state of struggle over their futures. These individuals can be characterized as being in "crisis."

Identity formation researchers point out that for most adolescents and young adults, identity formation is a progressive process, moving from more volatile identity states (e.g., moratorium) to identity achievement (Kroger, Martinussen, & Marcia, 2010). Although progress in identity formation is likely to be progressive (i.e., moving from a less stable to more stable identity), in some instances, it may be regressive (Kroger et al., 2010). That is, in some cases, an adolescent or young adult may reach identity achievement only to backslide into a less stable form of identity formation (e.g., moratorium).

Alan Waterman (1985) looked at identity status across eight cross-cultural studies of individuals of varying ages. Waterman found that identity achievement is most frequently found for college juniors and seniors. Foreclosure and identity diffusion are most common for younger children (sixth to tenth grade). Moratorium was less common for most age groups, except for individuals in their first two years of college where around 30 percent were in moratorium. Finally, once an identity has been formed, it may not be stable. Individuals typically fluctuate among identity statuses (for example, between moratorium and identity achievement).

STUDY CHECK

What is meant by "identity formation" in adolescence, and what factors influence its development?

THINKING CRITICALLY

Have you reached Marcia's stage of identity achievement? What factors have influenced your development and sense of self-esteem?

Development in Early Adulthood

The changes that occur during our adult years may not seem as striking or dramatic as those of our childhood and adolescence, but they are no less real. Many adjustments that we make as adults go unnoticed as we accommodate to physical changes and psychological pressures. As an adult, one's health may become a concern for the first time. Psychological adjustments need to be made to marriage, parenthood, career, retirement, the death of friends and family, and, ultimately, one's own death.

Following the lead of Erikson (1968) and Levinson (1986), we will consider adulthood in terms of three overlapping periods, or seasons: early adulthood (roughly ages 18 to 45), middle adulthood (ages 45 to 65), and late adulthood (over age 65). Presenting adult development in this way can be misleading, so we have to be careful. Although there is some support for developmental stages in adulthood, these stages may be better defined by the individual adult than by the developmental psychologist.

If anything marks the transition from adolescence to adulthood, it is *choice and commitments made independently*. The sense of identity formed in adolescence now needs to be put into action. In fact, the achievement of a sense of self by early adulthood is a good predictor of the success of intimate relationships later in adulthood. With adult status, there are new and often difficult choices to be made. Advice may be sought from elders, parents, teachers, or friends, but as adults, individuals will make their own choices. Should I get married? Which job/career should I pursue? Do I need more education? What sort? Where? Should we have children? How many? Most of these issues are first addressed in adolescence, during identity formation. But for the adult, these questions are no longer abstract. They now are real questions that demand a response.

Levinson calls early adulthood the "era of greatest energy and abundance and of greatest contradiction and stress" (1986, p. 5). In terms of our physical development, we are at something of a peak during our twenties and thirties, and apparently are willing to work hard to maintain that physical condition. Young adulthood is a season for finding our niche, for working through the aspirations of our youth, for raising a family. On the other hand, it is a period of stress, finding the "right" job, taking on parenthood, and maintaining a balance among self, family, job, and society at large. Let's take a look at two important decision-making tasks of young adulthood: the choice of mate and family and the choice of job or career.

Marriage and Family

Erikson suggests that early adulthood revolves around the choice of intimacy or isolation. Failure to establish close, loving, intimate relationships may result in loneliness and long periods of social isolation. Marriage is not the only source of interpersonal intimacy, to be sure, but it is the first choice of most Americans. More young adults than ever before are postponing marriage plans, but a majority of us eventually marry (at least once).

Young adults may value marriage, but the choice of whom to marry is of no small consequence. Psychologists have learned over the past 40 years that mate selection is a complex process. At least three factors influence the choice of a marriage partner. The first deals with *availability*. Before we can develop an intimate relationship with someone, we need the opportunity to establish the relationship in the first place. The second factor is *eligibility*. Here, matters of age, religion, race, politics, and background come into play. Once a partner is found who is available and eligible, a third factor enters the picture: *attractiveness*. Attractiveness in this context does mean physical attractiveness, but as we all know, judgments of physical beauty depend on who's doing the judging. Attractiveness also involves psychological traits, such as understanding, emotional supportiveness, and similarity in values and goals.

Psychologist David Buss reviewed the evidence on mate selection with a focus on the question of whether opposites attract. He concluded that, in marriage, they do not. He found that "we are likely to marry someone who is similar to us in almost every variable"

It is usually in early adulthood that couples make choices about a mate, marriage, and beginning a family.

Source: IVASHstudio/Shutterstock.

(Buss, 1985, p. 47). The most important factors are (in order) age, education, race, religion, ethnic background, attitudes and opinions, mental abilities, socioeconomic status, height, weight, and even eye color. Buss and his colleagues found that men and women are in nearly total agreement on the characteristics they seek in a mate. Buss found that there was a significant difference in ranking for only two: good earning potential and physical attractiveness. Males ranked physical attractiveness higher than females, and females ranked good earning potential higher than males.

Let's pause here and remind ourselves of two important points. First, the conclusions of the studies just cited are true only in general, on the average. There may be happy couples that share few of the traits identified by Buss. Second, these general conclusions are valid only in Western, largely Anglo, North American cultures. Buss and many others have been studying global preferences in selecting mates. In one report of their efforts, people from 33 countries on six continents were studied. There were some similarities among all of the cultures studied, but cultures tended to show significantly different rankings of preferences for mates. The trait that varied most across cultures was chastity.

Samples from China, India, Indonesia, Iran, Taiwan, and Palestine placed great importance on chastity in a potential mate. Samples from Ireland and Japan placed moderate importance on chastity. In contrast, samples from Sweden, Finland, Norway, the Netherlands, and West Germany generally judged chastity to be irrelevant or unimportant (Buss et al., 1990).

Interestingly, the mate-selection preferences for heterosexual and homosexual individuals do not differ all that much. For example, research shows that heterosexual and gay men do not differ significantly in their partner preferences (Burrows, 2013; Kenrick, Keefe, Bryan, Barr, & Brown, 1995). For example, Kenrick et al. found that heterosexual and gay men advertised for very similar characteristics in a partner in personal advertisements. They also found a slight difference between lesbian and heterosexual women, with younger women in both groups expressing interest in same-aged mates; however, with age, lesbians were more likely than heterosexual women to desire a younger partner.

Choosing a marriage partner is not always a matter of making sound, rational (cognitive) decisions, regardless of one's culture. Several factors, including romantic love and the realities of economic hardship, sometimes affect such choices. As sound and sensible as choices at the time of marriage may seem, approximately 50 percent of all first marriages end in divorce, and 75 percent of second marriages suffer the same fate. The average life span of a first marriage in the United States is about 10 years.

Beyond establishing an intimate relationship, becoming a parent is often taken as a sure sign of adulthood. For many couples, parenthood is more a matter of choice than ever before because of more available means of contraception and new treatments for infertility. Having a family fosters the process of generativity, which Erikson associates with middle adulthood. Generativity reflects a concern for family and for one's impact on future generations. Although such concerns may not become central until a person is over age 40, parenthood usually begins much sooner.

Generativity—a concern for family and for one's impact on future generations.

There is no doubt that having a baby around the house significantly changes established routines. Few couples have a realistic vision of what having children will do to their lives. The freedom for spontaneous trips, intimate outings, and privacy is in large measure given up in trade for the joys of parenthood. As parents, men and women take on the responsibilities of new social roles—of father and mother. These new adult roles add to the already-established roles of being male or female, son or daughter, husband or wife. It seems that choosing to have children (or at least choosing to have a large number of children) is becoming less popular. Although many people see the decision not to have children as selfish, irresponsible, even immoral, there is no evidence that such a decision leads to a decline in well-being or satisfaction later in life.

Marital satisfaction tends to increase after children leave the nest.

Source: Rawpixel.com/Shutterstock.

What changes occur in a relationship when a child is born? There is overwhelming evidence that marital satisfaction tends to drop during the child-rearing years of a marriage (Lawrence et al., 2008). There are three reasons for this drop in marital satisfaction. First, after a child is born, the marital partners spend less quality time alone together (Dew & Wilcox, 2011). Second, after a child is born, there is a less equal division of domestic chores, with most of the burden falling on the mother. This, too, is related to reduced marital satisfaction (Dew & Wilcox, 2011). Third, role conflict (having to play more than one role at a time, such as wife and mother) and role strain (the demands of a role exceed a person's abilities) both increase after a child is born (Bee, 1996). The competing demands of multiple roles and constantly changing demands contribute to increased stress in a marriage and dissatisfaction.

The good news is that marital satisfaction increases again once the children leave the nest. There has been no newer data to contradict Glenn's (1990) review of the literature in this area, in which he concluded that the U-shaped curve representing marital satisfaction before, during, and after the child-rearing years is one of the most reliable in the social sciences.

STUDY CHECK

How do psychologists characterize "early adulthood"?
What factors tend to influence the choice of a mate?
What are the consequences of young adults starting a family?

THINKING CRITICALLY

What characteristics do you (or did you) look for in a potential mate? How do you feel (or did you feel) about becoming a parent?

Career Choice

By the time a person has become a young adult, it is generally assumed that he or she has chosen a vocation or life's work. In today's marketplace, a person's initial career choice is not likely to be a life-long decision, as multiple career changes are commonplace. Choice of occupation and satisfaction with that choice go a long way toward determining self-esteem and identity. For women in early adulthood, being employed outside the home is a major determinant of self-worth (Stein et al., 1990). Dual-career families, in which both spouses work are quite common. In 2018, 48.3 percent of families had both spouses working (Bureau of Labor Statistics, 2018a). Women now make up more than half of the labor force in the United States (U. S. Department of Labor, 2018).

Selection of a career is driven by many factors; family influence and the potential for earning money are just two. Choosing a career path involves several stages. The following terminology is that of Turner & Helms (1987).

1. *Exploration*: There is a general concern that something needs to be done; a choice needs to be made, but alternatives are poorly defined, and plans for making a choice are not yet developed.
2. *Crystallization*: Some real alternatives are being weighed: Pluses and minuses are associated with each possibility, and although some are eliminated, a choice is not yet made.
3. *Choice*: For better or worse, a decision is made. There is a sense of relief that at least a person knows what he or she wants, and an optimistic feeling develops that everything will work out.
4. *Career clarification*: The person's self-image and career choice become intertwined. Adjustments and accommodations are made. This is a matter of fine-tuning the initial choice: "I know I want to be a teacher; but what do I want to teach, and to whom?"
5. *Induction*: The career decision is implemented, presenting a series of potentially frightening challenges to a person's own values and goals. "Is this *really* what I want to do?"
6. *Reformation*: A person discovers that changes need to be made if he or she is to fit in with fellow workers and do the job as expected. "This isn't going to be as simple as I thought it would be. I'd better take a few more classes or sign up for in-house training."
7. *Integration*: The job and the work become part of a person's self, and the person gives up part of himself or herself to the job. This is a period of considerable satisfaction.

Clearly, this list is idealized. Sometimes situational factors simply overpower a rational, well-thought-out procedure. "This farm (or business or shop) has been in this family for generations, and when we die, you will not abandon it. Period." Occasionally a person makes a poor career decision (a few seem to do so habitually). This is most likely to occur in the third stage of choosing a career path but probably won't be recognized until the fourth or fifth stage. In such cases, there is little to do but begin again and work through the process, seeking the self-satisfaction that comes at the final stage.

STUDY CHECK

What factors may be involved in making a decision about one's career?

THINKING CRITICALLY

What factors matter to you in choosing your "life's work"?

Development in Middle Adulthood

As the middle years of adulthood approach, many aspects of life have become settled. By the time most people reach the age of 40, their place in the framework of society is fairly set. They have chosen their lifestyle and have grown accustomed to it. They have a family (or have decided not to). They have chosen their life work. "Most of us during our forties and fifties become 'senior members' in our own particular worlds, however grand or modest they may be" (Levinson, 1986, p. 6). In reality, the notion of a mid-life crisis is mostly a myth (McCrae & Costa, 1990).

TABLE 15.2 Development in Middle Adulthood

Facts About Middle Adulthood
By age 40 most lifestyle, family and career choices have been made.
Adjustments must be made to physiological changes and physical activities may have to be modified.
Although there are challenges, the notion of a mid-life crisis is mostly a myth.
If career satisfaction is not attained, a mid-career job change is possible.
Dealing with family matters becomes an issue. For example, helping teenagers adjust to adolescence and prepare to "leave the nest," and caring for own aging parents.
One challenge is thinking about what one will do with what time is left and how one can leave a mark on future generations.

There are several tasks that a person must face in the middle years (see **Table 15.2**), and one of the first is adjusting to physiological changes. Middle-aged persons can surely engage in many physical activities, but they may have to be selective or modify the vigor with which they attack such activities. Heading out to the backyard for pickup basketball with the neighborhood teenagers is something a 45-year-old may have to think twice about.

While career choices have been made, in middle age one comes to expect satisfaction with work. If career satisfaction is not attained, a mid-career job change is possible. Of course, there are also situations in which changing jobs in middle age is more a matter of necessity than choice. In either case, the potential exists for crisis and conflict or for growth and development.

A major set of challenges that middle-aged persons face is dealing with family members. At this stage in life, parents are often in the throes of helping their teenagers adjust to adolescence and prepare to "leave the nest," while at the same time caring for their own parents. Adults in this situation have been referred to as "the sandwich generation." Individual responsibility and concern for the care of the elderly have not lessened in recent years. In fact, 80 percent of all day-to-day health care for the elderly is provided by family members.

One task of middle adulthood is similar to Erikson's stage, or crisis, of *generativity* versus *stagnation*. People shift from thinking about all they have done with their lives to thinking about what they will do with what time is left for them and how they can leave a mark on future generations.

Although all the "tasks" noted above are interdependent, this is particularly true of these last two: relating to a spouse as a person and developing leisure-time activities. As children leave home and financial concerns diminish, there may be more time for a person's spouse and for leisure. In the eyes of adults, these tasks can amount to enjoyment: enjoying each other, status, retirement, vacations, and travel. In truth, taking advantage of these opportunities in meaningful ways provides a challenge for some adults whose lives previously have been devoted to children and career.

STUDY CHECK

How is middle adulthood characterized?

THINKING CRITICALLY

If there is no such thing as a mid-life crisis, why do so many people use the concept to explain their behaviors and the behaviors of others?

Development in Late Adulthood

The transition to late adulthood generally occurs in our early to mid-sixties. Perhaps the first thing to acknowledge is that persons over the age of 65 constitute a sizable and growing proportion of the population. By the year 2030, nearly 20 percent of Americans will be over 65—about 66 million persons (Armas, 2003). According to a Census Bureau report, by the year 2050, the number of persons 65 years old or older will be 78.9 million—with an average life span of 82.1 years. The census data also tell us that aging is disproportionably a women's issue. The vast majority of those over age 80 are women who live alone, and the number of older ethnic minority adults is increasing more rapidly than for the population in general.

Ageism—discrimination and prejudice against a group on the basis of age.

Ageism is the name given to discrimination and prejudice against a group on the basis of age. Ageism is particularly acute in our attitudes about the elderly. One misconception about the elderly is that they live in misery. We cannot ignore some of the difficulties that come with aging, but matters may not be as bad as many believe they are. Sensory capacities may be diminished. But as B. F. Skinner (1983) suggested, "If you cannot read, listen to book recordings. If you do not hear well, turn up the volume of your phonograph (and wear headphones to protect your neighbors)." Some cognitive abilities decline with age, but others develop to compensate for most losses (Grady et al., 1995). Some apparent memory loss may reflect more of a choice of what one wants to remember than an actual loss. Mental speed is reduced, but the accumulated experience of living often outweighs any advantages of speed.

Children have long since left the nest, but they're still in touch, and now there are grandchildren with whom to interact. Further, the children of the elderly have reached adulthood themselves and are more able and likely to provide support for aging parents. Indeed, a majority of older adults live in family settings. In fact, only about 13 percent of Americans over the age of 65 live in nursing homes. However, the number of elderly living in nursing homes increases with age, reaching about 25 percent for individuals aged 85 and older (AAHSA, 2003).

One of the major challenges of late adulthood is the transition to retirement. This transition requires two developmental challenges: First is the adjustment to the loss of one's work role and the social relationships included in that role. Second is the development of a satisfactory postretirement life (van Solinge & Henkens, 2008). Some individuals dread retirement, but most welcome it as a chance to do things they have planned for years (Kim & Moen, 2001). Many people over the age of 65 become more physically active after retiring, perhaps from a job in which they sat at a desk all day. Reactions to retirement vary, with some individuals showing increased depression and loneliness and others showing increased well-being (Mo, Henkens, & H-Janna van, 2011). Four factors relate to how well a retiree adjusts to retirement (Mo et al., 2011): (1) level of financial resources available, (2) family variables (e.g., marital status, marriage quality), (3) retirement transition variables (e.g., voluntariness, preretirement planning), and (4) postretirement variables (e.g., part-time employment, leisure activities).

Until recently, almost all research on the effects of retirement focused on males. As more women enter the workforce and then retire from it, the study of retirement is changing. Two tentative conclusions seem warranted: First, women appear to have more negative attitudes toward retirement. Second, having an employed spouse extends the working life of both members of the couple.

Many people assume that old age necessarily brings with it the curse of poor health. However, only 22 percent of elderly individuals report their health to be fair or poor. That compares to a 10 percent rate for non-elderly individuals (Centers for Disease Control and Prevention, 2017). Also, only 6.4 percent of individuals over the age of 65 reported needing assistance for daily care from someone else (Clarke, Norris, & Schiller, 2017). That's not to say that older people do not have health problems; of course they do. According to the National Council on Aging (2018), 80 percent of the elderly have one chronic disease, and 68.4 percent have at least two. Twenty-three percent of individuals 60 and over have diabetes. But what matters most—as is true for all of us—is the extent to which problems can be managed successfully (Brod et al., 1999). Emerging evidence suggests that those older adults who do experience chronic illness (diabetes, arthritis, cardiovascular disease, and cancer, for example) can take significant strides in fighting off declining health by becoming actively engaged in their own care. Active control strategies (referred to as "health-engagement control strategies," or HECSs), such as investing time and energy in addressing one's health concerns, seeking help when it is needed, and making commitments to overcome threats to physical health can have remarkably helpful effects, not only on physical health but also for improving the simple

Young-old seniors are the majority of those over 65 years of age. They can still be productive and have fun!

activities of daily living (Wrosch & Schulz, 2008; Wrosch et al., 2007; Wrosch et al., 2006). Obviously, there are limits to getting elderly people with serious health problems engaged in their own care. One rule of thumb seems obvious: The sooner, the better. A time will come when health issues become so severe that successfully engaging in HECS is not likely.

Developmental psychologists find it useful to think about persons over 65 as members of one of two groups: the *young-old* and the *old-old*. This distinction is not made on the basis of actual, chronological age, but on the basis of psychological, social, and health characteristics. The distinction reinforces the notion that aging is not some sort of disease. The young-old group is the large majority of those over 65 years of age (80 to 85 percent). They are "vigorous and competent men and women who have reduced their time investments in work or home-making, are relatively comfortable financially and relatively well-educated, and are well-integrated members of their families and communities" (Neugarten & Neugarten, 1986).

STUDY CHECK

What are the major aspects of the last stage of human development, late adulthood?

THINKING CRITICALLY

Have you ever—seriously—contemplated your own death? Do you think that your attitudes and feelings about death will change as you get older?

Understanding Death and the Dying Process

Of the two sure things in life, death and taxes, the former is the surer. There are no loopholes. About 57 million people die each year, worldwide, with nearly 2.7 million in the United States. Dealing with the reality of our own deaths is the last major crisis we face in life. A century ago, most people died in their homes, and death was an experience witnessed by everyone, even children. During the nineteenth and early twentieth centuries, people even hired photographers to take portraits of their departed loved ones. This was known as memorial portraiture or postmortem photography. Now a majority of Americans die in hospitals (60 percent) and nursing homes (20 percent), although 80 percent say they would prefer to die at home (Stanford University School of Medicine, 2018). Many people never have to deal with their own deaths in psychological terms. These are the people who die young or suddenly. Still, many individuals do have time to contemplate their own deaths, and this usually takes place in late adulthood.

Much attention was focused on the confrontation with death in the popular book *On Death and Dying* by Elisabeth Kübler-Ross (1969, 1981). Her description of the stages one goes through when facing death was based on hundreds of interviews with terminally ill patients who were aware that they were dying. (Kübler-Ross herself died on August 24, 2004.) She suggested that the process commonly takes place in five stages:

1. *Denial*—a firm, simple avoidance of the evidence; a sort of "No, this can't be happening to me" reaction.
2. *Anger*—often accompanied by resentment and envy of others, along with a realization of what is truly happening; a sort of "Why me? Why not someone else?" reaction.
3. *Bargaining*—a matter of dealing, or bartering, usually with God; a search for more time; a sort of "If you'll just grant me a few more weeks, or months, I'll go to church every week—no, every day" reaction.
4. *Depression*—a sense of hopelessness that bargaining won't work, that a great loss is imminent; a period of grief and sorrow over both past mistakes and what will be missed in the future.
5. *Acceptance*—a rather quiet facing of the reality of death, with no great joy or sadness, simply a realization that the time has come.

Kübler-Ross's description may be idealized. Many dying patients do not fit this pattern at all. Some may show behaviors consistent with one or two of the stages, but seldom all five. Although she never meant her stages to be taken as a prescription, there has been some concern that this pattern of approaching death may be viewed as the "best" or the "right" way to go about it. The concern is that caretakers may try to force dying people into and through these stages, instead of letting each face the inevitability of death in his or her own way (Kalish, 1985).

Whether people go through the sequence of stages while dying suggested by Kübler-Ross, there is no doubt that dying is now conceptualized as a process that people go through. Researchers are investigating the attitudes of terminally ill patients toward death in order to better understand the process and improve end-of-life care to the dying. In one study, Schroepfer (2007) interviewed dying patients about their experiences and found that the patients identified four critical experiences in the dying process: (1) perceived insensitive communication of the terminal diagnosis, (2) experiencing unbearable physical pain, (3) unacknowledged emotions about chemotherapy or radiation therapy, and (4) dying in a distressing environment. Schroepfer points out that although the patients may have experienced one of these events, it is likely that a dying patient will experience more than one. These events can cause the dying experience to be more stressful than it needs to be. Schroepfer suggests that health professionals take these experiences into account when treating dying patients. Finally, the process of dying can be improved by providing the dying person a greater sense of control over the process (Schroepfer, Noh, & Kavanaugh, 2009).

Although elderly people have to deal with dying and death, they are less morbid about it than are adolescents. Older people may fear the process of dying, but they have much less concern about the event of death (Leming & Dickinson, 2002). In one study, adults over age 60 reported thinking about and talking about death more frequently than did the younger adults in the survey. However, of all of the adults in the study, the oldest group expressed the least fear of death, with some even saying they were eager for it (Fortner & Neimeyer, 1999).

Anxiety over death is fairly common and is experienced by elderly individuals facing death (Ron, 2010). However, how much anxiety people feel relates to their self-esteem and sense of mastery over their lives, with individuals higher on these two characteristics experiencing less anxiety (Ron, 2010). Additionally, women and individuals with less education experience higher levels of death anxiety (Azaiza, Ron, Shoham, & Gigini, 2010). These researchers report that having social support and raising self-esteem can reduce death anxiety.

Despite the presence of death anxiety, research suggests that dying people also express positive emotions and thoughts (Hack et al., 2010). In a study reported by Hack et al., the transcripts from dying patients undergoing "dignity therapy" were content analyzed for the emotions, thoughts, and values expressed. Hack et al. found that dying patients frequently spoke about family, children, the pleasure derived from life's activities, caring about others, and the friendships they made during their lives. Results such as these suggest that with the proper therapy, the end-of-life experience need not be an entirely negative and terrifying one.

There is an old saying that "there are no atheists in foxholes." Although it is not clear who first said it, the saying suggests that at times of great existential threat, people turn to faith to ease the anxiety over the experience. Of course, not everyone will turn to faith at such times. However, the saying raises the issue of the role of spirituality at the end of life. Research shows that at least some people turn to faith to help cope with serious illness and impending death (Moestrup & Hvidt, 2016; Thuné-Boyle, Stygall, Keshtgar, & Newman,

2006). In their review of the literature, Thuné-Boyle et al. found that in a number of studies, there was evidence that religious coping was successful in helping reduce distress and increase illness adjustment. In another study, Keeley (2004) analyzed the final conversations family members had with loved ones just before death. Keeley found that in 26 of 30 conversations, messages relating to faith and spirituality were part of those final conversations. An important element inherent in the spiritual messages was validation of the dying person or loved one's religious or spiritual beliefs. In only one final conversation was anger expressed toward God. Keeley found that in 15 final conversations, religious content served as a source of comfort. The notion of there being an afterlife was particularly comforting. For many dying patients, faith and spirituality were increased after they became seriously ill, and that faith provided a sense of comfort and support (Moestrup & Hvidt, 2016). These studies tell us that religion and spirituality can help a dying person better cope with death.

Chapter Summary

What are the major events in prenatal development?
Prenatal development begins at conception and ends (about 270 days later) at birth. The period between two and eight weeks after conception is the embryonic stage, during which development is rapid and the organs of the body are laid in place. From two months after conception until birth is the stage of the fetus, during which weight gain is rapid. Survival is possible if the fetus is born after the seventh month, the point of viability.

What are the consequences of a pregnant mother's behaviors?
To avoid the negative consequences of low birth weight, miscarriage, and retarded mental and physical development, it is important that pregnant women eat a balanced, nutritious diet, and avoid smoking, alcohol, and drugs.

What are the consequences of the father's behaviors for prenatal development?
Often overlooked in the past, scientists are now attending to paternal influences on prenatal development. The major impact of the father involves the condition of his sperm at conception. Paternal age is a significant risk factor for both schizophrenia and autism.

What are the basic features of Piaget's theory of cognitive development?
Piaget theorized that a child's mental development involves the formation of cognitive structures (schemas) of

what is known and functions (how one comes to know it). An important cognitive function is adaptation, the development of schemas to help meet the demands of the environment. Piaget proposed that development takes place in four successive stages and that these stages are universal.

What are the ages of, and characteristics of, Piaget's four stages of cognitive development?
During the sensorimotor stage (birth to two years) a baby develops schemas through an interaction with the environment by sensing and doing. The baby begins to appreciate cause-and-effect relationships, imitates the actions of others, and by the end of the period, develops a sense of object permanence. Egocentrism is found in the preoperational stage (two to seven years). The child appears unable to view the world from anyone else's perspective. In addition, children begin to develop and use symbols in the form of words to represent concepts. In the concrete operations stage (7 to 11 years), a child organizes concepts into categories, begins to use simple logic and understand relational terms. The essence of the formal operations stage (12 years and older) is the ability to think, reason, and solve problems symbolically or in an abstract rather than a concrete, tangible form.

What is the information-processing approach to cognitive development, and how does it differ from Piaget's theory?
The information-processing approach to cognitive development states that there are quantitative changes in

information-processing abilities with age. Piaget's theory suggested that there are qualitative changes in cognitive abilities with age. Evidence for the information-processing approach comes from research on the development of children's learning and memory abilities with age. Newborns show the ability to learn simple classically conditioned responses. Later, they benefit from operant conditioning, and later still, they benefit from sophisticated imitation skills. Memory also shows improvement with age. For example, young children do not use basic rehearsal strategies on their own, whereas older children do. The use of a sophisticated strategy like mental imagery is not common until a child is in adolescence.

What is gender identity, and when does it develop?
Gender identity is the sense or self-awareness of one's maleness or femaleness and the roles that males and females traditionally play in one's culture. Most children have a sense of their own gender by the age of two to three years, with gender identity most strongly reinforced by peer groups and play activities. A child's cognitive sense of gender stereotypes may flavor how new information is accommodated. In some cases, gender role concepts can become rigid, as evidenced by the pink frilly dress phenomenon.

What are the major—and conflicting—views of adolescence that have been put forward in psychology?
Physically, adolescence begins with puberty (attainment of sexual maturity) and lasts until the end of physical growth. Historically, the time has been seen as one of stress, distress, and abnormality. More contemporary views see adolescence as a period of challenges, but a period that most teenagers survive with no lasting negative consequences.

What characterizes the onset of puberty?
Two significant physical developments mark adolescence: a spurt of growth, seen at an earlier age in girls than in boys, and the beginning of sexual maturity, a period called puberty. As adolescents, individuals are for the first time physically prepared for sexual reproduction and begin to develop secondary sex characteristics.

What are the consequences of reaching puberty before or after one's age-mates?
The consequences of reaching puberty early are more positive for males than females. Being a late bloomer is more negative in its impact on teens of both sexes, although the long-term consequences for both are few and slight.

What is meant by "identity formation" in adolescence, and what factors influence its development?
The challenge of identity formation is to establish a personal identity (sense of self) that is separate from the parents. A major task of adolescence, then, is to define and integrate the sense of who one is, what one is to do in life, and what one's attitudes, beliefs, and values should be. According to James

Marcia, there are four stages of identity formation: identity achievement, foreclosure, identity diffusion, and moratorium. Resolution through identity achievement means that a person has gone through a period of decision-making and has settled on a self-chosen career and ideological path. An individual in foreclosure has had an ideological and career path chosen by someone else, most likely the parents. Individuals who have not yet chosen an ideological or career path, but may have gone through a decision-making phase, are said to be identity diffusers. Those in moratorium are in "crisis" and are in a state of struggle over the future. Identity achievement is most common among college juniors and seniors. Foreclosure and identity diffusion are most often seen in younger children in sixth to tenth grades.

How do psychologists characterize "early adulthood"?
Early adulthood (ages 18 to 45) is characterized by commitments and choices made independently. The young adult assumes new responsibilities and is faced with decisions about career, marriage, and family. For Erikson, the period is marked by the conflict between social relationships and intimacy on the one hand, and social isolation on the other.

What factors tend to influence the choice of a mate?
Mate selection and marriage are two issues that most young adults face. Individuals tend to "match" on a variety of characteristics (e.g., age, race, or education). Many marriages do fail, but most adults list a good marriage as a major source of happiness in their lives. Many factors determine the choice of a mate. There is little support for the notion that opposites attract, and the characteristics of desired mates vary among cultures.

What are the consequences of young adults starting a family?
There is a U-shaped function relating family status and marital satisfaction. Before the birth of the first child, marital satisfaction is high. During the child-rearing years, marital satisfaction declines, but it recovers again after the children leave the home. The birth of a child adds stress to a marriage via role conflict and role strain.

What factors may be involved in making a decision about one's career?
Choosing a career or occupation is a decision of early adulthood. Choosing the right career contributes in positive ways to self-esteem and identity. It is a process that often goes through several stages: exploration, crystallization, choice, career clarification, induction, reformation, and integration. From time to time, a person makes a poor career choice and may have to begin the process all over again.

How is middle adulthood characterized?
Middle adulthood (ages 45 to 65) may be troublesome for some, but most adults find middle age to be a period of great satisfaction and opportunity. Toward the end of the

period, the person begins to accept his or her own mortality in several ways. Tasks of middle age involve adapting to one's changing physiology, occupation, aging parents and growing children, social and civic responsibilities, and the use of leisure time.

What are the major aspects of the last stage of human development, late adulthood?
The number of elderly persons is growing rapidly—approaching nearly 66 million by the year 2030 in the United States alone. Although there may be sensory, physical, and cognitive limits forced by old age, fewer than 30 percent of elderly people rate health problems as a major concern. Although some elderly are isolated and lonely, fewer than 13 percent live in nursing homes. Older people may be concerned about death, but they are neither consumed by it nor morbid about it. With good nutrition, the development of a healthy lifestyle, proper social support, and the maintenance of some degree of autonomy and control over one's life, "successful aging" can become even more common than it is today. This is another way of saying that we can increase the already large percentage (80 to 85 percent) of those over the age of 65 who have been characterized as young-old, as opposed to old-old.

Key Terms

Prenatal period (p. 326)
Fetal alcohol syndrome (FAS) (p. 328)
Cognitive development (p. 329)
Schema (p. 329)
Adaptation (p. 329)
Sensorimotor stage (p. 329)
Preoperational stage (p. 330)
Concrete operations stage (p. 332)

Formal operations stage (p. 332)
Information-processing approach (p. 333)
Adolescence (p. 336)
Puberty (p. 337)
Menarche (p. 337)
Identity crisis (p. 339)
Generativity (p. 342)
Ageism (p. 346)

Glossary

A

Abnormal maladaptive cognitions, affects, and/or behaviors that are at odds with social expectations and result in distress or discomfort.

Accommodation changing of the shape of the lens in the eye.

Activation-synthesis theory a theory of dreaming stating that dreams are activated by physiological mechanisms in the brainstem, probably in the pons, and given meaning through a synthesis process.

Adaptation in Piaget's theory, developing the appropriate schemas so that one can manage the demands of the environment.

Adolescence the period of transition from the dependence of childhood to the independence of adulthood. It is the period of development that begins at puberty (sexual maturity) and lasts through the teen years.

Adrenal glands glands located on the kidneys that secrete a variety of hormones into the bloodstream.

Affect (af´-ekt) a term that refers to feelings, emotions, or moods.

Ageism discrimination and prejudice against a group on the basis of age.

All-or-none principle a principle stating that a neuron either fires or it doesn't.

Antianxiety drugs drugs (tranquilizers) that help reduce the felt aspect of anxiety.

Antidepressant drugs drugs that elevate the mood of persons who are depressed.

Antipsychotic drugs drugs that alleviate or eliminate psychotic symptoms.

Anxiety a general feeling of tension, apprehension, and dread that involves predictable physiological changes.

Approach-approach conflict a conflict in which an organism is caught between two (or more) alternatives, and each of them is positive, or potentially reinforcing.

Approach-avoidance conflict a conflict in which a person is in the position of considering only one goal and would like to reach that goal but at the same time would very much like not to.

Aqueous humor the fluid in the eye providing nourishment to the cornea and the other structures at the front of the eye.

Arbitrary symbolic reference the idea that there need be no resemblance between a word and its referent.

Arousal an organism's level of activation or excitement.

Association areas areas of the cerebral cortex where sensory input is integrated with motor responses and where cognitive functions such as problem solving, memory, and thinking occur.

Atonia muscular immobility observed in REM sleep.

Attitude a relatively stable disposition used to evaluate an object or event.

Audience inhibition the tendency to be hesitant about doing things in front of others, especially strangers.

Autism spectrum disorder a disorder characterized by impaired social interaction, problems with communication, and unusual or severely limited activities and interests.

Autonomic nervous system consists of neurons involved in activating the smooth muscles, such as those of the stomach and intestines, and the glands.

Avoidance-avoidance conflict a conflict in which a person is faced with several alternatives, and each of them is negative or in some way punishing.

Axon the part of a neuron that sends messages along its length to other neurons, muscles, or glands.

Axon terminals a branching series of bare end points of an axon.

B

Basal ganglia brain structures involved in the planning, initiation, and coordination of large, slow movements.

Behavior what organisms do—their actions and reactions.

Behavioral observation personality measurement that involves drawing conclusions about someone's personality on the basis of observations of his or her behaviors.

Biofeedback the process of providing information to an individual about his or her bodily processes in some form that he or she might be able to use to modify those processes.

Bipolar disorder episodes of depression are interspersed with episodes of mania.

Bisexual orientation individuals attracted to both members of the same and opposite sex.

Blind spot the place at which the nerve impulses from the rods and cones, having passed through many layers of cells, exit the eye.

Bottom-up processing organizing, identifying, and storing stimuli in our memory centers based on information derived from our senses.

Brightness constancy the perception that familiar objects retain their usual brightness regardless of amount or type of light under which they are viewed.

Bystander effect the suppression of helping behaviors when bystanders are present at an emergency situation.

C

Category relationship exists when the parties involved in a social situation are perceived to belong together in some way (e.g., siblings, boyfriend-girlfriend).

Cell body the largest concentration of mass in the neuron, containing the nucleus of the cell and other structures necessary for the neuron's life.

Central nervous system (CNS) a division of the nervous system that includes all neurons and supporting cells found in the spinal cord and brain.

Cerebellum the part of the brain that smooths and coordinates rapid body movements.

Cerebral cortex the large part of the brain that makes us uniquely human by giving us our ability to think, reason, and use language.

Chunk the representation in memory of a meaningful unit of information.

Ciliary muscles powerful muscles that expand or contract to reflexively change the shape of the lens that brings an image into focus.

Classical conditioning a learning process in which a neutral stimulus is paired with a stimulus that elicits an unconditioned response. After conditioning, the neutral stimulus alone elicits a new, conditioned response, much like the original unconditioned response.

Closure the process by which we fill in gaps in our perceptual world.

Cochlea the snail-like structure of the inner ear containing the actual receptor cells for hearing.

Cognitions mental events, such as beliefs, perceptions, thoughts, ideas, and memories.

Cognitive-behavior therapy (CBT) a cognitive therapy that has a joint focus: Change the way that you have been behaving, and change the way you interpret and think about the situations in which behavior change is required.

Cognitive development age-related changes in learning, memory, perception, attention, thinking, and problem solving.

Cognitive dissonance a state of tension or discomfort that exists when we hold and are aware of inconsistent cognitions.

Cognitive map a mental picture or representation of the physical environment, noting significant landmarks when possible.

Cognitive restructuring therapy a cognitive therapy that is less confrontational and direct than rational emotive therapy.

Cognitive therapist a therapist who believes that what matters most is a client's beliefs, thoughts, perceptions, and attitudes about himself or herself and the environment.

Color constancy the perception that the color of a familiar object is constant, despite changing lighting conditions.

Compulsions constantly intruding, repetitive behaviors.

Concepts mental categories or classes into which we place the events and objects we experience.

Concrete operations stage (7 to 11 years) Piaget's third stage of development, in which children begin to form many new concepts and show that they can manipulate those concepts.

Conditioned response the learned response made to a conditioned stimulus.

Conditioned stimulus a stimulus that comes to elicit a learned response after being paired with an unconditioned stimulus.

Cones photoreceptors for color vision that operate best in daylight conditions.

Conformity a direct form of social influence that occurs when we modify our behavior, under perceived pressure to do so, to make it consistent with the behavior of others.

Conscious a level of consciousness housing ideas, memories, feelings, or motives of which we are actively aware.

Consciousness the subjective awareness of the environment and of one's own mental processes.

Consummate love a type of love with high levels of passion, intimacy, and commitment.

Continuity (or good continuation) when we see things as ending up consistently with the way they started.

Contrast the extent to which a stimulus is physically different from the other stimuli around it.

Control group a group of participants receiving a zero level of the independent variable.

Convergence a binocular cue for depth involving the eyes turning toward each other when viewing something up close.

Cornea the tough, virtually transparent outer shell of the eye.

Corpus callosum a network of hundreds of thousands of fibers connecting the two hemispheres of the cerebral cortex.

Correlational research research involving the search for a relationship between variables that are observed and measured, but not manipulated.

Credibility the believability of a source of a persuasive communication.

Cross laterality arrangement of nerve fibers in the brainstem crossing from one side of the body to the opposite side of the brain.

Cutaneous senses senses providing the psychological experience of touch or pressure and of warm and cold.

D

Dark adaptation the process in which visual receptors become *more* sensitive with time spent in the dark.

Death instincts (Thanatos) the impulses of destruction.

Decibel scale a scale of sound intensity measuring perceived loudness.

Deductive reasoning reasoning leading to specific conclusions about events based on a small number of general principles.

Delusions false beliefs; ideas that are firmly held regardless of evidence to the contrary.

Dendrite the part of a neuron reaching out to receive messages, or neural impulses, from nearby neurons.

Dependent variable a variable providing a measure of the participants' behavior.

Depressants drugs that reduce awareness of external stimuli, slow bodily functioning, and decrease levels of overt behavior.

Depressive disorder a disorder involving a sad or depressed mood accompanied by physical and cognitive changes that make functioning difficult.

Deviation IQ a measure of intelligence using established group norms that allows for comparing intelligence scores across age groups.

Diagnosis the act of recognizing a disorder on the basis of specified symptoms.

Diathesis-stress model a model proposing that individuals inherit multiple genes, which may give rise to the tendency or predisposition to express certain behaviors, but these behaviors are expressed only if activated by stress or trauma.

Difference threshold the smallest difference between stimulus attributes that can be detected.

Diffusion of responsibility a process in which the greater the number of people present, the smaller is each individual's perceived obligation to intervene.

Discrimination biased, often negative, behavior directed at a member of a social group simply because of that person's group membership.

Discrimination learning a process by which an organism learns to discriminate between different stimuli, emitting the conditioned response (CR) in the presence of some stimuli and not others.

Dissociative amnesia the inability to recall important personal information that is too extensive to be explained by ordinary forgetfulness.

Dissociative disorder disorder in which a person seeks to escape from some aspect of life or personality seen as the source of stress, discomfort, or anxiety.

Dissociative identity disorder (DID) the existence within the same person of two or more distinct personalities or personality traits.

Drive a state of tension, arousal, or activation.

Drug abuse a condition involving (a) a lack of control, as evidenced by daily impairment and continued use, even knowing that one's condition will deteriorate; (b) a disruption of interpersonal relationships or difficulties at work that can be traced to drug usage; and (c) indications that maladaptive drug use has continued for at least one month.

E

Ego the part of the personality that develops through one's experience with reality. In many ways, it is our "self."

Elaboration likelihood model states that there are two routes to persuasion: the central route and the peripheral route.

Elaborative rehearsal rehearsal used to transfer information from short-term to long-term memory. It involves organizing, forming images of, attaching meaning to, or relating information to something already in long-term memory.

Electroconvulsive therapy (ECT) treatment that involves passing an electric current of between 70 and 150 volts across a patient's head for a fraction of a second.

Electroencephalograph (EEG) an instrument that measures and records the electrical activity of the brain.

Electromyogram (EMG) an instrument that measures a muscle's activity, tone, or state of relaxation.

Emotion an experience that includes a subjective feeling, a cognitive interpretation, a physiological reaction, and a behavioral expression.

Emotion-focused strategy a coping strategy in which you deal with how you feel and with finding ways to change how you feel.

Emotional intelligence intelligence characterized by four sets of skills: (1) *managing* emotions so as to attain specific goals; (2) *understanding* emotions, emotional language, and the signals conveyed by emotions; (3) *using* emotions to facilitate thinking; and (4) *perceiving* emotions accurately in oneself and others.

Encoding the process of putting information into memory, or forming cognitive representations of information.

Endocrine system a network of glands that affect behaviors by secreting chemicals called hormones.

Episodic memory storage system where we store the memories of our life events and experiences.

Excitatory neurotransmitter a neurotransmitter that stimulates the next neuron in a sequence to fire.

Experimental group a group of participants exposed to some value of the independent variable.

Experimental research research in which investigators actually manipulate a variable and then look for a relationship between that manipulation and changes in the value of some other variable.

Explicit attitude type of attitude that works on a conscious level; we are aware of these attitudes and how they occasionally influence our behaviors.

Explicit stereotype a stereotype that we are consciously aware of and that is under conscious control.

Extinction the process in which the strength of a conditioned response (CR) decreases with repeated presentations of the conditioned stimulus (CS) alone.

Extraneous variable a factor, other than the independent variable, that can influence the dependent variable of an experiment.

F

Family therapy a therapy technique focusing on the roles, interdependence, and communication skills of family members.

Fetal alcohol syndrome (FAS) a condition occurring when mothers drink during pregnancy, resulting in smaller babies with retarded growth, poor coordination, poor muscle tone, intellectual disabilities, and other problems.

Figure-ground relationship well-defined objects stand out against a relatively formless background.

Five-Factor Model a trait model of personality suggesting that there are five core traits making up personality.

Formal operations stage (12 and older) Piaget's fourth stage of development involving the logical manipulation of abstract, symbolic concepts.

Fovea a small area of the retina where there are few layers of cells between the entering light and the cone cells that fill the area.

Free association a technique in psychoanalysis where patients say aloud whatever comes into their minds.

Frustration-aggression hypothesis the hypothesis stating that frustration is the *only* cause of aggression.

Frustration the reaction to blocking or thwarting of goal-directed behavior—blocking that may be total and permanent or partial and temporary.

Fully functioning a person strives to become all that he or she can be.

G

Gender the social and sociocultural characteristics associated with one's sex.

Gender identity a person's subjective experience of his or her gender.

Gender role the cultural expectations for males and females.

Generalized anxiety disorder (GAD) a disorder involving distressing, felt anxiety. This disorder is characterized by unrealistic, excessive, persistent worry.

Generativity a concern for family and for one's impact on future generations.

Grammar the formal expression of the syntax of a language.

Group polarization effect occurs when group participation makes an individual's reactions more extreme, or polarized.

Group therapy a therapy technique in which several people are receiving therapy together.

Groupthink an excessive concern for reaching a consensus in group decision-making to the extent that critical evaluations are withheld.

Gustation the technical term for the sense of taste.

H

Hallucinations false perceptions; perceiving that which is not there or failing to perceive that which is.

Hallucinogens drugs that have unpredictable effects on consciousness. One obvious reaction to these drugs is the formation of hallucinations.

Heterosexual orientation individuals mostly attracted to members of the opposite sex.

Homeostasis a state of balance within our internal physiological reactions.

Human sexuality all of the emotional, cognitive, behavioral, and physical experiences of humans related to their sexuality.

Hypnosis a state of consciousness characterized by (a) a marked increase in suggestibility, (b) a focusing of attention, (c) an exaggerated use of imagination, (d) an unwillingness or inability to act on one's own, and (e) an unquestioning acceptance of distortions of reality.

Hypothesis a tentative explanation of some phenomenon that can be tested and then either accepted or rejected.

I

Id the totally inborn portion of personality. It resides in the unconscious level of the mind, and it is through the id that basic instincts are expressed.

Identity crisis the struggle to define and integrate the sense of who one is, what one is to do in life, and what one's attitudes, beliefs, and values should be.

Implicit attitude type of attitude that operates below consciousness, at nearly "gut" level.

Implicit stereotype a stereotype that operates on an unconscious level and is activated automatically, without conscious thought.

Incentives external stimuli that serve as motivating agents for behavior.

Independent variable a variable that the experimenter manipulates.

Inductive reasoning reasoning leading to a likely general conclusion based on separate, specific facts and observations.

Inferiority complex the feeling that we are less able than others to solve life's problems and get along in the world.

Information processing the process of finding out about the world, making judgments about it, learning from it, and remembering what we have learned.

Information-processing approach a view of cognitive development suggesting quantitative changes (changes in degree) in a number of information-processing systems, such as learning and memory.

Inhibitory neurotransmitter a neurotransmitter that prevents the next neuron from firing.

Insanity the legal concept that a person did not know or fully understand the consequences of his or her actions at a given time, could not discern the difference between right and wrong, and was unable to exercise control over his or her actions at the time a crime was committed.

Instincts unlearned, complex patterns of behavior that occur in the presence of certain stimuli.

Intellectual disability a disorder involving deficits of intellectual and adaptive functioning as well as deficits in conceptual, social, and practical domains with an onset during the developmental period.

Intelligence the capacity of an individual to understand the world around him or her and his or her resourcefulness to cope with its challenges.

Interneurons neurons within the spinal cord and central nervous system that transmit information between neurons.

Interview measurement of what people say about themselves, rather than what they do.

IQ (Intelligence Quotient) a measure of intelligence determined by dividing the person's mental age (MA) by his or her actual, chronological age (CA), and multiplying the result by 100.

Iris the colored part of the eye that can expand or contract depending on the intensity of light striking the eye.

K

Key word method a method of study that works by imagining a connection that visually ties a word to a key word.

Kinesthetic sense senses the position and movements of parts of the body and has receptors found in the joints, muscles, and tendons.

L

Language a large collection of arbitrary symbols that have a common, shared significance for a language-using community and that follow certain rules of combination.

Latent content the "true," underlying meaning of the dream that resides in a person's unconscious mind.

Latent learning a form of learning that is hidden and not shown in behavior until it is reinforced.

Learning a relatively permanent change in behavior that occurs as a result of practice or experience.

Lens a flexible structure in the eye that changes shape to focus an image on the back of the eye.

Libido the psychic energy through which the sexual instincts operate.

Life instincts (Eros) impulses for survival, including those that motivate sex, hunger, and thirst.

Limbic system a collection of brain structures controlling many of the complex behavioral patterns that are often considered to be instinctive.

Lobotomy psychosurgery severing the major neural connections between the prefrontal lobes (the area at the very front of the cerebral cortex) and lower brain centers.

Loneliness a subjective, psychological state that arises when there is a discrepancy between relationships we would like to have and those we actually have.

Long-term memory (LTM) memory for large amounts of information that is held for long periods of time.

M

Maintenance rehearsal (or rote rehearsal) rehearsal we use to keep material active in short-term memory that amounts to little more than the simple repetition of the information already in our STM.

Major depressive disorder depressive disorder defined as a period of at least two weeks during which the person experienced five or more of a list of specific symptoms nearly every day.

Mania a condition characterized as an elevated mood with feelings of euphoria or irritability.

Manifest content the content of a dream of which the dreamer was aware.

Matching principle the idea that we tend to become involved with a partner with whom we are usually closely matched in terms of physical attributes or social status.

Meaningfulness the extent to which information elicits existing associations already in memory.

Meditation a self-induced state of consciousness characterized by a focusing of attention and relaxation.

Medulla part of the brain that controls such functions as heart rate, respiration, blood pressure, coughing, sneezing, tongue movements, and reflexive eye movements.

Memory a set of systems involved in the acquisition, storage, and retrieval of information that can hold information for periods of time ranging from fractions of a second to a lifetime.

Menarche the first menstrual period.

Mental set a cognitive structure formed when we are psychologically predisposed or expect to perceive something.

Minnesota Multiphasic Personality Inventory (MMPI-2) a personality test that measures several personality dimensions with the same set of items.

Mnemonic device an encoding technique that aids retrieval by helping to organize and add meaningfulness to new material.

Modern racism racism that is not expressed openly but, rather, is manifested in an uncertainty in feelings and behaviors toward minorities.

Morphemes the smallest units of meaning in a spoken language; a collection of phonemes that means something.

Motivation the process that arouses, directs, and maintains behavior.

Motor area the area of the cerebral cortex located in strips at the very back of the frontal lobes that coordinates and initiates most voluntary activity.

Motor neurons nerve fibers that carry impulses away from the spinal cord and brain to the muscles and glands.

Multiple approach-avoidance conflict a type of conflict arising when an individual is faced with a number of alternatives, each one of which is in some way both positive and negative.

Myelin a white substance composed of fat and protein found on about half of the axons in an adult's nervous system.

N

Narrative chaining a technique that helps improve retrieval of otherwise unorganized material by weaving that material into a meaningful story.

Need a lack or shortage of some biological essential that is required for survival.

Need for affiliation a need to be with others, to work with others toward some end, and to form friendships and associations.

Need for intimacy a need to form and maintain close, affectionate relationships.

Need for power a need to be in control, to be in charge of both the situation and other people.

Need to achieve (nAch) the acquired need to meet or exceed a standard of excellence in one's behaviors.

Negative reinforcement delivering an aversive (i.e., something the organism doesn't like) stimulus *before* a response is made, with the intention of increasing or maintaining a response that removes it.

Negative symptoms symptoms of schizophrenia that involve a loss of or a decrease in normal functions.

Neural impulse a rapid, reversible change in the electrical charges within and outside a neuron.

Neural threshold the minimum level of stimulation required to fire a neuron.

Neuron a microscopically small cell that transmits information—in the form of neural impulses from one part of the body to another.

Neurotransmitters chemicals released into the synapse that act to excite or inhibit the transmission of a neural impulse in the next neuron.

NREM sleep a type of sleep characterized by fragmented thoughts rather than vivid dreams.

O

Obedience when we modify behavior in response to a command from someone in authority.

Obsessions ideas or thoughts that involuntarily and constantly intrude into awareness.

Obsessive-compulsive disorder (OCD) a disorder characterized by a pattern of recurrent obsessions and compulsions.

Olfaction the technical name for the sense of smell.

Operant conditioning a learning process that changes the rate, or probability, of responses on the basis of the consequences that result from those responses.

Optic nerve the collection of neurons that leaves the eye and starts back toward other parts of the brain.

Orienting reflex a simple, unlearned response of attending to a new or unusual stimulus.

Overlearning the process of practicing or rehearsing material over and above what is needed to learn it.

P

Panic disorder a disorder with the major symptoms of an unpredictable, unprovoked onset of sudden, intense anxiety, or a "panic attack."

Parasympathetic division division of the autonomic nervous system that is active when we are relaxed and quiet.

Parkinson's disease a disorder involving the basal ganglia in which the most noticeable symptoms are impairment of movement and involuntary tremors.

Perception a process that involves the selection, organization, and interpretation of stimuli.

Peripheral nervous system (PNS) a division of the nervous system that consists of all neurons in the body not in the CNS—the nerve fibers in the arms, face, fingers, intestines, and so on.

Persistent depressive disorder a milder, but chronic form of depression, involving recurrent pessimism, low energy level, and low self-esteem.

Personality the affects, behaviors, and cognitions of people that characterize them in a number of situations over time.

Personality disorder a disorder that involves a long-lasting pattern of perceiving, relating to, and thinking about the environment and oneself that is maladaptive and inflexible and causes either impaired functioning or distress.

Persuasion the application of rational and/or emotional arguments to deliberately convince others to change their attitudes or behavior.

Pheromones chemicals that produce distinctive odors affecting other members of the same species.

Phonemes meaningless language sounds that result in a meaningful utterance when put together in the proper order.

Physical attractiveness bias physically attractive people are thought to have a wide range of positive attributes.

Physical proximity effect the idea that we become friends with those whom we find ourselves in close physical contact with.

Pinna the outer ear.

Pituitary gland a gland often referred to as the master gland, reflecting its direct control over the activity of many other glands in the endocrine system.

Pleasure principle the idea that the major function of the id is to find immediate gratification and satisfaction for basic pleasurable impulses.

Pluralistic ignorance the belief on the part of the individual that only he or she is confused and does not know what to do in an emergency, whereas everyone else is standing around doing nothing for a good reason.

Pons a structure in the brain serving as a relay station or bridge, sorting out and relaying sensory messages from the spinal cord and the face up to higher brain centers and similarly relaying motor impulses from higher centers of the brain down to the rest of the body.

Positive reinforcement delivering a reinforcer after a behavior that is intended to increase or maintain the strength of a response.

Positive symptoms symptoms of schizophrenia involving thoughts and perceptions (largely hallucinations and delusions) that are not present in normal people.

Posttraumatic stress disorder (PTSD) a disorder that involves distressing symptoms that arise sometime after the experience of a highly traumatic event.

Pragmatics the study of how language is related to the social context in which it occurs.

Preconscious a level of consciousness containing aspects of our experience of which we are not conscious at any moment but that can easily be brought to awareness.

Prejudice a biased, often negative, attitude toward groups of people.

Prenatal period the period of development between conception and birth.

Preoperational stage (two to seven years) Piaget's second stage of development, in which a child's thinking is self-centered.

Primary drive a drive based on unlearned, physiological needs.

Primary reinforcer a reinforcer whose properties are unlearned and do not require previous experience to be effective.

Problem a discrepancy between one's present state and one's perceived goal state and no readily apparent way to get from one to the other.

Problem-focused strategy a coping strategy in which you look beyond how you feel at the moment to find the underlying situation causing your present feelings.

Procedural memory a storage system where we store motor responses and chains of motor responses that we have learned well.

Projective test a personality test that asks a person to respond to ambiguous stimuli. The stimuli can be any number of things, and there are no clearly right or wrong answers.

Prototypes members of a category that typify or represent the category to which they belong.

Proximity (or contiguity) events occurring close together in space or time are perceived as belonging together and part of the same figure.

Psychoactive drugs chemicals that alter psychological processes.

Psychoanalytic approach a personality theory relying on innate drives as explanatory concepts for human behavior and an acceptance of the power of unconscious forces to mold and shape behavior.

Psychological test an objective, standardized measure of a sample of behavior; used as an aid in the understanding and prediction of behavior.

Psychology the science that studies behavior and mental processes.

Psychosurgery surgical procedures, usually directed at the brain, used to affect psychological reactions.

Psychotic symptoms symptoms involving loss of contact with reality, such as delusions and hallucinations, and a gross impairment of functioning, inappropriate affect, or total loss of affect.

Puberty when a person becomes physically capable of sexual reproduction.

Punishment when a stimulus delivered to an organism *decreases* the rate, or probability, of the response that preceded it.

Pupil the opening through which light enters the eye.

R

Rational emotive therapy (RET) a therapy with the basic premise that psychological problems arise when people try to interpret what happens in the world (a cognitive activity) on the basis of irrational beliefs.

Reality principle the reasonable and rational way to satisfy the impulses of the id.

Reasoning the process of reaching conclusions that are based on either a set of general (cognitive) principles or an assortment of acquired facts and observations.

Recall a memory process where one produces information to which he or she has been previously exposed.

Recognition a memory process where we ask someone to identify material previously experienced.

Reflex an unlearned, automatic response that occurs in the presence of a specific stimulus.

Reinforcement the *process* of increasing the rate or probability of a response.

Reinforcer the actual stimulus used in the process of reinforcement that increases the probability or rate of a response.

Reliability the consistency, dependability, or repeatability of an observation.

REM sleep a stage of sleep characterized by rapid eye movements and clear, vivid dreams.

Repression the process in which anxiety-producing unresolved conflicts are forced out of awareness and into the unconscious mind.

Resistance the unwillingness or inability to discuss freely some aspect of one's life during psychoanalysis.

Reticular formation brain structure involved in determining our level of activation or arousal.

Retina the structure at the back of the eye where vision begins to take place. Light energy is transduced into neural energy here.

Retinal disparity a binocular cue for depth in which each eye gets a different view of the same object.

Retrieval the process of getting information out of memory.

Rods photoreceptors that are responsible for achromatic (not color), low light vision.

Romantic love a type of love with high levels of passion and intimacy but low levels of commitment.

S

Same-sex orientation (formerly referred to as homosexual) individuals mostly attracted to members of the same sex.

Schema a mental representation that children construct in order to make sense of the world in which they live.

Schizophrenia a disorder involving a distortion of reality; a retreat from other people; and disturbances in affect, behavior, and cognition.

Science a discipline with two characteristics: (1) an organized body of knowledge (published research articles), and (2) the use of scientific methods.

Scientific methods methods that involve observing a phenomenon, formulating hypotheses about it, making more observations, refining and re-testing hypotheses.

Secondary drive a drive derived from an organism's learning experience.

Secondary reinforcer a reinforcer whose properties are learned and may be referred to as a conditioned, acquired, or learned reinforcer.

Semantic memory memory where we store all our vocabulary, simple concepts, and rules.

Semantics the study of meaning in language.

Sensation the act of detecting external stimuli and converting those stimuli into nervous-system activity.

Sensorimotor stage (birth to two years) Piaget's first stage of development, in which children learn about the world by sensing (*sensori-*) and by doing (*motor*).

Sensory adaptation sensory experience decreases with continued exposure to a stimulus.

Sensory area the area of the cerebral cortex that receives impulses from the senses.

Sensory memory a storage system that stores large amounts of information for very short periods.

Sensory neurons nerve fibers that carry impulses toward the brain or spinal cord.

Sensory threshold the minimum intensity of a stimulus needed to operate a sense organ.

Sex one's biological status with respect to sexuality.

Sexual orientation one's pattern of emotional, sexual, and romantic attraction of those of a particular gender.

Sexually transmitted disease (STD) a contagious disease usually passed on through sexual contact.

Shape constancy the perception that objects maintain their shape even though the retinal image they cast may change.

Short-term memory (STM) a level, or store, in human memory with a limited capacity and, without the benefit of rehearsal, a brief duration.

Similarity grouping together in perception stimuli that are alike or share properties.

Size constancy the tendency to see objects as unchanging in size regardless of the size of the retinal image they produce.

Sleep a state of consciousness that reduces our alertness, awareness, and perception of events occurring around us.

Social anxiety a condition resulting when a person expects negative encounters with others.

Social cognition the processes used to think about and evaluate social situations.

Social facilitation when the presence of others improves an individual's performance on some task.

Social learning theory considers learning that takes place through the observation and imitation of models.

Social loafing the tendency to work less (to decrease individual effort) as the size of the group in which one works becomes larger.

Social psychology the field of psychology concerned with how others influence the thoughts, feelings, and behaviors of the individual.

Socioeconomic status (SES) a measure that reflects income, educational level, and occupation.

Somatic nervous system consists of those neurons that are outside the CNS and serve the skeletal muscles and pick up impulses from our sense receptors, such as the eyes and ears.

Spanking a form of punishment that is (a) physically noninjurious, (b) intended to modify behavior, and (c) administered with an opened hand to the extremities or buttocks.

Specific phobia a disorder involving a persistent and excessive fear of some object, activity, or situation that leads a person to avoid that object, activity, or situation.

Spinal reflexes simple, automatic behaviors that occur without conscious, voluntary action of the brain.

Split-brain procedure a surgical technique used to separate the functions of the two cerebral hemispheres.

Stereotype a rigid set of positive or negative beliefs about a group of people, especially members of a group we perceive to be different from us.

Stimulants drugs that stimulate or activate an organism, producing a heightened sense of arousal and an elevation of mood.

Stimulus generalization a process by which a conditioned response is elicited by stimuli similar to the original conditioned stimulus (CS).

Storage the process of keeping information and experiences in memory.

Stress a complex set of reactions made by an individual under pressure to adapt.

Stressor a source of stress.

Superego the part of the personality involving one's sense of morality or conscience.

Sympathetic division division of the autonomic nervous system that is active when we are emotionally aroused or excited.

Synapse the location at which a neural impulse is relayed from one neuron to another.

Syntax the rules that govern how sentences are formed or structured in a language.

Systematic desensitization a technique with the goal of gradually teaching a patient to associate positive feelings of relaxation with a previously feared stimulus.

T

Taste buds the receptor cells for taste located on the tongue.

Test norms results of a test taken by a large group of people whose scores are used to make comparisons.

Thalamus a brain structure acting as a relay station for impulses traveling to and from the cerebral cortex.

Theory an organized collection of testable ideas used to describe and explain a particular subject matter.

Thinking cognitive processes that build on existing cognitions, perceptions, ideas, experiences, and memories.

Thyroid gland a gland located in the neck that produces a hormone called thyroxin. Thyroxin regulates the pace of the body's functioning.

Timbre the psychological quality or character of a sound that reflects its degree of purity.

Top-down processing when what one selects and perceives depends on what the perceiver already knows.

Trait any distinguishable, relatively enduring way in which one individual differs from others.

Transducer a mechanism that converts energy from one form to another.

Transgender identity individuals whose appearance and/or behaviors do not conform to traditional, accepted gender roles.

Transsexual individual whose gender identity is opposite from his or her biological sex and is likely to seek medical intervention to change their sex.

Triangular theory of love theory stating that love consists of three interrelated components: passion, intimacy, and commitment.

Type A behavior pattern (TABP) a behavior pattern involving a person being competitive, achievement-oriented, and impatient; the individual typically works at many tasks at the same time, is easily aroused, and is often hostile or angry.

U

Unconditional positive regard the expression of being accepting and non-critical in humanistic therapy.

Unconditioned response the unlearned response to the unconditioned stimulus.

Unconditioned stimulus a stimulus that reliably elicits a response with no prior learning.

Unconscious the level of consciousness containing cognitions, feelings, or motives that are not available at the conscious or the preconscious level.

V

Validity the extent to which an observation reflects what is actually happening.

Vesicles incredibly small containers that are concentrated at axon terminals and hold neurotransmitters.

Vestibular sense the sense that tells us about balance, about where we are in relation to gravity, and about acceleration or deceleration.

Vitreous humor the thick fluid filling the interior of the eye behind the lens.

W

White light light of the lowest possible saturation, consisting of a random mixture of wavelengths.

References

A

AAHSA (American Association of Homes and Services for the Aging). (2003). *Nursing home statistics*. Retrieved from http://www.aahsa.org

Abdool Karim, Q., Abdool Karim, S. S., Frohlich, J. A., Grobler, A. C., Baxter, C., Mansoor, L. E., . . . CAPRISA 004 Trial Group. (2010). Effectiveness and safety of tenofovir gel, an antiretroviral microbicide, for the prevention of HIV infection in women. *Science* (New York, N.Y.), 2010 (5996), 1168–1174.

Abrahams, B. S., & Geschwind, D. H. (2008). Advances in autism genetics: On the threshold of a new neurobiology. *Nature Reviews Genetics*, *9*, 341–355. https://doi.org/10.1038/nrg2346

Acker, M., & Davis, M. H. (1992). Intimacy, passion and commitment in adult romantic relationships: A test of the triangular theory of love. *Journal of Social and Personal Relationships 9*, 21–50.

Adler, N., & Matthews, K. (1994). Health psychology: Why do some people get sick and some stay well? *Annual Review of Psychology, 45*, 229–259.

Adler, N. E., & Rehkopf, D. H. (2008). US disparities in health: Descriptions, causes, and mechanisms. *Annual Review of Public Health*, *29*, 235–252. https://doi.org/10.1146/annurev.publhealth.29.020907.090852

Aiken, L. R. (1984). *Psychological testing and assessment* (4th ed.). Boston, MA: Allyn & Bacon.

Ajzen, I. (2001). Nature and operation of attitudes. *Annual Review of Psychology, 52*, 27–58.

Ajzen, I., & Fishbein, M. (2000). Attitudes and the attitude-behavior relation: Reasoned and automatic processes. *European Review of Social Psychology, 11*, 1–33.

Albarracin, D., Durantini, M. R., & Earl, A. (2006). Empirical and theoretical conclusions of an analysis of outcomes of HIV-prevention interventions. *Current Directions in Psychological Science, 15*, 73–78.

Aleman, A., Kahn, R. S., & Selton, J. (2003). Sex differences in the risk for schizophrenia. *Archives of General Psychiatry, 60*, 565–571.

Alexander, J. (2015). The major ideologies of liberalism, socialism and conservatism. *Political Studies, 63*, 980–994.

Almeida, D. M. (2005). Resilience and vulnerability to daily stressors assessed via diary methods. *Current Directions in Psychological Science, 14*, 64–68.

Amaro, H. (1995). Love, sex, and power: Considering women's realities in HIV prevention. *American Psychologist, 50*, 437–447.

American Association on Intellectual and Developmental Disabilities. (2018). *Definition of intellectual disability*. Retrieved from https://aaidd.org/intellectual-disability/definition

American Cancer Society. (2005). *Cancer facts & figures for African Americans 2005–2006*. Atlanta, GA: Author.

American Psychiatric Association. (2000). *Diagnostic and statistical manual of mental disorders* (4th ed. Text Revision). Arlington, VA: American Psychiatric Publishing.

American Psychiatric Association. (2013). *Diagnostic and statistical manual of mental disorders* (5th ed.). Arlington, VA: American Psychiatric Publishing.

American Psychological Association. (2018). *Divisions*. Retrieved from http://www.apa.org/about/division/index.aspx

American Society of Addiction Medicine. (2016). *Opioid addiction 2016 facts & figures*. Retrieved from https://www.asam.org/docs/default-source/advocacy/opioid-addiction-disease-facts-figures.pdf

Anderson, B. L. (1997, July). Psychological interventions for individuals with cancer. *Clinician's Research Digest: Supplemental Bulletin 16*.

Anderson, C. A., & Bushman, B. J. (2002). Human aggression. *Annual Review of Psychology, 53*, 27–51.

Anderson, C. A., Shibuya, A., Ihori, N., Swing, E. L., Bushman, B. J., Sakamoto, A., ... Saleem, M. (2010). Violent video game effects on aggression, empathy, and prosocial behavior in Eastern and Western countries: A meta-analytic review. *Psychological Bulletin, 136*, 151–173.

Anderson, J. R. (1987). Skill acquisition: Compilation of weak-method problem solutions. *Psychological Review, 94*, 192–210.

Anderson, V., Spencer-Smith, M., & Wood, A. (2011). Do children really recover better? Neurobehavioural plasticity after early brain insult. *Brain: A Journal of Neurology, 134*, 2197–2221. https://doi.org/10.1093/brain/awr103

Anshel, M. H. (1996). Effect of chronic aerobic exercise and progressive relaxation on motor performance and affect following acute stress. *Behavioral Medicine, 21*, 186–196.

Anshel, M. H., Sutarso, T., & Jubenville, C. (2009). Racial and gender differences on sources of acute stress and coping style among competitive athletes. *Journal of Social Psychology, 149*, 159–178.

Anthony, M. V. (2002). Concepts of consciousness, kinds of consciousness, meanings of "consciousness." *Philosophical Studies, 109,* 1–16.

Anything Pawsable. (2018). *First five skills you should teach a service dog in training.* Retrieved from https://www.anything-pawsable.com/first-five-skills-service-dog-in-training/

Areh, I. (2011). Gender-related differences in eyewitness testimony. *Personality & Individual Differences, 50,* 559–563. https://doi.org/10.1016/j.paid.2010.11.027

Armas, G. C. (2003). Worldwide population aging. In H. Cox (Ed.), *Annual editions: Aging* (pp. 3–4). Guilford, CT: McGraw-Hill.

Armstrong, D. (1981). *The nature of the mind.* Ithaca, NY: Cornell University Press.

Aron, A., Aron, E., & Allen, A. H. (1998). Motivations for unrequited love. *Personality and Social Psychology Bulletin, 21,* 787–796.

Aronson, E., Wilson, T. D., & Akert, R. M. (2005). *Social psychology* (5th ed.). Upper Saddle River, NJ: Prentice Hall.

Asch, S. E. (1951). The effects of group pressure upon the modification and distortion of judgment. In H. Guetzkow (Ed.), *Groups, leadership, and men* (pp. 177–190). Pittsburgh, PA: Carnegie Press.

Asch, S. E. (1956). Studies of independence and conformity: I. A minority of one against a unanimous majority. *Psychological Monographs: General and Applied, 70*(416), 1–7.

Aserinsky, E., & Kleitman, N. (1953). Regularly occurring periods of eye mobility and concomitant phenomena during sleep. *Science, 18,* 273–274.

Ashby, F. G., & Maddox, W. T. (2005). Human category learning. *Annual Review of Psychology, 56,* 149–178.

Ashton, M. C., & Lee, K. (2001). A theoretical basis for the major dimensions of personality. *European Journal of Personality, 15,* 327–353. https://doi.org/10.1002/per.417

Association for Psychological Science. (2018). *Who we are.* Retrieved from https://www.psychologicalscience.org/about/who-we-are

Atkinson, R. C. (1975). Mnemotechnics in second-language learning. *American Psychologist, 30,* 821–828.

Auyenung, B., Baron-Cohen, S., Ashwin, E., Knickmeyer, R., Taylor, K., Hackett, G., & Hines, M. (2009). Fetal testosterone predicts sexually differentiated childhood behavior in girls and in boys. *Psychological Science, 20,* 144–148.

Azaiza, F., Ron, P., Shoham, M., & Gigini, I. (2010). Death and dying anxiety among elderly Arab Muslims in Israel. *Death Studies, 34,* 351–364.

B

Baars, B. J. (2003). Some good things about Crick and Koch's "Framework for consciousness." *Science & Consciousness Review, 3.* Retrieved from http://psych.pomona.edu/scr/editorials/20030303.html

Bachorowski, J., & Owren, M. J. (1995). Vocal expression of emotion: Acoustic properties of speech are associated with emotional intensity and context. *Psychological Science, 6,* 219–224.

Baddeley, A. (1998). *Human memory: Theory and practice* (rev. ed.). Boston, MA: Allyn & Bacon.

Baddeley, A. D. (2001). Is working memory still working? *American Psychologist, 56,* 851–864.

Baer, J. S., Sampson, P. D., Barr, H. M., Conner, P. D., & Streissguth, A. P. (2003). A 21-year longitudinal analysis of the effects of prenatal alcohol exposure on young adult drinking. *Archives of General Psychiatry, 60,* 377–385.

Baer, R. A., Smith, G. T., Hopkins, J., Krietemeyer, J., & Toney, L. (2006). Using self-report assessment methods to explore facets of mindfulness. *Assessment, 13,* 27–45.

Bail, C. A., Argyle, L. P., Brown, T. W., Bumpus, J. P., Haohan, C., Hunzaker, M. F., & . . . Volfovsky, A. (2018). Exposure to opposing views on social media can increase political polarization. *Proceedings of the National Academy of Sciences of the United States of America, 115,* 9216–9221. https://doi.org/10.1073/pnas.1804840115

Baker, T. B., McFall, R. M., & Shoham, V. (2008). Current status and future prospects of clinical psychology toward a scientifically principled approach to mental and behavioral health care. *Psychological Science in the Public Interest, 9,* 67–103.

Bandura, A. (1997). *Self-efficacy: The exercise of control.* New York, NY: Freeman.

Bandura, A. (1999). Social cognitive theory of personality. In D. Cervone & Y. Shoda (Eds.), *The coherence of personality: Social-cognitive bases of consistency, variability, and organization* (pp. 185–241). New York, NY: Guilford.

Bandura, A. (2001a). Social cognitive theory: An agentic perspective. *Annual Review of Psychology, 52,* 1–26.

Bandura, A. (2001b). *On shaping one's future: The primacy of human agency.* Paper presented at the annual meeting of the American Psychological Society, Toronto, Canada.

Bandura, A., Ross, D., & Ross, S. A. (1963). Imitation of film-mediated aggressive models. *Journal of Abnormal and Social Psychology, 66,* 3–11.

Barber, T. X. (2000). A deeper understanding of hypnosis: Its secrets, its nature, its essence. *American Journal of Clinical Hypnosis, 42,* 208–272.

Bargh, J. A., & Ferguson, M. J. (2000). Beyond behaviorism: On the automaticity of higher mental processes. *Psychological Bulletin, 126,* 925–945.

Barlow, D. H. (2002). *Anxiety and its disorders: The nature and treatment of anxiety and panic* (2nd ed.). New York, NY: Guilford Press.

Barlow D. H., & Durand, V. M. (2009). *Abnormal psychology: An integrative approach.* Belmont, CA: Wadsworth.

Barnier, A. J., & McConkey, K. M. (1992). Reports of real and false memories: The relevance of hypnosis, hypnotizability, and context of memory test. *Journal of Abnormal Psychology, 101,* 521–527. https://doi.org/10.1037/0021-843X.101.3.521

Barnier, A. J., & McConkey, K. M. (2004). Defining and identifying the highly hypnotizable person. In M. Heap, R. J. Brown, & D. A. Oakley (Eds.), *High hypnotizability: Theoretical, experimental and clinical issues* (pp. 30–60). New York, NY: Brunner Rutledge.

Barrett, L. F. (2006). Solving the emotion paradox: Categorization and the experience of emotion. *Personality and Social Psychology Review, 10,* 20–46.

Barrett, L. F., & Wager, T. D. (2006). The structure of emotion. *Current Directions in Psychological Science, 15,* 79–83. https://doi.org/10.1111/j.0963-7214.2006.00411.x

Bartoshuk, L., M., Fast, K., & Snyder, D. (2005). Differences in our sensory worlds. *Current Directions in Psychological Science, 14,* 122–125.

Baum, A., & Grunberg, N. E. (1991). Gender, stress, and health. *Health Psychology, 10,* 80–85.

Baumeister, R., Wotman, S., & Stillwell, A. M. (1993). Unrequited love: On heartbreak, anger, guilt, scriptlessness and humiliation. *Journal of Personality and Social Psychology, 64,* 377–394.

Baumeister, R. F. (2000). Gender differences in erotic plasticity. *Psychological Bulletin, 126,* 347–374.

Baumeister, R. F., & Bratslavsky, E. (1999). Passion, intimacy, and time: Passionate love as a function of change of intimacy over time. *Personality and Social Psychology Review, 3,* 49–67.

Baumeister, R. F., Catanese, K. R., & Vohs, K. D. (2001). Is there a gender difference in strength of sex drive? *Personality and Social Psychology Review, 5,* 242–273.

Beam, C. R., Kaneshiro, C., Jang, J. Y., Reynolds, C. A., Pedersen, N. L., & Gatz, M. (2018). Differences between women and men in incidence rates of dementia and Alzheimer's Disease. *Journal of Alzheimer's Disease, 64,* 1077–1083. https://doi.org/10.3233/JAD-180141

Bearman, P. S., & Bruckner, H. (2002). Opposite-sex twins and same-sex attraction. *Journal of Sociology, 107,* 1179–1205.

Beatty, J. (1995). *Principles of behavioral neuroscience.* Chicago, IL: Brown & Benchmark.

Beck, A. T. (1976). *Cognitive therapy and the emotional disorders.* New York, NY: International University Press.

Beck, A. T. (1991). Cognitive therapy: A 30-year retrospective. *American Psychologist, 46,* 368–375.

Beck, A. T. (1995). *Cognitive therapy: Basics and beyond.* New York, NY: Guilford.

Beck, A. T., & Freeman, A. (1990). *Cognitive therapy of personality disorders.* New York, NY: Guilford.

Becker, B., Wagner, D., Koester, P., Bender, K., Kabbasch, C., Gouzoulis-Mayfrank, E., Daumann, J. (2013). Memory-related hippocampal functioning in ecstasy and amphetamine users. *Psychopharmacology, 225,* 923–934. https://doi.org/10.1007/s00213-012-2873-z

Becker, D. F., & Grilo, C. M. (2007). Ethnic differences in the predictors of drug and alcohol abuse in hospitalized adolescents. *The American Journal on Addictions, 16,* 389–396.

Bee, H. (1996). *The journey of adulthood* (3rd ed.). Upper Saddle River, NJ: Prentice Hall.

Beeber, L. S. (2018). Disentangling mental illness and violence. *Journal of the American Psychiatric Nurses Association, 24,* 360–362. https://doi.org/10.1177/1078390318783729

Békés, V., Beaulieu-Prévost, D., Guay, S., Belleville, G., & Marchand, A. (2016). Women with PTSD benefit more from psychotherapy than men. *Psychological Trauma: Theory, Research, Practice and Policy, 8,* 720–727.

Ben Hamida, S., Mineka, S., & Bailey, J. M. (1998). Sex differences in perceived controllability of mate value: An evolutionary perspective. *Journal of Personality and Social Psychology, 75,* 963–966.

Bendak, S. (2015). Objective assessment of the effects of texting while driving: A simulator study. *International Journal of Injury Control & Safety Promotion, 22,* 387–392. https://doi.org/10.1080/17457300.2014.942325

Benenson, J. F., & Heath, A. (2006). Boys withdraw from one-on-one interactions, whereas girls withdraw more in groups. *Developmental Psychology, 42,* 272–282.

Benjet, C., & Kazdin, A. E. (2003). Spanking children: The controversies, findings, and new directions. *Clinical Psychology Review, 23,* 197–224.

Bennett, M. P., & Lengacher, C. (2009). Humor and laughter may influence health IV. Humor and immune function. *Evidence-Based Complementary & Alternative Medicine (Ecam), 6,* 159–164.

Ben-Porath, Y. S., & Tellegen, A. (2008). *Minnesota Multiphasic Personality Inventory-2-Restructured Form® (MMPI-2-RF®).* Retrieved from https://www.pearsonclinical.com/psychology/products/100000631/minnesota-multiphasic-personality-inventory-2-rf-mmpi-2-rf.html

Berkowitz, H. (1994). U.S. firms trip over their tongues in wooing the world. *The Journal Gazette,* June 21.

Berscheid, E. (1994). Interpersonal relationships. *Annual Review of Psychology, 45,* 79–129.

Bjorklund, D. F. (2000). *Children's thinking: Developmental function and individual differences* (3rd ed.). Belmont, CA: Wadsworth.

Blakemore, S. (2001). State of the art—the psychology of consciousness. *The Psychologist, 14,* 522–525.

Blass, E. M., Ganchow, J. R., & Steiner, J. E. (1984). Classical conditioning in newborn human infants 2–48 hours of age. *Infant Behavior and Development, 7,* 223–235.

Boles, D. (2005). A large-sample study of sex differences in functional cerebral lateralization. *Journal of Clinical & Experimental Neuropsychology, 27,* 759–768. https://doi.org/10.1080/13803390590954263Boles

Bond, R., & Smith, P. B. (1996). Culture and conformity: A meta-analysis. *Psychological Bulletin, 119,* 111–137.

Booth, A., Johnson, D. R., Granger, D. A., Crouter, A. C., & McHale, S. (2003). Testosterone and child and adolescent adjustment: The moderating role of parent-child relationships. *Developmental Psychology, 39,* 85–98.

Bootzin, R. R., & Rider, S. P. (1997). Behavioral techniques and biofeedback for insomnia. In M. R. Pressman & W. C. Orr (Eds.), *Understanding sleep: The evaluation and treatment of sleep disorders* (pp. 315–338). Washington, DC: American Psychological Association.

Bordens, K. S., & Abbott, B. B. (2018). *Research design and methods: A process approach* (10th ed.). New York, NY: McGraw Hill.

Bordens, K. S., & Horowitz, I. A. (2017). *Social psychology* (5th ed.). St. Paul, MN: Freeload Press.

Borinstein, A. B. (1992). *Public attitudes toward persons with mental illness*. Retrieved from https://www.healthaffairs.org/doi/pdf/10.1377/hlthaff.11.3.186

Bornstein, R. F. (1989). Exposure and affect: Overview and meta-analysis of research, 1968–1987. *Psychological Bulletin, 106*, 265–289.

Boss, P., Beulieu, L., & Wieling, E. (2003). Healing loss, ambiguity, and trauma: A community-based intervention with families of union workers missing after the 9/11 attack in New York City. *Journal of Marital & Family Therapy, 29*, 455–467. https://doi.org/10.1111/j.1752-0606.2003.tb01688.x

Bousfield, W. A. (1953). The occurrence of clustering in the free recall of randomly arranged associates. *Journal of General Psychology, 49*, 229–240.

Bower, G. H., & Clark, M. C. (1969). Narrative stories as mediators for serial learning. *Psychonomic Science, 14*, 181–182.

Bradley, R. H., & Corwyn, R. F. (2002). Socioeconomic status and child development. *Annual Review of Psychology, 53*, 371–399.

Bradshaw, J. L., & Nettleton, N. C. (1983). *Human cerebral asymmetry*. Englewood Cliffs, NJ: Prentice Hall.

Braun, K. A., Ellis, R., & Loftus, E. F. (2002). Make my memory: How advertising can change our memories of the past. *Psychology & Marketing, 19*, 1–23. https://doi.org/10.1002/mar.1000

Breedlove, S. M. (2017). Prenatal influences on human sexual orientation: Expectations versus data. *Archives of Sexual Behavior, 46*, 1583–1592. https://doi.org/10.1007/s10508-016-0904-2

Bregman, J., Dykens, E. Watson, M., & Leckman, J. (1987). Fragile X syndrome: Variability in phenotype expression. *Journal of the American Academy of Child and Adolescent Psychiatry, 26*, 463–471.

Brislin, R. W. (1993). *Understanding culture's influence on behavior*. Fort Worth, TX: Harcourt Brace.

Brockmeyer, T., Anderle, A., Schmidt, H., Febry, S., Wünsch-Leiteritz, W., Leiteritz, A., & Friederich, H. (2018). Body image related negative interpretation bias in anorexia nervosa. *Behaviour Research and Therapy, 10*, 469–473. https://doi.org/10.1016/j.brat.2018.03.003

Brod, M., Stewart, A. L., Sands, L., & Walton, P. (1999). Conceptualization and measurement of quality of life in dementia: The Dementia Quality of Life Instrument (DQoL). *The Gerontologist, 39*, 25–35.

Brougham, R., Zail, C., Mendoza, C., & Miller, J. (2009). Stress, sex differences, and coping strategies among college students. *Current Psychology, 28*, 85–97. https://doi.org/10.1007/s12144-009-9047-0

Brumbaugh, C. C., & Fraley, R. C. (2006). Transference and attachment: How do attachment patterns get carried forward from one relationship to the next? *Personality and Social Psychology Bulletin, 32*, 552–560.

Budge, S. L., Adelson, J. L., & Howard, K. S. (2013). Anxiety and depression in transgender individuals: The roles of transition status, loss, social support, and coping. *Journal of Consulting and Clinical Psychology, 81*, 545–557.

Bunde, J., & Suls, J. (2006). A quantitative analysis of the relationship between the Cook-Medley hostility scale and traditional coronary artery disease risk factors. *Health Psychology, 25*, 493–500.

Bureau of Labor Statistics. (2018a). *Employment characteristics of families summary*. Retrieved from https://www.bls.gov/news.release/famee.nr0.htm

Bureau of Labor Statistics. (2018b). Psychologists. In *Occupational outlook handbook*. Retrieved from https://www.bls.gov/ooh/life-physical-and-social-science/psychologists.htm

Burger, J. M. (2000). *Personality* (5th ed.). Belmont, CA: Wadsworth.

Burger, J. M. (2009). Replicating Milgram: Would people still obey today? *American Psychologist, 64*, 1–11. https://doi.org/10.1037/a0010932

Burke, S. M., Manzouri, A. H., & Savic, I. (2017). Structural connections in the brain in relation to gender identity and sexual orientation. *Scientific Reports, 7*, 17954. https://doi.org/10.1038/s41598-017-17352-8

Burrows, K. (2013). Age preferences in dating advertisements by homosexuals and heterosexuals: From sociobiological to sociological explanations. *Archives of Sexual Behavior, 42*, 203–211.

Buss, D. M. (1985). Human mate selection. *American Scientist, 73*, 47–51.

Buss, D. M. (1988a). Love acts: The evolutionary biology of love. In R. J. Steinberg & M. L. Barnes (Eds.), *The psychology of love* (pp. 100–118). New Haven, CT: Yale University Press.

Buss, D. M. (1988b). From vigilance to violence: Tactics of mate retention in American undergraduates. *Ethology and Sociobiology, 9*, 291–317.

Buss, D. M., Abbott, M., Angleitner, A., Asherian, A., Biaggio, A., Blanco-Villasenor, A., . . . Yang, K.-S. (1990). International preferences in mate selection: A study of 37 cultures. *Journal of Cross-Cultural Psychology, 21*, 5–47.

Butler, L., Waelde, L., Hastings, T., Chen, X., Symons, B., Marshall, L., Kaufman, A., & Nagy, T. (2008). Meditation with yoga, group therapy with hypnosis, and psychoeducation for long-term depressed mood: A randomized pilot trial. *Journal of Clinical Psychology, 64*, 806–820.

Byrne, P., Jones, S., & Williams, R. (2004). The association between cannabis and alcohol use and the development of mental disorder. *Current Opinion in Psychiatry, 17*, 255–261.

C

Cahn, B., & Polich, J. (2006). Meditation states and traits: EEG, ERP, and neuroimaging studies. *Psychological Bulletin, 132*, 180–211.

Campion, M. A., Palmer, D. K., & Campion, J. E. (1997). A review of structure in the selection interview. *Personnel Psychology, 50*, 655–702.

Canli, T., Desmond, J. E., Zhao, Z., & Gabrieli, J. D. E. (2002). Sex differences in the neural basis of emotional memories. *Proceedings of the National Academy of Sciences, 99*, 10789–10795.

Cannon, W. B. (1932). *The wisdom of the body.* New York, NY: Norton.

Cannon, W. B., & Washburn, A. L. (1912). An explanation of hunger. *American Journal of Physiology, 29*, 441–454.

Capellan, J. A., & Gomez, S. (2017). Change and stability in offender, behaviours, and incident-level characteristics of mass public shootings in the United States, 1984–2015. *Journal of Investigative Psychology and Offender Profiling, 15*, 51–72. https://doi.org/10.1002/jip.1491

Cargiulo, T. (2007). Understanding the health impact of alcohol dependence. *American Journal of Health-System Pharmacy, 64*, S5–S11.

Carnagey, N. L., Anderson, C. A., & Bartholow, B. B. (2007). Media violence and social neuroscience: New questions and new opportunities. *Current Directions in Psychological Science, 16*, 178–182.

Carroll, J. S., Padilla-Walker, L. M., Nelson, L. J., Olson, C. D., McNamara Barry, C., & Madsen, S. D. (2008). Generation XXX: Pornography acceptance and use among emerging adults. *Journal of Adolescent Research, 23*, 6–30.

Carroll, R. T. (2006). *Pseudoscience.* Retrieved from http://skepdic.com/pseudosc.html

Carter, M. M. (2002, September/October). Uncontrolled anxiety: Understanding panic disorder with agoraphobia. *Family Therapy Magazine*, 32–38.

Carver, C. S., & Scheier, M. F. (1999). Optimism. In C. R. Snyder (Ed.), *Coping: The psychology of what works* (pp. 182–204). New York, NY: Oxford University Press.

Caspi, A., Roberts, B. W., & Shiner, R. L. (2005). Personality development: Stability and change. *Annual Review of Psychology, 56*, 453–485.

Caspi, A., Sugden, K., Moffitt, T. E., Taylor, A., Craig, I. W., . . . Poulton, R. (2003). Influence of life stress on depression: Moderation by a polymorphism in the 5-HTT gene. *Science, 301*, 291–293.

Castro-Fornieles, J., Gual, P., Lahortiga, F., Gila, A., Casulà, V., Fuhrmann, C., . . . Toro, J. (2007). Self-oriented perfectionism in eating disorders. *International Journal of Eating Disorders, 40*, 562–568.

Catalá-Miñana, A., Walker, K., Bowen, E., & Lila, M. (2014). Cultural differences in personality and aggressive behavior in intimate partner violence offenders: A comparison of English and Spanish offenders. *Journal of Interpersonal Violence, 29*, 2652–2669.

Cattell, R. B. (1973). *Personality and mood by questionnaire.* San Francisco, CA: Jossey-Bass.

Cattell, R. B. (1979). *The structure of personality in its environment.* New York, NY: Springer.

Centers for Disease Control and Prevention. (2010). Vital signs: State-specific obesity prevalence among adults—United States, 2009. *Morbidity and Mortality Weekly Report (MMWR), 59*, 1–5. Retrieved from http://www.cdc.gov/mmwr

Centers for Disease Control and Prevention. (2013). *HIV and AIDS in America: A snapshot.* Retrieved from https://www.cdc.gov/nchhstp/newsroom/docs/factsheets/hiv-and-aids-in-america-a-snapshot-508.pdf

Centers for Disease Control and Prevention. (2014). *Monitoring selected HIV prevention and care objectives by using HIV surveillance/resource/reports.* Retrieved from https://www.cdc.gov/hiv/pdf/library/reports/surveillance/cdc-hiv-surveillance-supplemental-report-vol-22-2.pdf

Centers for Disease Control and Prevention. (2015). *Deaths and mortality.* Retrieved from https://www.cdc.gov/nchs/fastats/deaths.htm

Centers for Disease Control and Prevention. (2016). *Leading causes of death reports, 1981–2016.* Retrieved from https://webappa.cdc.gov/sasweb/ncipc/leadcause.html

Centers for Disease Control and Prevention. (2017). *Health, United States 2016.* Retrieved from https://www.cdc.gov/nchs/data/hus/hus16.pdf#045

Centers for Disease Control and Prevention. (2018a). *Drug overdose and death data.* Retrieved from https://www.cdc.gov/drugoverdose/data/statedeaths.html

Centers for Disease Control and Prevention. (2018b). *HIV in the United States: At a glance.* Retrieved from http://natap.org/2018/HIV/081018_02.htm

Centers for Disease Control and Prevention. (2018c). *Prevalence of autism spectrum disorder among children aged 8 years—autism and developmental disabilities monitoring network, 11 sites, United States, 2014.* Retrieved from https://www.cdc.gov/mmwr/volumes/67/ss/ss6706a1.htm

Centers for Disease Control and Prevention. (2018d). *Smoking & tobacco use: Data and statistics.* Retrieved from https://www.cdc.gov/tobacco/data_statistics/fact_sheets/index.htm

Centers for Disease Control and Prevention. (2018e). *Smoking & tobacco use: Tobacco-related mortality.* Retrieved from https://www.cdc.gov/tobacco/data_statistics/fact_sheets/health_effects/tobacco_related_mortality/index.htm

Centers for Disease Control and Prevention. (2018f). *Suicide rising across the U.S.* Retrieved from https://www.cdc.gov/vitalsigns/suicide/

Centers for Disease Control and Prevention. (2018g). *2017 Sexually transmitted disease surveillance: National profile.* Retrieved from https://www.cdc.gov/std/stats17/2017-STD-Surveillance-Report_CDC-clearance-9.10.18.pdf

Cepeda, N. J., Pashler, H., Vul, E., Wixsted, T. J., & Rohrer, D. (2006). Distributed practice in verbal recall tasks: A review and quantitative synthesis. *Psychological Bulletin, 132*, 354–380.

Chai, P. M., Krägeloh, C. U., Shepherd, D., & Billington, R. (2012). Stress and quality of life in international and domestic university students: Cultural differences in the use of religious coping. *Mental Health, Religion & Culture, 15*, 265–277. https://doi.org/10.1080/13674676.2011.571665

Chalmers, D. J. (1995). The puzzle of conscious experience. *Scientific American, 273*, 62–68.

Chambless, D. L., & Ollendick, T. H. (2001). Empirically supported psychological interventions: Controversies and evidence. *Annual Review of Psychology, 52*, 685–716.

Chan, A. S., Cheung, J., Leung, W. W. M., Cheung, R., & Cheung, M. (2005). Verbal expression and comprehension deficits in young children with autism. *Focus on Autism and Other Developmental Disabilities, 20,* 117–124.

Chan, D., K-S., & Cheng, G. H-L. (2004). A comparison of offline and online friendship qualities at different stages of relationship development. *Journal of Social and Personal Relationships, 21,* 305–320.

Chan, G., & Yanos, P. T. (2018). Media depictions and the priming of mental illness stigma. *Stigma and Health, 3,* 253–264. https://doi.org/10.1037/sah0000095

Chandola, T., Brunner, E., & Marmot, M. (2006). Chronic stress at work and the metabolic syndrome: Prospective study. *British Medical Journal, 332,* 521–525.

Chandrashekar, J., Hoon, M. A., Ryba, N. J., & Zuker, C. S. (2006). The receptors and cells for mammalian taste. *Nature, 444,* 288–294.

Chaudhari, N., Landin, A. M., & Roper, S. D. (2000). A metabotropic glutamate receptor variant functions as a taste receptor. *Nature: Neuroscience, 3,* 113–119.

Chekroun, P., & Brauer, M. (2001). The bystander effect and social control behavior: The effect of the presence of others on people's reactions to norm violations. *European Journal of Social Psychology, 32,* 853–867.

Cheslack-Postava, K., DPhil, K. L., & Bearman, P. S. (2011). Closely spaced pregnancies are associated with increased odds of autism in California sibling births. *Pediatrics, 127,* 246–253.

Chinman, M. J., Rosenheck, R. A., & Lam, J. A. (2000). Client-case manager racial matching in a program for homeless persons with serious mental illness. *Psychiatric Services, 51,* 1265–1272.

Chiolero, A., Fach, D., Paccaud, F., & Cornuz, J. (2008). Consequences of smoking for body weight, body fat distribution, and insulin resistance. *American Journal of Clinical Nutrition, 87,* 801–809.

Chodosh, J., Ferrell, B. A., Shekelle, P. G., & Wenger, N. S. (2001). Quality indicators for pain management in vulnerable elders. *Annals of Internal Medicine, 135,* 731–735.

Chomsky, N. (1957). *Syntactic structures.* The Hague, Netherlands: Mouton & Company.

Chow, R. M., Tiedens, L. Z., & Govan, C. L. (2008). Excluded emotions: The role of anger in antisocial responses to ostracism. *Journal of Experimental Social Psychology, 44,* 896–903. https://doi.org/10.1016/j.jesp.2007.09.004

Chressanthis, G. A., Gilbert, K. S., & Grimes, P. W. (1991). Ideology, constituent interests, and senatorial voting: The case of abortion. *Social Science Quarterly, 72,* 588–600.

Chua, H. F., Boland, J. E., & Nisbett, R. E. (2005). Cultural variation in eye movements during scene perception. *Proceedings of the National Academy of Sciences of the United States of America, 102,* 12629–12633. https://doi.org/10.1073/pnas.0506162102

Cinciripini, P., Blalock, J., Minnix, J. A., Robinson, J. D., Brown, V. L., Lam, C. Y., . . . Karam-Hage, M. (2010). Effects of an intensive depression-focused intervention for smoking cessation in pregnancy. *Journal of Consulting and Clinical Psychology, 78,* 44–54.

Clark, K. B., & Clark, M. K. (1939). The development of consciousness of self and the emergence of racial identification in Negro preschool children. *Journal of Social Psychology, S.P.S.S.I. Bulletin, 10,* 591–599.

Clark, L. A. (2009). Stability and change in personality disorder. *Current Directions in Psychological Science, 18,* 27–31.

Clark, L. A., & Watson, D. (2008). Temperament: An organizing paradigm for trait psychology. In O. P. John, R. W. Robins, & L. A. Pervin (Eds.), *Handbook of personality: Theory and research* (pp. 265–286). New York, NY: Guilford Press.

Clarke, T. C., Norris, T., & Schiller, J. S. (2017). *Early release of selected estimates based on data from the 2016 National Health Interview Survey.* Retrieved from https://www.cdc.gov/nchs/data/nhis/earlyrelease/earlyrelease201705.pdf

Clement, S. (2015). *Millennials are just about as racist as their parents.* Retrieved from https://www.washingtonpost.com/news/wonk/wp/2015/04/07/white-millennials-are-just-about-as-racist-as-their-parents/?utm_term=.41324afb1c35

Clemente, A. S., Diniz, B. S., Nicolato, R., Kapczinski, F. P., Soares, J. C., Firmo, J. O., & Castro-Costa, É. (2015). Bipolar disorder prevalence: A systematic review and meta-analysis of the literature. *Revista Brasileira De Psiquiatria (Sao Paulo, Brazil: 1999), 37,* 155–161. https://doi.org/10.1590/1516-4446-2012-1693

Cloos, J., & Ferreira, V. (2009). Current use of benzodiazepines in anxiety disorders. *Current Directions in Psychiatry, 22,* 90–95.

Cohen, J. (2010). HIV/AIDS: At last, vaginal gel scores victory against HIV. *Science, 329,* 374–375.

Cohen, S., & Pressman, S. D. (2006). Positive affect and health. *Current Directions in Psychological Science, 15,* 122–125.

Colucci, M., Cammarata, S., Assini, A., Croce, R., Clerici, F., Novello, C., & . . . Tanganelli, P. (2006). The number of pregnancies is a risk factor for Alzheimer's disease. *European Journal of Neurology, 13,* 1374–1377. https://doi.org/10.1111/j.1468-1331.2006.01520.x

Committee on Health and Behavior; National Institute of Medicine. (2001). *Health and behavior: The interplay of biological, behavioral, and societal influences.* Washington, DC: National Academy Press.

Conner, K. O., Copeland, V. C., Grote, N. K., Koeske, G., Rosen, D., Reynolds, C. & Brown, C. (2010). Mental health treatment seeking among older adults with depression: The impact of stigma and race. *American Journal of Geriatric Psychiatry, 18,* 531–543. https://doi.org/10.1097/JGP.0b013e3181cc0366

Conway, L. G., Gornick, L. J., Houck, S. C., Anderson, C., Stockert, J., Sessoms, D., & McCue, K. (2016). Are conservatives really more simple-minded than liberals? The domain specificity of complex thinking. *Political Psychology, 37,* 777–798. https://doi.org/10.1111/pops.12304

Cook, B., Creedon, T., Wang, Y., Lu, C., Carson, N., Jules, P., & . . . Alegría, M. (2018). Examining racial/ethnic differences in patterns of benzodiazepine prescription and misuse. *Drug and Alcohol Dependence, 18,* 729–734. https://doi.org/10.1016/j.drugalcdep.2018.02.011

Corballis, P. M., Funnell, M. G., & Gazzaniga, M. S. (2002). Hemispheric asymmetries for simple visual judgments in the split brain. *Neuropsychologia, 40,* 401–410.

Corker, R. (2001). *Science and pseudoscience.* Retrieved from https://physics.weber.edu/carroll/honors/pseudoscience.htm

Cosgrove, G. R. (2009). Cingulotomy for depression and OCD. In *Textbook of stereotactic and functional neurosurgery* (pp. 2887–2896). New York, NY: Springer.

Cosgrove G. R., & Rauch, S. L. (2003). Stereotactic cingulotomy. *Neurosurgery Clinics of North America, 14,* 225–235.

Costello, C. C., Wood, D., & Tov, W. (2018). Revealed traits: A novel method for estimating cross-cultural similarities and differences in personality. *Journal of Cross-Cultural Psychology, 49,* 554–586.

Cottone, J. G., Drucker, P., & Javier, R. A. (2002). Gender differences in psychotherapy dyads: Changes in psychological symptoms and responsiveness to treatment during 3 months of therapy. *Psychotherapy: Theory, Research, Practice, Training, 39,* 297–308. https://doi.org/10.1037/0033-3204.39.4.297

Cowan, N. (2001). The magical number 4 in short-term memory: A reconsideration of mental storage capacity. *Behavioral and Brain Sciences, 24,* 87–114.

Cowell, J. M., Lee, K., Malcolm-Smith, S., Selcuk, B., Zhou, X., & Decety, J. (2017). The development of generosity and moral cognition across five cultures. *Developmental Science, 20,* 1–12. https://doi.org/10.1111/desc.12403

Cramer, P. (2000). Defense mechanisms in psychology today: Further processes for adaptation. *American Psychologist, 55,* 637–646.

Cramer, R. E., McMaster, M. R., Bartell, P. A., & Dragna, M. (1988). Subject competence and minimization of the bystander effect. *Journal of Applied Social Psychology, 18,* 1133–1148.

Crandall, C. S. (1991). Do heavyweight students have more difficulty paying for college? *Personality and Social Psychology Bulletin, 17,* 606–611.

Craske, M. G., & Barlow, D. H. (2001). Panic disorder and agoraphobia. In D. H. Barlow (Ed.), *Clinical handbook of psychological disorders* (3rd ed., pp. 1–64). New York, NY: Guilford Press.

Crick, F., & Koch, C. (1998). Consciousness and neuroscience. *Cerebral Cortex, 8,* 97–107.

Crooks, R., & Baur, K. (2014). *Our sexuality* (12th ed.). Belmont, CA: Wadsworth, Cengage Learning.

Cross, W., Parham, T., & Helms, J. (1998). Nigrescence revisited: Theory and research. In R. L. Jones (Ed.), *African American identity and development* (pp. 3–72). Hampton, VA: Cobb & Henry.

Cuellar, N. G. (2005). Hypnosis for pain management in the older adult. *Pain Management Nursing, 6,* 105–111.

D

Dabbs, J. M., Carr, T. S., Frady, R. L., & Riad, J. K. (1995). Testosterone, crime, and misbehavior among 692 male prison inmates. *Personality and Individual Differences, 19,* 627–633.

Dal Cin, S., Gibson, B., Zanna, M. P., Shumate, R., & Fong, G. T. (2007). Smoking in movies, implicit associations of smoking with the self, and intentions to smoke. *Psychological Science, 18,* 559–563.

Dalenberg, C. J. (1996). Accuracy, timing and circumstances of disclosure in therapy of recovered and continuous memories of abuse. *Journal of Psychiatry & Law, 24,* 229–275.

Damasio, A. R., Grabowski, T. J., Bechara, A., Damasio, H., Ponto, L. L. B., Parviza, J., & Hichwa, R. D. (2000). Subcortical and cortical brain activity during the feeling of self-generated emotions. *Nature: Neuroscience, 3,* 1049–1056.

Dambrun, M., & Vatiné, E. (2010). Reopening the study of extreme social behaviors: Obedience to authority within an immersive video environment. *European Journal of Social Psychology, 40,* 760–773.

Dargie, E., Blair, K. L., Pukall, C. F., & Coyle, S. M. (2014). Somewhere under the rainbow: Exploring the identities and experiences of trans persons. *Canadian Journal of Human Sexuality, 23,* 60–74.

Dargis, M., & Koenigs, M. (2018). Personality traits differentiates of criminal offenders with distinct cognitive, affective, and behavioral profiles. *Criminal Justice & Behavior, 45,* 984–1007.

Darley, J. M., & Schultz, T. R. (1990). Moral rules: Their content and acquisition. *Annual Review of Psychology, 41,* 525–556.

Davidson, R. J., Kabat-Zinn, J., Schumacher, J., Rosenkranz, M., Muller, D., Santorelli, S. F., Urbanowski, F., Harrington, A., Bonus, K., & Sheridan, J. F. (2003). Alterations in brain and immune function produced by mindfulness meditation. *Psychosomatic Medicine, 65,* 564–570.

Davidson, R. J., Pizzagalli, D., Nitschke, J. B., & Putnam, K. (2002). Depression: Perspectives from affective neuroscience. *Annual Review of Psychology, 53,* 545–574.

Davis, M., Walker, D. L., Miles, L., & Grillon, C. (2010). Phasic vs sustained fear in rats and humans: Role of the extended amygdala in fear vs anxiety. *Neuropsychopharmacology, 35,* 105–135. https://doi.org/10.1038/npp.2009.109

Davis, P. J. (1999). Gender differences in autobiographical memory for childhood emotional experiences. *Journal of Personality and Social Psychology, 76,* 498–510.

de la Chica, R. A., Ribas, I., Giraldo, J., Egozcue, J., & Fuster, C. (2005). Chromosomal instability in amniocytes from fetuses of mothers who smoke. *Journal of the American Medical Association, 293,* 1212–1222.

de Macedo-Soares, M. B., Moreno, R. A., Rigonatti, S. P., & Lafer, B. (2005). Efficacy of electroconvulsive therapy in treatment-resistant bipolar disorder: A case series. *The Journal of ECT, 21,* 31–34. https://doi.org/10.1097/01.yct.0000148621.88104.fl

De Pedro, K. T., Gilreath, T. D., Jackson, C., & Esqueda, M. C. (2017). Substance use among transgender students in California public middle and high schools. *Journal of School Health, 87,* 303–309.

DeAngelis, T. (2010). "Little Albert" regains his identity. *Monitor on Psychology, 41*(1), 10.

Deary, I. J., Strand, S., Smith, P., & Fernandes, C. (2007). Intelligence and educational achievement. *Intelligence, 35,* 13–21.

Delaney-Black, V., Covington, C., Nordstrom, B., Ager, J., Janisse, J., Hannigan, J. H., … Sokol, R. J. (2004). Prenatal cocaine: Quantity of exposure and gender moderation. *Journal of Developmental and Behavioral Pediatrics, 25,* 254–263.

Denver Post. (2017). Exclusive: Traffic fatalities linked to marijuana are up sharply in Colorado. Is legalization to blame? Retrieved from https://www.denverpost.com/2017/08/25/colorado-marijuana-traffic-fatalities/

Deter, H., Weber, C., Herrmann-Lingen, C., Albus, C., Juenger, J., Ladwig, K., & . . . Orth-Gomér, K. (2018). Gender differences in psychosocial outcomes of psychotherapy trial in patients with depression and coronary artery disease. *Journal of Psychosomatic Research, 11,* 389–399. https://doi.org/10.1016/j.jpsychores.2018.08.005

Dew, J., & Wilcox, W. B. (2011). If momma ain't happy: Explaining declines in marital satisfaction among new mothers. *Journal of Marriage & Family, 73,* 1–12. https://doi.org/10.1111/j.1741-3737.2010.00782.x

DeYoung, C. G., Hirsh, J. B., Shane, M. S., Papademetris, X., Rajeevan, N., & Gray, J. R. (2010). Testing predictions from personality neuroscience: Brain structure and the Big Five. *Psychological Science, 21,* 820–828.

Dick, D. M., Rose, R. J., Viken, R. J., & Kaprio, J. (2000). Pubertal timing and substance use between and within families across late adolescence. *Developmental Psychology, 36,* 180–189.

Dickens, W. T., & Flynn, J. R. (2006). Black Americans reduce the racial IQ gap: Evidence from standardization samples. *Psychological Science, 17,* 913–920. https://doi.org/10.1111/j.1467-9280.2006.01802.x

Digman, J. M. (1990). Personality structure: Emergence of the five-factor model. *Annual Review of Psychology, 41,* 417–440.

Dijksterhuis, A., & Nordgren, L. F. (2006). A theory of unconscious thought. *Perspectives on Psychological Science, 1,* 95–109.

Dion, K. K., Berscheid, E., & Walster, E. (1972). What is beautiful is good. *Journal of Personality and Social Psychology, 24,* 285–290.

Dollard, J., Doob, L., Miller, N., Mowrer, O. H., & Sears, R. R. (1939). *Frustration and aggression.* New Haven, CT: Yale University Press.

Domjan, M. (2005). Pavlovian conditioning: A functional perspective. *Annual Review of Psychology, 56,* 179–206.

Donnellan, M. B., Trzesniewski, K. H., Robins, R. W., Moffitt, T. E., & Caspi, A. (2005). Low self-esteem is related to aggression, antisocial behavior, and delinquency. *Psychological Science, 16,* 328–335.

Donnerstein, E., Donnerstein, M., & Evans, R. (1975). Erotic stimuli and aggression: Facilitation or inhibition. *Journal of Personality and Social Psychology, 32,* 237–244.

Dougherty, D., Mathias, C., Dawes, M., Furr, R., Charles, N., Liguori, A., Shannon, E., & Acheson, A. (2013). Impulsivity, attention, memory, and decision-making among adolescent marijuana users. *Psychopharmacology, 226,* 307–319. https://doi.org/10.1007/s00213-012-2908-5

Drapalski, A. L., Youman, K., Stuewig, J., & Tangney, J. (2009). Gender differences in jail inmates' symptoms of mental illness, treatment history and treatment seeking. *Criminal Behaviour & Mental Health, 19,* 193–206.

Drews, C. D., & Murphy, C. C. (1996). The relationship between idiopathic mental retardation and maternal smoking during pregnancy. *Pediatrics, 97,* 547–553.

Drugabuse.com. (2017). *Ecstasy history and statistics.* Retrieved from https://drugabuse.com/library/ecstasy-history-and-statistics/

Dunston, A. (2003). *Kicking butts in the twenty-first century: What modern science has learned about smoking cessation.* New York, NY: American Council on Science and Health.

Durand, V. M. (2004). Past, present and emerging directions in education. In D. Zager (Ed.), *Autism: Identification, education, and treatment* (3rd ed., pp. 89–110). Hillsdale, NJ: Erlbaum.

E

Eack, S. M., & Newill, C. E. (2012). Racial disparities in mental illness. *Social Work Research, 36,* 41–52. https://doi.org/swr/svs014

Eagly, A. H. (1995). The science and politics of comparing women and men. *American Psychologist, 50,* 145–158.

Eagly, A. H., Kulesa, P., Chen, S., & Chaiken, S. (2001). Do attitudes affect memory? Tests of the congeniality hypothesis. *Current Directions in Psychological Sciences, 10,* 5–9.

Eastwick, P. W., Luchies, L. B., Finkel, E. J., & Hunt, L. L. (2014). The predictive validity of ideal partner preferences: A review and meta-analysis. *Psychological Bulletin, 140,* 623–665.

Eaton, N. R. (2010). Personality pathology in the *DSM-5*: Psychological science is changing the way we think about mental disorder. *APS Monitor, 23,* 33–36, 41–43.

Ebdlahad, S., Nofzinger, E. A., James, J. A., Buysse, D. J., Price, J. C., & Germain, A. (2013). Comparing neural correlates of REM sleep in posttraumatic stress disorder and depression: A neuroimaging study. *Psychiatry Research: Neuroimaging, 214,* 422–428. https://doi.org/10.1016/j.pscychresns.2013.09.007

Ebstein, R. P., Novick, O., Umansky, R., Priel, B., Osher, Y., Blaine, D., . . . Belmaker, R. H. (1996). Dopamine D4 Receptor (D4DR) Exon III polymorphism associated with the human personality trait of novelty seeking. *Nature Genetics, 12,* 78–80.

Eccles, J., Wigfield, A., Harold, R. D., & Blumenfeld, P. (1993). Age and gender differences in children's self and task perceptions during elementary school. *Child Development, 64,* 830–847.

Edleson, S. M. (2007). *Overview of autism.* Retrieved from http://www.autism.com

Edvardsen, J., Torgersen, S., Roysamb, E., Lygren, S., Skre, I., Onstad, S., & Oien, P. A. (2008). Heritability of bipolar spectrum disorders. Unity or heterogeneity. *Journal of Affective Disorders, 106,* 229–240.

Edwards, S. B., & Flynn, J. P. (1972). Corticospinal control of striking in centrally elicited attack behavior. *Brain Research, 41,* 51–65.

Eichenbaum, H., & Fortin, N. (2003). Episodic memory and the hippocampus: It's about time. *Current Directions in Psychological Science, 12,* 53–57.

Eisler, I., Dare, C., Russell, G. F. M., Szmukler, G., le Grange, D., & Dodge, E. (1997). Family and individual therapy in anorexia nervosa: A five-year follow-up. *Archives of General Psychiatry, 54,* 1025–1030.

Ekman, P. (1992). Facial expression and emotion: New findings, new questions. *Psychological Science, 3,* 34–38.

Ekman, P. (1993). Facial expression and emotion. *American Psychologist, 48,* 384–392.

Ekman, P., Levenson, R. W., & Friesen, W. V. (1983). Autonomic nervous system activity distinguishes among emotions. *Science, 221,* 1208–1210.

Elfenbein, H. A., & Ambady, N. (2002). On the universality of cultural specificity of emotional recognition. *Psychological Bulletin, 128,* 203–235.

Ellis, A. (1970). *Reason and emotion in psychotherapy.* Secaucus, NJ: Stuart.

Ellis, A. (1987). The impossibility of achieving consistently good mental health. *American Psychologist, 42,* 364–375.

Ellis, A. (1991). How can psychological treatment aim to be briefer and better? The rational-emotive approach to brief therapy. In K. N. Anchor (Ed.), *Handbook of medical psychotherapy* (pp. 51–88). Toronto, Canada: Hogrefe & Huber.

Ellis, A. (1995). Rational emotive behavior therapy. In R. J. Corsini & D. Wedding (Eds.), *Current psychotherapies* (5th ed., pp. 162–196). Itasca, IL: Peacock.

Ellis, A. (1997). Using rational emotive behavior therapy techniques to cope with disability. *Professional Psychology: Research and Practice, 28,* 17–22.

Ellis, L., & Ames, M. A. (1987). Neurohormonal functioning and sexual orientation: A theory of homosexuality-heterosexuality. *Psychological Bulletin, 101,* 233–258.

ElSohly, M. A., Ross, S. A., Mehmedic, Z, Arafat, R., Yi, B., & Banahan, B. (2000). Potency trends of delta-9-THC and other cannabinoids in confiscated marijuana from 1980–1997. *Journal of Forensic Sciences, 45,* 24–30.

Endler, N. S., Cox, B. J., Parker, J. D. A., & Bagby, R. M. (1992). Self-reports of depression and state-trait-anxiety: Evidence for differential assessment. *Journal of Personality and Social Psychology, 63,* 832–838.

Erickson, C. A., Posey, D. J., Stigler, K. A., & McDougle, C. J. (2007). Pharmacotherapy of autism and related disorders. *Psychiatric Annals, 37,* 490–500.

Erikson, E. H. (1963). *Childhood and society.* New York, NY: Norton.

Erikson, E. H. (1968). *Identity: Youth and crisis.* New York, NY: Norton.

Eskine, K. J., Kacinick, N. A., & Prinz, J. J. (2011). A bad taste in the mouth: Gustatory disgust influences moral judgment. *Psychological Science, 22,* 295–299. https://doi.org/10.1177/0956797611398497

Espie, C. A. (2002). Insomnia: Conceptual issues in the development, persistence, and treatment of sleep disorder in adults. *Annual Review of Psychology, 53,* 215–243.

Espy, K. A., Hua, F., Johnson, C., Stopp, C., Wiebe, S. A., & Respass, J. (2011). Prenatal tobacco exposure: Developmental outcomes in the neonatal period. *Developmental Psychology, 47,* 153–169.

Estelles, J., Rodriguez-Arias, M., Maldonado C., Aguilar, M. A., & Minarro, J. (2005). Prenatal cocaine exposure alters spontaneous and cocaine-induced motor and social behaviors. *Neurotoxicology and Teratology, 27,* 449–457.

Evans, C. J., & Cahill, C. M. (2016). Neurobiology of opioid dependence in creating addiction vulnerability. *F1000research, 5.* https://doi.org/10.12688/f1000research.8369.1

Everson, S. A., Kauhanen, J., Kaplan, G. A., Goldberg, D. E., Julkunen, J., Tuomilehto, J., & Salonen, J. T. (1997). Hostility and increased risk of mortality and acute myocardial infarction: The mediating role of behavioral risk factors. *American Journal of Epidemiology, 146,* 142–152.

F

Fairburn, C. G., Cooper, Z., Doll, H. A., Norman, P., & O'Connor, M. (2000). The natural course of bulimia nervosa and binge eating disorder in young women. *Archives of General Psychiatry, 57,* 659–665.

Farrelly, M. C., Davis, K. C., Haviland, M. L., Messeri, P., & Healton, C. G. (2005). Evidence of a dose response relationship between "truth" antismoking ads and youth smoking prevalence. *American Journal of Public Health, 95,* 425–431.

Farren, C. K., Snee, L., & McElroy, S. (2011). Gender differences in outcome at 2-year follow-up of treated bipolar and depressed alcoholics. *Journal of Studies on Alcohol and Drugs, 72,* 872–880.

Fazio, R. H., & Olson, M. A. (2003). Implicit measures in social cognition research: Their meaning and use. *Annual Review of Psychology, 54,* 297–327.

Feinstein, J. S., Adolphs, R., Damasino, A., & Tranel, D. (2011). The human amygdale and the induction and experience of fear. *Current Biology, 20,* 34–38.

Fell, C. B., & König, C. J. (2016). Cross-cultural differences in applicant faking on personality tests: A 43-nation study. *Applied Psychology: An International Review, 65,* 671–717. https://doi.org/10.1111/apps.12078

Felson, J. (2011). The effect of religious background on sexual orientation. *Interdisciplinary Journal of Research on Religion, 7,* 1–33.

Felson, R. B. (2002). *Violence and gender reexamined.* Washington, DC: American Psychological Association.

Fergusson, D. M., Boden, J. M., & Horwood, L. J. (2006). Cannabis use and other illicit drug use: Testing the cannabis gateway hypothesis. *Addiction, 101,* 556–569. https://doi.org/10.1111/j.1360-0443.2005.01322.x

Ferns, I., & Thom, D. P. (2001). Moral development of black and white South African adolescents: Evidence against cultural universality in Kohlberg's theory. *South African Journal of Psychology, 31,* 38–47.

Festinger, L. (1957). *A theory of cognitive dissonance.* Stanford, CA: Stanford University Press.

Festinger, L., Riecken, H. W., & Schachter, S. (1982). When prophecy fails. In A. Pines & C. Maslach (Eds.), *Experiencing social psychology: Readings and projects* (pp. 69–75). New York, NY: Knopf.

Fetvadjiev, V. H., Meiring, D., van de Vijver, F. R., Nel, J. A., Sekaja, L., & Laher, S. (2018). Personality and behavior prediction and consistency across cultures: A multimethod study of blacks and whites in South Africa. *Journal of Personality and Social Psychology, 114,* 465–481. https://doi.org/10.1037/pspp0000129

Fink, M. (1997, June). What is the role of ECT in the treatment of mania? *The Harvard Mental Health Letter,* 8.

Fink, M. (2000). Electroshock revisited. *American Scientist, 88,* 162–167.

Fink, M. (2001). Convulsive therapy: A review of the first 55 years. *Journal of Affective Disorders, 63,* 1–15.

Fiore, M. C., Bailey, W. C., Cohen, S. J., Dorfman, S. F., Goldstein, M. G., Gritz, E. R., . . . Wewers, M. E. (2000). *Treating tobacco use and dependence: Clinical practice guideline.* Rockville, MD: U.S. Department of Health and Human Services, Public Health Service.

Fischer, P., Greitemeir, T., Pollozek, F., & Frey, D. (2006). The unresponsive bystander: Are bystanders more responsive in dangerous emergencies? *European Journal of Social Psychology, 36,* 267–278.

Fisher, S., & Greenberg, R. P. (1977). *The scientific credibility of Freud's theories and therapy.* New York, NY: Basic Books.

Fiske, S. T., & Taylor, S. E. (1991). *Social cognition* (2nd ed.). New York, NY: McGraw-Hill.

Flavell, J. H. (1977). *Cognitive development.* Englewood Cliffs, NJ: Prentice Hall.

Flynn, F. J., & Wiltermuth, S. S. (2010). Who's with me? False consensus, brokerage, and ethical decision making in organizations. *Academy of Management Journal, 53,* 1074–1089.

Foa, E. B. (1995). How do treatments for obsessive-compulsive disorder compare? *The Harvard Mental Health Letter, 12,* 8.

Foerch, C., Misselwitz, B., Sitzer, M., Berger, K., Steinmetz, H., & Neumann-Haeflin, T. (2005). Difference in recognition of right and left hemispheric stroke. *The Lancet, 366,* 392–393.

Folkman, S., & Moskowitz, J. T. (2000). Stress, positive emotion, and coping. *Current Directions in Psychological Science, 9,* 115–118.

Folkman, S., & Moskowitz, J. T. (2004). Coping: Pitfalls and promise. *Annual Review of Psychology, 55,* 745–774. https://doi.org/10.1146/annurev.psych.55.090902.141456

Foote, B., Smolin, Y., Kaplan, M., Lagatt, M. E., & Lipschitz, D. (2006). Prevalence of dissociative disorders in psychiatric outpatients. *American Journal of Psychiatry, 163,* 623–629.

Ford-Gilboe, M., & Cohen, J. A. (2000). Hardiness: A model of commitment, challenge, and control. In V. R. Rice (Ed.). *Handbook of stress, coping, and health* (pp. 425–436). Thousand Oaks, CA: Sage.

Fortner, B. V., & Neimeyer, R. A. (1999). Death anxiety in older adults: A quantitative review. *Death Studies, 23,* 387–411.

Franco, P., Groswasser, J., Hassid, S., Lanquart, J. P., Scaillet, S., & Kahn, A. (1999). Prenatal exposure to cigarette smoking is associated with a decrease in arousal in infants. *Journal of Pediatrics, 135,* 34–38.

Frasure-Smith, N., & Lesperance, F. (2005). Depression and coronary heart disease: Complex synergism of mind, body, and environment. *Current Directions in Psychological Science, 14,* 39–43.

Freitag, C. M. (2007). The genetics of autistic disorders and its clinical significance: A review of the literature. *Molecular Psychiatry, 12,* 2–22.

Freud, A. (1958). *Adolescence: Psychoanalytic study of the child.* New York, NY: Academic Press.

Freud, S. (1900). The interpretation of dreams. In J. Strachey (Ed.), *The complete psychological works of Sigmund Freud.* London, England: Hogarth Press.

Freud, S. (1913). *The interpretation of dreams* (3rd ed.). New York, NY: Norton.

Freud, S. (1933). *New introductory lectures on psychoanalysis: Standard edition.* New York, NY: Norton.

Fried, P. A., & Watkinson, B. (2000). Visuoperceptual functioning differs in 9- to 12-year-olds prenatally exposed to cigarettes and marijuana. *Neurotoxicology and Teratology, 22,* 11–20.

Friedman, H. S., Tucker, J. S., Schwartz, J. E., Tomlinson-Keasey, C., Martin, L. R., Wingard, D. L., & Criqui, M. H. (1995). Psychosocial and behavioral predictors of longevity: The aging and death of the "Termites." *American Psychologist, 50,* 69–78. https://doi.org/10.1037/0003-066X.50.2.69

Friedman, M., & Rosenman, R. (1959). Association of specific overt behavior patterns with blood and cardiovascular findings. *Journal of the American Medical Association, 169,* 1286.

Friedman, S. (1972). Habituation and recovery of visual response in the alert human newborn. *Journal of Experimental Child Psychology, 13,* 339–349.

Friedman, S., & Schonberg, S. K. (1996). Consensus statements. *Pediatrics, 98,* 853.

Friedson, M. (2016). Authoritarian parenting attitudes and social origin: The multigenerational relationship of socioeconomic position to childrearing values. *Child Abuse & Neglect, 51,* 263–275. https://doi.org/10.1016/j.chiabu.2015.10.001

Fujita, F., Diener, E., & Sandvik, E., Fujita, F., Diener, E., & Sandvik, E. (1991). Memory performance intensity measure. *Journal of Personality and Social Psychology, 61,* 427–434.

Funder, D. C. (2001). Personality. *Annual Review of Psychology, 52,* 197–221.

G

Gabbard, G. O., Gunderson, J. G., & Fonagy, P. (2002). The place of psychoanalytic treatments within psychiatry. *Archives of General Psychiatry, 59,* 505–510.

Gallacher, J. E. J., Yarnell, J. W. G., Elwood, P. C., & Stansfeld, S. A. (2003). Is type A behavior really a trigger for coronary heart disease events? *Psychosomatic Medicine, 65,* 339–346.

Gallart-Palau, X., Lee, B. T., Adav, S. S., Qian, J., Serra, A., Park, J. E., . . . Sze, S. K. (2016). Gender differences in white matter pathology and mitochondrial dysfunction in Alzheimer's disease with cerebrovascular disease. *Molecular Brain, 9.*

Gallo, L., Shivpuri, S., Gonzalez, P., Fortmann, A., los Monteros, K., Roesch, S., Matthews, K. (2013). Socioeconomic status and stress in Mexican-American women: A multi-method perspective. *Journal of Behavioral Medicine, 36,* 379–388. https://doi.org/10.1007/s10865-012-9432-2

Gallo, V., & Robinson, P. (2000). *Is there a homosexual brain?* Retrieved from https://www.thefreelibrary.com/ Is+There+a+%22Homosexual+Brain%22%3f-a077712294

Gallup. (2017). *In U.S., estimate of LGBT population rises to 4.5%.* Retrieved from https://news.gallup.com/poll/234863/ estimate-lgbt-population-rises.aspx

Galton, F. R. S. (1879). *Psychometric experiments.* Retrieved from http://galton.org/essays/1870-1879/galton-1879-brain -psychometric-experiments/galton-1879-brain-psychometric -experiments.pdf

Gangestad, S. W., & Thornhill, R. (1997). Human sexual selection and developmental instability. In J. A. Simpson & D. T. Kenrick (Eds.), *Evolutionary social psychology* (pp. 169–195). Mahwah, NJ: Erlbaum.

Garcia, S., Stinson, L., Ickes, W., Bissonette, & Briggs, S. R. (1991). Shyness and physical attractiveness in mixed-sex dyads. *Journal of Personality and Social Psychology, 61,* 35–49.

Garcia, S. M., Weaver, K., Moskowitz, G. D., & Darley, J. M. (2002). Crowded minds: The implicit bystander effect. *Journal of Personality and Social Psychology, 83,* 843–853.

Gardner, H. (1993). *Multiple intelligences: The theory in practice.* New York, NY: Basic Books.

Gardner, H. (1999). *Intelligence reframed: Multiple intelligences for the 21st century.* New York, NY: Basic Books.

Gardner, H. (2003a). *Multiple intelligences after twenty years.* Invited address presented at the American Educational Research Association meeting, Chicago, Illinois.

Gardner, H. (2003b). Three distinct meanings of intelligence. In R. Sternberg, J. Lautrey, & T. I. Lubert (Eds.), *Models of intelligence for the new millennium.* Washington, DC: American Psychological Association.

Garland, H. (1990). Throwing good money after bad: The effect of sunk costs on the decision to escalate commitment to an ongoing project. *Journal of Applied Psychology, 75,* 728–731.

Gauthier, C., Hassler, C., Mattar, L., Launay, J., Callebert, J., Steiger, H., . . . Godart, N. (2014). Symptoms of depression and anxiety in anorexia nervosa: Links with plasma tryptophan and serotonin metabolism. *Psychoneuroendocrinology, 39,* 170–178.

Gay, M. C., Philippot, P., Luminet, O. (2002). Differential effectiveness of psychological interventions for reducing osteoarthritis pain: A comparison of Erikson hypnosis and Jacobson relaxation. *European Journal of Pain, 6,* 1–16.

Gazzaniga, M. S. (1998). The split brain revisited. *Scientific American, 279,* 50–55.

Gazzaniga, M. S., Ivry, R. B., & Mangun, G. R. (2002). *Cognitive neuroscience: The biology of the mind* (2nd ed.). New York, NY: W. W. Norton.

Ge, X., Conger, R. D., & Elder, G. H., Jr. (1996). Coming of age too early: Pubertal influences on girls' vulnerability to psychological distress. *Child Development, 67,* 3386–4000.

General Social Survey. (1999). Retrieved from http://www. icpsr.umich.edu/GSS99/home.htm

General Social Survey. (2010–2012). *White millennials' views of Blacks similar to Gen Xers, Baby Boomers.* Retrieved from https://www.washingtonpost.com/news/wonk/wp/2015/04/07/ white-millennials-are-just-about-as-racist-as-their- parents/?utm_term=.41324afb1c35

George, M. S., Ketter, T. A., Parekh, P. I., Horwitz, B., Herscovitch, P., & Post, R. M. (1995). Brain activity during transient sadness and happiness in healthy women. *American Journal of Psychiatry, 152,* 341–351.

Gershoff, E. T. (2002). Corporal punishment by parents and associated child behaviors and experiences: A meta-analytic and theoretical review. *Psychological Bulletin, 128,* 539–579.

Gettman, J. (2006). *Marijuana production in the United States (2006).* Retrieved from https://www.drugscience.org/Archive/ bcr2/cashcrops.html

Gilbert, P. L., Harris, M. J., McAdams, L. A., & Jeste, D. V. (1995). Neuroleptic withdrawal in schizophrenic patients: Review of the literature. *Archives of General Psychiatry, 52,* 173–188. https://doi.org/10.1001/archpsyc.1995.03950150005001

Gilligan, C. (1982). *In a different voice.* Cambridge, MA: Harvard University Press.

GLADD. (2015). *GLADD media reference guide—terms to avoid.* Retrieved from https://www.glaad.org/reference/ offensive

Gladue, B. A. (1994). The biopsychology of sexual orientation. *Current Directions in Psychological Science, 3,* 150–154.

Glanz, K. (1997). Behavioral research contributions and needs in cancer prevention and control: Dietary change. *Preventative Medicine, 26,* S43–S55.

Glanz, K., Lew, R., Song, V., & Cook, V. A. (1999). Factors associated with skin cancer prevention practices in a multiethnic population. *Health Education and Behavior, 26,* 44–59.

Glenn, N. D. (1990). Quantitative research on marital quality in the 1980s: A critical review. *Journal of Marriage and the Family, 52,* 818–831.

Glick, I. D., Berman, E. M., Clarkin, & J. F., Rait, D. S. (2000). *Marital and family therapy* (4th ed.). Washington, DC: American Psychiatric Press.

Global Leadership & Organizational Behavior Effectiveness. (2016). Retrieved from https://globeproject.com/results/ clusters/sub-saharan-africa?menu=list

Goldbach, J. T., Mereish, E. H., & Burgess, C. (2017). Sexual orientation disparities in the use of emerging drugs. *Substance Use & Misuse, 52,* 265–271.

Goldblum, P., Testa, R. J., Pflum, S., Hendricks, M. L., Bradford, J., & Bongar, B. (2012). The relationship between gender-based victimization and suicide attempts in transgender people. *Professional Psychology: Research and Practice, 43,* 468–475.

Goldstein, E. B. (2017). *Sensation and perception* (10th ed.). Boston, MA: Cengage.

Goldstein, I. L. (1991). *Training and development in organizations.* San Francisco, CA: Jossey-Bass.

Goleman, D. (1995). *Emotional intelligence.* New York, NY: Bantam Books.

Golub, M. S., Coollman, G. W., Foster, P. M. D., Kimmel, C. A., Rajpert-De Meyts, E., Reiter, E. O., . . . Toppari, J. (2008). Public health implications of altered puberty timing. *Pediatrics, 121,* S218–S230.

Goodman, G. S., Ghetti, S., Quas, J. A., Edelstein, R. S., Alexander, K. W., Redlich, A. D., Cordon, I. M., & Jones, D. P. H. (2003). A prospective study of memory for child sexual abuse: New findings relevant to the repressed-memory controversy. *Psychological Science, 14,* 113–118.

Gottfredson, L. S. (2004). Intelligence: Is the epidemiologist's "fundamental cause" of social class inequalities in health? *Journal of Personality and Social Psychology, 86,* 174–199.

Gottfredson, L. S., & Deary, I. J. (2004). Intelligence predicts health and longevity, but why? *Current Directions in Psychological Science, 13,* 1–4.

Gould, M. S., Kalafat, J., Harrismunfakh, J. L., & Kleinman, M. (2007). An evaluation of crisis hotline outcomes. Part 2: Suicidal callers. *Suicide & Life-Threatening Behavior, 37,* 338–352.

Grace, A. A. (2010). Ventral hippocampus, interneurons, and schizophrenia: A new understanding of the pathophysiology of schizophrenia and its implications for treatment and prevention. *Current Directions in Psychological Science, 19,* 232–237.

Gracheck, J. E. (2006). The insanity defense in the twenty-first century: How recent United States Supreme Court case law can improve the system. *Indiana Law Journal, 81,* 1479–1501.

Grady, C. L., McIntosh, A. R., Horowitz, B., Maisog, J. M., Ungerleider, L. G., Mentis, M. J., . . . Haxby, J. V. (1995). Age-related reductions in human recognition memory due to impaired encoding. *Science, 269,* 218–221.

Grant, J. M., Mottet, L. A., Tanis, J., Harrison, J., Herman, J. L., & Keisling, M. (2011). *Injustice at every turn: A report of the national transgender discrimination survey (executive summary).* Retrieved from http://endtransdiscrimination.org/PDFs/NTDS_Exec_Summary.pdf

Grant, R. M., Larna, J. R., Anderson, P. L., McMahan, V., Liu, A. Y., Varga, L., . . . Glidden, D. V. (2010). Preexposure chemoprophylaxis for HIV prevention in men who have sex with men. *New England Journal of Medicine, 363,* 2587–2599.

Gray-Little, B., & Hafdahl, A. R. (2000). Factors influencing racial comparisons of self-esteem: A quantitative review. *Psychological Bulletin, 126,* 26–54.

Graziano, A. M., & Raulin, M. L. (1993). *Research methods: A process of inquiry.* New York, NY: HarperCollins.

Greene, J., & Haidt, J. (2002). How (and where) does moral judgment work? *Trends in Cognitive Sciences, 6,* 517–523.

Greenwald, A. G., McGhee, D. E., & Schwartz, J-L. K. (1998). Measuring individual differences in implicit cognition: The implicit association test. *Journal of Personality and Social Psychology, 74,* 1464–1480.

Grinspoon, L. (Ed.). (1997). Mood disorders: An overview. Part I. *The Harvard Mental Health Letter, 14,* 1–4.

Groth, A. N. (1979). *Men who rape: The psychology of the offender.* New York, NY: Plenum.

Grundy, S. M. (1999). Primary prevention of coronary heart disease. Integrating risk assessment with intervention. *Circulation, 100,* 988–998.

Grysman, A. (2017). Gender differences in episodic encoding of autobiographical memory. *Journal of Applied Research in Memory and Cognition, 6,* 51–59. https://doi.org/10.1016/j.jarmac.2016.07.012

Guilford, J. P. (1959). *Personality.* New York, NY: McGraw-Hill.

Guthrie, R. V. (1976/2004). *Even the rat was white: A historical view of psychology* (2nd ed.). Boston, MA: Pearson.

Guttentag, R. E., Ornstein, P. A., & Seimens, L. (1987). Children's spontaneous rehearsal: Transitions in strategy acquisition. *Cognitive Development, 2,* 307–326.

H

Haas, A. P., Eliason, M., Mays, V. M., Mathy, R. M., Cochran, S. D., D'Augelli, A. R., . . . Clayton, P. J. (2011). Suicide and suicide risk in lesbian, gay, bisexual, and transgender populations: Review and recommendations. *Journal of Homosexuality, 58,* 10–51.

Haas, A. P., Rodgers, P. L., & Herman, J. L. (2014). *Suicide rates among transgender and gender non-conforming adults: Findings from the National Transgender Discrimination Survey.* Retrieved from http://williamsinstitute.law.ucla.edu/wp-content/uploads/AFSP-Williams-Suicide-Report-Final.pdf

Habermas, T., & Bluck, S. (2000). Getting a life: The emergence of the life story in adolescence. *Psychological Bulletin, 126,* 748–769.

Hack, T. F., McClement, S. E., Chochinov, H. M., Cann, B. J., Hassard, T. H., Kristjanson, L. J., & Harlos, M. (2010). Learning from dying patients during their final days: Life reflections gleaned from dignity therapy. *Palliative Medicine, 24,* 715–723.

Halama, P., & Strizenec, M. (2004). Spiritual, existential or both? Theoretical considerations on the nature of higher intelligence. *Studia Psychologica, 46,* 239–253.

Halim, M. L., Ruble, D. N., & Amodio, D. M. (2011). From pink frilly dresses to "one of the boys": A social-cognitive analysis of gender identity development and gender bias. *Social & Personality Psychology Compass, 5,* 933–949. https://doi.org/10.1111/j.1751-9004.2011.00399.x

Halim, M. L., Ruble, D. N., Tamis-LeMonda, C. S., Zosuls, K. M., Lurye, L. E., & Greulich, F. K. (2014). Pink frilly dresses and the avoidance of all things "girly": Children's appearance rigidity and cognitive theories of gender development. *Developmental Psychology, 50,* 1091–1101. https://doi.org/10.1037/a0034906.supp

Hall, G. S. (1904). *Adolescence*. Englewood Cliffs, NJ: Prentice Hall.

Halpern, D. F., Benbow, C. P., Geary, D. C., Gur, R. C., Hyde, J. S., & Gernsbacher, M. A. (2007). The science of sex differences in science and mathematics. *Psychological Science in the Public Interest, 8*, 1–51.

Hamel, M., Gallagher, S., & Soares, C. (2001). The Rorschach: Here we go again. *Journal of Forensic Psychology Practice, 1*, 79–87.

Hansen, N. B., Lambert, M. J., & Forman, E. M. (2002). The psychotherapy dose-response effect and its implications for treatment delivery services. *Clinical Psychology Science and Practice, 9*, 329–343.

Hansen, R. A., Gartlehner, G., Lohr, K. N., Gaynes, B. N., & Carey, T. S. (2005). Efficacy and safety of second-generation antidepressants in the treatment of major depressive disorder. *Annals of Internal Medicine, 143*, 415–426.

Hanyu, H., Sato, T., Hirao, K., Kanetaka, H., Iwamoto, T., & Koizumi, K. (2010). The progression of cognitive deterioration and regional cerebral blood flow patterns in Alzheimer's disease: A longitudinal study. *Journal of Neurological Sciences, 290*, 96–101.

Harding, J. F., Hughes, D. L., & Way, N. (2017). Racial/ethnic differences in mothers' socialization goals for their adolescents. *Cultural Diversity & Ethnic Minority Psychology, 23*, 281–290. https://doi.org/10.1037/cdp0000116

Harness, A., Jacot, L., Scherf, S., White, A., & Warnick, J. E. (2008). Sex differences in working memory. *Psychological Reports, 103*, 214–218. https://doi.org/10.2466/PR0.103.5.214-218

Harvey, J. H., & Weary, G. (1984). Current issues in attribution theory and research. *Annual Review of Psychology, 35*, 427–459.

Hasan, H., & Hasan, T. F. (2009). Laugh yourself into a healthier person: A cross cultural analysis of the effects of varying levels of laughter on health. *International Journal of Medical Sciences, 6*, 200–211.

Hastorf, A. H., & Cantril, H. (1954). They saw a game: A case study. *Journal of Abnormal and Social Psychology, 49*, 129–134.

Hatfield, E. H., Walster, G. W., & Traupmann, J. (1978). Equity and premarital sex. *Journal of Personality and Social Psychology, 36*, 82–92.

Hatsukami, D. K., Stead, L. F., & Gupta, P. C. (2008). Tobacco addiction. *The Lancet, 371*, 2027–2038.

Hausenblas, H. A., Campbell, A., Menzel, J. E., Doughty, J., Levine, M., & Thompson, J. (2013). Media effects of experimental presentation of the ideal physique on eating disorder symptoms: A meta-analysis of laboratory studies. *Clinical Psychology Review, 33*, 168–181. https://doi.org/10.1016/j.cpr.2012.10.011

Heatherton, T. F., & Sargent, J. D. (2009). Does watching smoking in movies promote teenage smoking? *Current Directions in Psychological Science, 18*, 63–67.

Hedman-Robertson, A. S. (2018). Undergraduate students' exposure, knowledge, utilization, and intended use of the national suicide prevention lifeline. *Crisis: The Journal of Crisis Intervention and Suicide Prevention, 39*, 110–118. https://doi.org/10.1027/0227-5910/a000480

Hemmingway, H., & Marmot, M. (1999). Psychosocial factors in the aetiology and prognosis of coronary heart disease: Systematic review of prospective cohort studies. *British Medical Journal, 318*, 1460–1467.

Henderson, C., Evans-Lacko, S., & Thornicroft, G. (2013). Mental illness stigma, help seeking, and public health programs. *American Journal of Public Health, 103*, 777–780. https://doi.org/10.2102/AJPH.2012.301056

Henriksen, L., Feighery, E. C., Schleicher, N. C., Haladjian, H. H., & Fortmann, S. P. (2004). Reaching youth at the point of sale: Cigarette marketing is more prevalent in stores where adolescents shop frequently. *Tobacco Control, 13*, 315–318.

Herbozo, S., Tantleff-Dunn, S., Gokee-Larose, J., & Thompson, J. K. (2004). Beauty and thinness messages in children's media: A content analysis. *Eating Disorders, 12*, 21–34.

Herlitz, A., Nilsson, L., & Bäckman, L. (1997). Gender differences in episodic memory. *Memory & Cognition, 25*, 801–811.

Herlitz, A., & Yonker, J. E. (2002). Sex differences in episodic memory: The influence of intelligence. *Journal of Clinical & Experimental Neuropsychology, 24*, 107.

Heun, R., & Kockler, M. (2002). Gender differences in the cognitive impairment in Alzheimer's disease. *Archives of Women's Mental Health, 4*, 129.

Hilgard, E. R. (1975). Hypnosis. *Annual Review of Psychology, 26*, 19–44.

Hilgard, E. R. (1978, January). Hypnosis and consciousness. *Human Nature*, 42–49.

Hilgard, E. R., & Hilgard, J. R. (1975). *Hypnosis in the relief of pain*. Los Altos, CA: W. Kaufman.

Hill, A. C., Laird, A. R., & Robinson, J. L. (2014). Gender differences in working memory networks: A BrainMap meta-analysis. *Biological Psychology, 10*, 218–229. https://doi.org/10.1016/j.biopsycho.2014.06.008

Hill, C. A. (1987). Affiliation motivation: People who need people. . .but in different ways. *Journal of Personality and Social Psychology, 52*, 1008–1018.

Hill, C. A. (2008). *Human sexuality: Personality and social perspectives*. Los Angeles, CA: Sage.

Hill, E. L. (2014). Linking clinical and industrial psychology: Autism spectrum disorder at work. *Industrial and Organizational Psychology, 7*, 152–155. https://doi.org/10.1111/iops.12125

Hill, W. F. (1985). *Learning: A survey of psychological interpretations* (4th ed.). New York, NY: HarperCollins.

HIV.gov. (2017). *HIV treatment overview*. Retrieved from https://www.hiv.gov/hiv-basics/staying-in-hiv-care/hiv-treatment/hiv-treatment-overview

HIV.gov. (2018). *Fast facts*. Retrieved from https://www.cdc.gov/hiv/statistics/overview/ataglance.html

Hobson, J. A. (1988). *The dreaming brain: How the brain creates both the sense and nonsense of dreams*. New York, NY: Basic Books.

Hobson, J. A. (1995). *Sleep*. New York, NY: Scientific American Library.

Hoeft, F., Watson, C. L., Kesler, S. R., Bettinger, K. E., & Reiss, A. L. (2008). Gender differences in the mesocortico-limbic system during computer game play. *Journal of Psychiatric Research, 42,* 252–258.

Hollis, J. F., Connett, J. E., Stevens, V. J., & Greenlick, M. R. (1990). Stressful life events, type A behavior, and the prediction of cardiovascular and total mortality over six years. *Journal of Behavioral Medicine, 13,* 263–281.

Hollon, S. D., Shelton, R. C., & Loosen, P. T. (1991). Cognitive therapy and pharmacotherapy for depression. *Journal of Consulting and Clinical Psychology, 59,* 88–99.

Holmes, D. S. (2001). *Abnormal psychology* (4th ed.). Boston, MA: Allyn & Bacon.

Holmes, T. S., & Holmes, T. H. (1970). Short-term intrusions into the life-style routine. *Journal of Psychosomatic Research, 14,* 121–132.

Hong, S., & Kim, S. H. (2016). Political polarization on twitter: Implications for the use of social media in digital governments. *Government Information Quarterly, 33,* 777–782. https://doi.org/10.1016/j.giq.2016.04.007

Hope, L., & Wright, D. (2007). Beyond unusual? Examining the role of attention in the weapon focus effect. *Applied Cognitive Psychology, 21,* 951–961. https://doi.org/10.1002/acp.1307

Hovland, C. I., Janis, I. L., & Kelley, H. H. (1953). *Persuasion and communication.* New Haven, CT: Yale University Press.

Howe, M. L. (2003). Memories from the cradle. *Current Directions in Psychological Science, 12,* 62–65.

Hoxha, E., & Hatala, M. N. (2012). A Cross-cultural study of differences in romantic attitudes between American and Albanian college students. *College Student Journal, 46,* 467–469.

Hubert, G., Tousignant, M., Routhier, F., Corriveau, H., & Champagne, N. (2013). Effect of service dogs on manual wheelchair users with spinal cord injury: A pilot study. *Journal of Rehabilitation Research & Development, 50,* 341–350. https://doi.org/10.1682/JRRD.2011.07.0124

Hudspeth, A. J. (1997). How hearing happens. *Neuron, 19,* 947–950.

Hull, C. L. (1943). *Principles of behavior.* Englewood Cliffs, NJ: Prentice Hall.

Hunt, E. (1995). *Will we be smart enough? A cognitive analysis of the coming workforce.* New York, NY: Russell Sage Foundation.

Hunt, E., & Carlson, J. (2007). Considerations relating to the study of group differences in intelligence. *Perspectives on Psychological Science, 2,* 194–213.

Hutchinson Marron, K., Marchiondo, K., Stephenson, S., Wagner, S., Cramer, I., Wharton, T., . . . Alessio, H. (2015). College students' personal listening device usage and knowledge. *International Journal of Audiology, 54,* 384–390. https://doi.org/10.3109/14992027.2014.986691

Hyde, J. S., Mezulis, A. H., & Abramson, L. Y. (2008). The ABCs of depression: Integrating affective, biological, and cognitive models to explain the emergence of the gender difference in depression. *Psychological Review, 115,* 291–313.

Hyde, Z., Flicker, L., Hankey, G. J., Almeida, O. P., McCaul, K. A., Chubb, S. A., & Yeap, B. B. (2010). Prevalence of sexual activity and associated factors in men aged 75 to 95 years: A cohort study. *Annals of Internal Medicine, 153,* 693–702.

I

Iervolino, A. C., Hines, M., Golomok, S. E., Rust, J., & Plomin, R. (2005). Genetic and environmental influences on sex-typed behavior during the preschool years. *Child Development, 76,* 826–840.

Ijsselstijn, L., Dekker, L. M., Stingl, C., van der Weiden, M. M., Hofman, A., Kros, J. M., . . . Luider, T. M. (2011). Serum levels of pregnancy zone protein are elevated in presymptomatic Alzheimer's disease. *Journal of Proteome Research, 10,* 4902–4910. https://doi.org/10.1021/pr200270z

Impett, E., & Peplau, L. A. (2003). Sexual compliance: Gender, motivational, and relationship perspectives. *Journal of Sex Research, 40,* 87–100.

Ingalhalikar, M., Smith, A., Parker, D., Satterthwaite, T. D., Elliott, M. A., Ruparel, K., Hakonarson, H., Gur, R. E., Gur, R. C., & Verma, R. (2014). Sex differences in the structural connectome of the human brain. *Proceedings of the National Academy of Sciences of the United States of America, 111,* 823–828.

Ion, A., Iliescu, D., Aldhafri, S., Rana, N., Ratanadilok, K., Widyanti, A., & Nedelcea, C. (2017). A Cross-Cultural analysis of personality structure through the lens of the HEXACO model. *Journal of Personality Assessment, 99,* 25–34. https://doi.org/10.1080/00223891.2016.1187155

Irvine, J., Garner, D. M., Craig, H. M., & Logan, A. G. (1991). Prevalence of type A behavior in untreated hypertensive individuals. *Hypertension (Dallas, Tex.: 1979), 18,* 72–78.

Isenberg, D. J. (1986). Group polarization: A critical review and meta-analysis. *Journal of Personality and Social Psychology, 50,* 1141–1151.

Izard, C. E. (1993). Four systems for emotional activation: Cognitive and metacognitive processes. *Psychological Review, 100,* 68–90.

Izard, C. E. (2007). Basic emotions, natural kinds, emotion schemas, and a new paradigm. *Perspectives in Psychological Science, 2,* 260–280.

Izard, C. E. (2009). Emotion theory and research: Highlights, unanswered questions, and emerging issues. *Annual Review of Psychology, 60,* 1–25.

J

Jackson, D. N., & Rushton, J. P. (2005). Males have greater g: Sex differences in general mental ability from 100,000 17- to 18-year-olds on the Scholastic Assessment Test. *Intelligence, 34,* 479–486.

Jackson, L. A., Zhao, Y., Witt, E. A., Fitzgerald, H. E., & Von Eye, A. (2009). Gender, race and morality in the virtual world and its relationship to morality in the real world. *Sex Roles, 60,* 859–869.

Jaffe, M. L. (1998). *Adolescence.* New York, NY: John Wiley & Sons.

Jain, H. C., Normand, J., & Kanungo, R. N. (1979). Job motivation of Canadian Anglophone and Francophone hospital employees. *Canadian Journal of Behavioural Science/Revue Canadienne Des Sciences Du Comportement, 11,* 160–163. https://doi.org/10.1037/h0081583

James, W. (1890). *Principles of psychology.* New York, NY: Holt, Rinehart & Winston.

James, W. (1892). *Psychology. The briefer course.* New York, NY: Henry Holt and Company.

James, W. (1904). *Does "consciousness" exist?* Retrieved from http://psychclassics.yorku.ca/James/consciousness.htm

Janis, I. L. (1972). *Victims of groupthink.* Boston, MA: Houghton Mifflin.

Janis, I. L. (1983). *Groupthink: Psychological studies of policy decisions and fiascoes* (2nd ed.). Boston, MA: Houghton Mifflin.

Jankowiak, W. R., & Fischer, E. F. (1992). A cross-cultural perspective on romantic love. *Ethnology, 31,* 149.

Jenkins, C. D. (1976). Recent evidence supporting psychological and social risk factors for coronary disease. *New England Journal of Medicine, 294,* 1033–1038.

Ježová, D., Juránková, E., Mosnárová, A., Kriška, M., & Skultétyovi, I. (1996). Neuroendocrine response during stress with relation to gender differences. *Acta Neurobiologiae Experimentalis, 56,* 779–785.

Jimenez, D. E., Bartels, S. J., Cardenas, V., & Alegría, M. (2013). Stigmatizing attitudes toward mental illness among racial/ethnic older adults in primary care. *International Journal of Geriatric Psychiatry, 28,* 1061–1068. https://doi.org/10.1002/gps.3928

Jobe, T. H., & Harrow, M. (2010). Schizophrenia course, long-term outcome, recovery, and prognosis. *Current Directions in Psychological Science, 19,* 220–225.

Johansson, P., Kerr, M., & Andershed, H. (2005). Linking adult psychopathy with childhood hyperactivity-impulsivity-attention problems and conduct problems through retrospective self-reports. *Journal of Personality Disorders, 19,* 94–101.

John, O. P., Naumann, L. P., & Soto, C. J. (2008). Paradigm shift to the integrative Big Five trait taxonomy: History, measurement, and conceptual issues. In O. P. John, R. W. Robins, & L. A. Pervin (Eds.), *Handbook of personality: Theory and research* (pp. 114–158). New York, NY: Guilford Press.

Johnson, N., Davis, T., & Bosanquet, N. (2000). The epidemic of Alzheimer's disease: How can we manage the costs? *Pharmacoeconomics, 18,* 215–223.

Johnson, Z. F., Diamond, B. J., & Goolkasian, D. Z. (2010). Mindfulness meditation improves cognition: Evidence of brief mental training. *Consciousness and cognition, 19,* 597–605.

Jones, M. C. (1924). A laboratory study of fear: The case of Peter. *Pedagogical Seminary, 31,* 308–315.

Jordan, J., Kaplan, A., Miller, J., Striver, I., & Surrey, J. (1991). *Women's growth in connection.* New York, NY: Guilford.

Jost, J. T., Glaser, J., Kruglanski, A. W., & Sulloway, F. J. (2003). Political conservatism as motivated social cognition. *Psychological Bulletin, 129,* 339–375.

Juslin, P. N., & Laukka, P. (2003). Communication of emotions in vocal expression and music performance: Different channels, same code? *Psychological Bulletin, 129,* 770–814.

K

Kahn, R. S., Fleischhaacker, W. W., Boter, H., & Davidson, M. (2008). Are all antipsychotics equal? *Lancet, 372,* 202.

Kaiser Foundation. (2016). *Opioid overdose deaths by race/ethnicity.* Retrieved from https://www.kff.org/other/state-indicator/opioid-overdose-deaths-by-raceethnicity/?currentTimeframe=0&sortModel=%7B%22colId%22:%22Location%22,%22sort%22:%22asc%22%7D

Kalish, R. A. (1985). The social context of death and dying. In R. H. Binstock & E. Shanas (Eds.), *Handbook of aging and the social sciences* (2nd ed.). New York, NY: Van Nostrand-Reinhold.

Kanwal, G. S. (2015). Indian culture and the experience of psychoanalytic treatment. *Psychoanalytic Review, 102,* 843–872. https://doi.org/10.1521/prev.2015.102.6.843

Kaplan, R. M., & Saccuzzo, D. P. (2001). *Psychological testing* (5th ed.). Monterey, CA: Brooks/Cole.

Kassin, S. M., Tubb, V. A., Hosch, H. M., & Memon, A. (2001). On the "general acceptance" of eyewitness testimony research: A new survey of the experts. *American Psychologist, 56,* 405–416.

Katerndahl, D. A., & Realini, J. P. (1995). Where do panic attack sufferers seek care? *Journal of Family Practice, 40,* 237–243.

Kaufmann, W. E., & Reiss, A. L. (1999). Molecular and cellular genetics of fragile X syndrome. *American Journal of Medical Genetics, 88,* 11–24.

Kaye, W., Fudge, J., & Paulus, M. (2009). New insights into symptoms and neurocircuit function of anorexia nervosa. *National Review of Neuroscience, 10,* 573–584.

Kazdin, A. E., & Benjet, C. (2003). Spanking children: Evidence and issues. *Current Directions in Psychological Science, 12,* 99–103.

Kazdin, A. E., & Blase, S. L. (2011). Rebooting psychotherapy research and practice to reduce the burden of mental illness. *Perspectives on Psychological Science, 6,* 21–37.

Kearney, C. A., & Trull, T. J. (2012). *Abnormal psychology and life: A dimensional approach.* Stamford, CT: Cengage Learning.

Kebbell, M. R., & Wagstaff, G. F. (1998). Hypnotic interviewing: The best way to interview eyewitnesses? *Behavioral Sciences & the Law, 16,* 115–129.

Keefe, F. J., Abernathy, A. P., & Campbell, L. C. (2005). Psychological approaches to understanding and treating disease-related pain. *Annual Review of Psychology, 56,* 601–630.

Keeley, M. P. (2004). Final conversations: Survivors' memorable messages concerning religious faith and spirituality. *Health Communication, 16,* 87–104.

Keller, D. M. (2012). Cingulotomy gives lasting relief to long-term OCD patients. Presentation at the American Association of Neurological Surgeons (AANS) 80th Annual Meeting, Miami, FL.

Kelly, G. A. (1955). *The psychology of personal constructs: A theory of personality* (Vols. 1 & 2). New York, NY: Norton.

Kelly, G. F. (1995). *Sexuality today: The human perspective.* Madison, WI: Brown & Benchmark.

Kelly, J. R., Jackson, J. W., & Huston-Comeaux, S. L. (1997). The effects of time pressure and task differences on influence modes and accuracy in decision-making groups. *Personality and Social Psychology Bulletin, 23,* 10–22.

Kenrick, D. T., Keefe, R. C., Bryan, A., Barr, A., & Brown, S. (1995). Age preferences and mate choice among homosexuals and heterosexuals: A case for modular psychological mechanisms. *Journal of Personality and Social Psychology, 69,* 1169–1172.

Kerr, N. L., & Tindale, R. S. (2004). Group performance and decision making. *Annual Review of Psychology, 55,* 623–655.

Kessler, R. C., Berglund, P., Demler, O., Jin, R., & Walters, E. E. (2005). Lifetime prevalence and age-of-onset distributions of *DSM-IV* disorders in the National Comorbidity Survey Replication. *Archives of General Psychiatry, 62,* 593–602.

Kessler, R. C., Stang, P. E., Wittchen, H. U., & Ustun, T. B. (1998). Lifetime panic-depression comorbidity in the National Comorbidity Survey. *Archives of General Psychiatry, 9,* 801–808.

Kiecolt-Glaser, J. K., McGuire, L., Robles, T. F., & Glaser, R. (2002). Psychoneuroimmunology: Psychological influences on immune function and health. *Journal of Consulting and Clinical Psychology, 70,* 537–547.

Kiefer, M. (2012). Executive control over unconscious cognition: Attentional sensitization of unconscious information processing. *Frontiers in Human Neuroscience, 6,* Article 61. https://doi.org/10.3389/fnhum.2012.00061

Kientzle, M. J. (1946). Properties of learning curves under varied distributions of practice. *Journal of Experimental Psychology, 36,* 187–211.

Kim, G., & Han, W. (2018). Sound pressure levels generated at risk volume steps of portable listening devices: Types of smartphone and genres of music. *BMC Public Health, 18.* https://doi.org/10.1186/s12889-018-5399-4

Kim, J. E., & Moen, P. (2001). Is retirement good or bad for subjective well-being? *Current Directions in Psychological Science, 10,* 83–86.

Kim, K., & Smith, P. K. (1998). Childhood stress, behavioral symptoms and mother-daughter pubertal development. *Journal of Adolescence, 21,* 231–240.

Kimble, G. A. (1989). Psychology from the standpoint of a generalist. *American Psychologist, 44,* 491–499.

Kingo, O. S., Berntsen, D., & Krøjgaard, P. (2013). Adults' earliest memories as a function of age, gender, and education in a large stratified sample. *Psychology and Aging, 28,* 646–653. https://doi.org/10.1037/a0031356

Kinsey, A. C., Pomeroy, W. B., & Martin, C. E. (1948). *Sexual behavior in the human male.* Philadelphia, PA: Saunders.

Kirk, K., Bailey, J., Dunne, M., & Martin, N. (2000). Measurement models for sexual orientation in a community twin sample. *Behavior Genetics, 30,* 345.

Kirsch, I. (2000). The response set theory of hypnosis. *American Journal of Clinical Hypnosis, 42,* 274–292. https://doi.org/10.1080/00029157.2000.10734362

Kirsch, I., & Braffman, W. (2001). Imaginative suggestibility and hypnotizability. *Current Directions in Psychological Science, 10,* 57–61.

Klassen, R. M., Usher, E. L., & Bong, M. (2010). Teachers' collective efficacy, job satisfaction, and job stress in cross-cultural context. *Journal of Experimental Education, 78,* 464–486. https://doi.org/10.1080/00220970903292975

Knox, P. L., Fagley, N. S., & Miller, P. M. (2004). Care and justice moral orientation among African American college students. *Journal of Adult Development, 11,* 41–45.

Kobasa, S. C. (1979). Stressful life events, personality, and health: An inquiry into hardiness. *Journal of Personality and Social Psychology, 37,* 1–11.

Kobasa, S. C. (1987). Stress responses and personality. In R. C. Barnette, L. Beiner, & G. K. Baruch (Eds.), *Gender and stress* (pp. 308–329). New York, NY: Free Press.

Kohlberg, L. (1981). *Philosophy of moral development.* New York, NY: HarperCollins.

Kohlberg, L. (1985). *The psychology of moral development.* New York, NY: HarperCollins.

Kosslyn, S. M. (1987). Seeing and imagining in the cerebral hemispheres: A computational approach. *Psychological Review, 94,* 148–175.

Kosten, T. R., & George, T. P. (2002). The neurobiology of opioid dependence: Implications for treatment. *Science & Practice Perspectives, 1,* 13–20.

Krantz, D. S., & McCeney, M. K. (2002). Effects of psychological and social factors on organic disease: A critical assessment of research on coronary heart disease. *Annual Review of Psychology, 53,* 341–369.

Kring, A. M., & Caponigro, J. M. (2010). Emotion in schizophrenia: Where feeling meets thinking. *Current Directions in Psychological Science, 19,* 255–259.

Kroger, J., Martinussen, M., & Marcia, J. E. (2010). Identity status change during adolescence and young adulthood: A meta-analysis. *Journal of Adolescence, 33,* 683–698. https://doi.org/10.1016/j.adolescence.2009.11.002

Krueger, R. F., & Eaton, N. (2010). Personality traits and the classification of mental disorders: Toward a more complete integration in *DSM-5* and an empirical model of psychopathology. *Personality Disorders: Theory, Research, and Treatment, 1,* 97–118.

Kübler-Ross, E. (1969). *On death and dying.* New York, NY: Macmillan.

Kübler-Ross, E. (1981). *Living with death and dying.* New York, NY: Macmillan.

Kumru, A., Carlo, G., Mestre, M. V., & Samper, P. (2012). Prosocial moral reasoning and prosocial behavior among Turkish and Spanish adolescents. *Social Behavior and Personality, 40,* 205–214. https://doi.org/10.2224/sbp.2012.40.2.205

Kurdek, L. A. (1991). The dissolution of gay and lesbian couples. *Journal of Social and Personal Relationships, 8,* 265–278.

Kurdek, L. A. (1998). Relationship outcomes and their predictors: Longitudinal evidence from heterosexual married, gay cohabiting, and lesbian cohabiting couples. *Journal of Marriage and the Family, 60,* 553–568. https://doi.org/10.2307/353528

Kurdek, L. A. (2005). What do we know about gay and lesbian couples? *Current Directions in Psychological Science, 14,* 251–254.

Kurdek, L. A. (2008). Change in relationship quality for partners from lesbian, gay male, and heterosexual couples. *Journal of Family Psychology, 22,* 701–711.

Kyung Hee, R., Hye Sook, S., & Eun Young, Y. (2015). Effects of laughter therapy on immune responses in postpartum women. *Journal of Alternative & Complementary Medicine, 21,* 781–788. https://doi.org/10.1089/acm.2015.0053

L

Labov, W. (1973). The boundaries of words and their meaning. In C. J. N. Bailey & R. W. Shuy (Eds.), *New ways of analyzing variations in English* (pp. 340–373). Washington, DC: Georgetown University Press.

Lam, L. T., & Kirby, S. L. (2002). Is emotional intelligence an advantage? An exploration of the impact of emotional and general intelligence on individual performance. *Journal of Social Psychology, 142,* 133–143. https://doi.org/10.1080/00224540209603891

Lamb, M. E. (2004). *The role of the father in child development* (4th ed.). Hoboken, NJ: John Wiley & Sons Inc.

Landhuis, C. E., Poulton, R., Welch, D., & Hancox, R. J. (2007). Does childhood television viewing lead to attention problems in adolescence? Results from a prospective longitudinal study. *Pediatrics, 120,* 532–537.

Laney, C., & Loftus, E. F. (2008). Emotional content of true and false memories. *Memory, 16,* 500–516. https://doi.org/10.1080/09658210802065939

Langer, S. K. (1951). *Philosophy in a new key.* New York, NY: New American Library.

Langlois, J. H., Roggman, L. A., Casey, R. I., Riesner-Danner, L. A., & Jenkins, V. Y. (1987). Infant preferences for attractive faces: Rudiments of a stereotype? *Developmental Psychology, 23,* 363–369.

Larson, R., & Pleck, J. (1998). Hidden feelings: Emotionality in boys and men. In D. Bernstein (Ed.), *The Nebraska Symposium on Motivation: Gender and motivation* (pp. 25–74). Lincoln: University of Nebraska Press.

Latané, B., & Darley, J. M. (1968). Group inhibition of bystander intervention in emergencies. *Journal of Personality and Social Psychology, 10,* 215–221.

Latané, B., & Darley, J. M. (1970). *The unresponsive bystander: Why doesn't he help?* Englewood Cliffs, NJ: Prentice Hall.

Latané, B., Williams, K., & Harkins, S. (1979). Many hands make light work: The causes and consequences of social loafing. *Journal of Personality and Social Psychology, 37,* 822–832.

Laurenceau, J. P., Barrett, L. F., & Pietromanaco, P. R. (1998). Intimacy as an interpersonal process: The importance of self-disclosure, partner disclosure, and perceived partner responsiveness in interpersonal exchanges. *Journal of Personality and Social Psychology, 74,* 1238–1251.

Lavond, D. G., Kim, J. J., & Thompson, R. F. (1993). Mammalian brain substrates of aversive classical conditioning. *Annual Review of Psychology, 44,* 317–342.

Lawrence, E., Rothman, A. D., Cobb, R. J., Rothman, M. T., & Bradbury, T. N. (2008). Marital satisfaction across the transition to parenthood. *Journal of Family Psychology, 22,* 41–50.

Lazarus, R. S. (1981). Little hassles can be hazardous to your health. *Psychology Today, 15,* 58–62.

Lazarus, R. S. (1991). Cognition and motivation in emotion. *American Psychologist, 46,* 352–367.

Lazarus, R. S. (1993). From psychological stress to the emotions: A history of changing outlooks. *Annual Review of Psychology, 44,* 1–21.

Lazarus, R. S. (2000). Toward better research on stress and coping. *American Psychologist, 55,* 665–673.

Lazarus, R. S., & Folkman, S. (1984). *Stress, appraisal, and coping.* New York, NY: Springer.

Leary, M. R. (1983a). *Understanding social anxiety: Social, personality, and clinical perspectives* (Vol. 153, Sage Library of Social Research). Beverly Hills, CA: Sage.

Leary, M. R. (1983b). Social anxiousness: The construct and its measurement. *Journal of Personality Assessment, 47,* 66–75.

Leary, M. R., Kowalski, R. M., Smith, L., & Phillips, S. (2003). Teasing, rejection, and violence: Case studies of the school shootings. *Aggressive Behavior, 29,* 202–214. https://doi.org/10.1002/ab.10061

LeDoux, J. E. (1995). Emotion: Clues from the brain. *Annual Review of Psychology, 46,* 209–235.

Lee, J., Lee, K. J., & Kim, H. (2017). Gender differences in behavioral and psychological symptoms of patients with Alzheimer's disease. *Asian Journal of Psychiatry, 26,* 124–128. https://doi.org/10.1016/j.ajp.2017.01.027

Lee, K., Ashton, M. C., Morrison, D. L., Cordery, J., & Patrick, D. D. (2008). Predicting integrity with the HEXACO personality model: Use of self- and observer reports. *Journal of Occupational & Organizational Psychology, 81,* 147–167. https://doi.org/10.1348/096317907X195175

Leinders-Zufall, T., Lane, A., Puche, A. C., Ma, W., Novotny, M. V., Shipley, M. T., & Zufall, F. (2000). Ultrasensitive pheromone detection by mammalian vomeronasal neurons. *Nature, 405,* 792–796.

Leming, M. R., & Dickinson, G. E. (2002). *Understanding dying, death, and bereavement* (5th ed.). Fort Worth, TX: Harcourt College Publishers.

Lempers, J. D., Flavell, E. R., & Flavell, J. H. (1977). The development in very young children of tactile knowledge concerning visual perception. *Genetic Psychology Monographs, 95,* 3–53.

Lerman, C., Rimer, B., & Glynn, T. (1997). Priorities in behavioral research in cancer prevention and control. *Preventative Medicine, 26,* S3–S9.

Lesage, A., Lemasson, M., Medina, K., Tsopmo, J., Sebti, N., Potvin, S., & Patry, S. (2016). The prevalence of electroconvulsive therapy use since 1973: A meta-analysis. *The Journal of ECT, 32*, 236–242.

Leserman, J., Petitto, J. M., Golden, R. N., Gaynes, B. N., Gu, H., & Perkins, D. O. (2000). The impact of stressful life events, depression, social support, coping and cortisol on progression to AIDS. *American Journal of Psychology, 57*, 1221–1228.

Lessem, J. M., Hopfer, C. J., Haberstick, B. C., Timberlake, D., Ehringer, M. A., Smolen, A., & Hewitt, J. K. (2006). Relationship between adolescent marijuana use and young adult illicit drug use. *Behavior Genetics, 36*, 498–506. https://doi.org/10.1007/s10519-006-9064-9

Levey, S., Levey, T., & Fligor, B. J. (2011). Noise exposure estimates of urban MP3 player users. *Journal of Speech, Language & Hearing Research, 54*, 263–277. https://doi.org/10.1044/1092-4388(2010/09-0283)

Levine, J. M., & Moreland, R. L. (1990). Progress in small group research. *Annual Review of Psychology, 41*, 585–634.

Levine, M. (1999). Rethinking bystander nonintervention: Social categorization and the evidence of witnesses at the James Bulger murder trial. *Human Relations, 52*, 1133–1155.

Levine, M. W., & Shefner, J. M. (1991). *Fundamentals of sensation and perception* (2nd ed.). Pacific Grove, CA: Brooks/Cole.

Levinson, D. J. (1986). A conception of adult development. *American Psychologist, 41*, 3–13.

Lewin, K. (1936). *A dynamic theory of personality.* New York, NY: McGraw-Hill.

Lewis, B. A., Singer, L. T., Short, E. J., Minnes, S., Arendt, R., Weishampel, P., Klein, N., & Min, M. O. (2004). Four-year language outcomes of children exposed to cocaine in utero. *Neurotoxicology and Teratology, 26*, 617–627.

Libman, E., Creti, L., Amsel, R., Brender. W., & Fichten, C. S. (1997). What do older good and poor sleepers do during periods of nocturnal wakefulness? The sleep behaviors scale: 60+. *Psychology and Aging, 12*, 170–182.

Lichtenstein, E., Zhu, S., Tedeschi, G. J. (2010). Smoking cessation quitlines: An underrecognized intervention success story. *American Psychologist, 65*, 252–261.

Lieberman, J. A., Jody, D., Geisler, S., Alvir, J. M., Loebel, A., Szymanski, S., . . . Borenstein, M. (1993). Time course and biologic correlates of treatment response in first-response schizophrenia. *Archives of General Psychiatry, 50*, 369–376.

Lieberman, J. A., Tollefson, G. D., Charles, C., Zipursky, R., Sharma, T., Kahn, R. S., . . . HGDH Study Group. (2005). Antipsychotic drug effects on brain morphology in first-episode psychosis. *Archives of General Psychiatry, 2005*, 361–370.

Life. (March 3, 1947). Psychosurgery: Operation to cure sick minds turns surgeon's blade into an instrument of mental therapy.

Light, K. C. (1997). Stress in employed women: A woman's work is never done if she's a working mom. *Psychosomatic Medicine, 59*, 360–361.

Lilienfeld, S. O. (2005). The 10 commandments of helping students distinguish science from pseudoscience in psychology. *APS Observer*, 18. Retrieved from www.psychologicalscience.org/observer/getArticle.cfm?id=1843

Liljenquist, K., Zohng, Z. B., & Galinsky, A. D. (2010). The smell of virtue: Clean scents promote reciprocity and charity. *Psychological Science, 21*, 381–383.

Linden, W., & Moseley, J. V. (2006). The efficacy of behavioral treatments for hypertension. *Applied Psychophysiology and Biofeedback, 31*, 51–63.

Lindholm, T., Christianson, S.-Å., & Karlsson, I. (1997). Police officers and civilians as witnesses: Intergroup biases and memory performance. *Applied Cognitive Psychology, 11*, 431–444.

Lindsley, D. B., Bowden, J., & Magoun, H. W. (1949). Effect upon EEG of acute injury to the brain stem activating system. *Electroencephalography and Clinical Neurophysiology, 1*, 475–486.

Liossi, C., & Hatira, P. (2003). Clinical hypnosis in the alleviation of procedure-related pain in pediatric oncology patients. *International Journal of Clinical and Experimental Hypnosis, 51*, 4–28.

Lipari, R. N., Williams, M., & Van Horn, S. L. (2017). *Why do adults misuse prescription drugs?* Retrieved from https://www.samhsa.gov/data/sites/default/files/report_3210/ShortReport-3210.html

Lisanby, S. H., Maddox, J. H., Prudic, J., & Sackeim, H. A. (2000). The effects of electroconvulsive therapy on memory of autobiographical and public events. *Archives of General Psychiatry, 57*, 581–590.

Littman, L. (2018). Rapid-onset gender dysphoria in adolescents and young adults: A study of parental reports. *Plos ONE, 13*, 1–41. https://doi.org/10.1371/journal.pone.0202330

Lock, J. (1690). An essay concerning human understanding: Book I. Retrieved from http://www.earlymoderntexts.com/assets/pdfs/locke1690book1.pdf

Lock, J., Le Grange, D., Agras, W., Moye, A., Bryson, S., & Jo, B. (2010). Randomized clinical trial comparing family-based treatment with adolescent-focused individual therapy for adolescents with anorexia nervosa. *Archives of General Psychiatry, 67*, 1025–1032.

Locke, K. D., Sadler, P., & McDonald, K. (2018). Cross-situational consistency of trait expressions and injunctive norms among Asian Canadian and European Canadian undergraduates. Advance online publication. *Cultural Diversity & Ethnic Minority Psychology.* https://doi.org/10.1037/cdp0000195

Loftus, E. F. (1993a). The reality of repressed memories. *American Psychologist, 48*, 518–537.

Loftus, E. F. (1993b). *Therapeutic memories of early childhood abuse: Fact or fiction.* Paper presented at the Annual Meeting of the American Psychological Association, Toronto, Canada.

Loftus, E. F. (2003). *Illusions of memory.* Presentation at the 25th Annual National Institute on the Teaching of Psychology, St. Petersburg Beach, FL.

Loftus, E. F. (2004). Memories of things unseen. *Current Directions in Psychological Sciences, 13*, 145–147.

Loftus, E. F., Loftus, G. R., & Messo, J. (1987). Some facts about "weapon focus." *Law and Human Behavior, 11*, 55–62.

Loyd, D., & Murphy, A. (2006). Sex differences in the anatomical and functional organization of the midbrain periaqueductal gray-rostal ventromedial medullary pathway. *Neurology, 496,* 723–738.

Luca, S., Blosnich, J., Hentschel, E., King, E., & Amen, S. (2016). Mental health care utilization: How race, ethnicity and veteran status are associated with seeking help. *Community Mental Health Journal, 52,* 174–179. https://doi.org/10.1007/s10597-015-9964-3

Lucas, R. E., & Fujita, F. (2000). Factors influencing the relation between extroversion and pleasant affect. *Journal of Personality and Social Psychology, 79,* 1039–1056.

Lucyshyn, J. M., Albin, R. W., Horner, R. H., Mann, J. C., Mann, J. A., & Wadsworth, G. (2007). Family implementation of positive behavior support for a child with autism: Longitudinal, single-case, experimental, and descriptive replication and extension. *Journal of Positive Behavior Interventions, 9,* 131–150.

Lynn, R. (2006). *Race differences in intelligence: An evolutionary analysis.* Augusta, GA: Washington Summit Books.

Lynn, S. J., Milano, M., & Weekes, J. R. (1992). Pseudomemory and age regression: An exploratory study. *American Journal of Clinical Hypnosis, 35,* 129–137. https://doi.org/10.1080/00029157.1992.10402995

Lytton, H., & Romney, D. M. (1991). Parents' differential socialization of boys and girls: A meta-analysis. *Psychological Bulletin, 109,* 267–296.

M

Maccoby, E. E. (1988). Gender as a social category. *Developmental Psychology, 24,* 755–765.

Maccoby, E. E. (1990). Gender and relationships: A developmental account. *American Psychologist, 45,* 513–520.

Maccoby, E. E., & Jacklin, C. N. (1974). *The psychology of sex differences.* Palo Alto, CA: Stanford University Press.

MacDonald, R., Anderson, J. Dube, W. V., Geckeler, A., Green, G., Holcomb, W., . . . Sanchez, J. (2006). Behavioral assessment of joint attention: A methodological report. *Research in Developmental Disabilities, 27,* 138–150.

MacKenzie, K. R. (1997). *Time-managed group psychotherapy: Effective clinical applications.* Arlington, VA: American Psychiatric Association.

MacKenzie, M. J., Nicklas, E., Waldfogel, J., & Brooks-Gunn, J. (2012). Corporal punishment and child behavioural and cognitive outcomes through 5 years of age: Evidence from a contemporary urban birth cohort study. *Infant & Child Development, 21,* 3–33. https://doi.org/10.1002/icd.758

Madhyastha, S., Latha, K., & Kamath, A. (2014). Stress, coping and gender differences in third year medical students. *Journal of Health Management, 16,* 315–326. https://doi.org/10.1177/0972063414526124

Malamuth, N. (1986). Predictors of naturalistic sexual aggression. *Journal of Personality and Social Psychology, 50,* 953–962.

Malamuth, N., & Check, J. V. P. (1980). Sexual arousal to rape and consenting depictions: The importance of the woman's arousal. *Journal of Abnormal Psychology, 89,* 763–766.

Mann, J. J., Apter, A., Bertolote, J., Beautrais, A., Currier, D., Haas, A., & . . . Hendin, H. (2005). Suicide prevention strategies: A systematic review. *JAMA, 294,* 2064–2074.

Manns, J. R., Varga, N. L., Trimper, J. B., & Bauer, P. J. (2018). Cortical dynamics of emotional autobiographical memory retrieval differ between women and men. *Neuropsychologia, 110,* 197–207. https://doi.org/10.1016/j.neuropsychologia.2017.07.010

Marchiano, L. (2017). Outbreak: On transgender teens and psychic epidemics. *Psychological Perspectives, 60,* 345–366.

Marcia, J. E. (1980). Identity in adolescence. In J. H. Flavell & E. K. Markman (Eds.), *Handbook of adolescent psychology* (pp. 159–187). New York, NY: John Wiley.

Marengo, J. T., & Harrow, M. (1987). Schizophrenic thought disorder at follow-up. *Archives of General Psychiatry, 44,* 651–659.

Markay, P. M. (2000). Bystander intervention in computer-mediated communication. *Computers in Human Behavior, 16,* 183–188.

Markman, A. B., & Genter, D. (2001). Thinking. *Annual Review of Psychology, 52,* 223–247.

Martin, T. L., Solbeck, P., Mayers, A. M., Daryl J., Langille, R. M., Buczek, Y., & Pelletier, M. R. (2013). A review of alcohol-impaired driving: The role of blood alcohol concentration and complexity of the driving task. *Journal of Forensic Sciences, 58,* 1238–1250. https://doi.org/10.1111/1556-4029.12227.

Maslow, A. H. (1943). A theory of human motivation. *Psychological Review, 50,* 370–396.

Maslow, A. H. (1970). *Motivation and personality.* (2nd ed.). New York, NY: HarperCollins.

Masuda, T., & Nisbett, R. E. (2001). Attending holistically versus analytically: Comparing the context sensitivity of Japanese and Americans. *Journal of Personality and Social Psychology, 8,* 922–934.

Masuda, T., & Nisbett, R. E. (2006). Culture and change blindness. *Cognitive Science, 30,* 381–399.

Matheny, K. B., Ashby, J. S., & Cupp, P. (2005). Gender differences in stress, coping, and illness among college students. *Journal of Individual Psychology, 61,* 365–379.

Matud, M. P. (2004). Gender differences in stress and coping styles. *Personality & Individual Differences, 37,* 1401–1415. https://doi.org/10.1016/j.paid.2004.01.010

Matud, M. P., Bethencourt, J. M., & Ibáñez, I. (2015). Gender differences in psychological distress in Spain. *International Journal of Social Psychiatry, 61,* 560–568. https://doi.org/10.1177/0020764014564801

Maxhom, J. (2000, February 12). Nicotine addiction. *British Medical Journal,* 391–392.

Mayer, J. D., Roberts, R., & Barsdale, S. (2008). Human abilities. *Annual Review of Psychology, 59,* 507–536.

Mayer, J. D., & Salovey, P. (1995). Emotional intelligence and the construction and regulation of feelings. *Applied and Preventative Psychology, 4,* 197–208.

Mayer, J. D., & Salovey, P. (1997). What is emotional intelligence? In P. Salovey & D. J. Sluyter (Eds.), *Emotional* development and emotional intelligence: Educational implications (pp. 3–34). New York, NY: Basic Books.

Mayer, J. D., Salovey, P., & Caruso, D. R. (2008). Emotional intelligence: New ability or eclectic traits? *American Psychologist, 63*, 503–517.

Mayet, A., Legleye, S., Falissard, B., & Chau, N. (2012). Cannabis use stages as predictors of subsequent initiation with other illicit drugs among French adolescents: Use of a multistate model. *Addictive Behaviors, 37*, 160–166. https://doi.org/10.1016/j.addbeh.2011.09.012

McAdams, D. P. (1982). Intimacy motivation. In A. J. Stewart (Ed.), *Motivation and society* (pp. 133–171). San Francisco, CA: Jossey-Bass.

McAdams, D. P. (1989). *Intimacy.* New York, NY: Doubleday.

McAdams, D. P., & Pals, J. L. (2006). A new Big Five: Fundamental principles for an integrative science of personality. *American Psychologist, 61*, 204–217.

McAngus-Todd, N. P., & Cody, F. W. (2000). Vestibular responses to loud dance music: A physiological basis of the "rock and roll threshold." *Journal of the Acoustical Society of America, 107*, 496–500.

McCaffrey, T. (2012). Innovation relies on the obscure: A key to overcoming the classic problem of functional fixedness. *Psychological Science, 23*, 215–218. https://doi.org/10.1177/0956797611429580

McCauley, C. (1989). The nature of social influence in groupthink: Compliance and internalization. *Journal of Personality and Social Psychology, 57*, 250–260.

McClay, R. N., & Spira, J. L. (2009). Use of a portable biofeedback device to improve insomnia in a combat zone, a case report. *Applied Psychophysiology and Biofeedback, 34*, 319–321.

McClelland, D. C. (1985). *Human motivation.* Glenview, IL: Scott, Foresman.

McClelland, D. C., Atkinson, J. W., Clark, R. A., & Lowell, E. L. (1953). *The achievement motive.* Englewood Cliffs, NJ: Prentice Hall.

McConahay, J. G. (1986). Modern racism, ambivalence, and the modern racist scale. In J. F. Dovidio & S. L. Gaertner (Eds.), *Prejudice, discrimination, and racism* (pp. 91–125). San Diego, CA: Academic Press.

McConkey, K. M., & Kinoshita, S. (1988). The influence of hypnosis on memory after one day and one week. *Journal of Abnormal Psychology, 97*, 48–53. https://doi.org/10.1037/0021-843X.97.1.48

McCown, J. A., Fischer, D., Page, R., & Homant, M. (2001). Internet relationships: People who meet people. *CyberPsychology and Behavior, 4*, 593–596.

McCrae, R., & Costa, P. (2008). Empirical and theoretical status of the five-factor model of personality traits. In G. Boye, G. Metthews, & D. Saklofske (Eds.), *The Sage handbook of personality theories and assessment. Vol. 1: Personality theories and models* (pp. 273–297). Thousand Oaks, CA: Sage.

McCrae, R. R., & Costa, P. T. (1990). *Personality in adulthood.* New York, NY: Guilford.

McDougall, W. (1908). *An introduction to social psychology.* London, England: Methuen.

McElree, B. (2001). Working memory and focal attention. *Journal of Experimental Psychology: Learning, Memory, & Cognition, 27*, 817–835.

McEwon, K., & Treit, D. (2010). Inactivation of the dorsal or the ventral hippocampus with muscimol differentially affects fear and memory. *Brain Research, 1353*, 145–151.

McGillicuddy-De Lisi, A. V., Sullivan, B., & Hughes, B. (2003). The effects of interpersonal relationship and character gender on adolescents' resolutions of moral dilemmas. *Applied Developmental Psychology, 23*, 655–669.

McGinty, E. E., Kennedy-Hendricks, A., Choksy, S., & Barry, C. L. (2016). Trends in news media coverage of mental illness in the United States: 1995–2014. *Health Affairs, 35*, 1121–1129. https://doi.org/10.1377/hlthaff.2016.0011

McGinty, E. E., Webster, D. W., Jarlenski, M., & Barry, C. L. (2014). News media framing of serious mental illness and gun violence in the United States, 1997–2012. *American Journal of Public Health, 104*, 406–413. https://doi.org/10.2105/AJPH.2013.301557

McGlone, J. (1980). (1980). Sex differences in human brain asymmetry: A critical survey. *The Behavioral and Brain Sciences, 3*, 215–227.

McGuffin, P., Rijsdijk, F., Andrews, M., Sham, P., Katz, R., & Cardno, A. (2003). The heritability of bipolar affective disorder and the genetic relationship to unipolar depression. *Archives of General Psychiatry, 60*, 497–502.

McHale, S. M., Updegruff, K. A., Helms-Erikson, H., & Crouter, A. C. (2001). Sibling influences on gender development in middle childhood and early adolescence: A longitudinal study. *Developmental Psychology, 37*, 115–125.

McKenna, K., Green, A., & Gleason, M. (2002). Relationship formation on the Internet: What's the big attraction? *Journal of Social Issues, 58*, 9–31.

McKenna, M. C., Zevon, M. A., Corn, B., & Rounds, J. (1999). Psychosocial factors and the development of breast cancer: A meta-analysis. *Health Psychology, 18*, 520–531.

McNally, R. J. (2001). The cognitive psychology of repressed and recovered memories of childhood sexual abuse: Clinical implications. *Psychiatric Annals, 31*, 509–514.

McNally, R. J. (2003a). *Remembering trauma.* Cambridge, MA: Belknap Press/Harvard University Press.

McNally, R. J. (2003b). Progress and controversy in the study of posttraumatic stress disorder. *Annual Review of Psychology, 54*, 229–252.

McRoberts, C., Burlingame, G. M., & Hoag, M. J. (1998). Comparative efficacy of individuals and group psychotherapy. *Group Dynamics, 2*, 101–117.

Mealey, L., Bridstock, R., & Townsend, G. C. (1999). Symmetry and perceived facial attractiveness: A monozygotic twin comparison. *Journal of Personality and Social Psychology, 76*, 151–158.

Meara, E. R., Richards, S., & Cutler, D. M. (2008). The gap gets bigger: Changes in mortality and life expectancy, by education, 1981–2000. *Health Affairs, 27,* 350–360. https://doi.org/10.1377/hlthaff.27.2.350

Meichenbaum, D. (1977). *Cognitive-behavior modification: An integrative approach.* New York, NY: Plenum.

Meiri, N., Ankri, A., Hamad-Saied, M., Konopnicki, M., & Pillar, G. (2016). The effect of medical clowning on reducing pain, crying, and anxiety in children aged 2–10 years old undergoing venous blood drawing—a randomized controlled study. *European Journal of Pediatrics, 175,* 373–379. https://doi.org/10.1007/s00431-015-2652-z

Meloy, J. R., Hempel, A. G., Mohandie, K., Shiva, A. A., & Gray, B. T. (2001). Offender and offense characteristics of a nonrandom sample of adolescent mass murderers. *Journal of the American Academy of Child and Adolescent Psychiatry, 40,* 719–728.

Melton, G. B., Petrila, J., Poythress, N. G., & Slobogin, C. (2007). *Psychological evaluation for the courts: A handbook for mental health professionals and lawyers.* New York, NY: Guilford.

Meltzoff, A. N. (1995). Understanding the intentions of others: Re-enactment of intended acts by 18-month-old children. *Developmental Psychology, 31,* 838–850.

Menezes, C. B., de Paula Couto, M. C., Buratto, L. G., Erthal, F., Pereira, M. G., & Bizarro, L. (2013). The improvement of emotion and attention regulation after a 6-week training of focused meditation: A randomized controlled trial. *Evidence-Based Complementary & Alternative Medicine (ECAM),* 1–11. https://doi.org/10.1155/2013/984678

Merikangas, K. R., He, J., Burstein, M., Swanson, S. J., Avenevoli, S., Cui, L., Benjet, C., Georgiades, K., & Swendsen, J. (2010). Lifetime prevalence of mental disorders in U.S. adolescents: Results from the National Comorbidity Survey replication—Adolescent Supplement (NCS-A). *Journal of the American Academy of Child & Adolescent Psychiatry, 49,* 980–989.

Merikle, P. M., & Daneman, M. (1998). Psychological investigations of unconscious perception. *Journal of Consciousness Studies, 5,* 5–18.

Mick, E., Biederman, J., Faraone, S. V., Sayer, J., & Kleinman, S. (2002). Case-control study of attention-deficit hyperactivity disorder and maternal smoking, alcohol use, and drug use during pregnancy. *Journal of the American Academy of Child and Adolescent Psychiatry, 41,* 378–385.

Mielke, M. M., Vemuri, P., & Rocca, W. A. (2014). Clinical epidemiology of Alzheimer's disease: Assessing sex and gender differences. *Clinical Epidemiology, 6,* 637–648. https://doi.org/10.2147/CLEP.S37929

Miklowitz, D. J., George, E. L., Richards, J. A., Simoneau, T. L., & Suddath, R. L. (2003). A randomized study of family-focused psychoeducation and pharmacotherapy in the outpatient management of bipolar disorder. *Archives of General Psychiatry, 60,* 904–912.

Milgram, S. (1963). Behavioral studies of obedience. *Journal of Abnormal and Social Psychology, 67,* 371–378.

Milgram, S. (1965). Some conditions of obedience and disobedience to authority. *Human Relations, 18,* 57–76.

Milgram, S. (1974). *Obedience to authority.* New York, NY: Harper-Collins.

Miller, D. T., & McFarland, C. (1987). Pluralistic ignorance: When similarity is interpreted as dissimilarity. *Journal of Personality and Social Psychology, 53,* 298–305.

Miller, G., Chen, E., & Cole, S. W. (2009). Health psychology: Developing biologically plausible models linking the social world and physical health. *Annual Review of Psychology, 60,* 501–524.

Mirabela, M., & Madela, A. (2013). Cultural dimensions and work motivation in the European Union. *Annals of the University of Oradea, Economic Science Series, 22,* 1511–1519.

Mirasol Recovery Centers. (2018). *Eating disorders statistics.* Retrieved from https://www.mirasol.net/learning-center/eating-disorder-statistics.php

Mischel, W. (1968). *Personality and assessment.* New York, NY: Wiley.

Mischel, W. (1973). Toward a cognitive social learning reconceptualization of personality. *Psychological Review, 80,* 252–283.

Mischel, W. (1999). Personality coherence and dispositions in a cognitive-affective personality system (CAPS) approach. In D. Cervone & Y. Shoda (Eds.), *The coherence of personality: Social-cognitive bases of consistency, variability, and organization* (pp. 37–60). New York, NY: Guilford.

Mischel, W., Shoda, Y., & Smith, R. E. (2004). *Introduction to personality: Toward an integration.* New York, NY: Wiley.

Mitchell, M., & Jolley, J. (2001). *Research design explained* (4th ed.). Belmont, CA: Thomson/Wadsworth.

Miyamoto, Y., Nisbett, R. E., & Masuda, T. (2006). Culture and the physical environment. *Psychological Science, 17,* 113–119. https://doi.org/10.1111/j.1467-9280.2006.01673.x

Mo, P. H., Ko, T. T., & Xin, M. Q. (2018). School-based gatekeeper training programmes in enhancing gatekeepers' cognitions and behaviours for adolescent suicide prevention: A systematic review. *Child and Adolescent Psychiatry and Mental Health, 12,* 1–24. https://doi.org/10.1186/s13034-018-0233-4

Mo, W., Henkens, K., & H-Janna van, S. (2011). Retirement adjustment: A review of theoretical and empirical advancements. *American Psychologist, 66,* 204–213. https://doi.org/10.1037/a002244

Moestrup, L., & Hvidt, N. C. (2016). Where is God in my dying? A qualitative investigation of faith reflections among hospice patients in a secularized society. *Death Studies, 40,* 618–629.

Monastersky, R. (2003, August 15). Whence wine? Blending chemistry and archeology, a researcher tracks the origins of grape fermentation. *The Chronicle of Higher Education,* A16–A18.

Money, J. (1987). Sin, sickness, or status? Homosexual gender identity and psychoneuroendocrinology. *American Psychologist, 42,* 384–399.

Montgomery, G. H., & DuHamel, K. N. (2000). A meta-analysis of hypnotically induced analgesia: How effective is hypnosis? *International Journal of Clinical and Experimental Hypnosis, 48,* 138–153.

Moon, C., & Fifer, W. P. (1990). Syllables as signals for 2-day old infants. *Infant Behavior and Development, 13,* 377–390.

Moriyama, Y., Mimura, M., Kato, M., & Kashima, H. (2006). Primary alcoholic dementia and alcohol-related dementia. *Psychogeriatrics, 6,* 114–118. https://doi.org/10.1111/j.1479-8301.2006.00168.x

Morris, C. (1946). *Signs, language, and behavior.* New York, NY: Prentice Hall.

Moruzzi, G., & Magoun, H. W. (1949). Brain stem reticular formation and activation of the EEG. *Electroencephalography and Clinical Neurophysiology, 1,* 455–473.

Moscovici, S., Mugny, G., & Van Avermaet, E. (1985). *Perspectives on minority influence.* New York, NY: Cambridge University Press.

Muchnik, C., Amir, N., Shabtai, E., & Kaplan-Neeman, R. (2012). Preferred listening levels of personal listening devices in young teenagers: Self-reports and physical measurements. *International Journal of Audiology, 51,* 287–293. https://doi.org/10.3109/14992027.2011.631590

Mulholland, A. M., & Mintz, L. B. (2001). Prevalence of eating disorders among African American women. *Journal of Counseling Psychology, 48,* 111–116.

Mulla, Z., & Krishnan, V. (2014). Karma-Yoga: The Indian model of moral development. *Journal of Business Ethics, 123,* 339–351. https://doi.org/10.1007/s10551-013-1842-8

Murphy, P. N., Bruno, R., Ryland, I., Wareing, M., Fisk, J. E., Montgomery, C., & Hilton, J. (2012). The effects of "ecstasy" (MDMA) on visuospatial memory performance: Findings from a systematic review with meta-analyses. *Human Psychopharmacology: Clinical & Experimental, 27,* 113–138. https://doi.org/10.1002/hup.1270

Murray, B. (2002, February). What a recovering nation needs from behavioral science. *Monitor on Psychology, 33,* 30–33.

Murray, H. A. (1938). *Explorations in personality.* New York, NY: Oxford University Press.

Musek, J. (2007). A general factor of personality: Evidence for the Big One in the five-factor model. *Journal of Research in Personality, 41,* 1213–1233. https://doi.org/10.1016/j.jrp.2007.02.003

Mustanski, B., & Liu, R. T. (2013). A longitudinal study of predictors of suicide attempts among lesbian, gay, bisexual, and transgender youth. *Archives of Sexual Behavior, 42,* 437–448.

Myles, B. S. (2007). Teaching students with autism spectrum disorders. *Remedial and Special Education, 28,* 130–131.

N

N. Broome, J. R., Orme-Johnson, D. W., & Schmidt-Wilk, J. (2005). Worksite stress reduction through the Transcendental Meditation Program. *Journal of Social Behavior & Personality, 17,* 235–273.

Nash, M. (1987). What, if anything, is regressed about hypnotic age regression? *Psychological Bulletin, 102,* 42–52.

Nathan, P. E., Stuart, S. P., & Dolan, S. L. (2000). Research of psychotherapy efficacy and effectiveness: Between Scylla and Charybdis. *Psychological Bulletin, 126,* 964–981.

National Alliance on Mental Illness. (n.d.). *Mental health by the numbers.* Retrieved from https://www.nami.org/Learn-More/Mental-Health-By-the-Numbers

National Alliance on Mental Illness. (2018). *Risk of suicide.* Retrieved from https://www.nami.org/Learn-More/Mental-Health-Conditions/Related-Conditions/Suicide

National Association of Anorexia Nervosa and Associated Disorders. (2018). *Eating disorder statistics.* Retrieved from http://www.anad.org/education-and-awareness/about-eating-disorders/eating-disorders-statistics/

National Council on Aging. (2018). *Healthy aging facts.* Retrieved from https://www.ncoa.org/news/resources-for-reporters/get-the-facts/healthy-aging-facts/

National Down Syndrome Society. (2018). *What is an intellectual disability?* Retrieved from https://www.ndss.org/resources/what-is-an-intellectual-disability/

National Eating Disorders Association. (2018). *Anorexia.* Retrieved from https://www.mirasol.net/learning-center/eating-disorder-statistics.phphttps://www.nationaleatingdisorders.org/statistics-research-eating-disorders

National Health Interview Survey. (2017). *Estimated prevalence of children with diagnosed Developmental Disabilities in the United States, 2014–2016.* Retrieved from https://www.cdc.gov/nchs/data/databriefs/db291.pdf

National Institute of Mental Health. (2016). *Major depression.* Retrieved from https://www.nimh.nih.gov/health/statistics/major-depression.shtml#part_155029

National Institute of Mental Health. (2017). *Mental illness.* Retrieved from https://www.nimh.nih.gov/health/statistics/mental-illness.shtml

National Institute of Mental Health. (2018). *Suicide.* Retrieved from https://www.nimh.nih.gov/health/statistics/suicide.shtml

National Institute on Alcohol and Alcoholism. (2018). *Alcohol facts and statistics.* Retrieved from https://www.niaaa.nih.gov/alcohol-health/overview-alcohol-consumption/alcohol-facts-and-statistics

National Institute on Drug Abuse. (2007). *Cocaine dependence and activation of the reward pathway.* Retrieved from https://www.drugabuse.gov/publications/teaching-packets/neurobiology-drug-addiction/section-iv-action-cocaine/5-cocaine-dependenceeactivation-reward-pa

National Institute on Drug Abuse. (2018a). *Opioids.* Retrieved from https://www.drugabuse.gov/drugs-abuse/opioids

National Institute on Drug Abuse. (2018b). *Sex and gender differences in substance use.* Retrieved from https://www.drugabuse.gov/publications/research-reports/substance-use-in-women/sex-gender-differences-in-substance-use

National Institute on Drug Abuse. (2018c). *What is the scope of heroin use in the United States?* Retrieved from https://www.drugabuse.gov/publications/research-reports/heroin/scope-heroin-use-in-united-states

National Institutes of Health, Review Panel on Coronary Prone Behavior and Coronary Heart Disease. (1981). Coronary-prone behavior and coronary heart disease: A critical review. *Circulation, 63,* 1199–1215.

National Intimate Partner and Sexual Violence Survey. (2017). *National Intimate Partner and Sexual Violence Survey: 2010–2012 report.* Retrieved from https://www.cdc.gov/violenceprevention/pdf/NISVS-StateReportBook.pdf

Nelson, G., Chandrashekar, J., Hoon, M. A., Feng, L., Zhao, G., Ryba, N. J. P., & Zuker, C. S. (2002). An amino-acid taste receptor. *Nature, 416,* 199–202.

Neubauer, P. J. (1992). The impact of stress, hardiness, home and work environment on job satisfaction, illness, and absenteeism in critical care nurses. *Medical Psychotherapy, 5,* 109–122.

Neugarten, B. L., & Neugarten, D. A. (1986). Changing meanings of age in the aging society. In A. Piter & L. Bronte (Eds.), *Our aging society: Paradox and promise* (pp. 33–51). New York, NY: Norton.

Newcomb, M. E., Birkett, M., Corliss, H. L., & Mustanski, B. (2014). Sexual orientation, gender, and racial differences in illicit drug use in a sample of US high school students. *American Journal of Public Health, 104,* 304–310. https://doi.org/10.2105/AJPH.2013.301702

Nguyen, H., & Ryan, A. (2008). Does stereotype threat affect test performance of minorities and women? A meta-analysis of experimental evidence. *Journal of Applied Psychology, 93,* 1314–1334.

Nickerson, R. S., & Adams, M. J. (1979). Long-term memory for a common object. *Cognitive Psychology, 11,* 287–307.

Nielsen, L. M., Christrup, L. L., Sato, H., Drewes, A. M., & Olesen, A. E. (2017). Genetic influences of OPRM1, OPRD1 and COMT on morphine analgesia in a multi-modal, multi-tissue human experimental pain model. *Basic & Clinical Pharmacology & Toxicology, 12,* 6–12. https://doi.org/10.1111/bcpt.12757

Nijholt, D. T., Ijsselstijn, L., vas der Weiden, M. M., Zheng, P., Sillevis Smitt, P. E., Koudstaal, P. J., & . . . Kros, J. M. (2015). Pregnancy zone protein is increased in the Alzheimer's disease brain and associates with senile plaques. *Journal of Alzheimer's Disease, 46,* 227–238. https://doi.org/10.3233/JAD-131628

Nisbett, R. E., Peng, K., Choi, I., & Norenzayan, A. (2001). Culture and systems of thought: Holistic vs. analytic cognition. *Psychological Review, 108,* 291–310.

Noor, F., & Evans, D. C. (2003). The effect of facial symmetry on perceptions of personality and attractiveness. *Journal of Research in Personality, 37,* 339–347.

Nuttall, G. A., Bowersox, M. R., Douglass, S. B., McDonald, J., Rasmussen, L. J., Decker, P. A., . . . Rasmussen, K. G. (2004). Morbidity and mortality in the use of electroconvulsive therapy. *The Journal of ECT, 20,* 237–241. https://doi.org/10.1097/00124509-200412000-00009

Nuttbrock, L., Hwahng, S., Bockting, W., Rosenblum, A., Mason, M., Macri, M., & Becker, J. (2010). Psychiatric impact of gender-related abuse across the life course of male-to-female transgender persons. *Journal of Sex Research, 47,* 12–23.

O

O'Connor, D. B., & Shimizu, M. (2002). Sense of personal control, stress and coping style: A cross-cultural study. *Stress and Health: Journal of the International Society for the Investigation of Stress, 18,* 173–183. https://doi.org/10.1002/smi.939

O'Haire, M. E., & Rodriguez, K. E. (2018). Preliminary efficacy of service dogs as a complementary treatment for posttraumatic stress disorder in military members and veterans. *Journal of Consulting and Clinical Psychology, 86,* 179–188. https://doi.org/10.1037/ccp0000267

Ortony, A., & Turner, T. J. (1990). What's basic about basic emotions? *Psychological Review, 97,* 315–331.

Ostovich, J. M., & Sabini, J. (2005). Timing of puberty and sexuality in men and women. *Archives of Sexual Behavior, 34,* 197–206.

Over, R., & Phillips, G. (1997). Differences between men and women in age preferences for a same-sex partner. *Behavioral and Brain Sciences, 20,* 138–140.

Ozer, E. J., & Weiss, D. S. (2004). Who develops posttraumatic stress disorder? *Current Directions in Psychological Science, 13,* 169–172. https://doi.org/10.1111/j.0963-7214.2004.00300.x

P

Packer, D. J. (2008). Identifying systematic disobedience in Milgram's obedience experiments: A meta-analytic review. *Perspectives on Psychological Science: A Journal of the Association for Psychological Science, 3,* 301–304. https://doi.org/10.1111/j.1745-6924.2008.00080.x

Pagnin, D., de Queiroz, V., Pini, S., & Cassano, G. B. (2004). Efficacy of ECT in depression: A meta-analytic review. *The Journal of ECT, 20,* 13–20.

Paivio, A. (1986). *Mental representations: A dual coding approach.* New York, NY: Oxford University Press.

Palmer, R. K. (2007). The pharmacology and signaling of bitter, sweet, and umami taste sensing. *Molecular Interventions, 7,* 87–98.

Palmiero, M., Nakatani, C., & van Leeuwen, C. (2017). Visual creativity across cultures: A comparison between Italians and Japanese. *Creativity Research Journal, 29,* 86–90.

Paludi, M. A., & Gullo, D. F. (1986). The effect of sex labels on adults' knowledge of infant development. *Sex Roles, 16,* 19–30.

Pasterski, V. (2017). Fetal androgens and human sexual orientation: Searching for the elusive link. *Archives of Sexual Behavior, 46,* 1615–1619. https://doi.org/10.1007/s10508-017-1021-6

Patel, K. R., Cherian, J., Gohil, K., & Atkinson, D. (2014). Schizophrenia: Overview and treatment options. *Journal of Pharmacy & Therapeutics, 39,* 638–645.

Patton, G. C., McMorris, B. J., Toumbourou, J. W., Hemphill, S. A., Donath, S., & Catalano, R. F. (2004). Puberty and the onset of substance use and abuse. *Pediatrics, 114,* e300–e306.

Patton, S. (2017). *Corporal punishment in black communities: Not an intrinsic cultural tradition but racial trauma.* Retrieved from http://www.apa.org/pi/families/resources/newsletter/2017/04/racial-trauma.aspx

Paunonen, S. V., & Jackson, D. N. (2000). What is beyond the Big Five? Plenty! *Journal of Personality, 68,* 821–835.

Pawaskar, M. D., Joish, V. N., Camacho, F. T., Rasu, R. S., & Balkrishnan, R. (2008). The influence of co-morbidities on prescribing pharmacotherapy for insomnia: Evidence from US national outpatient data 1995–2004. *Journal of Medical Economics, 11,* 41–56. https://doi.org/10.3111/13696990701817491

Pawlicki, R. E., & Heitkemper, T. (1985). Behavioral management of insomnia. *Journal of Psychosocial Nursing, 23,* 14–17.

Pearce, J. M., & Bouton, M. E. (2001). Theories of associative learning in animals. *Annual Review of Psychology, 52,* 111–139.

Peplau, L. A. (2003). Human sexuality: How do men and women differ? *Current Directions in Psychological Science, 12,* 37–40.

Peplau, L. A., & Perlman, D. (1982). Perspectives on loneliness. In L. A. Peplau & D. Perlman (Eds.), *Loneliness: A sourcebook of current theory, research and therapy* (pp. 1–18). New York, NY: John Wiley.

Perfect, T. J., Wagstaff, G. F., Moore, D., Andrews, B., Cleveland, V., Newcombe, S., . . . Brown, L. (2008). How can we help witnesses to remember more? It's an (eyes) open and shut case. *Law & Human Behavior, 32,* 314–324. https://doi.org/10.1007/s10979-007-9109-5

Perilla, J. L., Norris, F. H., & Lavizzo, E. A. (2002). Ethnicity, culture, and disaster response: Identifying and explaining ethnic differences in PTSD six months after Hurricane Andrew. *Journal of Social and Clinical Psychology, 21,* 20–45. https://doi.org/10.1521/jscp.21.1.20.22404

Pervin, L. A., & John, O. P. (2001). *Personality: Theory and research* (8th ed.). New York, NY: John Wiley.

Peters, J. W. (2014). *The decline and fall of the "H" word.* Retrieved from https://www.nytimes.com/2014/03/23/fashion/gays-lesbians-the-term-homosexual.html?_r=0

Petersen, J. L., & Hyde, J. S. (2010). Gender differences in sexual attitudes and behaviors: A review of meta-analytic results and large datasets. *Journal of Sex Research, 48,* 149–165.

Petty, R. E., & Cacioppo, J. T. (1986). *Communication and persuasion.* New York, NY: Springer-Verlag.

Pew Research Center. (2014). *Political polarization in the American public.* Retrieved from http://www.people-press.org/2014/06/12/political-polarization-in-the-american-public/

Pew Research Center. (2015). *Use of spanking differs across racial and education groups.* Retrieved from http://www.pewsocialtrends.org/2015/12/17/parenting-in-america/st_2015-12-17_parenting-09/

Piaget, J. (1932/1948). *The moral judgment of the child.* New York, NY: Free Press.

Piaget, J. (1952). *The origins of intelligence in children.* New York, NY: W. W. Norton.

Pierce, J. P., White, M. M., & Gilpin, E. A. (2005). Adolescent smoking decline during California's tobacco control programme. *Tobacco Control, 14,* 207–212.

Pihl, R. O., Assad, J. M., & Hoaken, P. N. S. (2003). The alcohol-aggression relationship and differential sensitivity to alcohol. *Aggressive Behavior, 29,* 302–315.

Pilgram, D. (2011). The hegemony of cognitive-behavioral therapy in modern mental health care. *Health Sociology Review, 20,* 120–132.

Piotrowski, C., Belter, R. W., & Keller, J. W. (1998). The impact on "managed care" on the practice of psychological testing: Preliminary findings. *Journal of Personality Assessment, 70,* 441–447.

Plaskon, L. A., Penson, D. F., Vaughan, T. L., & Stanford, J. L. (2003). Cigarette smoking and risk of prostate cancer in middle-aged men. *Cancer Epidemiology, Biomarkers and Prevention, 12,* 604–609.

Plomin, R., & McGuffin, P. (2003). Psychopathology in the postgenomic era. *Annual Review of Psychology, 54,* 205–228.

Pogue-Geile, M. F., & Yokley, J. L. (2010). Current research on the genetic contributors to schizophrenia. *Current Directions in Psychological Science, 19,* 214–219.

Polivy, J., & Herman, C. P. (2002). Causes of eating disorders. *Annual Review of Psychology, 53,* 187–213.

Pollack, H., Lantz, P. M., & Frohna, J. G. (2000). Maternal smoking and adverse birth outcomes among singletons and twins. *American Journal of Public Health, 90,* 395–400.

Pool, R. (1993). Evidence for homosexuality gene. *Science, 261,* 291–292.

Port, C. L., Engdahl, B., & Frazier, P. (2001). A longitudinal and retrospective study of PTSD among older prisoners of war. *American Journal of Psychiatry, 158,* 1474–1479.

Powers, S. I., Hauser, S. T., & Kilner, L. A. (1989). Adolescent mental health. *American Psychologist, 44,* 200–208.

Prati, G., & Pietrantoni, L. (2009). Optimism, social support, and coping strategies as factors contributing to posttraumatic growth: A meta-analysis. *Journal of Loss and Trauma, 14,* 364–388.

Pratkanis, A. R., & Aronson, E. (1992). *The age of propaganda.* New York, NY: Freeman.

Pressley, M., & Levin, J. R. (1980). The development of mental imagery retrieval. *Child Development, 51,* 558–560. https://doi.org/10.1111/1467-8624.ep12329684

Pressley, M., Levin, J. R., & Delaney, H. D. (1982). The mnemonic keyword method. *Review of Educational Research, 52,* 61–91. https://doi.org/10.2307/1170273

Price, C. S., Thompson, W. W., Goodson, B., Croen, L. A., Marcy, M., Eriksen, E., Bernal, P., & Davis, R. L. (2010). Prenatal and infant exposure to thimerosal from vaccines and immunoglobulins and risk of autism. *Pediatrics, 126,* 656–664.

Punch, J. L., Elfenbein, J. L., & James, R. R. (2011). Targeting hearing health messages for users of personal listening devices. *American Journal of Audiology, 20,* 69–82. https://doi.org/10.1044/1059-0889(2011/10-0039)

Pusswald, G., Lehrner, J., Hagmann, M., Dal-Bianco, P., Benke, T., Marksteiner, J., . . . Schmidt, R. (2015). Gender-specific differences in cognitive profiles of patients with Alzheimer's disease: Results of the prospective dementia registry Austria (PRODEM-Austria). *Journal of Alzheimer's Disease, 46,* 631–637. https://doi.org/10.3233/JAD-150188

R

Ramanathan, D. M., Wardecker, B. M., Slocomb, J. E., & Hillary, F. G. (2011). Dispositional optimism and outcome following traumatic brain injury. *Brain Injury, 25,* 328–337

Raz, A., & Shapiro, T. (2002). Hypnosis and neuroscience: A cross talk between clinical and cognitive research. *Archives of General Psychiatry, 59,* 85–90.

Reeder, G. D., Pryor, J. B., Wohl, M. J. A., & Griswell, M. L. (2005). On attributing negative motives to others who disagree with our opinions. *Personality and Social Psychology Bulletin, 31,* 1498–1510.

Regan, P. (1998). What if you can't get what you want? Willingness to compromise ideal mate selection standards as a function of sex, mate value, and relationship context. *Personality and Social Psychology, 24,* 1294–1303.

Regan, P. C., & Berscheid, E. (1999). *Lust: What we know about human sexual desire.* Thousand Oaks, CA: Sage.

Rego, S., Arantes, J., & Magalhães, P. (2018). Is there a sunk cost effect in committed relationships? *Current Psychology, 37,* 508–519. https://doi.org/10.1007/s12144-016-9529-9

Reich, D. A. (2004). What you expect is not always what you get: The roles of extremity, optimism, and pessimism in the behavioral confirmation process. *Journal of Experimental Social Psychology, 40,* 199–215.

Reichenberg, A., Gross, R., Weiser, M., Bresnahan, N. N., Silverman, J., Harlap, S., . . . Susser, E. (2006). Advancing paternal age and autism. *Archives of General Psychiatry, 63,* 1026–1032.

Reisner, S. L., Greytak, E. A., Parsons, J. T., & Ybarra, M. L. (2015). Gender minority social stress in adolescence: Disparities in adolescent bullying and substance use by gender identity. *Journal of Sex Research, 52,* 243–256. https://doi.org/10.1080/00224499.2014.886321

Reneman, L., Lavalaye, J., Schmand, B., de Wolff, F. A., van den Brink, W., den Heeten, G. J., & Booij, J. (2001). Cortical serotonin transporter density and verbal memory in individuals who stopped using 3, 4-methylenedioxymethamphetamine (MDMA or "Ecstasy"). *Archives of General Psychiatry, 58,* 901–906.

Rensink, R. A. (2002). Change detection. *Annual Review of Psychology, 53,* 245–277.

Rice, P. L. (1999). *Stress and health* (3rd ed.). Pacific Grove, CA: Brooks/Cole.

Rice, W. R., Friberg, U., & Gavrilets, S. (2012). Homosexuality as a consequence of epigenetically canalized sexual development. *Quarterly Review of Biology, 87,* 343–368.

Richards, A. (2015). Psychoanalysis in crisis: The danger of ideology. *Psychoanalytic Review, 102,* 389–405. https://doi.org/10.1521/prev.2015.102.3.389

Riedel, B. W., Lichstein, K. L., Peterson, B. A., Epperson, M. T., Means, M. K., & Aguillard, R. N. (1998). A comparison of the efficacy of stimulus control for medicated and nonmedicated insomniacs. *Behavior Modification, 22,* 3–28.

Riise, T., Nortvedt, M. W., & Ascherio, A. (2003). Smoking is a risk factor for multiple sclerosis. *Neurology, 61,* 1122–1124.

Ringhand, L. A. (2007). Judicial activism: An empirical examination of voting behavior on the Rehnquist natural court. *Constitutional Commentary, 24,* 43–102.

Ritterband, L., Thorndike, F., Gonder-Frederick, L., Magee, J., Bailey, E., Saylor, D., & Morin, C. (2009). Efficacy of an Internet-based behavioral intervention for adults with insomnia. *Archives of General Psychiatry, 66,* 692–698. https://doi.org/10.1001/archgenpsychiatry.2009.66

Robert, M., & Savoie, N. (2006). Are there gender differences in verbal and visuospatial working-memory resources? *European Journal of Cognitive Psychology, 18,* 378–397. https://doi.org/10.1080/09541440500234104

Roberts, B. W., Kuncel, N. R., Shiner, R., Caspi, A., & Goldberg, L. R (2007). The power of personality: The comparative validity of personality traits, socioeconomic status, and cognitive ability for predicting important life outcomes. *Perspectives in Psychological Science, 2,* 313–345.

Robinson, N. N., Zigler, E., & Gallagher, J. J. (2000). Two tails of the normal curve: Similarities and differences in the study of mental retardation and giftedness. *American Psychologist, 55,* 1413–1424. https://doi.org/10.1037/0003-066X.55.12.1413

Robinson, T. E., & Berridge, K. C. (2003). Addiction. *Annual Review of Psychology, 54,* 25–53.

Rochat, F., Maggioni, O., & Modgiliani, A. (2000). The dynamics of obeying and opposing authority: A mathematical model In T. Blass (Ed.), *Obedience to authority: Current perspectives on the Milgram paradigm* (pp. 91–110). Mahwah, NJ: Lawrence Erlbaum.

Rodriguez, C. G., Moskowitz, J. P., Salem, R. M., & Ditto, P. H. (2017). Partisan selective exposure: The role of party, ideology and ideological extremity over time. *Translational Issues in Psychological Science, 3,* 254–271. https://doi.org/10.1037/tps0000121

Rodriguez, K. E., Bryce, C. I., Granger, D. A., & O'Haire, M. E. (2018, April, 27). The effect of a service dog on salivary cortisol awakening response in a military population with posttraumatic stress disorder (PTSD). *Psychoneuroendocrinology,* 1–9. https://doi.org/10.1016/j.psyneuen.2018.04.026

Roediger, H. L., III, & Karpicke, J. D. (2006a). The power of testing memory: Basic research and implications for educational practice. *Perspectives on Psychological Science, 1,* 181–210.

Roediger, H. L., & Karpicke, J. D. (2006b). Test-enhanced learning: Taking memory tests improves long-term retention. *Psychological Science, 17,* 249–255.

Rogers, C. R. (1959). A theory of therapy, personality, and interpersonal relationships as developed in the client-centered framework. In S. Koch (Ed.), *Psychology: A study of science* (pp. 185–256). New York, NY: McGraw Hill.

Rogowski, J., & Sutherland, J. (2016). How ideology fuels affective polarization. *Political Behavior, 38,* 485–508. https://doi.org/10.1007/s11109-015-9323-7

Rohrer, D., Taylor, K., Pashler, H., Wixted, J. T., & Cepeda, N. J. (2005). The effect of overlearning on long-term retention. *Applied Cognitive Psychology, 19,* 361–374.

Roid, G. (2003). *Stanford-Binet Intelligence Scales* (5th ed.). Itasca, IL: Riverside Publishing.

Ron, P. (2010). Elderly people's death and dying anxiety: A comparison between elderly living in the community and in nursing homes in Israel. *Illness, Crisis and Loss, 18,* 1–17.

Rorschach, H. (1921). *Psychodiagnostics.* Bern, Switzerland: Huber.

Rosa, A. R., Andreazza, A. C., Kunz, M., Gomes, F., Santin, A., Sanchez-Moreno, J., Colom, F., Vieta, E., & Kapczinski, F. (2008). Predominant polarity in bipolar disorder: Diagnostic implications. *Journal of Affective Disorders, 107,* 45–51.

Rosario, E. R., Chang, L., Head, E. H., Stanczyk, F. Z., & Pike, C. J. (2011). Brain levels of sex steroid hormones in men and women during normal aging and in Alzheimer's disease. *Neurobiology of Aging, 32,* 604–613. https://doi.org/10.1016/j.neurobiolaging.2009.04.008

Rosario, M., Reisner, S. L., Corliss, H. L., Wypij, D., Calzo, J., & Austin, S. B. (2014). Sexual-orientation disparities in substance use in emerging adults: A function of stress and attachment paradigms. *Psychology of Addictive Behaviors: Journal of the Society of Psychologists in Addictive Behaviors, 28,* 790–804. https://doi.org/10.1037/a0035499

Rosch, E. (1973). Natural categories. *Cognitive Psychology, 4,* 328–350.

Rosen, D. S. (2010). Clinical report: Identification and management of eating disorders in children and adolescents. *Pediatrics, 126,* 1240–1253.

Rosenblum, L. (2008, May 8). Unobtrusive hybrid car "noise" being developed. *The Fort Wayne Journal Gazette,* 13A.

Rosenman, R. H., Brand, R. J., Jenkins, C. D., Friedman, M., Straus, R., & Wurm, M. (1975). Coronary heart disease in the Western Collaborative Group Study: Final follow-up experience of 8 1/2 years. *Journal of the American Medical Association, 233,* 872–877.

Rosnow, R. L., Skleder, A. A., & Rind, B. (1995). Reading other people: A hidden cognitive structure? *The General Psychologist, 31,* 1–10.

Ross, C. A. (1997). *Dissociative identity disorder.* New York, NY: Wiley.

Roth, S., Robbert, T., & Straus, L. (2015). On the sunk-cost effect in economic decision-making: A meta-analytic review. *Business Research, 8,* 99–138. https://doi.org/10.1007/s40685-014-0014-8

Ruscio, A. M., Brown, T. A., Chiu, W. T., Sareen, J., Stein, M. B., & Kessler, R. C. (2008). Social fears and social phobia in the USA: Results from the National Comorbidity Survey Replication. *Psychological Medicine, 38,* 15–28.

Russell, J. A. (2003). Core affect and the psychological construction of emotion. *Psychological Review, 110,* 145–172.

Russell, J. A., Bachorowski, J., & Fernández-Dols, J. (2003). Facial and vocal expressions of emotion. *Annual Review of Psychology, 54,* 329–349.

Russock, H. I. (2011). An evolutionary interpretation of the effect of gender and sexual orientation on human mate selection preferences, as indicated by an analysis of personal advertisements. *Behaviour, 148,* 307–323. https://doi.org/10.1163/000579511X556600

Ryabinin, A. E. (1998). Role of hippocampus in alcohol-induced memory impairment: Implications from behavioral and immediate early gene studies. *Psychopharmacology, 139,* 34–43.

Ryan, K. M., & Kanjorski, J. (1998). The enjoyment of sexist humor, rape attitudes, and relationship aggression in college students. *Sex Roles, 38,* 743–756.

S

Sacher, J., Neumann, J., Okon-Singer, H., Gotowiec, S., & Villringer, A. (2013). Sexual dimorphism in the human brain: Evidence from neuroimaging. *Magnetic Resonance Imaging, 31,* 366–375. https://doi.org/10.1016/j.mri.2012.06.007

Sahoo, F. M., Sahoo, K., & Das, N. (2011). Need saliency and management of employee motivation: Test of an indigenous model. *Vilakhsan: The XIMB Journal of Management, 7,* 21–36.

Salas, E., & Cannon-Bowers, J. A. (2001). The science of training: A decade of progress. *Annual Review of Psychology, 52,* 471–499.

Salovey, P., & Grewal, D. (2005). The science of emotional intelligence. *Current Directions in Psychological Science, 14,* 281–285.

Salthouse, T. A. (2004). What and when of cognitive aging. *Current Directions in Psychological Science, 13,* 140–144.

Salthouse, T. A., & Ferrer-Caja, E. (2003). What needs to be explained to account for age-related effects on multiple cognitive variables? *Psychology and Aging, 18,* 91–110.

Samuelson, F. J. B. (1980). Watson's Little Albert, Cyril Burt's twins, and the need for a critical science. *American Psychologist, 35,* 619–625.

Sanders, G. S., & Simmons, W. L. (1983). Use of hypnosis to enhance eyewitness accuracy: Does it work? *Journal of Applied Psychology, 68,* 70–77. https://doi.org/10.1037/0021-9010.68.1.70

Satir, V. (1967). *Conjoint family therapy.* Palo Alto, CA: Science and Behavior Books.

Saylik, R., Raman, E., & Szameitat, A. J. (2018, June, 29). Sex differences in emotion recognition and working memory tasks. *Frontiers in Psychology, 9,* 1–9. https://doi.org/10.3389/fpsyg.2018.01072

Schacter, D. L., Norman, K. A., & Koutstaal, W. (1998). The cognitive neuroscience of constructive memory. *Annual Review of Psychology, 48,* 289–318.

Schall, J. D. (2004). On building a bridge between brain and behavior. *Annual Review of Psychology, 55,* 23–50.

Schalock, R. L., Luchasson, R. A., & Shogren, K. A. (2007). The renaming of mental retardation: Understanding the change to the term intellectual disability. *Intellectual and Developmental Disabilities, 45,* 116–124.

Schechter, R., & Grether, J. K. (2008). Continuing increases in autism reported to California's Developmental Services System. *Archives of General Psychiatry, 65,* 19–24.

Scheier, M. F., & Carver, C. S. (1993). On the power of positive thinking: The benefits of being optimistic. *Current Directions in Psychological Science, 2,* 26–30.

Schichl, M., Ziberi, M., Lahl, O., & Pietrowsky, R. (2011). The Influence of midday naps and relaxation-hypnosis on declarative and procedural memory performance. *Sleep & Hypnosis, 13,* 7–14.

Schiffenbauer, A., & Schavio, S. R. (1976). Physical distance and attraction: An intensification effect. *Journal of Experimental Social Psychology 12,* 274–282.

Schilt, K., & Westbrook, L. (2009). Doing gender, doing heteronormativity: "Gender normals," transgender people, and the social maintenance of heterosexuality. *Gender & Society, 23,* 440–464.

Schilt, T., de Win, M. M. L., Koeter, M., Jager, G., Korf, D. J., van den Brink, W., & Schmand, B., (2007). Cognition in novice ecstasy users with minimal exposure to other drugs: A prospective cohort study. *Archives of General Psychiatry, 64,* 728–736.

Schmidt, U., & Asen, E. (2005). Editorial: Does multi-family day treatment hit the spot that other treatments cannot reach? *Journal of Family Therapy, 27,* 101–103.

Schimmel-Bristow, A., Haley, S. G., Crouch, J. M., Evans, Y. N., Ahrens, K. R., McCarty, C. A., & Inwards-Breland, D. J. (2018). Youth and caregiver experiences of gender identity transition: A qualitative study. *Psychology of Sexual Orientation and Gender Diversity, 5,* 273–281. https://doi.org/10.1037/sgd0000269

Schnall, S., Haidt, J., Clore, G. L., &. Jordan, A. H. (2008). Disgust as embodied moral judgment. *Personality and Social Psychology Bulletin, 34,* 1096–1109.

Schneider, R. H., Alexander, C. N., Staggers, F., Rainforth, M., Salerno, J. W., Hartz, A., Arndt, S., Barnes, V. A., & Nidich, S. (2005). Long-term effects of stress reduction on mortality in persons > or = 55 years of age with systemic hypertension. *American Journal of Cardiology, 95,* 1060–1064.

Schneiderman, N. (2004). Psychosocial, behavioral, and biological aspects of chronic diseases. *Current Directions in Psychological Science, 13,* 247–251.

Schneiderman, S., Antoni, M. H., Saab, P. G., & Ironson, G. (2001). Health psychology: Psychosocial and biobehavioral aspects of chronic disease management. *Annual Review of Psychology, 52,* 555–580.

Schoen, R., & Wooldredge, J. (1989). Marriage choices in North Carolina and Virginia, 1969–71 and 1979–81. *Journal of Marriage and the Family 51,* 465–481.

Schroepfer, T. A. (2007). Critical events in the dying process: The potential for physical and psychosocial suffering. *Journal of Palliative Medicine, 10,* 136–147. https://doi.org/10.1089/jpm.2006.0157

Schroepfer, T. A., Noh, H., & Kavanaugh, M. (2009). The myriad strategies for seeking control in the dying process. *The Gerontologist, 49,* 755–766. https://doi.org/10.1093/geront/gnp060

Schulkind, M., Schoppel, K., & Scheiderer, E. (2012). Gender differences in autobiographical narratives: He shoots and scores; she evaluates and interprets. *Memory & Cognition, 40,* 958–965. https://doi.org/10.3758/s13421-012-0197-1

Schwarz, S., & Hassebrauck, M. (2012). Sex and age differences in mate-selection preferences. *Human Nature, 23,* 447–466. https://doi.org/10.1007/s12110-012-9152-x

Schweinsburg, A. D., Schweinsburg, B. C., Medina, K. L., McQueeny, T., Brown, S. A., & Tapert, S. F. (2010). The influence of recency of use on fMRI response during spatial working memory in adolescent marijuana users. *Journal of Psychoactive Drugs, 42,* 401–412.

Scott, A., & Fraser, T. (2008). Decreased usage of electroconvulsive therapy: Implications. *British Journal of Psychiatry, 192,* 476.

Sears, P. S., & Barbee, A. H. (1977). Career and life satisfaction among Terman's gifted women. In J. Stanley et al. (Eds.), *The gifted and the creative: Fifty year perspective* (pp. 72–106). Baltimore, MD: Johns Hopkins University Press.

Sechrest, L., & Walsh, M. (1997). Dogma or data: Bragging rights. *American Psychologist, 52,* 536–540.

Segall, M., Dasen, P., Berry, J., & Poortinga, Y. (1990). *Human behavior in global perspective.* Elmsford, NY: Pergamon.

Segovia, F., Moore, J. L., Linnville, S. E., & Hoyt, R. E. (2015). Optimism predicts positive health in repatriated prisoners of war. *Psychological Trauma: Theory, Research, Practice, and Policy, 7,* 222–228. https://doi.org/10.1037/a0037902

Seidlitz, L., & Diener, E. (1998). Sex differences in the recall of affective experiences. *Journal of Personality & Social Psychology, 74,* 262–271.

Seo, D.-C., & Torabi, M. R. (2004). The impact of in-vehicle cell-phone use on accidents or near accidents among college students. *Journal of American College Health, 53,* 101–107.

Serbin, L. A., Sprafkin, C., Elman, M., & Doyle, A. B. (1984). The early development of sex differentiated patterns of social influence. *Canadian Journal of Social Science, 14,* 350–363.

Serpanos, Y. C., Berg, A. L., & Renne, B. (2016). Influence of hearing risk information on the motivation and modification of personal listening device use. *American Journal of Audiology, 25,* 332–343. https://doi.org/10.1044/2016_AJA-15-0062

Shackelford, T. P., Schmitt, D. P., & Buss, D. M. (2005). Universal dimensions of human mate preferences. *Personality and Individual Differences, 39,* 447–458.

Shadick, R., Dagirmanjian, F. B., Trub, L., & Dawson, H. (2016). Sexual orientation and first-year college students' nonmedical use of prescription drugs. *Journal of American College Health, 64,* 292–299. https://doi.org/10.1080/07448481.2015.1117469

Shadish, W. R., Navarro, A. M., Matt, G. E., & Phillips, G. (2000). The effects of psychological therapies under clinically representative conditions: A meta-analysis. *Psychological Bulletin, 126,* 512–529.

Shaffer, D. R. (1999). *Developmental psychology: Childhood and adolescence* (5th ed.). Pacific Grove, CA: Brooks/Cole.

Shaffer, D. R. (2002). *Developmental psychology: Childhood & adolescence* (6th ed.). Belmont, CA: Wadsworth.

Shaffer, D. R., & Kipp, K. (2007). *Developmental psychology: Childhood and adolescence.* Belmont, CA: Wadsworth.

Shattuck, P. T. (2006). The contribution of diagnostic substitution to the growing administrative prevalence of autism in U.S. special education. *Pediatrics, 117,* 1028–1037.

Shaw, B. F., Elkin, I., Yamaguchi, J., Olmsted, M., Vallis, T. M., . . . Imber, S. D. (1999). Therapist competence ratings in relation to clinical outcome in cognitive therapy of depression. *Journal of Consulting and Clinical Psychology, 67,* 837–846.

Sheehan, P. W., Green, V., & Truesdale, P. (1992). Influence of rapport on hypnotically induced pseudomemory. *Journal of Abnormal Psychology, 101,* 690–700.

Sheehan, P. W., Statham, D., & Jamieson, G. A. (1991). Pseudomemory effects over time in the hypnotic setting. *Journal of Abnormal Psychology, 100,* 39–44. https://doi.org/10.1037/0021-843X.100.1.39

Shiffman, S., Balabanis, M. H., Gwaltney, C. J., Paty, J. A., Gnys, M., Kassel, J. D., . . . Paton, S. M. (2007). Prediction of lapse from associations between smoking and situational antecedents assessed by ecological assessment. *Drug and Alcohol Dependence, 91,* 159–168.

Shotland, R. L., & Straw, M. K. (1976). Bystander response to an assault: When a man attacks a woman. *Journal of Personality and Social Psychology, 34,* 990–999.

Simons, D. A., & Wurtele, S. K. (2010). Relationships between parents' use of corporal punishment and their children's endorsement of spanking and hitting other children. *Child Abuse & Neglect: The International Journal, 34,* 639–646.

Simons, D. J., & Chabris, C. F. (2011). What people believe about how memory works: A representative survey of the U.S. population. *Plos ONE, 6,* 1–7. https://doi.org/10.1371/journal.pone.0022757

Sinai, M. J., Ooi, T. L., & He, Z, J. (1998). Terrain influences the accurate judgment of distance. *Nature, 395,* 497–500.

Singh, D., & Rani, A. (2017). A study of psychological (personality) correlates of criminal behaviour. *Indian Journal of Health & Wellbeing, 8,* 62–66.

Sinha, B. K., & Watson, D. C. (2007). Stress, coping and psychological illness: A cross-cultural study. *International Journal of Stress Management, 14,* 386–397. https://doi.org/10.1037/1072-5245.14.4.386

Sinha, B. K., Willson, L. R., & Watson, D. C. (2000). Stress and coping among students in India and Canada. *Canadian Journal of Behavioural Science/Revue Canadienne Des Sciences Du Comportement, 32,* 218–225. https://doi.org/10.1037/h0087118

Sinha, S. (2016). Personality correlates of criminals: A comparative study between normal controls and criminals. *Industrial Psychiatry Journal, 25,* 41–46. https://doi.org/10.4103/0972-6748.196058

Skinner, B. F. (1983). Intellectual self-management in old age. *American Psychologist, 38,* 239–244.

Skinner, B. F. (1989). The origins of cognitive thought. *American Psychologist, 44,* 13–18.

Slattery, M. L., Edwards, S., Curtin, K., Schaffer, D., & Neuhausen, S. (2003). Associations between smoking, passive smoking, GSTM-1, NAT2, and rectal cancer. *Cancer Epidemiology, Biomarkers and Prevention, 12,* 882–889.

Smetana, J. G., Killen, M., & Turiel, E. (1991). Children's reasoning about interpersonal and moral conflicts. *Child Development, 62,* 629–644.

Smetana, J. G., & Gaines, C. (1999). Adolescent-parent conflict in middle-class African-American families. *Child Development, 70,* 1447–1463.

Smith, B. N., Kerr, N. A., Markus, M. J., & Stasson, M. F. (2001). Individual differences in social loafing: Need for cognition as a motivator in collective performance. *Group Dynamics, 5,* 150–158.

Smith, K., & Parekh, A. (1996). A cross-sectional study of moral development in the South African context. *Psychological Reports, 78,* 851–859. https://doi.org/10.2466/pr0.1996.78.3.851

Smyrnios, K. X., & Kirkby, R. J. (1993). Long-term comparison of brief versus unlimited psychodynamic treatments with children and their parents. *Journal of Consulting and Clinical Psychology, 61,* 1020–1027.

Soldo, T., Blank, I., & Hofmann, T. (2003). (+)-(S)-Alapyridaine—a general taste enhancer? *Chemical Senses, 28,* 371–379.

Soloman, R. C. (2003). *What is an emotion? Classic and contemporary readings* (2nd ed.). New York, NY: Oxford University Press.

Somerfield, M. R., & McCrae, R. R. (2000). Stress and coping research: Methodological challenges, theoretical advances, and clinical applications. *American Psychologist, 55,* 620–625.

Sood, B., Delany-Black, V., Covington, C., Nordstrom-Klee, B., Ager, J., Templin, T., Janisse, J., Martier, S., & Sokol, R. J. (2001). Prenatal alcohol exposure and childhood behavior at age 6 to 7 years: I. Dose-response effect. *Pediatrics, 108,* e34.

Spanos, N. P. (1994). Multiple identity enactments and multiple personality disorder: A socoiocognitive perspective. *Psychological Bulletin, 116,* 143–165.

Spanos, N. P., Menary, E., Gabora, N. J., DuBreuil, S. C., & Dewhirst, B. (1991). Secondary identity enactments during past-life regression: A sociocognitive perspective. *Journal of Personality and Social Psychology, 61,* 308–320.

Sperry, R. (1968). Hemispheric disconnection and unity in conscious awareness. *American Psychologist, 23,* 723–733.

Sperry, R. (1982). Some effects of disconnecting the cerebral hemispheres. *Science, 217,* 1223–1226.

Springer, J. P., & Deutsch, G. (1981). *Left brain, right brain.* San Francisco, CA: Freeman.

St. Jacques, P. L., Conway, M. A., & Cabeza, R. (2011). Gender differences in autobiographical memory for everyday events: Retrieval elicited by SenseCam images versus verbal cues. *Memory, 19,* 723–732. https://doi.org/10.1080/09658211.2010.516266

Staddon, J. E. R., & Cerutti, D. Y. (2003). Operant conditioning. *Annual Review of Psychology, 54,* 115–144.

Stanford University School of Medicine. (2018). *Where do Americans die?* Retrieved from https://palliative.stanford.edu/home-hospice-home-care-of-the-dying-patient/where-do-americans-die/

Statista. (2018). *Percentage of U.S. adults that had ever received treatment for a mental health condition as of 2018.*

Retrieved from https://www.statista.com/statistics/872364/mental-health-treatment-adults-us/

Stein, J. A., Newcomb, M. D., & Bentler, P. M. (1990). The relative influence of vocational behavior and family involvement on self-esteem: Longitudinal analyses of young adult women and men. *Journal of Vocational Behavior, 36*, 320–328.

Steinberg, L., & Morris, A. S. (2001). Adolescent development. *Annual Review of Psychology, 52*, 83–110.

Stern, W. (1912). *The psychological methods of testing intelligence.* Retrieved from https://archive.org/stream/psychologicalmet00ster/psychologicalmet00ster_djvu.txt

Sternberg, R. J. (1986). A triangular theory of love. *Psychological Review, 93*, 119–135.

Sternberg, R. J. (1988). Triangulating love. In R. J. Sternberg & M. L. Barnes (Eds.), *The psychology of love* (pp. 119–138). New Haven, CT: Yale University Press.

Sternberg, R. J. (1997). The concept of intelligence and its role in lifelong learning and success. *American Psychologist, 52*, 1030–1037.

Sternberg, R. J. (1999). The theory of successful intelligence. *Review of General Psychology, 3*, 292–316.

Sternberg, R. J. (2004). Culture and intelligence. *American Psychologist, 59*, 360–362.

Sternberg, R. J. (2007). Who are the bright children? The cultural context of being and acting intelligent. *Educational Researcher, 36*, 148–155.

Sternberg, R. J. (2011). *Cognitive psychology* (6th ed.). Belmont, CA: Wadsworth.

Sternberg, R. J., Grigorenko, E. L., & Kidd, K. K. (2005). Intelligence, race, and genetics. *American Psychologist, 60*, 46–59.

Stokes, D., & Lappin, M. (2010). Neurofeedback and biofeedback with 37 migraineurs: A clinical outcome study. *Behavioral and brain functions, 6*, 9. https://doi.org/10.1186/1744-9081-6-9

Stoner, J. A. F. (1961). *A comparison of individual and group decisions involving risk.* Retrieved from https://dspace.mit.edu/bitstream/handle/1721.1/11330/33120544-MIT.pdf?sequence=2

Streissguth, A. P., Bookstein, F. L., Barr, H., Sampson, P. D., O'Malley, K., Kieran, M. B., & Young, J. K. (2004). Risk factors for adverse life outcomes in fetal alcohol syndrome and fetal alcohol effects. *Journal of Developmental and Behavioral Pediatrics, 25*, 228–238.

Szymanski, D. D., & Steward-Richardson, D. N. (2014). Psychological, relational, and sexual correlates of pornography use on young adult heterosexual men in romantic relationships. *Journal of Men's Studies, 22*, 64–82.

T

Tabarean, I., Morrison, B., Macondes, M.-C., Bartfai, T., & Condi, B. (2010). Hypothalamic and dietary control of temperature-mediated longevity. *Ageing Research Reviews, 9*, 41–50.

Takahashi, Y. (1990). Is multiple personality disorder really rare in Japan? *Dissociation, 3*, 57–59.

Tang, N., Bensman, L., & Hatfield, E. (2014). The impact of culture and gender on sexual motives: Differences between Chinese and North Americans. *International Journal of Intercultural Relations, 36*, 286–294.

Tashkin, D. P., Zhang, Z. F., Greenland, S., Cozen, W., Mack, T. M., & Morganstern, H. (2006). *Marijuana use and lung cancer: Results of a case-control study.* Paper presented at the American Thoracic Society International Conference, San Diego, CA.

Taurah, L., Chandler, C., & Sanders, G. (2014). Depression, impulsiveness, sleep, and memory in past and present poly-drug users. *Psychopharmacology, 231*, 737–751. https://doi.org/10.1007/s00213-013-3288-1

Taylor, C. A., Hamvas, L., & Paris, R. (2011). Perceived instrumentality and normativeness of corporal punishment use among black mothers. *Family Relations, 60*, 60–72.

Taylor, M. A. (2018). A comprehensive study of mass murder precipitants and motivations of offenders. *International Journal of Offender Therapy and Comparative Criminology, 62*, 427–449. https://doi.org/10.1177/0306624X16646805

Taylor, S. E. (1989). *Positive illusions: Creative self-deception and the healthy mind.* New York, NY: Basic Books.

Taylor, S. E., & Gollwitzer, P. M. (1995). Effects of mindset on positive illusions. *Journal of Personality and Social Psychology, 69*, 213–226.

Taylor, S. E., Kemeny, M. E., Aspinwall, L. G., & Schneider, S. G. (1992). Optimism, coping, psychological distress, and high-risk sexual behavior among men at risk for acquired immunodeficiency syndrome (AIDS). *Journal of Personality and Social Psychology, 63*, 460–473.

Taylor, S. E., Klein, L. C., Lewis, B. P., Gruenewald, T. L., Gurung, R. A. R., & Updegraff, J. A. (2000). Biobehavioral responses to stress in females: Tend-and-befriend, not fight or flight. *Psychological Review, 107*, 411–429.

Tenopyr, M. L. (1981). The realities of employment testing. *American Psychologist, 36*, 1120–1127.

Terpstra, S., Beekman, A., Abbing, J., Jaken, S., Steendam, M., & Gilissen, R. (2018). Suicide prevention gatekeeper training in the Netherlands improves gatekeepers' knowledge of suicide prevention and their confidence to discuss suicidality, an observational study. *BMC Public Health, 18*, 637. https://doi.org/10.1186/s12889-018-5512-8

Tetlock, P. E., Peterson, R. S., McGuire, C., Shi-jie Chang, & Feld, P. (1992). Assessing political group dynamic: A test of the groupthink model. *Journal of Personality and Social Psychology, 63*, 403–425.

Thapar, A., Fowler, T., & Rice, F. (2003). Maternal smoking during pregnancy and attention deficit hyperactivity disorder symptoms in offspring. *American Journal of Psychiatry, 160*, 1985–1989. https://doi.org/10.1176/appi.ajp.160.11.1985

The Free Dictionary (n.d.). *Ideology.* Retrieved from https://www.thefreedictionary.com/ideology

Thomas, J. L., Britt, T. W., Odle-Dusseau, H., & Bliese, P. D. (2011). Dispositional optimism buffers combat veterans from the negative effects of warzone stress on mental health symptoms and work impairment. *Journal of Clinical Psychology, 67*, 866–880.

Thompson, R. F. (2005). In search of memory traces. *Annual Review of Psychology, 56,* 1–23.

Thorsteinsson, E., & Brown, R. 2009. Mediators and moderators of the stressor-fatigue relationship in non-clinical samples. *Journal of Psychosomatic Research, 66,* 21–29.

Thuné-Boyle, I. C., Stygall, J. A., Keshtgar, M. R., & Newman, S. P. (2006). Do religious/spiritual coping strategies affect illness adjustment in patients with cancer? A systematic review of the literature. *Social Science & Medicine, 63,* 151–164. https://doi.org/10.1016/j.socscimed.2005.11.055

Tice, D. M., & Baumeister, R. F. (1985). Masculinity inhibits helping in emergencies: Personality does predict the bystander effect. *Journal of Personality and Social Psychology, 49,* 420–428.

Tice, D. M., & Baumeister, R. F. (1997). Longitudinal study of procrastination, performance, stress, and health: The costs and benefits of dawdling. *Psychological Science, 8,* 454–458.

Time. (November 30, 1942). Psychosurgery.

Time. (September 15, 1952). Mass lobotomies.

Tindle, H., Belnap, B. H., Houck, P. R., Mazumdar, S., Scheier, M. F., Matthews, K. A., Rollman, B. L. (2012). Optimism, response to treatment of depression, and rehospitalization after coronary artery bypass graft surgery. *Psychosomatic Medicine, 74,* 200–207. https://doi.org/10.1097/PSY.0b013e318244903f

TNS BMRB. (2015). *Attitudes to mental illness 2014 research report.* Retrieved from https://www.time-to-change.org.uk/sites/default/files/Attitudes_to_mental_illness_2014_report_final_0.pdf

Tolman, E. C., & Honzik, C. H. (1930). Introduction and removal of reward and maze performance in rats. *University of California Publication in Psychology, 4,* 257–275.

Tombs, S., & Silverman, I. (2004). Pupillometry: A sexual selection approach. *Evolution and Human Behavior, 25,* 221–228.

Torpy, J. M. (2005). JAMA patient page: Smoking and pregnancy. *Journal of the American Medical Association, 293,* 1286.

Torre, P. (2008). Young adults' use and output level settings of personal music systems. *Ear and Hearing, 29,* 791–799.

Tragesser, S. L., Beauvais, F., Burnside, M., & Jumper-Thurman, P. (2010). Differences in illicit drug-use rates among Oklahoma and non-Oklahoma Indian youth. *Substance Use & Misuse, 45,* 2323–2339. https://doi.org/10.3109/10826084.2010.484320

Trepka, C., Rees, A., Shapiro, D. A., Hardy, G. E., & Barkham, M. (2004). Therapist competence and outcome of cognitive therapy for depression. *Cognitive Therapy and Research, 28,* 143–157.

Triplett, N. (1898). The dynamogenic factors in pacemaking and competition. *American Journal of Psychology, 9,* 507–533.

Tschampa, D. (2014). Cue the engine rumble. *Bloomberg Businessweek, 4362,* 20–21.

Tuiten, A., Van Honk, J., Koppeschar, H., Bernaards, C., Thihssen, J., & Verbaten, R. (2000). Time course of effects of testosterone administration on sexual arousal in women. *Archives of General Psychiatry, 57,* 149–153.

Tulving, E. (1972). Episodic and semantic memory. In E. Tulving & W. Donaldson (Eds.), *Organization of memory* (pp. 382–402). New York, NY: Academic Press.

Tulving, E. (2003). Episodic memory: From mind to brain. *Annual Review of Psychology, 53,* 1–25.

Tulving, E., & Thompson, D. M. (1973). Encoding specificity and retrieval processes in episodic memory. *Journal of Experimental Psychology: Learning, Memory, and Cognition, 8,* 336–342.

Turnbull, C. (1961). Some observations regarding the experiences and behaviors of the Bambuti pygmies. *American Journal of Psychology, 74,* 304–308.

Turner, J. S., & Helms, D. B. (1987). *Contemporary adulthood.* New York, NY: Holt, Rinehart & Winston.

U

Unitarian Universalist Association. (1996–2015). *Sexual identity and gender identity 101.* Retrieved from http://www.uua.org/lgbtq/identity

U.S. Department of Health and Human Services. (2013). *Results from the 2013 National Survey on Drug Use and Health: Summary of national findings.* Retrieved from https://www.samhsa.gov/data/sites/default/files/NSDUHresultsPDF-WHTML2013/Web/NSDUHresults2013.pdf

U.S. Department of Health and Human Services. (2018). *What is the U.S. opioid epidemic?* Retrieved from https://www.hhs.gov/opioids/about-the-epidemic/index.html

U.S. Department of Labor. (2018). *Data & statistics: Women in the labor force.* Retrieved from https://www.dol.gov/wb/stats/stats_data.htm

U.S. Department of Veterans Affairs. (2018). *VA releases veteran suicide statistics by state.* Retrieved from https://www.va.gov/opa/pressrel/pressrelease.cfm?id=2951

V

Vaid, J., Rhodes, R., Tosun, S., & Eslami, Z. (2011). Script directionality affects depiction of depth in representational drawings. *Social Psychology, 42,* 241–248. https://doi.org/10.1027/1864-9335/a000068

Van den Pol, A. N. (1999). Hypothalamic hypocretin (orexin): Robust innervation of the spinal cord. *Journal of Neuroscience, 19,* 3171–3182.

van der Linden, D., Dunkel, C. S., Beaver, K. M., & Louwen, M. (2015). The unusual suspect: The General Factor of Personality (GFP), life history theory, and delinquent behavior. *Evolutionary Behavioral Sciences, 9,* 145–160. https://doi.org/10.1037/ebs0000027

van der Pompe, G., Antoni, M. H., & Heijen, C. (1998). The effects of surgical stress and psychological stress on the immune function of operative cancer patients. *Psychological Health, 13,* 1015–1026.

Van Gundy, K., & Rebellon, C. J. (2010). A life-course perspective on the "gateway hypothesis". *Journal of*

Health and Social Behavior 51, 244–259. https://doi.org/10.1177/0022146510378238

van Solinge, H., & Henkens, K. (2008). Adjustment to and satisfaction with retirement: Two of a kind? *Psychology & Aging, 23*, 422–434. https://doi.org/10.1037/0882-7974.23.2.422

VandenBos, G. R. (1986). Psychotherapy research: A special issue. *American Psychologist, 41*, 111–112.

Vander Wall, S. B. (1982). An experimental analysis of cache recovery in the Clark's nutcracker. *Animal Behavior, 30*, 84–94.

Vargha-Khadem, F., Gadian, D. G., Watkins, K. E., Connelly, A., Ban Paesschen, W., & Mishkin, M. (1997). Differential effects of early hippocampal pathology on episodic and semantic memory. *Science, 277*, 376–380.

Veenema, A. H., Blume, A., Niederle, D., Buwalda, B., & Neumann, I. D. (2006). Effects of early life stress on adult male aggression and hypothalamic vasopressin and serotonin. *European Journal of Neuroscience, 24*, 1711–1720.

Verde, P., Piccardi, L., Bianchini, F., Guariglia, C., Carrozzo, P., Morgagni, F., & . . . Tomao, E. (2015). Gender differences in navigational memory: Pilots vs. nonpilots. *Aerospace Medicine and Human Performance, 86*, 103–111. https://doi.org/10.3357/AMHP.4024.2015

Vest, R. S., & Pike, C. J. (2013). Gender, sex steroid hormones, and Alzheimer's disease. *Hormones and Behavior, 63*, 301–307. https://doi.org/10.1016/j.yhbeh.2012.04.006

Villalobos, B. T., & Bridges, A. J. (2018). Prevalence of substance use disorders among Latinos in the United States: An empirical review update. *Journal of Latina/o Psychology, 6*, 204–219. https://doi.org/10.1037/lat0000097

Voinescu, B. I., Szentagotai, A., & David, D. (2013). Internet-administered cognitive-behavioral therapy for insomnia. *Journal of Cognitive & Behavioral Psychotherapies, 13*, 225–237.

W

Wade, D., Varker, T., Kartal, D., Hetrick, S., O'Donnell, M., & Forbes, D. (2016). Gender difference in outcomes following trauma-focused interventions for posttraumatic stress disorder: Systematic review and meta-analysis. *Psychological Trauma: Theory, Research, Practice and Policy, 8*, 356–364. https://doi.org/10.1037/tra0000110

Wagstaff, G. F., Vella, M., & Perfect, T. (1992). The effect of hypnotically elicited testimony on jurors' judgments of guilt and innocence. *Journal of Social Psychology, 132*, 591–595.

Walker, E., Kestler, L., Bollini, A., & Hochman, K. M. (2004). Schizophrenia: Etiology and course. *Annual Review of Psychology, 55*, 401–430.

Wang, J., Wang, Y., Feng, J., Chen, B.-y., & Cao, J. (2013). Complex sleep apnea syndrome. *Patient Preference & Adherence, 7*, 633–641. https://doi.org/10.2147/PPA.S46626

Wang, M., & Kenny, S. (2014). Parental physical punishment and adolescent adjustment: Bidirectionality and the moderation effects of child ethnicity and parental warmth. *Journal of Abnormal Child Psychology, 42*, 717–730. https://doi.org/10.1007/s10802-013-9827-8

Wang, P. S., Lane, M., Olfson, M., Pincus, H. A., Wells, K. B., & Kessler, R. C. (2005). Twelve-month use of mental health services in the United States: Results from the National Comorbidity Survey Replication. *Archives of General Psychiatry, 62*, 629–640.

Wang, Q. (2013). Gender and emotion in everyday event memory. *Memory, 21*, 503–511. https://doi.org/10.1080/09658211.2012.743568

Warrior Canine Connection. (2018). *Mission based trauma recovery infographic.* Retrieved from https://warriorcanineconnection.org/how-we-help-warriors/infographic/

Washburn, M. F. (1908). *The animal mind: A text-book of comparative psychology.* New York, NY: MacMillan Company.

Waterman, A. S. (1985). Identity in the contest of adolescent psychology. *New Directions in Child Development, 30*, 5–24.

Watson, J. B. (1913). Psychology as a behaviorist views it. *Psychological Review, 20*, 158–177.

Watson, J. B. (1919). *Psychology from the standpoint of a behaviorist.* Philadelphia, PA: Lippincott.

Watson, J. B. (1925). *Behaviorism.* New York, NY: Norton.

Watson, J. B., & Rayner, R. (1920). Conditioned emotional reactions. *Journal of Experimental Psychology, 3*, 1–14.

Watson, P. W., & Thornhill, P. (1994). Fluctuating asymmetry and sexual selection. *Trends in Ecology and Evolution, 9*, 21–25.

WebMD (2018). *Sexual orientation.* Retrieved from https://www.webmd.com/sex-relationships/guide/sexual-orientation#1

Wechsler, D. (1939). *The measurement of adult intelligence.* Baltimore, MD: Williams & Wilkins.

Wechsler, D. (1975). Intelligence defined and undefined: A relativistic reappraisal. *American Psychologist, 30*, 135–139.

Weekes, J. R., Lynn, S. J., Green, J. P., & Brentar, J. T. (1992). Pseudomemory in hypnotized and task-motivated subjects. *Journal of Abnormal Psychology, 101*, 356–360.

Wegner, D. M., Lane, J. D., & Dimitri, S. (1994). The allure of secret relationships. *Journal of Personality and Social Psychology, 66*, 287–300.

Wehby, G. L., Prater, K., McCarthy, A. M., Castilla, E. E., & Murray, J. C. (2011). The Impact of Maternal Smoking during Pregnancy on Early Child Neurodevelopment. *Journal of Human Capital, 5*, 207–254.

Weinland, J. (1996). Cognitive behavior therapy: A primer. *Journal of Psychological Practice, 2*, 23–35.

Weintraub, Z., Bental, Y., Olivan, A., & Rotschild, A. (1998). Neonatal withdrawal syndrome and behavioral effects produced by maternal drug use. *Addiction Biology, 3*, 159–170.

Weisberg, M. (2008). 50 years of hypnosis in medicine and clinical health psychology: A synthesis of cultural cross-currents. *American Journal of Clinical Hypnosis, 51*, 13–27.

Weiss, M., Allan, B., & Greenaway, M. (2012). Treatment of catatonia with electroconvulsive therapy in adolescents. *Journal of Child and Adolescent Psychopharmacology, 22*, 96–100.

Wellman, H. M., & Gellman, S. A. (1992). Cognitive development: Fundamental theories of core domains. *Annual Review of Psychology, 43*, 337–375.

West, R. F., Meserve, R. J., & Stanovich, K. E. (2012). Cognitive sophistication does not attenuate the bias blind spot. *Journal of Personality and Social Psychology, 103*, 506–519.

West, V. (2003). Hypnotic suggestibility and academic achievement: A preliminary study. *Contemporary Hypnosis, 20*, 48–52.

Westen, D. (1998). The scientific legacy of Sigmund Freud: Toward a psychodynamically informed psychological science. *Psychological Bulletin, 124*, 333–371.

Westfall, J., Van Boven, L., Chambers, J. R., & Judd, C. M. (2015). Perceiving political polarization in the United States: Party identity strength and attitude extremity exacerbate the perceived partisan divide. *Perspectives on Psychological Science, 10*, 145–158.

Wheat, A. L., & Larkin, K. T. (2010). Biofeedback of heart rate variability and related physiology: A critical review. *Applied Psychophysiology and Biofeedback. 35*, 229–242.

Wheeler, M. A., & McMillan, C. T. (2001). Focal retrograde amnesia and the episodic-semantic distinction. *Cognitive, Affective, and Behavioral Neuroscience, 1*, 22–37.

White, M. A., McKee, S. A., & O'Malley, S. S. (2007). Smoke and mirrors: Magnified beliefs that cigarette smoking suppresses weight. *Addictive Behaviors, 32*, 2200–2210.

White, V., Tan, N., Wakefield, M., & Hill, D. (2003). Do adult focused anti-smoking campaigns have an impact on adolescents? The case of the Australian National Tobacco Campaign. *Tobacco Control, 12*, ii23.

Whitman, F. L., Diamond, M., & Martin, J. (1993). Homosexual orientation in twins: A report on 61 pairs and three triplet sets. *Archives of Sexual Behavior, 22*, 187–206.

Whyte, G. (1989). Groupthink reconsidered. *Academy of Management Review, 14*, 40–56.

Wickelgren, I. (2005). Autistic brains out of sync? *Science, 308*, 1856–1858.

Widiger, T. A., & Sankis, L. M. (2000). Adult psychopathology: Issues and controversies. *Annual Review of Psychology, 51*, 377–404.

Wijkstra, J., & Nolen, W. A. (2005). Successful maintenance electroconvulsive therapy for more than seven years. *The Journal of ECT, 21*, 171–173. https://doi.org/10.1097/01.yct.0000176018.63613.d0

Wilkes, J. (1986). Conversation with Ernest R. Hilgard: A study in hypnosis. *Psychology Today, 20*, 23–27.

Williams, J. E., & Best, D. L. (1990). *Measuring sex stereotypes: A multination study.* Newbury Park, CA: Sage.

Williams, J. M., & Dunlap, L. C. (1999). Pubertal timing and self-reported delinquency among male adolescents. *Journal of Adolescence, 22*, 157–171.

Williams, W. M., & Ceci, S. J. (1997). Are Americans becoming more or less alike: Trends in race, class, and ability differences in intelligence. *American Psychologist, 52*, 1226–1235.

Wilson, L. L., Ballman, A. D., & Buczek, T. J. (2016). News content about mass shootings and attitudes toward mental illness. *Journalism & Mass Communication Quarterly, 93*, 644–658.

Wilson, T., Lindsey, S., & Schooler, T. Y. (2000). A model of dual attitudes. *Psychological Review, 107*, 101–126.

Winner, E. (1996). *Gifted children: Myths and realities.* New York, NY: Basic Books.

Winner, E. (2000). Giftedness: Current theory and research. *Current Directions in Psychological Science, 9*, 153–155.

Witgen, B. J., Zhou, M., Cai, Y., Balaji, J., Karlsson, M. G., Parivash, S. N., . . . Silva, A. J. (2010). The hippocampus plays a selective role in the retrieval of detailed contextual memory. *Current Biology, 20*, 1336–1344.

Wolpe, J. (1958). *Psychotherapy by reciprocal inhibition.* Stanford, CA: Stanford University Press.

Wolpe, J. (1981). Behavior therapy versus psychoanalysis. *American Psychologist, 36*, 159–164.

Wolpe, J. (1997). Thirty years of behavior therapy. *Behavior Therapy, 28*, 633–635.

Wong, M. M., & Csikszentmihalyi, M. (1991). Affiliation motivation and daily experience. *Journal of Personality and Social Psychology, 60*, 154–164.

Wood, C. (1986). The hostile heart. *Psychology Today, 20*, 10–12.

Wood, J. M., Garb, H. N., Lilienfeld, S. O., & Nezworski, M. T. (2002). Clinical assessment. *Annual Review of Psychology, 53*, 519–543.

Wood, J. M., Lilienfeld, S. O., Nezworski, M. T., Garb, H. N., Allen, K. H., & Wildermuth, J. L. (2010). Validity of Rorschach Inkblot scores for discriminating psychopaths from nonpsychopaths in forensic populations: A meta-analysis. *Psychological Assessment, 22*, 336–349. https://doi.org/10.1037/a0018998.supp (Supplemental)

Woodworth, R. S., & Schlosberg, H. (1954). *Experimental psychology* (rev. ed.). New York, NY: Henry Holt.

Worchel, S., Cooper, J., Goethals, G. R., & Olson, J. M. (2000). *Social psychology.* Belmont, CA: Wadsworth.

Worchel, S., Rothgerber, H., Day, E. A., Hart, D., & Butemeyer, J. (1998). Social identity and individual productivity within groups. *British Journal of Social Psychology, 37*, 389–413.

World Health Organization. (2018a). *The top 10 causes of death.* Retrieved from http://www.who.int/news-room/fact-sheets/detail/the-top-10-causes-of-death

World Health Organization. (2018b). *Tobacco.* Retrieved from http://www.who.int/news-room/fact-sheets/detail/tobacco

World Health Organization. (2018c). *Global Health Observatory (GHO) data: HIV/AIDS.* Retrieved from http://www.who.int/gho/hiv/en/

Worringham, C. J., & Messick, D. M. (1983). Social facilitation of running: An unobtrusive study. *Journal of Social Psychology, 121*, 23–29.

Wrosch, C., Dunne, E., Scheier, M. F., & Schultz, R. (2006). Self-regulation of common age-related challenges: Benefits for older adult's psychological and physical health. *Journal of Behavioral Medicine, 29*, 299–306.

Wrosch, C., & Schulz, R. (2008). Health-engagement control strategies and 2-year changes in older adult's physical health. *Psychological Science, 19,* 537–541.

Wrosch, C., Schultz, R., Miller, G. E., Lupien, S., & Dunne, E. (2007). Physical health problems, depressive mood, and cortisol secretion in old age: Buffer effects of health engagement control strategies. *Health Psychology, 26,* 341–349.

Wyatt, R. J., & Henter, I. D. (1997). Schizophrenia: The need for early treatment. *The Harvard Mental Health Letter, 14,* 4–6.

Y

Yan, L. L., Liu, K., Matthews, K. A., Daviglus, M. L., Ferguson, F., & Kiefe, C. I. (2003). Psychosocial factors and risk of hypertension: The Coronary Artery Risk Development in Young Adults (CARDIA) Study. *Journal of the American Medical Association, 290,* 2138–2148.

Yarborough, B. H., Stumbo, S. P., Yarborough, M. T., Owen-Smith, A., & Green, C. A. (2018). Benefits and challenges of using service dogs for veterans with posttraumatic stress disorder. *Psychiatric Rehabilitation Journal, 41,* 118–124. https://doi.org/10.1037/prj0000294

Yuille, J. C., & McEwan, N. H. (1985). Use of hypnosis as an aid to eyewitness memory. *Journal of Applied Psychology, 70,* 389–400.

Yun, O. B., Kim, S., & Jung, D. (2015). Effects of a clown–nurse educational intervention on the reduction of postoperative anxiety and pain among preschool children and their accompanying parents in South Korea. *Journal of Pediatric Nursing, 30,* e89–e99. https://doi.org/10.1016/j.pedn.2015.03.003

Z

Zajonc, R. B. (1965). Social facilitation. *Science, 149,* 269–274.

Zalla, T., Koechlin, E., Pietrini, P., Basso, G., Aquino, P., Sirigu, A., & Grafman, J. (2000). Differential amygdala responses to winning and losing: A functional magnetic resonance imaging study in humans. *European Journal of Neuroscience, 12,* 1764–1770.

Zammit, S., Allebeck, P., Dalman, C., Lundberg, I., Hemmingson, T., Owen, M. J., Lewis, G. (2003). Paternal age and risk for schizophrenia. *British Journal of Psychiatry, 183,* 405–408.

Zebrowitz, L. A., Collins, M. A., & Dutta, R. (1998). The relationship between appearance and personality across life-span. *Personality and Social Psychology Bulletin, 24,* 736–749.

Zeidan, F., Johnson, S. Diamond, B. J., David G., & Goolkasian, P. (2010). Mindfulness meditation improves cognition: Evidence of brief mental training. *Consciousness & Cognition, 19,* 597–605.

Zillmer, E. A., & Spiers, M. V. (2001). *Principles of neuropsychology.* Belmont, CA: Wadsworth.

Zimbardo, P. (2007). *The Lucifer effect: Understanding how good people turn evil.* New York, NY: Random House.

Zimmerman, M., Posternak, M. A., Attiullah, N., Friedman, M., Boland, R. J., Baymiller, S., . . . Chelminski, I. (2005). Why isn't bupropion the most frequently prescribed antidepressant? *Journal of Clinical Psychiatry, 66,* 603–610.

Index

Note: Marginal glossary terms, defined upon their first appearance unless noted otherwise, are in bold type. Chapter Summaries, Study Checks, and Thinking Critically are not indexed.

outer ear, 60
oval window, 59
pinna, 59
stirrup, 59
tympanic membrane, 59
Earbuds, 59
Early adulthood development, 341–344
Eating disorders, 178
Echoic memory, 103
Ecstasy, 141–143
Educational, or instructional, psychologists, 15
Ego, 213
Eichmann, Adolph, 312
Ekman, Paul, 186
Elaboration likelihood model, 305
Elaborative rehearsal, 107
Electroconvulsive therapy (ECT), 280–282
suicide and suicide prevention, 281
Electroencephalograph (EEG), 128
Electromyogram (EMG), 128
Ellis, Albert, 289
Embryonic stage, 328
Emotional intelligence, 158
managing emotions, 158
perceiving emotions, 158
understanding emotions, 158
using emotions to facilitate thinking, 158
Emotions, 182–183
classifying, 182–183
defining, 182–183
emotion-focused strategy, 240
expressing emotion, 185–186
parasympathetic division, 184
physiology of, 183–185
sympathetic division, 184
Encapsulated nerve endings, 62
Encoding, 102
Encoding specificity, 113
Endler Multidimensional Anxiety
Scale, 225
Endocrine system, 27
Environmental frustration, 233
Episcotister, 114
Episodic LTM, 107
Episodic memory, 108
Equanil, 284
Erikson, Erik, 339, 341
Estrogen, 27, 274
Even the rat was white: A historical view of
psychology, 13
Evolutionary psychology, 203
Excitatory neurotransmitter, 25
Executive cognitive functions (ECFs), 127
Existential intelligence, 157
Experimental group, 8
Experimental Psychology, 150
Experimental research, 8
Expertise, 305
Explicit attitude, 304
Explicit stereotype, 307
Exposure and response prevention, 288
Expressing emotion, 185–186
Extinction, 84
Extraneous variable, 9
Extroversion/Introversion, 220
Eye, receptor for vision, 53–56
accommodation, 54
aqueous humor, 54
blind spot, 55–56
ciliary muscles, 54
cones, 54
fovea, 55
glaucoma, 54
lens, 54
optic nerve, 54
retina, 54–55

rods, 54
vitreous humor, 54
Eyewitness testimony, 110

F
Factor analysis, 220
False consensus bias, 302
False memories, 134
Family therapy, 291
Fatal attraction, 206
Fear appeals, 305
Female-to-male transgender person (FtM), 197
"Feminine" cultures, 174
Festinger, Leon, 176
Fetal alcohol effects (FAE), 328
Fetal alcohol syndrome (FAS), 328
Figure-ground relationship, 67
Five-Factor Model, 220–221
Flextime, 16
Formal operations stage, 330–331
Fovea, 55
Fragile X syndrome, 166
Free association, 285
Free morpheme, 154
Free nerve endings, 62
Freud, Sigmund, 12, 126–127, 130, 211–214, 284–285.
See also under Psychoanalytic approach
Frontal lobes, 36
Frustration, 233
Frustration-aggression hypothesis, 245
Frustration-induced stress, 233–234
Fully functioning, 218
Functional fixedness, 151
Functionalism, 11
Fundamental attribution error, 302

G
Galton, Sir Francis, 159
Gamma waves, 128
Ganglion cells, 54
Gardner, Howard, 157
Gatekeeper, 281
Gateway hypothesis, 140
Gay and Lesbian Alliance Against Defamation
(GLADD), 195
Gender, 191
gender differences
in Alzheimer's disease, 274
in memory, 111
in the brain, 41
gender identity, 191
development, 334–336
gender role, 191
General Factor of Personality (GFP), 226
General Social Survey, 307–308
Generalization, 84–85
Generalized amnesia, 267
Generalized anxiety disorder (GAD), 263
Generativity, 342, 345
Generic-parts technique (GPT), 152
Genovese, Kitty, 315, 317
Gestalt principles of form perception, 68
Gilligan, Carol, 332
Glaucoma, 54
Grammar, 154
Grapheme, 154
Grilo, Carlos, 143
Group approaches, 291–292
Group decision-making, 319–321
Group differences in measured intelligence, 162
Group polarization effect, 320
Group therapy, 291
Grouping stimuli
with bottom-up processing, 68–70
with top-down processing, 70–71
Groupthink, 320

Growth hormone, 27
Growth spurt, 337
Grysman, Azriel, 111
Gustation, 61
Guthrie, Robert, 13

H
Hair cells, 60
Hallucinations, 272
Hallucinogens, 137, 140
Hammer, 59
Han, Woojae, 59
Health psychologists, 15
Health-engagement control strategies (HECSs), 347
Healthy behaviors, promoting, 251–254
stop smoking, 251–252
Hearing, 57–61. *See also* Audition, sense of hearing
Help-negation, 282
Heroin, 29, 137, 139
Heterosexual orientation, 194–197
Heuristic solution, 151
HEXACO model, 221
agreeableness (A), 221
conscientiousness (C), 221
emotionality (E), 221
extroversion (X), 221
honesty (H), 221
openness to experience (O), 221
High discrepancy, 305
Hill, Craig, 191
Hippocampus, 34–35
Histrionic personality disorder, 269
Hobson, Alan, 132
Holmes, Thomas, 237
Homeostasis, 175
Hormones, 27
Horney, Karen, 215
Hull, Clark, 171
Human brain
structures, 32
Human immunodeficiency virus (HIV), 252
Human memory, 102
Human nervous systems, 26–28. *See also* Cerebral
cortex; Neurons
organization, 26
Human sexuality, 191–193. *See also* Sexuality and
relationships
varieties of, 194–199
affectional orientation, 195
cisgendered individuals, 197
female-to-male transgender person (FtM), 197
heterosexual orientations, 194–197
male-to-female (MtF) transgender person, 197
"queer", 198
same-sex orientations, 194–197
transgender identity, 197–199
Humanistic approaches, 218–219, 287
Humanistic psychology, 12
Hunger motive and eating disorders, 178
Hyperactivity, 266
Hyperthyroidism, 28
Hypnosis, 133–135
memory improvement and, 119
physical pain and, 134
susceptibility to, 133
Hypothalamus, 34–35
Hypothesis, 4

I
Iconic memory, 103
Id, 212
Identity achievers, 340
Identity crisis, 339
Identity diffusers, 340
Identity foreclosure, 340
Identity formation challenges, 339–340

storage, 102
test, 163
Menarche, 337
Mental age, 159–160
Mental health technicians, 15
Mental illness, 261
Mental processes, 2
  affect, 2
  behaviors versus, 3
  cognitions, 2
Mental retardation, 165
Mental set, 66
Mere exposure effect, 201
Methamphetamine, 138
Method of loci, 115
Middle adulthood development, 344–345
Middle ear, 60
Milgram, Stanley, 312–313
Miller, Neal, 217
Miltown, 284
Mindfulness meditation, 135
Minnesota Multiphasic Personality Inventory (MMPI-2), 225
  restructured form, 225
Mischel, Walter, 218, 227
Mnemonic device, 114
Modern racism, 308
Moniz, Egas, 279
Monochromatic light, 53
Moral reasoning, group differences in, 332
  conventional moral stage, 332
  postconventional morality, 332
  preconventional moral stage, 332
Moratorium, 340
Morphemes, 154
Motion parallax, 73
Motivated social cognition, 309
Motivation, 169–188
  arousal, 170
  balance or equilibrium, 175–177
  culture, needs, and job performance, 174
  explaining, 170–175
  hunger motive and eating disorders, 178
  incentives, 175
  instincts, 171
  Maslow's hierarchy of needs, 173
  motivational concepts, applying, 177–179
  needs and drives, 171–174
  physiological needs, 172
  primary drive, 171
  psychologically based motives, 179–182
  safety needs, 172
  secondary drive, 171
  sub-processes, 170
Motivational conflicts, 234
Motor area, 37–38
Motor neurons, 30
Multiple approach-avoidance conflict, 236
Murray, Henry, 180
Musical intelligence, 157
Myelin, 23

N
Naïve realism, 310
Nanometer (nm), 52
Narrative chaining, 114
Naturalistic intelligence, 157
Need, 171
  need for affiliation, 181
  need for intimacy, 181
  need for power, 181
  need to achieve (nAch), 180
Negative reinforcement, 90
Negative symptoms, 272
Neo-Freudians, 214

Nervous disorders, 12, 126, 284
Neural impulses, 24, 48
Neural threshold, 24
Neurodegenerative disorder, 130
Neurodevelopmental disorder, 265–267
Neurons, 22–26
  all-or-none principle, 24
  axon, 23
  axon terminals, 24
  as building blocks, 22–26
  cell body, 23
  dendrite, 23
  excitatory neurotransmitter, 25
  inhibitory neurotransmitter, 26
  interneurons, 31
  motor, 31
  myelin, 23
  neural impulse, 24
  neurotransmitters, 24
  receptor sites, 24
  sensory, 31
  synapse, 24
  synaptic cleft, 24
  synaptic transmission, mechanisms, 25
  vesicles, 24
Neuropsychologists, 14
Neuroticism, 221
Neurotransmitters, 24
Neutral stimulus (NS), 82, 86
Newborn, 327
Nicotine, 137–138
Non-anorexics, 179
Nondeclarative LTM, 107
Normal waking consciousness, 124–125
NREM sleep, 130

O
Obedience, 312–314
  to authority, 312–314
  destructive obedience, 312
Object permanence, 330
Objective reality, 17
Obsessions, 264
Obsessive-compulsive disorder (OCD), 264, 288
Occipital lobes, 36
Occupational therapists, 15
Old-fashioned racism, 307
Olfaction, 61
Operant chamber, 88
Operant conditioning, 87–95
  basics, 87–95
  parenting, ethnic and racial differences in, 94
  punishment, 89, 92–95
  reinforcement, 89–92
  reinforcer, 89
Opiates, 137, 139
Optic nerve, 54
Orientation, 194
Orienting reflex, 82
Ossicles, 59
Outer ear, 60
Oval window, 59
Overlearning, 117

P
Pain sense, 63
Panic disorder, 263
Paranoid personality disorder, 269
Parasympathetic division, 27
Parenting, ethnic and racial differences in, 94
Parietal lobes, 37
Parkinson's disease, 34
Partial schedule of reinforcement, 88
Partisan selective exposure, 310
Passion, 204

Pastoral counseling, 15
Pavlov, Ivan, 82–83
Peplau, Letitia, 193
Perceived collective efficacy, 174
Perception, 47–78, 148
Perceptual constancies, 74–75
Perceptual reasoning, 161
Perceptual selection, 63–67
  intensity, 64
  perceptual world, organizing, 67–75
    depth and distance, 71–74
    figure-ground perception, 67
    Gestalt principles of form perception, 68
    grouping stimuli, 68–70
  personal factors in, 66–67
    bottom-up processing, 66
  personal factors, 64
  stimulus factors in, 64–66
Peripheral nervous system (PNS), 27
Peripheral-route processing, 306
Persistent depressive disorder, 270
Personal constructs, 217
Personal factors, 64
Personal frustration, 234
Personal listening devices (PLDs), 59
  hearing loss and, 59
Personal unconscious, 215
Personality, 209–229. *See also* Trait approach
  assessment or measurement, 223–227
    behavioral observations, 223–224
    criterion-referenced test, 225
    Endler Multidimensional Anxiety Scale, 225
    interviews, 224
    projective test, 225
    psychological tests, 224–227
    Rorschach inkblot test, 225
    Taylor Manifest Anxiety Scale, 225
    Thematic Apperception Test (TAT), 226
    word association technique, 225
  behavioral/learning approach, 216–217
  cognitive approach, 217–218
  cultural differences in, 222
  Freud's psychoanalytic approach, 211–214. *See also under* Psychoanalytic approach
  humanistic approach, 218–219
  parts of, 213
  personality disorders, 268–270
  predicting criminality from, 226
  "Theories", 210–223
Person-centered personality, 218
Person-centered therapy, 287
Persuasion, 304–306
Peterson, Adrian, 94
Pheromones, 62
Phobias, treating, 86–87
Phobic disorder, 86
Phonemes, 154
Physical attractiveness bias, 202–204
Physical distance, 201
Physical exercise, 242
Physical health, psychological factors in, 246–250
  cynical hostility, 246
  optimism cure, 249
  Type A behavior pattern (TABP), 246–247
  unhealthy lifestyle, 247–250
Physical proximity effect, 201
Physiological needs, 172
Physiological psychologists, 14
Physiological responses, 262
Physiology of emotion, 183–185
Piaget, Jean, 329
Piaget's stage of cognitive development, 330
Pictorial cues, 72
Pinna, 59
Pitch, 58
Pituitary gland, 27

Plasticity, 39
Pleasure principle, 213
Pluralistic ignorance, 316
Political polarization, 309
Pons, 33
Positive behavior support, 266
Positive reinforcement, 90
Positive symptoms, 272
Postconventional morality, 332
Posttraumatic stress disorder (PTSD), 91, 244, 250, 264–265
Pragmatics, 155
Preconscious level, 126, 211
Preconventional moral stage, 332
Preference, 194
Pregnancy zone protein (PZP), 275
Prejudice, 306–310
Prejudicial attitudes, 306
Prenatal development, 328–329
  embryonic stage, 328
  stage of the fetus, 326–327
  stage of the zygote, 328
Prenatal period, 326, 328
Preoperational stage, 330–331
Primary drive, 171
Primary reinforcer, 89
Problem, 150
  problem-focused strategy, 240
  solving, 150–152
    algorithm, 151
    effective, 151
    functional fixedness, 151
    goal state, 150
    heuristic, 151
    ill-defined problems, 150
    ineffective, 151
    initial state, 150
    possible routes, 150
    strategy, 151
    well-defined problems, 150
Procedural LTM, 107
Procedural memory, 108
Processing speed, 161
Productivity, 153
Progesterone, 274
Projective test, 225
Prototypes, 149
Proximity, 68–69
Prozac, 283
Pseudomemories, 134
Pseudoscience, 10
  real science versus, 10
  Science versus, 10
Psychedelic amphetamine, 141
Psychiatric nurses, 15
Psychiatry, 15
Psychoactive drug therapy, 282–284
  antidepressant drugs, 283
  antipsychotic drugs, 282–283
Psychoactive drugs, 136
Psychoanalytic approach, Freud's, 211–214
  after Freud, 214–216
  conscious level, 211
  death instincts (Thanatos), 212
  ego, 213
  id, 212
  pleasure principle, 213
  preconscious level, 211
  reality principle, 213
  superego, 213
  unconscious level, 211
Psychoanalytic psychology, 12
Psycholinguistics, 154
Psychological disorders, 257–297. *See also* Biomedical treatments; Psychotherapy techniques

abnormal, 258–262
anxiety disorders, 262–264
bipolar disorder, 271–272
bipolar I disorder, 271
bipolar II disorder, 271
classifying, 259–260
depressive disorders, 270–271
diathesis, 271
diathesis-stress model, 271
dissociative amnesia, 267
dissociative disorders, 267–268
dissociative identity disorder (DID), 267
dysthymia, 270
gender differences in Alzheimer's disease, 274
generalized amnesia, 267
insanity, 260–262
manic depression, 271
persistent depressive disorder, 270
personality disorders, 268–270
  antisocial, 269
  avoidant, 269
  Cluster A, 268
  Cluster B, 268
  Cluster C, 268
  dependent, 270
  histrionic, 269
  paranoid, 269
  schizoid, 269
posttraumatic stress disorder, 264–265
schizophrenia spectrum disorder, 272–275
  negative symptoms, 272
  positive symptoms, 272
selective amnesia, 267
treatment for, 277–297
Psychological distance, 201
Psychological field, 227
Psychological test, 159, 224–227
Psychological Testing, 13
Psychological tests of intelligence, 159–164
Psychologically based motives, 179–182
Psychology, 2, 13
  applied/practitioner areas in, 15–16
  careers in, 13–16
  in our lives, 1–19
    history, 11–13
    research ways, 7–11
    Science and practice, 4–6
  minorities in, 13
  principles to guide, 16–17
    individual differences, 17
    interactions, 16
  scientific/research areas in, 14–15
  women in, 13
Psychometric psychologists, 15
Psychosurgery, 278–279
Psychotherapy techniques, 284–292
  aversion therapy, 288
  behavioral approaches, 287–289
  client-centered therapy, 287
  cognitive approaches, 289–291
  contingency contracting, 288
  contingency management, 288
  evaluating, 292–295
  free association, 285
  group approaches, 291–292
  humanistic approaches, 287
  latent content, 286
  manifest content, 286
  person-centered therapy, 287
  psychoanalytic approaches, 284–287
  reflective listening, 287
  Rogerian therapy, 287
  systematic desensitization, 288
Psychotic symptoms, 282
Puberty, 337
  challenges, 337–339

Punishment, 89, 92–95
Pupil, 53

R
Racism, 306
Rahe, Richard, 237
Rapid eye movement (REM) sleep, 129–130
  disorder, 130
Rapid-onset gender dysphoria, 198
Rational appeal, 305
Rational-emotive therapy (RET), 289
Rayner, Rosalie, 85–86
Real science, pseudoscience versus, 10
Reality principle, 213
Reasoning, 149
  categories, 149
  deductive, 149
  inductive, 149
Reasoning test, 163
Recall, 112
Receptor sites, 24
Recognition, 112
Reflective listening, 287
Reflex, 82
Rehabilitation psychologists, 15
Reinforcement, 89–92
  positive versus negative, 90
  Service Dog, 91
Reinforcer, 89
Relative size, 72
Relaxation techniques, 241–242
Reliability, 6, 159
Repetition, 65
Representativeness heuristic, 152
Repressed memory, 109
Repression, 285
Resistance, 285
Restructured form, 225
Reticular formation, 34
Retina, 54
Retinal disparity, 71
Retrieval of memory, 102, 112–120
  encoding, 112
  improving, 112–120
  information encoding affecting, 113–116
  key-word method, 116
  practicing, 119–120
  scheduling practice, 116–119
  storage, 112
Risky shift, 319
Rods, 54
Rogerian therapy, 287
Rogers, Carl, 218, 287
Role confusion, 340
Romantic love, 205
Roosevelt, Eleanor, 219
Rorschach inkblot test, 225
Rosch, Eleanor, 149
Rote rehearsal, 105
Rule-based moral system, 333
Rules of combination, 153

S
Safety needs, 172
Salovey, Peter, 158
Salthouse, Timothy, 163
Salty, 61
Same-sex orientations, 194–197
  factors relating to, 196–197
Saturation, 53
Savory-ness, 61
Sawyer, Diane, 197
Scheduling practice, 116–119
Schema, 329
Schizoid personality disorder, 269